ISLAND PEOPLE

ISLAND PEOPLE

THE CARIBBEAN
AND THE WORLD

Joshua Jelly-Schapiro

ALFRED A. KNOPF
NEW YORK
2016

THIS IS A BORZOI BOOK
PUBLISHED BY ALFRED A. KNOPF

www.aaknopf.com

Knopf, Borzoi Books, and the colophon are registered trademarks of
Penguin Random House LLC.

Page 453 constitutes an extension of the copyright page.

Portions of this book first appeared, in different form,
in *The New York Review of Books*, *The Believer*,
The Nation, the *Los Angeles Review of Books*, and on www.newyorker.com.

Library of Congress Cataloging-in-Publication Data
Names: Jelly-Schapiro, Joshua, author.
Title: Island people : the Caribbean and the world / by Joshua Jelly-Schapiro.
Description: First edition. | New York : Knopf, 2016.
Identifiers: LCCN 2016010673 (print) | LCCN 2016027814 (ebook) |
ISBN 9780385349765 (hardback) | ISBN 9780385349772 (ebook)
Subjects: LCSH: Caribbean Area—Civilization. | Caribbean Area—History. |
Caribbean Area—Intellectual life. | BISAC: TRAVEL / Caribbean & West Indies.
| HISTORY / Caribbean & West Indies / General. | HISTORY / Social History.
Classification: LCC F2169.J45 2016 (print) | LCC F2169 (ebook) |
DDC 972.9—dc23
LC record available at https://lccn.loc.gov/2016010673

Jacket design by Oliver Munday

Manufactured in the United States of America

First Edition

For my parents

and for island people everywhere

The indigenous Carib and Arawak Indians, living by their own lights long before the European adventure, gradually disappear in a blind, wild forest of blood. That mischievous gift, the sugar cane, is introduced, and a fantastic human migration moves to the New World of the Caribbean; deported crooks and criminals, defeated soldiers and Royalist gentlemen fleeing from Europe, slaves from the West Coast of Africa, East Indians, Chinese, Corsicans, and Portuguese. The list is always incomplete, but they all move and meet on an unfamiliar soil . . . in an unpredictable and infinite range of custom and endeavour, people in the most haphazard combinations, surrounded by memories of splendour and misery, the sad and dying kingdom of Sugar, a future full of promises. And always the sea!

—George Lamming

We're all in the Caribbean, if you think about it.

—Junot Díaz

CONTENTS

PART II: The Lesser Antilles

Sea of Islands

ISLAND PEOPLE

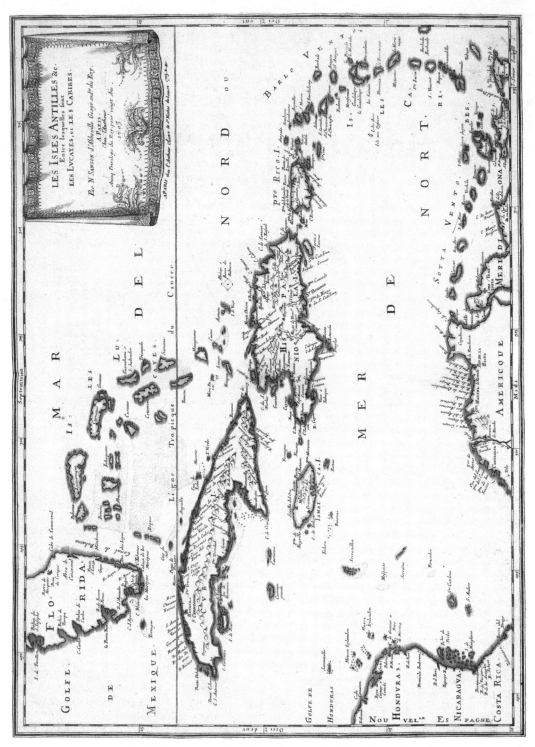

David Sanson and Guillaume Sanson, *Les Isles Antilles* (1703).

INTRODUCTION

IN NOVEMBER 1963, Vintage paperbacks published a new edition of *The Black Jacobins*, C. L. R. James's celebrated history of the Haitian Revolution. The book had first appeared in London in 1938, where James had arrived by transatlantic steamer from his native West Indies a few years before to launch a literary career. A quarter century later, *The Black Jacobins*—though already a touchstone for black intellectuals worldwide—had fallen out of favor and out of print. Its itinerant author had moved from England to the United States shortly before World War II, then had returned to Europe after being expelled from the U.S. as a subversive in 1953. Finally, in 1958, he returned to his home island in the southern Caribbean for the first time since he'd left his life there as a colonial schoolteacher.

Born in British-owned Trinidad in 1901, C. L. R. James was the son of a schoolmaster and a cultured mother whose bookcase of Victorian novels and Elizabethan drama occupied him when cricket didn't. He grew into a radical whose passion for dramatic narrative always equaled his yen for discourse on historical materialism. ("[Thackeray's] 'Vanity Fair' holds more for me than Capital," he said.)[1] Drawn to the classics and hugely ambitious, James sought to place the history of the Caribbean within the larger telos of not only modernity and capitalism but also humanity's struggle for democracy, reaching back to the Greeks. Perhaps more distinctively, he sought always to understand the cultures of his own day—cricket matches and calypso songs, Hollywood films and radio serials—within that larger story.

James Baldwin wrote, "I believe what one has to do as a black American is to take white history, or history as written by whites, and claim it all—including Shakespeare."[2] For C. L. R. James, growing up in Trinidad, this seems never to have been an issue. The grandson of slaves, he claimed from childhood not only Shakespeare but Virgil and Thackeray as his own. He embraced—and embodied in his black frame—ideas and principles normatively opposed. A passionate anticolonial who believed in something called "Western Civilization," he was a devotee of Aeschylus who also loved pulp novels; an intellectual who also played cricket; a Marxist materialist not immune to the charms of the bourgeois stage. A thinker whose "interdisciplinary" approach to history anticipated recent academic trends by decades, his peripatetic life and political engagements embody the core dramas of a century that "he sought to embrace in its dialectical whole," as the Guyanese writer Wilson Harris put it.[3]

James's return to the Caribbean was prompted by the promise of self-rule in Trinidad and the triumph of the Cuban revolution. And it was these same momentous developments that prompted his decision to publish a revised edition of his history of the epochal slave revolt, led by Toussaint L'Ouverture, through which "West Indians"—and not only Haitians—"first became aware of themselves as a people."[4]

James left the main text of *The Black Jacobins* unchanged, except for the addition of several lambent lines about Toussaint's sad demise. More substantively, James included a postscript "appendix" in which he offered a new interpretation of the Haitian Revolution's significance. This new afterword's thrust was conveyed in its title: "From Toussaint L'Ouverture to Fidel Castro." Rather than signifying "a merely convenient or journalistic demarcation of historical time," Toussaint and Fidel were joined because each man had led revolutions that were "peculiarly West Indian, the product of a peculiar origin and a peculiar history," no matter that they occurred 150 years apart and on different islands.[5] The Caribbean was a region whose "peculiar history," according to James, had not only produced a common culture on its islands but given them a special role to play on the world stage.

He sought, in his new afterword to *The Black Jacobins*, to explain why. "The history of the West Indies is governed by two factors, the sugar plantation and Negro slavery," he began.

> Wherever the sugar plantation and slavery existed, they imposed a pattern. It is an original pattern, not European, not African, not a part of the American main, not native in any conceivable sense of that word, but West Indian, *sui generis*, with no parallel anywhere else.[6]

The plantation and racial slavery had been present elsewhere in the Americas. But the Caribbean, James argued, was unique. Firstly because of sheer numbers: from the early 1500s through to the end of the Triangle Trade, three centuries later, the region's islands received some six million African slaves to their shores (England's North American colonies that became the United States, during that time, received scarcely 400,000). And secondly, the region stood out for the particular nature of the lives its slaves lived. Those slaves, as builders of island societies made for the express purpose of providing sugar for distant tables, had from the sixteenth century on "lived a life that was in its essence a modern life."[7] They had moved vast distances to toil at industry, and helped forge a new world economy. They had "lived together in a social relation far closer than any proletariat of the time," learned Europe's languages, and belonged to societies where "even the cloth [they] wore and the food they ate was imported"—in places both made for, and sustained by, international communication and trade from the start.[8]

For James, these facts were far from mere historical trivia; they were crucial to understanding the role that the Caribbean's people were fated to play in world history—and in the world-historical development that would define the postwar era: the dismantling of Europe's colonial empires across Africa, Asia, and the Americas, and the emergence of its old colonies' people as full-fledged members of the world comity of nations. It was not by accident, James argued, that West Indians had formed the vanguard of black thinkers driven to end colonialism worldwide—as evidenced, for example, by figures like Marcus Garvey, the Jamaican-born founder of the United Negro Improvement Association, and by Frantz Fanon, the Martinique-born author of *The Wretched of the Earth* (to say nothing of James himself). And it was not by accident, either, that the islands wherein the world's "first truly modern revolution"[9] took place (in Haiti) had also just witnessed a triumph for socialism and guerrilla tactics, in Cuba, that freedom's lovers everywhere were touting at the time as *the* model for how the earth's wretched should right history's wrongs.

James's arguments were driven by politics: an ardent leftist, he was also writing at a time when he, like many West Indian intellectuals, was still hoping the Caribbean's islands might confederate into a single regional nation. But what was at stake for him in arguing that the Caribbean's diverse territories shared a common history and culture was not merely that such an understanding was necessary for the Caribbean's "self-realization." It was what that self-realization might entail for the world at large. "Of all formerly colonial coloured peoples," James wrote, there in his new afterword to *The Black Jacobins*, "the West Indian masses are the most highly experienced in the ways of Western civilisation and most receptive to its requirements in the twentieth century."[10] The Caribbean and its diasporas were destined, in other words, to play a special role in the development of world culture at large in the twentieth century.

Mention the Caribbean today and most people think of beaches and poverty, not of the historical anthropologist Sidney Mintz's description of these islands, echoing James, as "modern before modernity"[11]—as places where phenomena we think of as belonging to our own age—mass migration and mass industry and transcontinental trade—have been facts of life for centuries. Many of the million-plus revelers attending London's annual Notting Hill carnival, like dancers at salsa clubs from Lima to Harlem, may have a vague sense of their parties' Caribbean roots. But few credit how essential the Caribbean has been to how we think about identity and difference, in the decades since Marcus Garvey seized on applying the Jewish concept of "diaspora" to black people, too. It's only over the past couple of decades, fully two centuries after the Haitian Revolution, that a critical mass of historians has caught up to James's argument that what happened in the French sugar colony of Saint-Domingue wasn't merely central to the rise of global capitalism but birthed a question that's still at the core of our politics now: How universal, really, are universal rights?

* * *

THE CARIBBEAN, as much as it is a place, is also an idea. In this, the Caribbean is not unique. Any good geographer will tell you that. The ways that we humans develop our sense for place—the ways in which we vest location with meaning—have to do always, in some sense, with experience and memory. Especially so, and in a direct way, if the place in question is a hometown or spot in which you've spent time. But even with towns or regions we know well, our conception of a place is also always shaped by the stories we hear or tell about it. The images or ills that attach themselves to the name of New York or New England or the Wild West, via songs and films and books, lodge in our minds. And such stories, more than merely informing how we imagine, say, Bruce Springsteen's New Jersey or Saddam Hussein's Iraq can both reflect and shape them. From ad campaigns to attract tourists to propaganda that shapes governments' decisions about whether to protect or aid or bomb places foreign or domestic—the ways in which a place is imagined, especially by those with power to act on it, matters. And if stories matter with regard to single places, they especially matter for those collections of places we know as regions: assemblages of towns or states that may or may not share anything beyond their proximity, but that some party or group of people has joined together, for better or worse, in a common story.

This is certainly the case with "Caribbean," a moniker in which lie many of the torturous turns that made its islands as they now exist. The sea that gives the region its name was, for the first two or three centuries after Columbus's arrival, basically nameless, registered by the Spanish as an undifferentiated part of the Mar del Norte (as they termed all parts of the western Atlantic), and known to English navigators as the Spanish Main (the term, confusingly, that they also used for the South American littoral to the sea's south—what the Spanish called Tierra Firme). When exactly the Caribbean Sea—a body of water more or less discrete, ringed by the Antilles and the Central and South American coasts, saltier than the Gulf of Mexico and the Atlantic Ocean it abuts—first began to be called the Caribbean is unknown. But in 1773, the British cartographer Thomas Jefferys published *The West-India Atlas*, in whose introduction he wrote, "It has been sometimes called the Caribbean Sea, which name it would be better to adopt, than to leave this space quite anonymous."[12] He did so on his maps. "Caribbean" referred to the indigenous group once predominant on the Lesser Antilles, the Carib, who according to Spanish lore were distinguished from the more peaceable Arawak, whom the Carib had driven from the islands in precolonial days, by their practice of cannibalism. Evidence of any Carib actually eating people is scant. But the phonetic resemblance of the word "Caribbean" to "cannibal" was noted by writers from Shakespeare on; it seemed a fitting tag for this savage sea of pirates and slaves far from civilization's mores. The name stuck.

While, to be sure, today the Caribbean may no longer be associated with cannibalism, the region was defined by fantasy and myth from the moment Columbus gazed out from the *Santa Maria*'s deck at what he mistook for an island off of India, and wrote in his journal of "the most beautiful land that human eyes have ever seen."[13] Islands quickly shorn of their native peoples, societies built to enrich Old Europe, the

Caribbean—and its literature—were for many centuries tied to imperial endeavor. From the diaries and strivings of conquistadors seeking El Dorado, straight through the fierce panoply of glossy websites
and guidebooks depicting the islands as unchanging places of smiling
natives and eternal sun—the Caribbean has long figured as a place to be
consumed, like the sugar it brutally produced, as commodity.

The Caribbean isn't the only world region shaped by its colonizers
to exist, in Old Europe's mind, as "a place of romance, exotic beings,
haunting memories and landscapes, remarkable experiences."[14] But
unlike the Orient of legend described by Edward Said in *Orientalism*,
the Caribbean has also long been full of something else. C. L. R. James
is anything but the first or last person from these islands to have made a
vocation of describing the region's attributes, and its "Caribbean-ness,"
for himself.

As a white kid who'd grown up in snowy New England, my early
ties to the islands themselves were strictly long-distance. By the early
1990s, ten years after Bob Marley's martyrdom from cancer in 1981,
the dreadlocked singer whose posters I stuck to my bedroom wall had
long since become a symbol of mellow moods and mellow music, extra
well suited to the countercultural hills of northern Vermont, where as
a teenager I shared my obsession with others of my generation. As an
icon of racial justice and wry romance, Bob Marley caught my teenage
aims and ideals through lovely melodies, from "Get Up, Stand Up," to
"No Woman, No Cry." More important, though, he translated deep
subjects like the Triangle Trade ("I remember on the slave ship / how
they brutalize our very souls")[15] into great pop—and, in so doing, sent
me less to smoke up than to read every book I could find on Jamaica and
its music and the history of the region.

When I moved south to college in New Haven, Connecticut, I
brought my Marley posters with me to hang first in a dorm room and
then in the off-campus apartment in a town where my quotidian life also
included—from the Puerto Rican bodega owners from whom I bought
my Cheerios, to the Jamaican promoters who brought the island's top
dancehall acts to Toad's Place, behind the Yale library—no small impri-
matur of the Caribbean. I had by then developed an inchoate sense that
would soon become a conviction: that it was in the Caribbean that many
of the salient characteristics of the Americas at large—traumatic histories of colonialism and genocide and slavery; migration and creolization
as facts of life; the persistent sense of cosmopolitan possibility and new-
ness inherent to a New World—were brought into starkest relief.

Which is when and how I began on a course of study and exploration of the Caribbean. I spent most of the next four years immersed in a tradition of storytelling and intellection that went from José Martí, the nineteenth-century Cuban patriot who argued that the Caribbean's creole cultures would be a source of native strength for all of the Americas; through the Dominican poet Pedro Mir's "Countersong to Walt Whitman" (1945) ("I / a son of the Caribbean / Antillean to be exact. / The raw product of a simple / Puerto Rican girl / and a Cuban worker, / born precisely, and poor, / on Quisqueyan soil. / Overflowing with voices, / full of eyes / wide open throughout the islands")[16]; to all the island thinkers, with surnames like Brathwaite and Brodber and Césaire and Walcott, who, in the decades after James released his revised version of *The Black Jacobins*, have described what was *"sui generis"* about the Antilles, and what, if anything, unites them. I was lucky to get to study under some of the leading scholars in the field, and in a new Yale program that became my major, in "Ethnicity, Race, and Migration," I studied the writings of Edouard Glissant, the great poet and thinker from Martinique who described the Antilles as informed by a "poetics of relation," and of Stuart Hall, the Jamaica-born doyen of British cultural studies, who wrote that the Caribbean was the "home of hybridity."[17] I wrote papers on great Cuban novelist Alejo Carpentier's idea of the "marvelous real" and on Jean Rhys's *Wide Sargasso Sea*.[18] I thrilled to the essays that Sylvia Wynter, the Cuban-Jamaican dancer-cum-novelist-cum-brilliant-cultural-theorist, wrote after the quincentennial of Columbus's arrival in the New World, contending that since the Caribbean was the place where all the planet's peoples were joined in a single world history, for better or worse, it was also the place where a "re-enchantment of humanism" could occur.[19]

In Trinidad, I spent happy days in the library at the University of the West Indies, where C. L. R. James's papers are housed just down the traffic-choked road from where he grew up. The village of Tunapuna is now a dusty stop along the highway between Trinidad's airport and its capital, Port of Spain. But in the cool back room of the concrete library where much of Tunapuna's favorite son's archive now lives, I sat at a wooden table near a portrait of the great man, unmistakable with snowy barnet and in his scarecrow suit. I looked through folders of his correspondence and notes, laid on by friendly librarians; I read his letters to understand the circumstance of his falling out with Eric Williams in 1960 ("Trinidad is like some Italian city state in Renaissance times," one said; "characters being assassinated, intrigues bubbling, informers informing").[20] I was also interested to find, in a sheaf of letters to the publisher who agreed to reissue *The Black Jacobins* in New York, that same year, his first note describing "an essay I should like to append to the book, linking what took place in the Caribbean in the 18th century with what is taking place there today."[21]

This ambition was infectious. I decided to trace James's thinking in that era as a way to then explore the work and stories of some Caribbean artists and events that spoke to them. I delved, in Jamaica, into the audio archive of the great folklorist Louise "Miss Lou" Bennett, from whom Harry Belafonte got much of his source material for *Calypso* in 1956. I looked, in Brooklyn and Barbados, into the form and source of the exemplary Bajan American writer Paule Marshall's pathbreaking immigrant novel, *Brown Girl, Brownstones*. I researched an intriguing "cultural congress" in Havana, in 1968, when Cuba welcomed a bevy of leading Caribbean intellectuals from across the region, including James, to discuss "The Integral Growth of Man." I examined the old and lasting question of how and why Bob Marley, with the help of the impresario Chris Blackwell and within the unique context of the stagflationary 1970s, not only became "the first Third World superstar," but also enjoys a posthumous stature as arguably the most pervasive musical and political icon on earth.

My investigations fulfilled certain scholarly needs. They happily allowed me, while traveling frequently between California and the Caribbean, to earn a degree. But they also convinced me, as I began also to work as a journalist reporting on many of the islands' travails and triumphs, that the way I most wanted to contend with James's ideas, and with the world that made him, was by writing in a more than incidental way about something I'd found to be true throughout the Antilles. In seeking out the friends or kin of the outsized global figures all the islands seem to produce in such abundance—the writers, the sprinters, the revolutionaries, and reggae stars—I was struck by it again and again: on small islands, these figures were rendered domestic. To Marley's cousins in St. Ann Parish, in Jamaica, the reggae king was a familiar "Bob." To the rum-drunks by the cricket oval in Trinidad, C. L. R. James wasn't the Black Plato but rather a nerdy guy in a coat who used big words but was no more nor less deserving of respect or ridicule than anyone, in this New World Place where everyone was making it up as they went along.

In this there was something of what one finds when visiting the homeplaces of any famous person who has grown bigger than where she's from. But there was, in the islands, something else. Not only were the larger-than-life figures made familiar; the people who comprised the familiar—the rum-drunks by the cricket oval; the attitudinal woman selling corn soup down the way—had a way of growing outsized, too, in their presentation of self, and in ways that went beyond the mere perceptions of an outsider. Derek Walcott once wrote, "All Port of Spain is a 12:30 show."[22] I suspected he was right, and that there was something to be gained from placing that fact at the center of what the great British travel writer Patrick Leigh Fermor described, after a swing through the Antilles just after World War II, as "the perceptible texture of [these islands'] existence."[23]

From that trip Leigh Fermor produced a book that's endured as a classic portrait of the West Indies at the start of their modern age. His *The Traveller's Tree* (1952) was pitched neither strictly at scholars nor at holiday makers; it's joined, on a brief list of such serious literary portraits, by V. S. Naipaul's *The Middle Passage* (1962). Those books, by two of the last century's most stylishly incisive writers, comprise essential entries in the Antilles bibliography. But read today, they also serve as key lenses through which to view how the islands of the Caribbean— and how one must write about them—have changed. Which isn't to say that Leigh Fermor and Naipaul are wholly similar figures. They are in fact very different—the one a curious voyager of a Hellenist mind, whose *Traveller's Tree* renders warm visions of a magical world he's seeing for the first time; the other, an ambitious Anglophile from the colonies whose distaste for his own childhood, in Trinidad, suffuses each line of *The Middle Passage* (no matter that Naipaul was commissioned to write that book by Dr. Eric Williams, Trinidad's first prime minister). But both their books couldn't help but betray their era's sense that these islands, whatever their maladies or charms, were thoroughly marginal to the larger story of Western civilization. "History is built around achievement and creation," Naipaul went so far as to say in his, "and nothing was created in the West Indies."[24]

One should never read statements like that, from Naipaul, without appreciating the underlying spirit of what, in his home island's oral culture, is known as *picong*—an utterance meant, in its overstatement or wrath, to cut or provoke. But that doesn't change the obligation one feels, in writing about the Caribbean now, to show how deeply Naipaul's provocation has been buried by history. When Leigh Fermor wandered the Jamaican ghetto of Trench Town, he emerged with a quizzical account of the ropy-haired eccentrics he met there. His was a portrait of obscure cultists whose ideas were unknown beyond their island, but a half century later few culture mavens can't recognize the iconography (and grooming practices) of a Rasta faith that Trench Town's reggae stars made world famous—just as few followers of world literature don't now know the name of the young writer who, forty years after penning *The Middle Passage*, won the Nobel Prize. The Caribbean today may in many ways remain "marginal" indeed; its fragile economies are dependent, in the main, on the fickle funds of tourists. But to visit these islands now also means meeting other travelers, or returning émigrés, who are more than aware of how the islands have crucially shaped the sounds and feel of major world cities like New York and London and thus of modern cultures everywhere.

* * *

THIS BOOK PONDERS NOT MERELY what the Caribbean is but *where* it is as well. On that by-no-means-simple point, scholars and politicians all seem at least to agree that the Greater and Lesser Antilles are Caribbean: Cuba, Jamaica, Hispaniola, and Puerto Rico line the sea's northern edge; the Lesser Antilles, tailing off in a curving string of islands reaching from Anguilla toward Trinidad and the old Spanish Main, also qualify. But depending on who (or which tourist agency) you talk with, "the Caribbean" may also include the Bahamas and the coastal cays of Venezuela and Mexico's Yucatán Peninsula; nearby nations that don't touch the Caribbean Sea but share its colonial past (like Guyana, Surinam, Bermuda); and even Faulkner's Mississippi or the "Caribbean city" of New Orleans—a place that certainly feels, especially at carnival time, like a kissing cousin of Trinidad and Haiti. The influential geographer Carl Sauer, for his part, termed the Caribbean "a natural region, though fuzzy around the edges," whose territories included both the islands and "the rim of land around a Mediterranean Sea."[25]

This book, though, centers on the islands. This fact doesn't come without regret: to glean the Caribbean's claim on its South American littoral, one need look no further than to Gabriel García Márquez: *One Hundred Years of Solitude* isn't set in the Andes but rather in a place—Colombia's Caribbean shore—replete with magic and slaves and monocrop agriculture and gypsies washed up from afar. And the concept of the "marvelous real" was invented by Alejo Carpentier, a Cuban obsessed with the Haitian Revolution. But, alas: Macondo is beyond my scope here, and so are Cartagena, Costa Rica, Bluefields, Nicaragua, and a hundred other places I'd have loved to skip through with James at hand. But in a project that's as much a journey through an idea as a portrait of this region, my focus on the Antilles has also proceeded from an understanding of the Caribbean as an archipelago: as a "sea of islands" whose status as such has acted as both a crucial shaper of the region's history and a key aspect of the Caribbean's grip on the world's imagination.

In his preface to *The Traveller's Tree*, Leigh Fermor described the difficulty of forging his own experience of the Antilles into a cogent book: "Short of writing a thesis in many volumes, only a haphazard, almost a picaresque approach can suggest the peculiar mood and tempo of the Caribbean and the turbulent past from which they spring."[26] I agree. But in baking my own Caribbean picaresque into a narrative, my aim has been to collate years of study with more years of Antillean expeditions, to explore if not explain how and why these islands' peoples and cultures have only seemed more determined in recent decades, as one Cuban writer put it, to "expand beyond their own sea with a vengeance."[27]

In the years after World War II, most of the Antilles passed from under the rule of Old Europe. They took their place beneath the "soft" umbrella of a new hegemon whose imperial sway was perhaps felt less in new military bases, as Leigh Fermor wrote in 1952, than in the creep of "Coca-Cola advertisements, frigidaires, wireless sets and motor-cars."[28] The Cuban revolution forcibly removed both Coca-Cola ads and the CIA from the region's largest island. But the United States grew only more determined, after that event, to maintain the Caribbean as an "American lake." In 1983, Ronald Reagan went so far as to send the Marines to Grenada to prevent the emergence, on that tiny island, of "another Cuba." But geopolitics aside, postwar Caribbean culture has been most crucially shaped by its people confronting all that their new nations lack: stable populations, shared ancestral tongues, "stable" cultures with ancient roots—all the qualities, in other words, that "nations" are traditionally supposed to have.

But the more time one spends in those nations, the more one realizes that these perceived lacks have often been the source of their cultures' riches. For people whose ancestors were brought to work strange islands in chains, the question of how to best salve history's wounds was key long before the challenges of modern "nation building." In the Caribbean, two features often invoked as uniquely modern in their effects on identity—the mixing of cultures and peoples from different continents, and migration and displacement as facts of life—have been plainly evident for centuries. The deep question those facts prompt, which has in many ways defined its arts, was posed by one of Kingston's great vocal groups, the Melodians, on their contribution to the soundtrack of the classic reggae film *The Harder They Come:*

> By the rivers of Babylon / where we sat down
> Ye-eah we wept / when we remembered Zion
> The wicked carried us away in captivity / required from us a song
> Now how shall we sing a song of joy / in a strange land?[29]

The search for "roots," and their figuring in culture, is, of course, not a theme unique to the Caribbean: all people are seekers after "that which binds, and with which one can relate," as Simone Weil put it.[30] But in an era of mass migration and the World Wide Web and globalization, when cultures everywhere are contending with "rootlessness," perhaps it makes sense that a region so versed in those challenges has found its season. In 1972, *The Harder They Come* introduced Jamaican music to the world. A few years later, reggae's biggest star supplied a potent answer to the Melodians' query. "We know where we're going / we know where we're from," sang Bob Marley on *Exodus*, the record that cemented his global fame. "We're leaving Babylon / we're going to our Father's Land."[31] The universality of human desire to feel that way, and the success with which the Caribbean's finest voices have translated it into the idiom of pop, are key reasons why, one suspects, their work has gained the global resonance it has.

A sense of place, as Marley suggested in those lines about heading for Zion, matters to humans. It's only in and through place—the places that we call home, or the ones to which we want to go—that we figure out who we are. And it's through place, too, that we route our lives and our hopes: the places we live and the ones we recall; the places we imagine; the places we want to be.

It's perhaps not hard to understand, given those truths, the fierce hold that islands have long seemed to exert on our imaginations. They're at once "places apart" and connected to everywhere by the sea. They have figured in our literature, from Homer on, as sites of desire and fear; as the loci of prisons or paradise; as places on which to be marooned, reborn, or transformed. "Western culture not only thinks about islands," observed the historian John Gillis, "but thinks with them" as well.[32] Islands are potent places, and for five hundred years this exemplary sea of islands in the imagination has proved irresistible to adventurers and poets and protestors and hedonists alike. As the place where "globalization" began, and the region, too, where the West's still-ongoing conversation about universal human rights began, the Caribbean has been anything but marginal to the making of our modern world.

PART I

The Greater Antilles

Jamaica: The Wages of Love

CHAPTER I

BRANDING

ON TV, IT LOOKED LIKE the others were jogging.

Halfway through the Olympic 100-meter final, Usain Bolt—Jamaican hero, fastest man in the world, performing in London before eighty thousand flashbulb-popping fans—pulled away. At six-foot-five, hurtling down the tile-red track, Bolt stretched his stride in a way none of his rivals—compact, muscular men all—could match. One moment, eight Lycra-clad figures were sprinting in a pack. Then there was one: long legs churning, face calm. In Beijing four years before, he'd turned this race, as one oft-quoted account had it, into "a palette on which an emerging and transcendent talent could splash his greatness."[1] Slapping his chest before the line, exulting as he crossed—Bolt charmed the world with his brash joie de vivre. Now, as he pulled away, TV replays caught him glancing at the stadium clock: in Beijing, he'd entered history; here, he wanted to make it. And so he did. The clock showed the time—a new Olympic record. And Jamaica's pride, his nation's black, yellow, and green flag draped over his broad back, grinned and danced as he circled the stadium, soaking up its warm lights' love.

For most of the few hundred million around the globe watching on TV, the scene showed what the Olympic Games, Visa-sponsored corporate dross aside, could still be. Here was a beautiful human, from a little nation, moving with supernal grace on the world stage. But to Jamaicans, this win meant much more. In Kingston that night, they'd ignored tropical storm warnings to gather in their thousands, by one of the city's main crossroads, at Half Way Tree, before a big screen to watch him run. Dressed in yellow or green, blaring plastic horns, they could be seen, on videos posted to YouTube, hopping in place as the race began—and then, when Bolt won (and as his young Jamaican teammate

Yohan Blake took silver for good measure), leaping higher. They raised their fingers to the sky, hands held like pistols, yelling out Jamaicans' favored expression for affirming joy, in this city as well known for gunplay as for Bob Marley. *Brap, brap, brap!* The sound mimicked the sound of shots fired in the air. Behind them, on a big screen, was Usain Bolt in London performing dance moves that may have looked, to the world, like so much wiggling; people here knew, though, that they were moves born at street parties nearby.

In Jamaica, at any time, Bolt's win would have been a big deal. In this athletics-mad nation of two and a half million souls, sprinting—the source of fifty-two of the fifty-five Olympic medals Jamaica has ever won—matters. But what made the resonance of this triumph, at these London Olympics, extra deep, was its timing. August 5, 2012, fell on the eve of Jamaica's Golden Jubilee. The very next night, in Kingston's National Stadium, the island would celebrate its fiftieth birthday as a sovereign state. At midnight on this date in 1962, Princess Margaret lowered the Union Jack, which flew over this island for 307 years, and watched Alexander Bustamante, independent Jamaica's first prime minister, raise a bright new standard in its place. As Jamaica's sprinters, in London, raised that standard in the old empire's capital—Bolt and Blake followed up their 100-meter sweep with one at 200 meters, and then helped Jamaica's 4 x 100 relay team win gold, too—Jamaica's anniversary celebrations, which had been building for months, were reaching a peak.

This, as one government official later put it to me, was a "cosmological convergence," impossible to ignore. And Jamaica's leaders, that August, didn't. Hailing Bolt's glory, they sought to dovetail Jamaicans' pride in their athletes with the prideful celebration they hoped "Jamaica 50" might represent for its people. (Naturally, they also sought, in ways subtle and less so, whether or not they belonged to the party of Prime Minister Portia Simpson-Miller, to leverage this all for political gain.) None of this was surprising. What I found striking, as I read Jamaica's papers online that month, and tuned in to watch the Jamaica 50 Grand Gala, was their language.

"Brand Jamaica," said an official from the Olympic committee praising Bolt's win, "has benefited tremendously from the exposure of our athletes in London."[2] The government's minister of youth and culture agreed. "Jamaica's Golden Jubilee," she proclaimed, "presents a glorious context in which to present the value proposition of Brand Jamaica."[3]

The prime minister, in an interview with *Time* magazine, praised "the brand the world recognizes so well."[4] During her speech at the Jamaica 50 gala, the subtext of her remarks, about how "in the area of sport and music, we are the toast of the world," was plain.[5] The leader every Jamaican calls "Portia" spent her first months in office urging, as her inaugural speech put it, that "Jamaica must remain 'a quality brand.'"[6]

I'd heard the term—"Brand Jamaica"—before. Mostly from tourism officials, during recent trips to the island, who sometimes invoked it when interviewed on Jamaican TV about their industry. Members of the film board, too, were fond of it: Brand Jamaica featured prominently on the website of their parent outfit, JAMPRO, the Jamaican Promotions Company, the agency charged with attracting foreign investment here. Since the government's release of a much-publicized report on the theme—its findings: Jamaica was "sitting on a treasure-house of natural brand equity"[7]—Brand Jamaica had become a popular subject. At dinner parties with island intellectuals, it was ridiculed. It was a much more intriguing curio, though, than a ubiquitous slogan.

But now, as Jamaica toasted its fiftieth, Brand Jamaica was everywhere.

* * *

THE PHRASE SOUNDED NEW, though Brand Jamaica dated from the 1960s, when the new country's Tourist Board was launched to help Jamacia make its mark on the world. Hiring a fancy New York marketing firm to help attract the world's tourists to its shores, the Tourist Board registered Jamaica's name, and brand identity (as "the most complete, diverse, and unique warm weather destination in the world"[8]), and aired ads everywhere. But then, in the 1970s, Jamaica's shores had become as well known for shootings as for sun. The island's rival political parties— Edward Seaga's Jamaican Labor Party, or JLP, backed by the CIA, and the People's National Party, or PNP, led by charismatic, Cuba-loving Michael Manley—enjoined a hot local variant of the Cold War. The parties armed their supporters and built them housing-projects-cum-patronage-communities, called "garrisons." No one talked much about Brand Jamaica. The garrisons' criminal lords, called "dons," became flush with drug money and grew to dominate the politicians to whom they'd once answered. And two years before Jamaica 50, that dynamic exploded, as it had before. State police stormed Tivoli Gardens, a historic community built by Seaga's JLP. The ensuing debacle saw seventy-odd Jamaican citizens die, underscoring in red the corruption that had killed Brand Jamaica in the '70s. It also furnished the lingering backdrop, amid a tanking economy, for Jamaica's fiftieth anniversary. But none of this stopped Jamaica's powers that be from resurrecting the term to tout the island's achievements at venues ranging from Kingston's National Stadium to the Clive Davis School of Recorded Music, at New York University, where old Edward Seaga turned up, one day that fall, to tout the release of a CD box set of Jamaica's "100 most significant songs."

Those "significant songs," as Seaga's presence at NYU signaled, have been significant far beyond Jamaica: their sounds sowed seeds for hip-hop; they permanently altered the texture of rock and pop and R&B. Jamaica's wiliest politician of its modern era, a white-maned hipster statesman in a dark suit, affirmed these truths to the Manhattan music mavens who came to see him. Seaga explained that before entering politics, he had worked as an ethnographer in Kingston's ghettos; that he'd helped launch Jamaica's record industry. Back in the 1950s, he had released not a few songs now included on the CDs he was here to hawk. Seaga's biography—Harvard-trained anthropologist; record producer and label owner; thrice-elected Caribbean head of state—was hardly imaginable anywhere but Jamaica. But here, he spoke most of using this box set, and birthday, to "rebuild Brand Jamaica." His island's brand had many facets. These included swift sprinters and shining sands. But "our music has been the greatest," he intoned at NYU, "because it has made us a brand name."

And so, "brand" language aside, it did. No Jamaican, apart from Bolt, because of his recent quadrennial bursts, has ever approached the fame of the reggae king whose "One Love" has long been the Tourist Board's anthem, and whose dreadlocked visage, thirty years after his death, still adorns dorm rooms everywhere. Bob Marley, who in 1973 recalled the Middle Passage like it was yesterday, became the "first Third World Superstar" by making historical links with no right to resound as pop hits. He hailed the prospect, on singles from "Slave Driver" to "Get Up, Stand Up," of redeeming our bloody histories. And then, in the tune that's endured as his epitaph, he distilled his art's thrust. "Redemption songs," he sang at his life's end, "are all I ever have." Those lines carried more than one meaning from this artist far cannier than the saintly stoner image projected onto his sharp-featured face, who came of age just as freedom's hopes were being dashed by poverty's violence. What Marley had, like the larger Third World, was less freedom's benefits than its promise. Songs of redemption, rather than the thing itself. These were the great product of a poor society where "development" has seemed an ever-receding dream. But none of this has stopped Jamaica's boosters from seeing the island's very history as a redemption song—or from hailing how "this little island," as Seaga recited at NYU, "changed the world."

A couple of months later, I booked a flight to Kingston. Boarding the plane at JFK with Jamaicans doffing puffy coats to do the same, I intended to spend some weeks on their island as its leaders tried, a half century into Jamaica's struggle to enjoy freedom's benefits, to turn their culture's riches into a "brand" for the world to consume.

Those weeks, this being Jamaica, turned into months.

* * *

"LADIES AND GENTLEPERSONS." The flight attendant's tuneful voice shook the canned air. "Is' yard we reach!" Four hours out of New York, the plane banked over Kingston's glinting lights. A pair of women in my row sporting magenta-hued hair and six-inch heels tittered at our steward's invoking their slang name for Jamaica, resonant of the grim "government yards" where many of our cabinmates—"yardies," in the parlance—grew up. We would not have heard that patois on a flight to Montego Bay. That's the purpose-built entrepôt, on Jamaica's north shore, that receives nearly all the million-plus tourists who still come here each year to rent time on chaise longues nearby. But we were flying to Kingston. I was the sole passenger without brown skin, apart from a couple of well-fed businessmen in first class, and this cabin full of returning migrants—teachers or cabbies, doctors or dealers—laughed along as another man's voice rang out from a back row, as we bumped aground, to keep the "yardie" riff going.

Brap, brap, brap!

In Jamaica, the language people speak, even more than many aspects of their culture, has tricky implications for its brand. Jamaican patois—now often simply called "Jamaican" here—has in recent years won increased acceptance: in schools, educators understand patois as a language in its own right, with English vocabulary but African syntax, and treat it as their pupils' first tongue; the nation's main newspapers, each

day, run "patwa" columns; its star sprinters speak it. (As the bronze med-
alist Warren Weir put it to the BBC, after Jamaica's 200-meter sweep:
"Nuh English, straight patwa!") It is the Queen's English, though, that
remains the language of Jamaica's ruling classes—of the people both
most keen to tout Jamaica's charms—its exuberance and rebel allure—
and most conscious of the fact that in places like the UK (where Jamaicans remain among the few Commonwealth citizens requiring a visa to
visit), "yardie" is as synonymous with "gangster" as it is with "Jamaican." Rising to open the luggage racks overhead, I helped my row mates
lower tied-together parcels, to their murmured "T'anks," and I recalled
hearing after the Olympics how, when the nation's Ministry of Youth,
Sports, and Culture had grown concerned with the image their young
patwa-speaking athletes might project abroad, they instituted a strict
training program in media English, to go with their wind sprints, so
their Bolts and Blakes and Weirs would be ready when the foreign cameras shone.

Some months had passed since the main celebration of Jamaica 50.
The blandishments of that time—including the "Nation on a Mission"
theme song its leaders had commissioned to go with it, with its patriotic
verses mouthed by reggae stars and sprinters—were starting to fade. I'd
timed my visit, though, to coincide with the island's annual celebration
of Black History Month. In the United States, we've grown used to
our cafeterias breaking out paper place mats each February depicting
Sojourner Truth and Martin Luther King. In Jamaica, Black History
Month also congrues with a yearly salute to the local music that's made
Black History its great theme: in 2008, the government proclaimed
that every February, forevermore, would officially be "Reggae Month,"
too. That week in Kingston, the University of the West Indies was to
host a conference on "Global Reggae, a' [at] yard and abroad,'" which
promised to attract a devoted tribe of scholars and obsessives outlin-
ing Jamaica's nation-branding efforts, and the culture behind them, in
panel discussion form.

Jamaica is hardly the sole world nation in the early twenty-first century to have embraced a branding agenda. England has its "Cool Britannia" ad campaign; Korea, its "K-Pop." In an era when the public
sphere can feel like a marketing consultancy, even artists and grade
schoolers know that it's not the product, it's the brand. But the branding
concept's uses and abuses, in a society whose forebears' flesh was once
singed like cattle's, was striking. Striking, for that history. Striking, for

how Jamaica's attempts to forge a Pavlovian link, in the world's mind, between the island's flag and its charms, involved a process of at once touting and quieting its foremost pathologies—for sex and sun, frenetic energy and violence. Brand Jamaica was striking for how all its facets, from sports to music to frolicking tourists, were implicated within the garrison complex that came during the 1970s and '80s to rule and ruin island life. And it was striking, too, because of what Brand Jamaica's story could maybe reveal about the larger fortunes of the old Third World.

Since the Cold War's end, many members of that fraternity of less have seen their economies, devalued and debt-ridden, advance little. When Marley sang, "Today they say are we free / only to be chained in poverty," in 1973, Jamaica had a dollar whose value still equaled that of a U.S. greenback. Now a single American dollar bought one hundred Jamaican ones. Yet Jamaica had demonstrated a remarkable gift, like many of its Third World peers, for exporting its people to First World cities. And those cities' cultures, if not their civil politics, have thrived on the toothsome frisson, "ethnic" or "exotic" (choose your queasy word), of those migrants' pepper and sounds. In this complex of fresh spring rolls and green tofu curries and cumbia-for-white-folks, Jamaican reggae's image and sounds held a prideful place. This is a fact, to Brand Jamaica's touters, that was extremely crucial. How and whether it mattered at all, or could be made to matter, to the Jamaicans with whom I filed off that flight in Kingston, not one of them a dreadlocked singer or a world-class sprinter, was another question.

* * *

WE STEPPED THROUGH the balmy night air to enter an arrivals hall bedecked with yellow, green, and black bunting. A large banner hung on a back wall. It was affixed with the hummingbird-adorned Jamaica 50 logo and a prosaic message—"WELCOME HOME"—that echoed our flight attendant's protocol breach and evinced how its hangers hoped Jamaica's birthday might resonate for this émigré nation. The line at immigration for JAMAICA/CARICOM entrants was, as usual in Kingston, much longer than the one for foreigners. At the customs desk, a uniformed agent stamped my passport with a perfunctory nod. His approach toward my magenta-haired friends was more dilatory. The women hoisted their bags onto the agent's steel table and glared daggers at his colleague, whose dog sniffed at parcels perhaps full of new Nikes for their cousins, or bras and cell phones to sell. With hustlers' mores and the outsized manner of a people about whom the song "Everybody Is a Star" might have been written, the members of Jamaica's émigré nation are certainly *on a mission*—if not, most times, the patriotic one their government had hailed in its Jamaica 50 theme song, and that the island's largest cell phone company, by the baggage claim, touted on another wall-sized mural. "NATION ON A MISSION," it yelled in 1,000-point type, above where the phone company Digicel's logo was affixed to a photomontage of Bolt spreading his seven-foot wingspan to the world, as Shelly Ann Frazer-Price, "di pocket rocket," who also won London gold, sprinted from the ghetto where she grew. Stepping beneath another banner hailing the nation's fiftieth, I paused after customs. There, by the money changers' booths, a more homely pantheon entombed its elder heroes in papier-mâché.

A man-sized figure in antique cottons, first in line, had "Sam Sharpe" inked on a plate at his feet: Sharpe led a rebellion of Jamaica's slaves, in 1831, that helped force its owners to abolish slavery throughout their empire. By Sharpe's side was Paul Bogle, the Baptist preacher who led another uprising, a few decades later, of ex-slaves now freed from bondage but still chained in poverty. Marcus Mosiah Garvey, next up, was unmistakable in his Horatio Nelson hat: he founded the United Negro Improvement Association in 1917 after emigrating from Jamaica to Harlem, and helped the world's black masses see themselves as a diaspora like the Jewish one. The two men here whose papier-mâché skin was painted lighter than the others had led Jamaica's drive to independence in 1962, and founded the two parties that define its politics still: Alexander Bustamente, the populist demagogue who formed the JLP (and Jamaica's first government), and his first cousin Norman Manley, the high-minded barrister (and father of the country's fourth prime minister, Michael Manley), who birthed the PNP. The last figure in this lineup was its sole woman. Recognizable for her gender and her head scarf, Queen Nanny of the Maroons was the eighteenth-century matriarch of the island's runaway slaves. She led the Maroons' fight for freedom—but she's a figure perhaps most recalled by school kids now, on this island of women-led households whose culture's mores can feel matriarchal and misogynist all at once, for her alleged ability, when faced with the redcoats' muskets, to catch their bullets in her cunny and fling them back.

Such are the nobler ghosts of Jamaica's past. Its popular heroes of now derive their fame from the rather different sources cited by my taxi driver when I asked him, as we pulled out of the airport, about the current "runnings" in town, and he eased us onto the road running down the sandy spit of land, jutting out and around Kingston Harbour, on which the airport sits. The Palisadoes, as this piece of land is called, has been a center of Jamaican civilization since the pirate Blackbeard beached his ships here and, in one of the taverns out by its tip, befriended a wise-cracking parrot called Jefferson, who clutched his shoulder till the end.

"Badness!" my cabbie cackled as he sped down the drive, shooting a knowing grin in his rearview mirror. "Badness and bad men! Dat's wha gwaan deh."

His tone was winking: a play both on the expectations visitors bring to his island and Jamaicans' mordant image of it. But his words' sense that Jamaica's great product, never mind its rum or reggae, was "bad men" and their doings is hardly rare on an island long dominated by pirates. Jamaica is located some ninety miles to Cuba's south and a similar-length sail west of Hispaniola and was first settled by Taino Indians, from the Yucatán; the island's indigenous paddled dugout canoes onto these croton-covered shores a couple of millennia before Columbus's men, lowering dinghies from his *Pinta* and *Santa Maria*, did the same. It is by a variant of the Taino's name for this lush land (Xamayca: Land of Woods and Water) that Jamaica is still known. Claimed for Spain by Columbus in 1494, the island remained in Spanish hands until it was wrested from their grip by the British in 1655, from which time the island's sheltered proximity to the sea-lanes by which Castile's ships ferried silver from mines in Mexico and Peru, across the Caribbean's aqueous heart, toward Havana and then Seville, meant that Jamaica's first notoriety on the world stage was as a haven for crooks.

So notorious was Port Royal, the privateers' rest where Blackbeard's men came to spend stolen coins on prostitutes and pints, that it became known, as Jamaica's Tourist Board now fondly cites, as the "wickedest city on earth." During one summer month here in 1661, the place's pirate governor, Henry Morgan, granted no fewer than forty new licenses for taverns in a town where the parrots, reported a scandalized Dutchman passing through, "drank from the large stocks of ale with as much alacrity as the drunks."[9] When Morgan's men returned from another raid on Spain's galleons with thousands of coins, in another niblet historians like citing, a group of them "gave a strumpet 500 to

see her naked, and . . . [*sic*] other impieties."[10] Such tales of rakish glamour, if not tawdry gangbangs, survived the centuries to inspire Disney's
Pirates of the Caribbean—and served, long before that, as the setting for a
passion play from which the New World's men of cloth won great mileage. At just past 11 a.m. on June 7, 1692, a massive earthquake struck
Jamaica's southern shore. The act of God rudely woke Port Royal's
rowdies from their hangovers, and liquefied the loose sand on which
their town sat. A massive tsunami overswept the Palisadoes' spit. By
noon, nearly all the buildings of the New World's Sodom, and some
thousands of the inhabitants, lay under the waves.

Today, Port Royal is a forlorn cluster of seaside shacks from whose
owners you can buy delicious roast fish best eaten, while gazing at
Kingston across the harbor's chop, with local pepper sauce and fry
bread called "festival." Back in the 1990s, the government announced
a redevelopment scheme, in partnership with the Walt Disney Corporation and aimed at boosting tourism, that would turn the Palisadoes' tip into a site-specific theme park. Two decades later, there's
nary a replica saloon or plastic parrot souvenir shop here. And absent
those mooted tourist traps, and the deepwater berths Disney wanted
for its cruise ships, the Palisadoes is still best known for the key bit
of infrastructure—Kingston International Airport—to which Jamaica's
émigrés return from their exploits abroad, and that welcomes its non-
tourist foreigners: businessmen like those from my flight, whether from
Milwaukee or Montreal, who fly down to check on their investments
in bauxite or gas, and perhaps to see the island whores still patronized,
three centuries after Port Royal's fall, by men from many lands.

Badness. Certainly, that was part of the story. Especially in the aftermath of the saga that saw Tivoli Gardens' notorious don, Dudus,
deposed. My cabbie, who said his name was Delroy, related that the
government's long-promised report on the massacre had been delayed
again. No one, in any case, imagined that the report would establish the
truth of what had happened. This is a country where asking too many
questions about such things, as Delroy said and journalists often repeat,
"is a good way to get dead."

"How is downtown these days?" I asked. How was Kingston's inner-
city zone of dons and gunplay faring with its kingpin gone?

"Is worse!" he yelled. "Use' to be you could park a car deh—now?
No mon. Who know who in charge, wit di presi him gone?"

"Di presi"? The president: that's what they called the don of dons.
Jamaica's FIRST President: Dudus—that's the title of a book I picked up,

a few days later, at a shop in town.[11] Hard to imagine a better indica-
tor than that, in this city with its ghetto districts named for war-ripped
places like Angola and Gaza, that Jamaica is a "failed state" whose top
gangster's path to power, and to winning his countrymen's esteem, corresponded precisely with their leader's dwindling ability to do the same.
Not only had the gangster won a monopoly on socially sanctioned violence; none of Jamaica's actual heads of state, as that book on Dudus
detailed, had been able to replicate it. They'd also proved considerably less good than the gangsters they'd helped create, in many areas,
at attracting revenue and tending the common good. Now a new set
of leaders, from the PNP, was facing a familiar problem on an island
whose descent into violence, in the 1970s, commenced when it took
on unpayable debts from the International Monetary Fund, that world
institution set up after the war to shore up the Third World's listing
little states and keep global capitalism humming along—but that then
ended up, as those little economies came to grief, playing far larger
roles in their citizens' lives than their elected leaders did.

Delroy passed me a copy of the day's *Gleaner*, Jamaica's main daily. Its
headline could have been from 2001, or '93, or '76: "IMF Visit Raises
Concerns."

The IMF was in town to "evaluate a new loan program . . . to help
Jamaica meet its obligations." Since Jamaica accepted its first IMF loan
in 1973, it has borrowed some US$19 billion. During that time, it has
paid back over $20 billion—and still owes $8 billion more. Most countries carry public debt; the richer ones' deficits make a little Caribbean
island's look Lilliputian. They haven't had to borrow, though, at rates
that have forced Jamaica's budget makers, for years, to spend some 45
percent of their internal revenue paying interest. This math, to a grad-
student freelancer with a wallet full of maxed-out plastic from Visa and
Discover, was familiar. It is also familiar to any member of Jamaica's
political classes born in the past half century. Their government's rising
debt payments, long ago outstripping what it spent on such trifles as
health care and schools, increase by larger degrees each year. (Later that
spring, the government would accept a new "rescue loan" of US$1 bil-
lion to help it "meet its obligations." Its creditors were surely chuffed.
Jamaicans, less so: the loan came with familiar conditions mandating
further cuts in already-gutted social spending.)

"You see dat?" Delroy glared in his rearview mirror. "We all mash'
up! Politician' mash up the country."

He asked my business in Jamaica; I told him.

"I'll tell you something to write about." He proffered his suggestion by saying that listening to the BBC World Service, on his cab's radio, was one of the few bright bits of a job he didn't relish. "You saw what happened in the Falklands?"

I wasn't sure. What of world-newsworthy note had occurred, of late, on those semi-British rocks in the South Atlantic? "You mean when Thatcher invaded?"

"No man! Dem just had a vote! Dey say: We wan' the queen back again."

It was clear from how he said it: his countrymen, he thought, should follow suit.

"You think Jamaicans want to rejoin the empire?" I asked.

"Guarantee!" he shouted in the rearview mirror. "You hold a vote tomorrow, we bring back di queen! Guarantee."

This seemed a stretch. Could the views of the Falklands' shepherds, vis-à-vis their British parents' home, ever match those of a nation founded by Britain's slaves? But here was one Jamaican, anyway, whose vision for Jamaica's good clashed with its leaders' rhetoric about a country where, he told me when I changed the subject, he'd grown up the son of farmer parents who still lived in "a lickle village way past Mandeville." The village was called Good Intent. His surname was Hibbert. Was he related to Toots Hibbert, the reggae singer of Toots & the Maytals fame? "Him me cousin!" Of course he was.

Delroy Hibbert dropped me at my hotel, and, nodding at the bored man in starched shirt and black pants whose job it was to open and close the carpark's creaking gate for guests, bumped away into the night.

* * *

KINGSTON IS SPREAD ACROSS a deep valley wedged between the harbor and the Blue Mountains, to whose slopes its better-off cling. The social geography of Jamaica's capital, like its social order, is divided strictly in two: where "downtown" is comprised of the city's blighted old business district and newer ghettos, "uptown" is defined by its denizens' loftier class position and their condescension. My hotel, if hardly posh digs, was squarely uptown. Hidden up behind the big clapboard house where Bob Marley lived, once he escaped downtown's streets, it sat amid ranch-style homes guarded by barred windows and barking dogs. Its hopeful name—the Prestige—was painted, in badly fading paint, on a cement wall by the gate.

The Prestige's dimly lit lobby was adorned with another version of that airport pantheon. This one featured green construction-paper cutouts of Garvey, Bogle, and Queen Nanny in her kerchief. It looked like it had been crafted by someone's school-age kid for the Jamaica 50 celebration. Such homey touches, along with a big mango tree–shaded patio out back and rates for "fan-only rooms" far cheaper than the cheapest Motel 6 back home, were part of why I remained a loyal patron of a place whose customer base seemed largely comprised, apart from wandering scribes, of Jamaican school kids in town for track meets, defecting Cubans passing through, and the only species of foreign tourist regularly spotted in Kingston: Japanese reggae nuts. A few of these, dreadlocked and murmuring in Japanese, sat huddled under the mango tree out back, perhaps plotting a visit to Marley's old house nearby (it's now a museum to his memory) or having just returned. They were sipping Red Stripes around plates of Mideastern *kibbe* served up here by reassuringly thickset Jamaican women who staff the Prestige and blare gospel in the lobby from a boom box that they turn up even louder when the place's surly Syrian owners aren't on-site. (The Prestige, like much property here that's not owned by Jamaica's whites or Chinese, is owned by descendants of a Semitic merchant class who arrived from Lebanon and Palestine and Syria and elsewhere, but who are all called "Syrian" now.) I dropped my bag in my fan-cooled room in front of a xeroxed sign, taped to the wall, that said "No Foot on Wall Surface" and headed out to dinner.

The Global Reggae Conference had wrapped for the day. Some friends in attendance, though, were debriefing over Chinese food up the road. I arrived at the restaurant to find Herbie Miller, the director of the Jamaican Music Museum, surrounded by a tableful of northern visitors. Herbie was an accomplished music scholar and music-biz vet; he had the savoir faire of many in that world, and the dark skin and beautiful bone structure of many of his countrymen. He began his career managing the affairs of a few reggae greats and then, during a decade's stint in New York, those of jazz heavies like Max Roach. Now his workdays were spent inveigling his bosses in government for nonexistent funds, to build his museum, and liaising, by night, with people like his companions here: foreign "collectors" and untenured researchers whose obsessions with Jamaica's music, and with its records, have made them the main chroniclers of its history in books and films. Herbie greeted me warmly, and I said hello to a reggae deejay and filmmaker from Minnesota, né Brad but who went by "Moses" here, whom

I'd met years before under the mango tree at the Prestige. Herbie introduced a shaggy-haired white man with deep smile lines around his eyes, with whom he was engaged, when I arrived, in a sotto voce chat (their subject, I gleaned, was a high-profile collector and "reggae archivist" in LA). Herbie's interlocutor told us, over beef and broccoli, how he'd had two guiding passions over the past couple of decades. The first was helping Bob Marley's mum win her fair share of Bob's estate. The second, which was occupying all his time now, was working to "free up the herb" about whose benefits Bob sang. He handed me a business card. It listed an address in Omaha, and cited his head counsel position with a group advocating the medical uses of marijuana, called Patients Out of Time—POT.

Not every devotee of reggae studies is a pothead "from foreign": the inchoate discipline is very much a field forged and embraced by the serious scholars at the University of the West Indies, who had founded its Reggae Studies Centre and were hosting this conference. Their endeavors, moreover, were embraced by Jamaican society at large. That weekend, they launched a companion book to the conference. An anthology of essays on "the globalization of reggae" (its "global dispersal and adaptation," that is, "in diverse local contexts"), this was the kind of abstruse volume whose launch would struggle to attract a dozen shabby Brie munchers to a bookshop in Berkeley. Here, its publishers' fete was held at a flashy nightspot run by Jamaica's hottest modeling agency. *The Gleaner* dispatched a photographer and ran a full-page spread on the event the next day that reminded me of *Vanity Fair*'s caption-heavy coverage of its own Oscars party. Local pride informs such fetes: "This lickle island changed the world." But that pride, and this storyline, comes with an inborn tension between Jamaicans' determination to shape their culture's serious study (and its crass exploitation) for themselves, on the one hand, and a deep awareness, on the other, that reggae's viability, as both pop genre and scholarly field, depends on the abiding love of foreigners. Reggae Studies, and the idea of "authentic culture" on which its subject music is based, is predicated on its rhythms' capacity for getting people far from reggae's wellspring, most in countries far richer than Jamaica, to nod along.

Lucky for reggae, then, the music's sheer ability to do so, decades now after Bob Marley's end, continues to astonish. For the culture maven given to pondering this music's persistent grip on everyone from Iowa frat boys to the 100,000 Spaniards who attend the Rototom reggae fest on the Costa Brava each summer, there are many ways to explain how and why, after Jimmy Cliff's *The Harder They Come* soundtrack became a UK hit in 1973, reggae went global. This music's inspired makers were youths impressed by '60s rock but still in love with '50s doo-wop. They found a needful way to wed the latter's sweet harmonies to the former's bass-and-drums-led edge; they offered a digestible soundtrack, sung in English, to colonial rule's end across Africa and the Third World. They gave the black people of those lands, as a Kingston guitarist who toured the continent told me they said to him in Kenya, a model for "how to be at once black and modern." Reggae's stars evoked the same elixir of electrified primitivity that Jimi Hendrix, with his wild-haired-ethnic-with-a-Stratocaster act, caught at Woodstock. This was the territory they claimed, in the confusing years after the counterculture's end, in global youth culture's matrix. And that's no small reason, along with reggae's espousing the '70s' great narcotic as a sacrament, why their figurehead's face came to be plastered, alongside Che Guevara's, in coffee shops everywhere. A latte-complected oval, ringed by regal ropes of hair, that singer's visage became that of the soul rebel who condoned, from his post on the dorm-room wall, our seasons of don't-worry-about-a-thing experimentation: the pothead as revolutionary.

Of course, simple Marley worship, for serious reggae fans, is naturally passé: every one of them can tell you, and will, that by the time Bob's locks grew long enough to take those photos on the posters, his finest work was past. The Marley tunes they love best were made with the two old friends, Peter Tosh and Bunny Wailer, with whom he grew up in Jamaica before becoming a slicked-up Londoner, and were produced by Kingston's mad Rasta genius of the mixing board, Lee "Scratch" Perry. To roots reggae diehards, "Three Little Birds" is late-period dross. But such Marley tunes, no matter, had likely served as the gateway for people like Minnesota Moses and the Nebraska pot lawyer who we came, that night, to call "Ganja Man." These characters' backstories no doubt featured scenes like my own teen ritual of tromping to a big farmer's field each summer of high school, along with a few thousand reggae nuts and other partyers committing the deep cosmetological sin of wearing dreadlocks while white, to dance along to whichever of Marley's kids the Vermont Reggae Festival's promoters could book that year. Such scenes, as one lived them, may have felt endearing or absurd. But replicated around the world, in many times and spots over recent decades, they provided the kernel of entrée into a larger culture whose makers did things with the English of the King James Bible, and the magic of amplified bass, that had a way of blowing earnest teens' heads clean off. Not only did Marley and his righteous peers set the muse of history to a beguiling beat. (Reggae's guiding question was posed by the singer Burning Spear: "Do you remember the days of slavery?") They looked cool doing it. And they vested every mundane speech act, whether describing being in trouble (that was to be "under heavy manners") or expressing impending arrival ("soon come," they said) with Old Testament weight. Never mind the confounding tenets of a Rasta faith that held up a vainglorious dictator who died in 1975 as their immortal God. Who could resist a culture that turned talking with your friends into "reasoning with your brethren"?

Roots reggae determined to square two primal passions—for righteous politics and good art—that the grown-up world often doesn't think can be squared. Its makers ticked a lot of teenage boxes. Many of its more ardent fans, through a hashy haze, are still ticking them. But as those fans devoted enough to come all the way to the source perhaps knew, one reason this world doesn't merely reward further study, but can bear the weight of academese, is that the story of how Jamaican music emerged on the world's stage is a history perhaps unexcelled in what it can teach about the larger exigencies of recorded sound, and their power, in the postwar age. That story, as classically told, begins on a sleepy island whose music-scape is made up of hymns sung in clapboard churches and folk ditties strummed by *mento* men on its docks. Its action commences after World War II, as the island's countrypeople begin crowding to Kingston's slums. There, their sonic lives are transformed. Firstly, by the fact that this English-speaking island is in range of the new fifty-thousand-watt signals of AM radio stations in New Orleans and Miami that beam Fats Domino and Louis Jordan out over the Gulf; and second, by the inspired Kingston entrepreneurs who sense an urbanizing people's thirst for such sounds and invent an institution—the "sound system"—to provide them. The "sound system men," with their grandiloquent sobriquets like Duke and King, attach turntables to huge speaker towers, which they mount on trucks, from whose beds they spin records and sing-speak, over the beats, of the day's news and boasts. They grant amplified sound perhaps a larger role, in Kingston's streets, earlier than anywhere on the planet, in the making of social life—and, if you were unlucky enough to challenge a leading deejay and lose, social death.

Sound clash! That's what the deejays crow over the R&B 45s they fly to America to find in the '50s, digging in crates in Chicago and Houston to return with discs whose labels they scratch off to hide their names from rivals. Scattering seeds that their emigrant kids, up in New York, will sprout as hip-hop, the sound system men also reach the logical decision, in their drive to best the competition and as their sources dry up, that they should make records themselves. Local musicians, tweaking the boogie-woogie they love, forge a buoyant new music—"ska"—by sounding the upbeats its tempos leave silent. A generation of Kingston kids become singing stars—and find, in ska, a sound to then tweak and slow further. "Rocksteady," as their next rhythm's called, is then transformed once more, by savants of four-track recording like Scratch Perry, into the beat that Toots Hibbert names in his hit single "Do the Reggay" in 1968. It's at this point, with the help of Jamaica's émigrés in the cultural capitals of London and New York, *The Harder They Come*, and a sandy-haired Jamaican son of privilege, Chris Blackwell, who has the foresight, when a young Bob Marley strides into his office, to know that this ragged yardie was a star, that reggae goes global.

But the larger saga of "Jamaican music, a' yard and abroad," didn't end in the '70s. It has moved on, since that rootsy apogee, from the Rastas' sanctimonies to the stripped-down sex songs of "lover's rock," and the rat-a-tat *riddims* of the producers Sly and Robbie; to the "slack" sex songs of King Yellowman and Lady Saw; to the still-faster, still-rougher, all-in-patois sounds of the modern "dancehall," to whose pulse Kingston's youth thrill today. An aggressively local sound, recorded in such poor quality as to never be Grammy-worthy, dancehall's records are sung in local diction unintelligible to foreigners. But its foremost exponents, from the still-active trickster feminist Lady Saw (her first big hit was a sex ditty called "Stab Out the Meat") to the enigmatic Vybz Kartel (a gruff-voiced wraith with bleach-whitened skin who was jailed in 2011 after a charred body was found in his yard), still attract the ears of pop and hip-hop producers, and hip kids everywhere, looking for *what's next*, and giving Global Reggae's exegetes here plenty to chew on.

This, in other words, is its own complete world, complex and full. And at the University of the West Indies that weekend, that world's various aspects and characters, from ska's greatest horn players to Vybz Kartel's authored-in-prison book, *Voice of the Jamaican Ghetto*, were the subjects of panel talks.[12] But if reggae is a world, it is also a world with a king, around whose story and model the whole culture can often still feel arranged. There is one figure, after all, to which this music owes the world knowing it exists: everyone here has a Bob Story. And the conference's keynote speaker, whom my companions from the Dragon Court, with a hundred-odd others, went to see speak the next day, was a figure whose identity and livelihood had derived, for forty years, from his having been as close to Bob as anyone. Alan "Skill" Cole, who earned his nickname for his prowess as a footballer, addressed us in UWI's open-air lecture hall. He reminisced about his days living with Marley in that big clapboard home on Hope Road that now houses the Marley museum. "Me and Bob," Skill said, "lived a life consistent with being a good athlete." His words were underscored by his healthy white locks and lithe physique. "We would wake up around four-thirty, five, and train," Skill said. "We'd go to the studio; then go sell records; come back, play some football, and, in the nighttime, write some music."

It was hard to say how interesting Skill's crowd found these revelations there at the Global Reggae Conference. Either way, his talk served these prideful experts with a welcome prompt, that afternoon, to spend some ensuing hours discussing what it really meant, being "Bob's closest spar"—a title, in Skill's case, tied to his notorious habit of turning up with Marley at radio stations or business meetings where they needed a song played or deal done, with a big baseball bat he rather liked swinging. This tidbit was affirmed by Moses and others, whose knowing looks underscored a larger truth about "Jamdown": that in the 1970s and today, bad men were the ones with *respeck*. That famous peace prophet Bob Marley, like all those who succeed in rising from the ghetto here, knew this well. He also knew the bad men themselves. And he too had wielded their world's stock-in-trade—violence—to make his way out of Kingston's Trench Town ghetto, and into that big uptown home, once shared with Skill Cole, up behind which Global Reggae's devotees, returning to the Prestige after Skill's speech on Marley's authentic life, went to parse its aftermath.

* * *

HERBIE HADN'T COME ALONG. He had business, pertinent to Brand Jamaica, with the Russian ambassador: at the World Track Championships in Moscow, he hoped to mount an exhibition on Jamaican music. Ganja Man was present, though. And he served the role of wizened elder well. Settling into a chair beneath the mango tree, he opened a plastic tackle box and, murmuring something about the "endocannabinoid system," pulled out a thick spliff. "I've been coming to Jamdown since '78," he said, pushing a forelock from his eyes. "I know the runnings here." He lit his spliff. And then, drawing deeply, he began telling stories of his dealings with the famously turbulent Marley estate. In one such, he recalled how Bob's estranged wife, Rita—a craven operator, to hear most tell it—forged her dead man's signature to empty his cash accounts in the Tortugas by writing "Bob Marley" (he only ever signed his name "Robert") on a dotted line. Another recounted how the only way he'd been able to help Bob's mum, Cedella Booker, gain anything from Bob's estate was by helping her become the legal guardian of one of his kids. (This was Rohan, the Marley son who gained notoriety first as a football player at the University of Miami and then for his long relationship with the musician Lauryn Hill.)

If Jamaican society can feel like a place drawn in rings around Mother Booker's son, the family he left behind naturally occupies a prideful, if pitiable, place: three decades into his heirs' often-tawdry struggle to live off Bob's memory, unhelped by his having refused to sign a will, his kids have helped sell concerns ranging from Marley brand coffee to Marley brand headphones and Marley's Mood energy drinks. Much more interesting than Marley's family to me were figures more peripheral to his life but central to his culture. And on the Prestige's patio that night, Moses and Ganja Man discussed a few of these, hatching plans that would result that weekend in a series of adventures that turned Kingston into a living museum. The museum's rooms included a Rotary Club gym where Marley's close friend Ernie Smith, sporting the round belly and waist-long locks of an aging dread, mouthed the chorus to his classic "We de People" ("Are we building a nation? / Or are we building a hut?"); a shaded front porch, out in the suburb of Portmore, where we met a bespectacled octogenarian, known as Mr. Edwards to his neighbors but whom Minnesota Moses knew as "King" Edwards, owner of one of the "big three" sound systems in the '50s (and who happily recounted the Greyhound journeys he'd taken to find records in America, posing for photos with some of his old 45s with their labels scratched off); and the famous "locals beach" at Hellshire, out past the entrance to Kingston Harbour, where Jamaicans go to "play domino" or laze on scrapwood lounge chairs by the waves. As Ganja Man rolled his car onto the beach, he concluded what must have been his eighth soliloquy of the weekend, on the delicate workings of the endocannabinoid system. A pair of hustlers, waving a shining fresh parrotfish in Ganja Man's windshield, absorbed his protests that he was just here to see a friend but still insisted on guiding him, waiving their usual fee, to a parking spot in the sand.

Hellshire is always worth the trip. That day, though, we'd come on a mission: to visit with an old friend of Marley's and Ganja Man's with a potent bit role in reggae's golden era. Countryman had first come to Marley's attention, our pied piper had recounted on the drive, when a young Bob had heard of a fellow Rasta, out by Hellshire, with a gift for expounding the virtues of what the Rastas called *ital livity* (pure living), and for exampling its benefits. The first time Marley met Countryman, Ganja Man recalled, Countryman swam so far out from Hellshire that he disappeared. (He showed up again that night in time to drum and smoke with Bob.) Countryman became a kind of resident mystic for Marley's minders, and his doing so resulted in an eponymous film produced by Chris Blackwell and directed by a fellow Jamaican white boy, Dickie Jobson, with similar love for Rasta *livity*. In *Countryman* (1982), the star plays himself. The film begins with him fishing under a full moon. He sees a flaming prop plane crash into Hellshire Swamp and, rushing to the scene, finds a pair of pretty white kids in the wreckage. He saves their lives and deposits them by his campfire, before then waging a convoluted struggle against conniving "agents of Babylon," who are hunting them down. At one point, Countryman runs the twenty miles into town, loping over hill and bush to the one-drop pulse of Marley's "Natural Mystic." Such sounds and images, if not the film's patchy plot, helped *Countryman* win cult-classic status. But its success, Ganja Man said, also had the less cheery effect for its star of introducing him to cocaine. Countryman spent much of the '80s wasted on blow; he'd lost the house and the Datsun his film work had won him. Now he'd wound up squatting back by the beach where he'd once impressed Marley with his feats as a swimmer.

"Bredren!" Country called out as we approached, rising to embrace Ganja Man from in front of his zinc-and-wood hovel. "Long time!" He hugged his old friend's chest. He was tiny. He wore a white undershirt, bright against his copper-dark East Indian skin. Ganja Man looked Countryman over and, apparently satisfied that he wasn't in a bad way with rum or the white drug most Rastas hate, reminisced about some good times they'd shared, riding Jet Skis in Negril. Country led us to the beach. I negotiated with one of the fish hustlers to see about roasting one of his parrotfish for this summit. "Me live natural," Country said, pulling out scrap-wood stools for his guests. "No current deh; jus' livity." No electricity here, just life. Which consisted, here, of a five-foot-nothing Rasta man who crouched over his sun-blackened feet and had lost little of the wiry charisma that had convinced his fellows to turn him into a film that, with its righteous rebel hero and backdrop of violence, perhaps begot by the henchmen of *CIA-ga* (as the Rastas dubbed Seaga), distilled much of reggae's appeal. Countryman accepted his old friend's offer of a spliff. And then he turned to his guests with a half smile. He fixed us with piercing eyes flecked the same yellow hue as his matted white locks and bid us sit.

The disquisition he delivered, over the next hour and more, would have been impressive even without the smoke. But what made it true theater was Countryman's lady. She introduced herself as Mama Delsy and stood off to the side, in the Rasta way, with kind eyes and poverty's gnarled teeth. But from there, she punctuated Countryman's speech, on life and livity as Country sees it, with the affirmations or annotations of a Greek chorus. "Seen!" she'd exclaim, when she agreed; "Evr'y time!" was another favorite. Country began with a riff on "how all of us, when you think on it, are going twenty-four thousand miles an hour, spinning roun' the sun." ("Plenty fas'! Ev'ry time!") He told us how he pled in court with its judge ("Am I innocent or guilty? That's what I'm here to find out!"), and delivered a cogent excoriation of the "discomfortable livity" ("Discomfortable!") to which Bashar Assad in Syria was subjecting his people—while Countryman's hovel had no current, he kept his battery-powered radio tuned to the BBC. He made no mention of Jamaica 50.

Sitting there with these avid pilgrims and their penniless oracle was tricky. Who, as the song goes, was zooming who? In the story of reggae culture's wider appeal, the imaginary Noble Savage has always hovered. But the bearing of our host, wholly undiminished by this meeting, abounded with the proud will to perform, and create a public self that one grows so used to encountering here. When Warren Weir won London bronze, Jamaicans' Twitter feeds echoed with his catchphrase—Nuh English, straight patwa!—and with the suggestion, too, that someone should sell T-shirts touting it. Some awareness of this entrepreneurial spirit, certainly, informed Brand Jamaica's boosters. Whether their addled plan to fix all this in place, and monetize it, could ever work was unclear. Either way, Jamaicans would continue evincing the words of Country's old friend from the beach. "We the survivors," as Marley sang, "the Black survivors." Countryman continued to listen to the radio as we ate our parrotfish. The news of a meteor crashing into Russia prompted a reflection about how "we create in darkness; we sleep in darkness; and when you dead, you go back to darkness." His chorus agreed: "Seen!"

CHAPTER 2

BADNESS

IT WOULD BE FOLLY to suggest that Kingston, at least on its surface, is a lovely place. "The center resembles the nastiest of London outskirts," wrote Patrick Leigh Fermor in 1948, "and the outskirts are equal to the most dreary of West Indian slums."[1] He'd be more damning now. Kingston has little in the way of the shaded squares or comely spires that describe the Catholic capitals of Spain's or Portugal's New World empires—places designed, at least in part, to exude the majesty of those imperiums' hearts. Unlike Havana or Rio, Kingston was never intended to be a capital of anything but its makers' crass commerce in sugar and people. Back in the island's Spanish days, Jamaica had the makings of a stately capital. Sited in a sheltered river valley a dozen miles to Kingston's northeast, the Spanish founded Villa de la Vega in 1534. The town sitting there now, which Jamaicans call Spanish Town, still has a few colonial buildings redolent of Seville. Outside one such, visiting academics hop from taxis to sift crumbling records in Jamaica's National Archives. But for most Jamaicans, the phrase "Spanish Town" evokes images not of Conquistadors Past but of a dusty suburb reached by the busy and slum-choked Spanish Town Road, which runs between here and the core of the city whose great modern laureate, Peter Tosh, dubbed "Killsome."

No, Jamaicans don't have a beautiful capital to love. They have Kingston, a concrete jungle founded across the harbor after Port Royal's fall. It was built from an old farmer's field with little rhyme or foresight, along a sloping road leading up from the waterfront and toward Halfway Tree, now Kingston's symbolic heart but then a crossroads named for a huge cotton tree that shaded a popular pausing place, in olden days, on the route between Saint Andrew's hinterland and its port. By the early twentieth century, the blocks between the sea and Parade, old downtown's central square, were lined with Syrian- or Chinese-owned shops selling armchairs and egg creams. Down by the water, Kingston's old downtown even boasted the Myrtle Bank Hotel, a handsome white-columned pile to rival Havana's Hotel Nacional. Never what one could call prosperous, though, downtown fared even worse under Jamaican rule than it had under the British. In 1960, the Myrtle Bank was razed to make way for the vast port complex now containing the notorious "free zone," surrounded by razor wire and created by the IMF, where foreign conglomerates like Hanes and Levi's pay Jamaican women US$6 a day to sew underwear that's then loaded onto nearby ships. After independence, downtown's fate was sealed when Kingston's monied classes hatched a plan to move its key functions elsewhere. That plan unfolded on the grounds of the old Knutsford Park racetrack, just beyond Halfway Tree and near the foot of uptown's hills, and resulted in what's now called New Kingston: a soulless thicket of medium-rise banks and expensive hotels where the business of the country, and of governing it, takes place. With that monstrosity allied to choking traffic on treeless boulevards cutting across it, the greater KMA—Kingston Metropolitan Area—is an urban planner's bad dream.

But as is the way with such things, downtown's abandonment by its rich also fed the ragged charm now exerted by the old byways, like King and Orange streets, along which I strolled a few days after that visit to Countryman, passing discount stores whose facades haven't been changed since 1962, along sidewalks, crowded with "higglers" peddling bananas and flip-flops, that buzz with the feel of West African market towns. Not long before the witching hour, at dusk, when the higglers disappear down potholed side streets that lead into the notorious garrisons bleeding westward from Parade, or hop into route taxis taking them back to country homes, I walked down the stretch of Orange Street once known as beat street. It earned its name for the density of old record shops and spaces where the old sound system men, rolling blaring speaker towers here most nights of the week, once ruled. I stopped by the crumbling facade of Forrester's Hall: this is where King Edwards's Giant Sounds used to clash with Duke Reid's Trojans. The front gate was locked, but some shadowy figures, inside the now-roofless space, were swinging hammers at wooden planks. "What are you making there?" I asked through the gate.

They replied over their shoulders: "Coffin."

There's a saying here: "Inna yard, dead everywhere." But in neighborhoods with few weddings and lots of funerals to dress up for, street dances still remain, sixty years after the sound system's birth, the thumping core of Jamaican culture. Most nights of the week, deejays from leading systems like Stone Love and Kilimanjaro erect their speaker towers by side streets or parking lots to boom dancehall hits at volumes evidently designed to test Marley's adage, from "Trench Town Rock," that when "music hits, you feel no pain." Since Bob's day, the cadences have quickened. The sounds have grown rougher. So, too, has the dance style known as "daggering," through which Jamaica's young, pantomiming rough sex in clothes, further the old process of transforming the body from an instrument of pain into one of pleasure, in this ex-slave society, amid an air of barely suppressed violence. In the early sound system era, the dances weren't guarded, as one of the first I attended was, by glowering sixteen-year-olds holding Uzis in the dark. But if this culture's sounds and settings have grown more extreme, its guiding tensions, I thought as I approached the old Ward Theatre on Parade, have remained the same. This was where, back in 1964, an eighteen-year-old Bob Marley, with the group he'd formed with his friends Peter and Bunny, had their first big gig. The Wailing Wailers had won an audition with Clement "Sir Coxson" Dodd, a leading sound system man, and signed for Dodd's label, Studio One. The first Wailers record Dodd released, "Simmer Down," had shot to the top of Kingston's charts, and stayed. Addressing themselves to the "rude boys" with whom they passed their teens on Parade, the Wailers called for calm amid the heady days of their nation's newfound freedom. "Simmer down," they sang on that first hit. "Oh control your temper."

Simmer down, for the battle will be hotter
Simmer down, and you won't get no supper
Simmer down, and you know you bound to suffer
Simmer down, simmer, simmer, simmer right down

Here in the Ward in 1964, when the young Wailers performed "Simmer Down" in public for the first time, they affected shiny suits and shinier dance moves. Loud claps and yelps filled the hall. The raining applause was joined, Peter Tosh would recall, by a shower of coins. "Me look at some two and six-pence piece lick me head," he said years later. "So I stop sing and just go and pick them up . . . two pockets full!" For young singers being paid a pittance, if they were lucky, by their label, this was a lot of coin. Sadly for them, they didn't get to keep it. "Before I come offstage," Tosh said, "it was begged out. Every man in the audience come beg it back."[2]

Five decades on, the Ward's white-and-blue facade was crumbling; dirty paint peeled from the walls. I asked a large woman out front, squatting by a rack of plastic sunglasses with too-large Ray-Ban logos stenciled on their sides, what had befallen the Ward. "Hurricane!" she said, looking up briefly before returning to her wares.

"Which?" I asked. "When?"

"Gustav," she said to my shins. That storm had blown up the Caribbean in 2008, and taken care of the Ward's roof and once-shining marquee. Lord knew when it would be fixed. I handed her a bill for JA$500 ("Continued devaluation of JA's currency," said the IMF, "is good for the economy"), and slid a pair of eyeshades—they'd cost US$5—over my nose before continuing across Parade, in the afternoon's fading glare. I walked down King before pausing, outside the courthouse, by a large monument. The statue included a big obsidian head, ten feet tall. Onto its cheeks were welded two brass tears. Its base was engraved, like Maya Lin's wall in Washington, with rows of names and numbers—Joshua Hill, 6; Shanna-Kay Robinson, 1; Tia Murray, 15. The numbers were ages. The statue's larger title, engraved on its base, explained its meaning in this town whose tabloids are filled, every day, with stories about the bad things that happen among destitution-damaged people trying to rear kids in an "afflicted yard." The memorial said this: "In Memory of Children Killed Under Violent/Tragic Circumstances."

The phrase and its punctuation (what was up with the slash?) were striking, for its conflation of two concepts—violence and tragedy—sometimes linked in life, but often not. The monument was also striking, though, for what it said about this movie-mad town whose young have had a shortage of neither experience with violence nor the narrative conventions of tragedy. The theaters where Kingston's ska stars shone, back in the '60s, were also the movie houses where "rudies" flocked to shoot-'em-up Westerns and joined the action by shooting their pistols at the screen. Perhaps the second most memorable of early Wailers gigs, after their debut at the Ward, was at the Palace Theater, now vanished but long near where I stood. A few months after "Simmer Down" hit, they headlined a packed Christmas concert. Again, coins pummeled the stage. But just as they kicked off "Simmer Down," the house lights went dark. The blackout was citywide. The crowd, though, didn't know. A notorious rudie called Big Junior, his head swollen from a cameo appearance in the film version of sometime-Jamaican Ian Fleming's novel *Dr. No*, smashed his wooden chair on the floor. The Wailers escaped the ensuing riot only by barricading themselves in a backstage toilet. In a young country where the rule of law was as inchoate as its electrical grid, a song urging self-control may have made street-tough youths into singing stars. But it was their town's outlaws, like Big Junior, who remained its favorite folk heroes.

* * *

"BADNESS! AND BAD MEN." They're still around, in this weary, wary city where plastic shopping sacks are called "scandal bags" and where the only sure way to have regular electricity is to live in the precinct of a big enough bad man that he extorts or pays for "yuh current," and your fealty, himself. But downtown, by now, is not the sort of place where people can flock to old-style bijous or shoot their pistols at their screens: there are no cinemas, and few businesses targeting anyone with real disposable income farther down than Half Way Tree. When I went to a film one night, it wasn't being screened in a cinema, but in a more homey venue on downtown's western edge. Earlier that year, the long-awaited documentary *Marley* had reached cinemas here and worldwide. The film I headed downtown to see was related, but different. *Marley* had been the result of a decade-long saga that began as a project helmed by Martin Scorsese, and then, once he'd wearied of dealing with Rita and the gang, chewed up another fancy director—Jonathan Demme. Finally the film was completed by a young Scotsman called Kevin Macdonald. Macdonald was previously best known for *The Last King of Scotland*, a drama about the mad Ugandan dictator Idi Amin. His achievement with *Marley* was to allow all the living principals in the great man's story to share their refractive memories of his life and end. It included such nuggets as Rita, sitting poolside in regal Asante robes, informing us that Bob's cancer "came from his white blood." Macdonald had his pick, with the family's full support, of a great array of archival footage of Bob in concert and repose. There was one key bit of old tape, though, that he hadn't been able to use. And it was to see this tape, edited together in a new film called *The Making of a Legend*, that I went all the way downtown, to an abandoned old building by the water that someone had converted into a kind of extra-rootsy art space for events like this.

I parked by the building and headed up to the second floor, arriving to find the film's maker, a onetime paramour of Marley's, standing at the front of the room. She was now a tired-looking sixtysomething woman, dressed in made-in-China Rasta regalia. She explained the story of her film. Forty years before, she'd been a young model enjoying a fling with a hot young star. She had lugged a primitive Super 8 camcorder into their briefly overlapping lives. For thirty-odd years, the resulting footage was mislaid in a friend's Toronto garage. When it was found, she had refused to part with it or license it to anyone else. Instead, she had made the film we were about to screen in this space that a white woman from foreign had turned into a wood-working studio for local youths and, rumor said, a place for seducing them. Who knew if it was true. But Kingston is like that: leave no good turn unpunished. The space, in any case, was cool. And though the tech, with dodgy wires hooked up to tinny-sounding laptop speakers, was wanting, the footage was something.

There, flickering on the wall, were the three members of the trinity—Bunny, Peter, Bob—right On the Cusp. When our filmmaker met them, the Wailers had just released *Catch a Fire*, the 1973 album into whose raw reggae mix their new producer, Chris Blackwell, hoping to win them careers in England and beyond, had overdubbed electric rock guitars. The album was received with rapture by the critics. In *The Village Voice*, Robert Christgau wrote that "half these songs are worthy of St. John the Divine." But the jury was still very out as to whether Blackwell's scheme to turn these raw yardies into rock stars would actually come off. Back on their home island, they were writing songs for a new record. The girl who photographed them doing so was a sometime publicist and full-time hustler. She had beat Marley and Co. to London by a few years, and her light brown glamour had won her film work and a role with Blackwell's Island Records. She had returned to Jamaica, with Bob, to shoot video and stills of the group for their label (her photo of a shirtless Bob smoking his morning spliff came to adorn *Catch a Fire*'s cover), in that big clapboard home, Island House, that Marley would later own but that was now known as the Kingston HQ of Blackwell's label.

We watched the trio lazing about, their matted Afros just turning into dreadlocks. This was the moment of grace before the Wailers blew up—and split apart. Captured with one of the first-ever camcorders, our filmmaker's images showed the men lying around with guitars. Playing riffs back and forth. Trading lines. The moments of creative spark that we who are interested in art making wonder at. Also, plenty of stoned conversation whose stoned profundity maybe wasn't so profound ("Belief can live and belief can kill," we watched Bob intone), but that we nodded along to, nonetheless. Marley's charisma-filled cheekbones leapt from the screen: the man, as this PR flack and all his brand's builders learned, never took a bad picture. The same, alas, couldn't be said of the film's maker, whose sad need to insert herself into the narrative found her ludicrously staged, in between these lovely spells of footage, by an ornate Victorian mantel in a chunky necklace, recounting how she helped her lover write "I Shot the Sheriff." The coughs and fidgeting in the audience during these passages were loud. But for us to whom the friendships captured by the old footage were the subject of obsessive thought, the moments of filial love were thrilling. Here they were, the lanky brown-skinned Marley and the darker Tosh trying, as friends do, to make each other laugh. The looks exchanged between chords were all the more poignant for us watching from the future. Mere months later, Marley would step onto a path, at the front of a band that could have only one front man, that made him into the kind of rock star in England he and his minders envisioned. Soon enough, he won the kind of fame that made him a figure who belonged as much to the world as to his friends.

After Bob blew up, Peter and Bunny did enjoy their own fame. Each made great records. Tosh, with the help of rabble-rousing hits like his pro-ganja ode "Legalize It," became a figure even more dearly embraced in Jamaica than Marley. Many still call him "Jamaica's greatest music man." It's not hard, playing back Tosh classics like "Stop This Train" and "400 Years," to understand why. Peter, who much more closely resembled most Jamaicans than Bob, also came much closer than his pal, during what remains Kingston's most-famous-ever concert, to voicing most Jamaicans' feelings on their postcolonial state. The One Love Peace Concert, convened between the bloody election seasons of 1976 and 1980, was aimed to convince members of the capital's PNP- and JLP-affiliated gangs to stop shooting each other. The event is best recalled for Marley's enjoining the party's two leaders, Seaga and Manley, to join hands above his head during an extra-long rendition of "Jamming," to "show the people that we got to unite." That was the night's takeaway image. But it was another moment, little recalled beyond Jamaica, that distilled the lasting distinction between two figures who have resounded since as rough equivalents of Martin Luther King and Malcolm X: one an inspired conciliator with a prophet's smile (never mind how key the juxtaposition of "screwface" scowl and lover's grin were to Bob's appeal); the other an icon of black rage, glowering behind dark glasses (never mind the goofy strain central to Peter's manner and hits). On the night Marley provided his great tableau of music's peace-making power, Tosh capped his own set by lighting an enormous spliff onstage. He defied the "shitstem" to arrest him.

"I am not a politician," he intoned before the bloodiest election yet, "but I suffer the consequences."

* * *

PETER MACKINTOSH WAS BORN in a small seaside village in Westmoreland. He was reared, like most Jamaicans, by his mother. He learned to play piano and sing, like most of the country's musicians, in her church. Peter's father was little seen in the village of Belmont ("a bad boy, a rascal," Tosh described him, who "just go around and have a million and one children").[3] Gainful work was scarce too. Peter left the provinces to make a life in Kingston's slums. When he met Bob and Bunny, his fellow Wailers-to-be, he was selling sugarcane juice from a cart by Parade. When his life later ended under decidedly "violent/ tragic circumstances" (he was shot in his home at the age of forty-one), his body was brought back to the sleepy town where he was born. Belmont is a teeny village by the turquoise sea, not far from the old Spanish slave port of Savanna-la-Mar, whose most notable site is its favorite son's tomb. Tosh's mausoleum is a cement box painted red, gold, and green. It sits by the water, on the road that hugs Jamaica's sleepy south coast, in a shaded yard by the tidy little house that Peter bought his mother in the 1970s. It's a quiet tourist trap, most days, where the young men who work the rum shop by the yard's gate rouse themselves from their dominoes, when the few Tosh-obsessed Germans and Japanese who make it here turn up, to demand ten dollars apiece from visitors. Marley's tomb, across the island in St. Ann Parish, is patronized not only by scores of such pilgrims daily but also by busloads of casual vacationers who sign up, in plush north coast resorts nearby, to visit the reggae king's home. Belmont, by contrast, remains outside the tourist circuit. But as perhaps befits its great son's contrasting place in Jamaica's memory, it does serve, as I saw visiting one Peter Tosh Day, as a pilgrimage site for Jamaicans. More especially, for believers of the born-in-Jamaica faith that island boosters claim is "the only major world religion born in the twentieth century"—in whose pantheon Peter resides, ever blacker and just a touch *badder* than Bob, too—it is the resting place of an enduring saint.

Rolling into Belmont, I turned my rental car's radio to 107.1, Irie FM. The deejay said that Jamaica's "roots radio" had been broadcasting live from Peter's gravesite since 6 a.m. "Tha sisdren and bredren," he said, had been arriving since dawn. He introduced a snippet of recorded speech from Tosh's Red X Tapes, a posthumously released spoken-word album whose digressions Peter's admirers know by heart. "I don't smoke marijuana." His baritone filled the car. "Marijuana is a girl from Cuba. I smoke HERB." Tosh pronounced the last word with a hard H, emphasizing the sacrament it was. "Lawmakers make every name illegal, to incriminate the underprivileged. . . . But herb, and music, is the healing of the nation. Key to the doors of inspiration. Without herb, any other thing cause distortion, and confusion. Seen?"

Seen. Into Peter's yard and through its gates, the sisdren and bredren streamed. Elder Rastas in army fatigues and colorful headwraps. A tattooed young woman wearing a gold necklace whose shape spelled "BAD." A young man, shirtless and resting a flagpole on his shoulder, carrying a great banner in Rasta's colors of red, gold, and green. On a fence outside, someone had painted a big marijuana leaf, captioned with Tosh's most famous lyric. "Legalize It." Right in front of it, a uniformed policewoman and policeman stood in their colonial-looking black caps. Jamaica's anti-cannabis laws are far stricter than most spring breakers here think. But this pair seemed little interested in enforcing them. I stepped into the yard to see a striking woman, six feet tall and wearing burlap robes accented with Rasta-colored trim. In her arm she cradled an immense bundle, like a baby, of pungent green herb. On a dais nearby, Mutabaruka, the deejay from Irie FM, wore his own robes to describe how in the 1760s the veterans of Jamaica's Maroons journeyed to Haiti and played crucial roles there in fomenting history's only slave revolution. Here, in their thousands, was a great convention of the Rastafari of Jamaica. Actual followers of this faith still amount to only a fraction of the number of Jamaica's Adventists or Baptists. But the Rastas' particular riff on Christian scripture, and the charismatic reggae-star apostles who've embraced it, has played an outsized role in shaping Jamaica's external image and internal culture. And here, by the resting place of one of their great apostles, the sisdren and bredren had come to praise their lord, Jah.

The roots of Rasta, like many strains of Jamaican culture, came from its makers' imaginative interpretation of mediated images from abroad. In Jazz Age Harlem, Marcus Garvey founded and built the Universal Negro Improvement Association. His stirring rhetoric—"Africa for the Africans, at home and abroad," he said—attracted many admirers on his home island. A few of these, watching a newsreel in Kingston's Carib Theatre in 1930, saw footage of a black king being crowned Ethiopia's new emperor, amid *nuff* pomp and pageantry. They grew convinced that one of his prophecies had come true. "Look to the east," Garvey was supposed to have said, "for the crowning of an African king."[4] Developing an elaborate eschatology built from the King James Bible, the Rastafari (named for Haile Selassie's Amharic honorific, Ras—Prince—Tafari) espoused the smoking of ganja as a sacrament ("He causeth the grass to grow for the cattle, and herb for the service of man," Psalms 104:14), and eschewed the eating of meat and the cutting of hair ("They shall not make baldness upon their head," Leviticus 21:5). For most of the next few decades, they remained an obscure, if visible, feature of Jamaican life. And then, in April 1966, Selassie visited the island.

Among the thousands driven that day to worship Selassie as a living god were Peter Tosh and Bunny Wailer. Marley, having joined his mother in Delaware to "work some money" as a custodian and assembly-line worker at a Chrysler plant there for some months, wasn't present. But he received a letter from his sweetie Rita, back home, about how when the emperor waved to her from his motorcade, she'd glimpsed Christ's stigmata on his palm. All three, upon Bob's return, stopped cutting their hair and began spending much of their time at the Trench Town yard of Mortimo Planno, the prominent Rasta who had hosted Selassie on behalf of Jamaica's government. Whatever their personal reasons for embracing the faith, Rastafari gave the Wailers a liturgical language that, in an era of Black Power and African freedom struggles, bespoke connections among black people everywhere. Their success in setting those links to music made them stars—and forced Jamaican leaders like Michael Manley, in the 1970s, to embrace a sect whose adepts his father's generation had suppressed. In 1962, military police raided a Rasta camp in the hills over Montego Bay, beating and jailing its inhabitants—a few were killed—to signal the new state's determination that these unkempt cultists weren't welcome. A decade later, as that nation's dreadlocked singers won fame at home and abroad, this changed. Michael Manley traveled to Ethiopia and returned with a long staff he called the "rod of correction." He played hard to the Rastas, who called him "Joshua," even advocating for laws allowing the Rastas their sacred herb. His government's main patrons in Washington, at the IMF and in the White House across Pennsylvania Avenue, put the kibosh on that. But this history may help gloss the reply supplied by the woman in burlap robes, there at Peter Tosh Day, when I asked her, as she cradled her weed amid the reggae filling the air around Tosh's tomb, why she wasn't concerned about the police outside. She looked at me hard. "Di music mek it legal."

In the decades since Rasta gained something like mainstream tolerance, if not full acceptance, in Jamaica, its faithful have weathered many crises, including the dawning realization on the part of many that their "immortal" god was an earthly despot unrevered by his subjects. More challenging still was the fact that, a mortal man, and a frail old one at that, he up and died in 1975. Had the latter event occurred before reggae's greats "went Rasta," one wonders if Rasta would have survived. But luckily for the faithful, and Selassie's memory, those greats were already selling millions of records in 1975, when Marley wrote his response to his Jah's demise: "Jah no Dead." By the time Selassie passed, the cult he'd inspired had spawned singing saints with prophecies of their own. And infelicities of earthly history aside, "the larger point of Rasta," a musician friend told me in Kingston, was that "we needed to connect some dots—between now and our past, between here and Africa." Which, no matter the squiggly lines it used, was true. And there in Belmont, it was plain that Rasta was still furnishing a usable language and worldview for poor people seeking ways to grasp the larger history that made them poor, and to reject the larger "Babylon system"— the entire white capitalist West—that keeps them that way. And it still offered ways and means, with the help of excellent vibes and *ital* goods, to live outside Babylon's walls.

Beneath the breadfruit and mango trees in old Tosh's yard, vendors peddled some of these. In front of *ital* food stalls, they hawked low-salt corn porridge and green callaloo. A juice stall's bottles were tagged with aphrodisiac names like "Mannish Wata" and "Front-End-Lifter," and bore ingredient lists rich in Irish moss, ginger, and ra-moon bark. Next door, the turbaned proprietor of I-Nation Books and Necessities stood over tables stacked with not a few of the titles one sees lining the racks of "black book" peddlers on 125th Street in Harlem. Perusing a comic-book biography of Marcus Garvey and another of Nanny of the Maroons, I passed over Eric Williams's *Capitalism and Slavery* and Elijah Muhammad's *Fall of America*. Eschewing a few others pertaining to numerology and *Candle Burning Magic*, I picked up a volume called *Olympic DNA: Birth of the Fastest Humans*. Its cover was done in the colors of the Jamaican flag. Its argument, I found when I read it, posited that all of Jamaica's world-class sprinters, for a complex mash of reasons pertaining to chromosomes and history, owed their gifts to the runaway Maroons whose resistance to slavery, and physical feats in Jamaica's jungle, helped their progeny develop insuperable speed—and become the modern-day heroes of people like the man dressed in flowing golden robes who stopped me as I walked by with my purchase to point at "Usain!" on its cover.

I inspected the *ital* "jewels" the man in gold robes was peddling, and complimented the tray of necklaces he'd laid on a cloth on the ground. They were made from dried bits of carrot and mango, accented with fish skin, and covered with clear rosin. His golden robes, he told me, signaled "uplifment, yuh know." His name was Rasta Shaw, and he had come here from Sav-la-Mar, just up the coast, "where di slave ships come," because "Peter a revolutionary. Seen?" Seen. "Him stand up for equal rights. Equal rights . . . and justice." He sang the last words, as Peter did in a famous song whose chorus continued where Marley had left off in "Get Up, Stand Up." Tosh demanded not just equal rights now, but redress for past wrongs as well. This may have been what distinguished Tosh, most of all, to his admirers here. The flyer Rasta Shaw handed me agreed. "Commemoration Coral Gardens," it read, in gold ink. "Atrocity Against Rastafari." Coral Gardens is the name of the old Rasta camp by Montego Bay that was devastated by the "Bad Friday" massacre in 1962. In a couple of weeks, many of those gathered here would reconvene for "cultural presentations, drumming," and a stage show featuring a pair of performers called Mackie Conscious and Ranking Punkin. On the flyer, an outline of the African continent was overlaid with a slogan that was also a statement of faith. "Victory of Good Over Evil," it said.

I took the flyer from Rasta Shaw's hand, with thanks, and moved on.

Down by the stage, a few dozen Rastas sang and drummed along with one of Peter's sons. Dressed in camo pants and a black T-shirt printed with the block-lettered phrase "BABYLON CAN'T WIN," he mouthed his dad's songs into a mic. At the yard's other end, I approached a small house on whose porch a stooped old woman sat. She was dressed in a high-necked gray blouse and an ankle-length skirt. I mounted her porch's stairs to pay respects. This was Mrs. Coke: Peter's mum. Her unseeing eyes were mostly shut; whiskers ringed her chin. I told her how pleased I was to meet her, touching her hand, and she smiled gently. I asked her how it felt to welcome all these thousands of people to her yard, to honor her son. "Bless," she nodded. "Joy." Which seemed about right for a ninetysomething woman. As I took my leave, I pressed a small bill into her palm, as seemed to be the custom here, and turned to greet a man, standing on the porch nearby, whom I'd noticed before.

He wasn't the only other white person here. Ganja Man, naturally, was also on the scene. He was everywhere. He'd spent much of the afternoon on the dais with Irie FM's deejay, reasoning with passion on air about the *ital* importance of ensuring balance in your endocannabinoid system. There were also a few aging bohemians, led by the ex-wife of the novelist Russell Banks, who kept winter homes in the area and whom I recognized from meeting at a restaurant down the way. This fellow, though, was different. He was youngish, but with a proprietary air. He had the shabby-chic facial hair and skinny stylish girlfriend of an LA hipster. James Baldwin wrote, "One Negro meeting another at an all-white cocktail party . . . cannot but wonder how the other got there."[5] The same, but different, could have been said about us. But this man's alibi, and larger hustle, became clear when I shook his hand. He was the person now in charge of Tosh's estate. It was his dollars, rather than Peter's mum's, that were underwriting this free celebration of a figure whose brand's star, he was convinced, could rise even higher than Bob's. He'd worked closely with the family since winning the estate manager's role a couple of years before, to get a new "Peter biopic" off the ground, and, more generally, to leverage the departed's memory, and tunes, for good and for cash. "The Beatles had McCartney and Lennon," said Mr. LA. "But one of them—Lennon—will always feel cooler. Peter is that. Marley is McCartney; Peter is John. That's what we want to do." I wished him luck.

I wasn't sure if Tosh's avowedly black act, and message, had the same crossover potential twenty years after his death as the mixed-race Obama-ite figure his old friend Bob became. But at this party, where, Peter's estate manager told me, everyone was performing for free, the reverence accorded "the Toughest" by the sisdren and bredren singing his songs, anyway, was clear. For them, the question of how the great

Peter Tosh could be sold to kids in Peoria was as irrelevant as Babylon's impertinent queries about their god's end. And up onstage, the Rastas were pounding their drums, dozens strong, with open palms. The elders waved their flags in time, and then parted behind them to allow a new party to come to the fore.

A diminutive figure, stepping from between two bearded drummers, shuffled onstage. He was spectacularly attired. He wore a mock policeman's outfit, made of pink cloth, topped off by a matching pink sailor cap with gold and green piping. Down his back, a single cord of braided dreadlocks hung, reaching nearly to his knees. It was the last of the Wailers. Bunny. In a pink sailor cap and all. Burdened with the weight of being both the least charismatic and the least successful of Jamaican culture's holiest trinity, Bunny is also the only Wailer not to have been martyred before middle age. When he left the group, he took their name as compensation: he has gone, for forty years, by "Bunny Wailer." He is a tricky figure. Given to reclusive paranoia and mad pronouncements, he is a man more warily respected, even among his fellow Rastas, than actively loved. But on this day, his pro bono appearance at what felt like a family reunion shook with meaning. Bunny embraced Peter's son, in his black T. Taking the mic in hand, he extended a pink-sleeved arm.

"Get up, stand up!" The elders beat their drums, good and slow. Bunny growled. "Stand up for your rights." The song is known as Marley's, but it was one of the last songs the original Wailers recorded together—and its most searing verse, as all Jamaicans know, and as Bunny sang, loud and strong, by its author's grave, was penned by Peter Tosh.

> We're sick and tired of your ism-schism game
> Dyin' 'n' goin' to heaven in-a Jesus name, Lord
> We know when we understand
>   Almighty God is a living man

The last living Wailer, his sailor hat bobbing in the fading light, conducted his flock.

> You can fool some people sometimes
> But you can't fool all the people all the time

We all sang along.

So now we see the light (what you gonna do?)
We gon' stand up for our rights!

As the sun dipped into the waves, I piled back into the rental car with
Ganja Man and pair of new Rasta pals who I watched flick their half-
smoked spliffs into the sea. The music might have legalized the herb for
the afternoon, but not now. "Too much Babylon on di road." We pulled
out into traffic. And then, after pausing in Sav-la-Mar, where old Tosh's
forebears were unloaded as slaves and our friends took a pee break by a
seawall scrawled with the phrase "Don't Piss Yah," we hopped back in
the car and rolled on toward Jamaica's western tip.

* * *

ONCE, WESTMORELAND WAS BEST known for the slave ports
where Africans were delivered to this island where the roots of badness,
as every hack reggae writer and historian parrots, reach back centuries. Now another species of *arrivant* crowds the once teeny town at
Westmoreland's end, providing the parish with its dodgy lifeblood. As
recently as the 1970s, Negril was reachable only by dirt track. The tourist mecca's famed "seven-mile beach" was inhabited by a few fishermen
and a growing colony of counterculture types from the capital, who
came to live out their own "Countryman" fantasies or join the area's
main industry at the time. Negril and Orange Hill, in the bush nearby,
were famous for their weed. In those days, before the United States'
own production of the plant had become a cash crop to rival corn,
smugglers used grassy airstrips out past the coral cliffs north of town
to toss loaded duffel bags into prop planes bound for Florida. Such
was Negril's outlaw air, in that era before electricity reached the beach,
that those days' veterans are full of stories about how Babylon's soldiers
turned up, more than once, to arrest their friends and sack tent cities
lousy with Castro-ite Rastas, the authorities claimed, and commie plots.
In the 1980s, all that changed. That was when the developers moved in,
along a new road from Mo' Bay they paved for the purpose, to exploit
Negril's super sunsets for themselves. Among them was Butch Stewart,
a white Jamaican who began his career as an air-conditioning magnate
before switching industries to invent such crucial tourism technologies,
at his resorts, as couples-only guest policies and swim-up bars. Stewart
built an outpost of his Sandals chain here in 1988. Since it opened,
Negril's famous beach has been so built up that scarcely an inch of its

west-facing shore, for five miles on either side of its teeny town center, isn't filled with resorts, ranging from Stewart's old Sandals to Hedonism II, a clothing-optional "sandbox for your inner child," its website says, "where the word 'no' is seldom heard."

For the sun-starved honeymooners and others who come here for three to eight days of all-inclusive fun, the smooth road down from the Montego Bay airport, traversed by courtesy shuttle or chauffeured SUV, proffers few visions of "the real Jamaica." Approaching West-moreland's tourist hub from the south, however, reveals more typi-cal Jamaican byways, riddled with potholes, on which the first rule of Third World Driving is strictly observed: If there's a car in front of you, you pass it. Whether the fatalism feeding that rule is a simple epi-phenomenon of poverty or comes from some deeper historical well, it's hard to say. But either way, and especially when careening around a tight corner or crossing a one-lane bridge at night, it can lead to some close calls, and, naturally, to tale telling about times when the close calls didn't work out. Times like the night, on the road past Sav-la-Mar, when Ganja Man said he happened on the aftermath of an awful accident that had taken the arm of a car's driver—and then watched a couple of bystanders, before the police turned up, run out to lift a gold watch off that severed limb. Or the time, after an evening church ser-vice like one of the many we passed on that road, when another of our party watched some addled motorcyclist, for reasons unknown, barrel into the crowd outside, killing four—and then ending up, after some-one walked over to where the motorcyclist lay and hurled rocks at his head, "getting dead" himself. (The next day's newspaper, like the police report, read, "The driver died at the scene.") Such were the stories fill-ing our car as it passed dusky hillsides dotted with the half-done houses that émigré Jamaicans build in piecemeal fashion by sending a bit of money back each year. With bits of rebar sticking skyward from their flat roofs, these homes awaited second stories that may or may not ever be completed by owners who, after thirty-two or forty years working in Brooklyn or Brixton, may or may not come to retire on their native isle. Jamaica was known in slavery days as a place synonymous with death, and the name that a leading historian of that era gave it—"the Reaper's Garden"—may still fit.[6]

If the ghosts of colonial violence are never far away here, they've cer-tainly found a home in the other trade, alongside tourism, that makes Negril go. At huge all-inclusive resorts owned by Spanish and other foreign conglomerates on the island's north shore, the assumption is that guests will spend their three to eight days lounging behind their hotels' barbed wire walls, that they'll not glimpse a Jamaican beyond the ones pouring their drinks or cutting the grass. On the white sands fronting Hedonism II in Negril, by contrast, part of the allure likely derives from the prospect of closer contact. There's a reason why Terry McMillan, the American author of bougie-black-women's fantasy *par excellence*, set *How Stella Got Her Groove Back* in Negril. There's also much to be gleaned from the real-life truth that the man on whom McMillan based the book, a gorgeous green-eyed Jamaican she met while vacationing here and then brought home to wed, later divorced her. Her fantasy man, when not performing for a green card, was rather more into romancing fellow young men than women twice his age.

For a man walking down the beach here, any innocent query for Wi-Fi or directions can win a reply proffering something else: "Nice girls!" The dreads peddling shell bracelets or Red Stripes say, "Yuh need nice girls? Nice and clean." If you're sitting in a nearby beach bar to use the internet, the hustling women aren't shy. "I need to get back to Bog Walk," says a buxom young woman with sad eyes. "You sure you don' wan a massage?" The attention from local males toward foreign women is even more overt. The swimsuited youths playing football in the sand, all bouncing pecs and sidelong glances, always keep an eye on passing quarries. They're players in an elaborate pantomime in which tourists and natives both play their part, their "yah mon"s and "no problem"s sounding less like their countrymen's and more like those spouted by vacationing white boys in dreadlock wigs. But on this beach where "rent-a-dreads" flourish, so does the trade in the ra-moon bark and ginger juices meant to fortify the "big bamboo." I stopped by a shop advertising "shot glasses, T-shirts, sunglasses," and, less predictably, "Bob Marley." Inside, the man himself wasn't for sale. Nor was the stuff for which his name was code in tourist Jamaican. ("Bob Marley!" the weed sellers crow. "You need some Bob Marley?") The place's shelves were stocked with the typical panoply of Marley T-shirts and Jamaican-flag towels. But against a back wall stood a wooden statue, four feet high, that made a rather succinct point about another aspect of Bob's memory and the crucial aid it's been to the many thousands of Jesus-haired men it has helped get laid. A smiling fetish fashioned from dark brown wood, the figure had ropy hair hanging to his shoulders. He was a wild-eyed all-purpose "ethnic." He had sculpted muscles and, protruding from his middle, an immense erect cock.

Subtle, Negril isn't. There's something to be said, though, for the place's way of stripping culture's transactional uses, and the tourist trade's full-contact aspect, down to the essence. Sipping a Red Stripe at Alfred's, one of Negril's seedier beach bar/guesthouses, one wins a new sense of what the wag who wrote a book on Las Vegas called *The Last Honest Place in America* may have meant. There is, at least, a certain clarity of motive emitting from the characters plying this VD-breeding dish, from the rent-a-dreads and sex tourists to the hustling taxi men and working girls who convene each Friday night at a Canadian-owned hotel, the Seastar Inn, where a local troupe of dancers perform for hotel guests and debauched local expats who know it's the best show in town. The Seastar Dancers worked out a mélange of West African moves and beat their djembes with expert force, leaping and spinning in loincloths for the only people—horny foreigners—who'll pay to see them. After the show, I complimented one of the dancers and asked her how, as a performer plainly devoted to her craft, she felt toward her gig here. "Dancing is my passion," she said. "And here, I get paid to dance."

The built-in tension between art making and the often tetchy exigencies for artists of earning a living is hardly unique to Jamaica. But that tension perhaps finds extra force here, as in other places where performing for tourists is one of the few reliable ways musicians and others have ever had to make a living. The homegrown record industry, now such a symbol of the Jamaica brand, began the same way. The first musicians to be recorded for sale here, by island impresarios, were the *mento* and jazz men who made their living playing by the pool at the Myrtle Bank in Kingston or Mo' Bay's Half Moon Hotel. Years before Bob Marley strode into Chris Blackwell's London office, the latter had captured the tinkly stylings of a Bahamian piano player named Laurel Aitken, who spent three months each winter playing at the Half Moon. From that first effort, Blackwell grew Island Records—whose roster eventually included Roxy Music, the Police, and U2—into "music's greatest independent label." What he understood about Marley's rebel allure—"He looked like the real character from *The Harder They Come*," Blackwell recalled—was both rooted in Jamaican culture and always crucial to his genius for pop. Since selling Island for $300 million in 1989, Jamaica's greatest entrepreneur has dabbled in producing films and distilling rum (his Blackwell's brand of tipple is delicious). But it makes a kind of sense, given where he began, that now he pours the bulk of his energy into building Brand Jamaica's other key industry: tourism.

Among the properties Blackwell owns with his company, Island Out-post, are Strawberry Hill, a Georgian-style retreat high over Kingston, and the Caves hotel, in Negril, a Tolkienesque warren built into Negril's coral cliffs by some of his old hippie friends who escaped here in the '70s. But Blackwell's greatest passion, and general home base, is the place he's developing on a property he's known even longer. In the quiet village of Oracabessa and near the old banana port of Port Antonio, that property—GoldenEye—was named by its first owner: Ian Fleming. When Patrick Leigh Fermor visited the elegant clifftop home Fleming built there, he dubbed it a "model for new homes in the tropics." This is where the famed spy novelist wrote all fourteen of his novels about that suave agent for the MI6, James Bond, whose name he borrowed from the author of a 1936 guidebook, *Birds of the West Indies*. Blackwell's mother, the noted island socialite Blanche Lindo, belonged to an old Portuguese Jewish family whose forebears came to Jamaica in the seventeenth century to make their fortune, during the era of slavery, in sugar and rum. Blanche was a close friend of both Fleming's and Noël Coward's. It was from her family's old lands that Blanche carved out a plot for Coward to build his famous Jamaican retreat, Firefly, and it was Blanche, too, who found Fleming the splendid sea frontage on which he built GoldenEye.

* * *

I FOUND BLACKWELL on his teak deck by the lush green lagoon. There down below the original Fleming villa, I watched a pair of resort guests paddle up, mistaking their host's stoop for a bar, and ask for a beer. "Some people did that earlier," Blackwell chuckled. "I just gave them a drink, and off they swam." Dressed in his daily uniform of bright T-shirt and shorts, he looked years younger than seventy-six; he could as easily have been GoldenEye's well-sunned barkeep as its boss. His delight in his guests' occasional error was grounded in something important to him. Forging a relaxed vibe is as crucial to resort making, in his eyes, as it was in making records. During his thirty years running Island Records, he said, "we never tried to appeal to the majority. You don't want the 80 percent. You want the 20 percent who get what you're going for. That's all you need."

He should know. These days, though, the great tastemaker had largely moved from promoting pop stars to touting a place. Intent on marketing the island where he grew up, Island Outpost's hotels are "like artists on a label," Blackwell told me over tall glasses of coconut water. "Each with its own feel." All of them, though, were meant to serve a larger passion. Chris Blackwell, the man once responsible for bringing Jamaican music to the world, was now driven to bring the world to Jamaica. "Jamaica isn't a country that can manufacture plastic chairs, you know, and compete with anyone," he explained. "But what it has . . . it's such a beautiful country, with incredible people—funny, smart. And it has its own soundtrack!" His eyes shone. "A country with its own frigging soundtrack! Imagine that." Blackwell's first experience with that soundtrack came in childhood. "I was a sickly boy," he said, smiling at a housekeeper as she refilled his glass, "so I spent a lot of time inside, with the staff—I got to know them, what they liked." His first job in the record business, as a teen, required him to ride a motorbike around the island's countryside to change out the records in its rum bars' jukeboxes. As a location scout on the first James Bond film, in 1962, Blackwell found the beach where Ursula Andress, dripping in her bikini-and-dagger suit in *Dr. No*, became a star. But it was in England that he made his mark.

"When we won independence in 1962," Blackwell said, "I didn't really know what I could do for Jamaica as a white person. I thought I could contribute more in England." So he went. Having founded Island Records in 1959 to distribute Jamaica's music among its emigrants abroad, Blackwell now delivered his wares from the boot of his Mini Cooper to West Indian shops from London to Birmingham. And then he decided, with trademark foresight, that one of those records could win white kids' acclaim, too. In 1964 he arranged to have thousands of copies of a chirpy tune by a sixteen-year-old girl from near Montego Bay, Millie Small, pressed onto 45s. Millie's cover of "My Boy Lollipop," an obscure R&B record from the 1950s, didn't just become the first Jamaican single to reach number one in the UK; worldwide, it sold six million copies. Blackwell accompanied his young charge to all the hot parties and broadcasts. He got to meet all the players and promoters, too. "Pretty quickly," he said, "you go from being one in ten thousand to being one in a hundred." Island Records, leveraging its owner's new ties and energy, became home to Cat Stevens and Traffic in the late '60s, before it broke Marley's reggae to the world in the '70s. Later that decade, Blackwell glimpsed a photo of a young model with an androgynous style in a magazine and exclaimed, "We need to make a record that sounds like *that*." A fellow Jamaican who'd grown up in Spanish Town before making her way to New York, Grace Jones was quickly signed. Jones's records with Blackwell, once he became her producer, included the enduring post-disco classics *Nightclubbing* and *Living My Life*.

In the meantime, Blackwell had helped Marley buy Fleming's sea-front home—before Marley then pronounced GoldenEye "too posh," and signed it back over to his producer. Blackwell seems to have agreed with his friend: beyond loaning the place to assorted Rolling Stones and other pals in need of a spot to dry out or write (a gold record hanging there, signed by Sting, says "'Every Breath You Take'—written at GoldenEye"), he didn't really know what to do with it—until he decided, in the 1990s, to turn the house into a plush vacation rental. Blackwell added a few more tasteful villas to the grounds, and his GoldenEye resort was born—and with it, his ongoing effort to revolutionize Jamaican tourism.

For Blackwell, the "all-inclusive" model that's guided most efforts to sell Jamaica's sun and sand, since the 1960s, is anathema. "These massive hotels who warn you, 'Don't go outside,' with their food precut and pre-portioned, flown in from Florida—they're killing the country." His aims were different. "We encourage people to go out and about—to meet locals, to meet the producers. Because I'm convinced that that's what makes long-term business sense, for us—and for Jamaica to thrive." And it was here at GoldenEye, and in the neighboring village of Oracabessa, where he was focusing his efforts. After striding across a new suspension footbridge over the lagoon, we plodded down a white sand beach lined with tasteful cottages, toward where Blackwell, on a promontory the government built to make a new port here, was planning to expand GoldenEye further. He gestured over the bay, and toward St. Mary's hills beyond. "When I was a boy, I used to watch the banana boats anchor here." Those boats' workers, loading the boats by night, wished for the daylight that would let them go home. "Day-o!" they cried, giving Harry Belafonte the inspiration for what became, when he released his *Calypso* LP in 1956, history's first million-selling LP—and launched a career that inspired Blackwell's own. It was the title of Belafonte's 1957 film, *Island in the Sun*, based on Alec Waugh's novel, that inspired the name of Island Records. "That's where it started," Blackwell murmured in the breeze. "And now, there are three musics that you hear everywhere in the world. American, English, and . . . Jamai-

can." We arrived to an open-air restaurant whose decor featured col-
laged photos of Blackwell's musician pals, and sat down to lunch.

Since the completion of the first of Blackwell's planned expansions, a
couple of years before, GoldenEye had won raves in luxury travel rags
for its easy elegance. It wasn't hard to see why, as I admired the callaloo
and pepper that came from Pantrepant, Blackwell's own organic farm.
Across from me at the table sat a striking black woman, laughing in her
big red hat. It took a few beats to realize she was the selfsame "Grace"
whose image hung nearby. In the early '90s, Grace Jones introduced
Blackwell to his wife, the designer Mary Vinson. (Vinson, whose fabrics
and ideas are all around GoldenEye, died in 2004.) Jones had come
home for vacation, as she often did, and to see her old friend. She nodded as Blackwell explained how Island Outpost had begun organizing
farm-to-table meals and tours of Pantrepant. I wondered if patrons of
this paradise would ever want to leave GoldenEye's premises, having
paid upward of US$1,000 a night to stay. But Blackwell was undeterred.
He was convinced that "the 20 percent" of Jamaica's visitors who both
covet authenticity and can afford to pay are out there—and would further his goals. "I love the island, I love the people. That's why I'm doing
my work here," he said. "And if I'm successful in what I'm trying to pull
off, it will genuinely make a difference." And then he excused himself
to partake in an afternoon ritual he never forgoes. Minutes later, a poof
of white hair bobbed past: a proud Jamaican on a Jet Ski, tracing a bit
of the St. Mary's coast he first fell in love with as a boy, and where, now,
he was building his legacy.

* * *

FROM ST. MARY'S BANANA FIELDS to the famous statue in St.
Thomas of the rebel preacher Bogle; from Westmoreland's beaches, and
weed, to the Karst convolutions of Trelawny's "cockpit country" which
sheltered the Maroons; from Portland's Blue Lagoon to the arid shores
of St. Elizabeth, from whence a pair of lovelorn slaves offed themselves,
when they couldn't wed, at a place called Lover's Leap—each of Jamaica's fourteen parishes, like America's states or the countries of Spain, has
its own identity and fame. The "garden parish" of St. Ann, comprised of
fecund peaks tumbling down to the sea, was for most of its history best
known for a stretch of coast called Discovery Bay: this is where Christopher Columbus brought history's first whites, and his conquistador's

particular breed of badness, to Jamaica. In the past couple of decades, though, word has gotten out that the peaks above Disco Bay were also where, 450 years later, history's most famous Jamaican was born, and where, 36 years after that, he was laid to rest in the little hillside hamlet of Nine Miles. St. Ann's identity changed. Today the parish may as well be known as Bob Marley Parish. But as I learned the first time I visited Marley's birthplace, by way of another hamlet a few hilltops over, St. Ann's hills and quays have shaped not a few of Jamaica's greatest modern exponents.

The village of Aboukir, St. Ann, was like many obscure outposts of the British Empire named for a famed battle long ago and far away—in the case of Aboukir, the site on Egypt's Nile where Commodore Horatio Nelson routed Napoleon's army in 1798. Not that this matters to the people of a hamlet whose denizens pronounce its name "Ah-boo-kah," and who live in a place where the sight of a white man in shorts, to judge from the quizzical stares my presence earned from kids walking home from school, is pretty uncommon. In the town rum shop, I chatted with a few old-timers passing their afternoon in dominoes and booze, and soon found what I had come for—an aging cousin of Aboukir's favorite son, Harry Belafonte. The singer's Jamaican mother, emigrating from here to Harlem, found work there as a maid, but grew wary of the trouble her rambunctious son might find in the cold city's streets. She sent him away, on one of the United Fruit Company boats the boy's father worked on as a cook, for "safekeeping" in her own mum's home. And so it was in St. Ann's hills that Belafonte, who spent parts of each year with his grandmum here, absorbed the songs and stories to which he'd later turn, as a struggling young actor back in New York, to launch the new vocation—as a folk singer—that made him a star. His *Calypso* record of Caribbean folk tunes, released in 1956, didn't merely become the first long-playing record to sell a million copies. It made Belafonte America's "first black matinee idol," and earned him the royalties he then used, over the next decade, to bankroll his friend Martin Luther King Jr.'s civil rights movement. Not bad for a kid from Aboukir. But it wasn't surprising to his cousin, whose name was Norman and who shared Harry's light brown skin (their grandmother, he said, was a Scotswoman) and with whom I chatted, fortified by bush rum, about all this and more. Norman dilated on his and Harry's boyhood mango-throwing exploits, and also recounted, when I asked, how their uncle Callbeck had sold off their grandmother's shack, "down by

Old Bethany," when he went to work for Kaiser Aluminum in St. Ann's Bay—the town where I was going to end that day. Not, that afternoon, to pay respects to Uncle Callbeck, but because that sleepy port was the natal home of yet another massive figure—Marcus Garvey—in the modern history of black culture and politics.

Watching the sun set from the town's ancient jetty, I pictured a young Garvey doing the same, before he emigrated to Harlem and from there spread his message to a global flock of followers that included Belafonte's mother. "Garvey's model was everything to us," Belafonte told me back in New York, after I wrote him a letter about my time in Aboukir and we met at a seafood place on the Upper West Side. "That constant striving, for more than we were given." As he sipped cranberry juice with his clams, the old singer's voice was gravelly, his presence immense. He thought that this outlook, and its particular badness, was crucial to how he and his best friend, Sidney Poitier, won a sort of fame previously unthinkable to American blacks. "When me and Sidney were coming up, people took the way we carried ourselves as proud, imperial; they said we were special." Belafonte laughed. "But that's every fucking Jamaican I know! And a lot of them are a pain in the ass!"

That was one impact of Garvey's rhetoric. Another was to furnish Bob Marley, born a few hilltops over, with the liturgical language to become his turbulent century's greatest translator of history's muse into the idiom of pop. Garvey, Belafonte, Marley. This out-of-the-way parish, on this poor little island, birthed not one but three totemic figures in the great twentieth-century story of black freedom. Astonishing, when you think about it—and even more so when you're standing in the middle of St. Ann's hardscrabble poverty. But then, this was Jamaica, where punching above one's weight is a kind of national sport, and where, passing through Aboukir's quiet, years after that first visit, I watched the uniformed school kids walk across their old field, now lined with a wavy-lined running track, on which they could train to become their island's next gold-winning star. I wound through blue-green hills crosscut by the ochre gashes of bauxite mines to find the town where Bob Marley, like the Age of Three Worlds he so shaped, was born in 1945.

* * *

HIDDEN IN THE HILLS above the larger market town of Brown's Town, Nine Miles is a dusty hamlet as remote as it sounds. Its one main street winds past sloping plots, planted with dasheen and yams, that Marley's maternal kin have tended for centuries. His mother, when he became her firstborn, was a sixteen-year-old peasant girl, dark-skinned and homely. His white father, employed as a surveyor of Crown Lands in the area, was the short outcast son of a prominent Kingston family. He was past sixty when he rode into Nine Miles on a white horse and chatted up young Ciddy, who soon thereafter bore Captain Marley's son. Christening her little half-caste boy Nesta Robert, Ciddy raised him here; then, after she brought him to the capital when he was twelve, he finished the job himself. Rising from the Trench Town streets, where in his teens he earned the nickname Tuff Gong for his scrappy prowess as a fighter, he became a man so revered by the time he died that every mile of the winding road to Nine Miles was lined with mourners when his hearse passed. That route is still traversed by old lorries carrying bananas and sugarcane and by shared roto-taxis carrying kerchiefed country women, stuffed five across in rattly Toyotas' backseats, heading home from town with their shopping. Now, though, these vehicles have been joined by white-paneled tourist buses which bump up the rough road from Ocho Rios and disgorge their sunburned cargo within the high-walled gates of the compound that's been built up around Marley's refurbished birth shack and the rather grander mausoleum, alongside, where he's interred. Outside the walls, affected Rastas mill about, trying to sell visitors mix CDs and "Bob Marley weed!" Offput or scared by the poverty glimpsed through the bus windows, few of their prey experience much of Bob's world beyond the disembodied voices or hands that, reaching through slats in the wall, proffer those CDs and herb. The tourists prefer patronizing the overpriced gift shop, strategically located between the parking lot and the bar, with its stuffed monkeys with dreads, Rasta-colored water shoes, with little sockets for your toes, and shelves full of all you might need—rolling papers, all kinds; a metal "herb grinder"; a six-inch "Marley's mood" lighter—to craft a spliff to puff while kicking about the hacky-sack affixed with Bob's face, also for sale here. Nine Miles can be a gnarly scene. Until, that is, you move beyond the several square feet of transactional nastiness around its one tourist trap to stroll through a place exuding the mellow air of little mountain towns everywhere.

Having had the fortune, this time, to arrive with a man who lawyered for Bob's mom, and fought to win her wing of the family their piece of Bob's posthumous pie, I listened to Ganja Man ring up "Bob's brother Richard"—one of Ciddy's other sons; he lived in Miami—to see about crashing in the family's home by the mausoleum, which he managed "from foreign." We rolled into town. Ganja Man lowered his window to greet one kindly local after another, identifying them all as "Bob's cousin." His phone rang. It was Richard: "It's cool." Sleeping spot sorted, I stepped from the car and walked down a main street lined with the familiar features of country life here. Outside the little Yah Suh Nice Store, a cheery higgler was selling "gunga rice and peas" in Styrofoam trays, "wit chunks if yuh like." ("Chunks" are a soy-based meat substitute that some development scheme somehow worked into Jamaicans' diet long ago.) Down farther, outside a crooked wooden house that sat just below the Marley mausoleum, a hand-painted sign advertised "Mount Zion Apostolic Ministries Incorporated." Nearby, a rough concrete retaining wall was painted with a fresh mural, of a sort one sees all over Jamaica, showing a round-faced local potentate who'd recently passed. "In Memory of Karl 'Busta' Brown," it said. "Our Father Our Hero Our Strength." I poked my head into an open door by the wall that led onto a darkened barroom. Inside, a low stage was equipped with a metal stripper pole and decorated with a metal street sign. The sign said "Pimpin' Ave." I asked a young woman outside where we were. "Is Busta Brown place," she explained. Whatever else the biggest local bad man was up to, this country go-go bar, it seemed, was among his holdings. She pointed behind the bar to a cement structure guarded by faux-Doric columns, likewise freshly painted, in saffron. This, she explained, was Busta Brown's mausoleum. That Friday would be his "nine night"—the all-night ritual, rich with music and rum, by which Jamaicans mark their fellows' passage from this plane to another. It was clear, from how she said it, that Busta's nine night was a big deal.

The young woman outside the bar, with her big eyes set in a wide face over a button nose, bore more than a passing resemblance to the photos of a young Ciddy, Bob's mother, that hang in her mausoleum. (She died here in 2008, after returning from Florida and opening a school in her old hometown.) Were they related? To some degree, probably. Omeriah Malcolm, Bob's maternal granddad and a local grandee of his day, fathered dozens of kids. The kinship ties that bind this bit of St. Ann's to itself, with Omeriah's offspring still hoeing his lands, are hardly rare in rural Jamaica. What distinguishes Nine Miles, though, is that not a few of Marley's darker cousins earn their living from his memory. This fact, it's fair to say, doesn't occur to most tourists who come here picturing their hero's latte-colored face. But back at the compound, on old Omeriah's land, which has been built up in Bob's name, it is various of his cousins who work there as tour guides, and who prod visitors with their own theme song: "One love, one heart / Tip your tour guide, and feel alright!" They lead visitors up the hill to show them the little shack where Bob was born (his childhood bed is decorated with a marijuana-leaf flag reading "A Spliff a Day Keeps the Doctor Away"). They point to a rock outside that may or may not have inspired his verse, in "Talkin' Blues," about how "rock stone was my pillow too." They take their charges through the handsome marble chapel where Bob is buried, right next to the newer one where his mother is. By day, this Temple Mount felt overrun. But that night, after the cruise shippers cleared out and the compound's high gates were locked, I accompanied Ganja Man up the path to the mausoleum that he called "Zion," to a nodding night watchman called Chicken, to "smoke with Bob."

There in the chapel, around a marble plinth two tombs high, lay the offerings of pilgrims from the four corners: a charcoal drawing of Malcolm X; a small Canadian flag on a wooden dowel; a book emblazoned with Marley's face and the title, in what looked like Serbo-Croatian, "Boba Marlija." From the road below, the plaintive sounds of singing people drifted up: the congregants of Zion Apostolic Ministries Incorporated were praising Jesus. On one of the chapel's walls, a large black-and-white photo showed Mother Booker smiling and hugging a handsome young man who shared her smile. This was another of her sons—a bodybuilder in Miami named Anthony, who, like her firstborn, died too young. Ciddy had ordained that he be interred here, with Bob: it was Anthony, rather than the woman for whom the tomb's second berth was first built—Rita Marley—who lay next ot Bob in the two-slot tomb. The presence of the matriarch's less-famous son here, though, wasn't the only bit of intrigue surrounding the tomb—nor, Ganja Man revealed, did Anthony's quiet interment mark the tomb's last opening. Puffing his spliff, my companion looked over as the hymns floated up from below. "You know they cut him out," he said through the haze. "Bongo Joe—he took Bob out; put him back again."

There was only one thing, the next morning, to do. Find Bongo Joe. We found Bongo Joe sitting on the porch of a sturdy split-level ranch house on the edge of Brown's Town. Out front, a few of his bredren sat by a fire, roasting bits of the breadfruit they helped him farm in the backyard. Bongo Joe waved hello. He was a wiry little Rasta man with smiling eyes and his locks tucked into a knitted tam. He showed me into a home whose rooms were furnished with a few mattresses on the floor, an old antique globe, and an old unplugged refrigerator being used, with its doors open and absent of "current" to cool its shelves, for simple storage.

"Give thanks." Our host offered the traditional Rasta greeting. He bid me sit on a bag of fertilizer. I asked him his name. "My name Bongo." He paused. "My other name—my Babylon name—it's Gilbert Powell." He chuckled gently. And then he told me his tale.

Born here in Brown's Town, he had adopted Jah as lord in the late 1960s and taken his nom de Rasta around the same time he "met a lady, yuh know, from up in the hills." Said lady was from Nine Miles. It was in renting a house there, from Bob Marley's aunt, that he got to know the local kid who always made time, Bongo Joe said, to drive his Land Rover up from town and, tending to one of the family plots, to fill his jeep with "plenty punkin and yam." Bongo Joe was a trusted fellow Rasta in the rural homeplace where Marley returned, even after growing world famous, "when him want to relax hisself." The men became close. And when the end came, Bongo Joe was there. The hearse that carried the Gong up from the capital, he said, had broken down around the town of Ewarton; Bob's bredren, following in one of the departed's trucks, slid his coffin from one carrier into the next. They continued into St. Ann's and, once they reached Nine Miles, slid the box containing Bob's battered body and his Gibson guitar out of the pickup's bed and into his marble tomb—without remembering, some said later, to turn the coffin around again. No one knew for sure. But the prospect that "Bob went in wrong way" set the stage for the secret drama in which Bongo Joe, who worked with the Marley family and served as a tour guide at Zion for years, played his indispensable role.

"We always tell people," he recalled, "that Bob Marley head face east, face the star." The heads of the dead, in Jamaica, must face the rising sun. Tombs on the island, no matter their context, are angled that way. It matters. "But we never sure," Bongo continued. "And then Bob mother and him lawyer start having dreams. Having dreams that Bob not happy in him tomb."

"They thought he was faced the wrong way?"

"Yeah mon. And so one day, Bob brother Richard, he say, Bongo! Come up here." Up by the tomb, Bongo found Bob's brother standing with their mother and a robed priest from the Ethiopian Orthodox

Church. "'We need to get in there,' Richard say. 'We need help to dig Bob out. We need to turn him round.'" Bongo, there on his porch in Brown's Town, lifted a pantomime hammer and chisel. "So I start to dig. Dig and dig and dig and dig. The whole of me face white up. Dust flying in me nose. I couldn't leave it, cause they wanted me to do it. So I dig and dig."

Back in Nine Miles that night, as the townspeople gathered by Busta Brown's bar to toast the bad man's life, I walked up the Temple Mount to Bob's tomb once more. The praiseful sounds of Zion Apostolic Ministries floated up in the dark. I sat by the tomb's western end, crouching by the little Canadian flag and a burning stick of incense. I moved aside a bit of the gauzy cloth hung over its end. I could see, through the haze, a wide seam of rough stone where someone had chiseled an opening and then, working in cement, covered it up again.

CHAPTER 3

REDEMPTION SONGS

"BADNESS! AND BAD MEN. Dat's wha gwaan deh." It's certainly
true in Nine Miles, where Busta Brown's wake was the party of the
year; it's true all over Jamaica. But most of all, it's true in the capital,
where the forging of the Jamaican state corresponded with the building
of a garrison complex whose construction, housing scheme by housing scheme and brick of coke by brick of weed, made the state Jamaicans know today: a twisting concatenation of overlapping interest and
contested concern whose presiding logic and larger course are perhaps
nowhere better distilled than in the story of the first garrison. That tale
is inextricable, like Jamaica's history as a sovereign nation, from the
career of the politician who became known as the "bigges' bad man of
all." Edward Seaga, the man who built Tivoli, and who used the garrison as a springboard to becoming Jamaica's elected leader long before
the gangster Dudus became its "first president," was never one to let
holding office stand in the way of wielding real power. Seaga never let
his background or views—he was born to a prominent Syrian family
from Kingston's merchant class—prevent his winning its poor's love.
A pro-Washington right-winger who was born in Boston (his parents
were there for school), he was long chided by supporters of his great
rival, Michael Manley, with a tune touting their man's native-born
cred: "He was born here." But the man PNPers called *CIA-ga* grew
up in Kingston. Seaga attended Wolmer's Boys School there before
earning his BA at Harvard and returning home, in the mid-1950s, to
settle—surprisingly, for a young man of his class—by downtown's poor
western edge. His career as a politician, even before he was one, began
brilliantly.

Seaga worked as an ethnologist in the downtown slums of Denham

Town and Back-o-Wall, becoming one of Jamaica's leading scholars of black religion. He also became a record producer and promoter whose ties to downtown's poor, and recordings of their songs, made him a crucial figure in building Jamaica's music industry. When "independence time" came, Seaga became West Kingston's first member of Jamaica's parliament—and Jamaica's first minister of development and welfare. Still in his early thirties, he was perhaps the only figure in Jamaica's new government who could have pulled off convincing his constituents and friends in Back-o-Wall to abide the ministry's bulldozing of their neighborhood. He oversaw the razing of the zinc-sheet and cardboard-walled shacks where they lived, and directed the building of the new community—Tivoli Gardens—into which these once-and-future supporters of his JLP, thrilled to join the era of cement walls and indoor plumbing, moved in 1965. Legend says the garrison's walls were laid out with their ramparts aligned for armed defense. Whether or not that's so, Tivoli soon became the potent base of its builder's growing sway.

In Seaga's early years downtown, his most crucial source of support came from the congregation of a Revivalist preacher named Mallica "Kapo" Reynolds, a charismatic figure whose talents as an artist—Kapo was also a prolific sculptor and painter of folk-mystic scenes in an elemental style—made him one of Jamaica's most noted artists. After Tivoli rose in Back-o-Wall's place, Kapo remained a loyal Seaga ally and JLP Stalwart. But as the garrison system took shape, and with it the violent mores of a new island politics, Seaga's patronage also began flowing to the top-ranking street toughs who rivaled such preachers' power on the ground. By the early 1970s, area bad men like Claudie Massop commanded foot soldiers with names like "Tek Life" and "Ba Bye," and were being furnished with arms by the parties whose garrisons they controlled. Men like Massop and his PNP-affiliated counterpart, Bucky Marshall, were responsible for overseeing the copious bloodletting that accompanied Jamaica's elections in 1972 and '76. It was also Massop and Marshall, though, whose mutual friendship with the most famed downtown tough—Bob Marley—helped them convince the singer to take part in the One Love Peace Concert.

That show, in 1978, which forms such a crucial part of the Gong's legend, was Marley's first appearance in his homeland in nearly two years. He had fled the island eighteen months before after an attempt on his life. His second and third records for Chris Blackwell had won him fame and money, and in early 1975, he'd bought Island House from Blackwell and moved himself, and his entourage, to Hope Road. In moving uptown, though, Marley didn't so much leave the ghetto behind as bring it with him. And in December 1976, downtown came calling. One warm evening, Marley stood in his kitchen peeling a grapefruit. He was talking with his manager, Don Taylor, when a car turned off Hope Road and rolled through his gates. A pair of gunmen leapt from the car. They spotted their target through his open kitchen door and emptied their rounds in his direction, before then hopping back in the car and, screeching through Island House's gate, tearing off toward downtown. Inside the kitchen, Don Taylor lay slumped in a corner. His lap was full of blood; he'd been shot in the groin. Rita Marley was unconscious, but alive; a bullet had struck her skull, but only grazed it. Her husband clutched his arm. He was lucky too. A shot that might have killed him had only glanced by his chest, lodging in his biceps. That night, Marley and Co.'s security whisked them up, by way of the hospital, to Chris Blackwell's retreat on Strawberry Hill. A couple of days later the Gong insisted on performing, with his arm in a sling, at a show for peace called "Smile Jamaica," the key template for the later One Love concert. He stepped down from the stage and straight into a car for the airport, then flew straight to the Bahamas, and from there to London, where he recorded the album—*Exodus*—that *Time* magazine later named the "Greatest Album of the Twentieth Century."

Marley's assailants, according to street wisdom if not the courts (no charges were ever filed in the attack), were "Labourite ta Ras"— hard-core JLP men. Marley was a savvy ghetto kid with close bredren from both sects: he always sought to project a public image of prophetic nonalliance—and to maintain juice, behind the scenes, with all parties. But after the PNP's Michael Manley became prime minister, in 1972, that image grew harder to maintain. Manley allied himself, during his winning campaign, with the Rastas. This risky move proved prescient; in the 1970s, the faith's icons and argot became the lingua franca of island culture. For Seaga's JLP, a party nominally in thrall more to Christ and capitalism than to "social living" and reggae, this remained a problem throughout the decade (Manley was reelected twice). Perhaps it also convinced some of Seaga's soldiers, if not the "Big Man hisself," that offing the biggest Rasta of all might be a good idea. That offing didn't work. But neither, sadly, did the One Love Peace Concert Marley came home to play in 1978. The show's aftermath comprised a bloodier-than-ever election season during which both Bucky Marshall and Claudie Massop were slain. The peacemaking "shottas" heirs, now armed with M16s (guns provided them, if they were tied to the JLP, by the CIA), were responsible for some eight hundred deaths, during the campaign that saw Eddie Seaga installed in Jamaica House for the first time. Among those who abetted that win, in 1980, was a new don of Tivoli. That figure's rise made him a hero for would-be bad men across Jamaica and heralded an era in which the garrisons, and their dons, would grow more powerful than the politicians who had made them.

The man they called "Jim Brown" was born Lester Coke in Denham Town and first won notice in his teens on the blocks he would rule as a soccer player.[1] The legend of his rise began one day when he was walking home from a kickabout. Jim Brown (who chose his sobriquet in homage to the American football star whose "bad strength and pride" he admired) was jumped by a gang of assailants, affiliation unknown, and found bloodied and dying in the street. His friends brought him to a new free health clinic in nearby Tivoli Gardens—whose doctors were installed by the area's JLP member of parliament, Eddie Seaga. Jim Brown built his career and fearsome rep from there, at the side of JLP bad men like Claudie Massop. And then he gained control of Tivoli just as Seaga was helping, inadvertently or no, and in his first term as prime minister, to vastly increase the Jamaican underworld's power and wealth. In the '70s, Jamaica had earned its reputation as America's great source for marijuana. In the supply chain that made this so, the best-armed and best-connected segment of Jamaica's populace—its bad men—had naturally become big players. After Seaga took power in 1980, his own patrons in Washington, D.C., leaned on him to curtail the stream of ganja-fueled prop planes and boats departing Jamaica for Miami. His success at doing so, in the '80s, had two effects above all. One was to help spur an explosion, still ongoing, in ganja production stateside. The other was to help push Jamaica's gangsters toward a much more lucrative and dangerous replacement.

That replacement was cocaine. And among those who moved aggressively to make Jamaica a key node in the hemisphere's trade was Jim Brown. Working with a close émigré associate named Vivian Blake, Jim Brown built an international cartel based in the Kingston garrison he now ruled. His syndicate network of smugglers and hit men reached from his Tivoli headquarters south to Colombia's coca fields and north to Brooklyn and the Bronx, through Miami, Baltimore, Toronto, and

Texas. His cartel was called the Shower Posse. It was perhaps named for a JLP slogan, but the gang's tag also evoked its members' predilection for showering their enemies with lead. In conjunction-cum-rivalry with the PNP-affiliated Spangler Posse, centered mere blocks from Tivoli in the adjoining burg of Matthews Lane, Jamaica's cartels became the hemisphere's only ones to rival the Colombians' impact. They perhaps gained an even larger one: it was the Shower Posse's Vivian Blake, who, while looking for more profitable ways to push cocaine, and foisting what he cooked up on poor addicts in the Bronx, is alleged to have invented crack.

Such activities on U.S. soil have a way of attracting federal heat. The FBI and the State Department both built huge dossiers on a ring alleg-edly responsible for more than two thousand murders by 1992, many of them grisly. Eventually, the investigation brought Jim Brown down. In 1991, he was imprisoned in Kingston's castle-like General Penitentiary. But with U.S. agents waiting at the airport to extradite him to the States for indictment on a raft of charges, the cell of "don dadda" was engulfed in a mysterious fire. Jim Brown died in the fire at the age of sixty-four. Whether the flames were set by a don who preferred silence by suicide to being asked to squeal on his cronies or by cronies or enemies who feared that he would is still debated. But Brown's funeral march saw Eddie Seaga lead thirty thousand mourners through Kingston's streets. It was the sort of thing to keep conspiracy theorists talking for years. (Many naturally posit that since the autopsy photos of Jim Brown's charred body have never been released, he's still alive.) But it also set the stage for Jim Brown's youngest son to take his place—and go further.

The man all Jamaicans learned to call "Dudus" was a short, pudgy youth of just twenty-one when his father died. Christopher Coke was not only the youngest of Jim Brown's sons; he was also born to a woman who was not the don's wife—hardly a rare story in context, but a certain handicap for his prospects. (The alleged source for his moniker was his favoring African-style shirts that were also worn by the '70s-era Jamai-can statesman Dudley Thompson.) During the weeks and months after Jim Brown's death, not a few pretenders to his throne were subjected to a "Tivoli funeral," their bullet-riddled bodies deposited in front of the Denham Town Police Station. During this interregnum, Dudus dis-played deft cunning. Helped by the fact that Jim Brown's eldest son, Jah T, had been murdered in mysterious circumstances days before his dad's death, Dudus outmaneuvered his rivals to secure rising-don status. He ultimately won power, in an apt wrinkle on this incestuous isle, with the unwitting help of another son of a 1970s icon.

Bob Marley's eldest son, Ziggy, is a singer who has enjoyed a modicum of success internationally—though not in Jamaica—that has often seemed to depend on his striking resemblance, especially as beheld by stoned reggae fans abroad, to his famed father. As a spoiled son of privilege, Ziggy grew up far from Bob's home ghetto and its ways. In 1994, he endeavored to "give back" to Trench Town's people by building a recording studio for local kids and seasoned pros who wanted to soak up the vibes of his father's home slum near Tivoli's edge. Unfortunately, he neglected to call the area's new don to kick the construction contract his way. Maybe Ziggy was determined not to deal with the progeny of men who had tried to murder his father (Jim Brown was long rumored to have been one of Marley's assailants in 1976), but in any case, this wouldn't do, and it was Dudus's swift campaign to show as much—a couple of Ziggy's associates ended up prone in front of the Denham Town Police Station—that concretized his rule as the new don dadda. (It may be no accident that the only one of Marley's offspring with much cred or popularity on the Jamaican street is Damian. "Junior Gong," as he's known, is the son of Cindy Breakespeare—Miss World 1976—who, after the Gong's death, partnered with a prominent "garrison lawyer" who was intimately tied to the leaders of the Tivoli garrison, and made sure her son spent much of his youth downtown.)

Dudus was as unflamboyant as Jim Brown was flashy; "Short Man" (another nickname) was a study in wily discretion—and a keen businessman. He moved quickly to open a new construction firm. That outfit, Incomparable Enterprise, soon had a portfolio of rich public contracts from such agencies as Jamaica's National Heritage Trust and the Ministry of Education. Its projects didn't just include bread-and-butter local jobs like rebuilding Tivoli's drainage gully; Dudus's firm was also responsible for such prominent gigs as the long-delayed refurbishment of the Ward Theatre and the incredible boondoggle that is the Downtown Kingston Transport Centre. Completed not long before Dudus's death in 2010, the center consists of a huge maze of concrete barriers and Plexiglas bus shelters. It's sited right between downtown proper and Tivoli's eastern edge, and was intended to be the main hub for buses and roto-taxis linking Kingston to its suburbs and beyond. Today, the completed complex sits empty: its smooth pavement is used much more for pickup soccer than transport, and is eschewed by Kingstonians, who still prefer to line up for buses and roto-taxis—as someone in power may or may not have known they would—where they always have: by Parade. With his wealth from these other less visible gangster trades, Dudus furnished financing for Tivoli's young women to open beauty salons and other businesses; he bought their kids toys at Christmas; he provided the entire garrison—whose twenty-thousand-odd tenants have always lived there rent-free—with water and power. He also became the de facto don of Jamaican music. Through his production company, Presidential Click, Dudus promoted shows that launched the careers of dancehall stars like Vybz Kartel. He also underwrote Passa Passa, the street dance held each Wednesday right outside Tivoli's gates, for a decade from the late '90s, which made his garrison the twerking heart of Jamaica's youth culture. Dudus, as the don dadda also responsible for organizing other JLP garrisons (and, as such, for what might be called get-out-the-vote efforts across the island), was also crucial to helping the first JLP government in a generation take power, in 2007, under the leadership of the new-sullied politico, Bruce Golding, who succeeded Seaga as both Tivoli's MP and his party's titular head.

All of which may help explain why, when the United States pressured Golding into detaining Dudus by force, in 2010, not a few Jamaicans were shocked that he agreed. Goldings party's power derived from the gangsters it relied on for votes. The dons, whose sway in the ghetto far excelled the government's, had long since usurped their makers. Could this JLP lifer, Golding, really invade his own constituency by force, to arrest its don? In the end, it seems that he had no choice: his government's chief patron, and indispensable creditor in Washington, had decided that it was time to the haul the Shower Posse's head to jail. The ensuing set-to pitted Jamaica's military police against the don's well-armed supporters, many of whom erected burning barricades and fired on their assailants from within Tivoli's walls. When Golding's soldiers shot back with bigger weapons and indiscriminate fire, the result was at least seventy-four civilians dead, and a country in chaos. (Two police officers also died in the violence.) Dudus was eventually captured, stopped at a roadblock in a disguise comprised of an old lady's hat and glasses, but not before Kingston burned once more, and not without disgracing a prime minister who lost all credibility not merely in his brutalized constituency but across the country. Golding was ushered from power, and Tivoli Gardens, the garrison he had both represented and destroyed, was returned to the wizened hands of its creator. Edward

Seaga, fifty years after creating Tivoli, and never having really relinquished it, became the garrison's MP once more and the scars from this "incursion," as I found hopping a cab downtown two years later, still linger large amid Kingston's more general state of emergency.

I pointed, as we rolled down King Street from the Half Way Tree, at a hulking concrete building with blue trim. "That's KPH, no?" My query to my cabbie was more about making conversation than confirming the identity of this place. We were passing Kingston Public Hospital, whose emergency room during the Tivoli incursion became a hellish blood den. His short reply, though, contained a memorable tale.

"Yes, sir," murmured the cabbie, whose head, I noticed, was as large as his thick neck. "I was there."

He reached across my lap to open the glove compartment, and pulled out a bit of folded paper. "Dem shot me," he said softly. "Darkness." He handed me the paper. It was a clipping from *The Gleaner:* "'Fat Head' Survives Head Wound," read its headline.[2]

The story described how "the taxi driver Anthony Nicholson, also known as 'Fat Head,'" had been jumped by three "youths," who, after demanding money and ganja, had shot him in the head. It continued: "While Nicholson cannot remember the month or year, Nicholson is definite that he was shot between 4:30 and 5 pm." Fat Head, as we rolled past KPH, confirmed the information to me.

"Have you thought of leaving the taxi business?" I asked.

"No sir." Fat Head drove his cab six days a week—every day but Saturday. He was a Seventh-day Adventist, and Saturdays were reserved for Jesus.

We passed a church called Redeemer's Moravian. Fat Head turned onto Marcus Garvey Drive, down by the sea, and stopped his cab. I stepped out.

"You take care," he said. He smiled faintly as he pushed his hat back on his iron dome. "Bless."

* * *

IT IS CLEAR EVERYWHERE one looks that little in Jamaica remains untouched by its two parties' fractious rivalry. Along the waterfront, a hot wind blew off the sea to buffet the dusty palms and turn Kingston Harbour, as usual, into a choppy tub dotted with rusting freighters and no pleasure craft. I paused by an outsized bit of bronze that was, until recently, the island's most famous bit of art. A blocky figure whose metallic brown head, with angular art deco lines, is thrown back to the sky, *Negro Aroused* was sculpted by Edna Manley, the artist wife of founding father Norman. She was inspired by the labor unrest in the 1930s that grew into Jamaica's drive for independence—and lived to see her work erected outside the state institution where I was to meet my ride to an engagement in the nearby garrisons that make that state go. Jamaica's National Gallery of Art is housed in a boxy 1950s-style hovel that began its life, before high-end retail left downtown, as a department store. The gallery boasts scores of impressive works by the likes of Isaac Mendes Belisario, whose depictions of the "John Canoe" dances of slavery days, and the colorful costuming associated therewith, have been invaluable to scholars connecting those traditions to today. Its permanent collection also contains two galleries, and two alone, dedicated to individual artists. One is devoted to Edna Manley, white-woman icon of bien-pensant PNP socialism. The other is filled with the "intuitive" paintings and sculpture of Kapo, the Pocomania preacher who, when not making art, delivered to Seaga's JLP its first partisans among the "sufferahs."

The parties' animus, though modeled in the layout of the National Gallery, finds deadlier form in the built environs of the nearby blocks I was heading for. I had been invited to visit with a youth group in Trench Town run by one of the neighborhood's most devoted servants. I stepped from the gallery to climb into the backseat of a white SUV. At the wheel was Nando Garcia, an expat Spanish filmmaker whose passion for Jamaican culture led him to make such useful movies as *Why Do Jamaicans Run So Fast?*, a winning vox-pop documentary, and *Hit Me with Music*, a portrait of dancehall culture's vibrant state at Passa Passa's height. In Garcia's passenger seat sat his producer. Shirley Hanna was an elegant uptown lady whose main notoriety in Jamaican society, apart from this film work, came of her being the mother of Lisa Hanna, the last Jamaican Miss World and the current minister of youth and culture. Our driver, excited as a schoolboy, rolled off from the gallery toward the west.

Garcia guided his SUV up Matthews Lane, the longtime stronghold of Spangler Posse and its PNP thugs. He turned a corner by Coronation Market to pass higglers peddling green dasheen and gritty-sweet naseberries. The center of the JLP's downtown cosmos rose into view. Tivoli's cement walls, two years after the incursion, were still pocked with divots from its invaders' bullets. On one gray-white wall was a green-tinted mural of a big U.S. dollar bill. The portrait at its center, in place of George Washington's, was Jim Brown's. We rolled past the Denham Town Police Station, and Garcia pointed to the spot on Span-ish Town Road where Passa Passa once ruled, but no more. During the 2010 state of emergency, the government moved to enforce old "noise abatement laws"; two years later, they were still in force. We passed the huge May Pen Cemetery, where many of those slain in Dudus's deposi-tion now lay, and where a young Bob Marley and his friends, training themselves to "sing wid duppy," rehearsed. Then we turned up Collie Smith Boulevard to enter the ghetto that the most famous Wailer made Jamaica's best known.

"Trench Town! It's an even stronger brand than Brand Jamaica." That's what our host, Junior Lincoln, exclaimed soon after we hopped out of Garcia's car. We were standing in his neighborhood's heart. An esteemed music impresario who got his start organizing dances here in his teens, Lincoln had light brown skin and a manner at once gentle and firm. He made his way from Jamaica to London in the 1960s and played a key role there, as a concert promoter and producer, in sell-ing Trench Town's music to the world. After thirty years abroad, he returned home, and now he was spending his dotage trying to "put Trench Town on the map." He handed me an actual map. Its title was printed in bold red ink: "Musical Celebrities from Trench Town: To Di Root." The map charted an area, to downtown's west, cross-hatched with a ladder of streets numbered 1 through 7 and jutting off of Collie Smith. Trench Town was built in soggy lowlands uninhabited until World War II. It became a landing place for the rural poor who crowded the capital after the war's end, among them little Nesta Robert Marley and Bunny Wailer and Peter Tosh: each had a spot on Junior's map. But this was also a borough, as the map showed in numbered red dots, which were clustered with astonishing density along these blocks, whose shanties nurtured the rise of assorted Heptones and Maytals, ska greats like Ernest Ranglin, and Alton Ellis, the rocksteady king. Kapo's Zion Revival Chapel, on Junior's map, sat around the corner from the 2nd Street yard where Marley hit puberty. The latter site is home now to the Trench Town Culture Yard, a would-be tourist destination where adventuresome pilgrims can come to take snapshots of the burned-out VW bus near which Bob wrote "No Woman, No Cry" ("I remember / when we used to sit / inna government yard in Trenchtown"). If they're more brave still, they can take up one of the scowling hustlers outside on their offer to buy some Marley weed, or check out the surrounding blocks. (Few do.) I found the dot, on Junior's map, corresponding to the low-slung cement building, with slatted windows and yellow walls, before which we stood. This was Boys' Town, an old Anglican community center where many of the greats on Junior's map came as kids to escape the grim yards where they lived. Junior had invited a few guests here today to speak with some of the area kids who do the same now. Inside, he pointed out a battered old piano where Tosh and Marley learned harmony.

There in the main hall, a testament to "The Cricket 'Immortals' of the West Indies" hung alongside a portrait of Father Hugh Sherlock, the kindly mid-century parson who founded Boys' Town and also wrote his secular nation's rather Christian national anthem ("Eternal Father, bless our land, / Guide us with Thy mighty hand"). Boys' Town sits right between JLP- and PNP-controlled blocks; it has long been a sanctuary where wearing the parties' colors (green and orange, respectively) is banned. On a chalkboard, someone had scrawled a plaintive slogan in blue chalk: "Revenge Restrained Is a Victory Gained." Restive kids sat teasing each other in their chairs. Most were skinny or fat in the way poor kids everywhere tend to be; a few looked undernourished-gaunt. I took my place, in a plastic seat, with the other interlopers Junior had asked to "say some words to the youth." My role, as the "professor from foreign," was to offer some sincere noises about how I knew they may have heard how their neighborhood changed the world, but that I was here to tell them that well, it was true. I did so. Then I handed the microphone to the reggae-pop singer Shaggy, whose string of world hits in the early aughts, from "Boombastic" to "Angel," saw him sell more records than any Jamaican since Marley. Shaggy was dressed in designer jeans; he'd hung his expensive sunglasses from the V-neck of his shirt. He crooned a verse for the kids; the girls giggled. He told them to "follow they dreams." And then Junior Lincoln, who'd told us he was trying to raise funds to build the "top-class recording studio" here that Ziggy Marley never did, followed with a slightly-more-real urging that "in the music business, we need more than stars; we need engineers and stylists and roadies." This information was received by the kids with only a few more nods than the remarks of another of our party: Shirley Hanna expounded the uplifting powers of "positivity" and good posture.

In the hall afterward, we sipped powdered lemonade from paper cups. A few of the boys followed Shaggy's lead, taking turns singing songs or showing off with the mic. A few of the girls played at perfecting their beauty-queen walks while laughing with Shirley. I chatted with some kids in knockoff Man United jerseys about a subject—Premier League Soccer—in which children everywhere but America can converse. Back out on Trench Town's ragged streets, feral dogs were skulking past. It wasn't hard to despair of a country whose privileged, when met with its poor, have naught to offer but blandishments about following dreams and a good carriage's uplifting force. But as I walked up the boulevard with Junior Lincoln, it was also true that the lines playing in my head had been written by a ghetto kid who strode from these blocks with a beauty queen's bearing, and with dreams and positivity to burn.

> Natty dread, natty dread now
> A dreadlock congo bongo I
> Natty dreadlock inna Babylon
> Roots natty, roots natty.

This is the chorus of "Natty Dread," the title track to Marley's beautiful third album. It begins as kid's-verse homily to Rasta living, and being a locksman "inna Babylon." But then it gets interesting.

> Then I walk up the 1st Street
> And then I walk up to 2nd Street to see
> Then I trod on, through 3rd Street

What's the singer aiming to see? He goes on:

> And then I talk to some dread on 4th Street
> Natty dreadlock inna 5th Street
> And then I skip one fence to 6th Street

He talks to a Rastaman, before pausing, on 5th, to check himself before treading on to 6th Street, and telling us where he's going.

> I've got to reach 7th Street

He's got to reach 7th Street. Why? Walking up Collie Smith with Junior, I felt a possibility arise. Across 7th, we could see another block of low-rise projects. Arnette Gardens was this garrison's official name;

unofficially, it's known as "concrete jungle," per another Marley tune ("Concrete jungle / Where the living is harder"). On a wall by its entrance, I could see an orange-tinted mural. A bit higher up, another building-side image featured the face of Portia Simpson-Miller, leader of the PNP and a big bad man herself. Here was an area loyal to the party of Portia, Manley, and Marshall. Back toward Tivoli, green was everywhere; here it was all about orange. And 7th Street, not a few times in its history, and especially at election times, has comprised a frontier not to be crossed. Pondering Marley's lines by the road that inspired them, I found it easy to imagine young men here, caught on the wrong side, thinking just what he sang. "I've got to reach 7th Street."

Reaching safe turf, as any ghetto kid knows, is a worthy subject for song. If that simple muse was the subject of "Natty Dread," though, the theme of its bridge, like his larger oeuvre, was the grander problem of how, whether with music or otherwise, to transcend the brutal "politricks" that made the concrete jungle tick. And in this respect, the home Marley figured wasn't mere blocks away, or even up in Kingston's hills. "Natty 21,000 miles away from home," he sang. "And that's a long way for Natty to be from home." Redemption, as the Rastas said, lay over the sea. Rarely was their greatest voice so literal about it, though. Marley's best songs—and this was his greatness—refused to ground Zion in the vulgarities of blood or land. In the tune that endured as his epitaph, he distilled his art's essence. "Redemption songs / are all I ever have." The line's double meaning, and his image of music's subtler salvations in this place where daily life was a hurtful grind, were of a piece. "One good thing about music," went the chorus to "Trenchtown Rock," "when it hits you, you feel no pain." And that song, fittingly enough, was the one Junior Lincoln invoked as we reached 7th Street and, approaching the dusty site of one of music's most aqueous springs, stepped across.

"Tell: What music was playing when the Berlin Wall fell?" Junior pulled a key from his pocket. "Trench Town rock!" We were standing by a large building's curving concrete wall, freshly painted white; only a small "PNP" someone had tagged, off to our side, sullied its surface. Lincoln pushed his key into a heavy padlock on its gate and, removing the chain, led me inside. The place's roof was long gone. But the distinct shape of a large theater's proscenium and deep stage was plain. "And right here," Junior said, "is where it began." He pointed to the spot where he'd stood as a boy when Alton Ellis was discovered by Sir Coxsone Dodd; when the Wailers played "Simmer Down" for their friends; when Jimmy Cliff, years before being cast as a gun-flashing folk hero in *The Harder They Come*, got his start chirping ska ditties during the Vere Johns Opportunity Hour. We were standing on the floor of the Ambassador Theatre. This was "hallow' ground in the story of this music." The revitalization of "the 'Bas," Junior said, would be a main feature of Trench Town's future.

How was that going? A buzzard flew overhead. "Tough road." Butch Stewart, the package-tourism magnate, had invited Junior onto his yacht to express support for his aims of leveraging Trench Town's brand. He couldn't get anyone in government, though, to back his plans. But Junior, who'd been key to spreading the music born here to its old ruler's heart, wasn't terribly surprised.

"You saw what a mess they made of the Olympics? Jamaica 50, in London—all the culture England *has* comes from us! And you saw what they did?"

I had not seen it.

"That's right! Because they had some little ting in a theater, two thousand people. It should have been the party of the year. All the stars; Hyde Park. But it was a higgler's shop! A bloody higgler's shop."

This, Junior thought, was a huge opportunity lost for Brand Jamaica. But part of why the government hadn't been able to get it together was familiar. After Bruce Golding's catastrophic campaign to bring Dudus to justice, new elections were called. Months before the Olympics, the JLP was swept from power and a new government installed. The transition's timing couldn't have been worse. Any chance for an effective large-scale touting of Brand Jamaica in London was lost.

Junior Lincoln stepped into the sunlit scrubland around the 'Bas and the 7th Street frontier. "Perhaps," he sighed, as he replaced the roofless theater's lock, "we can do better here."

* * *

JAMAICA'S POWERS THAT BE were not enthused about ferrying tourists to the ghetto districts that supply both their power and their shame. This wasn't shocking. But if their idea wasn't to help Junior Lincoln bring tourists to Trench Town, what did they mean, after all, by Brand Jamaica, and what might they do with it? A couple of weeks after visiting the 'Bas and Boys' Town with Junior Lincoln, I went to another event that promised some answers at Emancipation Park in New Kingston.

Emancipation Park lies about as far from the 'Bas as one can get in

Kingston's geography of power. Since opening in 2002, it has become Jamaica's chosen venue for official showcases of "national culture" and attendant conflicts. This was the place, for example, where the gala Jamaican premier of Kevin Macdonald's *Marley* was almost canceled after Bunny Wailer, arriving to the film with a delegation of Rasta elders, saw the red, gold, and green carpet laid out at the park entrance, protested that no one should trod on the holy colors, and demanded its removal. (A plain red one was found instead.) This is also the bit of Jamaican public space that boasts the piece of statuary that's supplanted Edna Manley's *Negro Aroused* as Jamaica's most famed. Unmistakable for its location and size, the piece guards the park's entrance, where it's set in a low circular pool. It is comprised of two nude figures, twelve feet tall and with their thighs emerging from the water, their eyes gazing up from bondage. Sculpted by another white female artist from Kingston's upper classes, it was called, predictably enough, *Redemption Song*. But the statue's local notoriety derives less from artistic merits than from a feature that is impossible to miss. Walking by and casting your eyes at these obsidian figures, you are met, right at eye level, with the figures' colossal genitals. Big Bamboo, indeed.

On the day of the prime minister's Youth Awards for Excellence, hundreds of uniformed school kids streamed into the park, pointing at Mr. Jamaica's Brobdingnagian bits, and giggled loudly. I joined the throng of well-dressed parents and kin who'd come straight from church; it was a Sunday afternoon. I'd spent some weeks speaking with people from the Tourist Board, the Film Board, and the Institute of Jamaica; it was clear that none of them, no matter the ways they all spoke of Brand Jamaica, could talk about what comprised best brand practice. This event was put on by the prime minister and had the official motto "Youth on a Mission . . . Project 2062." It was presided over by then minister of youth and culture Lisa Hanna and promised to distill, in one grand tableau of live-action propaganda, how Portia's administration saw the brand and its uses. Loitering inside the park, I looked for the new friend who had told me about it.

Seretse Small was a veteran of Jamaica's culture industries with a secondary role in their official staging. He was a noted jazz guitarist and arranger whose career had taken him from studying music theory and composition at Edna Manley College of the Visual and Performing Arts, just up the road, to touring the world with reggae's biggest stars. He had told me, the evening we'd met through a mutual friend, about backing up Shaggy on *Saturday Night Live*, and about how, when he'd gone on tour to Kenya with someone else, the people there had told him how it was Jamaican music men like him who "showed them how to be both modern and black." Now Seretse had mostly retired from performing. But he was still in the music game, managing a band of young men from his alma mater whose reggae-tinged guitar pop seemed aimed at appealing to the boy-band fan base of One Direction. His group, Da Blueprint, had bested a few thousand rivals in a "World Battle of the Band Contest" in the UK earlier that year, and thus garnered a spot on the bill at the Youth View Awards back home. A couple of nights before, I'd stopped by Edna Manley College to watch them rehearse. The school's '70s-idealist architecture placed domes and trees amid little amphitheaters and shaded groves. It seemed almost a carbon copy of the analogous school Fidel Castro built in Havana in the '60s on the grounds of an old country club to train the youth who would build Caribbean socialism. This made sense: Michael Manley's PNP took its cues from Cuba in the '70s. To judge by the official who stopped by that night to look in on Da Blueprint's rehearsal, today's PNP still takes them from there. The official was an affable if unctuous fat man in a tie, backed up by two aides, similarly attired. He pronounced the band's two covers of classic reggae songs "okay." He was less sure about a bubble-gum ballad, "Your Love," on which the skinny guitar player harmonized with his bassist brother. Was it too risqué to include in their nine-minute set? He'd let Seretse know.

At Emancipation Park, one party who had needed no pre-show vetting was the woman who gazed into the crane-mounted camera sweeping over the crowd, to welcome us to the show. Lisa Hanna was no stranger to TV. She first passed before the public eye hosting local programs as a teen before ascending, after she became Miss World in 1993, to the status of Brand Jamaica icon. When flying out for that pageant in South Africa, Lisa's mother told me, the nineteen-year-old budding politician made a point of showing local news cameras how, at the nape of her neck, she had grown a single little dreadlock, wrapped in Rasta-colored string, that she would hide beneath flowing tresses abroad but that people back home, secure in her Jamaican-ness, would know was there. Twenty years on, Shirley Hanna's daughter had traded her tiara for a prim suit. Now she lent her poise and perfect grooming to this PNP government as its minister of youth and culture. It was her job, baring pearly teeth below high cheekbones, to launch this pageant put on by her boss. She said we were there to honor young Jamaicans who, "like the stars up above," had a "brilliance [that's] allowed Jamaica to shine and provide light for the rest of the world." And then those young stars—a young man who'd won London bronze at 200 meters; a young woman who won the same colored medal, in "Fashion Technology," at something called the WorldSkills Competition, in São Paulo—mounted the stage. They took their plaudits from the prime minister, who smiled serenely from the front row, doting on her children. One of them, a proud pigtailed schoolgirl in this society where twice as many girls as boys finish high school, delivered the day's "vote of thanks." She described how the honorees gathered onstage weren't merely proud to be honored, and proud of Jamaica's great leaders; they felt that "Portia" wasn't just a leader, she was "our mother too, the mother of our people. And for her love, which we can feel so dear, we are so grateful." Amen.

Seretse's boy band was allowed to do their song; another young singer, I learned, drew harsh reprimand for wiggling his hips overmuch. I'd seen his act. His moves might have been risqué on *The Ed Sullivan Show* in 1954; in this city where kids' dominant dance was called "daggering" for a reason, they seemed gentility's height. But such wiggling wasn't in accord with the aims of what was, at bottom, a political rally whose producers left nothing to chance. This was unshocking. So were the leagues of remove from actual youth culture its youth culture awards cited. What was striking, here, was the larger vision of Brand Jamaica, and culture's role in it, espoused by Minister Hanna as she closed the proceedings. "The excellence of the next generation," she told us and the cameras, "would herald a new time of courage, passion, resilience, and fortitude, for Jamaica to remain the best cultural capital, and country, in the world." She wasn't done there. Remaining "the best cultural capital" wouldn't be easy. She flashed those pearly teeth to conclude with a call to arms. "What we need," the former Miss World intoned, "is a cultural revolution."

The Chairman Mao phrasing was striking. But it wasn't new. She'd used it before. "Cultural revolution" had also been the takeaway phrase from a speech she'd delivered in the heady days of Jamaica 50, in which she'd outlined her ministry's new cultural policy, high in the mountains of the cockpit country, where the Maroons won self-rule from the British. The larger aspect and resonance of the venue for that speech, the Maroons' old capital of Accompong, suggested much about its contents. This village was described by the American choreographer Katherine

Dunham in her 1946 book, *Journey to Accompong*,[3] based on Dunham's research as a grad student in anthropology, as home to a kind of "Africanity" unknown in North America. Dunham's ideas helped inspire a postwar folk revival whose builders included Louise "Miss Lou" Bennett in Jamaica and, in New York, a folk singer—Harry Belafonte—who married one of Dunham's dancers. That generation's art was premised on performing a kind of "authenticity" that may be regarded, by sophisticated kids now, as imbued with the same artifice all performing is. But Accompong's resonance, in the Dunham-Bennett-Belafonte vision of folk culture's political uses, certainly allied with the vision of cultural revolution Lisa Hanna proclaimed in a place whose ties to its past I'd glimpsed when, after driving up to Accompong myself, I met the curator-cum-foreman of its town museum. That thin man with a wily air told me he was descended in a direct line from Queen Nanny and insisted on posing, with her *abeng* horn, for a picture. And then he showed me around a tidy mountain town whose access to public funds, and the sympathy of international NGOs, was plain in its gleaming new school and the good, drivable road I'd arrived on—built by the PNP, he said, for their loyal supporters here. "Di only green me deal with," he volunteered, "is di vegetation and grass deh."

That avowed Maroon's reasons for enacting a past that was also his livelihood, and for rejecting the JLP's colors, were plain. Could it really be, though, that his party's new leaders, invoking their cultural revolution and Brand Jamaica in the same breath, saw the same pastward-looking thrust as Jamaica's path ahead? As I stood in Emancipation Park, listening to Lisa Hanna try to instill in the youths the spirits of the elders, it certainly seemed so. And when I went to see her ministry's chief consigliere and speechwriter, he confirmed it. Resplendent in his silk Rasta-colored tie and braces, he shrugged off the phrase's Beijing ring. "What we mean by 'cultural revolution,'" he explained, "is activity awakening the memory of Bogle, and Nanny, and Sam Sharpe and the Maroons." The efflorescence of those figures' images, on hotel walls and in airports, had found their source. "That culture of resistance *is* Brand Jamaica," he concluded. "And we are a uniquely cultural people." I didn't have the heart to ask, as I'd planned to, why this government so committed to Jamaica's "uniquely cultural people" was actively engaged in constricting the main space—street dances—within which their culture now grows.

The answer was implicit. The only ways that Jamaica's leaders, so aware of their peoples' visibility and keen to tout it, had been able to work out how to do so were stuck, if not in the seventeenth century, then certainly in the 1970s. What the policymakers didn't see, or couldn't, was that what makes Jamaica cool was not it "activating the past." It was about young people from Tokyo to New York looking here, as they have been learning to do for some decades now, to see what will be cool next week, or next year. Jamaica's brand had juice precisely for the bits of culture that governments are traditionally good not at supporting but suppressing. And it had juice because of how its most gifted exponents don't "activate" the past so much as play with it. In the manner, say, of the martyred street dancer Bogle, whose name did just that, and whose funeral march, featuring a glass casket adorned with the Sesame Street characters he loved, brought thousands of decked-out mourners to "jiggy jiggy" wakes, in the garrisons where he was a hero. ("A lie!" they yelled as his hearse passed.)[4] Or in the manner of, say, Lady Saw, whose reign as the Queen of the Dancehall has lasted better than twenty years, and who told me, when I met her one night at TGI Friday's in Kingston, about how she saw her work as building on the best folk tradition of Louise Bennett.

"How did Miss Lou put it, about 'Jamaican 'oman'?" asked Lady Saw in our corner booth. "Look how long dem liberated and de man dem never know!" Wearing white sneakers, and dark sunglasses perched atop an auburn wig, Lady Saw laughed. We sat across Hope Road from the Marley museum, in this chain restaurant full of Jamaicans who, perhaps getting a jump on their dream to one day dwell in a Florida suburb, were downing iridescent drinks from big plastic cups. Their island's queen of raunch, sipping a daiquiri and eating fries, told me of being born to a large family in a small country town, and of how her father went to America, and though he never got papers to bring his family, did send home country records she loved. ("You know Loretta Lynn's 'Woman Enough to Take My Man'—that's gangster!") She told me of coming to Kingston to work as a sweatshop seamstress in the Free Zone, where she met the lover-producer who "put her on." ("First hit was 'Half-and-Half Love Affair'—it was about having an affair with a man when he's someone else's man.") She explained the over-sexed "slack" persona she performs onstage—"The guys were doing it, why couldn't a woman do it?"—and she recounted how the American pop-punk band No Doubt came to Jamaica to record their Grammy-winning hit "Underneath It All," and called her to lend them a verse.

("It was done in a minute, and then: Boom! It was a hit. I loved that.") She chatted graciously with fans who walked over to pay respects, and told me about how much she loved Louise Bennett—but how she'd also felt compelled, in a remake of Miss Lou's "Under the Sycamore Tree," to tweak her hero. ("It's about getting her first kiss under that tree. But you know she got laid under there!") She told me about how lots of young pretenders had come at her crown but that she "spits harder than any of these young chicks coming up; I don't have competition" (it was true); and also about how, when she's placed in social set-tos with Jamaica's "uppity uppitys" among whom she now lives in a big house uptown, they are often shocked to find that Marion Hall, the lovely, bright woman Lady Saw is when she's not singing tunes they abjure, "actually wasn't a rude person at all."[5]

Here, in short, was a real, live exemplar of what makes Jamaica cool as hell. But here, also, was a remarkable person whose appeal to officialdom, and to a minister of culture who closed her Youth Awards for Excellence with the hope that "God continue to bless this country, as we move forward, to bless the world with who we are," was beyond nil. That spring, Lady Saw, after an extended raunch sabbatical during which she'd performed only gospel and country tunes, had just returned to heavy radio play and cultural relevance, with a tune Miss World wouldn't touch with a bamboo pole.

The title of her latest hit was this: "Fuck Me with My Heels On."

* * *

THE BIRTHLAND OF the great Lady Saw, of course, is hardly the sole country whose uppity uppitys struggle to commandeer the songs and styles of their lowers, for the ends of an establishment that fucks them. One is tempted, as a general rule, to echo the dictum of a great island culture maven about what happens when officialdom butts in. "Anytime you get government involved," says Chris Blackwell, "it's a fuckup." Which, with the exception of building schools to train art makers, or create spaces for them to play—and then getting out of the way—may obtain everywhere. So may the gap between culture as it happens on the street and "cultural policy" as decreed from on high. That Jamaica's powers that be should turn Marley's "Redemption Song," a tune as subtly aware of art's limits as music's power, into a gravely unsubtle monument in stone isn't surprising. But part of what's striking about these gaps' breadth, in this country whose brand's boosters speak of "our uniquely cultural people," and whose Miss World minister of culture believes she lives in "the best cultural capital, and country, in the world," is that even on their discourse's own terms, Brand Jamaica's strength is middling to poor.

Not in terms of Jamaica's outsized impress on global pop: by now, that's both undeniable and widely known. But in terms, as a prominent local blogger pointed out after the Youth Awards, of its "brand strength's" putative relation to real economic growth. In a report by an outfit called FutureBrands that aimed to quantify growth potential as tied to countries' reputations for "quality of life," "good for business," and "history and culture," the Jamaican author Diana McCaulay noted on her Facebook page, Jamaica wasn't merely nowhere on the list of top entrants.[6] It lagged far behind such island peers as Mauritius (20), and Bermuda (24), not to mention such diverse rivals as Namibia (46) and Belize (48). In the Caribbean, Jamaica's "brand strength" was soundly bested by Barbados (29) and the Dominican Republic (53). Even Trinidad and Tobago (54) and, most galling of all, socialist Cuba (57) trumped the world nation perhaps most invested in, and high on, using its "brand strength" for growth. Jamaica came in 62nd.[7] FutureBrand's algorithm may have been hazy. But as Jamaica's wakeful citizens began to assert with rising force, banking on the ineffable currency of "cool" seemed about as wise a tack for battling poverty as bottling sin. Brand Jamaica, as McCaulay and others noted, was perhaps most useful as a politicians' slogan for demeaning democracy. They had seen how their minister of culture, when she caught some negative press, maligned a group of concerned citizens for harming Jamaica's brand: they had signed a simple petition voicing concern over state care provided to youths by her ministry. By that spring's end, as I readied to leave the island, it was unclear how long Brand Jamaica would dominate the country's chats with itself. Either way, one felt sure, Jamaican culture would survive. Its makers would continue, with their outsized will to perform, to enact their past and their now, by means loud and funny and inspired and mad, forever.

On one of my last days in Jamaica that spring, I walked by Emancipation Park, past the Herculean nudes of *Redemption Song*, and turned up New Kingston's main road. I passed a building-sized Digicel billboard featuring Usain Bolt's familiar torso ("Millions of Dreams," read its flag-colored caption, "Need Strong Shoulders"), and stepped into an outlet of Tastee, the fast food restaurant whose morsels of fatty dough, air-fried around ground meat, are dispensed from franchises around the island and have become free Jamdown's national dish. I took the bag my pattie came in. "Buy Jamaica," it said on the greasy brown paper. "Brand We Love." I continued up the road, to where the same flashy modeling agency that hosted the *Global Reggae* book launch in its bar was hosting a similar fete tonight. This one toasted the release of a book of photos of "reggae's golden age," published by the same outfit that put out Edward Seaga's *100 Most Influential Songs* box set. Word was that the Dark Lord Seaga, who'd had a hand in this project, too, might turn up.

At a table by the bar, I recognized Seaga's partner in releasing many old records Pat Chin. Earl "Chinna" Smith, an eminent Rasta guitarist whose chicken-scratch tones graced all the greats, was accepting the adoration of a pair of Japanese girls in saddle shoes. On the bar's walls, and in an adjacent room, hung large-format images of the late-'70s moment that Jamaica's boosters can't seem to leave behind. There was Marley in full flight; Toots in repose; a smiling Peter Tosh, skinny and locked, riding a unicycle on Martha's Vineyard during a U.S. tour. At the bar I chatted with a tall young woman in a royal-blue dress and zebra-print heels, from whom I gathered that the duty-cum-perk of signing with the modeling agency she represented was that you had to adorn the bar at functions like these. She said she had a manager in Zurich; she'd spent last summer in Ibiza, "working." She bore a striking resemblance to Rihanna. She asked if I'd like to pay her rent. I paid for her wine, instead (she frowned when the barkeep said he had no moscato; she settled for Chablis). This was a timely reminder that the only sure way Jamaica seems to have found for "monetizing" its "uniquely cultural people" in a new era that maybe wasn't so new was to offer the more exceptional of their bodies, whether belonging to models or sprinters, for sale. I joined a tableful of culturati I'd grown used to seeing at these things.

Seaga, it seemed, wasn't coming after all. At his name's mention, though, someone at the table presented an intriguing theory about the Tivoli incursion. "You know it' Seaga doing," he said. Tivoli was Seaga's garrison; what better way for the old CIA hand to tie up his loose ends, near his life's end, than by taking out a don who'd outgrown his control and, in the same swoop, making the position of his loathed successor as PM untenable? (Golding and Seaga had a notorious falling-out.)

"Where Seaga now?" We knew. "He' back! And the people still love him!" True enough. "Politricks," or the wary perception thereof, knew no bounds in this city where Vybz Kartel's just-released book contained some sage conclusions. In *The Voice of the Jamaican Ghetto*, the dancehall king had argued that the nation's first step to betterment was to ban its two ruling parties. "As a people," he wrote, "we should insist that we will not vote for the PNP or JLP in the new Republic. Those two bodies are synonymous with too many deaths."[8] Perhaps there'd be a new constitutional convention. Now, though, the photographer being feted here had risen behind a microphone at the end of the patio to speak.

He wore a knit skully and a tie-dyed T-shirt. These weren't the only traits, in this hunched sixtysomething white man with kind eyes, to scream "aging hippie." He thanked us for coming to see the pictures that had made him the don of reggae photogs, and told us about how, after growing up in Westchester County as a scion of the family behind Simon & Schuster publishing (and the brother of Carly Simon), he fell in love with Jamaican music. "It all started when I went to see *The Harder They Come*," Peter Simon recalled. "I'd been following American rock 'n' roll for many years, but got bored with it; it became too commercial. So when I saw that film with Jimmy Cliff in '73, it hit me like a wave. A wave of compassion, love, and reggae rhythm." The film and its soundtrack inspired him. He won a book deal, he explained, to come down and start shooting the snaps we were toasting tonight. And then he introduced a special guest, by way of a story about how he'd met his wife, one fall night in 1975, just after the Red Sox, as usual, had lost the World Series. "I've got two tickets for Toots and the Maytals!" he'd said to a bar full of downcast friends in Boston. No one knew who he was talking about; one shy girl, though, raised her hand. By the time they reached the club, Toots had already played. "But it was Toots," Simon said, "that brought on my romance with my wife. And I'm so grateful to Toots for playing that night, and we've been friends ever since, and he's the best." Applause. "And now, I'd like to welcome him to the stage."

A small man I'd noticed before but not recognized—his head was cloaked in a do-rag and dark glasses—ambled onstage. The reason I'd noticed him, apart from his leather pants, was that he seemed to be attracting more than his share of well-wishers. Now, holding an acoustic guitar by his leather-pantsed leg, he gave Simon a hug, and I understood. The short man plugged in the guitar, and began to play.

Stick it up, mister!
Can you hear what I'm saying now, yeah
Get your hands in the air, sir!

It was Toots. The leather pants and round belly made it hard to tell. But the voice was all his.

I said yeah (I said yeah)
Listen what they say (listen what they say)
Can you hear me say, yeah? (yeah yeah)
Listen what they say (listen what they say)

He swayed like Stevie Wonder, he crooned the words to his great song about being locked up—everyone has one—in Kingston's jail for badness (or, in Toots's case, on weed charges that saw him spend a year there in '66). His photographer pal, off to the side, swayed happily, too.

You give it to me, one time!

We knew how to reply. "Huh!"

You give it to me two times (huh-huh!)
You give it to me three times (huh-huh-huh!)
You give it to me four times (huh-huh-huh-huh!)

We gave it to him. And his familiar voice, floating over the heads of the Red Stripe- and Chablis-sipping crowd, shook the hot Kingston night.

54-46 was my number, was my number, man
Right now, someone else has that number
54-46 was my number, well
Right now, someone else has that number . . .

Cuba Libre

CHAPTER 4

CUBA SÍ

PLUNKED ON AN IMPOSING BLUFF by the sea, Cuba's Hotel Nacional remains Havana's best place for gazing over its seawall and pondering the city's present and past. First opened in 1930, the stately cream-colored hotel was built to house Prohibition-era American tourists, who came to quaff rum cocktails invented by the hotel's bartenders to separate *yanquis* from their dollars. Since that time, the Nacional's rooms have hosted even more stars and statesmen than evidenced by the hundreds of cracked photos watching over the lobby, which is as dusty as you'd expect of a once-luxe place that's been managed for decades by the Cuban Communist Party. But with its patio still stalked by emerald peacocks and waiters in faded black-and-whites, the grounds are lovely. And it's not hard, sipping a mojito in a wicker chair here, to imagine the scene on a fateful day in December 1946, when the Nacional was closed for a private meeting.

On that afternoon a few days before Christmas, a group of distinguished foreign visitors tucked into a feast of ersatz local delicacies. There were crab and queen conch enchiladas from the southern archipelago, swordfish and oysters from the nearby village of Cojímar, roast breast of flamingo and tortoise stew and grilled manatee, all washed down with añejo rum. It is unknown whether the attendees—whose number included about twenty of North America's most notorious gangsters—ended their meal with a cake like the one served at their feast's fictional rendering in *The Godfather: Part II*. But as in the film, the purpose of the gathering was clear: to divvy up shares in the empire of vice they were busy establishing in Havana.

During the next decade, the Mafia built a seaside gambling resort, which soon rivaled, in profits and glamour, its sister project in dusty

Las Vegas. Under the canny direction of Meyer Lansky, the Jewish don who'd risen from the streets of New York's Lower East Side, members of the Havana mob became fabulously wealthy. So too did Cuba's U.S.-backed dictator, Fulgencio Batista, whose stake in the mob's affairs exceeded the sacks of cash delivered weekly to the presidential palace. With Lansky and fellow mobsters like Santo Trafficante employed as "tourism experts" in his government, Batista eliminated taxes on the tourism industry, guaranteed public financing for hotel construction, and even granted responsibility for Cuba's infrastructure development to a new mob-controlled bank, Bandes. In December 1957 the opening of the Riviera, a $14 million Mafia show palace just down the seawall from the Nacional, was celebrated by a special episode of *The Steve Allen Show* on U.S. television and a gala in Havana featuring Ginger Rogers. Three months later, the twenty-five-story Havana Hilton—mortgage holder: Bandes—became Cuba's biggest hotel yet.

The party ended on New Year's Day 1959. Fidel Castro's *barbudos* had built support for their cause, in Cuba's countryside, by decrying the capital's occupation by mobsters. Now they advanced on Havana. Batista fled the island, and Castro's bearded rebels established their headquarters in the Havana Hilton. They loosed a truckload of pigs on the sleek lobby of the Riviera. Castro announced the "socialist nature" of his revolution. Nikita Khrushchev sent Soviet missiles. President John F. Kennedy—who, during a visit to Havana the previous year as a senator, had spent an afternoon with three mob-supplied prostitutes under the gaze, from behind a two-way hotel room mirror, of Santo Trafficante—instituted the embargo which would for decades define U.S.-Cuba relations. And Cuba, once coveted by Thomas Jefferson as "the most interesting addition which could ever be made to our system of states," became an enduring thorn in that system's heel.[1]

When I first stepped into the garden at the Nacional, I was an American student chuffed to be visiting a place that in the late 1990s my government would rather I didn't. Since then, the sharpness of Cuba's thorn—blunted first by the fall of the Soviet Union and then by the senescence of Havana's leaders—has now also been softened by the warming waters issued from a new American president in Washington. Barack Obama's restoration of Washington's formal diplomatic ties with Havana, just before Christmas in 2014, also included a partial end to the ban on U.S. travelers coming here, if not an actual tearing up of the decades-old embargo that was still described, on a billboard I passed a year after the announcement, as "El Genocidio Mas Largo En La Historia": the longest genocide in history.

Such state-sponsored propaganda messages, which supplanted old placards for Coca-Cola and Esso Gas at the start of the embargo, have long dominated Cuba's visual landscape. Artifacts of blunt lefty moralizing, if not of Cold War kitsch, they were once manna to those "internationalist" visitors who came here to cut sugarcane and do volunteer work in solidarity with this anti-capitalist wonderland whose billboards didn't tell people that they were ugly or that they should buy Crest toothpaste to be happy. Instead, these signs proclaimed Cuba's devotion to the cause of Nelson Mandela or to proudly touting a society in which "no Cuban child sleeps in the streets." That claim can remarkably still be made, in a country with huge problems but also a functioning social safety net.

What kept a rusty state-run economy afloat for the decades after the revolution here was never the volunteer work of crusty Bolivians or Berkeley-ites. It was the patronage of the Soviets. When that patronage ended after the fall of the USSR, Cuba lost 90 percent of its revenue. But Cuban officials determined to keep their social safety net working and the state vaguely solvent. They realized that the funds had to come from somewhere—and so they came from European and Canadian tourists. Attracting tourists' dollars became official policy.

The fantasies that foreigners now come here to fulfill with those dollars, especially now that the foreigners' numbers are set to include more Americans, are usually a lot less noble than those carried by old members of the Venceremos Brigade. They include both the dodgy visions of sex tourists who've always found exploitative joy here and of befuddled beret-sporting admirers of Che Guevara's legend. They include the pretensions of NPR-listening parents and their German peers, who turned *Buena Vista Social Club* into not merely the best-selling record in the history of "world music"; played by monied northerners to warm their wine parties, the *Buena Vista* record comprised a kind of greatest-hits reel from the mob-run heyday of Havana's dance-band peak in the 1950s. Its cuts were performed by survivors of that era who were no more or less charming, in their perky pageboy caps, than most older citizens of an extroverted nation where it's not just performers who perform, and the job of sexiness is never left solely to the young. The album conjured a world, especially for U.S. listeners, sundered from them by politics and time. It furnished the perfect aural accompaniment to a certain image of Havana that need never be sullied for the sort of visitor here who rolls around town in a convertible cab, treating a city that's home to two million actual humans as a kind of sepia set. For such visitors, Havana's art deco lines and old autos, if not those cars' actual riders, feed an especially unearned form of nostalgia.

What's wrong with that particular form of nostalgia, when projected onto today's Cuba from outside, is obvious. The charm of a '55 DeSoto, if you're its owner, dwindles fast when it's breaking down every few blocks, or if it catches fire because it's been refitted to run on propane. A crumbling tenement's faded pastel hue, won by being blasted by salt air and unmaintained for five decades, isn't as cute when its roof caves in (as occurs to an average of three buildings a day in Havana, says an oft-quoted statistic here). But what's more knottily interesting about nostalgia here is its larger role in Cuban life, both on the island and abroad. For particular kinds of longing on which fierce nostalgia feeds have found in Cuba a plenipotent source at least since the November week in 1492 when Columbus poked around its northern shore and promptly began eulogizing "the most beautiful land that human eyes have ever seen."

For some decades now similar sentiments have been especially audible among Cubans who take their morning *café* not in Havana's Vedado but in Styrofoam cups outside the Versailles Restaurant in Miami. The nostalgia of Florida Cubans who after the Castros' revolution left behind memories or gorgeous palm-fringed homes is easy to explain. But it's not just the Cubans who've left who speak like this. If one ever needs affirmation that this emotion's targets aren't limited solely to the past—that one can also be nostalgic for the present and for the future, or simply for life while you're alive—Cuba is the place to learn. Perhaps Columbus sensed a love for superlatives, by means of some mysterious Genoese intuition, in this island's very soil. Whatever the source, his first effusive appraisal clocked the abiding tone of much conversation in a country that remains in love with over-the-top endearments, and with diminutive ones, too. Here where the woman at the lunch counter will address you as "mi vida" (my life's devotion), and apologize for running out of cheese sandwiches by sighing, "Disculpe, mi amor" (I'm sorry, my love), every Pedro's a Pedrito and every Ana an Anita. Here where every drama contains hints of melodrama, the unbearable— the too much or too little; the too beautiful, the too painful, the too sweet—is to be cherished too, at least in its retelling. There's a reason

Cuba is the home of the bolero: one of many Cuban song forms to conquer the Americas in the twentieth century, it's a form of ballad devoted not merely to rending the heart but to making it bleed, as well. And it fits. Whether you're from here, or were from here once, or would like to be again. The island as obsession, the island as wound—it's a not-uncommon way, for all those who touch Cuba, to engage it.

Meyer Lansky was once asked why he remained fixated on Cuba during the decades between his first visit here, in the 1920s, and when he opened the Riviera in 1957. He replied with a gangster's concision: "I couldn't get that little island off my mind."[2] Neither has any Cuban who's ever been here and then left, or has parents who've done the same. With its balmy breezes and sherbet sunsets and *tres leches* ice cream and rumba to kill, there's a lot for which to build affection, and upon which to base one's own understanding—whether personal or received—of what's known here as *cubanidad*: Cuban-ness. Only people from nations with a healthy sum of self-regard see fit to devote blood and thought to the idea not merely that they possess an ineffable nation-ness, but that their country's essence has contours that are discoverable—and that those contours' essence is something for which one can, and maybe should, really suffer. But Cuba is one of those nations: it's not just the intellectuals who stake hopes and careers, here, on arguing about the meaning and contents of *cubanidad*.

Of course, part of Cuba's outsized self-regard, *pace* Meyer Lansky, is that it's not a little island at all: at fully eight hundred miles from tip to tail, it's huge. Its claims to kingliness are based firstly on amplitude. But being the greatest of the Greater Antilles does not a major player in world power make. This big island is also a small country that wants to be a macho-sized nation. That desire—linked always to the aim of not having its big, looming neighbor flick it about—has molded Cuba's story from Jefferson's age through the Castros'. And it has led, at moments like the crisis that ensued after Khrushchev sent his missiles, to some tricky spots. Tricky spots will happen, as Quixote learned, when tilting at windmills or superpowers.

For a brief time in the 1960s and after, and whatever one felt for its bearded leaders' revolution, those *barbudos'* egos and aims gave Cuba a seriously macho profile on the world stage. In an era when dozens of ex-colonial states joined the United Nations, but also in the context of the Cold War whose contending powers forced them to choose sides, Castro's Cuba became a chief source of inspiration, if not of actual power, for the quixotic dreams of the Nonaligned Third World. That era and Cuba's role in it were bound to be short-lived. But if politics are momentary, culture is forever. And Cuba's self-regard, like Cubans' general pride in their *cubanidad*, has never derived as much from its politicians' rhetoric as from daily life—from the cultural fruits and quirks of quotidian streets whose collective ethos, wrote their first determined scholarly excavator, Fernando Ortiz, has always been "creative, dynamic, and social."[3] And from their justified pride, too, in *cubanidad*'s impacts not merely on their own lives but on others' lives, too, in the audible impress that its rhythms have long had on the soundscape of the wider world.

For far beyond the sunsets and ice cream and royal palms, the inevitable core of *cubanidad* has been this: how it sounds. And it's been this, too: how its sounds have spread. Long before an aging LA guitarist met Ibrahim Ferrer and heard about a defunct social club in the Havana suburb of Buena Vista, it was here in Cuba's capital that a series of dynamic idioms and patterns took root and were then shipped, north and south and east and west, to vibrate the globe. In Cuba, this was thanks as well to down-island Afro tributaries in places like Matanzas and Santiago de Cuba, the southeastern seat of island soul. But from the "Spanish tinge" that made the syncopation of New Orleans jazz, to the "clave" rhythmic core of salsa, from Caracas to Manhattan, to the *cha-cha-cha* figure upon which "Louie, Louie" and other early rock 'n' roll was built—it was here in the Antilles' great beachhead, the meeting ground for the lifeways of Congo and Yoruba-land and Andalucía, that the sounds of "Latin America," and of the Afro-Americas at large, took perhaps their most potent shape.

For well over two centuries, beginning in the mid-1500s, it was here in Havana that the great treasure fleet of Spain gathered to transport gold and silver from Mexico and from Potosí back across the Atlantic to Seville. Cuba's role in Spain's empire was fixed less as a center of production than as the key way station and gathering point for the New World's riches. It was inscribed in Madrid's empire, and the larger Atlantic world that empire helped create, as a great port, rich in the kinds of interchange upon which culture's evolution thrives—and whose riches in that regard only increased after Havana was opened to traders from all nations in 1790. For it was in the decades after that event, as free trade first brought an abundance of African slaves here, and then later saw them freed, that Havana also became the great metropolis of manumitted blacks who rolled their drums and families into Cuba's capital from its fields to give Havana its lasting stature as the great Caribbean city.

And the great Caribbean city, make no mistake, is what it remains. Because what you learn, over repeated visits and in absorbing its history, is this: if in 1820 Havana was the most intriguing and beautiful and rhythmic city in the New World, which is to say in the world, it was also those things in 1920—and it remains so, beneath the crust of decay and of politics, as we near 2020, as well.

Havana, like the island it incarnates, will break your heart.

* * *

IT DID MINE, from the moment I alighted here for my first unhurried stay. I was twenty-two and had just sprung from a college apartment with a Che photo on the wall and a worn CD of Cachao's *Descargas* on the hi-fi, but with just one previous visit to Cuba under my belt. I'd come down, during college, in one of the few legal ways one then could: with a delegation led by lefty Jesuits who were sympathetic to Cuba's ruling party because they were lefties but kosher to the U.S. because they were Christian. Our officially sanctioned itinerary, organized by our very *nomenclatura* Cuban hosts, included visits to places like a model psychiatric hospital with a sign over its playing field, out front, that read "Sports: For a Healthy Mind," and a little museum area, as we entered, on whose walls were hung big photos depicting "the era of capitalist psychiatry"—people chained to beds, abused kids, lobotomized patients, that sort of thing. This exhibition led onto the gracious grounds of a place where the mentally compromised, treated not with capitalist brutalism but with socialist care, were encouraged to paint pictures and to dance ballet and to belong to bands like the rock ensemble, with its earnest savant belting off-key opera out front, whom we watched to affirm with our applause these good works, anyway, of Cuban communism. This appealing place, our humorless guide intoned to drive the point home, had all been made possible by the revolution—that mythic event, in 1959, that had occurred in the past but was also still going on in a country where every neighborhood still had a Committee for the Defense of the Revolution. Near the Museum of the Revolution, which Fidel's government built into the old dictator's palace to commemorate this triumph, a big sign proclaimed, "We Have and We Will Have Revolution."

But that was then. And this, now, was me returning to Havana for a year's stay aimed not at touring the revolution's official showpieces but at living its daily life. I'd won a fellowship to study language and culture and also to forge "people to people" ties, however I might, by researching and perhaps helping out with a number of what were here called "popular education" projects—sundry community development efforts, run not by the state but by private citizens with initiative. Aimed, for example, at helping older people to read more or young people to make art, they were led by people I'd met through the lefty priests.

Less grandly, I wanted to live in Havana to see what it was like. My first brief visit had included, alongside the official hospital tours, enough long walks through the city—one—to convince me that walking around Havana, tuning my ear to its Spanish and its ways, was about my favorite thing to do in the world. That visit had also included a brief stroll by the grand main campus of the University of Havana, a neoclassical Parthenon set atop a low hill dividing the pleasantly noisy streets of Centro Habana, the city's treeless but jangling core, from the leafier district of El Vedado—once Havana's first suburb, now an urban zone of mossy mansions and elegant apartment houses that since the 1930s had hosted most of the city's cinemas and jazz and modern hopes. It was in this area that I had decided, or fantasized, that I'd like to live. In returning to Havana now, it was to the university and a contact in its school of architecture that I went to see if I could.

The University of Havana was founded in 1728 and moved to its current location in 1901; it's an institution through which very many of Cuba's historical notables have passed. Like many landmarks here, though, even and especially the older ones, its resonance in the cityscape has a way of according with its role in the revolution—or with moments in Fidel's younger life, more specifically, to which it played host. There's a reason that, when climbing its great granite steps, you may call to mind the young Fidel, back when he was a prolix law student here in the 1940s, haranguing his peers about one or another constitutional abuse by some corrupt senator. Once the strapping first son of a rich landowner from the countryside, the onetime law student now ran a country that's full of billboards praising his revolution but whose only piece of lasting graffiti—at least that I've ever seen—is a red scrawl on a wall across from the university steps. The graffiti, in a city where such spontaneous expressions from the young aren't much tolerated, is carefully preserved from the era of Fidel's own youthful rebellions. It reads "Batista Asesino"—Batista is a killer.

What Batista's deposing by kids like Fidel, back in the '50s, had now led to was a society with its own contradictions. But among the most vexing when I arrived in the fall of 2002, not too long after the end of what Castro had dubbed the "Special Period in Peace Time"—the lean season of scarcity after the fall of the USSR—was a whole set of problems arising from allowing U.S. dollars into the Cuban economy. Fidel's government, needful of cash and having to pursue it from foreign sources, had recently made it legal for Cubans—people whom they directed to hate the United States and its capitalism with a passion—to possess and use U.S. dollars themselves. What this policy had meant, in the few years since they took this astonishing step, was the emergence of a bipartite economy. While state salaries were paid in Cuban pesos—a currency still usable here for unpackaged staples like rice and eggs and Chinese bike parts—the packaged goods and bottled sodas and TVs that everyone really wanted, so that they might live like their cousins in Miami, required dollars. (A few years later, the U.S. dollar would again be outlawed and replaced with something pegged to it but called the "convertible peso"; the dual economy remained.) What it also meant was that people like the gray-haired architecture professor whom I went to see at the university, a man with an advanced degree and an air of authority befitting his station at the nation's top institution, was earning a state salary worth the equivalent of maybe twenty dollars a month. But when I asked him if he knew anyone with a room to rent, he didn't pause; he scrawled an address on a torn edge of that day's *Granma*, the official communist daily that was many Cubans' best source for scrap paper. He sent me, a ready source of dollars, to an old student of his who he thought could use them.

Address of former architecture student in hand, I walked past the Habana Libre and the great Coppelia ice cream park, where many Cubans had spent much of the 1990s queuing up to consume the cheap calories, four and five bowls at a sitting, of state-funded sweets. Continuing down 23rd Street into Vedado, I passed its iron statue of Don Quixote, and turned off 23rd onto F. I found the address in my hand and called up to a third-floor balcony until my soon-to-be host, Carlos, leaned over its rail. His third-floor flat had high ceilings and chipped-tile floors and a terrace with a view over terra-cotta roofs, downhill. Carlos was a gentle round-faced man with gold-brown skin; he may have earned a degree in architecture, but his worn-in flip-flops and shirtlessness indicated a fellow who'd realized, like many Cubans by then in a broken economy, the rather large disincentives to holding an actual job. He welcomed me to his home and accepted his old mentor's regards just as his wife, a determined-looking woman with freckles and bright blue eyes, cut in to betray her glee at having an unexpected *yuma*—the Cuban slang term for Americans (perhaps deriving from the popularity here of the old Western *3:10 to Yuma*)—land at their door. "You can pay for a room?" she asked before saying hello.

"Dagdelay," he said, "es muy capitalista." Carlos apologized by way also of introducing a woman whose typically unpronounceable Cuban name took me weeks to learn. Dagdelay, I'd later learn, was from way out in Villa Clara Province—Cuba's Kansas. She came from a farming family whose roots, like many of those in the Cuban *campo*, were in the Canary Islands; she couldn't pronounce my name, either (it came out sounding like "Jax"). But the price she quoted was more than fair— $10 a night, for a comfy bedroom in the back of their flat along with hot milk and bread in the morning and rice and rich beans at night, often supplemented with a fried egg or tomato from the farmers' market down the block. And the months I spent with them there (especially after I seized on the necessity, during a quick trip to Mexico to renew my Cuban visa, of bringing back a bottle of hot sauce to liven the bland Cuban palate) were almost euphorically happy.

Apart from their *yuma* boarder—to whom it was made plain straightaway that, if any nosy parties wanted to know, I was Dagdelay's cousin visiting from the Canarys—their household included their demonic little son, Carlitos, and Carlos's aging mother, who suffered from dementia and shuffled from her room only at mealtimes. Some nights Carlos's brother Gustavo, a charming *malandro* who usually lived with his girlfriend across town, would bunk here too: on nights when the girlfriend kicked him out or he came this way looking for other action, in scenarios that perhaps weren't unrelated, he would crash here solo or with some stiletto-wearing conquest, in the spare room off the balcony.

The only member of the household with a job was Dagdelay. She did regular shifts in a state-owned cigar factory whose primary utility for her, to judge by the raw brown tobacco leaves she brought home and stacked in boxes by a table in the living room, was to furnish the material she'd use to roll her own cigars, sometimes in the shape of baseball bats, to sell to tourists. Dagdelay was a hustler to her core, a *capitalista* indeed—a striving provincial who'd come to the city with the hope not merely of making it in the capital, but also of getting out of Cuba. Carlos was different; he'd grown up playing baseball on Vedado's peaceful blocks. He loved both his neighborhood and reminiscing about the good old days of his youth, in the '80s, when there was a Russian-bought chicken in every pot. Now his passive role in their home economy was to put on a shirt, sometime past midmorning, and wander out in his flip-flops to *buscar el pan* (look for bread) at the state-run shop-cum-supply-depot down the street. Here payment was made by getting a little check in your *libreta* ration book, and here he'd also use the passive phrasing of communists everywhere—"Hay huevos?" (Are there eggs?)—to ask whether the rusted works of Cuban communism had managed, this day, to get any foodstuffs, beyond the cooking oil and sugar one could always count on, to this corner of the realm. Carlos was no party-line naïf. He just traversed both the mellow indignities and the small benefits of his country's system with a wry sense for humor: raising his fist with a wink, as he passed by a billboard bearing a familiar bereted figure and the slogan "We Will Be Like Che!," he would pick up Carlitos at his kindergarten. The school, a state-run place called the Heroic Vietnam School, was housed in a mansion abandoned by this area's old overclass, whose porch was now hung with a sign depicting not Mickey Mouse or Elmo but a little cartoon member of the Viet Cong in a pointy hat. Back home, Carlos and Dagdelay spoiled Carlitos, a catty little boy who liked sitting in the middle of the living room floor crashing toy cars into each other, within an inch of his life, and then would complain with a sigh, on the rare occasions when they asked him to do something, that he was "un poquito malcreado" (a little badly made). I loved them dearly, and they stayed in my life for years.

But if the homey feel of sharing Carlos and Dagdelay's Vedado days was one happiness of life at *19 y F*—19th Street and F—what also made life there a joy was the ideal base it made for exploring the city on foot.

* * *

HAVANA WAS BUILT by the narrow entrance to the sheltered bay that was long its lifeblood. It's a maritime town whose historic core is built onto a musty bulkhead guarding the harbor's gate. Each evening at

9:00 Old Havana still pauses at attention, as cannons are fired from near the base of its Morro lighthouse, marking the old hour of its closing to new boats wishing to enter from the sea. Along the water, old forts guard the cobbled streets and shaded plazas fronted by old churches built from coral by Spanish monks and by the great storehouses made from stone by old hidalgos to keep the gold and other treasure, plundered or mined from across the Indies, that was gathered here to ship home. Havana was the port through which all people and goods bound for the Spanish Americas, or returning from Spain's colonies to Europe, had to pass until the era of the U.S. revolution.

But as the empire declined, Havana's island began to produce wealth itself—first from cultivating tobacco in the eighteenth century, and then from sugar's brutal trade in the nineteenth—and Havana expanded west and south from the old port. Gobbling up land along the great Malecon seawall over which gray waves now crash during winter storms, Havana grew clear to the mouth of the Almendares River—five miles distant—and then crossed the river, to colonize its newer suburbs of Miramar and Cubanacan and to fill in the humbler zones, tucked in behind, of Marianao and La Lisa. With strong ties to its vast hinterland having emerged during that period of rapid expansion, it grew as linked to Cuban towns like Santiago and Camagüey as it had long been to Cartagena, Cádiz, and the Bight of Benin. But like a devoted servant of Yemaya, the Yoruba goddess of waters, whom women here praise at dusk by the Malecon with beads and songs, it remains a city preternaturally focused on the sea: a place built to overlook the great invisible current coursing just a mile or so offshore, into which Spanish sea captains angled their convoys to slingshot out through the Bahamas and then to catch the mighty Gulf Stream that sped them home to Seville.

Nowadays the closest that many of Havana's two million inhabitants get to boarding a seagoing vessel may be hopping a raft for Florida. But with Havana's *brisa* blowing off the water to salt the air and buff its homes' pigments into that mottled pastel so loved by cameras, this is still a sea-loving place whose inhabitants, on hot summer nights, empty onto its seawall to flirt or fight or ponder or make love. An atavistic attachment to the sea, however, isn't the sole reason people here hang out on the Malecon. Havana's a warm-weather city where many kids live for decades in their parents' homes, and where no one has any money to hang out *except* in the street. And as I settled into life at Carlos and Dagdelay's, waking to her bread and hot milk and looking forward to enjoyable classes or visits to community projects to occupy my days, I made it my business to learn as much of the city's squiggly grid as I could.

Changing my U.S. dollars into Cuban pesos to explore Havana allowed me to see what was still possible to do with the island's currency—which was, it turned out, quite a lot. It was from Havana's peso economy that I developed, with the help of vendors selling small cups of thick and sweet *café* from their stoops for one peso (about four cents), my first taste for coffee. I learned, too, to lunch most days on *pan con tortilla*, the basic but filling egg sandwich those same vendors laid on for about thirty cents (and occasionally the less desirable *pan con jamon*—bread and ham, served dry with no fixings of any kind—that they also peddled, in a country mad for pig meat in all its forms). If ever I was stranded across town or in need of getting someplace more quickly than my feet or a bus allowed, all I needed to do was to hold up a hand along a main boulevard and flag down one of the big lumbering *maquinas*—old American cars that trundled down set routes on main drags, their old engines replaced with newer Korean numbers or burping motors borrowed from tractors. I'd then hand the driver ten pesos (about forty cents), and sink into a cavernous backseat with an old *abuela* or a pair of young lovers or whoever else was going the same way. *Maquinas*, though, were only for when I was in a rush. And I was rarely in a rush. So usually I walked.

Vedado was a world in itself. Its sloping grid of fern-lined streets reached down to the sea. The once-exclusive bastion of Havana's sugar rich was laid out in the late 1800s as an urban garden whose every *parterre* between curb and sidewalk had by law to contain a green strip of grass or shrub, and whose every intersection was inlaid with a little granite pyramid, as if in advance readiness for the monumental memories these streets' denizens would form around the fragrant corner of *17 y F* or *21 y C*. Built by Cuba's rich, Vedado was given over, after the revolution, to the ideas of its Communist Party and the fierce will of tropical nature. Many of its sidewalks were now a treacherous tangle of concrete slabs, pushed up and askew by the surging roots of its banyan trees. With no funds in the public budget to repair the sidewalks, it was often better to walk instead down side streets that, given the general paucity of cars beyond the city's main drags, were blessedly free of both traffic and noise beyond the happy cries of playing kids and chatting mothers and the groups of men in flip-flops who crowded around rickety tables to slap down dominoes and talk jovial shit in the shaded yards of crumbling mansions. Many of the grander homes, abandoned by their owners or seized by the state after 1959, were converted into multi-family dwellings. Other of the more baroque examples were taken over by the state or leased to foreign powers for their embassies.

Two of these in easy range of Carlos and Dagdelay's apartment were the North Korean embassy, by whose vaulted gate a glass-encased billboard featured photos of Kim Jong Il "greeting his people," and the magnificent gabled mansion, a few blocks down 17th, that since 1959 has housed the headquarters of UNEAC, the national union of writers and artists. In that lush tiled garden, old party-line poets in berets gathered in the afternoons to sing along to old boleros. (The menu pointedly did not include discussing the rather more trenchant work of nonunion writers like Pedro Juan Gutiérrez, whose *Dirty Havana Trilogy* had recently exposed for the world the seamy underside of Special Period life.)

Another porticoed palace nearby had a front hall hung with a big portrait of Fidel. Its porch welcomed patients to a cardiovascular hospital, the best one in the country. Years later, I was walking home from a night out with a friend who'd recently had heart surgery and wasn't feeling well, and we stopped in to rouse the sleeping guard. We were swiftly ushered in, at 1 a.m., to see an impressive young doctor. He checked my friend's vitals and gave him a thorough checkup, with no fuss and no demand for pay, before sending us home with a smile. Maintaining sidewalks had never been a priority for the revolution. But expending resources on its vaunted system of socialized medicine still was. That system had its problems—round-the-clock checkups are one thing; actually having medicine to prescribe is another. But it was still cherished by Cubans like Carlos, who looked deeply confused whenever I tried to explain to him that no, Americans couldn't just wander into a free clinic, like the one he frequented down the block, whenever they had a headache.

That was Vedado. But at least a couple of days a week, I made sure to head down to the university, onto San Lázaro and past the bit of anti-Batista graffiti at its great steps' base, to take the two-mile walk down through Centro Habana to where the city began.

In Centro, buildings crept right up to the street, their fronts studded with ladders of balconies. Women in tank tops lowered old buckets on frayed ropes, raising bread or plantains from friends or vendors below and hanging laundry from their edges. Their habit of dumping their washbasins' gray-water contents off their *balcones* meant the sidewalks were best avoided. Luckily, most cars and buses in Centro Habana were limited to a few main drags too. I shared its streets' middles with sweaty onion vendors pushing wooden carts and with women sauntering to market toting little plastic sacks and dressed in bright Lycra bodysuits. The latter outfit, a look indicative less of ostentation than informality, was only in keeping with the deeply undemure norms of self-presentation in this country. Here, uniformed customs agents at the airport welcome you to Cuba in clingy skirts and, no matter their age or shape, black fishnet stockings. Here, where the general rule for female evening wear has long been the higher the hemline and the higher the heel, the better, the modern Cuban love affair with spandex crosses genders: rare is the younger man who doesn't wear his T-shirts sleeveless and as tight as possible (or who, for that matter, doesn't also sport eyebrows as carefully tweezed as any young woman's). Here, comfort in one's skin and with one's looks is less a tactic for social advancement than a necessity. In a place where every skinny boy is called *flaco* by strangers and every fat woman is fondly dubbed *gorda* to her face, many forms of body shame and attendant politesse familiar to the neurotic North feel entirely absent.

The vendors pushing their carts cried out as they went, with full-throated *pregones*, to hawk their pork rinds or peanuts ("Maniiiii!" the peanut vendor said). It was the cry of *el manisero*, the peanut seller, that inspired the Jazz Age composer Moisés Simons to pen the eponymous tune that became, after the era's great singer Rita Montaner brought it to New York, both one of Cuba's best-loved songs and one of the most-recorded melodies of the twentieth century. Watchful bystanders, usually male and often sitting on a wooden box or car bumper and utterly unconvinced of the foreign custom that says staring is rude, offered more spontaneous cries. The speech act that's known here as a *piropo* is prompted by its speakers' admiration for the curved waist or sway-hipped strut of some passing *muchacha*. The customary response to *piropos*, bouncing off their ever-dignified objects like flies and carrying little of the implied violence of northern "harassment," is the same as with a *pregón*: they're ignored—until some lout crosses a line that his *piropo*'s target will signal by letting fly a withering volley of insults to undress her accoster, in front of his fellows, shrink his manhood, and make plain that his prowess could never match hers.

As a male person of evidently foreign hue, I was largely spared the necessity of building up my *piropo* defenses (unless you count the lewd propositioning that invariably follows foreign men, especially, from the *jinetera* hookers down Dragones as dusk nears). But on a Cuban street, no one is free of the need to hone both one's body language (to convey ease) and one's verbal defenses in those situations—and there are many—where there's nowhere to hide. I learned how to deal with annoying touts who'd made being a *jinetero*—literally, a jockey—a new form of Cuban street hustle. The *jinetero*, whose aim is to attach himself to a wandering tourist and not let go, commonly begins by approaching the unwary foreigner and making some busted-up reference to the Buena Vista Social Club or calling out, "My friend! Where do you from?" The reply I learned to give, to start another kind of conversation, was to say in jesting Spanish that I was from Bauta or Diez de Octubre or some other provincial town on Havana's outskirts where no tourist ever treads.

Growing fully attuned to Cuban Spanish—a variant of Castilian marked by extreme volume and speed—I picked up idiosyncracies pertaining, for example, to the varied meanings one can attach here to the word for "penis." In a country whose phallocentrism goes far beyond the great granite pillar of the monument by the Plaza de la Revolución (dedicated to nineteenth-century Cuba's greatest mustachioed espouser of *cubanidad*, José Martí, but from whose base Fidel used to harangue his people for hours), it's not uncommon to hear a person or song or thing described as *de pinga* (of the penis). The crux is in how it's said: *¡de pinga!* means something's awful; *de pinga*, said without the exclamation mark and with a warmer timbre, means it's great. In Centro Habana neighborhoods like Cayo Hueso, there was never any shortage of sights or sounds or smells that one could reasonably describe as *de pinga* in either sense. The warm scents of frying garlic and cumin mixed with rum and diesel fumes and rotting fruit and cheap shampoo. Many blocks also bore the unmistakable scent, from behind some door or down an alley, of dead cat.

Wandering through Cayo Hueso, which allegedly won its name from the surfeit of migrants from Key West who once settled here, I continued down San Lázaro and into the barrio called Colón. There I often stopped by a historic recording studio where some *rumberos* I knew banged out astonishing polyrhythms on their *tumbadoras* and *cajón* box drums. Melding Congo figures with accents of Yoruba and Calabar into only-in-Cuba patterns, they painted astonishing figure-eights in sound, far deeper in complexity and spirit and drive than any other rhythm-based music I'd ever heard. The studio where they played had moldy egg-cartoned walls and was named for Ignacio Piñeiro: a local sonic pioneer who incorporated Afro-Cuban accents—notably songs from the Calabar-derived secret society known here as Abakuá—into his dance band's repertoire in the 1920s. Adding a singing trumpet to the traditional "son cubano" lineup in that same era, it was Piñeiro who evolved the basic sound with which the outside world grew smitten, after *Buena Vista*'s release, seven decades later.

I passed under the ornate paifang arch guarding what's here called Havana's *barrio chino* to find blocks that now boasted far more Chinese restaurants than Chinese people, but that once hosted (thanks to the workers who came in the 1830s to build Cuba a railroad before Spain had one) the Americas' largest Chinatown. I walked into the historic barrio Jesús María, abutting Old Havana's southern edge and the train station where many of this zone's Afro-Cuban residents arrived by train a century ago, from the sugar fields around the old slave port of Matanzas, where the rumba took root. Through a friend I met a *santera*, a priestess in the syncretic Yoruba faith that's the closest thing Cuba has to a national religion. She took me to her home, which was decked with yellow and green beads and bells for the *orisha* who was her spirit mother, Oshun, and invited me to attend the initiation of one of her goddaughters into the path: a last day of drumming and drinking and convivial time that also marked the culmination, for the shy young woman at its center, of having spent a year dressed like one of the many people—black or olive-skinned and all the browns in between—who walk Havana's streets dressed in white from their shoes to their umbrellas. Proving their devotion and their capacity to live in purity for a year, they are readying to accept Oshun or Changó or Elegba less as their personal savior than as a kind of guiding ally whose *aché*, or force, along with that of all the *orishas*, they may have use for in facing obstacles attending both this and the spirit world.

North from the train station and past the Parque de la Fraternidad's waterless fountains, I passed Cuba's immense but mothballed Capitolio—built here to resemble the U.S. Capitol in the 1920s but where no legislators have met since 1959. Beyond the Capitolio, I skirted the rococo edifice of Cuba's opera house, the gleaming Gran Teatro that was the hemisphere's biggest theater when it opened in

1838; Caruso sang, and Alicia Alonso, the half-blind grand dame of Cuban ballet, danced here. By the hedge-lined benches of the Parque Central, men played chess and talked more shit. I paused for coffee or to read *Granma* on the broad terrace of the elegant Hotel Inglaterra and ambled onto the grand Prado Boulevard's promenade, guarded by a pair of cast iron lions. It was down that median's marble tiles that *haute* Habaneros paraded in the nineteenth century to court new mates or gossip in muslin frocks or cravats.

The Prado and its surrounds are artifacts of bourgeois Cuba's obsession in the 1800s, shared with most of Latin America, with Italian opera and belle epoque Paris. But the narrower streets of the old city, running off the boulevard to its east, bespeak a different era and nation. Their more medieval widths funnel pedestrians down toward the bay and to the old plazas whose coral churches were built by Galician friars but which also still ring with the ghostly echoes of the slaves who were always allowed, under Spain's more liberal if hardly more humane slave regime, to do two things that England's slaves never were: to keep their drums, and to play them in public on Sundays. That first winter in Havana, on the Twelfth Day of Christmas, which was as big a deal here as *la navidad* itself, I joined a *comparsa* troupe from Jesús María on their traditional walk into the old town's heart. Its members played drums and cornets and walked on stilts or dressed in the hooded leopard-skin garb of the Abakuá, to tout their gods and their blocks in the same way their ancestors have done here on January 6 since the 1700s (except when banned from doing so, as they periodically have been, in a country whose leaders' attitude to its blacks has often been deeply schizophrenic—and whose most recent revolution's attitudes toward Christmas, for its first several decades, were just plain negative).

Old Havana's streets and squares were recognized by UNESCO, in 1982, as a world heritage site. Its buildings' piecemeal restoration commenced soon after. But with Cuba's government lacking anything like the cash or the will to be able to shore up all the bones and facades corroded by the *brisa*, most of this sprawling zone's blocks remained every bit as decrepit—and as communist—as any blocks in the city. Along the main shopping street, Obispo, a few new places had popped up to sell Ray-Bans and way-too-pricy souvenirs. But these stood right next to local offices of the Committee for the Defense of the Revolution and peso places whose vendors slung four-cent *cafecitos* and odd soft-serve ice cream, dispensed from rusty machines, with a slightly medicinal taste.

New dollar establishments nearby sold nice plates of chicken or lobster to tourists, for a hundred times the price of a common *pan con jamon*. A cafeteria listing prices in pesos tried to acknowledge the disjuncture but likely made it worse: in its window over the racks of stale ham-and-bread sandwiches on a dirty tray, it menacingly promised "Ofertas y Servicios de Excelencia en Moneda Nacional"—offerings and services of excellence, that is, in Cuban pesos.

Since those days in Old Havana, and as was already under way behind the scenes but has now become visible, a few local potentates with requisite ties both to the Cuban state and to foreign cash have worked out how to capitalize on their district's UNESCO status. They've turned many of its squares into alfresco shopping malls accepting foreign cash and, less regrettably, restored many more of its stunning old buildings. In 2002, there were already a few must-avoid bars pitching expensive drinks to cigar-chomping *yumas* in thrall to stories about how Papa Hemingway used to down a dozen daiquiris on one of their stools after a day of marlin hunting in the Florida Current. This foreign-celebrity-got-drunk-here-and-you-should-too trait of the tourist trade has now gotten out of hand. But in those days it was possible to head down Obispo to the elegant Hotel Ambos Mundos near the water, where Hemingway lived before buying his finca across the bay, and to take the old iron elevator up to its then-secret roof. The little bar there, fifteen years later, is mobbed at all times with tourists. In 2002, after reaching the end of a long walk from Carlos and Dagdelay's in Vedado, I rarely found more than one or two other guests atop the Ambos Mundos. Sipping a Hatuey beer, I gazed over to where the bay's narrow neck spread into a broad expanse of calm water—now crossed by a rusty little ferry heading to Regla but once filled with up to three hundred galleons bobbing in the waves. I didn't find it hard to understand why the Spanish set up shop here or why this place was of enduring allure.

* * *

THAT HAVANA WAS EXPLORABLE in this way to my twenty-two-year-old self—that it felt so uniquely open to the open-minded visitor—was, of course, due to its rather unique political economic station. Cuban communism had by the turn of this century proved itself to be as uniquely bad at wealth creation and feeding the full range of its citizens' ambitions as communism anywhere. But it had also managed, through its uncommon attention to the common good—along with its success at keeping this town, with its strict laws and cops on every other corner, almost completely free of guns and drugs harder than rum—to create in Havana what surely remains the most peaceful big city in the hemisphere. That peace came at a psychic cost. All the forms of ennui and longing endemic to actually-existing-socialism were only exacerbated by the fact, then, that the government still refused to grant exit visas to most everyone who wanted them. But the inhabitants of an island where time and nice weather were the only things in big supply were also blessed to live in a place whose climate and calm allowed them to spend much of their lives outdoors and to feel safe even when walking home, anywhere, at 2 a.m. Homes that would have been sequestered behind concertina wire and Rottweilers in Rio or Kingston here snoozed calmly behind nothing but ferns.

With its dearth of cars and big highways and other high-modern infrastructure tearing at its urban fabric, Havana remains a city whose organic development—the ways in which one neighborhood relates to the next, how one historical layer suffuses what follows—is visible to the sensitive looker. A city whose harmful holding in place is also its beauty, and its lesson. Even Old Havana's annuated charms are owed, in a sidelong way, to the revolution. In the late 1950s a group of Harvard-trained local architects led by a man named José Luis Sert, and evidently in thrall to a dastardly mix of Robert Moses's and Le Corbusier's worst ideas, proposed a new master plan for Havana's core that would have razed colonial blocks to put in highways and turned its plazas into parking lots. Those plans were put paid by the rise of a state economy whose scant cement and scanter construction budget has for forty years left only a marginal impact on its capital's physical plant—and then only on a few stadiums and Soviet-style apartment blocks on its outskirts. Havana is a heaven for the urbanist and the walker—a city where getting around on foot, as in all the great walking places, can yield the sensation of walking around in your own mind. A city, also, where there's a reason one of its finest writers, Alejo Carpentier, described its aspect as "a marketplace of columns, a jungle of columns, an infinity of columns."[4]

Ionic or fluted or Tuscan or Doric or plain—Havana's columns render the city a *mezquita*-like forest of plaster and stone. Holding up porches or roofs or nothing at all, they also support one feature of this cityscape that must be Havana's signal contribution to a certain ideal of urban design in the tropics: the great porticoes that don't just front many houses here but also line public byways on main drags from Infanta in Centro to Agramonte by Old Havana's edge to long stretches of those blocks facing the Malecon. The porticoes mimic Bologna's arcades but also provide shade, which in summer is much less a luxury than a necessity. Around the garden at the Hotel Nacional, over the wicker couches where I loved to go sit, the porticoed patio can strike one as merely a grand riff on Old World Luxury, of the sort such grand New World structures always contain. But it also reminds you, after you've spent some time in Havana, of the sidewalk chess players sheltering on the porticoes off Infanta or the *pregones* and *piropos* that bounce off roofed columns by the Prado and off their round-hipped targets as well. The prevalence of Havana's porticoes may be as contingent or random as any other of its features. But they have a way, like much here, of feeling inevitable to the way people live—as if they fit, in ways one can only grasp at, into some larger way of being that the city's form both reflects and shapes.

Life that happens out of doors, open windows and carless streets, the outsized characters of its people—the sheer exultant immodesty of it all, only expanded by the lack of privacy at home, meant that much making out and music making took place in public. It meant also that the music pouring from open windows, angular and buoyant, clung to poor people who didn't so much walk as prance down their blocks, and always found a way, when it was someone's birthday, to do so while carrying a big frilly cake—it meant that all this together amounted to the *cubanidad* with which Cuban partisans and intellectuals from José Martí on have been obsessed. How did this all come to be; how had it changed or not since 1959? How did a New World city built with an idea of its own magnificence, and in love with its own urbanity, come to shape a public culture of the street that was above all, as Fernando Ortiz described it, "creative, dynamic, and social"? How did *cubanidad*—the very stuff that predated the revolution, and will outlive it—inform the political climate?

The Cuban revolution, before it was Marxist or socialist or anything else, was nationalist. It was devoted to a belief in *cubanidad* that's shared by Castro's foes in Miami (even if they don't always agree on its contents). What I came to understand while living in Havana that first year was the intractability of *cubanidad* across the political spectrum, even though I could not yet fully articulate what it was.

CHAPTER 5

CUBAN COUNTERPOINTS

THE TERM *CUBANIDAD* IS generally credited to José Antonio Saco, a prominent white *criollo* nationalist of the mid-nineteenth century. It gained a new currency when the island's blacks—notably the freed slaves who made up a large part of the army that launched Cuba's long series of wars against Spanish rule in 1868—embraced their leader Antonio Maceo's call to "ask for nothing as a black and everything as a Cuban."[1] To conceive of being sovereign, all worldly countries must first conceive of themselves as nations. And *cubanidad*, as such, first crystalized as an important, if still vague, idea when the cause of Cuban independence found its foremost apostle, in the 1880s and '90s, in the florid pen and speech making of José Martí. Addressing enthused émigré crowds in Tampa or New York, Martí evoked a sweet land of palm trees and sincere men to solicit contributions to his cause. He told Cubans abroad that their island was an enlightened place where "on the field of battle, dying for Cuba, the souls of whites and Negroes have risen together into the air."[2] Martí's high-minded *cubanidad* was estimably antiracist. But it was also more a rhetorical tool, useful in the run-up to the war that martyred him, than a definable good.

It wasn't until some years after Martí's soliloquizing helped spark the final phase of Cuba's struggle for independence, which saw the apostle killed in an early battle, that there emerged in Cuba a concerted and sophisticated effort to examine the question of how myriad African and Iberian and other strands combined to make Cuban culture. For though Cuba did gain its independence from Spain in 1898, that freedom came at a cost. The greatest Antille immediately became a quasi-colony of a nearer-by superpower, which swooped in as Spain was leaving. The United States forcibly inserted the so-called Platt Amendment into independent Cuba's first constitution, arrogating to itself the right to oversee and intervene in Cuban affairs however it wished. And it was under the series of corrupt and corrupted Cuban leaders, in the tawdry dependency that the Americans helped create, that Cuba's progressive intellectuals turned in earnest to parsing the substance and import of *cubanidad*. C. L. R. James appraised what happened in Cuba during those years—and the importance of that story's leading figure not just to Cuba but across the Caribbean.

It was just one year after the Platt Amendment that there first appeared what has turned out to be a particular feature of West Indian life—the non-political writer devoted to the analysis and expression of West Indian society. The first was the greatest of them all, Fernando Ortiz. For over half a century, at home or in exile, he has been the tireless exponent of Cuban life and *Cubanidad*.[3]

Fernando Ortiz, the most iconic of Cuban anthropologists, was a figure whose work and ideas—as James's homily suggests—resonated far beyond Havana. Ortiz was a son of Spanish immigrants who began his career right around the time of Platt, by earning a law degree and training as a criminologist interested in what he at first called "Brujeria Afro-Cubana" (Afro-Cuban witchcraft).[4] But he soon outgrew such pejoratives to produce a long shelfful of works on every aspect of Cuban music and religion and custom and politics, a body of work that was always notable, as James put it, for "the number of solid volumes he . . . devoted to Negro and Mulatto life in Cuba." To be sure, there were monographs on Cuban dance, Cuban instruments, Cuban storytelling, and a famous dictionary of "Cubanisms," but Ortiz's oeuvre culminated in the great book recalled as his masterpiece: *Contrapunteo Cubano* (1940) was a lyric opus of historical erudition expressed in imagistic prose whose overarching argument concerned the best way to understand the interplay of cultures not merely in Cuba but everywhere. Ortiz's *Cuban Counterpoint* interpreted, through the story of his island's economy's two most iconic products, tobacco and sugar, their broader ties to the story of race and culture in Cuba. In this country it's still not uncommon, when one visits the home of a member of its cultured classes, to find a bookcase that, in addition to volumes by Martí, features the collected works of Ortiz. There is a saying: "Cuba had two discoverers: after Columbus, there was Ortiz." C. L. R. James echoed it.

A quarter of a century before the Writers' Project of the New Deal began the discovery of the United States, Ortiz set out to discover his native land, a West Indian island. In essence it is the first and only comprehensive study of the West Indian people. Ortiz ushered the Caribbean into the thought of the twentieth century and kept it there.[5]

James, in his at times polemical historical essays, wasn't above exaggerating to make a point. By the time he wrote those words about Ortiz, the ranks of Caribbean scholars devoted to the "study of the West Indian people" already included influential figures doing groundbreaking and significant work across the islands. But Ortiz's contributions were immense. Describing his work's larger genesis, he would recall his days as a young man fascinated by his country: "I began to research, but I soon understood that, like all Cubans, I was confused."[6] As a white Cuban raised in a society whose culture's mores were nominally Spanish but whose people knew they certainly weren't European, he endeavored to find the source for that difference—and soon determined that it lay, most of all, in the "various lineages, tongues, musics, instruments, dances, songs, traditions, legends, arts, games, and folkloric philosophies . . . of the African cultures that were brought to Cuba."[7] Ortiz became the first Cuban writer to recognize that there were more than a hundred African ethnic groups among Cuba's blacks, and he popularized the term "Afro-Cuban." The grand home where he lived, across from the University of Havana, now houses the Fundación Don Fernando Ortiz and makes his works available to Cuban students in cheap peso editions. This was where for fifty years he explored the meaning and origins of such characteristic Cuban symbols as the danzón, the cigar, the rum drinker, and the rumba. And it was also where he decided, in examining those icons' emergence in conjunction with the island's historical role as the great Caribbean port of Spain's New World empire, that Cuba's development unfolded most crucially through what he called "transculturation"—the mutual transformation of cultures and "human groups" by others. His argument about how and why this was so was distilled in his *Cuban Counterpoint*'s most quoted line: "The real history of Cuba is the history of its intermeshed transculturations."[8]

Ortiz's concept of transculturation was formed against the then-dominant idea about how migrants, whether arriving in Europe or New York, "acculturate" to their new home. Ortiz saw that this model hardly applied to the creole lifeways of his island's people, who had for centuries been less engaged in accommodating to an existing culture than in creating something new. "Transculturation" never really caught on beyond the academy—perhaps partly because Ortiz's central argument about it in *Cuban Counterpoint* could not but strike most modern readers as almost banal. (What place's culture *isn't* the result of mixing between and among its constituent individuals and groups?) But what was important about Ortiz's larger work and contentions for a reader like C. L. R. James, serious observer of the Cuban scene that he was, was that Ortiz acknowledged long before peers in the United States did so, let alone those in Europe, that his island's culture was the product of intermixing. The culture's African strands weren't merely add-ons but were foundational. And Cuba's particular "intermeshed transculturations" had produced something exceptional, even in the larger context of the New World. "Songs, dances, and tunes came and went from Andalucía, America, and Africa," was how Ortiz put it, "and Havana was the center where they melted together with the greatest heat and the most colorful spectrum."[9]

About the latter point, partisans of Rio de Janeiro or New Orleans may plausibly disagree. But the heat that accrued in Havana isn't arguable. And the story of how Cuba became the special forge for a new world culture of such astounding variety and force began in earnest when the huckster explorer whom the Spanish called Cristóbal Colón and we call Columbus shoved off from the Bahamian sandbar where he first touched land in the New World in November 1492. Pointing his *Santa Maria* south, he approached the coastline of a mysterious landmass.

* * *

TODAY THE PEOPLE Columbus met here are recalled as "Taino," but that wasn't their name for themselves: *Taino* was their word for "noble." Their word for "dwelling place," *Cubanacan*, became the basis for the name by which the Spanish—after abandoning their first name for the place, Fernandina—came to call their home. They were a Neolithic people with stone tools and sophisticated agriculture whose ordered fields of sweet potato and yucca and tobacco and maize gave them "everything they needed for living, with many crops well-arranged," wrote their most sensitive early Spanish observer, Bartolomé de las Casas.[10] But without livestock or other domesticable mammals, they also lacked any antibodies to the germs that the Spanish, who'd shared their yards with pigs and goats for millennia, brought ashore. Here as on most nearby islands, their population declined quickly—from an estimated 350,000 to nearly nil within a few decades.

After parting with Cuba for the more populous and perhaps promising island of Hispaniola, Columbus decided to focus Spain's efforts at colonizing the Indies there. He returned to Cuba only for brief visits. Men he'd dispatched to explore its interior returned with word of a "magical weed" the Taino called *tobaco* and an ingenious cloth for sleeping that they called a *hamaca*, but no rumors of gold. At the time of his death in 1506, Columbus still thought Cuba was a continent. It wasn't until three years later that a Spanish sailor circumnavigated Cuba, thus proving it was an island. Sebastián de Ocampo traced its two thousand miles of coastline to discover a sheltered deepwater bay on its northwest coast whose narrow entrance and calm waters made it an ideal place, better than any yet glimpsed in the Caribbean, to pull a ship from the water and repair its hull. Ocampo dubbed the bay "Carenas" because of its suitability for such "careening." It would soon be renamed Havana and turned into the raison d'être for the larger colonization of the island, which began in earnest with the arrival, in 1511, of the conquistador who became its first governor.

Diego Velázquez pacified the Taino by defeating the native leader, Hatuey, who is now immortalized on beer bottles and by statues hailing "the first rebel in America." But it was in relation to a more famous epic of conquest, and a more famous native leader, that Havana won its lasting role in Spain's imperial system. When in 1521 Velázquez's lieutenant Hernando Cortés set out from Cuba on a wild freelance mission to mainland Mexico, he had the approval of neither the island's governor nor the Spanish crown. In the wake of Cortés's epoch-making defeat of the great emperor of the Aztecs, Montezuma, and his stunning seizure of Montezuma's shining capital, Tenochtitlán, he needed to get word of his feat home to his king before his nemesis Velázquez could arrest him, or claim Mexico's glories himself. The man Cortés dispatched to do so, a canny navigator called Alaminos, recalled how Ponce de León, during his recent venture to find the fountain of youth in what was later named Florida, had seen one of his boats swept out to sea by a mysterious current. Cortés's captain gambled on catching that same marine river off Cuba. Hugging the island's north cape, he managed to catch the Florida Current and then the Gulf Stream, which he rode all the way home in record time—and made Cuba's colonial administrators, in the process, aware of the advantages of moving the island's capital to the sheltered bay at Carenas, in Cuba's far northwest, that sat in easy range both of Mexico and of that fast current home.

In 1558, Spain designated Havana as its only New World port allowed to engage in transatlantic commerce, and then launched its system of fleets: two immense flotillas, comprised of up to one hundred cargo boats loaded down with gold and guided by naval escorts to guard against pirates, that for the next two centuries sailed between Havana and Seville twice per annum. With a port town's typical reputation for moral corruption, Havana wasn't a place, unlike the empire's viceregal capitals in Lima and Mexico City, to which respectable Spanish women ever really migrated. Rich in the bars and brothels that all great music towns have, Havana was always a place where gambling and gangsterdom and prostitution all thrived. Its sex trade and demographic mix early on birthed the figure who would become Cuba's patron saint. The mixed-race *mulata* sex worker, common to Havana's dens of iniquity, was a Cuban icon long before the Virgen de la Caridad became Cuba's copper-skinned *santa*. And "Spanish" Havana was a place whose populace and mores were shaped most not by Madrid but by the Moorish-inflected customs of Seville, in Andalucía—the city to which it was conjoined and whose distinct approaches to both slavery and racial difference it inherited.

In Iberia, slavery was a fact of life long before the Atlantic slave trade, and its practice there came with a modicum of regulations more humane than those in the English or French colonies. This truth was not unrelated to the fact that many light-skinned Iberians, during the centuries the Moors ruled Spain and afterward, too, were slaves themselves. The Moors' approach to slavery included the expectations that slaves should retain their freedom of movement when not at work and that they should also be able, through a process known as *coartación*, to buy their own freedom via piecemeal payments to their masters. All of this helps to explain why one hears some Cubans now talk of an *esclavitud mas suave*, a "softer form of slavery." Sugar slavery was as brutal here as anywhere. But these customs, especially during the centuries before the late arrival of industrial-scale agriculture here in the nineteenth century, and when most slaves lived in town, set an important tone—as did the visible presence in Havana, very early on, of a variety of hustling impresario known as the *negros curros*.

Like most who arrived from Europe in the early days, these *negros curros* hailed from Seville—around 10 percent of whose populace in the seventeenth century was black. Many of these freedmen became professionally active in the vices that thrived in Havana, as managers of taverns or gambling establishments, or as pimps, or in import-export trades. Always remarked upon for their flamboyant dress, many of them were also musicians whose rhythmic sense was North African. Before Cuba became an agrarian society—most of its Spanish peasants had yet to arrive; they came largely in the nineteenth and early twentieth centuries—it was an urban and profoundly "interracial" one. In the late 1500s, Havana was a town in whose dance halls the stylish black man, showy and proud, was already a fixture.

* * *

THE ERA OF the Spanish fleets set in motion the engine that made Cuban culture. But it was only as the age of the fleets declined, and as Cuba became an economic power and a destination in its own right, that the island developed what its inhabitants could come to recognize as a culture of its own. And that new era was launched, in a sense, less by Cuba's owners than by their English rivals who invaded Havana in 1762. The resulting British occupation lasted just eleven months, but it augured big changes, awaking creole Cubans to the benefits of being allowed to trade with any foreign merchant they pleased, rather than simply loading boats bound for Seville—and also to the riches to be made from producing sugar. The English imported expertise and equipment from nearby Jamaica, and brought slaves to cut sugarcane as well. When Spain finally opened its colonies to free trade in the 1780s, there were already a few dozen sugar plantations ringing Havana. Cuba's sugar era was under way. And just in the nick of time. An island over, on the French half of Hispaniola, an epoch-making slave revolt began in 1791.

The destruction of Saint-Domingue and its rebirth as Haiti left a gaping hole in the sugar market, which Cuba, already off to a running start, was perfectly placed to fill. From the early 1700s, Cuba had built an export economy based on its capacity for growing great tobacco leaves and for rolling them into cigars, and then, later, into cigarettes too. But tobacco remained more an artisanal than an industrial crop; its cultivation, even at a broad scale, didn't have the capacity to alter landscapes or populations in a major way. Sugar, as Fernando Ortiz would note in *Cuban Counterpoint*, was different. "Sugar is not made from patches of cane but from plantations of it," he wrote. Sugar was an industry whose sources of profit and nature of production required ever "more elaborate mills, more canefields, more land, greater investments and reserves—in a word, more and more capital."[11] And so it proved, as the sugar *centrales* first filled the plains around Havana, and then spread east to Matanzas.

The appetite for new labor was huge. When, after 1820, the steam engine revolutionized sugar production and made it more lucrative still, the system required an even greater number of workers. Cuba ended up importing more enslaved Africans between the opening of its ports to free trade in 1790 and 1867, when the last slave boat arrived in Havana, than anywhere else in the Americas, save Brazil. Some 800,000—to a country whose total population in 1790 wasn't much over a quarter million. These slaves were brought to Matanzas and Havana largely from a few ports in West and Central Africa—from Calabar, in what's now Nigeria; from the Lomboko slave fort, in what's now Sierra Leone; from the mouth of the Zaire River, in Congo. But just as key to the evolving course of the island's population and its politics were other flows of migrants to the huge and now burgeoning island during an era that signaled what Ortiz called "the real colonization of Cuba."[12]

Cuba's owners were already terrified, like all the owners of sugar colonies in the age of Haiti's revolution, of a Saint-Domingue-style slave revolt in Cuba—but especially so as their own slave populace sharply rose. They deemed it necessary to maintain some kind of racial balance. A concerted effort was made, beginning in the 1790s, to populate those parts of the Cuban *campo* not under sugar with Galician and Asturian peasants, paid to come over from Spain to grow tobacco and raise cows. Whether their presence attenuated the prospect of slave revolts is hard to say. But what's easier to judge is the impact of another influx in those years—the flood of thirty thousand terrified French planters who turned up from Saint-Domingue, after fleeing their homes by raft or boat or by any means they could manage, to reach Cuba's east in 1803. These planters, outrunning a final assault by Haiti's General Dessalines on his country's old masters, transformed Cuba's east.

With both their French love for coffee and their expertise at growing it, they installed hundreds of shaded coffee plantations in the mountains around Santiago, thereby implanting in Cuba a new industry and a new taste: cafés soon dotted Santiago and Havana. Many of Saint-

Domingue's refugees continued on, after spending a decade in Santiago, to New Orleans. But many of these French Antilleans also stayed.
They implanted in Cuba what their slaves' descendants still call the
tumba francesa—a mix of Bantu percussion with dancing that mimics old
French masters. They also brought to Cuba their love of the *contradanse*
quadrilles and line dances, which Cubans renamed "contradanza" and
took to with avidity as their island, and Havana especially, exploded in
both population and wealth.

The contradanza hit Havana at a time when the majority of its working musicians were creolized Africans. And these musicians, steeped
not in the steady march tempos of Europe, but in more syncopated
approaches to organizing sonic time, transformed the music's rhythms.
They built songs around the repeated rhythmic figures that musicologists trace to the looping thumb-piano melodies of south-central Africa,
and which would later become known here, in Cuban tunes, as their
montuno or tumbao. The creolizing collision of the contradanza with
West African time—and the collision of both with a certain Spanish
love for dramatic theater and lyric poems—would shape the emergence,
over the next century, of all those Cuban styles to come, from the danzón to the habanera, bolero, and cha-cha-cha.

But before and alongside the story that unfolded in the dance halls of
Havana was another history, related but moving along its own distinct
track that's as key to the making of Cuban music. That history involved
Cuba's huge new numbers of African slaves in its countryside and in
places like Matanzas, the great sugar port sixty miles to Havana's east.
Those slaves' arrival here was always bound, no matter what existed
in Cuba beforehand, to have huge implications for its culture. But the
customs these Carabalís and Mandingas and Yoruba and Bantu speakers
found here, and the way Spain treated its slaves, were essential to the
success they had not merely in retaining key parts of their ancestral cultures but in evolving a fine-tuned sense both of their commonalities and
differences among them. Delusions of "a softer slavery" aside, the particular traits and quirks of Spain's approach to bondage were felt even
on its slave ships. In the voluminous oral histories that Fernando Ortiz's
sister-in-law, Lydia Cabrera, the other legendary Cuban anthopologist
of their era, began compiling in the 1920s, one of her old informants put
it this way: "If there had been no drum on board, there would have been
no slavery. Because not one negro would have arrived alive."[13] Never
mind that in nearby English colonies like Jamaica and many other places

in the New World, where drums and drumming were strictly banned, slavery thrived. All the same, Cuba was an island where slaves were always allowed to keep and play their drums—big open-ended cylindrical ones from Congo, conical *ekpe* ones from Calabar, hourglass-shaped *batás* from Yorubaland. Drumming was a source, for people from those places, of both social and spiritual health. And beyond the policy of allowing drums, the island's Spanish owners tolerated a more institutional form of cultural preservation and communal power.

Cabildos, in most places in Spain's New World empire, were municipal councils through which well-born colonists made decisions for the common (or at least their own members') good. The cabildos of Cuba's Africans, granted their charters by the colonial government, were slightly different. They functioned as fraternal orders and mutual aid societies, providing for such essentials as the funerary costs of members. They also existed, much like the "social aid and pleasure clubs" of black New Orleans, for their members to make music together and dance in the streets on certain special occasions, like the Twelfth Day of Christmas. But unlike in New Orleans, they were never organized around simple affinity or residence; nor were they named for imaginative ties to a mythic African past (like New Orleans's Zulu Social Aid and Pleasure Club). Instead the black cabildos of Cuba brought people together based on their shared *nación*—their common bonds to Carabalí (Calabar), or Lucumí (Yoruba), or Congo, or any number of others.

Even today and especially in the countryside, it's anything but rare to meet a black Cuban who can tell with exactitude and feeling just where on the continent—based on the *batás* her uncle keeps, or the particular *regla* of deities followed by his mom—her people came from. The cabildos are a big reason why. They're also a big reason why the main Afro-Cuban religions—of which the Yoruba-derived Santeria is the most popular of many—developed as they did. Cabildos were required to register with the Catholic Church; they often displayed Christian symbols in their headquarters. It was in the Lucumí cabildos of Havana that Yoruba Cubans noted a kind of congruence between Rome's saints and their own deities, and created a syncretic faith wherein Santa Barbara accords with their gods' king Changó, San Pedro is Ogun, and San Lázaro, the purple-clad patron of all who are ill and aiming to heal, is Babalú-Ayé. Other cabildos helped nurture the *regla de palo*—the Congo-based faith that puts great store by the power of trees and whose practitioners here, called *paleros*, gather bundles of sticks and organic matter called *nganga*. Still other cabildos played a part in shaping the emergence—or, rather, the nurturing behind closed doors—of the male secret society of Abakuá: a kinship at once worldly and religious whose members came from the Carabalí *nación* and whose symbologies and function derive from the Egbo leopard society of Calabar, an ancient city in the watery region near what's now the border between Nigeria and Cameroon. Once recognizable in public for their tradition of filing their teeth to sharpened points, the Abakuá practice secret rites and wear garb not meant to be seen by others—except on those occasions when its members donned hoods to hide their faces and take to the street at carnival time. The Abakuá were long particularly active—and particularly feared—on Havana's rough docks and in the heavily Afro-Cuban towns of Regla and Guanabacoa, across its bay. These neighborhoods, still home to many dockworkers today, are also known as *barrios de babalaos:* home to many priests, called *babalaos*, of what's long been the prevalent Afro-Cuban religion. Today, the followers of Santeria now include Cubans of every ethnicity: its language and iconography are a lingua franca; and even non-adepts, whatever else they might or might not believe in, feel compelled to engage, hedging their bets. (Fidel Castro is said to be a son of Eleggua, the messenger-*orisha* who opens and closes paths.)

But if Santeria is the island's most visible cabildo-bred tradition, the others are also ever present. Hang around Cuba long enough, and you will be shown, by an old man or his young niece or both, a little bundle of sticks or bones and what looks like a crumbling wad of dirt that its owner will pull from the back of a closet or shack to explain that this is the *nganga* around which their household's spiritual power is centered. And one hardly need be a nosy ethnologist poking at secrets to encounter the Abakuá. Afro-Cuban religions, as they exist behind closed doors and as epiphenomena on the Cuban street, are, of course, also everywhere in Cuban music. In the nineteenth century, as the music took shape, the rhythms of Afro-Cuban religion fed the newly syncopated timbre of Havana's dance bands. And Cuba's blacks, both enslaved and free, also created their own born-in-Cuba musical idioms, the most important of which were the family of styles known as rumba that emerged in Matanzas after slavery's end.

Rumba was invented on the street and honed in the shared court-yards of *solares*—multi-family homes built around a shared yard—where poorer blacks lived. Its ties to the docks, and to the always large portion of stevedores among its players, was signaled by the *cajón*—a wooden box like the ones that smoked cod came in—that one of those players often sat on, to play like a drum between his legs. A strictly percussion-based music, rumba was also improvised for dancers whose movements both responded to and shaped what the drummers played. That dance, whether now performed by the national folkloric dance company or in the street, is typically a jousting simulacrum of dynamic courtship, performed by a couple whose male makes symbolic attempts, with hand or kerchief, to conquer the sex of the woman, who must react quickly to cover up, or exit the circle.

If rumba has a baseline ingredient from among the sundry *naciones* of Afro-Cuba, it's suggested by its Bantu-sounding name. Rumba is most often played on open-bottomed drums, akin to those of the deeply poly-rhythmic music of Congo's forests—the source for more Cuban slaves than anywhere else. Its birth also evolved a new kind of drum, waist-high and bowing outward like a barrel, that's called the tumbadora here but is now known wherever "Latin music" is played as the conga. One of rum-ba's key early forms, the yambú, was strongly based on the Congo baile yuka. The larger rumba complex, like black Cuban culture at large, is perhaps more Congo than anything else. But it contained strong strains of Lucumí and Ganga and Arara polyrhythms, too. Its players now sum-mon *orishas* of all the *reglas*. And in the style of rumba that became most popular in the twentieth century, the guagancó, its polyrhythmic figures were built around the "clave" spine now shared by most Cuban dance music—a way of organizing sonic time wherein each basic click isn't equally spaced, as you'd get with a metronome, but instead follows a more motive flow: two solid hits first, often, followed by three quicker ones (*UH-UH, uh-uh-uh*). Clave soon came to be kept on the invented-in-Cuba instrument that shares its name: the pair of clave sticks that Fernando Ortiz claims were invented on Havana's docks. The rumba, as much as it's African, is a New World music. And it's Cuban.

In the 1930s in the United States, an ersatz "rhumba" craze swept the hipper ballrooms of New York and Los Angeles. The music at that craze's core was a pastiche of Cuban son and big band jazz that had as little to do with real Cuban rumba as Carmen Miranda's fruity head-dress had to do with whatever hats people actually wear in Brazil. But as with that other Cuban-based music that begat another U.S. dance craze later on—the mambo—one suspects that part of why such words caught on, along with the exciting music they described and as Ned Sublette, the most rigorous excavator of Cuban music's vectors to the north, has observed, was the sheer deliciousness of their sound. That intervocalic "mb," round and rhythmic in one's mouth, is one of the signature phonemes of the Bantu family of languages; it's a sound toothsome to say, whether falling in the middle of rumba or mambo or tumbao or quimbombo (the Congo word for okra, still current in Cuba).

* * *

CUBA'S AFRICANITY MAY HAVE been essential, from the start, to what *cubanidad*'s espousers loved about their land. But the feelings of elite Cubans toward the human beings behind what might glibly have been called their culture's Congo tinge were of course more mixed. The island's colonial administrators feared its blacks and often loathed them. And the new class of local patriots who began flirting with the idea of separating from Spain in the early 1800s, like many Latin American creoles, also viewed blacks with ambivalence at best. After Simón Bolívar rallied a generation of *criollo* Spaniards to claim their independence from a weak Madrid in South America, his Venezuelan allies asked their Cuban counterparts if they'd like to join in doing the same. But Havana's best demurred. A Spanish minister distilled the reason: "The fear which the Cubans have of the blacks is the most secure means which Spain has to secure her dominion over this island."[14]

For much of the nineteenth century, that proved prescient—Cuba and Puerto Rico, alone among Spain's old American colonies, remained under the sway of Madrid, and those island's white elites' "fear of the blacks" was a big reason why. But it's also true that when Cubans finally did launch an armed campaign for independence, the army that did so in 1868 was comprised of slaves freed by onetime slaveholder Carlos Manuel de Céspedes, in whose forces many of those ex-slaves first became officers and then black revolutionaries known as mambises. It was the model of mambises like the "bronze titan" Antonio Maceo that José Martí, ten years old in 1868, carried with him over his decades abroad, as he wrote journalism from New York and poems about the royal palms back home (one such poem became the lyrics to "Guantanamera"), and eventually raised the funds and enthusiasm to return to Cuba, in the 1890s, to launch the last phase of Cuba's war for independence.

In his seminal 1891 essay "Nuestra America," Martí famously declared that *el mestizo autoctano* (the native-born half-breed) had "vanquished the exotic creole" as the embodiment of authentic *cubanidad*.[15] He continued:

> The rachitic thinkers and theorists juggle and warm over the library-shelf races [*razas de libreria*], which the open-minded traveler and well-disposed observer seek in vain in Nature's justice, where the universal identity of man leaps forth from triumphant love and the turbulent lust for life.[16]

Martí arrogated to Cuba, and to the larger *mestizo* America it represented, a degree of racial enlightenment that would soon lead the way for all humanity. Neither the nobility of sentiment nor the dreamy light in which he placed his isle were atypical for Martí. But both that sentiment and this light were wielded at some remove from reality. He was invoking "Nature's justice" barely five years after the end of slavery. And his oft-repeated claim that "there will never be a war between the races in Cuba" would be proven wrong in 1912: that year, some three thousand black members of Cuba's Independent Party of Color, for seeking racial justice, were massacred by the forces of President José Miguel Gómez. But Martí's *mestizaje* was emblematic of a larger dynamic that had run through Cuban nationalism long before him, and has persisted long after: the tendency of creole elites to valorize coloredness—or "mixedness"—as the wellspring of authentic Cuban identity, while eliding the racism under which actual dark-skinned Cubans still lived their lives. The Cuba of Martí and of the holy Virgen de la Caridad was and long remained a society that found little place for actual *mulatas* save for in its brothels and kitchens.

Before Cuba could work all that out, though, and before Cubans could do so on their own terms, they had to secure their island's freedom. And the war they fought to do so, which saw Martí shot on his horse, didn't ultimately yield a result that would have pleased him. The Cuban war of independence, though it did expel Spain from the island, did not end with the satisfaction of sovereignty for Cuba. If Ortiz's transculturation—the intermixing of peoples and cultures, to make something new—is "the true story of Cuba," then the story of Cuban politics in the twentieth century, and of the music that has so informed the island's own sense of *cubanidad*, is about something else: Cuba's old and deep and at times traumatic relationship with a northern neighbor with which it shares, as the leading historian of U.S.-Cuba relations, Louis A. Pérez, put it, "ties of singular intimacy."

* * *

THE UNITED STATES GAINED de facto control over Cuba as a result of the war for independence that's gone down in American history—because of the U.S. swooping in for the last three months of a four-year conflict—as the Spanish-American War; the war's result, from the vantage of Washington, was long overdue. With Spain's empire sunk in long decline, many in Washington, D.C., for much of the nineteenth century viewed the United States' eventual possession of Cuba as inevitable. And as Cuba's fight for freedom came to a head near that century's end, the yellow press in New York helped stoke the urge to intervene. In August 1897, William Randolph Hearst's *New York Journal* began running stories about Evangelina Cosío Cisneros, the eighteen-year-old daughter of a Cuban rebel leader allegedly arrested for sedition who was also, according to Hearst's paper, "the most beautiful girl in the island."[17] Evangelina's picture became a tabloid staple, her ordeal at the hands of her captors the topic of regular lurid updates. The melodrama ended only when Hearst's paper announced, that December, that it had arranged for Evangelina's escape to the United States. To celebrate her arrival as a "Cuban Joan of Arc," Hearst organized a mass rally to which more than seventy-five thousand New Yorkers arrived, chanting, "Viva Cuba Libre!"

Two months later, in February 1898, the warship USS *Maine* mysteriously exploded while docked at Havana. The United States had its pretext for invasion. That spring, Cuban rebels and invading U.S. forces pushed Spain from the island, and Cuba (along with Puerto Rico, Guam, and the Philippines) was annexed to the United States. "We went to war for civilization and humanity," as President William McKinley eulogized the conflict, "to relieve our oppressed neighbors in Cuba." Humanity's gains were hazy, but what the United States certainly gained was a de facto colony. Near Cuba's eastern tip, the U.S. Navy established a base supposedly "to enable the United States to maintain the independence of Cuba" (but also conveniently positioned to protect what would soon be a key sea-lane to the Panama Canal).[18]

In the Spanish-American War's wake, the U.S. agenda changed from justifying invasion to legitimizing a continued military and eco-

nomic presence. Accordingly, the representation of Cuba as a comely
woman in distress—usually depicted, like Evangelina, as white in complexion (and thus a fair reflection of American virtue)—changed too.
The mixed-race isle was now depicted in tabloid cartoons as a pitiable
black child holding the hand of a beneficent Uncle Sam on the path
to progress. Previously, U.S. opponents of annexing Cuba had often
based their arguments in racism. "The white inhabitants form too small
a proportion of the whole number," as one diplomat put it in 1825.[19]
"The Spanish-Creole race . . . ," explained a congressman in 1855, "are
utterly ignorant of the machinery of free institutions."[20] Now the same
logic justified a strong imperial hand. The Cubans, the commanding
U.S. general in the 1898 war declared, were "no more capable of self-
government than the savages of Africa."[21]

If once Cuba had figured as a virtuous lady in need of saving by an
imperial enterprise engaged in a civilizing mission, it soon came to be
seen as a different sort of woman, one whose mission was servicing
others. "We gave Cuba her liberty," declared a U.S. Army veteran on
holiday in Havana in 1925, "and now we are going to enjoy it."[22] As
the tourist trade grew, so did Havana's old reputation as the brothel
of the New World. The island "was like a woman in love," touted a
typical travel writer's account, and "eager to give pleasure, she will
be anything you want her to be."[23] At once overseas and right next
door, Cuba became the place where Americans—especially American
men—went to escape the stolid mores of wife and home. With the
passage of Prohibition in 1919, legal booze fortified Cuba's libertine
lure. *When It's Cocktail Time in Cuba* was the title of a popular U.S.
tourist guide, and Havana bartenders concocted those new rum-based
elixirs to coax more from visitors. A short cruise from Florida—or
an even shorter plane ride, after Pan American Airways launched its
first international passenger route with Key West–Havana flights in
1928—Cuba was, by the 1930s, receiving more U.S. visitors than even
Canada.

* * *

WHEN JOSÉ MARTÍ LAUNCHED what he hoped would be "a brief
and generous war" for Cuba's freedom, his hopes for brevity were strategic: his reasoned fear was that if the war were allowed to drag on,
the United States would find some pretense to intervene. ("I have been

inside the monster and I know its guts," went his oft-quoted summa-
tion of why, in the last letter he ever wrote.)[24] In this, he of course
was proved correct. To the Americans who arrived to run Havana in
the war's wake, Martí's antiracist aims mattered not at all. In the first
"free election" organized in the country, the Americans extended suf-
frage to all males on the island—provided they could read and write
or owned US$250 in property. That this excluded most blacks was the
point. Fitzhugh Lee, Cuba's first American governor, was a nephew of
Robert E. Lee's who'd begun his career as a general in the Confederate
army and had racial attitudes to match.

The society the Americans aimed to build here was based on the
Jim Crow South. It was also designed to be as welcoming as possible
to rich Americans who, colluding with Cuban elites, swept in to buy up
property and build new sugar mills and finance a new building boom
in Havana. The series of Cuban presidents who followed the Platt
Amendment's passage, each more corrupt than the last, all shared the
basic brief, vis-à-vis the island's American overlords, to ensure Cuba's
amenability to U.S. business interests by welcoming "investment from
abroad" and quashing dissent at home. These leaders' basic tactic for
maintaining a modicum of support from Cubans was to make their government, and its ambitious new program of public works, the country's
main source of middle-class employment. Blacks were largely excluded
from the jobs attached to such projects as building Havana's new seawall
and waterworks. Too, they were excluded from the new power structure
built by white Cuban leaders at a time when hundreds of thousands of
new immigrants arrived from Spain as a result of a concerted "whit-
ening" campaign after 1906. All of this informed both the poisoned
racial atmosphere attending the awful "race war" of 1912 and the rise
of the worst of the Plattist presidents, Gerardo Machado, who presided
over Havana's Jazz Age peak in the late 1920s. Bilking the treasury
with gusto, Machado commissioned the building of huge new projects
like Havana's grand new Capitolio more to enrich his friends than to
advance Cuban democracy. By enforcing bans on drumming in public,
and on the percussive *conga* processions that had been a feature of Afro-
Cuban carnival parades across the island, he also built a reputation as
Cuba's most racist leader yet. But in so doing, he also managed not
merely to alienate the darker-skinned working classes (whose general
strike in 1933 would eventually relieve him of power) but also to out-
rage a critical mass of intellectuals of all colors—among them Fernando

Ortiz and his friend Alejo Carpentier. Carpentier began writing his first book, which was called *¡Écue-Yamba-ó!* and whose main character was Abakuá, while imprisoned for protesting Machado's rule in 1927.

The "Afro-Cubanist" strain in Cuba's elite arts found expression not only in literature but also in music, by composers like Alejandro García Caturla and Amadeo Roldán, whose symphonic pieces incorporated accents from the same Congo and Carabalí sources with which Carpentier laced his fiction. Such borrowings were in one sense little different from the similar nods to African rhythms and form fed the Paris-born modernisms of Picasso and Matisse—except that in Havana, such rhythms and forms were audible and visible right down the block. And Afro-Cubanism also influenced makers of more popular entertainments who filled Havana's theaters during the Machado era. Rita Montaner, that era's standout singer, was a light-skinned *mulata* capable of playing a white girl onstage whose look recalled the zarzuela musical stars of the 1800s. Her 1928 recording of "El Manisero" made that ode to the peanut seller Cuba's best-known melody. But Montaner and her act, along with that of her longtime accompanist and long-suffering friend, the marvelous pianist and singer Bola de Nieve, reflected Fernando Ortiz's "confusion" and his passions. She came to be most associated with a kind of Afro-Cubanist cabaret singing that invoked Afro-Cuban rites and *lengua* for the nightclub set—but whose referents both Montaner and Bola de Nieve, a gentle and round black man whose nickname ("Snowball") ironized his appearance, both knew intimately from growing up in Guanabacoa, the historic barrio across Havana's bay that's famous for the density of its *santeros* and *paleros* and Abakuá.

If the presence of Afro-Cuba, ersatz or sincere, continued to be prominent in Cuba's concert halls, the Machado government's general approach to Afro-Cuban music's presence on the streets was exemplified by the president's minion in Santiago, the mayor Desiderio Arnaz. He moved to ban *conga* parades, full of hand percussion and raucous Afro-Cubans, from his city's streets. After Arnaz was run out of the country on Machado's coattails, he settled in Miami and watched his charming firstborn son—a tall young man also named Desi Arnaz—launch a career in show business by teaching Florida supper club–goers to follow him, as he later recalled, on "a flashback to the yearly carnivals in Santiago, when thousands of people in the streets form a conga line, and they go all over the town, singing and dancing for three days and nights."[25] Those people in Desi's hometown were precisely *not* allowed, thanks to his dad, to hold their percussion-driven parades. And when they did, it looked nothing like the safely exotic *one-two-three, KICK!* bit of cheesiness he popularized. But the larger career of the man who played Ricky Ricardo suggested much about the outward hostility but inward investment of some elite Cubans in Afro-Cubanidad. For if real street-style rumba wouldn't make it onto Havana's concert stages or those abroad for decades (it wouldn't even be properly recorded until after World War II), its crucial impact on Cuban music at large only grew all that time—witness its key role in the emergence, in the 1920s, of what became son cubano, the "mother form" of Cuban popular music in the twentieth century.

This son evolved less from danzón in the capital than from more flexible dance-band styles in the countryside out east, which combined the *guajiro*'s guitar and language with Bantu-style percussion and the Cuban clave's pulse. Music historians generally say that the classic son's sextet lineup was fixed around 1920; it included a guitar and bass instrument, along with maracas and claves played by the band's singers, and two instruments invented in Cuba not long before the son's birth. One was the tres: a kind of six-string guitar whose strings weren't tuned to six different notes but were instead grouped in three widely spread pairs of two, each repeating the same note, an octave apart. The tres wasn't made for playing melody or chords, like the guitar; it was perfect for playing montunos, the repeated melodic-rhythmic figures around which son songs, more than any other Cuban genre before, were built. The second were the bongo drums: a pair of compact open-bottomed tambores, played with the hands, whose loud report cut through any band's sound and whose taut-skin aspect allowed their player to quote from, and riff on, any number of rumba figures or Abakuá tropes.

The son's typical song form was as deliciously adaptable—and expandable—as its band's lineup. Songs were comprised of two verses followed by a chorus and a free-flowing section known by its basic building block's name; such tune's "montuno" sections built around the groove of a repeated melodic-rhythmic cell, allowing both a band's singer and its instrumentalists to stretch out and play to where its crowd wanted to go (the same role that the montuno still plays in son's famous offspring, salsa). The son montuno's sound proved an endlessly rich base for expansion and growth from a core at once flexible and simple. It would soon take on more elements of rumba. It also absorbed a piercingly sweet top layer, evoking the sound of Louis Armstrong's Hot

Seven, when Ignacio Piñeiro added a trumpet to his Septeto Nacional in 1927.

Once Machado was gone, and drums were again made legal on Havana's streets in 1934, city bandleaders would add still more elements to son's sound. These included a piano to play montunos by mimicking the tres's double-noted sound, but also more trumpets and another percussionist to play conga drums. Though invented for playing rumba on the street, those drums were now brought, through the son, onto the ballroom stage. Some of the bands playing those ballrooms in Havana, like the all-white ensemble Casino de la Playa, added violins and saxophones to suggest the texture of American big bands. But notwithstanding the complexion of its members, Casino de la Playa's sound—and most especially the vocal stylings of their great *sonero* Miguelito Valdés—was in other ways as deeply rooted in Afro-Cuba's old cabildos as the rumba was.

Valdés, who grew up in the Havana barrio of Cayo Hueso, was the first singer really to show what could be done over the montuno. Improvising gymnastic sixteenth-note ostinatos over those extended grooves, Valdés may have been olive-skinned with a Mexican mom, but his impromptu shout-outs to the *orishas* he'd grown up with, steeped in the *lenguas* and rites of Palo and Abakuá and of Santeria most of all, became a key part of the *sonero*'s vocal repertoire. When, in June 1937, a team of RCA Victor engineers turned up to record Havana's hottest act, they had no idea that the date was bound to be eulogized as "the beginning of the modern tradition of Cuban dance music."[26] But it was no surprise that Miguelito Valdés, that day, sang out not in an ersatz version of the bozal *lengua* of Cuba's enslaved, but in the prideful real thing. "Yo son carabalí," the white Cuban sang. "Negro de nación" (I'm Carabalí, the black man of a nation).

Miguelito Valdés's rendition of "Babalú," his best-known song, was full of antic vocals and playful charm. It described a scene less sexy than serious: a *santero* priest's preparations for a *toque de santo* honoring Babalú-Ayé, Santeria's purple-clad *orisha* of healing and rebirth. Syncretized with San Lázaro—Saint Lazarus—Babalú-Ayé is commonly depicted as an old man toting a crutch and covered in sores: clad in sackcloth, he understands suffering. Which is why he's also a figure whom tens of thousands of Cubans honor, each year on December 17, by walking or crawling on their knees to a small chapel outside Havana in hopes of healing themselves or a loved one. These images are what

Babalú-Ayé's name evokes in Cuba. But Miguelito Valdés was neither old nor covered in sores. He was a handsome young singer whose invocation of Babalú, over an effervescent son beat, turned black-feeling rhythm and tasty-sounding words into a touchstone of sexiness for everyone—much as Elvis Presley would do fifteen years later, as Ned Sublette noted, in the United States.

And it was Valdés's model, no doubt, that drew Desi Arnaz, the émigré son of Santiago's Machado-ite mayor, to his tune in the 1950s. When Arnaz began performing "Babalú" for millions of TV viewers on the hit show in which he starred with his American wife, Lucille Ball, he was no barrio boy steeped in the *reglas* from birth. He was the privileged son of a right-wing mayor who'd brought his son to Miami at sixteen. His performance of "Babalú," like his dubious version of the conga line, outlawed by his dad back home before Desi seized on using it as a part of his nightclub act, was more akin to an insulting party trick than honest expression. But through him "Babalú," like the ersatz conga line brought from his hometown's streets to bar mitzvahs and wedding parties in Miami, became a curious fixture of U.S. popular culture.

* * *

BY THE 1950S, Havana had acquired its cachet for American consumers as both brand and idea. On television Desi Arnaz was the all-purpose Latin Lover. Advertisements hawked Havana perfume, Havana soft drinks, Havana lingerie. "Waving palms, a cool island breeze," went the slogan for El Paso brand Cuban Black Bean Dip. "Visit a forbidden paradise of silky black beans, sweet red pepper and an undercurrent of rich gold rum, resulting in a Cuban sensation that may taste mild, but is definitely hot, hot, hot!"[27] Such was the context and fuel for the golden era of Cuban music that got under way after the Platt Amendment's repeal reached something of an apogee in the 1950s in the person of Benny Moré. Cuba's biggest star of that era was a poor black kid from the countryside, a joyous *sonero* with an amazing tenor voice who could sing fast like Valdés and slow like Montaner and who mastered every Cuban style to rule Havana with his Banda Gigante. But Moré's success, and his band's repertoire, built upon the great period of innovation from the 1930s on, when American record companies arrived in Havana to record the city's top groups. It was in this era that bandleaders like Arsenio Rodríguez turned their conjuntos into laboratories for exploring how rhythmically complex and emotively alive an ensemble of virtuosic musicians, playing hard-driving son around the clave spine, could get. Rodríguez, the blind grandson of a Congo slave, was a forceful and inventive tres player who was also a composer and arranger of vast gifts. His first great contribution to Cuban music came when he wrote the song for Miguelito Valdés in which Valdés declared himself, at that famous session in 1937, a "Negro de nación." But soon enough, Rodríguez had his own band, complete with congas and piano and trumpet, which ruled Havana. Between Rodríguez's group and that of his great rival, Antonio Arcaño, virtually every one of the era's musical greats passed through on their way to local or New York fame or both. Among them was Chano Pozo, a wild boyhood pal of Valdés's, who was known in their neighborhood for leading comparsas down the street and as a virtuoso conga player. Pozo's encounter with Dizzy Gillespie, once he got to the Big Apple and was introduced by the Cuban trumpeter Mario Bauzá, both helped birth "Latin jazz" and shaped bebop.

But among those who stayed in Cuba, at least until 1959, to keep evolving the music there in ways that reverberated across the hemisphere, was the bassist who manned the low end in Arcaño's band for some two decades—and who has often been called, for the variety and astonishing impacts of his innovations in that perch, "the most important bassist in twentieth-century popular music."[28]

Israel "Cachao" López was born in 1918 in the same Old Havana house as José Martí, but he cut his musical teeth across the bay in Guanabacoa. Hired as a boy by Bola de Nieve to help him accompany silent films in a local theater, he also learned classical technique in the Havana Philharmonic. With his brother Orestes "Macho" López, a prodigious fellow composer who played cello in Arcaño's group, Cachao penned hundreds of danzóns—often doing so on the spot to shout out the dance halls or local venues they played across Cuba. (One of these danzóns, improbably famous later on, was Cachao's "El Social Club de Buenavista.") Cachao's compositions revived what had seemed an almost dead genre—the danzón—by transforming it. To a song form that typically followed its opening and "paseo" sections with a main theme in the same easy tempo as the two preceding it, the López brothers added a new kind of third movement whose template was the Afro-Cuban-style montuno. Their montunos lent a different urgency in 2/4 time and were carried not by a tres but by Cachao's funky upright bass.

Their innovation was at first termed the *danzón nuevo ritmo*, but was later named for their 1938 composition "Mambo." Thusly have the López brothers often been co-credited with inventing the most famous genre in mid-century Cuban music. But Cachao's achievement, more broadly, was to transform the bass's role in Cuban pop by turning it into an instrument not merely for keeping time or playing chords-in-walking form, but for sounding his trademark tumbaos—repeated rhythmic-melodic figures that both undergirded a song's low end and drove it irresistibly forward. These tumbaos' feel would filter out into early rock 'n' roll; they now inform hits in genres ranging from reggae-ton to hip-hop to house and R&B.

Cachao's innovations made him a cult figure among musicians and musicologists who still obsess over the small-group *descarga* recordings he began making in the late 1950s. Given the extent to which "mambo" became in the 1950s a kind of catch-all term for Afro-Cuban music at large, like "rhumba" before it, it was perhaps inevitable that the fulsome obituaries meeting Cachao's death, a few years back, hailed him as "the inventor of the mambo." The story wasn't quite that simple, of course. Some of the López brothers' Havana contemporaries, notably Arsenio Rodríguez, laid their own claims to having been first to have the idea of turning the stately third movement of a standard danzón into an Afro-Cubanist playground in 2/4 time. What's not debated, though, are the hundreds of brilliant tunes and tropes the López brothers gave the form in the 1940s, and the fact that by that decade's latter half—after the style had been dubbed mambo by its most obliquely modern innovator, the eccentric pianist-cum-bandleader-cum-showman Dámaso Pérez Prado—it had leapt from Havana to the hemisphere.

Famous for the almost-profane sounding grunts he'd let loose when his arrangements reached their peak, it was Pérez Prado who seized on the idea, with a few Havana colleagues in the mid-1940s, of add-ing a saxophone section to play a repeated "submontuno" under the trumpets on new-style danzón numbers. And it was also Pérez Prado who, after going to Mexico to get his music heard in 1948, was most responsible for spreading it from Cuba's shores. Mexico City, in the late 1940s, became the center of a burgeoning Latin American film industry whose output was comprised mostly of noirish thrillers and smoky brothel melodramas to which Cuban music had become the de rigueur score. Many Cuban musicians, including great singers like Bola de Nieve and Olga Guillot and a young Benny Moré, decamped for the

Mexican capital. And it was there, selling out Mexico City's greatest halls with his uniquely energetic sound, enervating and dramatic and slyly dissonant all at once, that Pérez Prado became a sensation who "made the Americas dance," wrote the scholar Alexandra Vazquez, by "grunting their violent undercurrents."[29] Pérez Prado was omnipresent on the radio and in films in Mexico, and thus across Latin America, and his international smash "Mambo #5" reached New York—whose own era of "mambo madness" was just then taking off—in early 1950.

Decades later, Pérez Prado wearied of an interviewer who was prodding him to recall how and why he'd called his music "mambo." "Do you believe that my music became popular because I called it mambo?" he replied. "I could have called it La Chunga or El Dengue and it still would have caught on."[30] This may well have been so. But the very sound of the word—*mambo*—along with its roots and meaning in Afro-Cuba also mattered, in ways Arsenio Rodríguez explained: "The word mambo is African, of the Congo dialect. One singer says to the other: 'abre cuto güirí mambo,' that is: 'open your ear and listen to what I'm going to tell you.'"[31] "Mambo" described serious sonic business. And serious sonic business is what it came to represent, certainly, in the famous Midtown Manhattan nightspot where it took on New York. In the Palladium Ballroom, Mario Bauzá's cousin Machito and his band were joined by a young Puerto Rican timbales player and bandleader, Tito Puente, and his namesake, Tito Rodríguez, to launch a now much-mythologized era of mambo mania. The music they played there would eventually morph, in the 1960s, into the new genre-cum-marketing tag—salsa—that repackaged Afro-Cuba's rhythms for a new generation of Latino New Yorkers. But Puente, for one, whose career spanned both these eras, never lost track of where the music came from: "Salsa's for eating," he'd insist. "What I play is Afro-Cuban music." And among the tunes in that tradition that Puente made famous was a song he called "Oye Como Va" but whose repeated tumbao he borrowed from one Cachao had played on a tune called "Chanchullo" in 1942 (and which a Chicano guitarist from San Francisco named Carlos Santana retooled again, in 1969, to alert members of America's Woodstock generation, with his own hit version of "Oye Como Va," to the joys of moving to a Cachao tumbao).

After Cachao's death brought half of Miami out to his funeral, I took the ferry across Havana's bay to the hometown that he shared with Bola de Nieve. Guanabacoa's central square was fronted by dilapidated buildings, and had an air, like many such Cuban places, of importance that lay in the past. I soon found the old Cine Carril. The local movie house where Bola de Nieve gave a ten-year-old Cachao his first gig, and where he'd stood on a wooden crate to play his bass, was still in operation. Its mosaic entry hinted at past grandeur, but its doors' cracked glass suggested a place kept open only by the grace of the state. The theater, said a sleepy old woman earning her peso salary by sitting at a desk in its dusty lobby, didn't show films at all anymore. Movies were instead shown from VHS tapes on a TV wheeled in to where the band once played. In the window a paper printout announced that a new Russian film called *Stalingrado* would be shown at 5:30, and that a puppet show of Hansel and Gretel, for the kids, would be mounted that weekend. A few blocks away a little state-run museum devoted to the Afro-Cuban traditions of this *barrio de babalaos* contained rooms filled with Abakuá ceremonial robes and petrified frogs and bundles of sticks. An old *palero* named Enriquito lit up when I asked him, there, if he knew where the house that Bola de Nieve grew up in was. He did. "You know Bola de Nieve was gay," he said, apropos of nothing. "But his father was Abakuá. And his mother was one of the best *rumberas* in Guanabacoa."

I walked down Calle Martí, and turned toward Maceo to find the place. The house was a one-story porticoed number. It had no plaque or anything else touting its famous onetime occupant. It also had no roof—which perhaps explained why a group of jovial men were there enjoying their afternoon during the dead week between Christmas and New Year's, sitting on broken-down chairs and crates to pass around a plastic bottle of cheap peso rum. The roof, one of them explained, had come off in a hurricane a few years ago, and the family that had been living here had moved out. One of them offered me a plastic cup of rum. "*Claro!*" he said. The sounds of someone's holiday rumba, just getting under way somewhere nearby, were background for the tuneful rhythms of his speech. "Everyone knows Bola de Nieve lived here. The Snowball! *Fresco como lechuga.* Fresh like lettuce. He's great, you know. But he's not the only one. Guanabacoa's still got the best musicians in the world."

CHAPTER 6

AUTUMN OF THE PATRIARCH

"I HAVE THE MOST delicious mangoes here, my love."

I accept a piece of fruit from the woman's basket and hand her what amounts to about four U.S. cents, as she moves on to entice the others assembled by the deserted coastal roadway. My traveling comrades and I are huddled under acacia trees or clutching worn bags in the broiling sun. An old Russian truck sits motionless by the shoulder, steaming. Up until a half hour before, we were all riding in the truck's back, hunkered against its steel payload's sides or standing in the wind like cattle. But the *camión*'s engine, wheezing as we rounded a bend amid the lush scenery of Cuba's remote southeast, ground to a clunking halt. The truck's driver has been bent under its hood since. Now he throws up his wrench in defeat and, releasing a volley of curses, wanders down to the beach. There's nothing to do, for the rest of us, but sit and wait for another lift to come down the road.

I'm on my way to Santiago de Cuba, the island's second city and the capital of a hot and rural region Cubans know as "Oriente"—the East. The road we're standing by is perched between the sea and the high peaks of the Sierra Maestra, the mountains where Fidel Castro's merry rebels famously launched a revolution. This littoral overlooks not the breezy Straits of Florida, as Havana does, but the warmly placid Caribbean. On clear nights in Santiago, you can gaze south or east to see the dim lights of Jamaica and of Haiti, places with which this "most Caribbean" of Cuban regions shares much in terms of both climate and culture. I've been on the road for a week, having covered much of the distance from Havana, some five hundred miles distant, by traveling *por bortella*—going "by bottle" is what Cubans call hitchhiking, in reference to the shape your thumb and hand make when you're trying to catch a ride. It's something Cubans, especially in the countryside, do a lot of.

Here where fuel shortages are endemic, and car shortages even more so, hitchhiking isn't just allowed but encouraged. In fact, it's illegal for state-owned vehicles—which is to say pretty much every rusty truck or cracked-window bus on the road—*not* to stop for hitchhikers. In provincial towns, there's even a civic profession that amounts to finder-of-rides-for-the-people. The ride finders are easy to spot in their yellow coveralls. They're known colloquially as *amarillos* (yellows), and they sit under trees or by highway on-ramps with a clipboard. Asking travelers where they're going, and taking note of how many are in their party and who got there first, they then re-summon the same riders, whenever some diesel-powered relic rumbles along, to send them on their way to Bayamo or Holguin or Ciego de Avila.

Over recent days of traversing Cuba's vast countryside, I've accrued grateful debts to more than a few *amarillos*. But here on this remote road beneath the peaks of the high Sierra Maestra and the sea, in ways reminiscent of Big Sur, there were no *amarillos* to be found. Not more than a couple of rattling old American cars had passed, in the half hour since we've been stopped. Learning, though, from one of my fellow strandees that there is a town a couple of kilometers down the road, and fancying the idea of a walk more than sitting still, I pull on my backpack and, to the confounded stares of my *por botella* comrades, to whom I've now outed myself as a gringo crazy enough to walk in the midday heat, I set off in the direction we'd been heading. The "town," in the event, turns out to be a desultory cluster of seaside shacks whose most notable feature, beyond its weedy baseball field, is a large stone monument to a small skirmish here, in May 1957, when Fidel's ragged little force, still numbering only a few dozen bearded men, captured an army post, controlled by the dictator Batista, to win some much-needed supplies. From there, I do eventually find an onward ride to Santiago. But there is a more memorable moment from my walk down Cuba's State Highway 20, in this region of Oriente that Fidel Castro's government renamed "Granma Province," back in the '70s, to remind Cubans for all time that this was the part of the island where he and his men crashed ashore in a little motorized yacht named the *Granma*, to make a revolution.

One of the idiosyncratic charms of the Cuban countryside under socialism, apart from the simple lack of traffic (when you're not hunting a ride, anyway), has long been the propaganda billboards, which, in the absence of ads for Burger King or gas, mark time and welcome you to each province and town on the highway, most often by proclaiming that Cienfuegos or Santa Clara or Holguin is "FIEL!" or "PRESENTE!" (Faithful or Present, that is, for the revolution presumably). Others trumpet old slogans like "PATRIA O MUERTE" (Fatherland or Death) or bear the visage of the martyred Che Guevara and proclaim "SEREMOS COMO EL CHE" (We'll Be Like Che) or remind Cubans they live in a country where there's "SALUD PARA TODOS" (Health for All). The more poetical among these signs, though, are the ones that offer wry pleasure when appearing on some green hillock or by a dingy interchange to trumpet more oblique or muse-ful thoughts like "EDUCAR ES CREAR" (To Educate Is to Create) or simply "EL PODER DE IDEAS" (The Power of Ideas). At a certain point, of course, and once you've seen the same canned phrase on eight different billboards around the island, they begin to seem less intriguing than banal. But never before nor since have I been so stopped short by one of these as I was when, rounding a curve there on Highway 20 on the gorgeous southeast coast, I encountered a sign that, whether it was placed there by some befuddled party bureaucrat looking to blow his yearly signage budget or a closet art theory student who had penetrated the propaganda ministry far enough to get this sign built and have herself a laugh, was striking.

The sign was plunked by a high bend in the road. Its site offered stunning vistas over the sparkling sea below, and of the curved folds of mountainous ridges that faded ad infinitum to the horizons, tumbling steeply to the waves. It was an amazing spot. But the sign's boards were placed in such a way as to directly obstruct the view. Rather than affixing Che's bereted head or a caricature of Uncle Sam as a Nazi, however, the image affixed to the boards was decidedly site-specific. Whether the sign's message amounted to a tacit apology for its presence or a profoundly thick attempt to exploit its locale was impossible to say. But either way, what it depicted was this: a crude painting, done almost in the style of a child with blotchy colors but unmistakable in its representation, with green mountains at the right and a shining sea to the left and, yellow sun up above, of precisely the landscape behind it. And the sign had a caption.

"CUBA," it said, "AQUI ESTA SU OBRA."

CUBA, HERE IS YOUR OEUVRE.

* * *

FOR THE STUDENT OF both Cuban nationalism and the Cuban revolution (to say nothing of Baudrillard's *Simulacra and Simulation*, for instance), that billboard was something. On the one hand, it seemed to suggest a very basic pride in Cuba's beauty. But encountered there in Granma Province, near the end of a trip across the island in 2003, it also evoked something else: an aging revolution's flailing attempt to claim for itself, in the eyes of Cubans, that everything that was good and fine about their nation was the purview and achievement of Fidel Castro's revolution.

By this juncture in that revolution, convincing people of that ludicrous notion was the least of Fidel's government's worries. Any country where a majority of people have to break the law to have what they want is a country whose political system, to say nothing of its economic one, is in trouble. With the Soviet Union's collapse, 90 percent of Cuba's overseas trade and revenue disappeared. How Cuba's government, not to mention its people, survived the resulting "Special Period" of scarcity and hardship remained as much an astonishing mystery as a plucky triumph. The general feel in Havana, where I'd just spent several months, was of a place recalling the Girondists' old line about a revolution that devoured its young. "Revolution and youth are closely allied," wrote Milan Kundera. "What can a revolution promise to adults?"[1] In Cuba, many now saw a revolution that had not only reached stolid adulthood but also come out the other side to enter, with its gray *comandante*, a deluded old age.

But as I'd also found in traveling to Oriente from Havana, the Communist Party still enjoyed significant support in the countryside— where peasants fifty years ago lived in dirt-floored huts and still do so today, but now regarded free health care for their parents and good schools for their sons as birthrights. It remained open to debate, of course, whether the Cuban state's solicitude toward its kids and its aged was "worth" the repression too often endured by everyone else. But the story of the revolution's victory, in 2003 just like today, remains a kind of biblical narrative through or against which all of Cuban politics has had to refer, for over sixty years now. And it's a story that's especially alive, whether it is recounted or loathed, in Cuba's east—where the war was fought, and also where its chief protagonists were born and grew up.

Raúl and Fidel Castro's father was a Galician immigrant who arrived here poor in the early 1900s and settled north of Santiago. Ángel Castro grew rich by buying land and selling sugarcane, cut for pennies by hard-driven workers, to the United Fruit Company. Raúl and Fidel were raised in the country village their father turned into a personal fief, and attended a top Jesuit boarding school in Santiago. Fidel, the older and bigger and more extroverted of the brothers, launched his relationship with America's presidents, and one of the more discussed political biographies of the twentieth century, by writing a letter to Franklin Delano Roosevelt at fourteen in which he asked FDR to send him $10. He matriculated to the University of Havana to study law and grew involved in politics, becoming an acolyte of Eduardo Chibás, whose radio broadcasts bewailing the malfeasance of Cuba's corrupt president in the late 1940s, Ramón Grau San Martín, made him a notorious public figure. After Chibás's death in 1951, Fidel became a leading member in the underground organization determined to remove Grau from power, and then, once the loathed army colonel Batista staged a coup to return to power himself, in 1952, to unseat Batista.

It was after Fidel planned and helped lead a brazen assault on a government army barracks in Santiago—a mission that killed nine of his comrades and twenty-three of Batista's soldiers—that Fidel was charged with treason and gave the speech that won him national fame. He took up his own defense before the court and declared of his actions, "History will absolve me." He was jailed for two years on the Isle of Pines, but was unwisely granted amnesty by Batista in 1955. He promptly went to Mexico City and joined the long tradition of Cuban freedom fighters plotting from abroad to change their land. In Mexico, he met Ernesto "Che" Guevara, a young Argentine doctor who'd been radicalized by having been present in Guatemala for the United States' awful intervention to unseat a democratically elected leader, Jacobo Arbenz, whose aims ran counter to those of U.S.-owned United Fruit. Joining with other Cuban comrades, the Castros and Guevara trained for an attack on Cuba, obtaining the yacht *Granma* in Veracruz, in October 1956, to sail across the Gulf with eighty men. They made a disastrous crash landing, failing to take Batista's soldiers by surprise. Their force was reduced to just a dozen men—a terrible starting point from a military point of view, but ideal for the mythology that quickly surrounded the story of these apostles of revolution who launched a war, in the mountains of Oriente, for Cuban freedom.

* * *

WHEN FIDEL TRUNDLED INTO Havana in January 1959, three years after that little war's start, few in or outside Cuba knew much about him beyond his magnetism and rousing oratory. Apart from his loathing of Batista and idolizing of José Martí, his politics—as the Eisenhower administration's "watch and wait" approach to his government showed—were vague even to close observers. Soon enough, his strident nationalism and messianic bent were clear. But even as Castro's government began seizing lands owned by U.S. companies as part of its first agrarian reform in June 1959—and powerful Washington interests began urging Eisenhower to respond by ending the long-standing U.S. agreement to purchase most of Cuba's sugar—few foresaw the antagonism to come.

With Cuba's continued access to the chief market for its main crop looking unsure, and radicals like Che Guevara at Fidel's ear, whatever doubts Castro had about Leninism vanished. In February 1960 a delegation of Soviet ministers arrived in Havana and signed an agreement to purchase much of Cuba's sugar; Che traveled to Moscow to secure Havana's ties to the Eastern Bloc. Three years after Khrushchev had promised "We will bury you," the Soviets had established a communist beachhead in easy range of Florida. In Washington, the trauma was deep. The flurry of panicked recriminations over how this could have been allowed to happen is what led, in April 1961, to the CIA's fiasco of a covert invasion at the Bay of Pigs. That debacle did Fidel the great favor of allowing him to oversee the defeat of imperialist invaders on Cuba's beaches. In the months following, the Kennedy administration hatched a tragicomic series of attempts to kill Castro with explosive seashells and poisoned cigars (a job for which the CIA contracted the president's old Havana pimp, Santo Trafficante, now in Miami). But no matter. In October 1962, Washington's worst fears were realized when a U.S. spy plane over Cuba snapped photos of Soviet missile launchers nestled amid royal palms.

Whether or not the Cuban missile crisis was the most dangerous and direct confrontation of the Cold War, it's clear that Cuba's role was that of pawn or prop. This did not comfort Castro, who harbored deep resentment when Khrushchev failed to consult him before Moscow agreed to remove its nuclear missiles—a reaction that perhaps signaled the particularly Cuban pathos of this puffed-up leader of a smallish

island driven by the need to be treated and seen as head of a big powerful nation (or at least a sovereign one). Never much for affirming
that dictum from Thucydides that undergirds the think-tank school of
"political realism"—the principle that "the strong do what they can and
the weak suffer what they must"—Castro's role as not merely a blatant,
but also a historically reckless, affronter of American power was set.

For three decades, of course, a large part of how Cuba "stood up"
to the U.S. empire lay in its becoming the client state of another
empire. This truth did not prevent Cuba from becoming a new kind
of symbol across a Latin America long frustrated by the condescension of its northern hegemon. Across the hemisphere, the mythic story
of Cuba—a miraculous fable about a righteous band of longhairs who
went into their country's mountains and a few years later swept into
its capital on the shoulders of its poor—was one that women and men
who loved justice would seek to re-create from El Salvador to Peru. In
Washington, conversely, a new guiding metaphor for Cuba emerged:
that of a malignant cancer whose spread had to be contained at all costs.
And so it was that many thousands of those Latin Americans who went
to the continent's jungles during the '60s, '70s, and '80s, some toting
photos of Che and Fidel in their knapsacks, died awful deaths alongside
those whose cause they raised, often as the "disappeared" victims of
U.S.-backed dictatorships and death squads.

During that same era it was often claimed by Washington that Cuba
was actively supporting various of those movements—a fact true enough
in the case of Nicaragua's Sandinistas and, for a brief time, the National
Liberation Army (ELN) of Colombia. But among the more intriguing
of transcontinental "solidarities" Cuba fostered derived from Havana's
ties to, or at least fondness for, radical movements in the United States.
Not that Fidel ever FedExed grenades to the Black Panthers in Oak-
land. But the Cubans did grow notorious, especially in that wild era in
the early '70s when a plane a week was being hijacked in the United
States, for granting harbor to self-identified revolutionaries. One such
figure who landed here was Charles Hill, a member of the Republic of
New Afrika, a militant group, who famously outran federal marshals
in New Mexico by burying himself in the desert sand and breathing
through a straw, before commandeering a commercial jet to Havana.
As the last remnants of Vietnam-era radical organizations entered their
ultimate phase in the late '70s, Cuba made it official policy to accept as
political refugees U.S. activists who had become wanted as criminals,

by the U.S. government, for their more extreme acts on behalf of social and racial justice. During the first fall I lived in Havana, in 2002—a time when the number of Americans living in Cuba for any reason remained low indeed—those political exiles' conviviality and comfort was such that when I attended an "Anti-Imperial Thanksgiving" celebration at the home of a friend, his guests included Assata Shakur, the famous activist and memoirist sprung from a New Jersey prison by her comrades in 1979, and Charles Hill. The latter handed me a business card as we ate beans listening to Otis Redding. It listed his name as Fela, and cited his occupation as "Tigers Tamed, Ladies Loved, Justice Won."

* * *

THAT THE SUBJECT of race should have been central to Fidel's revolution from the start, and in at times vexed ways, isn't surprising. For at least as much as that revolution was socialist or anti-imperial or anything else, its leaders have always presented their cause as tied to Martí's odes to the island's "half-breed soul" and Ortiz's erudite riffs on tobacco and transculturation. Fidel's revolution, before it was Marxist-Leninist or Castroist or anything else, had always been framed and experienced in Cuba as a nationalist struggle. Accordingly, it was not solely on the grounds of Marxian virtue but also of *cubanidad* that Fidel battled cocaine and prostitution as "un-Cuban" in the 1960s (never mind that sex for pay held a prominent place in Cuban society long before its exploitation by *yanquis*) and contended, during the '70s, that Cuba's military involvement in Angola and Mozambique was driven by Cuba's core identity as an "Afro-Latin" nation.

Fidel's custodianship of *cubanidad* had its own roots in the longer history of Cuban men of privilege defining the nation's identity. Batista was a mulatto cane cutter's son; Fidel and Raúl were the children of Spanish landowners—putative members, that is, of a class of Cubans who thought the déclassé rule of an uneducated army colonel a national shame. Not every member of Cuba's elite who came to support Castro against Batista in the 1950s was driven by prejudice; Fidel has always been a strong antiracist, in his way. But the *machista* worlds of elite Cuban politics and culture have also always been paternalistic, whether in Martí's wishful 1891 declaration that in Cuba "[t]here are no races," or the long-standing tradition—from Nicolás Guillén's iconic 1930 poem "Mulata" to innumerable paintings of the copper Virgen—of holding up the comely *mulata* as embodiment of *cubanidad* while granting less respect to actual brown-skinned Cuban women in the society, or fewer opportunities for advancement, than anyone.

After his revolution officially banned racial discrimination in 1960, Fidel blithely declared that racism was defeated in Cuba. As in 1891, the actual situation was more complex. The masses of Afro-Cubans who'd lived in illiterate destitution since slavery—and seen three thousand of their forebears massacred in the awful 1912 race war—had the most to gain from socialist projects in housing, health care, and education. That Cuba's four million blacks still provide a key base of Communist Party support is a measure of how much their lives have improved under Fidel. But his blind spots with regard to race have at times also been pernicious.

Carlos Moore, a black Cuban writer who has focused on those blind spots, described their impacts on his own life in a memoir called *Pichón*. The book took its title from a Cuban slur for Jamaican and Haitian laborers who survived the Depression by scrounging for slaughterhouse scraps in the manner of ugly black buzzards, or *pichones*. The book begins with Moore recounting a rural Cuban childhood of being tormented by the fists and epithets of white schoolmates, before then recounting his personal epic: leaving for New York City at sixteen in the late 1950s and falling into the black radical demimonde of Maya Angelou and Malcolm X, before then returning to Cuba as an ardent Fidel admirer in the early 1960s, only to be imprisoned and exiled by Fidel's revolution for daring to protest the race prejudice of some of its ministers.

After meeting his mentor Angelou in a Harlem bookshop in 1958, Moore directed an occupation of the UN General Assembly, two years later, to protest the U.S.-sponsored killing of the Congolese freedom fighter Patrice Lumumba. It was during Castro's own 1960 visit to the UN—during which Fidel stayed at the Hotel Theresa in Harlem to convey solidarity with those oppressed by the U.S. empire at home—that Moore decided it was his revolutionary duty to join the cause. Returning to Havana in June 1961, Moore sought to put his skills as an English speaker to work at the Foreign Ministry. He became convinced that the bureaucrat denying his requests for a job was doing so on account of his dark skin, and he took the audacious step of traveling to a provincial army barracks to demand a meeting with the only Afro-Cuban member of Fidel's inner circle, the guerrilla hero Juan Almeida. Almeida indulged the headstrong youth with a warning to "Stop talking as you do," but once back in Havana, Moore was "detailed" by the revolutionary police and tossed into a new jail made from a converted mansion on the city's outskirts. He was released a few weeks later with no charge or explanation and eventually found work in another branch of the government. But in late 1962, after some months of increasing disquiet about the revolution's puritanical excesses—with police sending homosexuals to labor camps and forcibly shuttering Afro-Cuban social clubs—Moore encountered his old nemesis in the Foreign Ministry. Furious that the young *negrito* was still at large, the bureaucrat promised to ensure that Moore was "take[n] care of" for good. That afternoon Moore knocked at the door of the Havana embassy of the new West African nation of Guinea and requested asylum; a few weeks later he left Cuba on a freighter bound for Africa. He eventually settled in Paris, and went on to write *Castro, the Blacks, and Africa* (1989), a controversial radical critique of the revolution's race mores whose exaggerated animus's source came clear in the experiences related in Moore's more personal memoir.

When Moore went into exile in the early 1960s, most Cubans who fled the island belonged to its white upper classes. The arch right-wingers among them nurtured a deep anger about Castro's "giving it all away" to the riffraff and *pichones*. Their story is perhaps less tragic than that of exile families with more liberal pasts like the Bacardis, of the eponymous liquor empire, whose kids attended the same Santiago school as Fidel and Raúl. The Bacardis' family epic began in the 1860s, when a penniless Catalan immigrant named Facundo Bacardi discovered a new way to distill sugarcane into clear white rum. His son Emilio Bacardi became a key ally to Martí in the fight for independence in the 1890s, and the Bacardis' 1950s heirs were fervid Fidel supporters—but then left the island and became fervid Castro haters when he ordered a state takeover of the company they'd spent a century building from scratch. Such sagas about seized storehouses and abandoned mansions still compose the sacred text of mainstream Cuban exile politics. But as stories like Carlos Moore's show, belonging to a class of Cubans whose lot the revolution improved granted no exemption from being tyrannized by party discipline and hierarchy.

And similar contradictions concerning race have persisted to the present. I gained a purchase on those from certain of the guests at that Anti-Imperial Thanksgiving, in 2002, with whom I became friends. Many political asylum holders in Cuba spent years working regular state jobs as schoolteachers or doing yearly stints in the sugar fields. But the remarkable Nehanda Abiodun, a onetime member of the organization whose signal achievements in the '70s included springing Assata Shakur from jail, landed in Cuba in 1990—and had by the early 2000s, when we met, become established in Havana's cultural scene as the *"madrina"* of Cuban hip-hop. We grew close over long bonding sessions and dance parties at her apartment east of Havana, or in one of the many venues around town where talented young Cubans were then trying their hand at performing U.S.-style hip-hop.

After Abiodun arrived in Cuba, her hosts at first hoped she'd take a job here teaching English. But she carved out a niche advising and helping to foment the inchoate "hip-hip movement" among young Afro-Cubans in Havana. Their music was at first viewed with skepticism by Cuba's Ministry of Culture. But a few of Abiodun's mentees convinced the ministry (perhaps with an assist from Harry Belafonte, who, it was said, had convinced Fidel that hip-hop wasn't only about expressing bravado; it could be revolutionary, too) to support their art rather than trying to shut it down. So grew a vibrant scene into which I fell as a college-aged devotee of Nas and Dead Prez. One result of Abiodun's encouraging Havana's young rappers to narrate their society's own problems in song was their calling out racist practices by Havana's cops, who were notorious, among young black Habaneros, for being more assiduous in asking to check their IDs, or booking them for petty offenses, than they were with their lighter-skinned peers. Such critiques were not only tolerated but abetted by the Cuban state, by the early 2000s. This signaled significant shifts in Cuba's cultural policy—if also the fact that race prejudice, as sympathetic American blacks well knew, still existed here.

* * *

IN THE LEAN YEARS of the Special Period and after, rappers weren't the only people in Cuba setting flight from the island as their life's main goal. In a state-run economy where all the old structural problems identified by Janos Kornai in the Eastern Bloc—"the economy of shortages," and hoarding, forced substitution, and "the soft budget constraint"— were abundant, the post–Special Period years had introduced a new set of incentives for leaving Cuba.[2] The immense carrot of the United States' old "wet foot, dry foot" policy was still in place: it prescribed that any Cuban who reached U.S. shores be granted immediate residency. But now the legalizing of dollars in Cuba itself meant also that going abroad, so as to be able to send money home, was the best way to help one's family. Visiting Cuba over a period of years, one grows used to returning to the home of a friend or calling their old number only to learn that they too have left for *la yuma*, or for someplace else.

Keeping up with my friends Carlos and Dagdelay, with whom I stayed in 2002 and 2003 in Vedado, I watched Carlos's brother Gustavo emigrate to Germany, thanks to his seduction of a woman from Cologne. Their cousin Lisette went to Miami. Dagdelay herself, the old cigar-rolling hustler, didn't leave Cuba for good. But she began traveling back and forth to Ecuador—one of the few countries in Latin America where Cubans didn't need a visa to visit—to buy sacks of socks and other clothes to bring back to Cuba and sell for dollars. When in 2013 I went to find her and Carlos in the old apartment where I'd stayed with them on 19th Street, a neighbor told me they'd left—but hadn't gone far. A few blocks away, I found Carlos in a much less nice apartment building. He told me that Dagdelay had traded their apartment for this one, plus a good bit of cash, to fund her Ecuador schemes. Ecuador was where she was just then, in fact, Carlos said. When I remarked on how skinny he looked since last I'd seen him, without his wife around to cook, he chuckled. "You should see Dagdelay now. I think I lost all this weight and gave it to her. She's huge."

During the Cold War, U.S. policy toward the island had been neither humane nor effective, but it did grimly accord with the apocalyptic logic of that period's geostrategy—as did all the dark deeds that Washington either allowed or abetted, elsewhere in the hemisphere, to prevent the emergence of another Soviet satellite in its "backyard." But what the years since the USSR's fall have also laid bare is the extent to which Washington's approach to Cuba itself has been driven by other than simply rational aims like containment. "Castro is not merely an adversary, but an enemy," a 1993 report from the U.S. Army War College observed, "an embodiment of evil who must be punished for his defiance of the United States. . . . There is a desire to hurt the enemy that is mirrored in the malevolence that Castro has exhibited towards us."[3] For U.S. politicians in national campaigns, being "tough on Cuba" long ago took its place alongside being "a friend to Israel" as a sine qua non of victory. But even more than that, as Cuba's potential threat to U.S. security progressively dwindled to nearly nil, U.S. antagonism toward its government only grew.

In 1992, a new Cuban Democracy Act codified the embargo as U.S. law. Four years later, it was toughened by the Helms-Burton Act that

Bill Clinton made official in 1996, which prohibited U.S. companies from dealing with foreign firms engaged in business with Cuban property seized by the revolution, and also mandated that the embargo could not be lifted until such time as Cuba is run by a government "that does not include Fidel Castro or Raúl Castro." And then George W. Bush, who owed his presidency to South Florida votes, won the White House.

Bush used his office in 2004 to funnel $59 million in new funding to no-bid Miami-Cuban boondoggles like the propaganda networks Radio and TV Martí. He moved to close one of the embargo's few loopholes by introducing strict limits on remittances Cuban Americans could send to family members on the island and on the number of trips they could take to visit them. He placed Cuba on the U.S. list of "state sponsors of terror"—thanks in part to those political exile pals of mine from the Anti-Imperial Thanksgiving. He also established, at the heart of the executive branch and under the chairmanship of Secretary of State Colin Powell, the Commission for Assistance to a Free Cuba, which was charged with determining how "to hasten the end of the dictatorship." In May 2004, the commission produced a report recommending that in the wake of an anticipated violent transition, Cuban schools should be kept open "in order to keep children and teenagers off the streets."[4]

Castro's government, in reply, grew gravely concerned that Cuba's involvement in Bush's "war on terror" would go beyond the United States' use of its imperial relic at Guantánamo Bay to hold certain prisoners beyond the jurisdiction of U.S. courts. "The Cubans were really worried," Lawrence Wilkerson, longtime chief of staff to Colin Powell, would recall of a visit he made to Havana just after leaving the State Department in 2005. "They wanted me first of all to assure them that we weren't going to invade."[5] In the spring of 2003, Fidel Castro—practiced in paranoia, always more comfortable on a war footing than not—responded to the new provocations by ordering the trial for treason of some seventy-five "dissidents," some of whom were indeed Cubans being paid by the United States to tweak (if hardly, in practice, to destabilize) their government, but most of whose offenses amounted to writing articles and circulating petitions.

* * *

MORE SIGNIFICANT TO CUBANS than Washington's long-standing obsession with upending their government were concerns over what that government might do to repair a broken economy. Many Cubans remained proud, then as now, that theirs was a poor country in which "no children sleep in the streets." The Communist Party still enjoyed support in the provinces. But either way, from the standpoint of a failed fifty-year attempt by the United States to change the island's government by isolation, the salient facts about Cuba, in those first years of the new century, were that it enjoyed good relations and strong economic ties with every other country in the hemisphere, including Canada (not to mention China and the European Union), and that it had a stable government, in evidently firm control of its military and police, which carried off its next major transition—the move to post-Fidel life—with minimal apparent fuss.

With rumors of Fidel's demise long a recurrent feature of Miami gossip, the guiding assumption both there and in Washington had long been that he'd never relinquish power without some sudden emergency, like death. In late June 2006, Fidel traveled to Argentina for a meeting of South American presidents during which he took the opportunity, there in Córdoba, to visit Che Guevara's boyhood home. A few weeks later, he appeared at the traditional anniversary celebrations of his and his youthful comrades' storming of the Moncada barracks on July 26, 1953. He must then have already been quite ill with the intestinal ailment—thought to be diverticulitis—that would require emergency surgery, a few days later. He was seventy-eight years old, and had been looking frail; after giving a speech in 2004, he'd tumbled from his podium to break an elbow and knee. His famed bush of beard was now frizzy white. Decrepitude was setting in. Still, no one expected his announcement, read on Cuban state TV by his personal secretary on July 31, 2006, in which Fidel explained to the Cuban people, in typically prolix fashion, that

> [d]ue to the enormous effort made to visit the Argentine city of Córdoba, participate in the MERCOSUR meeting, in the closing session of the Summit of the Peoples in the historical University of Córdoba and the visit to Altagracia, the city where Che lived as a child, and in addition to that immediately attending the commemoration of the 53rd anniversary of the assault on the Moncada and Carlos Manuel de Céspedes garrisons on July 26, 1953, in the provinces of Granma and Holguín, compounded by days and nights of continuous work with barely any sleep have all resulted

in my health, which has stood up to every test, being subjected to extreme stress and breaking down.[6]

He further explained that, in the wake of surgery, he had to contend with "an acute intestinal crisis . . . the operation has obliged me to take various weeks of rest, at a remove from my responsibilities and duties." And then, underscoring that since "our country is threatened in circumstances like this by the government of the United States," he declared: "I provisionally delegate my functions as president of the Council of State and the government of the Republic of Cuba to the first vice president, comrade Raúl Castro Ruz."

On the first July 26th celebration that Fidel was unable to attend, I traveled out to the provincial city of Camagüey, to watch Raúl—longtime leader of Cuba's army, dour military man—try to rally his troops. In a concrete plaza outside this central Cuban city whose colonial core is now surrounded by Soviet apartment blocks, I joined perhaps ten thousand people walking to the square to be handed little paper Cuban flags, long the customary accessory to events like these, to wave at the right times and for the state TV cameras set up by the concrete riser soon to be mounted by an unimposing man in green fatigues.

Raúl Castro was still acting in a provisional capacity; he was then the first vice president of the Councils of State and Ministers and maximum general of the Cuban armed forces. But with his thick eyeglasses and customary cap, he officially stood in for his ill older brother. Never known for his charisma, and not fond of public speaking, Raúl extolled his people's fortitude. He urged increased milk production, decried the high price of chicken, and described the meaning of revolution— "the profound conviction that there is no force in the world capable of crushing the strength of truth and ideas."[7] Beyond those platitudes, there was no stirring oratory forthcoming in the soupy Camagüey air. As Raúl's last cries of "Viva Fidel!" and "Venceremos!" faded from the loudspeakers, affable campesinos and flirting students filed from the square. Their conversations turned to the rum and dominoes promised by this holiday afternoon. The speech seemed to resonate little save for Raúl's definition of revolution and his surprising "willingness to discuss on equal footing the prolonged dispute with the United States."

* * *

IF YOU'D TOLD SOMEONE in the 1960s that Raúl Castro, the man then regarded as the most hard-line Stalinist in his brother's government, would one day be cast as the man to lead Cuba's halting embrace of the free market, you'd have been laughed out of Havana. But the role of reformer was precisely what Raúl took on when, in February 2008, he was formally installed as Cuba's president, succeeding his sick brother, by a unanimous election of the National Assembly. By then, he'd already used his speech in Camagüey—and in particular his call "to criticize what needs criticizing"—to launch an unprecedented process in Cuba: a program of community meetings, all across the island, in which citizens were invited to make proposals and air grievances about their government. Precisely what political game was behind this process wasn't clear initially. But it soon became apparent that at least one of its aims was to give Raúl the cover required to follow up on initial gestures at reform he'd made upon taking over Fidel's duties, which included the opening of the grounds of tourist hotels such as the Hotel Nacional to ordinary Cubans. Now Raúl also released most of the seventy-five political prisoners arrested in the wake of Fidel's Bush-provoked crackdown of 2003, and made the extraordinary suggestion, on which he indeed followed through, that all Cubans would soon be issued titles to their state-owned home. And he continued to insist on his willingness to address, in some form, "the prolonged dispute with the United States."

Whether Raúl was at this point simply shooting in the dark or playing domestic politics or had some larger agenda in mind, vis-à-vis who might ascend to the presidency, is hard to say. But in any event, during the U.S. presidential campaign that saw Barack Obama seize history in 2008, Obama called Raúl's bluff.

In his debates first with Hillary Clinton and then with John McCain, Obama stated his willingness to sit down with Cuba's new leader with a view toward improving relations. Realists predictably pooh-poohed this prospect as a nonstarter: Obama's future secretary of state, Hillary Clinton, back when she wasn't his chief diplomat but his primary rival, called his desire to meet with "foreign dictators" like Raúl Castro "irresponsible." But during Obama's first weeks in office, his administration—cognizant of polls showing that younger Cuban Americans voiced little support for the hard-line stance of the past, and that even a symbolic thaw with Cuba would be an easy way to improve relations with the rest of Latin America—successfully marshaled a bill through Congress overturning Bush-era restrictions on family visits and remittances. All this move did was return the United States' Cuba policy to its 2003 status. But it was a key signal that a larger overhaul of the policy would be on the table in Obama's Washington. At his first Summit of the Americas, in Trinidad and Tobago in April 2009, Obama observed that Cuba's thousands of doctors dispersed throughout the region were "a reminder for us in the United States that if our only interaction with many of these countries is . . . military, then we may not be developing the connections that can, over time, increase our influence." He also declared, though few paid him much mind then, that "a new beginning with Cuba" could be near.

In 1891, José Martí, who wasn't just Cuba's most articulate nationalist but also perhaps his generation's most perceptive writer on inter-American relations, wrote in "Nuestra America," "One must not attribute, through a provincial antipathy, a fatal and inbred wickedness to the continent's fair-skinned nation simply because it does not speak our language, or see the world as we see it, or resemble us in its political defects, so different from our own."[8] For many Cubans, the election of Obama represented an overcoming of political defects, and in his brown face they saw not a "fair-skinned nation" but something of themselves; their hope was that Obama would be a leader free of many of his country's old neuroses. The ultimate test of those hopes would come in ending the long-running embargo, which Lawrence Wilkerson, expressing a widely held but rarely stated Washington view, told *GQ* was "the dumbest policy on the face of the earth."[9] No less incontestable was an old remark from an ailing *barbudo* in Havana, who expressed doubt, after Obama's election, that he'd live to see the end of Obama's first term. "We cannot move, nor can the United States," Fidel Castro had told an interviewer in 1974. "Speaking realistically, someday some sort of ties will have to be established."[10]

* * *

WHEN THOSE TIES WERE at last restored, six years into Obama's term and six years after Raúl's speech in Camagüey, I happened to be in Havana. December 17, 2014, fell on a Wednesday—and also on El Día de San Lázaro: the day reserved, by Cuban adepts of Santeria, for the patron saint of healing and rebirth, whom they also call Babalú-Ayé. Each year on this day, thousands of Cubans stream toward a little church in the village of Rincón, twenty miles from Havana, to honor a figure depicted, in little statues and on key chains sold along the route, as a hunched *viejo* wearing purple. Even in the early years of the revolution, when Fidel's secular Marxism made religion forbidden, this ritual persisted.

As the pilgrims approached Rincón on that typically bright but cool December morning, there was little hint of the new resonance the day would carry. In *Juventud Rebelde*, the official organ of the youth wing of the Cuban Communist Party, a simple notice stated that at noon, on state TV, Raúl Castro Ruz, president of the Council of State and president of the Council of Ministers, would make an announcement. The line was hardly notable: such notices usually precede nothing more exciting than news of a trade pact with Caracas or China. But at midday, in a statement timed to coincide with a similar one made by President Obama from the Oval Office, Castro made history. "I have reiterated on many occasions our willingness to hold a respectful dialogue with the United States," he intoned, doffing his familiar ball cap but still wearing his glasses. "We have been able to make headway in the solution of some topics of mutual interest."[11]

On that patio behind the Hotel Nacional, where I'd gone to check email from my Wi-Fi-less flat nearby, there was little to suggest the moment. No drivers honked the horns of their decades-old American cars to celebrate the news that Cuba and the United States, after half a century of belligerence, were reestablishing diplomatic ties. Hustlers still ambled after tourists, as usual, and old ladies toted *libreta* ration books and plastic sacks full of state-supplied rice. The juxtaposition between these scenes and my laptop screen, aglow with urgent messages and headlines from afar, was stark. In the garden behind the Nacional, I looked up to see maids and bellhops going about their work in uniforms unchanged since 1959. The same old pair of friendly docents stood by, waiting to show curious visitors the network of tunnels and bunkers, built into the grounds, from which Fidel commanded soldiers during the missile crisis in 1962, when Havana and Washington's historic animus found its gravest depth.

On the afternoon, five decades later, when that animus was tentatively salved, it was already clear what the response among Cubans would be. As at other moments perceived from abroad as dramatic watersheds—the demise of the Soviet Union in 1991, an ailing Fidel's handoff of power in 2006—the news was met in Havana, by and large, with calm.

Wandering the quiet streets that evening, I hopped into an old Lada cab, whose driver pointed happily at a pair of Cuban and U.S. flags he'd anchored to his dashboard. He told me he hoped that he might soon get to see his twin sister, who'd left the island years earlier by raft, and who now lived in Boston. He dropped me by the beautiful art deco Mella Theatre, where the city's famed yearly jazz festival had opened the day before. Inside, a veteran scat singer and bandleader named Bobby Carcassés added some topical lines to a rumba number praising Changó. "The Five have returned!" he cried. "And *el bloqueo* has little time left!" The hall, whose orchestra seats were filled with several hundred American visitors in town on licensed tours for the festival, stood and erupted.

The story of "the Five," or Los Cinco, hadn't been one in which the U.S. media had shown much interest, but it was one that Cubans knew extremely well. The Five were agents whom Cuba has always maintained it sent to Miami, in the 1990s, to keep tabs on extremist Cuban exiles, of the kind who were responsible, for example, for blowing up a Cuban jetliner off Barbados in 1976. Their subsequent imprisonment by U.S. authorities has been a central component of the Cuban state's domestic propaganda since 1998, when the Five were first arraigned in the U.S. on various charges, including federal espionage charges. Across the island, billboards depict their faces under a simple caption: "¡Volverán!" (They will return!) And now Los Cinco had. Three of the prisoners, Gerardo Hernández, Antonio Guerrero, and Ramón Labañino, were returned to Cuba as part of a prisoner exchange announced along with the other measures; the other two, René González and Fernando González, returned to Cuba in 2013 and in early 2016, respectively. On December 18, both of Cuba's dailies led not with the larger agreement with Washington but with big photos of Los Cinco standing, beaming, with Raúl Castro, beneath a huge one-word headline: "¡Volvieron!" (They have returned!) (*Juventud Rebelde* and *Granma*, the Cuban Communist Party's official organ, also printed the full texts of both Castro's and Obama's speeches.)

Among most Cubans I spoke with, joy at the Five's return was real. But uncertainty prevailed about Carcassés's other assertion: that *el bloqueo*—the blockade, Cuba's term for the U.S. embargo—would expire soon. The announced restoration of diplomatic ties included some measures that would lessen the economic effects of *el bloqueo* for many people here, notably quadrupling the amount of money their émigré relatives could remit home from the States, from $500 to $2,000 per quarter.

But it was unlikely that the U.S. Congress would vote anytime soon to repeal the main piece of legislation—the Helms-Burton Act, signed into law by Bill Clinton in 1996—that undergirded the embargo.

Nor was it clear how the new measures would affect the vast changes already under way in Cuba. The country's cash-poor government has long seemed intent on following China's lead by maintaining firm control over the military and huge social service bureaucracy, while introducing free market measures to keep its economy afloat. For many Cubans, happiness at the new thaw with America was tempered by questions concerning the pace and implication of whatever reforms Raúl Castro would introduce next. At the same newsstands peddling state papers and party gazettes, you can now buy a booklet whose existence was until recently unthinkable: a compendium of classified ads, called *Papelito*, that lists homes for sale by their owners. (How does a colonial-style townhouse with marble columns and twenty-foot ceilings for US$20,000 sound?) The paper was only made possible after the central government, in 2011, issued deeds to every home in the country, all of which were formerly owned by the state. It seemed unlikely that Americans would be able, anytime soon, to turn their gazes toward owning Havana's stunning old buildings, as they've done since Thomas Jefferson said he fancied adding Cuba to "our system of states." It was unthinkable—at least then—that a government founded on the idea that Cubans should own Cuba would lift its proscription, in place since the revolution, on nonresidents owning Cuban property.

The changes, even then, were extending to private enterprise, in ways that boded well for what might be an increasing number of permitted American visitors in future years—but that also threatened to exacerbate new divisions. To a visitor returning to Havana after a couple of years away, the capital's efflorescence of new tapas bars and other swank spots was already shocking. Since Castro had approved the issuing of licenses to private business owners in 2010, some 300,000 Cubans had obtained them. And most of these, especially in Havana and other sites favored by tourists, listed their prices in the CUCs—"convertible pesos"—that only Cubans with access to foreign currency could afford. The contradictions and new class divisions were plain in a place where the people responsible for inspecting these posh new restaurants were still earning $20 a month. Rumors of bribes were rife, as were stories about pizzerias or bars being shut down by those inspectors for underreporting income or for keeping two sets of books.

But evidence of new spaces, and new ambitions, abounded. On the Friday night after the announcement, I headed to a former cooking oil factory that had been converted, by some enterprising young artists, into an impressive arts complex, containing galleries, performance spaces, and an airy screening room. There, hip young Cubans (who'd paid the same cover as the smattering of foreigners: $2) flirted and danced before a big screen playing music videos by the likes of Skrillex and Kanye West. Though the Fabrica de Arte Cubano was launched with help from the government's Ministry of Culture, the art on its walls included large photos of a propaganda billboard ("We have and will have SOCIALISMO") that was falling over.

The night's promised entertainment, a show by the hirsute red-state rockers ZZ Top (who have reportedly been vacationing here for years), had been called off: the Texan group had apparently decided that this tumultuous week might not be the best time, with the world's media descending on Havana, to play what was supposed to have been an under-the-radar show. But Ivan Vergara, one of the Fabrica's directors, was unperturbed. "They'll come again, and many more will, too," Vergara told me. "Our basic aim here is to create a world-class space, for everyone," he said, before showing me to a stylish restaurant on the old factory's roof. At the restaurant, a big table of what looked like Miami Cubans home for the holidays embraced old friends and tucked into a pricy meal.

The new influx of American dollars will test Cuba's socialist mores in ways—as liberal foes of both communism and the U.S. embargo have long contended—that the Soviets' fall never could. But Raúl Castro, for his part, gave a ringing speech on that Saturday, declaring that Cuba had "won the war" and proclaiming, on the eve of the revolution's fifty-seventh year, that Cuban communism "can last another five hundred and seventy years."[12]

That evening, near sunset, I trekked past the Plaza de la Revolución, the vast cement expanse where Fidel used to harangue his people for hours, to a scraggly park in the proletarian district of Cerro. There, outside Havana's main baseball stadium, a stage was being set up for a free concert by Silvio Rodríguez, Cuba's leading singer-songwriter since the '60s, whose poetic odes to unicorns and hope are akin to official hymns here. The show had been announced weeks earlier, but Cubans far beyond Cerro had recently become interested, thanks to rumors that the Five, who had yet to appear in public, would attend.

And, sure enough, as the park filled with Cubans, a retinue of officials parted the crowd, accompanied by TV cameras and exultant cheers, to make way for five men in polo shirts, looking far older than they did on their posters. They beamed with joy, soaked in the applause, and kissed babies in the warm night.

Few nations, let alone revolutionary states, are fortunate enough to have a musician as fine and as ideologically devoted as Silvio Rodríguez on hand for occasions like these. The many thousands filling the park sang along to every lyric he trilled from the stage. After he invited the Five onstage with him, one of the men, Antonio Guerrero, explained how, during their long years in solitary confinement, and on the rare occasions when they got to see each other, it was a Rodríguez song, "La Era Está Pariendo un Corazón," that they sang to lift their spirits. When Rodríguez launched into the tune, the men sang along, their microphones strategically turned down for the occasion. A couple of them wiped away tears, and another grabbed the mic to salute the crowd. "Fidel promised we'd return," he bellowed. "And here we are!"

Mirta Guibert, an older woman in attendance with whom I spoke after the show, saw fit to thank another couple of political figures for the men's return. "We're only separated by ninety miles," she said as she sat on a curb nursing her feet, sore from standing for the hours-long show. "There's no reason we can't be connected. So I thank Obama for doing something worthy of his Nobel Prize. And I think he might have gone to see San Lázaro, too."

* * *

BY THE TIME I made it back to Havana later that year, both the U.S. and Cuba had followed through on various of the steps promised in the wake of détente. Secretary of State John Kerry, in a gala ceremony in the spring of 2015, had alighted in Havana to oversee the rebranding of the notorious Interests Section by the Malecon. As I walked past the ugly edifice on one of my first days back in town, it was almost shocking, even though I'd known to expect it, to see the new sign affixed above the front door proclaiming the building an embassy of the United States. Perhaps even more radical, though, were those changes the Cubans had made in the plaza outside. Gone was the old billboard proclaiming "Señores Imperialistas, We Have No Fear of You!" Gone, too, were those 138 black flags that had been raised during the grim days of George W. Bush's post-9/11 provocations. At the plaza's rear, the statue of Martí still pointed an accusatory finger at the Yankees' lair. But the heavy air of antagonism that had for so long oppressed this part of the city in particular felt lifted.

Meanwhile, for most Habaneros the city's quotidian life was unchanged. Perhaps the most notable change Cubans had seen here was the appearance around town, by various public thoroughfares, of little flying saucer–like Wi-Fi routers, around which clusters of illuminated faces sat on curbs and benches, gazing at smartphones to Skype with relatives or trying to construct, despite abysmally slow broadband speeds, new online identities with El Feisbu—Facebook. That the internet was becoming less prohibitive to everyday Cubans was a big deal. But one of the reasons the speeds remained so slow—to the frustration much more of new gringo tourists than Cubans, who were accustomed to waiting—suggested how ingrained the effects of the U.S. embargo were: with no undersea cable joining Cuba to the nearby mainland, per U.S. wishes, every one of the emails and Facebook updates posted to Cuban computers was still traveling through a single wire to Venezuela.

Those here still earning state salaries lived as they always had—or discussed trying to take advantage of the old U.S. immigration law allowing them into *la yuma* by way of Mexico or anywhere else, before thawing relations got rid of that loophole. Which is to say that whatever changes were afoot at a policy level, their concerns remained the same. Six years after Fidel officially stepped down, there were new and louder rumors that senior officials in the government—and especially men tied to Raúl Castro's army—were jockeying to secure rich concessions, or previously public property, through impending market reforms on a much larger scale than simply allowing private restaurants and giving private citizens titles to their homes. But what had most changed about Havana, really, wasn't to do with its residents at all.

The most profound change in the months after the announcement was the palpably larger presence of foreigners, and Americans especially, striding its streets and filling its hotels. With American airlines having announced the resumption, within months, of frequent direct flights to José Martí International Airport, there was also a vibrant sense among many of those foreigners that they'd arrived here just in time—less to see Cuba "before it was too late" than to get in on the ground floor of what was coming next. At swish new restaurants in Miramar and Vedado, nightclub owners from Los Angeles rubbed elbows with Manhattan art dealers, London hucksters proposed new hotel ventures, and a critical mass of movie stars and sundry other representatives of the self-consciously hip took selfies in a city whose uses as a backdrop had been strongly evinced the month before in a *Vanity Fair* pictorial, shot by Annie Leibovitz, that found Rihanna posing as a prostitute in central Havana. It was impossible not to hear from one of these characters, at one of those establishments they frequented, about the various spectacular homes or seaside apartments they'd been shown by "realtors" in a town where selling property to foreigners was still in most cases quite illegal. At a great rumba gig I'd been attending for years in a weekly midnight set in the small club above Miramar's Casa de la Musica, the usual crowd of Cuban *rumberos* and hustlers were now joined in the front row by a well-known blond movie actress from Los Angeles. It was hard not to feel like Havana was coming full circle to the 1950s, when every Hollywood starlet and Manhattan wag with a yen for color and rhythm came to Havana for their kicks.

One evening on the newly redone veranda at the Hotel Telegrafo, a middle-aged man whom I at first mistook for a sex tourist sat down one table over from mine with a pretty young Cuban woman. When the woman left a few minutes later, he informed me in Russian-accented English that she was a lawyer whom he'd retained to advise him on changing real estate laws, and then summed up his appraisal of Havana just now: "Is like Russia, 1986." Real estate was one thing, but other prospecting already happening on a bigger scale pertained to the problem of that single wire to Venezuela through which Cuba got its internet: just weeks earlier, big U.S. telecom companies and venture capitalists alike had exulted at Obama's announcement that they'd soon be allowed to enter the Cuban market and perhaps even join it by cable to Key West. The subtext of this excitement was the hope, mirroring the Monopoly-like frenzy that attended the end of the Spanish-American War, that U.S. firms might again dominate the dormant Cuban market. Of course, what all this rather blatantly ignored was that whatever changes Cuba allowed, or economic reforms Raúl Castro effected, it was hardly likely that anyone in power here would consider, let alone rubber-stamp, any form of "foreign investment" not set to benefit either Cuba's ruling party or themselves.

Where this was all heading was hard to say, at least for now. The Russian's mention of 1986 implied its own timetable for how long Cuban communism might last. The larger direction of the island's opening economy, and its cultural scene as well, may or may not have been set to follow what one artist told me with regard to the government's plodding yet significant steps to date. "You can't melt one corner of an iceberg," he said, "without letting the whole thing go."

It was also plain that many Cubans, not least an ailing but still alive Fidel Castro and his brother, remained strongly determined to uphold both some semblance of sovereignty and the better-loved aspects of its socialist system. But what made things especially hard to judge at this juncture was that Raúl Castro's retiring form of leadership had only grown more retiring in the past year. After he announced that he would cede the presidency when his term ended in 2018, his general approach to governing, and to narrating for his people the reforms he was quietly enacting vis-à-vis the United States and otherwise, was to issue quiet communiqués and announcements in the state newspapers. In Havana that Christmas, there was a visible dearth of any new propaganda billboards extolling the revolution, and a visible rise in Christmas decor and other bits of capitalist kitsch long anathema here. The hope that Cubans might still affirm the revolution's ideals may have remained, but the aim of retaining their blind faith in its rhetoric seemed at last to be quietly exiting the stage. When on New Year's Day Raúl didn't deign to give a speech, it was anything but a surprise. What perhaps lay in wait for Cuba, though, if the new contradictions weren't managed well, was suggested in a drama that unfolded in the Plaza de la Catedral on New Year's Eve.

Not three months later, Barack Obama would arrive in a rainstorm with his lovely family to visit this, one of Old Havana's prettiest squares, as he readied to give a speech in which he proclaimed, "I am here to bury the last remnants of the Cold War in the Americas." But on New Year's Eve, a large group of well-heeled tourists was promised a night of dinner and dancing under the stars. Nothing was necessarily amiss about this, on its face. But in a city and a neighborhood where free access to public space has long been sacrosanct—especially on a night when Habaneros greet the new year by washing water from their homes and walking their barrio's blocks at midnight—the organizers of this event, clearly in some sort of cahoots with local authorities, had taken the unwise step of barricading off the square. The streets of Old Havana have, of course, been no stranger, for some years now, to wealthy foreigners rubbing up against some of the city's humbler citizens. But this marked something new.

For the cool price of US$200 per person—an amount equal to what people in the surrounding apartments earned in a year—guests in the plaza were to enjoy the superb backdrop of Old Havana without the bother of its locals. Their night began well enough. But it took a fateful turn when those wealthy tourists went to leave the square to board their air-conditioned tour buses. The one exit from the plaza, they found as they went to leave, was blocked by a few dozen angry Habaneros accustomed to hanging out here whenever they pleased. The locals snatched at the little paper bags, full of party favors, that the tourists were toting from the square. An angry crowd, doubtless tipsy on New Year's rum, began yelling obscenities as well. The police arrived and, sensing a serious situation, unleashed a pair of German shepherds. Many of the Cubans dispersed, but one of the dogs managed in his ardor to knock over a small, elderly man who belonged not to the crowd of locals but to the bag-toting tourists. A woman in the latter camp, witnessing the incident, grew so frightened of what lay beyond the square that she refused to leave. When her tour's minders finally convinced her to go, she walked with some friends back to their bus—but they were accosted by five or six young local men who demanded their bags and went so far as to follow them onto their bus. When one of the group's Cuban chaperones confronted the boys, they punched him in the face. Everyone made it home, eventually, relatively unscathed. But by night's end at least two of the older women in the tour group were shaken and hyperventilating at the sight of any Cubans, and at their own old fear of unrest and upset, being again loosed on the Havana night.

On Puerto Rico

CHAPTER 7

BORICUA AND THE BRONX

ISLANDS, SAID FERNAND BRAUDEL, are dream laboratories for the social scientist. To visit Puerto Rico is to glimpse his claim's source—especially if you've been to Cuba. These two islands' affinity was famously hailed by the Puerto Rican poet Lola Rodríguez de Tío's view, in the late nineteenth century, that "Cuba and Puerto Rico are two wings of the same bird."[1] They're deeply congruent in their shared Caribeño accent and colonial streets and the pork-fat *sabor* of their black beans and rice. But the contrasting fortunes and history of these islands, over the course of the long American Century since they managed to wriggle free from Spain's grip, has yielded two societies whose deep distinctions are visible the moment one arrives.

In Cuba, the roadway from José Martí International Airport into Havana has for decades been lined by billboards depicting Martí's aphorisms or Che's bereted face. On the analogous bit of roadway leading into San Juan, thickets of American logos and fast food spots rival any similar strip in Orange County: placards for Pantene and Pepsi hover above Subways and Baskin-Robbinses by the score. And the strip malls of greater San Juan are marked, even more than by the presence of these U.S. chains, by concentrations and combinations of them that one won't even find in the States. Nowhere in the U.S. can you see California-based Carl's Jr. hard by a southern Sonic and White Castle hamburgers from the Midwest. In Puerto Rico, you can.

Puerto Rico is as defined by its bonds to the mainland as Cuba is by its resistant alienation—and not only in terms of its old and total prostration to the whims and penetration of U.S. capital. As an American colony in all but name, Puerto Rico also became, during the decades when Cuba was forcefully removed from U.S. vacationers' itinerary, the territory in the Caribbean most visited by tourists. Each year, some four million Americans—who require only a driver's license to visit—alight here by cruise ship or plane to sunbathe and lunch on the same Whoppers they eat at home. But what makes Puerto Rico even more notable, in the context of the wider Caribbean, is the duration and power with which its bonds to North America, like the island's own culture, have been forged by people moving in the opposite direction.

It was on July 25, 1898, two months after the U.S. bulled into the Cuban War of Independence, that American forces landed in Puerto Rico, too. In the treaty Spain signed to relinquish its empire, Cuba was prevented from becoming a formal American colony by the Teller Amendment. Attached to Congress's declaration of war on Spain, the amendment was written by a Colorado senator who was concerned to protect the interests of beet sugar makers in his home state, and it prevented the U.S. from "exercising sovereignty over Cuba." Soon enough, another amendment—this one sponsored by Orville Platt—devised the formal means by which the U.S. could still control Cuban affairs. But no law protected Puerto Rico, and it became, six months after winning its freedom from Spain, and along with Guam and the Philippines, a colony of the United States. Its people would endure decades of misrule and exploitation only partially compensated for by the Jones Act of 1917, a law that made Puerto Ricans U.S. citizens—and thus able to travel north, unlike any other residents of the Greater Antilles, without passport or visa.

Aided by the advent of cheap air travel in the 1950s, when they left their island in greatest numbers, Puerto Ricans got a decade's head start on other immigrants to New York from the Caribbean, who began arriving en masse here after changes to U.S. immigration law in 1965. New York's Puerto Ricans established a community in the swath of East Harlem that was already called "El Barrio" by the end of the 1920s, and soon branched out to include meaningful chunks of the nearby Bronx, Brooklyn, and Manhattan's Lower East Side. The city's metro region is today home to more than a million people who identify with Puerto Rico by birth or heritage. The presence of these "Nuyoricans" in the United States, and the lives they've made there, have had a profound impact not only on New York but on their home island—a place whose culture has long been shaped at least as much by those who have left the island as by those who have stayed. In the 1960s and after, emigrants' kids reimagined Afro-Cuban music on their parents' congas to make "salsa" became the sonic lingua franca of "Latin New York." The music traveled back to Puerto Rico, by boat and by record, to dominate the soundscape of a city where during a visit in the winter of 2014 I learned that Rita Moreno, star of the film *West Side Story*—which won the Best Picture Oscar in 1961, and which pitted the Jets, a gang of delinquent white kids, against the Sharks, their Puerto Rican rivals—was set to perform, at the age of eighty-two, for the first time in her native land, at San Juan's Condado Vanderbilt Hotel.

The Condado Vanderbilt overlooks the sea from the posh Condado district, just down the capital's coast from where Old San Juan's colonial center—once a warren of sailors' brothels and bars built behind the great El Morro fortress—was restored into what amounts to an open-air mall crowded with tourists. San Juan stretches south and east from the old town, which sits on a raised island peninsula that guards the city's bay. It's a sprawling expanse of distinct neighborhoods, divided by modern expressways and chasms of class and aqua lagoons that are the remnant of a stretch of coast once comprised largely of mangrove swamps. Condado's art deco condos and beachside fro-yo shops put one in mind of Miami Beach. Leafy Miramar's elegant apartment homes, tucked in behind the Condado lagoon, feel more staidly urbane. Farther along the littoral sits Ocean Park, with its distinctly LA-like bungalows and surf, and then to-be-avoided Isla Verde, a tacky tourist zone whose big hotels' guests patronize outlets of Denny's and IHOP without ever venturing, if they can help it, across the highway and into the broad and labrynthine barrio of Santurce, which is larger in size and in its contribution to Puerto Rican culture than any of the seafront zones. Santurce is also a place down whose narrow streets, lined with tightly packed houses, shirtless men play dominoes by cars on blocks, and Orlando Cepeda and his proud daughters, the first family of the Afro–Puerto Rican musical idiom of bomba, run a community school devoted to island tradition. It's in places like these, and out along the pocked road to Los Piñones, past the airport, where delicious octopus salad is dished into paper cups to blaring reggaeton at the rickety beachside *barras* touting "MARISCOS DE TODOS CLASES," that something approximating San Juan's soul resides. But on Valentine's Day night in 2014, I joined a crowd of local dignitaries and aging couples who could afford to pay $200 apiece to fill the Condado Vanderbilt's dimly lit ballroom, to watch a tiny but spry silver-haired woman, wearing a sequined gown to match, emerge to exclaim, into her wireless microphone, "Aquí soy yo!" Here I am.

"It's been a long time," Rita Moreno said in English. Indeed, it had been. She was born here Rosa Dolores Alverio, at the start of the Depression, before she left her provincial hometown of Juncos, some thirty miles southeast of San Juan by El Yunque rain forest, as a little girl. Her young mother was fleeing an unfaithful husband and small-town life. She brought the then five-year-old Rosita on a boat to the Bronx in 1936, and enrolled her pretty daughter in the dance class on 57th Street that helped launch her showbiz career, as a child dancer and performer on Broadway. This led Louis B. Mayer to offer her a contract, while she was still in her teens and still called Rosita, to join MGM Pictures' stable of starlets. She was renamed Rita Moreno by one of Mayer's casting directors and turned into a kind of all-purpose ethnic; she earned a living in the 1950s playing Tahitians and Indians and Persian princesses in the costume musicals that were how Hollywood, in those days, engaged with difference. She really made her name, and launched what would turn into a glittering career, by playing an immigrant seamstress in the film version of *West Side Story* whose story precisely mirrored her mother's. The larger casting of that rendering of Arthur Laurents's masterpiece, and the identity and background of the performers hired to enact Jerome Robbins's stellar choreography, showed how far Hollywood still had to go. Among the film's "Puerto Ricans"—including the Greek American George Chiakiris's Bernardo and the Russian-born Natalie Wood's Maria—Moreno was the only lead who was actually the real thing. Moreno took over a role that Chita Rivera had made her own on Broadway, to win the Oscar for Best Supporting Actress, for her portrayal of Anita. Now, here in San Juan's swankiest room, her accompanist on piano was a doleful bald man, whom she said had been with her for thirty years. And he tinkled along as the still-vital diva crooned and strutted her way through a slate of milquetoast show tunes like "I Like a Piano," which she punctuated with patter delivered in Spanglish ("Conjo! Se me callo un shoulder pad") for a crowd of island worthies that included the latest corrupt governor and more beloved figures like the great *salsero* and bolero singer Cheo Feliciano, a suave smiling figure whose brown skin shone against his white jacket from the front row.

Some in this crowd weren't much impressed with the night's entertainment, which unfolded mostly in English. A woman in a leopard-print dress at my table fidgeted with attitude, to the bemusement of her rich-looking date, as they both studiously ignored the odd single guy who had been seated at their rose petal–covered banquet table. But the Puerto Rican Success at the room's front won warm applause for her fond, if unseasonal, rendition of the Christmas song "Aguinaldo," on this *navidad*-mad island where at each year's end revelers traditionally spend many days carrying bottles of coconut-and-cream-rum-punch *coquino* from house to house, singing. The laughter was even warmer when Borscht belt–style patter found Moreno recounting how her immigrant mother, after they settled in the Bronx, never managed to learn to pronounce the word "sheets" without having it sound like *shits*, and how when her New York–raised daughter first brought home a nice Jewish man, her mother asked him, "Are you a yew?" (The punch line is what made it: "My mother always said, 'You know I have trouble with my *bowels*.' ") The homey laughter of this aging crowd on an island where every family's story includes tales about heading for America, or returning home, was of the knowing kind—acknowledging that this woman was no less authentically Boricua for having built much of her career performing Puerto Rican-ness for gringos.

Or such was the sentiment of one kind couple at my table, anyway. In their seventies, they said they lived in Brooklyn but had in their retirement taken to spending much of each winter in Isla Verde. They'd been married fifty years. He was Puerto Rican—from Juncos, the same town as Moreno—and she was from Queens. Their daughter had bought them tickets to the show for their anniversary. I mentioned that I'd recently read Moreno's lively memoir, which, alongside dishy chapters about her cataclysmic years-long affair with Marlon Brando, included warm recollections of a paradisiacal Juncos of old that "blossoms like a flower in memory"—a world of "ice cream houses" and chirping coqui frogs and from which leaving for New York felt like leaving an Oz of "brilliant Technicolor to grit-gray, black and white."[2] When I asked the man if he went back there, his reply was the same as Moreno's when I also asked her after the show. Neither of them had been back. And when I drove out to see Juncos myself, a week later, it wasn't hard to see why. On the island that week, the newspapers featured news of a fresh tragedy—Cheo Feliciano, so vital-looking at Moreno's show, had wrapped his Jaguar around a telephone pole days later. But dominating the news were stories that have featured here for years: the steadily declining population of an island whose people continue to leave in droves, and the not-unrelated financial ruin of a government whose ever-rising debt had long ago attained junk bond status. Central Juncos still had the "ice cream houses" of Moreno's youth, pale pink or baby blue or cream. I found the bleached-white square where in her memoir she recalled being "aware of being shown off," and describes how "the prayers and praise mingle in my memory," to make her "feel sacred." But the faded pastels were now moldy. Juncos's streets, like many on this island named by Spain for its presumed riches, felt nearly deserted. The most happening and populous spot, in the old hometown of Rita Moreno and of my tablemate at her gig at the Condado Vanderbilt, was the Wendy's hamburgers on its edge where I found lunch.

* * *

THE BIG ISLAND that the Taino called Boriquen was first reached by Columbus during his second voyage, when he briefly alighted here in 1493. His party continued on to nearby Hispaniola, where the admiral had set up Spain's first New World beachhead—and where his preoccupation with exploring the rest of the Indies, and then with the political conflicts that embroiled Spain's first colony in the later 1490s, saw him sent home in chains from Santo Domingo in 1502. Boriquen was largely left alone until an ambitious conquistador called Ponce de León, then in charge of Santo Domingo's eastern reaches, convinced the colony's new governor to approve a simple voyage—the quick sail across the Mona passage to Boriquen—that the local Taino made every day. In 1508, de León landed on the northern shore of an island the Spanish then called San Juan Batista. He built a stone house there, and was chuffed to find, within weeks of arriving and with the help of an obliging cacique whose name is usually transcribed as Guaybana, an encouraging lode of gold.

Ponce de León returned to Santo Domingo to report his findings, and won approval from its administrator, and in turn from King Ferdinand, to become the island's provisional governor and to coerce the requisite labor from the island's natives, through Spain's old system of *encomienda*, to mine its metal. The latter task met predictable resistance; one uprising by Guaybana's people, in 1511, saw them slay two hundred Spaniards under the command of one called Sotomayor—only for his comrades to retaliate by killing many more of the Indians and forcibly branding survivors, whom they sent straight back to work in the mines, with a large "F," for Ferdinand, on their foreheads. The gold they did extract from the island, in those early years, was no small part of why Columbus's son Diego, who had been locked in litigation with the crown over his rights to lands found by his father, battled hard to win suzerainty over San Juan Bautista—and in 1513 forced Ponce de León to accept the consolation prize of a rather less valuable island in the Bahamas, Bimini, along with royal leave to explore the flowered territory north of Cuba that he named Florida (where, after searching in vain for the Fountain of Youth, he was killed by a Seminole's arrow, in 1521).

With the Indians dying off at shocking rates through the 1510s and '20s, African slaves were imported to work in the mines and also to help launch the island's halting production of sugar and ginger root. Diego Columbus moved the island's first inland capital to a site by the mouth of the Loiza River. His dubbing the place a rich port—"Puerto Rico"— signaled the role that its fortified anchorage, by what's now called San Juan, played in shaping the island's identity. But Spain's conquistadors realized that gold and silver here were limited, and moved on to the greater stores in Mexico and in Peru. Francisco Pizarro's conquest of the Incas was enabled by horses he'd grazed in Puerto Rico. As the first sizable territory the Spanish reached after crossing the Atlantic, this sheltered port might have been expected to play a larger role in the empire's maritime function. But it was Havana, not San Juan, that became the chief Caribbean hub for Spain's fleets; the biannual *flota* often bypassed Puerto Rico altogether. Cattle ranching and ginger-growing were the main "industries." By 1700, when the colonization of its hinterlands really began, the sleepy isle's population had dwindled to just a few thousand inhabitants.

During the long eighteenth century, when sharply rising populations in Europe abetted mass migration to the Americas, Puerto Rico was menaced by French corsairs and English pirates and others. The island could easily have passed from Spain's hands more than once; at the conclusion of the Seven Years' War in 1763, the only reason it didn't become British was that English planters in Jamaica and Barbados resisted the addition of a sugar-growing competitor to their realm. Here as across the region, the Haitian Revolution was a watershed: French refugees arrived here in numbers to begin growing coffee in its cool mountains, and acquisitive Spaniards looked to fill the gap in the world sugar market, just as they did in Cuba, by importing more Africans to work new plantations. It was partly in response to the growing number of blacks that the island's ownership class backed Madrid's issuance of a royal Cédula de Gracias, in 1815, whose aim was to increase the white population. Ensuing decades saw the arrival of thousands of Spanish peasants who settled the island's countryside to became its much-mythologized *jibaros*. There was also a major influx of motley strivers from Iberia's more cultured edges and from elsewhere in Europe. Catalans and Majorcan *chuetas*, descended from converted Jews; French and Corsicans; and Irish and Genoese—all came in numbers. Many adopted creolized names and made fortunes from coffee or sugar and turned the lovely southern city of Ponce into a bustling center. The city's 1882 Ponce Fair, modeled on the recent World's Fair in Paris, opened with the inauguration of a municipal electrical grid that was one of the Americas' first.

Puerto Rico's patriotic history began in earnest, like Cuba's, in the 1860s. That's when high-minded liberals like Ramón Emeterio Betances grew peeved at Madrid's attempts to levy new taxes on its last American colonies and began penning *proclamas* like his "Ten Commandments of Free Men," based on the French Revolution's Declaration of the Rights of Man. Betances's words helped spark an armed uprising in the mountain town of Lares in 1868. The Grito de Lares didn't succeed in winning Puerto Rico its independence, but it did give the island its first flag and also saw Lola Rodríguez de Tió, later famed for her lines about those "two wings of the same bird," write the lyrics to "La Borinqueña," which became its national anthem ("Beautiful Puerto Rico must follow Cuba / you have brave sons who wish to fight"). The revolt at Lares was defeated for prosaic reasons: Spain's forces intercepted five hundred guns that Betances was aiming to ship home from the nearby Virgin Island of St. Thomas. But the best explanation as to why it failed was perhaps offered by Betances himself: "Puerto Ricans don't want their independence."[3]

By this he didn't mean *all* Puerto Ricans—members of his organization's revolutionary cells, along with educated creoles and mixed-race islanders with roots here, were driven nationalists. But Puerto Rico in the nineteenth century possessed a Spanish peasantry and growing national bourgeoisie whose "foreign" members—Majorcan or Corsican or French Dominguen—were less interested in abstract politics than in making money. Perhaps most crucial of all, in terms of Puerto Rico's difference from Cuba, was its far smaller populace of freshly arrived African slaves—people for whom the fight for Cuba's independence, which they joined with gusto and indeed led, was a fight for their freedom, too. Some Puerto Rican nationalists, heading into exile, joined Cuba's *mambises* in battle. Lola Rodríguez de Tió became a devoted ally and acolyte of José Martí's in New York. It was from the stage of Havana's great Teatro Tacon, in 1890, that she first recited her famous line about these islands' mutual affinity—and its less-well-known second verse: "Cuba and Puerto Rico are two wings of the same bird / they receive flowers and bullets to the same heart."

Fond as that sentiment was, the bird evoked by Rodríguez de Tió was a metaphor with much to be desired—Puerto Rico is less than a tenth of Cuba's size, and is one thousand miles from Florida, not one hundred. And most of the bullets fired to win the islands' freedom were fired in Cuba. It was Spain's travails there led Madrid's diplomats to agree, in November 1897, to grant Puerto Rico self-rule. But just as Cuba's war of independence prompted the United States to swoop in and claim the island for itself, Puerto Rico, too, attracted American attention. "Give my best love to Nannie, and do not make peace until we get Porto Rico," wrote Teddy Roosevelt to Senator Henry Cabot Lodge, misspelling the island's name as was common in Washington for decades.[4] In May 1898, the same month a free Puerto Rico's newly elected legislature was meant to take office, a convoy of U.S. battleships steamed into San Juan's harbor. They began shelling the city to launch an American occupation which has lasted, for all intents and purposes, ever since.

* * *

YANKEE IMPERIALISM was evident variously, in the first decades of the twentieth century: English instruction was now mandatory in schools, and eugenicist doctors from the mainland subjected the island's women, in the 1920s, to involuntary sterilization on a wide scale. Later on, the brute authority of the colonizer was nowhere more insistent than in the little out-island of Vieques, Puerto Rico's *isla nena* that later became such a symbol of the American empire and of Puerto Rican resistance to it.

When two-thirds of its landmass was acquired by the U.S. Navy by dubious means in 1941, Puerto Rico's little-sister island—a twenty-two-mile-long sliver of mangrove and scrub, six miles to the big island's east—was turned into a bombing range and training ground for the U.S. military. For sixty years, the Pentagon used the island's low hills and beaches to test munitions and enact war games they didn't play anywhere else. Dropping untold tons of bombs on its reefs and strafing its shores, the Marines rehearsed their invasions of Vietnam and Bosnia and Iraq here. With ten thousand civilian inhabitants wedged between the two ends of the island reserved for the Navy, the people of Vieques—fisherfolk and ex-*machateros* who'd worked its now-defunct sugar fields—were compelled to live through constant, nerve-racking massive explosions. For decades they suffered shockingly high cancer rates, no doubt related to the poisoning of the soil and water by rusting ordnance and chemical explosives. At the end of the 1990s, a protest movement demanding the island's relinquishment became a cause célèbre for Puerto Ricans everywhere. In 2003, the Navy finally left, and many of the beautiful sugar-sand beaches it used for training—if not the polluted bombing range itself—were returned to civilian use.

When American soldiers first turned up in Puerto Rico, its working classes may have welcomed their new rulers, according to some accounts, as a chance to "settle scores" with the islands' old owners.[5] But the new occupiers had an outlook that was suffused with casual racism suggested by *The New York Times* when it appraised Puerto Rico, in 1899, as a place full of simple people "only interested in wine, women, music, and dancing."[6] The Americans' general approach to ruling the island was consistent with the economic aims outlined by the first of the colonial governors, one of a series of opportunistic if not venal members of the American ruling class sent here from Washington beginning in 1900. "Porto Rico is a beautiful island [whose] population [is] unfitted to assume the management of their own affairs," Charles Herbert Allen wrote home to President McKinley. "With American capital and American energies, the labor of the natives can be utilized to the lasting benefit of all parties."[7] What benefit the "natives" saw from putting their labor at the service of American capital, over the next few decades, is debatable; but benefit is certainly what Allen and the Americans got.

During his brief tenure, Allen came to understand that the best way to reap fortunes from Puerto Rico was to devote vast swaths of the island to growing sugar. He wasted little time, once he returned to New York and took a plum job on Wall Street at J. P. Morgan & Co., in setting up the American Sugar Refining Company—a conglomerate that we know as Domino Sugar, and that quickly came to control fully 98 percent of the U.S. sugar market. Allen coordinated and oversaw the rapid spread of U.S.-owned sugar plantations with the assistance of other American governors of the island keen to authorize the land foreclosures and railroad building and grant water rights that he and his agents needed. By the end of the 1920s, sugar accounted for fully half of Puerto Rico's arable land. By then, the U.S. Supreme Court had declared that the U.S. Constitution didn't apply to the island; nor did labor regulations or the right to collective bargaining. Abetted by this climate and the simple caprice of economic policies that had seen U.S. bankers declare by fiat, shortly after arriving here, that the Puerto Rican peso was worth a mere sixty cents against the dollar, American Sugar was decidedly in the money. It also succeeded in turning the island's old rural populace of *jíbaros* and peasants—farmers who'd once grown a variety of crops—into monocrop wage slaves, living in company-owned housing, and in hock to the company store. Their hard existence is well described through the example of Don Taso Zayas, the subject of the anthropologist Sidney Mintz's classic account of life in the sugar fields of Puerto Rico's southern plain, *Worker in the Cane*.[8]

Puerto Rico's pauperization by sugar's spread prompted many rural Puerto Ricans to head for the humbler barrios of greater San Juan, like Santurce, or to board steamers to New York. But as Don Taso's recollections of the labor unrest of the 1930s also signals, Big Sugar's depredations were what sparked Puerto Rico's modern nationalist movement, and eventually shaped a changing relation to the U.S. In early 1934, cane workers across the island went on strike—bewailing both their wages, which had fallen to seventy-five cents for a twelve-hour day, and the corrupt labor leaders who'd managed their contract. Seeking new leadership, sugar workers settled on the impassioned head of the new Nationalist Party of Puerto Rico, a fiercely articulate lawyer from Ponce named Pedro Albizu Campos. He oversaw the strike that resulted in the formation of a new national union of workers, closely allied to Albizu Campos's Nationalist Party, and a remarkable victory: an increase of sugar workers' wages to $1.50 a day.

Albizu Campos was a short, slight, mustachioed man whose life reads like a tall tale. He suffered considerably in the wake of that early victory and for his ideals. As a champion of nationalism, he is Puerto Rico's closest answer to José Martí. Born poor and orphaned as a toddler, Albizu Campos began school only at age twelve. But he so excelled that a few years later he won full scholarships to study in the United States. He did so first at the University of Vermont and then at Harvard, where he became the first Puerto Rican graduate, in 1919. He went on to Harvard Law School. One gathers much about Albizu Campos's worldly intellect and political imagination from this: in Boston he helped organize and spoke on behalf of Éamon de Valera's cause of Irish freedom; he both grasped and articulated, in debates at Harvard and in those years following the Easter Uprising, the commonality between the plight of Ireland and that of Puerto Rico. Turning down the job

offers you'd expect of a top graduate from Harvard Law—law and corporate jobs in the north; offers of judgeships back home—he instead
returned to Ponce to do pro bono work on cases more in accord with
his ideals, and spent much of the 1920s on barnstorming speaking tours
across Latin America, seeking to raise funds and ignite ardor for the
cause of Puerto Rican freedom. As long as Albizu Campos's activities
were limited to that, and to losing elections for public office (he tried
and failed to win a place in Puerto Rico's senate in 1932), the Americans
took little notice. But then Albizu Campos came into his own with the
sugar strike, and all that changed.

Puerto Rico's American owners, confronted with an island leader
clearly able to rally his fellow countrymen, first tried to buy Albizu
Campos off. The chief of the island police at the time of the strike,
Colonel E. Francis Riggs, was a scion of the powerful Riggs Bank of
Washington, D.C. The Riggs Bank's involvement in imperial statecraft
reached back to its loaning the U.S. government the funds it needed, in
1847, to wage war on Mexico; its close ties to the United Fruit Company had more recently seen Colonel Riggs orchestrate the political
killing, in Nicaragua, of the leftist leader Augusto Sandino. Riggs summoned Albizu Campos to San Juan's swankiest beach club, offering the
fiery leader a sum of $150,000 for his Nationalist Party, and assurances
that he could see to it that, if Albizu Campos allowed him to "handle the
strike," he would win his next race for senate and even be made governor
of the island within a decade. The strings attached to the offer would
have amounted to Albizu Campos's becoming Washington's puppet. He
told Riggs that Puerto Rico wasn't for sale. Within months, he was in
prison, jailed on charges of sedition. He would spend the rest of his life
hounded by J. Edgar Hoover's FBI, in and out of prison. In 1936, island
police commanded by Blanton Winship, a brutal new U.S.-appointed
governor who'd been brought in to straighten out the "anarchy" into
which Puerto Rico seemed to be descending, opened fire on a peaceful
march of Nationalist Party cadets in Ponce, killing nineteen civilians.
The atrocity's eventual fallout helped convince Franklin Delano Roosevelt, and many others in Washington, that a new approach to Puerto
Rico was needed. The way was paved for the island to elect its own
governor—and perhaps to gain its full autonomy from the U.S. But
sadly for Puerto Rico, the patriotic figure whose integrity and patriotic gifts perhaps made him the man most qualified to guide the island
through those years was festering in a Georgia jail. The job, instead of
going to Albizu Campos, went to the man who became his nemesis.

In Puerto Rico today, Luis Muñoz Marín is as hallowed as Albizu Campos—or so you'd think, if you judged by how the name of Puerto Rico's first democratically elected governor is affixed to San Juan's airport and on postage stamps in the "Great Americans" series issued by the U.S. Postal Service. But it's hard not to feel that Muñoz Marín, a leader as well recalled for corruption and compromise as for his devotion to the nation during the crucial stretch of years when he led (he was reelected governor four times, occupying the post from 1948 to 1965), is an apt icon of Puerto Rico's political classes precisely for that muddiness. Muñoz Marín was the privileged son of a newspaper magnate who had helped win Puerto Rico's autonomy from Spain. He was raised partly in Washington, D.C., and spent his young adulthood in New York's Greenwich Village, where he wrote poetry and developed a taste for opium that he may or may not have kicked when he returned home, in the 1920s, to launch a political career with the help of his dad's newspapers. Throughout the Depression-era tumult of massacres and strikes, Muñoz Marín backed the *independentista* cause, but dramatically changed his tune after assuming the leadership of Puerto Rico's senate in 1940.

Muñoz Marín had won the backing of the island's *jíbaros* based on his backing for the ideal of a *"Puerto Rico Libre!,"* and made independence a central plank of his Popular Democratic Party's platform. But when in Washington a U.S. senator named Millard Tydings at last introduced a bill to give Puerto Rico its full independence—a bill backed by virtually every politician on the island—Puerto Rico's most powerful political figure shocked many of his countrymen by coming out, vociferously and repeatedly, against it. Now claiming that the island "was not ready for self-government," he traveled to Washington in 1943, and again in 1945, to convince its legislators of the same thing. The reasons informing this flip have long been debated. In recent years, at least one historian has propounded the theory that Muñoz Marín's change of heart had a tragically simple root: the discovery and corroboration of the fact, by J. Edgar Hoover's FBI—which had made building detailed intelligence dossiers on all of Puerto Rico's leading political figures its business since the chaos of the middle '30s—that Puerto Rico's leading political figure was not merely "known to be completely personally irresponsible," but also a known "narcotics addict."[9] Whether or not the threat of this information's unveiling, by Hoover's FBI, directly dictated the future governor's stance on Puerto Rican independence, as Nelson Denis has argued, is hard to say. Muñoz Marín's more prosaic ties to Washington, and knowledge of what its largesse could yield, included his having convinced FDR to extend the New Deal's benefits, in the form of roads and other infrastructure, to his island. Having won great popularity for his success in doing so, he had other reasons to fear severing the cord. Either way, Muñoz Marín managed the delicate political chore of maintaining his popularity at home while also appeasing Washington. As chief architect of the island's modernity—its status as an *estado libre asociado* (a free-associated state) of the United States—he became the commonwealth's first freely elected governor but also its repressor-in-chief, from that date until he finally left office in 1965, of his island's Nationalist Party.

By the 1950s Albizu Campos's party had been functioning as a largely underground organ for some time. Its leadership had resolved to absent itself from electoral politics as long as Puerto Rican politics were corrupted by the oversight of the United States; they turned to armed struggle to advance their goals, in an era when Muñoz Marín pushed a piece of legislation through Puerto Rico's senate in the same year that he became its governor. Law 53, better known as the gag law, echoed the red-baiting timbre of the United States' McCarthyite Smith Act: it made the airing of pro-independence views, in voice or print, and the displaying of Puerto Rico's flag crimes punishable by ten years in jail. Not for the first time, the question was raised of whether freedoms guaranteed by the U.S. Constitution to all U.S. citizens actually extended to Puerto Ricans. But the gag law was used by Muñoz Marín to imprison opponents of all stripes—and helped prompt Albizu Campos, finally freed from jail for his old charge of sedition after eleven years, to hasten his and his comrades' plan to launch an armed revolt against the island's new status as a U.S. Commonwealth. That revolt, when it came in October 1950, saw Nationalist cadres seize and briefly hold the mountain towns of Jayuya and Utuado; others launched deadly but doomed attacks on the governor's mansion in San Juan, the Fortaleza, and on the temporary residence of President Harry Truman in Washington, D.C.

Albizu Campos didn't take part in the attacks himself; like other Nationalist leaders, he lived under constant surveillance. But he was rounded up at party headquarters in Old San Juan. He was placed in La Princesa, the notorious prison just down from the lair of a governor he loathed, where he would see out most of his remaining days. In the fall of 1964, the great Puerto Rican patriot was at last pardoned by Muñoz Marín; he died in April 1965, outside the prison's walls. By then, his treatment inside the empire's jail, where his declining health bore injuries consistent with some seriously bizarre and scary treatment by his captors, had become part of his legend. Whether or not Albizu Campos was actually subjected to prolonged and intentional atomic radiation, as he and his doctors contended, has never been proved. But in prison his limbs turned horribly black and swollen. He endured splitting headaches he sought to combat by wrapping his head in damp towels, provoking the prison's guards to jokingly dub him the "Towel King." It hardly seems a leap to conclude, as many have, that those afflictions were connected to his fellow prisoners' accounts of a strange humming machine in the jail in the early 1950s—a time, as has now been revealed, when U.S. Army doctors and the Department of Energy conducted experiments on prisoners and others.[10]

Today in Puerto Rico, there's an Albizu Street in nearly every town and a celebration staged each year on his birthday in the Pedro Albizu Campos Park in Ponce: he's an unsullied symbol of freedom, and a martyr for the atomic age who remains to many a prouder icon of Boricuaness than the leader who "modernized" the country, but whose legacy is defined less by national pride than by the acquiescence to U.S. capital involved in Operation Bootstrap—the program Muñoz Marín launched to encourage American manufacturers to set up shop in Puerto Rico in exchange for not having to pay taxes or decent wages, and that has offered a template for most development schemes in the country since. Among the other ways Muños Marín served as a model for the procession of corrupt governors who've followed is suggested by one of his major projects as governor. He used the recently created Puerto Rican Industrial Development Corporation, PRIDCO, to funnel millions in public funds to contractor cronies to build a big new Condado hotel—before handing the keys to what became the Hilton Caribe, and whatever profits might derive from it, to Conrad Hilton's U.S.-based firm. The only lasting benefit for Puerto Ricans not in the governor's circle, as with so many other projects meant to attract investment by any means necessary, were the crumbs of some low-wage jobs for maids and bellhops.

This is why at the largest yearly celebration of Boricua-ness—the Puerto Rican Day Parade that occurs not in San Juan but New York, and that brings hundreds of thousands of Nuyoricans and their admirers to Manhattan's Fifth Avenue each June—it's the Puerto Rico of Albizu Campos, an island of pride but also suffering, that's evoked by the masses waving a flag that Muñoz Marín made illegal in the 1950s.

Processing up the Upper East Side and toward El Barrio's historic seat above 96th Street, the parade has been held each year since 1958. It now attracts well over a million participants and spectators to wave their flag and display its colors on bandanas and booty shorts and beer cozies, too. They proclaim with their raucous presence, on New York's toniest blocks, the parade's unofficial motto: "Yo soy Boricua, pa' lo que sepa"—I'm Puerto Rican, so that you know.

* * *

THE STORY OF Puerto Rican nationalism—and of Puerto Rican culture—was set in New York in key ways even before the era when the island became a colony. But with island immigrants settling in a part of East Harlem that in the early 1900s was largely Italian, their experience of becoming New Yorkers, and of the battles attending that process, meant that "Puerto Rican politics," from very early on, were shaped as much by experiences and ideas absorbed on Manhattan's streets as on the tropical island sixteen hundred miles to the south. It was episodes like the cigar rollers' strike of 1919, described by the essential memoirist of that era, Bernardo Vega, as *the* key builder of *boricuas* as a constituency and a cause in New York.[11] But if New York shaped Puerto Rican–ness, so too did Puerto Ricans shape New York, and the look and sound of black New York in particular. Part of the rationale for and result of the passage of the Jones Act in 1917 was to allow Puerto Ricans to fill out the ranks of U.S. soldiers who fought in World War II. One result of their doing so, and of being placed in mostly black regiments, was that when Harlem's top enlisted bandleader, James Reese Europe, organized his famous 369th Infantry Division Hellfighters Band—an ensemble often credited with bringing jazz to Europe—fully half of his reed section was comprised of Puerto Rican doughboys, trained in the military bands of *la isla*. When the Hellfighters made their triumphant return to New York in 1919, they led a ragtimey march up Lenox Avenue that's recalled as the start of Harlem's Jazz Age. And from the moment Reese Europe's Puerto Rican saxophonists swayed through Harlem, there's been no style of black music in New York, from swing to bebop to hip-hop, to whose making Puerto Ricans haven't been central.

It was after the 1950s, though, when a massive new influx of islanders arrived in the city, that they solidified El Barrio not merely as their zone in the city but as the heart of Puerto Rican-ness everywhere—and as the psychic and physical home space of an urbane and brash breed of Nuyorican immigrant who would play a leading role in shaping the sound and feel of *latinidad* all across the hemisphere.

The signal musical idiom by which they did so, from the late 1960s, was salsa—a style whose songs were based in the rhythmic style of Cuba's son, but lent fresh impetus and a new trombone-led drive in the city. Salsa was sold to the world by Manhattan-based Fania records, owned by Johnny Pacheco, a Dominican flautist and bandleader, and Jerry Massuci, an Italian American businessman. The Fania-led "salsa boom," launched in the early seventies and fueled by records by the company's stars, from Willie Colón to Héctor Lavoe to the Cuban singer Celia Cruz, also inspired a dance style that swept Latin America from Caracas to Lima to Mexico City. New York, in the decades after the Cuban revolution, in many ways replaced Havana as the great source for the sounds to which "Latinos" everywhere moved. And the story about how that happened was crucially enabled by the urban Hispanophone world built by Puerto Ricans in El Barrio, and then across the Harlem River in the Bronx and everywhere else where they were later joined, after the elimination of national quotas in U.S. immigration law in 1965, by new influxes of Spanish-speaking migrants from the Dominican Republic, and from Colombia and Ecuador and elsewhere. Before and leading up to the salsa boom, though, Nuyoricans were also indispensable to the other "Latin music craze" that paved the way for it, in the form of the mambo mania that Manhattan experienced in the 1950s. This was a key episode in the cultural history of New York, with sonic implications for all of the Americas, one that, like the later salsa explosion, was in large measure effected by New York–based Puerto Ricans playing Cuban-born rhythms for a diverse dancing public.

In May 1947, an Italian music promoter named Federico Pagani convinced the owners of Manhattan's Palladium Ballroom, an old dance hall on 53rd Street with declining attendance and a declining vibe, to begin featuring Latin music on Sunday nights. Pérez Prado's mambo had just caused a sensation in Mexico City, and Havana's son heyday was soaring to the vital sounds of Arsenio Rodríguez and Miguelito Valdés. Pagani hired two of those players' New York–based peers—the *sonero* Machito (né Frank Grillo) and his storied saxophonist and bandleader, Mario Bauzá, late of Cab Calloway's group and the man perhaps most responsible for melding Cuban rhythms to the horn-arranging style of Ellingtonian swing. Machito's Afro-Cubans began to play the Palladium on Sunday afternoons. They appeared there along with Machito's sister, the exciting singer Graciela. They were soon joined, on a weekly bill that became immensely popular and packed the Palladium with exultant dancers for the next several years, by the great bands of two Puerto Ricans—the great *sonero* and bandleader Tito Rodríguez (born in Santurce, San Juan, but resident in El Barrio, New York, from the age of thirteen) and Rodríguez's *timbalero* namesake, Tito Puente.

Puente was born to Puerto Rican parents on 116th Street in Manhattan. He took piano lessons as a boy from Victoria Hernandez, the sister of Rafael Hernandez, who, after coming to New York and to El Barrio as a member of James Reese Europe's Hellfighters, became the author of some two thousand songs that made him "the king of Puerto Rican popular song." Puente himself served in the Navy during World War II, then attended Juilliard on the GI Bill. He was a devoted student of jazz and classical composers alike, but his great passion was for the Afro-Cuban styles evolved by heroes like Cachao and Arsenio Rodríguez. Long before he became the mugging character as well known for his cartoon appearances on *The Simpsons* and for his showmanship as for his gifts as a musician, Puente brought his timbales to the center of the Palladium's stage to establish the standard rhythm-section template for Latin dance bands in the city and beyond for decades—timbales, conga, and bongos in polyphony.

The last new rhythm to leave Havana for the mainland after Cuba's revolution, the pachanga, reached New York in the early 1960s. That era also saw two of the city's finer purveyors of "Latin jazz," the Bronx-based Cuban percussionist Mongo Santamaria and his Nuyorican colleague Ray Barretto, score unlikely pop hits with the *tumbadora*-tinged renditions of "Watermelon Man" (Santamaria) and the sui generis "Watusi" (Barretto). But by the time the Palladium closed in 1966, the city's economy of sound was shifting—big dance bands were on the way out; small combos and selling records were the new way. Many of Havana's leading musicians had by then come north; a new generation of Latinos in New York, from the Caribbean, was coming of age not in the islands but on New York's chill streets. The time was ripe for a new sound. The space for it was filled, for a brief time, by what's now called boogaloo. A kind of clave-tinged soul-rock hybrid, excellently pitched to the riot-filled summers of the mid-'60s, boogaloo's best-known cuts included simple sung-in-English refrains: "I'll never go back to Georgia (never go back)," "I like it like that (I like it . . . like that)"; its Nuyorican singers made explicit nods, in their tunes, to the black Americans with whom they shared joys and sorrows, in Upper Manhattan. But boogaloo's day was short. And the sound that soon came to represent El Barrio, with resonance throughout the hemisphere, is usually said to have been born, at least in recorded form, back in 1962.

That's when two piano-playing brothers with roots in Ponce, but who grew up in the South Bronx, Eddie and Charlie Palmieri, formed a band whose horn section ws comprised solely of brawny trombones. That stripped-down horn section was soon to become the signature of Eddie Palmieri's path-making ensemble La Perfecta. La Perfecta eschewed the tight harmonies of Palladium-style big bands for a sound that, in the words of one of salsa history's essential narrators, the Venezuelan radio deejay and scholar César Miguel Rondón, "stopped being glamorous and became feisty."[12] The Palmieris' sound, which other small groups in the Bronx and El Barrio soon adapted, was meant less for the ballroom than for the ghetto street. It's the music that Nuyorican radio deejays like Izzy Sanabria began calling "salsa." Its brashness was exemplified by trombonist and singer Willie Colón, another kid from the burned-out tenements of the South Bronx, whose almost punk approach to musicianship included a willful refusal to tune his horn on his name-making 1967 album, *El Malo*. The other key to salsa, in musical terms, was its borrowing of the Cuban son montuno—the clave-based song form that, since busting out of Cuba's Oriente to conquer Havana in the 1920s, had already proved its elastic adaptability to so many timbres and towns. It now also proved the ideal medium for young singers like Willie Colón's partner in crime on *El Malo*, the Ponce-born *sonero* Héctor Lavoe, through which to add their own flourishes and narrative beats on their tune's open-ended montunos. Salsa was a made–in–New York style, and its exponents reflected the city's ethnic mix. Among those on the bandstand at Manhattan's Cheetah Club during the famous August 1971 performance, by the Fania All-Stars, that became the classic salsa film *Our Latin Thing (Nuestra Cosa)*, the Jewish American pianist and producer Larry Harlow was prominent—he was always a key member of the Fania family. And before Celia Cruz made her signature call to add some sugar to the music's mix ("*¡Azúcar!*"), salsa's queen honed her craft in 1950s Havana, with the seminal Cuban son troupe Sonora Matancera. But the big majority of salsa's breakout stars in New York, from the Palmieris to Colón to Pete "El Conde" Rodríguez, were Puerto Rican. And that gave the music a special life— and distinct resonance—back in Puerto Rico.

Fania's plan for world domination naturally included distributing their top-selling records back in San Juan. They did so through Rafael Viera, the owner of Santurce's storied Viera Discos record shop, who

I found during a recent visit still sitting in the shop's back office. Now elderly, he paused from eating a grilled cheese sandwich to recall how "those Fania records, the good ones, changed everything here," before eyeing the stack of used Olga Guillot LPs I'd picked from his racks to tell me, with a dismissive wave, just to take them ("*un regalo*"). Puerto Rico did produce a few salsa stars who never decamped for New York. Ismael Rivera was an Afro–Puerto Rican from Santurce whose fond odes to barrio life, and to a "black Jesus" he resembled, informed the rise of black Puerto Rican pride also inspired by the success in baseball of Roberto Clemente. Tito Curet, another local hero, was a humble postman who in his off hours wrote hundreds of classic songs. But the man who best symbolizes both the salsa era at large and the pains of modern Puerto Rican history is Héctor Lavoe, who turned "Mi Gente" (My People) into his most lasting hit.

Lavoe was born in Ponce in 1946, and raised in the city's barrio of Machuelo Abajo, before heading to New York at sixteen. He fell in with Willie Colón and first won fame for singing their shared hits like "El Malo" and "Canto a Borinquen." He was a slight man with a large voice and a rare talent for improvising who wore chunky '70s glasses. Lavoe was famous for missing gigs, turning up late, or disappearing for months on end to battle mysterious demons or seek treatment, for his ailments or heartaches, from a Santeria priest (when he wasn't attempting suicide by jumping off a ninth-floor balcony in Condado). He was also a refractive artist for whom the magic of his "Mi Gente" was its expansiveness—Spanish speakers everywhere could feel included. So could the people of Kinshasa, Zaire, when Lavoe turned up at the "Rumble in the Jungle," between Muhammad Ali and George Foreman, resplendent in high-waisted red pants. There he was embraced by an adoring mass of Congolese who were his *gente*, too. He was martyred by AIDS in 1993. But he was a towering figure in life—and remains one in death—whose suffering was the source of people's identification with him. On "Todo Poderoso," he sang,

Ay, cómo lo escupieron
cómo lo empujaron
cómo lo llevaron a crucificar.

How he was spit on
How he was pushed around
How he carried the cross.

The figure might have been Pedro Albizu Campos; it might, too, have been Héctor Lavoe. But for all his own suffering, Lavoe, too, resonates as a great symbol of joy, as I found when I drove down to Ponce in the spring of 2015, not long before Puerto Rico's government defaulted on its huge debt and hit rock bottom, to find the man who led the charge there to build a bronze statue of the town's favorite son by its seafront.

Winding across Puerto Rico's central mountains from San Juan, I listen to the reggaeton and 1990s American R&B that's as common on the radio here now as salsa, and descended onto the arid southern plain. After crossing old sugar fields baked brown by the sun, I entered the town's center. Ponce's shaded square and grand museums still bespoke the old grandeur of a place whose motto is *"Ponce es Ponce,"* though the town felt as populated by ghosts as people. The statue of Lavoe, down by its waterfront, wasn't too impressive—a short man, life-sized and holding maracas, he was easy to miss. But it didn't take long, asking around, to find one of the men who'd helped raise the $68,000 required to build this. He was seated by a *pincho* stand. *Scarface* was playing on a TV behind him. Eric Rivera, the head of the Comité Pro Monumento a Héctor Lavoe, wore a backward Kangol cap and a smile. Rivera was pleased I'd found him: he would spend much of the next day showing me around—from a donut shop in the barrio where Lavoe was born, to the municipal cemetery where he's buried—and recounting how, when he'd fulfilled his dream to befriend "El Cantante" after moving to the Bronx, Lavoe had told him that "the point of music isn't to emphasize the sad things in life, but to be happy." It was for this reason, Rivera said, that he hated the movie that the Bronx's favorite daughter, Jennifer Lopez, had made about Lavoe with her singer-husband. "J-Lo and Marc Anthony didn't even come to Ponce; they got it all wrong," Rivera said, before then recounting how when he'd gone to see Lavoe on his deathbed, in New York, Lavoe again told him to be happy. As to why the town built the statue, Rivera said: "There's three other statues of El Cantante. . . . In San Juan, in Colombia, and in Peru. But all of those are only half of him, from the waist up—we wanted to do the whole man. So we did."

Hispaniola:
Mountains Beyond Mountains

CHAPTER 8

THE MASSACRE RIVER

ON DECEMBER 5, 1492, two months from first glimpsing the Bahamas and fresh from concluding that Cuba was richer in trees than gold, the admiral pointed his *Santa Maria* east. Crossing the slim Windward Passage, he approached another big island. He thought it might be Japan. But he gave it another name, too, to be safe, which honored his Iberian patrons. La Española—"the Spanish One"— proffered no quicker riches than Cuba did. But its blue bays and tall peaks were impressive. And on Christmas Eve, Columbus's weary men's spirits were high enough, or low enough, that they toasted *la navidad* with too much wine as their captain handed the boat's wheel to a cabin boy, and went to rest—before then bumping awake, with his tipsy crew, near midnight. The admiral's flagship, just offshore of what is now Cap-Haïtien, in northern Haiti, had crunched aground.

The *Santa Maria* wouldn't budge. Its crew relieved the sixty-foot ship of its food and cannon, and made for shore. On Christmas morning, on the beach, they showed off for some watching Taino by using their old vessel for target practice, and then salvaged its timber to build a crude fort they dubbed La Navidad. By the fort's walls, Columbus left thirty-nine luckless seamen; he boarded one of his mission's smaller craft, and told them to sit tight. The admiral, now aboard the *Niña*, continued east. He glimpsed Hispaniola's broad mountains and fields and also heard rumors of gold in a fertile valley, not far inland, that its natives called Cibao. This was the larger Indie, he grew convinced, to colonize. Back in Spain, he reported as much to his patrons, and won Isabela and Ferdinand's backing for the second voyage that saw him tacking back here, the next year, with seventeen laden-down boats. By then, the poor minders of La Navidad had perished from infighting or provoking their neighbors. But it seemed auspicious, in any case, to set up shop a bit farther east, nearer to the Cibao Valley's alleged gold. And so it was that in December 1493, Columbus's men alighted at a site near where tourists now sun themselves in Puerto Plata, in the modern Dominican Republic, and, with a settlement named for their queen, founded old Europe's first lasting colony in its New World.

La Isabela, their colony's first village, didn't last long—Columbus's men soon moved to the island's calmer south shore, by the deep mouth of the Ozama River. But the colony, which they named Santo Domingo for the Dominican friars sent here to save its Indians' souls, grew into a chaotic outpost of Castile in the tropics whose Genoese founder was made official governor—never mind that Columbus was far better at launching hubristic voyages than at politics. The eccentric mariner enlisted his brothers to help run things; he was resented by the Spanish ranchers and roustabouts who came here hunting riches. And when Columbus returned from exploring the Lesser Antilles in 1498, having left his brother Bartolomé in charge, he found a colony in revolt. The colonists were sick of the Colón brothers' capricious rule; their complaints included Bartolomé's having zealously applied, for such crimes as petty thieving, "punishments like mutilation."[1] Bartolomé had also ordered a woman, alleged to have questioned the legitimacy of his big brother's birth, to be paraded through town naked. The Spanish crown saw that their Admiral of the Ocean Seas, who'd now been named viceroy of the Indies as well, had lost control; they dispatched a successor-administrator to restore it. In July 1500, the cruel conquistador Francisco de Bobadilla arrived at the Ozama's mouth. Bobadilla forcibly relieved the admiral of his post, and then sent him home, bound in chains, on a boat to Seville.

Columbus did regain sufficient favor with his patrons in Spain, soon enough, to return to the Indies to claim the riches he was due—10 percent of all revenue from the lands he discovered, according to his old deal with Ferdinand and Isabela. But the fate he met on his last voyage west may underscore how Columbus himself wasn't exempt from the curse some say grew in Hispaniola's soil from the moment he hit it. For Dominicans, Columbus is a hero but also a figure whose Spanish name still resounds as a swearword ("Colón!" they'll exclaim when things go wrong). It was at the moment that his *Santa Maria* crunched aground, says the legend of a curse believers call the *fucú*, that he opened the "nightmare door" through which all the horrors of the Americas' history—from its First Nations' genocide to racial slavery to their worst modern *dictaduras*—have flowed.[2] In June 1502, Columbus passed back by the Ozama's mouth, aiming to join a convoy of treasure boats readying to return to Spain. But the port's new rulers denied him entry. The treasure fleet's captains, as Columbus stewed down the coast, sailed into a brewing storm, and most of the first riches sent home from the Indies to Spain were lost at sea. The admiral himself did make it home. But he died embittered back in Valladolid.

Columbus couldn't have nurtured many warm thoughts, by his life's end, for this island where history's earth-changing "Columbian exchange" began. But that fact has mattered little to those bosses of the modern state that occupies Hispaniola's eastern two-thirds, who have for generations made the fact of Columbus landing here a touchstone of national feeling. The Dominican Republic is a country whose culture, said its political identity's chief modern architect, Joaquín Balaguer, is "addicted to Iberia."[3] And as such it's also a place whose political class, led by the hack-scholar-cum-president Balaguer during the run-up to Columbus's quincentennial here, saw fit to devote much energy and treasure to erecting the great pharaonic monument that's loomed over the city's poor eastern suburbs since 1992 to welcome Santo Domingo's visitors, after they land at the grandly named Airport of the Americas and then roll, on a highway lined with pay-by-the-hour sex motels, to old Spain's first American city.

The Faró Colón—the Columbus Lighthouse—sits on a barren expanse of treeless cement. It is a monstrosity in concrete whose dimensions rival Yankee Stadium's and whose form mimics a huge crucifix lying on its side. The plan for the structure's great bisecting slabs, each open at the top, was that they'd exude a great beam of light into the heavens, like Batman's logo over Gotham but shaped like a cross. The lighthouse was meant to be a grand beacon and testament, for passing ships and all of the Americas' peoples, to what Balaguer termed "the radiance with which Spanish character projects its star in the American territory." It was a grim thrust at greatness, even at the concept stage, from a nation that's not great. But the Faró Colón has never even functioned as planned. The scheme of burning untold kilowatts, each night, to tout Christendom's beachhead on a heathen continent, was never likely to come off in a poor city whose humbler barrios' TVs blink dark, most days, in rolling blackouts.[4] Nowadays, the monument is lit up, some years, only on special occasions like New Year's Eve. It has resonated, since it opened, as a ruin—and as a repository for its namesake's curse, a *fucú* whose enduring power was also felt during the quincentennial celebrations the Columbus Lighthouse was built to mark. During those celebrations, dissenting young Dominicans voiced their support for the values of the twentieth century, rather than the sixteenth, by dressing as Indians, and rowed out to the replica Columbus boats that their reactionary president, Balaguer, brought to the Ozama's mouth. One of the protestors was a recent law school grad named Rafael Efrain Ortiz. Ortiz led a chant that went "Colón, fucú, aquí no cabes tú!" (Columbus, curse, there's no place here for you!)[5] He was helping lead a march through the old town when he was shot in the head, in images played and replayed on the news here, by soldiers of a regime less concerned with the lives of modern Dominicans, evidently, than with their rulers' vexed delusions of grandeur past.

In the DR of the twenty-first century, the nude repressions of blind old Balaguer, who rode to power on the scaly coattails of the infamous dictator Trujillo, who long defined its politics, have given way to subtler corruptions. But the Columbus Lighthouse remains: a ghostly ruin where, on the gray day I went to see it up close for the first time, the bored young guards who fondled shotguns around its base, under a typically heavy Santo Domingo sky, outnumbered the bored tourists inspecting the admiral's words on the *faro*'s plinth. "Cry tears for me," says the inscription. "Those of you who have truth, charity, and justice."

The words are curious. Especially so to those, one suspects, who don't know the great Colón's diminished end. Isn't this a monument to a triumph? But the inscription, in other ways, seems to fit its setting—the words match the penchant for the self-dramatizing pity of the macho men, in these parts, who still carry themselves like they get around on strutting horses and who seem "addicted to Iberia" indeed. The Caribbean's most populous island by far, Hispaniola is a place of firsts. The island where Columbus first resided in the New World was home to the Americas' first cathedral, their first university, their first library, and their first dairy farm, too. This is also the island where sugarcane and racial slavery first touched American soil—and where history's sole successful slave revolution, on its western half, sparked. But split among the Spanish Dominican Republic and the proud descendants of those enslaved Africans who seized their freedom from Frenchmen who controlled the Spanish One's west in the eighteenth century, it is an island whose twenty million souls have for half a millennium seen their historical life suffused, more than any in this region, by violence.

* * *

THAT VIOLENCE HAS TAKEN sundry forms—ranging from the Spaniards' genocidal wars against the Indians, to the astonishment, three centuries later, of the Haitian Revolution: that great cataclysm of history that saw a half million slaves who had turned French Saint-Domingue into the earth's most lucrative and awful plantation colony rise up to kill their owners and then declare, in 1804, the founding of a nation "where . . . no white man shall set foot as master."[6] That event's carnage was sown over a century of brutality during which few Africans imported to serve French Saint-Domingue, after that colony's formal launch in 1697, survived more than a few horrific sugar harvests. Those slaves' fierce revolt and its doomed repression released spirits so acrid that the cloud produced by the cane and bodies left smoldering around Cap-Haïtien, said Haiti's vodou priests, would hover for centuries. It's not hard, given Haiti's torrid history since, to credit that they're right. Haiti was saddled with unpayable debts by its old owners; it was scorned, by its American neighbors, for the simple hubris of being a black nation in a white world. Over its poor *bidonvilles* today, the lingering scent of wood smoke attests to the fact that few Haitians' cooking needs, even now, are met by gas or electric current. Their poverty derives more from iniquitous geopolitics and race hate than from metaphysics. But it has long seemed that Haiti's people, whose revolution posed a question that still dominates our politics now—How universal are universal rights?—have been fated to suffer for that service ever since. The Haitian Revolution's tragic aftermaths have been many. But perhaps the most tragic of all of them has played out not on a global scale but on this island. For the Haitian Revolution didn't just birth a new black nation. It also augured that nation's lasting animus toward those motley Spanish creoles, across Hispaniola, who in 1844 declared their independence not from Spain but from the Haitian generals who also seized control of their sleepy eastern ranches, in the early 1800s.

In a book Joaquín Balaguer wrote about the twenty years when Haitians were in power here, and about those years' lessons for Dominicans, he warned his countrymen against "the vegetable-like growth of the African race." Balaguer also claimed that though "Haitian imperialism" changed tactics after 1844—by moving from armed campaigns to threats of a "biological nature"—Haiti has remained bent, ever since, on controlling all of Hispaniola.[7] This would be news to Haitian heads of state, who've had their hands more than full over the last century tending to their own people, or their own power. But these nations' entwined histories can feel like textbook versions of what Benedict Anderson, the scholar of nationalism, called "imagined communities." Each country's contrasting conception of its past, and of the identity born from that past, suggests why. Both Haitians and Dominicans avow the old inhabitants of an island the Taino called Quisqueya. They agree on the myth-shrouded greatness of Quisqueya's last warrior-princess, Anacoana, for whom songs are sung on both of the island's ends. But though Haiti's very name derives from the Taino's term for mountainous land—*ayti*—its culture's base is Africa, and its story is about how Africa's memory was made new by the Jacobin ideals of Toussaint L'Ouverture. The whiter custodians of Dominican nation-ness, by contrast, have swung from claiming to comprise "spiritually the most chosen and physically the most homogeneous [race] in the Americas," to teaching all Dominicans—the great majority of whose roots meld West Africa and Spain—to refer to themselves, and their skin color, as *Indio* (Indian). This notwithstanding the truth that here as on most nearby islands, the Taino were wiped out by disease within a few brief decades of 1492.

It's hardly uncommon here to encounter a Dominican who'll inform you, with swelled Ibero-pride, that his or her copper-dark skin stems not from an African source but some lost Noble Savage from closer by. This casual racism isn't altogether the fault of the young soldier by the Columbus Lighthouse, say, whose complexion nears Michael Jordan's but who'll begin heaping scorn, if you mention Haiti, on *los morenos*—the dark ones. He lives in a state that until very recently issued national ID cards whose entry for "race" wasn't merely filled, in most cases, with a faux-racial label—*Indio*. Those labels also varied, in its taxonomy of skin colors ranging from J-Lo's to Jordan's, from *Indio claro* to *Indio oscuro* (from "light Indian," that is, to "dark Indian").

The Dominican Republic, in matters of color, can be confounding. But that isn't altogether the Dominicans' fault, either. For though it is true that it was the cursed Columbus who first brought sugar here, Hispaniola's Spaniards did not know how to turn the fresh-cut cane that grew better in its fertile valleys than just about anywhere else, into mountains of cash. That trick was instead turned a couple of centuries later, by the French, who plowed the island's remote northwest, near where the *Santa Maria* crashed, to build their greatest plantation colony. But French Saint-Domingue didn't spark until 1697. And what Castile's minions set out to do, on Hispaniola's other half, was something else. These rough men from La Mancha soon realized that they'd never pull much gold from the Spanish One's rivers. They built their colony around neither big mines nor the Big House; they built it around far-flung cattle stations where *caballeros* on horseback ranged over big tracts of palm-dotted plains to make Santo Domingo a going concern, if never a wealthy one, in Spain's imperial system. Built on a sprawling island whose basins and ranges can evoke an Antillean cousin of North America's Old West, the colony's economy revolved around raising cattle.

This ensured Santo Domingo's marginal status in a far-flung empire devoted to ferrying its great mines' ore, from Mexico or Potosí, homeward through Havana. But it also ensured the forming of a unique set of relations, between its Spanish owners and the Africans they imported to tend their ranches. "Slavery in a plantation society works differently from slavery in a cattle ranching society," explained the modern DR's historian laureate, Frank Moya Pons: this was a colony where both "the master and slave rode horses [and] wore machetes."[8] Cooperation was required between the land's owners and those who worked it. There was also the simple demographic fact that Santo Domingo's ranchers were never going to achieve their ambitions or staff their farms, in this gold-poor place to which few Spaniards were drawn, without other help. Their governors decreed as such that whites *should* mingle with their slaves to grow the populace. And the result of those truths is a curious case, a "racial formation" remarkable even for the New World: an impoverished race that identifies with their *caudillo* masters and, contrary to their appearance and their genes, insist on calling themselves *blancos de la tierra*, "whites of the land."

Many a nation of the Americas has now and then, here and there, taken pride in its racial hybridity—from Brazil's *mestizagem* to Cuba's *mestizaje* to the influential belief espoused by José Vasconcelo, in Mexico, that Latin America's is a "cosmic race," the examples abound. But not in the DR. This country where modernity's golden babies were compelled to see themselves as "whites of the land," is run by *tigueres* who live by their wits and by their cruelty. It's animated by the cockfights these men love and the whores they fuck. It gets around on the *motos* these men steer—their old horses having been replaced, in recent decades, by a million 125cc pony-like motorbikes, ridden by males from pubescence to middle age, often with a passenger or three hanging off their bike's back. Such is the DR nowadays, a country whose greatest heroes, curiously enough, are black baseball players who have amassed fame and riches in the United States.

"Bienvenido," your airline steward will cry out, "al secreto más guardado del Caribe!" He'll be speaking to a cabin that's mostly full (especially if you're not arriving in tourist season; especially if you're flying into the capital) of Dominicans sporting singed-flat hair or Jordans, who'll clap loudly when the plane lands safely in a place where things that can go wrong often do. "This is the home of Sammy Sosa, Vlad Guerrero, David 'Big Papi' Ortiz, Pedro Martínez, and Robinson Cano!" This is the island, the steward crows, of "Los mejores peloteros en todo el mundo!" The best baseball players in the world. Hailed here with a Spanish word—*pelotero*'s literal translation: "baller"—that feels especially fitting in a country whose culture has a strong claim, even on its *machista* continent, to being the most *machista* of all. This country often feels like it's built around the coarser aspects of masculinity—and around that masculinity's capacity for degrading whatever it deems different, or weaker, than itself.

It feels, spreading over two-thirds of its big island, like a Texas-style state of ranches with Texas-style delusions of being a great big nation. And the DR's is a culture informed by the same dynamic that the scholar of American studies Richard Slotkin identified as animating Americans' lasting love for cowboy films, guns, and the open road—that is, the "closing of the frontier." More than that, though, the frontier in the DR is an actual border that, as one of its island's exemplary modern novelists put it, "exists beyond maps, that is carved directly into the histories and imaginaries of a people."[9] It's a frontier, that is, that can be closed time and again. To be sure, the border between the DR and Haiti is fixed, and has been since the U.S. Marines, who occupied both of Hispaniola's countries for much of the early twentieth century, delineated it in 1929. Yet in the high mountains through which the border winds, more often unmarked than visible, it has always been much more porous than secure. For many people along its unguarded 220-mile length, both Haitian Kreyol and Spanish remain lingua francas. At official crossings, young men in the Dominican military take their border postings as an opportunity to grab market-rate bribes or blow jobs from passing Haitians. The porousness of the border doesn't alter its reality as the dominant fact of life on an island cut in two. Whatever the Dominican Republic might be, there's one thing, in the minds of its people, that it's not. That thing is as much an idea as a country. And the historical source for Dominicans' lasting hate of Haiti's name—as much a swearword here, in its way, as "Colón"—was well caught by a bespectacled fellow I stopped to chat with on the Avenida Independencía, not far from where Bartolomé Colón once presided over the *zona colonial.*

"Italiano? Portugues?" His accent was good, in both languages. His glasses were round and he carried a worn leather Bible. "My name's Francisco." Seeing that I was neither Italian nor Portuguese, he spoke English. "I'm an evangelical." He was also a benign street hustler, of a type familiar to anyone who's wandered the edges of poor cities' tourist zones: an autodidact who'd taught himself five languages and didn't proffer bogus cigars or *chicas* but rather aimed to forge a deeper tie by citing his love for the bits of his quarries' home culture he knew, which in my case included the Chicago Bulls, Aerosmith, and the rather improbable literary pair of "Joan Didion and Philip K. Dick—I've read all their books!" Which was enough, certainly, to ensnare me for a brief chat there on Independencía, during which I told Francisco that I'd come here, this visit, to look into how his country's anti-Haitian xenophobia seemed to be reaching new depths: the Dominican government had just threatened, earlier that fall of 2013, to deport from the country a half million Haitian-born workers—on whose low-paid toil the DR's building contractors and sugar plantations have long depended—to their home country. Francisco wasn't having it. "Everyone thinks we have a problem with Haiti," he said. "But you know it's them who came here and messed with us." It was hard to tell, at first, whether he was talking about the Haitian shoe-shine boys down the block or about past events. But Francisco quickly cleared that up. "They were here for twenty-two years. From 1822 until February the 27th, 1844." He said it like it was last week. "And they're still coming." And then this Christian whose charity only went so far wandered away. A foreign-looking woman had just strolled past in sunglasses. *"Italiana?"*

* * *

OLD SANTO DOMINGO'S stone plazas and old churches help it resemble, in many ways, the Spanish Caribbean's more touristy capitals. But where the well-scrubbed squares of Old San Juan, in Puerto Rico, now front shiny Starbucks branches patronized by cruise shippers, and Old Havana's UNESCO-led face-lift lends its main blocks the feel of an alfresco museum, this colonial zone, older than both of them, retains the ambience of an actual neighborhood whose faint scent of sewage and humbler denizens' poverty, as much as its physical plant, hint at late medieval Spain. Modern Santo Domingo spreads west and north from this old core. It features shopping malls and Miami-like condos for its monied classes and swarming slums for everyone else. The underemployed pass days in *calmado* corner-shop bars, the epicenter of much of Dominican life. In Havana the belle époque mansions and art deco towers outside its antique center convey an abiding sense of New World magnificence; in Santo Domingo the Inquisition feels a beat away. Here where old-style Galician tapas are considered haute cuisine, men in pointy loafers and women in crocheted hairnets reply to expressions of thanks, even at the cheapest lunch counters, not with the familiar *de nada* common across Latin America, but with unnerving formality. "Siempre, señor. A su orden." Always, sir. At your service.

Most foreign visitors looking for business or pleasure stay in one of the big new hotels overlooking the seafront Malecon's cement benches and open-air gyms where muscle-bound young men, lifting sea-rusted weights, hope to become the next David Ortiz. In flashing casinos attached to the Sheraton and the Gran Hotel Jaragua, sunburned Yanks ring felt blackjack tables or walk with caramel-colored lovelies whom they've perhaps picked up at some nearby *casa de chicas* in a town where any windowless "bar" might be a whorehouse. The complexity and import of the sex economy here, along with its stock characters, are suggested in the smoothly insistent verses of the comely guitar music, bachata, that emerged from Santo Domingo's brothel bars, in the 1990s, to hymn the pain of lovelorn *tigueres* and noble *putas* with hearts of gold or malice. But when I arrived that fall amid intensifying DR-Haitian hostilities, I didn't check into the Jaragua. I made my way, rather, to a calm little *pensión* near the old town's edge to which I'd been drawn for its good rates and location. The place's decor featured glass vats of mysterious green water, but it proved an excellent place from which to start delving into the larger causes, and implication, of the recent decision, by the DR's highest court, that had just made headlines worldwide.

In September 2013, the DR's Constitutional Tribunal ruled that the full rights and responsibilities of Dominican citizenship should be extended only to persons who could prove that each of their forebears, reaching back to 1929, were legal residents here when their progeny were born. It revised the DR's own *jus soli* standard of granting citizenship to all persons born on Dominican soil and threatened to contravene the Universal Declaration of Human Rights, to which the DR is a signatory, by stripping hundreds of thousands of people—many of whom had never set foot in Haiti, and had no claim on Haitian citizenship—of their right to a nationality. Verdict 168-13 had quickly become known, to those it menaced, by a simple and foreboding nickname: *la sentencia*. It seemed to herald an alarming final solution to the old problem Balaguer described in warning against population increase among the African race. Already in 2010, a new Dominican constitution emphasized the DR's right to deny citizenship to anyone whose parents were "in transit" at the time of her or his birth. The *sentencia* of 2013 interpreted that law to mean that the vague "in transit" tag didn't apply merely to visiting diplomats or tourists giving birth on vacation; it now applied to anyone whose ancestors' presence in the country hadn't been properly recorded in its civil registry. A vast number of people, one suspected, in a country whose government even now fails to provide birth certificates to nearly one in five newborns. The ruling's target was plain: all Dominicans of Haitian descent or Haitian birth. Their status in the country was looking dire when I checked into the little *pensión* on the edge of the *zona colonial*, a couple months after the *sentencia* came down, and called my man Carlos.

I'd met Carlos when I was hunting a ride to the Columbus Lighthouse a year before. He was a sixtysomething dark-skinned Dominican with a waddling walk and a pate of white hair he called his *caña*, his head of sugar, who showed me to his little yellow Nissan minivan, with its cracked windshield and expired Michigan license plate, before telling me, as we puttered over the river, about how he'd once been in the navy and then worked as a seaman. He kept his radio locked to the salsa station at all times. He explained his love for un-Dominican salsa by recounting a day's shore leave in Miami in 1978, when he made it to Calle Ocho, in Little Havana, for a concert featuring El Gran Combo and Cheo Feliciano that remained, thirty-five years later, one of his life's highlights. Carlo sensed on our first day together that his client might not be interested only in conventional tourist sites like the Faro Colón: he threw in a bonus visit to the notorious La Victoria prison, across town, to show his curious fare where the worst *tigueres* in the country lived. It was months later, though, during my next visit, that our bond was cemented. Walking near the Plaza España where I'd first met him, I heard a cry. "At least this time you wore pants!" It was Carlos. He was glad, since we'd been denied entrance to Victoria's prison yard on account of my wearing shorts, as did the prisoners, with whom we had to chat, as a result, through the fence.

Carlos wasn't a good driver: his habits included swerving the Nissan while making kissing noises at shapely ladies in the street. ("Ay que culazo! Abusadora!" Loosely: Stop abusing me with that ass!) In his mind he always had right of way, so he was always yelling and cursing at other drivers. Still Carlos had deep smarts and rich homespun stories for his scribbler friend, especially of the sporting kind. Carlos took me to a barrio tire shop run by David Ortiz's cousin in the barrio of Villa Juana. ("Big Papi was just here," cousin Ortiz confirmed, waving his tire iron. "He comes home and just hands out bills!") He drove me to the training camp for young ballplayers, run by the Los Angeles Dodgers, that's now been imitated by every major-league club and also to the country's center for a pastime—cockfighting—even more beloved than baseball. At the capital's Coliseo Gallistico—the Coliseum of Cockfighting—we watched the land's best-bred chicken gladiators being lowered, in clear plastic boxes from the ceiling as pump-up music played, into a sand-floored ring where white-coated attendants readied the birds for battle by slapping their beaks and then released them to fight, unto death. Baying bleacher jockeys around us cried out their bets as the cocks' owners, down in padded ringside seats, looked on. On the Sunday we visited, one such owner, a fat man with pale skin and gelled-back hair, who wore a yellow shirt with purple cuffs, also sported a surgical face mask. "He's the owner of the Gran Jaragua," Carlos murmured as the man rubbed his hands together with glee after one of his birds, down in the ring, finished pecking its rival into a blood-and-feathers mess.

Carlos loved discussing both cocksmen and Haitians—his capacity for doing the latter, in not typically Dominican ways, was why I really stuck with him—and we ended up, many afternoons, at a *calmado* he favored to share *jumbo* bottles of Presidente Light, poured nearly frozen into plastic cups. Carlos shared sea tales and cursed the bachata that his favorite place, like all such corner spots selling beer and chips and cans of condensed milk in the DR, now blared from big speakers at all times. Once it might have been the propulsive merengue to which the DR has long danced. But bachata's suave arpeggios have trounced not merely merengue here; on Spanish-language radio in the United States and beyond, bachata has now even bested salsa itself, thanks to smooth young exponents from the Bronx of a music which, though drawn from the *decima* tradition of old Spain's serenading farmhands, was evolved by rural Dominicans who migrated to their country's capital in the 1970s and '80s to become *guachimanes*—night watchmen—or habitués of those brothel bars. Bachata's key early stars like Luis Vargas evoked tender wants like those I heard Vargas voice one night when I trekked to the poor northern barrio of Villa Mella to watch the veteran singer, wearing a white suit and dark glasses at night, croon his hit "Loco de Amor" for a swooning crowd. Carlos refused to come.

But if bachata wasn't his jam, Carlos remained one of the few people I'd met, in a country where most people treat Haiti as Mordor, who had traveled to Port-au-Prince. It was only to help extract a sailor friend from a sticky romantic situation, but still. Carlos was a Dominican to whom not all Haitians were the devil. And he joined me on sundry errands to Santo Domingo's Little Haiti to befriend wary peddlers of mangoes and flip-flops by the old Modelo market there, after *la sentencia* came down, and to meet with a group of lawyers at a Jesuit-affiliated "center for reflection and action," nearby, who were gravely worried about its effects. The lawyers were Dominicans of Haitian descent. They were trying to make sense of the new law so as to figure out not merely how to fight it, but how to avoid the prospect of their families being forcibly deported to a country where they'd never set foot. And it was through them that I met the remarkable woman who would become the main face and public voice, over the next year, for their plight. "My parents came here from Haiti," said Ana Maria Belique in pure Dominican Spanish, "but I was born here and I'm a citizen of the Dominican Republic. I have rights."

Ana Maria's eyes beamed with intelligence, and her skin was deep brown. She wore the sandals and woven Mayan-style bag of a young activist and the self-possession of a woman far older than twenty-four. She carried a worn BlackBerry that she never went more than a few minutes without checking for the flood of messages, from allies and skeptics of a cause for which, because of her gifts for articulation and presence, she became a spokesperson. Ana Maria told me about how her father had declared her birth at their town's registry just after it occurred. How she'd been baptized in the Dominican Catholic Church and had a Dominican picture ID. How she'd been able, as such, to complete both primary school and high school. Ana Maria's troubles began when she went to enroll in the university and tried to obtain the duplicate birth certificate that she'd need to do so, only to be told, at the Civil Registry Office, that this wasn't possible. "My life was put on hold," she said, "because of this social exclusion. And I, of course, am just one face representing many—from my brother, who's been trying, for five years, to get an ID and works odd jobs to survive; to those who can't marry or own property; to all those who can't move their lives forward, however they wish. We have been placed, in this society and by this civil genocide, in a situation of extreme vulnerability."

As Ana Maria's prominence grew over the ensuing months and in this place where social capital is all, she was able to get her birth certificate. I saw the evidence of her will and ability to speak for the many when Carlos parked the Nissan by the presidential palace and I joined Ana Maria and a hundred of her peers as they marched in a circle, singing songs, on the pavement outside. Kids of Haitian descent, these were also Dominicans as in thrall to *béisbol* and bachata, to judge from their cell phone ringtones and ball cap logos, as anyone in this country. They all wore black T-shirts, screen-printed for the occasion with block letters declaring what their presence here also said: "SOY DOMINICANO, Y TENGO DERECHO"—I am Dominican, and I have rights. The young people were joined by a couple of kind-faced monks in habits, protesting these un-Christian laws, and by a number of TV crews with reporters in heavy makeup who circled around Ana Maria to inquire, for the evening news, what these poor "Haitians" were upset about now. "We are here because we are proud citizens of the Dominican Republic," she told the cameras, "and until we're respected as such, we'll keep coming back." The news ladies blinked their fake lashes blankly. Ana Maria's tone made it clear that her people would, indeed, keep coming back. Less clear was how or when their government would do what she and her peers demanded—and what would become of the many thousands of people in the DR living lives far more vulnerable than those of these kids in the capital.

* * *

DOMINICANS ARE WEDGED between one nation to which they can condescend (Haiti) and another, just across the shark-filled Mona Passage, to whose prosperity, relative as it may be, they aspire (Puerto Rico). For while Puerto Rico may be twice as poor as Mississippi, the DR is twice as poor again, with a per person GDP comparable to Angola's. This is a dirt-floored nation where boys who dream of the majors swing sticks at bottle caps and too many of their sisters peg their hopes on selling themselves, on the sex-trade beaches of Boca Chica and Sosua, to shady Germans or Florida cops who they hope will one day send them a plane ticket to Miami or Munich. The DR is squarely a member of what used to be called the Third World—a nation from which a preponderance of people are trying to escape. And as those who board leaky skiffs to brave the Mona Passage well know, and those who make it all the way to the Bronx do, too, Puerto Ricans have never evinced much love for their poorer *primo*s lacking Puerto Ricans' automatic access to U.S. citizenship and its welfare state. Those old resentments, moreover, have been compounded by the tension between Dominicans' ascendance in Nueva York, with their bachata and baseball stars, and Puerto Ricans' historical role as head-Hispanics-in-charge of New York City. But those frictions, in the DR itself, are much less dwelled on than Dominicans' relation to the people they can hit.

Poverty, like hate, is relative. And if in the DR "poverty" still signifies tin roofs and potbellied parents with strong-limbed kids, in Haiti it means sleeping under leaky tarps and skeletal malnutrition. This is why modern Haitians, like residents of all poor countries next to less-poor ones, stream to the DR to work. It's a story we know, or should, anyway, in Europe and the United States and everywhere where immigrants are resented and oppressed for doing what is necessary to survive. But one thing that marks the DR-Haiti antinomy as unique is the role that Santo Domingo's most notorious dictator played, from the 1930s to the '60s, both in stoking Dominicans' anti-Haitian animus and in giving the two countries' shared frontier, both on the ground and in each one's collective mind, its ugliest form.

Rafael Trujillo, that "once and future dictator," got his start as an overseer beating Haitians on a sugar plantation.[10] Later, during the years when he turned the DR into a deranged personal dreamland, he woke to powder his soft face, each morning, with makeup meant to hide the tinge of a Haitian grandmother. It's not easy to parse the lowest legacies of a soldier who was trained by the U.S. Marines and rose through the Dominican military, before seizing control of the capital that he renamed Ciudad Trujillo in 1936; who forced the residents of its barrios, as Carlos recounted to me in his old neighborhood, to hang signs over each of their doors saying "Viva Trujillo"; who required any girl in the country to whom he wished sexual access to join his degraded harem. His legacy's most imaginative interpreter described him as "our

Sauron, our Arawn, our Darkseid, our Once and Future Dictator." And indeed: Generalissimo Rafael Leónidas Trujillo Molina, Great Benefactor of the Nation and Father of the New Dominion, was, as Junot Díaz described him, "a personage so dreadful that not even a sci-fi writer could have made his ass up."[11]

In August 1937, Trujillo visited the northern border town of Dajabón to attend a banquet in his honor. For months rumors had been swirling about Haitian "incursions" into a border region whose fields had until recently been at least half Haitian. The Depression, moreover, had wrecked the world sugar market: Haitian cane cutters who'd been welcome here in the 1920s, when sugar went for twenty cents a pound, were unwanted when that same sack fetched only a couple of pennies. That summer, Trujillo had announced a new law whose thrust would become familiar: all foreigners now had to register with migration officials. If their papers were found wanting, they would be deported. At the banquet in Dajabón, where Trujillo was plied with good local rum by his loyal hosts, he claimed that eight thousand Haitians, under the new law, had been rounded up and dropped over the border. He also acknowledged that some of those he'd booted from their homes had apparently begun to trickle back. The rum-drunk dictator had a solution, though, inspired by his avowed model Adolf Hitler. "I have learned here that the Haitians have been robbing food and cattle from the ranchers," he proclaimed. "To you, Dominicans, who have complained of this pillaging committed by the Haitians who live among you, I answer: I will solve the problem. Indeed, we have already begun. Around three hundred Haitians were killed in Bánica." He pounded his fist on the table. "The solution must continue."[12]

The ensuing horrors were hidden even as they happened. Trujillo's soldiers, cloaked in rain and darkness, were evidently aware that the mass murder they committed would be described by their leader as the result of a "peasant uprising," of innocents defending their land. The soldiers didn't use their guns, or leave corpses full of army bullets. They were more intimate. They reportedly asked Haitians to pronounce the Spanish word for parsley (*perejil*). If respondents betrayed a Kreyol accent, they were swiftly killed with a machete chop to the neck. Exactly how many of these inquisitions happened as a part of the genocide is as unclear now as the precise number of those slaughtered in what was called, like the yearly sugar harvest, *el corte*—the cutting. But the killings made the aptly named Massacre River, running by Dajabón, either run red with its victims' blood or, depending on which account you read, grow stagnant with corpses. These were murders committed by illiterates, and suffered by people worse off than them. One of the few written accounts by a witness to what happened, or at least to its aftermath, was by a visiting American journalist, Quentin Reynolds, of *Collier's* magazine. He arrived days after the killing to describe the mass brutality of an operation that had resulted, among the survivors he met, in horrifying numbers of hacked-off limbs and awful wounds. Whether Trujillo's *corte* resulted in fifteen thousand slain or thirty thousand, it was the largest modern killing of its kind in the hemisphere. And it saw Trujillo use "a horrifying ritual of silence and blood," as Díaz put it, "that inflicted a true border on the two countries, a border that exists beyond maps, that is carved directly into the histories and imaginaries of a people."[13]

The signal horror of the *corte* of 1937, as with many such spectacularly evil events, can obscure the history the dictator's evil didn't just make but continues to express: Trujillo's psychic border existed long before him, and it has been built and rebuilt after him—by his old consigliere Balaguer, certainly, but also by their successors. In the new democratic age, some degree of anti-Haitian xenophobia, for any Dominican politician aiming for national office, remains a basic prerequisite. And the depth of amnesia surrounding that political fact's correlative history of violence is suggested by the truth that *el corte* wasn't memorialized at any public site anywhere here until 2011, when a crucial but curious place opened on a quiet street in the capital's *zona colonial*. The Museum of the Dominican Resistance was organized and built by a committee of old subversives' kids, led by a woman whose father was martyred by Balaguer's henchmen in 1967. Luisa de Peña Díaz and her colleagues shamed their government into providing most of the US $2 million it took to build the museum. The museum's thorough account of Trujillo's brutality and reign, rendered in photos and news clippings and in awful images of his torturers' victims and tools, depicts the 1937 *corte* as one of his greatest abuses, while also tracing the story of subversions bred by his reign. Its rooms include a holographic image, laced with 3D butterflies, of the best-known enemies of "the Goat," as he was known: the dear departed Mirabel sisters, Maria, Patria, and Minerva, who were forced off a dark road by Trujillo's thugs one night in 1960, for too publicly decrying his rule, and whose murder prompted wide public anger that perhaps hastened his demise. Its rooms also contain an animatronic model of Minerva Mirabel's also-martyred lefty husband, Manuel Tavárez Justo, haranguing an imaginary loving crowd in his Ray-Bans, and a model of the concrete bench on the capital's Malecon by which the hated Goat was at last gunned down, in May 1961, by his young foes. These exhibits, paid for with public funds, convey a bien-pensant public consensus that the Generalissimo was rather worse than his grandson claimed to *The New York Times* when the paper reached L. Ramfis Dominguez-Trujillo after the museum opened in 2011, and he insisted from Miami that while his misunderstood grandpa may have committed "a number of excesses," he was only human.[14]

In the winter of 2014, President Danilo Medina announced a new "National Regularization Plan for Foreigners," designed not only to address the fact that it would be impossible for his government to comply with the letter of the 2013 anti-Haitian laws but to appease international censure, in *la sentencia*'s wake. That censure was led, locally, by the UN High Commission for Refugees, headed by Gonzalo Vargas Llosa—son of the Nobel laureate. Medina's plan supposedly gave "foreigners" the chance to formally register their presence in the DR, and to begin the process to secure permits to remain. It also claimed to provide a route, for Dominicans of Haitian descent, to regain their citizenship. All of which was well enough and good, on the surface. But the plan contained a few wrinkles. The first was its directive that Dominican nationals of Haitian ancestry now had to declare themselves Haitian, to their government, to begin their redemption. The second was that the documents required for them to do so were rarely in their possession.

The day the plan went into effect, I joined Ana Maria Belique's crew of protestors outside the Presidential Palace. "We welcome the government's attempt to protect its citizens' rights," she told the news cameras. "But why must we register as foreigners in our own country?" The government's implied answer to that question, over ensuing months, never grew less distressing. As the plan got under way, its bureaucracy's dysfunctions were joined to threats that its registration deadline wouldn't be extended. Medina's interior minister assured the nation that deportations of those who failed to register in time would "start with people who roam the streets," before then moving on "to the interior [and] farming areas."[15]

* * *

NEITHER THAT MINISTER nor Medina ever did quite explain, as the plan progressed, how exactly the targets of these deportations would be found, save for random sweeps of "Haitian-looking" folks by local police or federal soldiers, who could be counted on to ask for either documentation or beer money, from those they picked up, to set them free. The new law's enforcement could only be selective. And it would begin, it seemed clear, by ignoring a subset of Haitians in the country—those "in the interior and in farming areas"—who worked on sugar plantations, as they had for generations, owned by the country's rich.

The sugar trade on Spanish Hispaniola, considering that it is the place where *la caña* first reached the Caribbean, was slow to flourish. With the DR's early settlers focused first on looking for gold and then on their cattle, Spain largely left sugar cultivation in the region to the English and French; it was only in the later 1700s that they entered the game, in Cuba. And it wasn't until Cuba was beset with civil war, after 1868, that its big landowners turned toward the expansive DR as an alternative. In the late nineteenth century, one corrupted Dominican leader after another granted generous concessions to foreign tycoons from Europe or America, or procured loans to build new *ingenios* themselves. The industry bloomed. By 1900, most of Santo Domingo's outskirts were under sugarcane, and so were the low rolling plains around the new southeastern port of La Romana. At first, these fields were worked by Dominican locals and the same imported *cocolos*—West Indian cane cutters from Jamaica and elsewhere—on whom Cuba also relied. But after the century's turn, both the DR and Haiti saw their chronically unstable politics devolve into unrest. The U.S. Marines arrived to occupy Haiti in 1915; they came to the DR a year later. With the Marines there also protecting U.S. firms' interests in an era when sucrose was fetching record prices on the world market, the 1910s and 1920s witnessed the large-scale recruitment to the DR of Haitian cutters who fled their own country's turmoil to perform jobs that became known, in sugar zones here like La Romana or in San Cristobal, on plantations Trujillo worked as a guard, as "Haitian work."

The DR's stance toward those workers and their kin has since the 1930s been shaped by forces beyond the workers' control: just as Trujillo's *perejil* massacre was partly prompted by the bottom falling out of the world sugar market, so has this century's new "civil genocide" been tied to broader shifts. In recent decades, the United States and other wealthy nations have turned to corn syrup or chemicals to sweeten their pop; sugar has declined in both import and price. The result, in Dominican towns around the capital and elsewhere whose sugar mills have shuttered, are defunct old *bateyes* comprising pockets of black poverty whose social isolation, like their provenance in larger economic shifts, share much with Detroit's postindustrial ghettos—except they're far poorer. At the same time, Haiti's own "push factors" have only grown with its birthrate—especially after its catastrophic 2010 earthquake. Many Haitians now stream east not to cut cane but to work construction jobs or just hustle. But in places like the old sugar heartland of La Romana, the harvest called the *zafra* remains a huge deal. And as I absorbed when I rented a car in the capital that spring, just before the harvest's end, to roll east to La Romana, the DR's old sugar core—and its rural *campo* in general—still remains at the crux of Hispaniola's battles with itself.

* * *

IF THE DR'S CAPITAL can feel like an unholy cross between medieval Spain and modern Miami, its great hinterlands more recall 1850s Mississippi. There peasants' wooden huts dot soft-lit, waving fields of cane also punctuated with old-*barracoon*-style barracks for black workers which recall, with vivid force, the days of slavery.

La Romana, the eponymous company town at this zone's heart, was founded only in 1897. But after the South Puerto Rico Sugar Company built a huge *ingenio* here in 1917 it became the DR's third-biggest city. The mill was later sold to Gulf & Western, which in turn sold it to its current owner, the Central Romana Corporation—a subsidiary of Florida's Fanjul Corp., an outfit owned by two controversial Cuban-born brothers from Miami, "Alfy" and "Pepe" Fanjul, whose jocular nicknames belie their iron grip on the Americas' sugar trade. The Fanjuls' portfolio of brands includes Florida Crystals, Domino Sugar, and the old British giant Tate & Lyle. In La Romana now, they own not only the great mill whose cloying smell sticks to everything here, but also the great web of railroads whose freight cars, stenciled with the familiar C-R logo, snake through the fields to bring cut cane to the mill. Central Romana also owns the province's hospital, its port, and the company stores where its workers spend their paychecks on marked-up cooking oil. The Fanjuls' fief also includes a huge country-club complex, called Casa de Campo: a gated world of tacky villas and marinas that's

touted by its boosters as "the Caribbean's finest resort community," and
that also includes, within its bounds, a mock "Mediterranean village,"
among whose buildings is a huge Roman-style amphitheater, perched
above the Chavón River and made from cut stone, that's used for gala
concerts by the likes of Julio Iglesias.

On the afternoon I paid the $20 entrance fee that keeps Casa de
Campo beyond most Dominicans (never mind Central Romana's workers, cutting cane nearby), the place was packed with cruise-ship passengers snapping iPhone photos of old-looking buildings that had nothing
to do with here but that did bespeak "vacation." Some sat for portraits
done by young sketch artists, working for tips, who I later learned were
students at the Altos de Chavón art school—one of the DR's only such
institutions, and perhaps the Fanjuls' one gesture toward redeemability
here. The alum from whom I learned about the school was a young
Dominican woman who introduced herself as Cookie, from behind
the bar in Brooklyn where I met her, who told me as she mixed drinks
that she'd just left the DR and was never going back. "The country's
like one big *calmado*," said Cookie, with a shake of her art school buzz-
cut, before she recounted, when I mentioned I'd recently been to La
Romana, how she'd attended Altos de Chavón but spent most of her
time there, when she wasn't drawing tourists with her classmates,
tromping down by the river to find a local flower whose stem, when
you ground it up like the Indians did, produced "a vodou powder that'll
make you trip your head off, I swear, for like nine hours."

La Romana's heart of darkness is surreal, but its geography is stark.
Beyond Casa de Campo and extending for fifty miles in every direction
are dirt tracks through the cane fields that lead to communities that
few non-Haitian Dominicans, let alone Casa de Campo's guests, ever
see. Leaving the resort's confines, I drove out into the cane, and it took
but twenty minutes to happen upon a little weigh station, by one of
Central Romana's railroad tracks, where a young Dominican foreman
held a clipboard to direct darker-skinned men decades his senior, who
moved their ox-pulled carts of cut stalks of cane, eight feet long, onto a
scale. The foreman explained, as one of the older men smiled in agreement, that "they get paid by the weight and they always have." I continued past clusters of shacks marked by road signs reading Batey 89 or
Batey 36, as two men argued, on the radio, over whether the number of
doubles hit by Moises Alou in 1994, when he was with the Expos, were
really Hall of Fame numbers, before pulling over to talk with a young

man who waved me down. The young man was skinny and twelve years old, with a warm smile. He told me, as he asked for a ride, that his name was Fernando. Fernando also told me, after he hopped in, that he went to school in the nearby village of Guaymete and that math was his favorite subject; that his grandfather, whose surname was Challi, came here from Haiti decades ago and lived in Batey 22; that he, Fernando, lived with his mother and her common-law husband in Batey 106; that when he played baseball, he fancied himself a right fielder, like Vlad Guerrero. "Soy Dominicano"—I'm Dominican—he said with the confidence he might have if he were Guerrero himself. He directed me to turn off the main road and onto the rutted track to the *batey* where he lived. Leaning out his window to wave at his most-impressed friends, barefoot and chasing the car, Fernando pointed us through the cluster of barracks and wandering chickens and told me to stop by a tin-roofed shack. From inside stepped a wiry woman with bright eyes whose age, in the Haitian way, was impossible to tell beyond that she was somewhere between twenty-five and fifty.

"This is my mother," said Fernando as the woman hugged her son and, offering a bemused smile to the visitor he'd brought home, extended her hand.

"I'm Annette." She pulled me into her home and onto a rickety chair and made the offer of hospitality that any Hispaniolan, no matter how poor, will. "Would you like coffee?"

Annette Challi handed me a tin cup of sweet delicious sludge, and then recounted, in Spanish, how she'd grown up in Mirebalais, a town on Haiti's central plateau, but had come here in her teens to follow her dad. How she worked, while her man here cut cane, farming beans and yucca to eat and to sell. How she'd given her son a "Dominican name" on purpose, but also how when she'd given birth to him in a clinic run by Central Romana, she'd "asked them for a birth certificate, but they said no." Months later, I returned to Batey 106, and Annette would grin as she showed me the paper proving that she'd registered her family in the regularization plan: officials from Central Romana had brought their workers to an office in town, to ensure all their workers did so. What the paper she held meant, though, wasn't very clear—either then or later. And the fact that she'd registered Fernando in the new process didn't change the fact that her son—who seemed to grow a foot between those two meetings, and who on the second one did a passable imitation of a teenager when he posed by my rental car for pictures—

still didn't have his birth certificate or a Dominican *cédula*, the crucial photo ID that you need to do much of anything in the DR. Which is to say that this bright kid, who loved math and baseball, but was soon to start working the same fields as his grandfather, likely wouldn't be able to continue school past that year.

Annette and Fernando Challi were charges of Central Romana and thus of the Fanjuls: in an economy run by favors exchanged among the powerful or bequeathed to their lowers, it was unlikely that some government trucks would pull up to the *batey* and load up its residents to dump them in Haiti. The full rights of citizenship were another question. But the residents of Batey 106 were certainly better off, in the short term anyway, than the many Haitians in the DR who lacked paternal protection, like those depicted in a video that one of Annette Challi's neighbors showed me on his smartphone.

I stared at an angry mob in the province of Moca. They were dragging what looked to be a Haitian man down the street by his short dreadlocks, as a woman cowered and the mob, brandishing bats and mugging for their pal's camera, clubbed dishes and smashed shelves in the home of this poor family they were running out of town. Ugly scenes. The video recalled the Haitian novelist Jacques Stephen Alexis's description of the border near Dajabón, in October 1937, where "such horrors took place . . . that your mouth tasted of ashes . . . and the flavor of all life indeed was repugnant." Alexis continued, "You would never believe that such things could come to pass on Dominican soil."[16] This was perhaps true in 1937, but it hasn't been true since. And in a country where communal justice remains as often a matter of communal action as judicial writ, what transpired in Moca (a young man had died; his friends, lacking better suspects, turned on their neighbors) was in many ways common: it's hardly rare, in the Dominican *campo*, for pedophiles or thieves to be "dealt with," with dispatch, by parties other than the police. It was only predictable that vigilantes would begin enforcing immigration policy, too.

Standing in Batey 106, I recalled a story I first read not long after the *sentencia* came down in *El Listín Diario*. That initial report, soon to be amplified by the DR's other main dailies, described the wanton murder of "two poor old coffee farmers," in the mountains over the border town of Neyba. It also described the ensuing revenge killing, by the couple's neighbors, of one of their suspected assailants—before also noting that "several dozen Haitians in the area, seeking protection, appeared at the Neyba Army Barracks."[17] The Haitian papers covered the story, too. Their slant was a bit different in that sad season when people there were only too ready to credit that lynch mobs were roving the land (as indeed they were). They reported that the 347 Haitians who turned up at the army barracks looking for protection were summarily loaded on trucks, instead, and dumped across the border. Hazier reports from the border's forests, long said to be haunted by malevolent wolf-spirits called "loup garou" but now stalked by more human *tigueres* too, also said that as many as thirty-five people, among hundreds more fleeing through the trees, were rumored to have been killed as they fled.

* * *

I RETURNED TO THE DR in the spring of 2015, and found Ana Maria Belique outside the Presidential Palace. She and her crew of young demonstrators were marking the one-year anniversary since the regularization plan's start. They were marching, in their "TENGO DERECHO" T-shirts, to highlight its failures. Their platoon's number hadn't grown much. With the plan's deadline approaching, though, the huddle of newswomen crowding Ana Maria certainly had. The newswomen pressed her to answer a question they'd asked her umpteen times before, despite its flagrantly missing the point ("Why are you still complaining if you yourself have your papers?"), and also raised new ones prompted by a story that had just run in *El Listin Diario* that proved her status, in the eyes of the state, as a threat. "The Central Electoral Commission has determined, after an internal investigation," the paper quoted that body's head, "that the parents of the activist Ana Maria Belique, at the time of her birth, made false statements about their status."[18] Ana Maria stepped from the fray, outside the Presidential Palace, to explain what was going on. "It's a smokescreen, of course, to distract from the larger issue. My parents never claimed to be anything but what they are—Haitian; and they declared my own birth, here, as they were meant to do at the time. The commission's actions show that their audit of the registry, like this whole process, is a sham."

Of the estimated 200,000 Dominicans of Haitian descent menaced by the new laws, just 8,000 of those whose ancestors' births hadn't been noted in the civil registry, by that spring, had been able to begin Medina's process. Of these, just a few hundred had been granted an actual *cédula* that would help them convince an inquiring policeman or vigilante, after the deadline passed, that they shouldn't be deported. Those in the still more vulnerable camp—actual Haitian-born immigrants—were still lining up outside one of six registration centers around the country, in hopes of joining Fernando Challi and his kin from Batey 106 who at least possessed a piece of paper marking them as "registered." By the deadline, some 280,000 had done so in spite of poor staffing at the registration centers, unconscionably long lines, and almost perverse bureaucratic complication. Days before the deadline, the DR's army chief assured that deportations would begin promptly after its expiry. Many Haitians made the same decision as a construction worker I met, outside their embassy, who'd been pouring concrete in Santo Domingo for a decade but who had no documents, beyond an outdated employee ID from some company for which he'd worked, listing his name as Jhonny Jean. Jhonny Jean had little hope of getting the other documents he'd need, on time, so he'd bought a bus ticket home to his Haitian hometown of Gonaïves. "I don't want to be thrown in a truck without my things, or my kids," he said. "I'm going to my country now." He didn't want to leave by the scary means I saw outside the Migration Ministry, nearby: a row of schoolbuses whose windows had been retrofitted with iron bars. I asked a young soldier guarding the buses who they were for. His answer was simple: "*los morenos*"—the dark ones.

In Little Haiti, Carlos and I tried to find the mango and flip-flop peddlers we'd befriended months before. They'd vacated their posts, like many in a neighborhood where most were staying inside. A contact in a *batey* community outside the capital said that police patrols were increasing. "Usually the cops come by a couple times a week to check papers and get bribes. But now they're coming two or three times a day." And outside the Interior Ministry, in the last days, the mood grew dark. The restive line of Haitians were menaced by riot cops gripping shields and clubs. They waited to enter the tower that was officially named the Juan Pablo Duarte Government Offices, after a nineteenth-century hero of the Dominican war of independence, but that everyone called by its more evocative nickname. That name, Huacal, was drawn from Dominicans' slang term for the idle public servants perceived to work there; *huacal* refers to an empty rack of bottles. Now Huacal was a hub of activity—at least for the exhausted people clutching their photocopied documents outside, hoping to get in. And on the last night, as it became clear that many of them wouldn't do so, the grim mood worsened. It wasn't helped by the nationally televised speech delivered by President Medina that Carlos and I repaired to a nearby *colmado* to watch. Medina made no mention of the national drama reaching a head outside Huacal, but did launch his bid for reelection, by congratulating the Dominican people on "everything that we've conquered together."

* * *

THE LONG-THREATENED DEPORTATIONS, with observers from the Organization of American States and Amnesty International circling, didn't happen on the scale or with the speed that many had feared; they would happen later, and more quietly. But with the climate growing alarmingly less secure, for Haitians in the DR now at the mercy of both the Dominican government and emboldened thugs in the *campo*, I headed for Haiti by way of the place—the border by Dajabón—whose barbed wire perhaps most concentrates the mind on the ghostly demarcations of Dominican history. I rolled northward past Santiago, and across the broad Cibao to reach a bustling market town centered around the iron bridge that, spanning the muddy Massacre River, joins Dajabón to Haiti. By this river that ran red in 1937—and whose name refers to the slaying of some French pirates here in the eighteenth century—the sole memorial to history lies south of town. It has nothing to do with either massacre. But the Loma de Cabrera monument does share much with the Columbus Lighthouse, both in its outsized form and its clarity as a massive boondoggle in concrete— this one commemorating the little-known "restoration" of 1866, when the DR ended its flirtation with Spain. That event is marked here, in the middle of nowhere and the middle of Hispaniola, with a grandiose pile whose helipad stands ready for politicians wishing to buzz in for a frontier photo op, but that on the afternoon I stopped by was completely deserted except for a skinny white horse, grazing by its side, and a couple of pensive cows.

Dajabón's more utilitarian bits of border infrastructure, back in town, abutted its ghost-filled river. Dominican youths raced motos and bachata blared over nearby blocks on a Thursday night, before the big Friday market that would see thousands of Haitians stream across the river, looking to buy goods that they couldn't at home, and to sell some of their own, at Dajabón's twice-weekly International Market. Dropping my things at the Massacre Hotel, I explored this frontier town with its de rigueur cockfighting ring and love motels on its outskirts, but also a grassy field by the border river where, when I went to speak to a Haitian woman hanging her laundry from the other side of the barbed wire by its bank, two baby-faced soldiers appeared to tell me that this was a restricted zone and then made jokes, after one pulled a little rapier from his waist, about killing Haitians. Across the Orwellian "friendship bridge" that joins Dajabón with its Haitian sister city of Ouanaminthe, a small Haitian kid ran playfully, ignored by guards to whom he was clearly a known person. The guards' own discretion, or mood, seemed the main criterion upon which people were allowed to enter here from Haiti. They did let across a clean-cut young man of about twenty who told me, as he stepped off the bridge in a polo shirt, that his name wss Edro and that he came from Fort Liberté, in Haiti, but that he'd been studying for two years at the Polytechnic College in Dajabón and so all the border guards knew him. Edro showed me around his school's campus. He smiled at a young *dominicana* classmate whom he sometimes helped with her homework, and whom he'd even got to make out with, but who would never publicly date him, "because Dominican girls, you know, are very materialistic." I bought Edro a Presidente Light in the little restaurant by the Hotel Massacre. On the news on its TV, Ana Maria Belique, back in the capital, was answering the same old questions. The place's manager pointed his clicker at the TV to switch to the MLB Channel's broadcast of some special on the Milwaukee Brewers. I returned to the hotel to wake early for a market day in Dajabón when by 6 a.m. the next morning thousands of Haitians would already be backed up behind the rusted blue gate leading onto the bridge, waiting to cross.

When I reached the bridge, at 6:45, the happy border kid was already there. Running about in the chute-like DMZ that led off the bridge and toward the market, lined with barbed storm fencing and concertina wire, and that would soon fill with entering Haitians, he was joined today by an assortment of police and soldier types. Some wore jeans and T-shirts along with small guns or nightsticks at their waists. Others were in Desert Storm–style camouflage and carried M16s—these were members of CESFRONT, the new U.S.-trained force working the border. One swarthy fellow in plain clothes, a tall and stout David Ortiz look-alike except for his mean look, walked up to the blue gate carrying a wooden bat. He exchanged a few cruel laughs with the defiant women behind, and then swung his bat at the metal with sadistic glee— *clang!*—to make them jump. Two other men, gentler of vibe and hanging back, wore green vests labeled "Ministry of Health." Their brief was to ensure that no Haitian entering here brought in too much unbottled water: the recent cholera outbreak in Haiti, loosed by some careless UN soldiers from Nepal who had emptied their base's sewage into a Haitian river, was no joke. The only other person apart from me loitering in the DMZ without official purpose, before the gates opened at 7, was a short man wearing a Detroit Tigers cap. His name was Manny, and he lived in the far-off town of Mao, he said, which he'd left at 3 a.m., as he did most Fridays, to get here by 6. Manny's hustle involved buying secondhand pants and sneakers from Haitian vendors here and selling them for profit in Mao; it had seen him turn the hundred dollars he'd shown up with, at Christmastime, into four hundred back in Mao. "*Buen negocio,*" he explained—good business. Indeed. Manny liked turning up early to watch the Haitians run, he said, but he'd never been across the river. "No way! They're a *tipo*, how to say—Africano." When the gate was opened, the tide of Haitians broke. Young men sprinted ahead, rushing through the barbed chute to stake out the market's best spots. Toters of wheelbarrows, right behind, pushed crates of saltfish and socks. Women from age ten to eighty laughed and walked and talked with huge loads on their heads—bundles of T-shirts or baskets or plastic soap jugs, wrapped in bulbous sacks.

The Madam Saras, as Haiti's market women are known, take their name from the migrant sara birds, who line Hispaniola's trees in chattering groups and are known for their ability to find food wherever they go. These Madam Saras dodged the attentions of Dominican customs agents with nightsticks who pulled women from the stream, at random, to play tug-of-war with their bundles even as they tried to drag them into a hut marked "Aduana/Customs," to pay capricious duties. In the river below us, people waded across, too. Going this way required pressing a little something into the palm of one of the fatigued soldiers stationed there, before scurrying to join the thousands of people who were turning the market into a teeming ecosystem of alleys and avenues of goods. When, twenty minutes after the gate's opening, I entered the market proper, this pop-up supermart by the Massacre River was already almost full. It was ringed by a rope line, manned by soldiers whose job it was to prevent the Haitians—who were here to sell their wares but also to buy what the Dominicans here were selling— from entering Dajabón. Above Haitians' tables, tarps with the logo of USAID on them, remnants of old foreign aid, fluttered over high piles of tropical-weight army boots; knockoff Converse and Fruit of the

Loom underwear; tubes of shampoo and bottles of Aqua Net hair spray and wooden boxes of smoked herring stamped "Product of New Brunswick." A woman in a T-shirt offering "FREE HUGS" across its chest tried to sell me a pair of someone's secondhand slippers whose toe-box embroidery declared "WALKING WITH JESUS." Manny the racist pants flipper fondled some black wingtips. "Son Chinos." They were Chinese. He bent the sole in half, to the table owner's distress, before putting them back and moving on.

The Dominicans here, for the most part, came to peddle foodstuffs—beans, cooking oil, GMO garlic, and, most visibly, five-pound bags of the unenriched spaghetti that has become a Haitian staple—which the Madam Saras would carry back to Haiti to sell, at market or to smaller merchants there, for a profit. Much of the stuff the Haitians pushed here, of the secondhand variety, had reached Haiti as donations from church groups or foreign governments. Some also sold mysterious bottles of liquor with Brit-sounding names, but slightly off—Chancellor's, Black's. The peddlers of this hooch seemed to be targeting the raging new desire in the DR, as in many poor countries aiming not to be, for Johnnie Walker Black. This was "scotch," that is—but its provenance, as I learned from a five-dollar bottle of Black's I procured from a young Haitian in a Real Madrid jersey, wasn't Scotland. On the label of this whiskey-flavored stuff whose main ingredient was actually grain alcohol, near where it said "BLENDED FOR MAXIMUM SMOOTHNESS" it also said "Bottled in Bangalore."

That night, back at the little resto-bar by the Hotel Massacre, the MLB channel was airing "The 20 Most Overlooked Plays in Baseball History." I woke again the next morning at dawn, after a fitful night's sleep, and walked toward Dajabón's DMZ, with its concertina wire and plainclothes cops and the border kid playing amid them all. I walked up to the rusted blue metal gate that led onto the bridge over the Massacre River and into Haiti. I stepped across.

CHAPTER 9

THE CITADEL

HAITI'S RUINED CAPITAL—a sprawling city of ten thousand cooking fires, smoldering on the floor of a broad canyon between the parched ridges of Hispaniola's southern mountains—is all browns and grays. Nine of every ten foreigners coming to Haiti arrive by air, to the Toussaint L'Ouverture International Airport. For the first-time visitor, gazing through a plane window's dusty oval at Port-au-Prince, it's not hard to project onto the scene below all the images that were stuck to Haiti, even before its catastrophic 2010 earthquake, like clingy ash: the people living in tents; the UN trucks rolling through the rubble; the kinds of corruption that none of the missionaries wearing shorts can solve. Even the encircling Caribbean's aqua sheen is sullied, by the muddy mouth of Rivière Momance that pushes the hazy beige tendrils of Haiti's topsoil, like floating smoke, out to sea.

From above, Haiti looks like the place that has long occupied the world's mind: the nation that has served as an icon of both our planet's bleak future and its brutal past. On the ground, the picture changes. The poverty, of course, astonishes. But so, too, do the riches of a culture born from the country's proud but awful history as the world's sole nation founded by its slaves. One aftershock of those slaves' heroism—the heroism of people long shunned by their neighbors and saddled, by their onetime owners, with unpayable debts—is Haiti's legacy of poverty. But another is the ravishing color and depth of their culture's vodou religion and Saint Soleil paintings and performative arts, all informed by an awareness of history's honor and the tragedy that places Haiti's epic not merely at the core of the Caribbean story, but near the heart of the larger epics of America and of modern history. But visitors don't discover this until they land (or perhaps not at all, depending on their predilections).

There is a photo, or a version of it, that is familiar to every high school geography student or casual web surfer enticed to click on one of those banner ads touting "The World's 10 Craziest Borders." The photo suggests what Haiti is by showing what it's not. It is taken from a plane, by a camera facing north. It captures a landscape whose left half is comprised of nude brown hills; its right side, beyond what seems an invisible fence bisecting the frame, is lush and green. The photo, its caption says, depicts the line between Haiti and the Dominican Republic. The question it begs—and that is seen answered by a thousand online pedants and "development theorists"—is this: Why do some countries stay poor and others prosper?

There are a thousand ways, dumb and smart, informed or less so, to answer that question. In 2010, Pat Robertson suggested that Haiti's poverty is due to its people having made a pact, in having chosen vodou over Christ, with the devil. In this view the huckster preacher is hardly alone: many of the missionaries coming here to save souls spout the same things. Yet the more execrable replies to the Haiti-DR question share at least one feature with the saner ones: both elide the truth that, by any reasonable measure and in the context of our twenty-first-century world, both Dominicans and Haitians are poor. Using the word "prosper" in connection with the mass of people from either of Hispaniola's nations, unless you're referring to the monied overclass of both countries, is an insult.

There's a further elision at work, too, in this photo whose common caption suggests that the Haiti-DR border is this starkly visible along its whole length. For along most of those 240-odd miles, not even a fence marks the line that was arbitrated by the U.S. Marines in the 1920s. What does is a hardly forbidding daisy chain of little granite pyramids, laid in the ground and placed up to a mile apart. Along most segments of this border, it's impossible to tell, until you wander into a nearby town, which country you're in. In the fecund north, many hills on either side are equally green. In the desiccated south, both sides are dry and the line is as invisible from above as it is on the ground. From where exactly that most common picture comes is hard to say. One suspects it's near the hills over Port-au-Prince—one of the few stretches of the border where there's actually a fence. This is the place, at Hispaniola's narrow waist and just twenty miles from downtown Port-au-Prince, where ten million Haitians crowd onto their slice of an island that they share with an equal number of Dominicans who are spread across a country whose mass is twice as large and whose population is concentrated, in the main, around centers of habitation a hundred miles from the border. The aerial border photo of the line between these countries, like many such blunt images, misleads as much as it reflects truth.

Which isn't to say that Haiti doesn't have nude hillsides—or that there aren't many ways to understand the real phenomenon that this picture, in its blunt way, suggests. Haiti is a country where widespread deforestation began in the eighteenth century, as avaricious Frenchmen sought, in the roaring 1770s and '80s, to plant as much sugarcane and coffee here as they possibly could. And where, in recent decades, deforestation has become an ongoing crisis in a country whose poor still have no fuel source but the charcoal made from their hilly homeland's stands of hardwood and pine. It is the yanking of these trees, from barren hillsides, that loosens the topsoil, which is then washed from the slopes during the rainy season and into the ambling brown waters of the rivers that carry it off to dissipate in the sea. The grand forests of mahogany and blue mahoe that once spread over 80 percent of Haiti's land now shade just 2 percent of it.

But what Haitians call their *pwoblem pyebwa*—their tree problem—is a problem, like many on this island, in which the DR is involved: there's a booming black market here for Dominican fuel wood. And what's most striking about the Haiti-DR border is less what separates the two countries than what sutures them together. Jean-Baptiste Azolin, a lawyer with the Haitian NGO devoted to assisting refugees from the Dominican Republic, put it this way: "The island of Hispaniola doesn't have two countries, it has three. There's Haiti, the Dominican Republic, and the border country mixing the two: a zone that extends for many miles on either side of the line."

When entering the Dominican Republic from Haiti, one grows used to negotiating a gauntlet of acquisitive cops or ball-capped *tigueres*. These figures, grabbing at your passport, will point you to the office of the actual border guards, often demanding bribes for their "help." Crossing into Haiti is different. As I stepped from the bridge across the Massacre River into Ouanaminthe, I conversed not with *tigueres* or border guards but Haitian kids looking for handouts or volunteering, if they were of moto-riding age, to tote me into town. To get my passport stamped and my entry recorded by Haitian officers of state, initiative was required not from those officials but from me. And when I did find the right official, the stamp he issued wasn't accompanied by any tapping at a computer keyboard or recording the information in some larger database linked to a central bureaucracy in Port-au-Prince. That official, rather, was a soft-spoken civil servant who asked me to sign a big vinyl-bound book whose musty pages looked as if they'd been in use in this dingy office since some U.S. Marine, back in the age of Herbert Hoover, left it here after America's first occupation of Haiti.

My presence thus registered on Haitian soil, and with a stamp in my passport to prove it, I walked down Ouanaminthe's bustling main street to find a ride to the nearby capital of Haiti's historic north—Cap Haïtien—to begin digging into how the country's old animus with its neighbor, now reaching uncharted depths, was playing on the ground.

* * *

IN OUANAMINTHE, THE STREET bore more scars than across the river, but the same bachata blared from *borlette* huts selling lotto tickets, and young men zoomed around on DR-style bikes. One of the kids, a young man in a wool skully and with a little Brazilian flag tied to his Hao Jin's handlebars (Neymar and other of Brazil's soccer stars are very popular here), insisted that the ninety-minute ride on the bumpy highway to Cap-Haïtien, with me hanging on to him and on to my bags and his little 110cc bike, was one he'd love to take. In the few years since Chinese manufacturers began exporting these cheap bikes—they retail for about US$500 here—and a few enterprising Syrian-Haitian businessmen began importing them to Haiti in bulk, such motos have revolutionized transport in a country where most people know firsthand what Bob Marley meant when he sang "My feet is my only carriage." The other main mode of getting around here has long been tap-taps—privately owned share taxis whose name means "quick quick" and which come in the form of buses or pickup trucks painted with bright colors, often featuring religious sayings or portraits of pop stars on their sides. When there's no tap-tap in sight, you can hop on one of thousands of bikes driven by kids who lease them for a day-fee, often, to operate as taxis. The moto ride, obvious hazards aside, is a splendid way to get across town—but also rather inadvisable for long hauls, given the lack of safety gear and unforgiving roads. I declined the offer of the skinny moto kid in his skully and found a minibus with "Le Cap" painted on its glass. I climbed in next to a bald-headed driver whose typical insistence that the *blan* sit up front with him, rather than wedged in back with the owners of the copious bundles and bags tied to our roof, was less an echo of subservience than an exemplar of typical Haitian hospitality toward foreigners who aren't soldiers (and who, no matter their skin color, are called *blans*). Once each of the bus's seats was filled, and its aisles were, too, we trundled off toward Cap-Haïtien.

The fields we passed, now covered in patchy grass, were once under sugar but haven't been since 1804. We also passed a low prison-like fort on whose walls was affixed a big UN logo. "That one's full of soldiers from Uruguay," the driver explained. The UN's multinational "stabilization force" is referred to in Haiti by its acronym, MINUSTAH—the Mission des Nations Unies pour la Stabilisation en Haïti. It's been present here since 2004, but grew in profile, and declined in Haitians' esteem, when after the 2010 earthquake some of its sloppy members opened their base's sewer to pour cholera into Haiti's Artibonite River. As we passed the fort, some of my bus-mates, laughing softly, *bah*-ed like goats. MINUSTAH's soldiers had a reputation, explained our driver, as goat fuckers. We rolled into a town that was once among the world's most important ports but where now women crouched over piles of onions for sale by the roadside, as big ash-colored pigs, nearby, rooted in muddy piles of trash.

That week, unlike most weeks, Cap-Haïtien was actually making world news. An undersea explorer from Cape Cod had just claimed, from a reef offshore, to have found the five-hundred-year-old wreck of Columbus's *Santa Maria*. The explorer's claim was perhaps made with an eye more toward a TV deal with the Discovery Channel than toward scientific truth. Still, newspapers in the DR were full of quotes from Dominican nationalists whom his claim had predictably piqued. ("We are closely following this news," said the country's minister of culture, "about a piece of our underwater patrimony." He cited the skepticism of a Dominican organ called the Permanent Commission of Ephemera of the Fatherland, whose head reminded his countrymen that the great Columbus's flagship, "as everyone knows, was destroyed before he founded Santo Domingo.")[1] But even before the explorer's claim was debunked the next week—the wreck's corroded copper bolts, it turned out, suggested not a Spanish galleon from the fifteenth century but some much newer craft—few here seemed to be paying the controversy, or his claim, much mind. Cap-Haïtien's main streets, with their pigs and moto boys, were lined with handsome houses whose iron railings were imported from Nantes in the eighteenth century. The town retained the feel of what it is: a place whose peak in worldly wealth and import, if not in human freedom, lay far back in its past.

Founded as Cap Français, this was French Saint-Domingue's capital, and the colony's main city for most of its history. After Haiti won its independence, though, a more secure-feeling southern entrepôt was made Haiti's capital and "Le Cap" began its long decline. The city's replacement as Haiti's center of economic and political life, Port-au-Prince, has long preyed on its hinterland like a parasite, sucking ever more of Haiti's rural poor, along with whatever wealth their country cousins still produce, into its maw, to become what a leading scholar here called the country's "Republic for the merchants."[2] In the nineteenth century, this dynamic enriched the new capital's importer-exporters; it also filled the vaults, in the twentieth, of the notorious, corrupt dictatorship of François "Papa Doc" Duvalier and his successor-son, Jean-Claude. The Duvaliers retained power for three decades, from 1957 to 1986, and the costs of their regime's doing so were many. But among the more prosaic, from the vantage of Le Cap, was their redoubled will to concentrate all their country's power and wealth in Port-au-Prince—and Papa Doc's decision, not long after becoming president, to halt plans to build a proper airport in Le Cap. That project was delayed for the next forty years. It wouldn't be completed until 2014, when the Hugo Chávez International Airport, named for the foreign leader who finally got it built, began receiving daily flights from Miami. As I wandered through Le Cap to its lowest-priced tourist hotel, though, that boost to its economy and life was still a few months off. It remained a sleepy place where the sole foreigners to be seen were the blue-helmeted UN soldiers at whom the kids *bah*-ed like goats, the occasional missionary or aid worker, and the sole other guest in the hotel I found down a narrow lane near the edge of town. Outside its gates, several dozen people were gathered around a little TV airing a soccer game involving Real Madrid. Beyond the gates and on the hotel's porch a squat white man with an Australian accent and a gruff manner was drinking a local Prestige beer and reading a novel by John le Carré.

The Aussie had an aura of prodigal exile. He said his main errand here was to visit the sight that most qualifies as an actual tourist attraction near Le Cap: the famous Citadel that this town's once-and-forever king, Henri Christophe, built onto a nearby mountain when he ruled over Haiti's north in the early 1800s. Christophe's fortress is a gargantuan edifice to whose making a dozen years and thousands of lives were sacrificed. It was built to repel any attempt to recolonize a country that the French insisted, for decades after Haiti's founding, on calling Saint-Domingue. The Citadel never saw military action. But it endures as a monument to Haitian pride, and to its builder's will to behave and be respected like a real king, in an era before France or the United States or any other world power recognized Haiti as sovereign. "They say it's the biggest fort in the world," the Aussie growled through his beard. "Figured I'd better have a look."

He now made his living when not traveling, he said, driving buses between Melbourne and Sydney. But his wanderlust had seen him hold down more exotic jobs, too, like during the years he spent driving retrofitted Bedford trucks full of adventuresome Brits on gap years clear from Cairo to Capetown—a gig that had won him not a few colorful tales about how, for example, it was the third time he got caught in a war in the Central African Republic that was the hairiest. We heard a loud cheer from the street outside: Real Madrid, Haiti's favorite team, had scored. "I don't know why more people don't come here," said the Aussie, finishing his Prestige. "Lovely country." He asked the elegant young barman, who was dressed in formal black and white though the bar was made from cracked plastic, for another beer. "And the Haitians are lovely little buggers."

In light of this solitary Australian tourist with his unintentional condescension and penchant for war zones, I wondered how Haiti's efforts to attract more tourists, as part of its post-earthquake "recovery" plan, were going. The country's tourism ministry had commissioned the design of a new national logo, with the *T* in "Haiti" doubling as the stamen of a stylized hibiscus blossom. It was meant to lure foreigners with the slogan "Haiti . . . experience it!" For now, though, five hundred years after Columbus ran aground off a beach now choked with trash, no sunbathers joined the gray pig rooting in the waves. There was little to suggest that the crumbling town where we sat was once one of the world's busiest ports—and the place where France sought, for a few frenzied decades in the late 1700s, to make up for starting slower than its Old World rivals in the Caribbean game.

* * *

WHEN COLUMBUS FIRST BUMPED ashore here, his backers' French counterpart was more focused on Europe than across the sea. Louis XII was busy, in the 1490s, trying to grow his domain by wresting control of two city-states he fancied—Naples and Milan—from the Holy Roman Empire. His cousin, Francis I, continued Louis's ruinous

Italian wars, but he was also aware of what his Habsburg rivals might gain from their New World. He built a new Atlantic port named Franciscopolis (seamen now call it Le Havre), and sponsored the Florentine navigator Giovanni da Verrazzano's attempt, in 1524, to find a westward way to China. Verrazzano poked around what became New York Harbor, before ranging north to the Maritimes, and the mouth of the St. Lawrence, to blaze a watery trail for the French cavaliers who later settled Quebec. The French soon realized, though, that the New World's real riches lay farther south. And they did try, starting with a doomed effort to settle an island off of Rio in Brazil, to challenge Iberian dominance there.

But the Portuguese already had a firm hold on Brazil's coast. They ended the hope of "France Antarctique's" Huguenot founders, in the 1550s, for establishing a toehold. And French luck was little better vis-à-vis the Spanish, whose conquistadors had by the 1560s forged the basic lineaments of an imperium joining their lucrative mines in Mexico and Peru to Puerto Rico and Havana. On the most minor of the Greater Antilles, Jamaica, England's seadogs loosened Madrid's hold; they also settled a remote coral island—Barbados—far from Castile's concern. But the French corsairs who persisted in sniffing around the Caribbean's "Spanish lake" were limited to living as parasites. They built camps on the Antilles' remoter beaches, grilling meat in a way the Taino called *barbacoa* and that they dubbed *barbeque* as they lay in wait, with their kings' backing, to raid Spanish gold.

In 1600 the only Antilles under even quasi-French control were the small Leeward Island of St. Christophe (later St. Kitts), which they shared with the English, and a little rock off Hispaniola's northeast shore, called La Tortue, home to a camp of barbecuing buccaneers. But then in 1635, a notorious new power behind the French throne chartered a new Compagnie des Iles de l'Amérique. Cardinal Richelieu was charged with expanding France's hold on the islands. Its owners dispatched men to nearby St. Barthélemy and St. Martin, and also moved to settle some forbidding isles, farther south, that Columbus had claimed for Spain but whose steep sides and fierce natives dissuaded his sponsors, with their bigger fish and islands to fry, from ever settling. Two of these would become Martinique and Guadeloupe—which are still-French bastions of the Lesser Antilles today, and whose import to France in 1763 was such that at the end of its Seven Years' War with England, Paris agreed to release all claims to Canada, dismissed by Vol-

taire as "a few acres of snow," to be able to keep these two little Antilles.[3] Yet as prized as Martinique and Guadeloupe came to be, France's
most prized colony of all would grow on Hispaniola. And that colony
fell into French hands thanks not to the actions of Richelieu's *Compagnie* but of the freelance pirates from the little island off its coast—La
Tortue—which now serves as a launching point for emigrating Haitians
who board leaky little sailboats here to try to reach the Bahamas.

The pirates of La Tortue took advantage of Spain's loose grip on
huge Hispaniola, beginning in the 1670s, to settle its northeast plain.
Their filibuster was backed by their king and then by the treaty his
diplomats signed with Madrid, in 1697, that gave them leave to continue farming the island's eastern third. The trajectory of the colony
they founded there was fixed when Spain's first Bourbon king, Philip V,
granted France an *asiento* to supply his American colonies with African
slaves. Gaul's mariners grew ascendant in the slave-trading game just as
Europe's ex-serfs and gentry alike were becoming hooked on sugar. The
French would leverage this new era, to more outsized and scary effect
than anywhere else, in the fertile fields around Le Cap.

The owners of French Saint-Domingue, there in Hispaniola's
remote northeast, were inspired by the fortunes that England's planters were wrenching from Barbados and Jamaica. They purchased the
same great iron grinders and copper stills, from Amsterdam's Dutch
merchants, that the Portuguese brought to Brazil. And then they began,
at a rate that rose slowly at first before shooting rapidly skyward, to
import slaves from Congo and Dahomey, where in the eighteenth century warring kings sold their enslaved enemies to European merchants
in numbers. Saint-Domingue soon surpassed not just Barbados and
Jamaica in the amount of sugar it produced, but also Brazil. Such was
the volume its enslaved Africans made that, by the time of the American Revolution, Saint-Domingue was furnishing fully two-thirds of
France's overseas trade. Its slaves' toil supported the livelihoods of a
few million Frenchmen directly dependent on its profits, and afforded
the building of many a Loire chateau. It also abetted the rise of that new
class—the bourgeoisie—that would enact the French Revolution. The
sugar trade's factories in the fields filled the northern plain. Ambitious
Saint-Dominguens—among them the colony's thirty thousand free
people of color—began planting coffee on its mountains' slopes, too;
that enterprise they spread down to Port-au-Prince and past its adjoining peaks, to the colony's southern-facing anchorage at Jacmel. But it
was on the northern plain, near Le Cap, whose plantations were home

to thousands of slaves who "live[d] together in a social relation far closer than any proletariat of the time," as C. L. R. James wrote, where the Saint-Domingue experiment both reached its brutal apogee and sowed its own undoing.[4]

* * *

AS THE 1780S PROGRESSED and profits soared, the plantations' absentee owners and their agents rushed to grow a trade that amounted, from the vantage of Bordeaux and Nantes, to printing money. The awful work of cutting cane, and of grinding its stalks in machines as likely to crush their operators' limbs, meant that it was always more efficient for the factory owners to import new adult slaves than to rear new ones. Between 1779 and 1790 alone, 400,000 Africans were unloaded at Saint-Domingue's docks. In 1789, fully 4,000 of those ships left the colony carrying sacks of coffee and sugar whose combined value—some 11 million livres worth of tropical stimulants—comprised a haul worth more than double what England gained from all its colonies combined. That this frenzied trade reached its height in the selfsame year that the Bastille's *vainqueurs* took Paris is a historical conjuncture that would grow fateful. But in Saint-Domingue, the demographics that made this frenzy whir had two key implications. One was that a mere thirty thousand whites were tasked with maintaining control—by sheer violence, or its threat—over half a million blacks. The other was that many of those blacks were not merely African born but also battle-ready veterans of the African wars whose dispensations had sent many of them here. In Saint-Domingue, those slaves also inhabited a society where, as C. L. R. James wrote, "even the food they ate was imported," and where "they lived what was in essence a modern life."[5] This latter truth was key to James's argument in *The Black Jacobins* that colonial Saint-Domingue's blacks comprised a modern proletariat—and that this was key to how and why, to his Marxist eyes, their revolt became a revolution of world-historical import. Whether or not that's so, these facts about Saint-Domingue's society were all central to the larger tale of a mass movement that began in a small clearing a few miles from Le Cap that I visited my second day in town. For this ride I sought out a moto, now emboldened to hop on its back seat and hold on to the driver's waist as we turned on to the main road from Le Cap.

Rattling past a man selling *klerin* sugar liquor from gas jugs, we turned on to a rutted track, unmarked by any sign, and soon reached a dusty glen. The glen's ground was patchy and goats munched thorns by its sides; it looked like most such clearings here except for the telling fact that its grass was shaded by a thick-trunked mapou tree that had been spared the fate of being chopped up for charcoal. By the tree's side was a little shelter that looked like a Hebrew sukkah; its roof was made from woven palm fronds and its one wall was painted with a Kreyol phrase announcing we were in *Bwa Kayiman*. There was no sign, beyond that, to announce that we were indeed on holy ground. The mapou tree's presence, though, was clue enough to this site's specialness for Haitians: they come here each year on the 14th of August to hail the place where on that date in 1791, a slave called Boukman summoned fieldhands and freedmen around a noble fire on a stormy night. From behind the tree, a spry man stepped forward to confirm that we were in the right place.

"Welcome to Bois Caiman."

The man spoke in his forebears' Kreyol but wore baggy jeans and a hand-me-down T-shirt whose Cross Colours logo recalled the streetwear era of *House Party 2*. His name was Etienne and he seemed to be the self-appointed guide and host for those rare history nerds, or travelers, who found their way here. "This is where Boukman lit his fire," he gestured around us, before walking out of the glen a ways to point at what looked like a crumbling stone aqueduct, overtaken with vines. "Sa a se pon an Ewopeyen an." This was the European bridge. "People from Morue and Macaya all crossed," Etienne explained, "to reply to Boukman's call." We turned back to the clearing, and Etienne recalled how Boukman had summoned his fellows here, to drink the blood of a pig killed by a female vodou priest, or *mambo*, named Cécile, who consecrated the potent gathering. Then he recited some famous words.

"Bondié blancs mandé crime, et part nous vlé bienfets." Etienne gazed at the mapou's top.

> mais dié là qui si bon, ordonnin nous vengeance
> Li va conduit bras nous, la ba nous assistance,

The words are some of Haiti's best known.

> The God of the whites pushes them to crime, but ours wants
>   good deeds.

That God who is so good orders us to vengeance.
He will direct our hands, give us help.[6]

This was the poem with which Boukman is said to have launched the summit-cum-ceremony held here on August 14, 1791. Of course Boukman left no written record of his speech. He was also soon killed by the fighting his words launched—what exactly he said is unknown. What isn't unknown is that a week after that first gathering, attendees of Boukman's rites effected a revolt—planned brilliantly in secret, and prosecuted with deadly efficiency—that brought down Saint-Domingue.

On the night of August 21 and the one following, slaves across the northern plain moved on their masters' homes. They torched the source of their misery, and the terrified screams of their owners launched a war whose beginning's details we know of thanks largely to a mulatto journalist from Port-au-Prince who in 1824 traveled north to record those people's memories of Haiti's revolution. It seems that Hérard Dumesle's rendering of Boukman's words, which he wrote down after that trip, were as likely born of the writer's mind as from anything he took down from an informant who was actually present at Bois Caiman in 1791. But like the Gospels of Matthew and Luke, these words' veracity and source matter less than how they've lived on. In Haiti, it's not at all uncommon to enter a conversation about current politics that ends up being a discussion of the minute details of some not-forgotten double cross or intrigue from the age of Boukman. Here where "Haitians walk in history," as one of their essential modern chroniclers put it, the tension between history as it's written and history as it's lived is ever present.[7] And as Etienne and I again reached the main clearing in Bois Caiman, my host in his Cross Colours T-shirt, accepted the crumpled bill I put in his palm and smiled farewell.

"Sa a se kote Ayiti te fèt," he said. "Out 14, 1791"—This is where Haiti was born, on August 14, 1791.

* * *

AND SO IT WAS. In a sense. The date to which historians peg Haiti's independence, and on whose anniversary Haitians eat pumpkin soup to mark it, came thirteen years after Boukman's fire. It was on January 1, 1804, at the end of a very long and bloody and complex war, that General Jean-Jacques Dessalines constituted a new state whose name was borrowed from the Taino. The war at whose end he did so had not only pitted Dessalines and comrades like his mentor, Toussaint L'Ouverture, against successive invasions by the French and Spanish and English, but also against each other. It finally ended with Haiti's founding, in 1804. But Etienne's assertion wasn't inaccurate, either.

For it was perhaps at Bois Caiman that the *nation* of Haiti—the larger community forged with the Kreyol melding of French vocabulary to Fon syntax and through a vodou faith that joined the gods of Kongo and Dahomey into a new pantheon—was born. The thirteen-year gap between 1791 and 1804 contained dramas that have haunted Haiti since, and that shaped a core conflict in its politics that the Haitian anthropologist Michel-Rolph Trouillot described in an essential book on Haitian history called *Haiti, State Against Nation*.[8]

The tension between state and nation, or at least the related conflict between city elites and the countryside's black masses, was implanted here during colonial days. It was the makers of Haiti's revolution who James called the Black Jacobins, but the first claimants to the Jacobin mantle here, after the Bastille's storming, were neither plantation slaves nor Maroon runaways. They were free *gens de couleur*—offspring of French masters' liaisons with their chattel, or manumitted blacks—who invoked the First Republic's new rhetoric, from Paris, to demand that they be accorded rights equal to those enjoyed by Saint-Domingue's whites. They sought an end to rules in the colony that banned them from, among other things, wearing sabers and practicing law. Had their demands been met more readily, many of Saint-Domingue's owners later agreed, the fire among their slaves might have been slower to spark. But the "mulattoes" were denied full satisfaction. And with Republican rhetoric circulating throughout the colony, there soon arrived a revolt of people "seeking their salvation in the most obvious way," as James put it, "[by destroying] what they knew was the cause of their sufferings."[9]

The violence provoked by that suffering, when it came, was total. It had to be. Here, after all, was a system of exploitation wherein slaves who dared eat in the fields were fitted with muzzles and where those who ran away had their hamstrings severed. Moreau de Saint-Méry, the crucial firsthand chronicler of daily life in old Saint-Domingue, described a country in which a specialized freelance profession developed, whereby crueler Frenchmen sold their ability to mete out depraved punishments on troublesome slaves for a fixed schedule of fees. Their services ranged from simple brandings or cutting off ears to performing more baroque experiments with gunpowder and sodomy. A simple hanging cost thirty pounds, but the planter wanting to make a more grisly example in his yard, and willing to part with sixty *livres*, could have a slave slowly burned at the stake. After the once-enslaved torched the fields, France tried mightily—notably when Napoleon determined to reinstate slavery in the Antilles, in 1801, and sent forty thousand troops to do so—to enslave them again. But long before then, something had clicked. The revolt destroyed forever the "kind of magic," said one exiled planter, "that made it so that three or four whites could sleep in complete security with their doors open on a property on which there were four or five hundred blacks."[10] That sudden shift—on the part of half a million slaves in the New World's most lucrative colony—is the primal fact, and starting point, of a stunning historical drama. The political story of how its initial revolt's makers came to frame their aims around the ideals of Robespierre and Raynal, and to help form the first and only worldly nation created by its slaves, is one of deep intrigue and vast historical import.

That tale's great protagonist is the ex-slave who united Boukman's motley bands into a potent army that, by late 1793, controlled much of Hispaniola's west. Toussaint Breda had been born a slave on a plantation near Le Cap. He was the son, according to apt legend if hazy record, of an Arara prince who'd been sold away from Dahomey after his own father lost at war. Toussaint was a coachman and lettered member of the colony's servant class. He was also, by 1791, a free man who owned his own slave. He joined Boukman's revolt a few weeks after its start, but then built his army's power through a strategic alliance with the Spanish, who shared his aim of weakening the French, and whose guns and powder helped Toussaint build a force that convinced the French Republican general Léger-Félicité Sonthonax to declare, in August 1793, the end of slavery in Saint-Domingue. That winter, the colony's new legation to the National Convention in France—a white Republican, a "yellow" man of mixed race, and a black ex-slave—went to Paris to convince Sonthonax's political bosses to follow suit, and free the slaves in all of France's colonies. They urged a willing convention to extend the rights and responsibilities of French citizenship to all persons, everywhere, whom "the tricolor flag [had] called to liberty."[11] And the convention, to rapt cheers and in what comprised a stunning step forward for both the idea and the upholding of universal human rights, agreed. Slavery, in February 1794, was outlawed throughout the French Empire.

By then Toussaint had acquired the nom-de-guerre L'Ouverture, which referred either to his gift for always finding an opening or, say other accounts, to the opening between his front teeth. Short and homely with bowed legs, he crisscrossed Saint-Domingue by thorough-bred, riding a hundred miles a day by switching among a network of steeds and turning up wherever his people, who called him "the Cen-taur," needed him. Early on, he'd issued an assurance to them—"I want Liberty and Equality to reign in St Domingue, [and] I am working to make that happen" and they believed him until his end.[12] He cut his ties with Spain, whose guns and powder he kept but whose help he no longer needed, to raise the tricolor over a still-French colony of which Sonthonax and his Republican colleagues, in 1796, soon made Tous-saint both the titular and military head. French Republicans appreci-ated him as an ally both in the fight against the royalists and in the fight for "nature's liberty" everywhere. But Toussaint was also a firm leader; when the radical French general Sonthonax—who became a fierce advocate for black rights—grew too outspoken on the blacks' behalf, and against the old planters whom Toussaint aimed to placate, too, Toussaint ordered his friend home to France. (Sonthonax as a kind of proto-wigger who wed a *mulâtresse* and claimed his dearest hope was to be reborn a black, had taken to urging Toussaint simply to massacre Saint-Domingue's old masters, and be done with it.)

* * *

HE WAS ABLE TO DO all this while not merely quoting from Abbé Raynal's discourse on liberty, but retaining the support of his island's masses. Toussaint also succeeded—mostly—in keeping a lid on the fierce rivalries among and between those masses' various leaders and a so-called mulatto class, whose interests and aims, signaled by their repeated rebellions and assertions of right, were not always in concert with his own. Raynal had written, in his description of how "nature's liberty" would be implanted and upheld across the world, that "[a] cou-rageous chief only is wanted." The Lumières' abbot asked, "Where is he, that great man whom Nature owes to her vexed, oppressed, and tormented children?"[13] Toussaint L'Ouverture was that man, judged contemporary admirers ranging from Wordsworth to the important French abolitionist Victor Schoelcher, who also became Toussaint's first biographer. And this is what C. L. R. James, over the course of what remains the classic narrative of Toussaint's life in the context of his time, also spelled out: "No single figure [has] appeared on the historical stage more greatly gifted than this Negro."[14] The claim sounds like typical Jamesian hyperbole. But it was more than borne out by James's account in *The Black Jacobins*, a book not merely attuned to the hamartia of Toussaint's tale, but also animated by the topical interest of a Pan-African Trotskyist's concern to understand, as the old colonies of Africa and the West Indies crept toward freedom in the middle of the twentieth century, when he wrote it, how and why Saint-Domingue's slaves were able to "throw up the leaders they needed in [such] profusion."[15] James was concerned to explain how and why Toussaint proved so specially able to "incarnate the determination of his people never, never to be slaves again." He did so by narrating for all time how Toussaint's was a political talent of genius—and by showing how his tragedy was that of a proud black man who was also proudly French.[16] Toussaint's gifts as a leader relied on his troops' love and his people's faith. But his skill as a rhetorician and the fineness of his mind were perhaps best glimpsed in the oath he composed and sent to Paris, amid the tumult of 1797 and as the forces unleashed by the French Revolution threatened to implode it. Toussaint swore, to Vaublanc's new Directory and even as he faced huge challenges at home, to continue honoring "those arms, which France confided to me, for the defence of its rights and those of humanity."[17]

* * *

FOR SEVEN-PLUS YEARS Toussaint upheld his oath. He retained control of Saint-Domingue for France and emancipated its blacks. He fought off and outmaneuvered the invading English (with whom he signed a treaty promising not to export revolt to their islands) and bested the Spanish (whose portion of Hispaniola he also took over, in 1801). He shared power with varied configurations of French generals, contending with periodic disquiet from the ex-slaves and with open revolt from so-called mulattoes whose grip over Saint-Domingue's south, and whose resentment of its black generals, would long bedevil its unity. Toussaint performed the political balancing acts of a leader of free people in a place that wasn't. And he did so in the context of a society whose very social structure, and very existence, was built to the end of growing unnutritious foodstuffs for export.

He concluded that maintaining the nation's old economic base—growing sugar—was crucial to its viability. This now looks like a misstep. When he directed ex-slaves to cut sugarcane for pay, under forced threat if they refused, he met with the same ultimate result as all such attempts, by Haitian leaders after him, to relaunch the sugar trade: he failed. (Coffee was and remains another story: it's still grown here, and brewed into blue-black sludge that remains a deep, tasty pleasure on Haitian mornings.) Even in Toussaint's day, what these ex-slaves began to do on their old plantations was to set up communal farms devoted to growing not sugar but food. They built new social structures based around what the Haitian sociologist Jean Casimir has called the "counter-plantation system," forging the fierce and lasting will of a peasant nation determined not merely never to be slaves again, but also to be able to shape its collective life.[18] And this they did, from the early 1800s on, against the dictates of the Haitian state that has perhaps never again been blessed, as the student of Haitian history quickly learns, with a leader equaling its progenitor's sagacious talent.

Many of Toussaint's modern admirers may now recall him as an uncompromising icon of black freedom. Many may not know that part of why he attracted many white fans in his own day ("Toussaint, the most unhappy of men!" began Wordsworth's eponymous sonnet from 1802),[19] was the well-known fact that before he joined Boukman's rebels, Toussaint ensured that his own old plantation's owners were safely out of the colony. He also advocated for bringing other plantation owners back to Saint-Domingue, in the interest of know-how, as part of his effort to relaunch its sugar trade. Whether these decisions attest to his apologism for Haiti's old masters or his deeper humanism or both, they also speak to the challenges he faced in shepherding a revolution that was centuries ahead of its time. The dynamics informing Toussaint's rise and the context in which he sought to govern shaped the contradictions faced by Haitian leaders who came after. For example, he embraced French as his government's official language, even though it wasn't spoken by 90 percent of its people, whose lingua franca, then as now, was Kreyol. He was also a committed Catholic, who failed to appreciate the importance of vodou to his people and how the ancestral memory that informed their faith's rites—"the memory of Africa; unity against a cruel and hostile world; survival," in one sensitive observer's words[20]—was intrinsic to how they sought in their revolution to remake their world. Vodou formed the ineluctable core of a place where flag-bedecked *houmfort* temples still dot the landscape today, and where on the Day of the Dead cemeteries are full of people who've been "mounted"—possessed—by vodou's black-suited *lwa* of the graveyard, Baron Samedi.

Haiti is a country where at a party a saucy flirt may berate you for having ignored her for years, even though you've never met her, prompting a friend's explanation that "that's just Erzulie Fredá"—the jealous *lwa* of femininity and compassion who's liable, at any time, to inhabit any of her daughters. It's a country where, when riding a moto into the hills above Jacmel on a moonlit night, you may find a mountain clearing where a convivial group is gathered around an aluminum pot, full of goat parts being cooked for the genial and hungry *lwa* of the harvest, Azaka Medeh, who has in exchange mounted a man who bucks and sways to the sharp tones of the *maman* drums. It's also a country where as you coast downhill in the moonlight from that feast, what looks like someone's dropped cell phone, glowing by the road, will prompt your friend on his moto to ask: "Did you see that?" A query to which you might reply that, yes, you had, and that it looked like a cell phone, before being corrected by your friend who'll insist, "No man—that was a jumbie," in a tone sufficient to impress you with the basic truth that Haiti is a place where jumbie sprites, to say nothing of far more potent *lwas* who reside beneath the sea and connect every Haitian to An Guinée—Africa—are very alive to those who believe they are, and as such are crucial to public and private life.

Toussaint L'Ouverture was a man of the Enlightenment and of science. That he disavowed much of the spiritual life of his people, as they sought to connect their past to their present while imagining their future, was in keeping with his values. But Toussaint's ultimate tragedy, as a man who sought freedom with the best that France had to offer, was his betrayal by France—or, rather, by the French figure against whom he would have to battle, and of whom C. L. R. James wrote "not Shakespeare himself could have found such an embodiment of fate."[21] Napoleon's counter-revolution took Paris in 1800, and Napoleon made re-instituting slavery central to his imperial policy. He swore "not [to] rest until I have torn the epaulettes off every negre in the colonies," and dispatched a huge force to the Antilles.[22] The force was helmed by his brother-in-law, Charles Leclerc, who was entrusted with "ridding us of these gilded negroes." Leclerc's orders were to make quick work of that task in Saint-Domingue, and then continue on to New Orleans. He was to tighten the empire's grip on Louisiana, too.[23] He sailed with his wife, Pauline, and all the chefs and jesters he'd need overseas to establish a new imperial court.

Leclerc's orders were based on racist presumptions that these "gilded negroes" were hopelessly inept at statecraft, and that their hold on power would necessarily be tenuous. His men were able, in Saint-Domingue, to seize some towns and plantations. They also managed to co-opt some of Toussaint's generals—by offering to make them French officers instead. But Leclerc's forces also suffered many defeats, and ceaseless harassment from Toussaint's soldiers and his subjects. Leclerc wrote his brother-in-law; "[w]e have in Europe a false idea of the country in which we fight, and of the men we fight against."[24] The rainy season came, and yellow fever ripped his ranks; the disease would soon claim Leclerc himself. But Toussaint seemed unable, for reasons that touch the core of his enigma, to believe what these exponents of Republican France, however degraded, were here to do. He didn't press the advantage, or seem to realize that a force of this size could have but one purpose. That purpose would be proved that summer in Guadeloupe. There, Leclerc's comrade Antoine Richepanse brutally restored slavery to the French Lesser Antilles. Still Toussaint chose, for reasons his biographers have argued about since, and in what James called the one emergency "in his political life . . . which he failed to meet with action bold and correct," to ride into town to meet Leclerc. He agreed, there, to "cease hostilities."[25]

In exchange, Leclerc told Toussaint that he and his generals would be allowed to keep their epaulettes, and their ranks. No sooner did Toussaint return to his farm outside Le Cap, and settle in, than did imperial troops turn up to slap him with chains. Loading Toussaint onto a boat bound for France, the ill Leclerc sent a letter with his prisoner, in one of his last acts before dying, advising Napoleon that "you cannot keep Toussaint at too great a distance from the sea, or keep him too safe."[26] Toussaint was placed in a frigid fortress in the Jura Mountains. He wrote beseeching letters to his deaf captor, insisting to Napoleon, "I have had the misfortune to incur your anger; but as to fidelity and probity, I am strong in my conscience, and I dare to say with truth that among all the servants of the State none is more honest than I."[27] He endured a terrible winter during which he was denied blankets and care. And on the seventh of April, 1803, despite the protestations of Wordsworth and other admirers in Europe who urged he be freed, Toussaint died.

That same week in Saint-Domingue, Toussaint's brave lieutenant Jean-Jacques Dessalines set their people on the course—toward independence—that they now craved.

* * *

TODAY IN HAITI Dessalines's likeness and name are even more common than Toussaint's: it was Dessalines, a leader as fiercely incisive as his mentor was sage, who in that spring of 1803 ripped the white strip from France's tricolor to make a new red and blue standard that, erasing the stain of whiteness on his country, remains the basis of Haiti's flag today.

Where here a common image of Toussaint depicts a noble horseman, carrying a roll of parchment, Dessalines's likeness usually finds him wearing a bicorn hat and standing erect, ever ready for battle. Dessalines is as imposing, on his two upright feet, as Toussaint is on his steed. He's the man, from history and in Haiti's mind, who does the violence that needs doing. The prosecutor of famous campaigns against both the mulattoes of the south and the French, Dessalines became the leader, after Toussaint's arrest, who fought off the empire's last charge— and ordered his men to kill all the whites they could find. He was a leader unschooled in books but his force of will and its entwinement with "the masses" was at the key moment decisive, as he declared the revolution's final victory: "Peace to our neighbors. But anathema to the French name," proclaimed Dessalines. "Hatred eternal to France. This is our cry."[28]

The sentiment was as blunt as the phrasing. But Dessalines was the leader that the final crisis demanded. The reason why, and his difference from his mentor, was described by C. L. R. James:

> If Dessalines could see so clearly and simply, it was because the ties that bound this uneducated soldier to French civilization were of the slenderest. He saw what was under his nose so well because he saw no further. Toussaint's failure was the failure of enlightenment, not of darkness.[29]

A year later, in 1804, Dessalines declared himself Haiti's emperor. His reign didn't last long. The same imperious will that helped him to power, once gained, perhaps fed his undoing. Dessalines was ambushed by his own lieutenants in ways that would become familiar here after less than two years in power. He was killed and dismembered by men who'd learned such brutality from the fierce campaign he himself had ordered against Haiti's *blans*. The father of the Haitian nation was martyred by infighting. But Dessalines's sundered body parts were gathered for proper burial, says the pregnant legend, by a now-famous woman named Défilée: he won a place in Haitians' hearts as a figure of not merely historic but spiritual magnitude. Dessalines found his way into the vodou pantheon. He's the *lwa* known here to vodouisants as "Ogou Dessalines." In his death's immediate wake, though, Haiti's rule was left to be fought over by the light-skinned southern officer who had led the plot to bring Dessalines down—Alexandre Pétion—and another of his ex-colleagues in Toussaint's corps of generals: the Le Cap waiter turned trusted Toussaint deputy, Henri Christophe. I went to visit Christophe's base of power with my gruff Aussie confrere, before leaving Le Cap.

* * *

ON A CLEAR DAY Christophe's citadel is visible from all over the northern plain. It looks like a prow-shaped rock sprouting from its green peak, three thousand feet up, menacing in the Haitian sky. An edifice that's as much symbol as garrison, the Citadel was built by thousands of Christophe's workers who hauled tons of stone, some of it salvaged from burned plantations, uphill. The man who ordered this construction was a king who holds his own vexed place in the mythography of Haiti, after beginning his career as a maître d' at his master's inn in Le Cap. Five miles outside town, we reached the hamlet of Milot, where at the base of the Citadel's mountain Christophe also built a grand palace that he conceived, a brief decade after Haiti won its independence, as a shrine to living *sans* pain.

He did so at a time when the country was wracked by civil war, divided between a southern part run by Pétion and the northern part of which Christophe declared himself not merely king but also "Destroyer of tyranny, Regenerator and benefactor of the Haitian nation, Creator of its moral, political and military institutions."[30]

Christophe was nothing if not imaginative. He was driven by his own flair both for theater and for a quirky brand of royalist antiracism. He believed deeply in the worldly virtue, and benefit for his Haiti, of his becoming "the first monarch crowned in the New World." He enjoyed a warm correspondence with leading English abolitionists like Thomas Clarkson. He wrote letters to fellow monarchs like Russia's emperor Alexander, to whom he insisted that "too long has the African race been unjustly calumniated."[31] He set up his kingdom with nobles and crests for families of all colors and he modeled his court's symbols less on Revolutionary France than on a mélange of manners borrowed from *ancien* aristocrats, African myth, and the indigenous Taino (with whose own bygone chiefs he claimed a dubious kinship, too). The retinue of Christophe and his queen included a corps of maidens dubbed the Society of Amazons, a royal police force known as the Royal Dahomets, and a personal guard unit for the king known, more or less solemnly, as the Royal Bonbons. But the signal symbol of Christophe's regal affections was the palace that the Aussie and I reached by the tap-tap we'd caught in town, at the end of the road to Milot. Sans-Souci may now be in ruins—it was mostly destroyed by an earthquake in 1842. But the grand palace's still-standing columns and graceful arches are still so impressive as to be moving, rising from the valley in a baroque rebuttal to what Christophe described as the world's outmoded notion that his race "was scarcely susceptible of civilization."[32]

Christophe has often been recalled, by modern commentators, as a buffoonish trader in ersatz glitz: Aimé Césaire, in his 1963 play *La tragedie du Roi Christophe*, offered an unflattering portrait of a deluded regent. And certainly Christophe's pharaonic ambition fed the outsized scale and aims of the great fortress he built atop a peak behind his palace. But he was hardly the first or last Haitian leader who saw fit, with ample reason, to devote a huge portion of Haiti's treasure to defense. He led a nation whose sovereignty had yet to be recognized by France or the United States (which wouldn't do so until the 1860s), and a country, as a prominent group of its exiled slave owners threateningly put it, "whose existence is shameful for all colonial governments."[33]

Haiti became a symbol, in early nineteenth-century Paris, of Jacobin excess and of all that needed reeling back in. For much of the rest of the white world, it was a risible anomaly, unworthy of respect. Christophe had every reason, as did his rival Pétion and generations of Haitian leaders to come, to fear foreign invasion. Hence his obsession with an impregnable fortress that could withstand and provide for a prolonged siege. And impregnable indeed the Citadel looked, amid wispy clouds, as the Aussie and I trudged uphill with a strapping fellow who'd attached himself to us, at the start of the road up from Sans-Souci, as our self-appointed guide. About accepting his services, there wasn't a choice: the Citadel's approaches seemed to be controlled by a local cartel of guides who took turns showing visitors uphill, for a modest fee. The imposing man wore new Nikes and the prepossessing air of someone with access to foreign cash or local power. Down by Sans-Souci, he had summoned three young moto drivers with a quick flick of his hand, who'd bumped over on their Hao Jins from across the glen, and bid us hop on. We wound uphill for twenty-five minutes, before they deposited us at the place in the road, a couple of miles up, beyond which all traffic, save on horse or foot, was banned.

Now we trudged up the cobbled path, followed by a retinue of kids leading ponies with threadbare ropes. Their hope was that we *blans*, upon realizing the route's steepness, might accept a ride. It was only after we'd been hiking for a mile, and as the dark walls of Christophe's citadel emerged from the clouds, that they peeled off. We entered the cool damp of those walls, twenty feet thick and even more imposing from up close than afar, and wandered its eerie ramparts. Unlike most sites declared human patrimony by UNESCO, this was a historic relic not refitted for tourists. No safety rails lined the cliff-like edges of the Citadel's outer walls. Staying well back from the edge, I inspected knee-high piles of iron balls—pyramids of cannon shot that had been placed here at the ready, it seemed, in Christophe's day. We passed the great hall for ammunition, where, after lightning struck the building and its gunpowder in 1818, a huge explosion damaged one of the fort's walls and killed many of Christophe's men. And then we found the covered keep in the fort's center where the king himself lies interred. When Christophe's own soldiers decided that they no longer wanted a king in 1820, and launched a revolt that saw Christophe surrounded by rivals in his palace down the hill, he turned a pistol on himself.

After Christophe's demise, Pétion's successor in the south, Jean-Pierre Boyer, quickly retook the north. Boyer was a mulatto officer like his predecessor, who'd briefly sided with Napoleon's General Leclerc during the revolution. But it was under him that a reunited Haiti took its lasting form, and gained most of the characteristics that have defined its politics ever since: the trappings of constitutional democracy but effective rule by a lighter-skinned merchant elite; the firming up of Port-au-Prince as undisputed capital; an autocratic president whose power derived from, and depended on, the allegiance of his troops—all these traits, inchoate when Boyer took office, would be concentrated during the remarkable twenty-five years, between 1818 and 1843, in which he retained power. His regime's form would be replicated and perpetuated in basic outline, if usually for far briefer duration, by dozens of successors. But Boyer's most concrete legacy derived from his agreeing, in 1825, to accept a fateful royal decree from France whose form—it suggested that "the French part of Saint-Domingue" still belonged to Paris—was as telling as its content.

The decree to which Boyer agreed dictated that his government pay an indemnity of 150 million francs, in recompense for what France's economy had lost to Haiti's revolution. In exchange, France would finally recognize Haiti's independence. But the massive debt Boyer thus contracted—which he began tending immediately, by taking out a loan for thirty million francs, from a French bank that charged a fee of six million additional francs just to issue it to Haiti, on top of a compound interest rate of 6 percent—would be one Haitians would pay for generations.

Today the names of Toussaint and Dessalines, Christophe and Boyer and Pétion still haunt Haiti's public life. They're synonymous with contending ideas, and qualities and actions, in a country whose singular birth presaged its stormy adolescence and the forging of a singular political vocabulary. Over the stormy course of Haiti's story since its founding, and especially in the decades after Boyer's death, the dizzying procession of colonels and merchants and policemen who gained power, whether by electoral chicanery or coup d'état, gave rise to a set of only-in-Haiti expressions ranging from *politique de doublure* (the common practice of the lighter-skinned elite emplacing a dark-skinned leader in power to resemble the majority's phenotype while enforcing minority interests); to *dechoukay* (whose literal meaning in Kreyol— "to uproot"—implies the necessity, after deposing an unwanted leader, of also eliminating his power base); to *parenthèse* (the period after one leader has been deposed but before a new one ascends to power, often typified by violent tumult).

* * *

TWO CENTURIES OF HAITI'S history have passed since Toussaint read his Raynal. And still a surprise was in store for us as we walked down from the Citadel with our guide in his Nikes.

I asked him who had restored the well-done cobbled road we were striding down, to meet up with the moto men. His reply's implication was less than genial.

"The president," he said. "The *best* president."

It was clear he didn't mean the current one. I took his bait. "Who was that?"

His voice grew forceful as he leapt downhill. "Duvalier."

This would have been scandalous a few years before. It still was now, to a visitor whose first exposure to Haiti as news, and as history, was framed by the news, back in 1986, that the Duvaliers' brutal tyranny had slunk to its end. I recalled reading of that dim morning in 1986 when Jean-Claude "Baby Doc" Duvalier rolled onto a tarmac at the airport in Port-au-Prince, with his glamorous wife, Michèle, and her ill-gotten furs, to flee the country, amid cheers from Haitians and from haters of tyranny everywhere. I could think of only one reason for our guide's sentiment. But the question "Were you, or maybe more likely your dad, a Tonton Macoute?" wasn't one that it felt wise to ask. The Tonton Macoutes were the Duvaliers' militia, answerable to the dictatorship and not to the thousands across the country they tortured or killed during its reign. The Macoutes were named for a scary character in Haitian folklore who steals kids from their homes, when they're naughty or otherwise, in a sack. Their name, to most Haitians I knew in the United States and here, was synonymous with devilry and fear. Yet there are nearly as many Haitians today who have personal ties to the Macoutes—the militia's hierarchy involved upward of 300,000 people—as who lost relatives to them. Our guide's seeming openness about his ties, nonetheless, surprised me into silence.

What he'd said about the road was shocking, too. Perhaps it shouldn't have been. The Duvaliers were far better known for directing Haiti's ducats to their own Swiss bank accounts than for tending its infrastructure, much less building roads. But Papa Doc's interest in Christophe's fort, which is to say in Haitian grandeur, made sense. Duvalier, before he became a dictator, won popular support as a dark-skinned rebuke to the *politique de doublure*. He was a country doctor who espoused the *noiriste* school of ethnology, which valorized the African ways and proud history of Haiti's masses. He drew many Macoutes from the ranks of their vodou houngans. He evinced their affinities by fashioning himself in the black bowler hat and dark suit of Baron Samedi. But even before and then especially after Papa Doc declared "I am an immaterial being," in 1962, he visited unconscionable pain on his people—and then he passed his power, in what seemed a final cruelty, to his idiot son. Duvalier *fils* was a chubby nineteen-year-old when he took over from his dad in 1971, with the Macoutes on his side. But then in 1986, amid a resurgent movement against Baby Doc's repression, innocent students in the northern town of Gonaïves were killed, sparking the groundswell. Foes like the popular priest Jean-Bertrand Aristide urged Haitians "to send the devil from here!": they eventually succeeded in sending Baby Doc and his wife away on that early-morning plane. His departure, for the liberal patriots for whom his reign had been hell and for foreign observers, was supposed to herald Haiti's dawn. It would have been hard to imagine anyone casually praising Duvalier in public in the late '80s and '90s, especially to a foreign visitor. But times, as my maybe-Macoute guide's utterance showed, had changed. And so had the Duvaliers' reputation, over the thirty often-chaotic years since Baby Doc's flight.

In fact, as we walked sweatily down the mountain, Jean-Claude Duvalier wasn't very far away at all. He was living peacefully, astonishingly, in the hills of Pétionville near the capital. He'd been allowed to return to Haiti, in January 2011 and after twenty-five years in exile, a development that those who'd fought for his flight could scarcely fathom. When Baby Doc stepped back onto the tarmac whence he and Michèle had fled, the old dictator looked hollow-eyed and far thinner than he once was. Newly arrived from Switzerland, he was zombie-like. But even stranger than Duvalier's presence in Pétionville now was the fact that he'd been joined, two months after his return, by another once-exiled leader, the man who was supposed to redeem Duvalier's abuses.

Jean-Bertrand Aristide was elected by a landslide in 1990. He was a parish priest from the Port-au-Prince slums, a tiny man who espoused the theology of liberation to emerge as Duvalier's most eloquent foe. His election came on the heels of a new constitution that made Kreyol an official language of the state for the first time. It signaled the rise of a leader who truly represented the concerns of the poor. But scarcely eight months after his election, Aristide was deposed by a military coup, before being restored to power by Bill Clinton and the U.S. Marines three years later. He was elected to the presidency again in 2000, amid allegations of fraud, but was then removed from the country, under fishy circumstances and perhaps with help from a United States now wearied of his erratic populism, in 2004. And now his saga had come to a bizarre end. Aristide had returned to Haiti, like Duvalier, under the condition that he'd remain out of public life. He now lived squirreled

away in a complex near the airport. He is now a complicated and compromised figure, as likely to be associated by young Haitians with street
gangs from the slums he once ran, whose guns are rumored to have
been provided by his party, as with the fight for freedom.

The whirligig of Haiti's history continues. All of this, as we descended
from the Citadel, perhaps helped explain my maybe-Macoute guide's
praise for Duvalier. For as much as Haiti remains in a post-Duvalier
age, it has entered a fuzzy post-Aristide age as well. Its leader in 2014
was a former carnival crooner turned neocon hack named Michel Martelly, who had made a show of reviving such old Duvalierist traditions
as the Carnival of Flowers—and had perhaps encouraged the country's
hidden right wing, after the awful earthquake in whose wake he took
power, to emerge from hiding.

Or so I pondered, anyway, as we continued down from Christophe's
citadel in silence.

CHAPTER 10

HAITI CHERIE

THREE HUNDRED THOUSAND, and likely more. That's how many perished when North America's continental crust slid into the Caribbean plate, where their friction has long shaped Haiti's peaks, and crunched forward to release a roiling pair of temblors that lifted Port-au-Prince with a start, in the soft light of a late tropical afternoon, and then, giving her a rough shake, laid her flat. In a country where building codes aren't even a rumor and streetwise builders mix their concrete mostly with sand and dispense with rebar altogether, the homes and habitations of most of this city's three million people stood no chance. The quake that measured 7.0 on the Richter scale rendered their black metropolis, as the sun set on the 12th day of January 2010, into smoking rubble. Those not buried wandered dazed through the debris, hunting loved ones or decrying the fates. The nation was bloodied. The shape of the state was suggested by the condition of its symbol—the proud domes of the vodou-white National Palace. The palace lay crumpled in two, destroyed, like a collapsed wedding cake.

The terrible aftermath of the earthquake—whose strength was comparable to the famous 1989 San Francisco seism that messed up the Bay Bridge but killed only sixty-three people—resulted in a spate of international intervention: the 82nd Airborne flew in the next day, and quickly took control of the airport; UNICEF and Oxfam and Save the Children and the Red Cross raised funds to address the disaster; "helping Haiti" became the cause du jour for soul-saving preachers and multinational corporations alike. The Church of Scientology sent a plane, owned by John Travolta, full of food and disciples intent on "touching people through their clothes." Haiti became the site, once again, for many of the world's most privileged to try, through donations or delusions, to balance their moral checkbooks. Amid this frenzy of humanitarian assistance, the country's ineffectual president, René Préval, was largely sidelined.[1] The leadership of the "recovery commission" was handed over to Bill Clinton, who had the distinction of being loathed by many Haitians across the political spectrum. His own investment in Haiti, moral and otherwise, perhaps derived from all the ways he'd mucked the place up as president. It was Clinton who'd sent in the Marines to restore Aristide to power, before forcing him to accept an economic policy that required Haiti to import cheap U.S.-grown rice from Arkansas, undercutting Haitian producers and harming the country's ability to feed itself. Clinton was now in charge of a recovery effort whose ideology and agenda "made the country sound like some place entirely outside the West," as the historian Laurent Dubois noted, rather "than as a place whose history has been deeply intertwined with that of Europe and the United States for three centuries."[2]

Within a year of the quake, it was clear even to Clinton's people that this new effort to "build Haiti back better," as the president put it, would result in disappointment. The work of many determined people, Haitians and foreigners, to help victims of the earthquake was hindered by the fact that only a mere fraction of the $10 billion in aid promised to Haiti, by governments worldwide, had actually come through. Five billion dollars were actually raised but too little reached the sufferers of the disaster. Two years after the quake, when I first visited Port-au-Prince, a half-million people here were still living in tents; some fifty thousand were bunking on the old Pétionville golf course under tarps, even as the gonzo, bleeding-heart paternalism of actor-turned-aid-worker Sean Penn, the administrator of that camp, was in full bloom.

Now, three years later, as I flew down to the capital in time for the quake's fifth anniversary, both Clinton and Penn—not to mention the once outsized flow of donations from abroad—were gone. And leading the country was an unprepossessing politician named Michel "Sweet Micky" Martelly. I went to see him preside, on a parched hillside outside the city, over the country's somber commemoration of the calamity of 2010.

* * *

TITANYEN LIES PAST the airport north of town. It's a sprawl of sloping wasteland creeping up the Morne Cabrit, whose desolation fits its historic reputation in the capital—as the place where bodies are dumped. Port-au-Prince has always had its share of corpses, and among those buried here are the victims of Duvalier's torturers in Fort Dimanche, and nameless kids, more recently, who've managed through hubris or bad luck to cross one of the gangs who run the poor *bidonvilles* nearby. After the quake, it was only natural that this would be the place where many of the dumptrucks conveying corpses from town brought their grisly cargo—and where now the government had chosen, atop the bleached-white pebbles of a mass grave, to erect its official memorial to the dead. An odd little structure of welded steel pipes, the memorial resembled a bit of scaffolding arching over a boulder onto which is bolted a little bronze plaque. In Kreyol, it reads "12 Janvye—Nou Pap Janm Bliye": January 12—We'll never forget.

This memorial and the mass grave for 150,000 or so bodies that it marks hadn't been the sole additions to Titanyen's landscape. The area had also become a complex of new settlements, with aptly Old Testament names like Canaan and Jerusalem, for hundreds of thousands of people who had lived for months after the quake in tents in the capital's parks or by its boulevards, and who now had either been forcibly removed or paid a pittance to repair miles away. This was the place, on a blinding bright morning five years after Haiti's worst day, where I stood to watch a staggered progression of rolling land-tanks that bespeak power in Haiti—hulking Toyota 4Runners or Nissan Patrols, their windows tinted black—wend its way across the barren plain. The vehicles turned upward off the road and up a boulder-strewn track to the memorial site to disgorge the well-starched members of the diplomatic corps, from the EU to Canada and Washington, and the representatives of the larger world NGOs, from Oxfam to UNICEF and the Red Cross.

A hundred or so people in blinding-white T-shirts cheered, as one black SUV eased up the hill and stopped. A dark-suited attendant opened a rear door for a light brown man with a shiny shaved head to hop down. He wore a starched white guayabera, and hailed the crowd as it unfurled a banner: "Prezidan Martelly Nou Avéw Toutian" (President Martelly We're Always With You). The man touched the hands of his paid admirers. Haiti's president wore a half smile more dutiful than joyous as he waved and pressed his hand to his chest, at once trying to project the happy-go-lucky vibe that won him power and to grant this occasion a solemnity belying the political crisis he was now facing. Michel Martelly brushed past where I stood to press the palms of other

dignitaries. He found his place in the front row of folding chairs that
had been set up, for the days' attendees, beneath a flimsy white tent that
would threaten, more than once as the windy ceremony progressed, to
fall on their heads.

Prezidan Martelly will always be known to Haitians as Sweet Micky—
the *konpa* crooner who wore MC Hammer pants on his old album covers and who flashes a giddy grin, in a hundred photos still circling the
internet, as he grinds lewdly with some lady admirer onstage. In the
late 1990s, Martelly recorded a song called "Prezidan" that became a
top carnival hit. His song about how what Haiti needed was to elect a
konpa singer president, when he made it, seemed tongue-in-cheek. But
when a decade later his traumatized country went to the polls to choose
a leader to replace René Preval, the liberal but ineffectual rum-drunk
who'd been intimidated by the worldly glare of the "international community" after the earthquake, Martelly's joke was no longer a laughing
matter.

The odd campaign from which he emerged victorious also featured
an abortive candidacy by another famous musician. Wyclef Jean, the
New Jersey–bred rapper-impresario left Haiti as a kid and grew famous
as the head of the late '90s hip-hop supergroup the Fugees that he
built around the talents of Miss Lauryn Hill. But this CV didn't help
him among Haitians, who loved mocking Wyclef's busted-up émigré
Kreyol. Martelly's main foe was the soberly progressive but unexciting
Mirlande Manigat, the schoolmarm candidate who would have seemed
the natural choice for sincere Haitian patriots and peasants. But, as one
friend told me, Sweet Micky "made people move their waists, where
others made them merely nod." That, and the fact that he'd plainly
managed, from his longtime home near Miami, to pull to his cause certain key businessmen and key figures in the U.S. embassy and in Hillary
Clinton's State Department, allowed him to emerge from an election
that required much more than receiving the most votes to win. The
election's results and legitimacy were contested, as is typical in Haiti, by
all involved except the victor. Martelly, since his election, had revealed
few clear policies—his leanings were vaguely right-wing—but had evidenced incompetence and a fondness for crony corruption. His term
had been a mixed bag of modest expectations, and even more modest achievement, which after five years was now set to reach its climax.
At midnight on the anniversary of the quake, the country's senate was
due to be dissolved. When it was, Martelly—who'd been engaged in a
months-long dispute with political foes about how and when to sched-

ule new elections—would begin ruling by decree. In recent days protesters had been burning tires in the capital's streets to demand new
elections. But whether they liked it or not, Haiti's executive branch
was set to become its government; the *konpa* singer, like the Duvaliers
before him, would become the Haitian state.

If the president was concerned about all this at Titanyen, it didn't
show. (To many of us here it was unclear whether "midnight on January
12" meant that the parliament had been dissolved the night before or
would be that night.) Martelly looked serene in his chair. Haiti's official
memorial for the earthquake's dead commenced with benedictions from
three representatives of the cloth. The first was a bishop of the Haitian
Catholic Church. The second wore a white suit with a Pentecostal purple tie and represented Haiti's evangelicals. Last was Errol Josue, the
head of Haiti's association of vodou priests. Josue was a red-brown man
in flowing white robes and an ocher scarf whose hue matched his dyed
coppery hair. He moved with the epicene beauty that seems common to
that brand of healer whose performative authority derives in part from
evincing the strength to draw on powers both female and male. He welcomed the assembled, spread his arms to sing-chant in Kreyol and other
tongues, too, his trust that the *lwa* who reside beneath the water—the
place beneath the sea that joins all Haitians to their African kin—were
abiding this summit, and the travels of those souls upon whose earthly
bones we now stood, too.

A choir composed of teens in T-shirts touting the Institut National
de Musique d'Haiti gave a wobbly rendition of a song that seems to
have become, since its inclusion on the soundtrack for Disney's *Shrek*,
a worldwide invitation to impersonal grief. The choir's performance of
Leonard Cohen's "Hallelujah" earned their director a hug from President Martelly. He took the lectern himself as members of the foreign
press scrambled to crouch at his feet, cameras clacking.

"This is a sad day," he said, "a day of mourning, a day where a lot of
people remember what happened." Haiti's president nodded to those
gathered under the flimsy tent and then to the hired supporters, out
beyond the rope line. "It didn't keep us on the ground," he said of the
quake. "We stood up stronger." The *konpa*-king-turned-president,
who'd won fame urging dancing women to *balanse* (sway) and *souke*
(shake), also used this occasion to blame the protesters clogging the
streets for his government's dysfunction. "Enough is enough," he told
them. "Give the country a chance, in the name of the victims who died
five years ago." Martelly didn't say much more than that. He stepped

from the dais to join the line of ambassadors and bigwigs walking slowly toward the boulder with flowers. He joined an elegant light-brown woman in an ivory pantsuit who, when she handed me her business card from his Ministry of Culture a few minutes later, made sure also to write her yahoo.com email address on the back. ("The government one doesn't always work," she explained.) Martelly laid a wreath of white roses by the rock. And then the *Prezidan*, waving warmly to his people, climbed into the backseat of his black Toyota and bumped off toward town, where his government was falling apart.

On my own way back to town, I stopped a mile down the road. There the self-built wilderness of Canaan baked in the midmorning heat. Most of its residents' homes were made from cardboard or frayed tarps stamped with the logo of USAID. Some others, farther down the slope, were solidly built little wood and metal cubes that had been erected here by the International Refugee Organisation or Japan's Social Development Fund. Their residents awaited the arrival of the jobs or services or schools that might make inhabiting the settlement bearable. There were no water mains or electrical lines, let alone paved roads, for the tens of thousands who'd arrived here to construct their own shelter with the help of men like the fellow I came across in Canaan 3, outside of a little hovel on which he'd painted, on a bit of cardboard, "Location de Materieux de Construction." The man's name was Pierre Monfort and he wore a T-shirt touting the University of Northern Florida Lady Panthers volleyball program. His zinc-roofed shack contained small piles of scrap wood and PVC piping he obtained on trips to town to sell here for a small profit. Monfort was from Cité Soleil, the notorious portside slum that was now run by a gang called Boston but that also helped birth the Lavalas movement of Aristide. He'd lost his home there, along with his brother and a sister and his wife and their child, in the quake. He said he'd lived in a tent city off the Boulevard Dessalines, near his old home, "yon kèk mwa" (for some months), but it sounded more like years. He'd moved here after some official, he wasn't sure from which agency or when, pressed five hundred gourdes (about ten dollars) into his hand and herded him with a bunch of his old neighbors from the tent city onto a bus, which deposited them by the dusty slope. "There's nothing for us here," he said. "But what life says, you have to believe."

Uphill from Pierre Monfort's was a big plastic cistern. There, another squatter camp entrepreneur was storing purified water that he then sold to his neighbors—this was their sole source of *dlo*—for five gourdes a bucket. There was also a neighborhood dentist whose office I found by following a series of hand-painted signs, hung on the shanties, depicting a crudely painted tooth and a grinning mouth over an arrow and the word "DENTISTE." The dentist's typically splendid Haitian name, Florial Osnel, was painted on a sign by the shack where he worked. Whether "Dr. Osnel" was a school-trained professional who'd lost his practice in the quake or a self-taught operator who'd conducted his practice with the help of *klerin* firewater, I didn't learn. A little girl playing with rocks by his gate confirmed that he was out. But here in Canaan, as so often is the case across this country, Haitians were doing for themselves. And they were doing for themselves in other ways, too, back on the streets of a capital in whose bright sky I could see, on the ride back into town, telltale plumes of acrid black smoke, rising over downtown. The forces of reaction—whether foes of Martelly demanding his immediate resignation, or supporters of aspiring heirs—were afoot.

* * *

ESPECIALLY NOWADAYS, Port-au-Prince is hardly among the beautiful capitals in the Caribbean. Even before the 2010 quake, the old centers of provincial Haitian towns like Le Cap and Jeremie boasted more colonial buildings. In the quake that Haitians call the *garou garou*, in onomatopoeic Kreyol, older structures and remnant "gingerbread" gables were pulverized. Downtown Port-au-Prince retained the look, years later, of a war zone. Down by the water, muddy slums seemed at risk of sinking into the sea. The old shopping district's eponymous Grand Rue was lined less by bustling shops than their memory. Their faded signs touting hardware or dresses now guarded darkened interiors that quartered squatters. The shop's commercial function was taken over, on the sidewalks outside, by peddlers selling everything from bedframes to parakeets as well as secondhand clothing shipped here by charity groups in big fabric bales that Haitians call *pepe*.

Haiti's capital more so even than nearby Kingston, its fellow island metropolis backing into high hills facing the sea, is a place whose low center was abandoned by its betters. Around Champs-de-Mars, the great square facing where the National Palace stood before the quake, a few key bits of national patrimony and civic infrastructure huddle under high palms. The national museum that's home to a marvelous collection of dozens of fine artists' visions of Toussaint and Dessalines, and to

Saint Soleil paintings by the likes of Tiga and Levoy Exil, is still housed here in a kind of mid-century concrete bunker facing Ha Mangone's famous statue of a willowy *Neg Mawon* (black Maroon), whose ankle is in chains and who raises a conch to his lips to signal revolt. Across the square sat a new concrete amphitheater. It had been built into the park with EU money after the quake and had recently hosted huge free concerts, by the likes of Chris Brown and Lil' Wayne, whose million-dollar performance fees President Martelly had controversially seen fit to pay with public funds.

On Avenue John Brown, proletarian tap-taps shared the road with SUVs shoving past them. The transition from Port-au-Prince's ruined downtown up to Pétionville's heights charts Haiti's raw topography of power. In between the route's ends, the hillside neighborhoods of Pacot and Haut-Turgeau offered intriguing nuance. Once-gracious zones whose homes' molding grandeur was left behind, in many cases, for Montreal or New York, they are inhabited now by the more upwardly mobile poor or stubborn members of Haiti's educated class. Their winding streets drip with bougainvillea and once-splendid homes whose yards offer still-splendid views, through their blooms, over downtown and of La Gonave, the little island out in its bay.

One such old manse was my hotel: with its creaky porch and spookily lush grounds, the Hotel Oloffson is a crumbling pile of atmosphere where Graham Greene set *The Comedians*. The Oloffson, even after the earthquake, retained its long-standing role as the meeting place, *par excellence*, for a certain brand of local intellectual, and foreign journalists who still come to absorb the mix of insight and cant laid on by the place's proprietor, Richard Morse, a prominent *mizik razin* musician and purveyor of "vodou rock" whose Anglo name belies the fact that he comes from an old Haitian family. Among his relations on his mother's side was Michel Martelly. After his cousin's election, Morse had in fact accepted an appointment from Martelly, to become Haiti's minister of culture before growing disillusioned with Micky's lies and resigning his post with the release of a song for carnival—"That's Not What You Said."

* * *

IT WAS THANKS TO one of the habitués of the Oloffson that I'd met my friend Richard Miguel, the professional translator and "fixer" who'd driven me to the memorial ceremony and with whom I now climbed the hotel's steps. That habitué, Daniel Morel, was seated at his usual table on the veranda, holding a camera. A soft-spoken Haitian man with salt-and-pepper dreads, he chided us for having attended the official memorial. Daniel had spent the morning, along with the Canon 5D he was never without, wandering downtown's streets to monitor the protests. "But people are all heading home now," he reassured us with a smile. "I think everyone's respecting the anniversary."

Daniel is an esteemed photojournalist who grew up in Port-au-Prince and whose photos have appeared in newspapers and on websites around the world. He was raised by a baker on the Grand Rue and has been documenting the lives of its people since he witnessed one of Duvalier's signal early atrocities, as a boy of thirteen, with his own eyes. In 1964, he was standing in the crowd before which two young dissidents, Marcel Numa and Louis Drouin, were executed by Papa Doc's goons. He picked up Drouin's cracked glasses, after the firing squad dragged the bodies away, and found them spattered with the young man's brains. He decided to become a photojournalist, not merely "to document Haiti's history," as he has said, but "so that I won't be afraid of anyone or anything."[3] With the camera he then bought, and all those he's owned since, Daniel estimates that he's taken well over a million photos of Haiti and its people in moments of both crisis and quotidian calm. By doing so, he has become a key figure in larger conversations about photography's vexed role in documenting life in a poor country like Haiti. After the earthquake here, one notorious and widely circulated candid image of photography at work here highlighted those dilemmas. That photo depicted a crew of white photojournalists wearing fancy vests full of gear. They were jostling one another to get a shot, reeking of exploitation as they fought to photograph a young girl who lay dead on the ground—the representative of Haiti they wanted to show to the world. Daniel's own photographic practice was different. As a professional who represents Haitian life not merely for the world but for Haitians, he was more focused on his people's humanity than their abjection.

When the quake hit, Daniel was walking down the Grand Rue near where he grew up. He had his Canon around his neck. "The earth moved like a wave and all was ruined," he told me of that day. "But I believe in continuity, and aftermaths—that you have to keep shooting." The thousands of frames Daniel caught that day comprise a crucial record of its tragedy. They've also had a remarkable life since.

The night of the quake, Daniel walked home to the Oloffson to find the hotel, as if by a miracle, both still standing and with still-working internet. He uploaded a quick edit of the scenes he'd shot of both horror and mutual aid—of people pulling bodies from the rubble, carrying strangers to safety, comforting their neighbors. One of the pictures showed a crying girl with her face caked in dust and her forehead bloodied, looking up at her rescuer, and at Daniel's lens, from the quake's debris. It appeared on magazine covers and in newspapers worldwide though frequently credited to someone else: some hack in Santo Domingo evidently ripped the image from Daniel's Twitter stream and succeeded in selling it to both Getty Images and Agence France Presse as his own. That theft of Daniel's photo, in the days after the quake, was key to his story. But so was the fact that he'd recently won a historic judgment against Getty and AFP, in U.S. federal court, for willfully stealing his work. Now today, five years after the quake, he was preparing his own form of remembrance.

* * *

BEYOND THE GOVERNMENT'S MEMORIAL to the victims of the 2010 earthquake in Titanyen, there are at least two other places, in Port-au-Prince proper, that serve the same function. There's a monument in the National Cemetery. It's not far from the dark stone cross that's dedicated there to Baron Samedi, where thousands gather on All Saints' Day to toast their dead and be mounted, perhaps, by the *lwa* of the necropolis. The statue recalling the earthquake there is a stylized woman made of iron, crying aluminum tears. Another memorial lies not far along the ridge from Pacot but in an area that's grown notorious, of late, for warring gangs. This one was largely funded by a dynamic foundation here, FOKAL, that's staked by George Soros's billions. And it, too, sits on historic ground: the lush acreage of what was once Habitation Leclerc—the historic home of Napoleon's general Leclerc and his wife Pauline, that was better known here for several decades in the mid-twentieth century as the Haitian base of Katherine Dunham. Dunham, the American choreographer and doyenne of modernism, was smitten with the forms of Africanity and New World rites she found in Haiti after visiting for the first time in the 1930s. The culture of the place informed her choreography and fed her soul. Dunham made her home here, off and on, for thirty years.

She was also the author of what remains one of the finer books on Haiti as both experience and place. Dunham's *Island Possessed* includes a vivid account of her initiation into the first rung of vodou initiates, the *lavé-tête*, a process that involved spending three days and nights lying on the floor of their houngan's home waiting, in piss and in hope, to be mounted by whichever *lwa* might make them a *hounci* in said *lwa's* service. It also includes vividly elegant recollections of her life here, during Haiti's pre-Duvalier moment of grace, and of such adventures as her interesting affair with future president-in-exile Dumarsais Estimé. *Island Possessed* still stands as a revelatory account—alongside similar books by fellow visiting devotees like Zora Neale Hurston and Maya Deren—of vodou's deep resonance for a thinker concerned with the form and practice of rites forged as survival techniques in the African-Americas. It's also a vivid study of all the ways that the lwa furnish "a kind of unifying and vitalizing force to Haitian life."[4]

The grounds of Dunham's old home here were turned, under the Duvaliers, into a luxury hotel. Now they've been refashioned again, into a lushly landscaped park meant not for Tonton Macoutes but for the public. The park is planted with native shrubs of curative and symbolic worth, a site meant for contemplating the present and past—and an ideal place for school kids, on the afternoon I visited, to do their homework under the trees. But as evening approached on the quake's fifth *anniversaire*, neither this site nor the cemetery nor Titanyen could hope to best, in poignant humility and power, the photographic memorial that Daniel Morel staged on the Grand Rue. There in the historic core of both Port-au-Prince life and the earthquake's destruction, his show began at precisely the moment—4:53 p.m.—the quake struck.

This event's venue was the outdoor atelier of the artist André Eugène. Eugène is a dynamic trickster-sculptor whose creations—forged from old car parts and real human skulls and tires and vodou motifs, all soldered together—have formed the guiding aesthetic for the "ghetto biennial" that he and his collaborators, working artists who paint tap-taps or barbershops in nearby yards, helped launch in 2009. That endeavor has grown to attract a certain breed of adventuresome foreign art-lover to Port-au-Prince, when the biennial's on. By contrast, this photo show was an event, as Daniel told me, "meant for the people who lived its images." Its concept was simple: Daniel had mounted large prints around the walls of Eugène's yard of several dozen of the photos he'd taken on this same block, precisely five years before. Most of the prints were just a foot or two across. A couple of them, though, were eight feet high and covered whole walls.

The photos had been shot when the darkness that now gathered on the Grand Rue was also descending, five years before. They showed people screaming and running through the street. Crumpled buildings. Clouds of dust. Brightly painted tap-taps lying on their sides or crushed like the bloodied bodies also here. The faces in the photos were terrified or calm. The biggest image showed two dust-covered men. One of them was screaming loudly, presumably for help, as he carried in his arms a man who to judge from the pain on his face has perhaps had a leg or two rendered useless by a crash. This tableau of photos, on their own or displayed in any context, would have been potent. But after Daniel called for a simple moment of silence, at 4:53 p.m., the project's aims and resonance gained in force. People from the street outside, perhaps attracted by the lights or perhaps drawn by the images, began to trickle into the yard. Stopped short by the photos or simply taking them in, they pointed at people they knew, or at themselves. Some simply stared. One young man wearing a Chicago Bulls cap gazed with pride at one image. He pointed out his brother, a dust-covered teen who wore a confused look in the picture as he gazed at one of those tap-taps lying on its side. The young man told me that he and his brother still operated a tap-tap that made the long haul from here to Jérémie. They'd been readying to leave that afternoon, five years ago, when the quake hit. "That's him by the bus," he said. "If it flipped the other way, he'd have died."

An old woman pointed with wonder, in one of the photographs, at her own bloodied head. She still had, as she showed with her hand, the mean ridge of a scar where some bit of rubble hit her. "I've not been the same since," she said. "Look at why."

Daniel Morel looked on quietly, but he was pleased. "That's the power of photography," he murmured. "To not be afraid of history, as you live it."

The next day, the protests would be back. I would roll with Richard Miguel past Cité Soleil, toward the smoke again choking the Grand Rue. Richard—whose perfect English was a result of his having been raised mostly in New York, before he was deported to his birth country in the 1980s—would cue up the CD of classic American rock he loved for such occasions and, as we crawled behind a crowd of rock-throwing protestors soon to be dispersed with tear gas, sing along with gusto to

Guns N' Roses' "Welcome to the Jungle." Haitians were entering a new year, and a new battle for political succession, in familiarly stormy fashion. For that night, though, anyway, there was a way to recall, with peace, where they had recently been.

* * *

THE YEAR FOLLOWING the earthquake's fifth anniversary, a year that included the Dominican government's deadline by which every "foreigner" was meant to register their presence with Santo Domingo, was stormy even by Hispaniola standards. When the Dominican deadline hit that June, Martelly was still ruling Haiti by decree. His power to offer anything like a firm or cogent response to the situation, without a sitting senate able to approve or pass laws, was severely limited. After the June deadline, the DR didn't immediately begin its threatened mass deportations of Dominicans of Haitian descent. But the more informal and insidious expulsion of a more vulnerable population—Haitians living in the DR without any papers at all—began in earnest. That summer I visited a refugee camp comprised of these poor people, near the remote southern border town of Anse-à-Pitres. I found a destitute settlement of several thousand where everyone I spoke with reported that they'd been rounded up by scary cops, in one fashion or the other, or chased from their homes by an angered mob in some forsaken corner of the DR, before being dumped by the border of a country that had no ability, or evident will, to receive them. A couple of the refugees reported that some or other Haitian government officer had visited them here once early in the summer. But their sandy camp remained completely devoid of water or sustenance or health care or anything; most reported never having seen any government official or humanitarian worker of any kind here at all. These people's invisibility to their own state, as horrifically unhumanitarian as the Dominican state's behavior was in forcing them here, was its own tragedy.

The next fall I returned to Port-au-Prince. The city I found, in the run-up to All Saints' Day on November 1, was one in which dark-clad protestors in the streets mirrored the *gedé* messengers of Baron Samedi crowding the cemetery. It was a place readying for what felt, to most observers, like a new bout of chaos.

The first round of elections, in October, had not produced a clear winner. Martelly, though, had thrown his weight behind one candidate—a "pro-business" plantain magnate from Le Cap whose name was Jovenel Moïse but whom most called "Nèg Bannann"—the Banana Man. Many people feared that other candidates like the thoughtful Jude Celestin, an Aristide heir from the south, and the populist firebrand Jean-Charles Moïse, whose campaign posters dubbed him "Pitit Dessalines," might be shut out. Moïse was already alleging that Martelly's minions had stuffed ballots on a massive scale. Rumors of other electoral shenanigans, per usual, were rife. Moïse's supporters were marching through Pétionville, even before the results were announced, with fake wooden muskets. At night, they or someone else was decorating the capital's soundscape with staccato bursts, all too real, of machine gun fire.

To make things stranger, the foreign press—with the earthquake receding farther and farther into history—wasn't here at all. The correspondent from the *Miami Herald*, the one U.S. paper to pay for regular Haiti coverage, was reporting on the election's attendant conflicts. But the only other foreign correspondent I encountered on my first days in town worked for one of those dodgy but monied new web news services. It was anyone's guess what would happen—especially if Jovenel was declared the outright winner without a runoff. My perception of things wasn't helped by a young tap-tap painter I spoke with down by the Grand Rue, in a zone likely to be engulfed by violence if things got messy; I asked him if he thought serious unrest, or even civil war, was in the offing. "If people vote how they're supposed to, everything will be fine," went his perfectly vague but also profound response. My plan, for before the results were announced, was to head south for Jacmel and then catch the boat to Anse-à-Pitres, to check in on how things were playing by the border. Before doing so, though, I called a friend in the capital who'd been trying for a year to show me an antique map of where the border once lay—and where, perhaps, it still should.

* * *

I'D MET GEORGES MICHEL at the Oloffson. He was a radiologist and a lecturer in the medical school here, whose business card also cited his position as a special adviser to the Haitian Ministry of Defense. With cinnamon skin and a wispy white goatee, he was a well-fed man who wore the guayabera shirts common to Caribbean intellectuals who came of age in the 1970s, with their breast pockets full of ballpoint pens. He liked to unwind after completing his rounds among the capital's hospitals, on the Oloffson's porch. The evening we met, he was holding court for a table of journalists and bemused peers who appreciated both his deep knowledge of Haitian history and his talent for delivering, in French-accented English, vivid metaphors for Haiti's present. One imagined him trying them out to himself as he made those rounds, going to inspect X-rays in his dented SUV.

"What you must glean about Martelly is that he governs like a rich boy with a fancy car." Georges was buttering his bread with gusto, speaking to a female listener with a notebook. "He sits in his Porsche but doesn't know how to drive. He should hire a driver and just ride. But he is stubborn. He insists on driving himself." Georges put down his bread and, sitting in his chair, took the wheel of an imaginary car. "He bumps forward." Georges lurched forward, eyes wide. "He bumps back." Georges did the same. "But he still wants, because he's unwise, to drive." He paused to let the image sink in, that first night I met him, before explaining its thrust. "We have long lived, though, in a society where the mediocre rule. And it is our job as Haitians, though we often fail, to try to pull them the right way."

Georges Michel himself was by no measure "a mediocre man." He was a doctor and professor who'd also earned a law degree for fun and was a licensed airplane pilot ("Flying, as Antoine de Saint-Exupéry said, gives another dimension," he explained) who had also authored, in his spare time, a shelfful of books on Haitian history and affairs. Among these were monographs like *The Railroads of Haiti*, *A Panorama of Haitian-Dominican Relations*, and a study of the mostly forgotten historic figure Charlemagne Péralte, the doomed hero who led Haiti's resistance to the first U.S. occupation, in 1918 and 1919.[5] Georges was a polymath and politico. He was possessed of that particular will common to island boys who desire to excel not in one realm but in all of them. Which is to say that he was also a member of a social and intellectual class that has largely left Haiti. But as I learned over the several dinners I shared with him in Port-au-Prince after that first meeting, Georges was above all a Haitian patriot—and it was for patriotic reasons, as well as scholarly ones, that he was so keen to show me the artifact we went to see one afternoon when the whole city, with election results about to be released, seemed on edge. Georges stopped, en route to his boyhood home in Turgeau, at an old barbershop. He said he'd been visiting its cracked vinyl chairs since he was eight years old; he wanted to be sure to get a haircut before the results were announced, in case street riots would soon force him to remain housebound. We continued on and pulled up, after his haircut, to a solid steel gate. Georges fished for his keys, calling through the gates' slats, "Bonswa, Leonel!" A thin young man in worn cutoffs approached from across the yard and gripped the gate to help Georges pull it open.

"Leonel's family ran a shop"—Georges nodded toward the boy—"in the house's first floor." The patchy lot where we stood was weed-choked; it had no house on it save Leonel's one-room shack. "Once it fell down in the quake, we let them stay." Georges leaned down to pick up some crumbled bricks: they were from the front patio of what must have been a grand home when he was growing up. He sighed deeply. Then he led me toward an old concrete outbuilding off to one side, which had evidently survived the quake and whose iron-grilled door, guarded with a padlock, he and Leonel yanked ajar, revealing a windowless room. This had once been his grandfather's office; later, Georges explained, "It was where I brought girls." He looked wistful. But then he skirted a rusted metal desk to shine his cellphone light toward a cracked rear wall, illuminating what we'd come here to see—the historic map of the island that Georges's great-grandfather, Alexander Poujol, drew with a French cartographer and surveyor named Henry Thomasset. The map's cartouche bore the date: 1908. "CARTE PHYSIQUE ET POLITIQUE DE L'ILE D'HAÏTI," read its title plate. "Dressée par l'Ingénieur H. THOMASSET, de l'Ecole Centrale de Paris et Msr. A POUJOL."

The map was seven feet across, with precise lines and exquisite labels in script. Its detail was staggering. Each river and hillock on Hispaniola was rendered with fine shading and contoured lines. So were known mineral deposits (manganese was marked with a little Mn; zinc, a Zn), subterranean oil (a little black derrick), and every fort and military outpost along the border between Haiti and the DR. Each was color-coded in accord with whether it was occupied, circa 1908, by soldiers loyal to Santo Domingo (black) or Port-au-Prince (red). The map was the most exacting and beautiful representation of Great Antille I'd ever seen.

"We don't know whether my great-grandfather was commissioned to do it, or if he endeavored, with Thomasset, to do it himself." Georges said. "But this is an extraordinary document: the last authoritative rendering of the Haitian-Dominican border's contours from a Haitian perspective, before the U.S. Army made a map in 1910 to supplant it. And also before Louis Borreau allowed the Americans to take responsibility, from the 1920s on, for the border's fixing." He said Borreau's name with a scowl: he was the puppet the Americans appointed to run Haiti, after Georges's great-grandfather turned them down, in 1921. "Look."

Georges pointed to the map's string of Haitian-controlled forts. The border they traced was a dotted red line that followed the Massacre River, in the north, before squiggling down the central mountains' spine to bound past Jimani-Malpasse, in the crook of the Enrequillo Valley, and to touch the southern coast well to the east of the current frontier at Anse-à-Pitres. "You see this red mark by Beladaire?" Georges pointed to a Dominican town some miles east of the large crossing at Malpasse. "Well, Beladaire, in 1908, was as Haitian as its name." The map was plainly more generous to Haiti, at several spots, than current ones are. The story of why lay in sundry negotiations and capitulations, most of them forgotten, effected by grabby Dominicans or dictatorial U.S. Marines—many of whom turned up here in the 1920s from the Jim Crow South and had minimal interest Haitians' rights. But even the Poujol-Thomasset map, Georges explained, wasn't as generous to Haiti as international law suggested it could be. The last legally defensible boundary between the two countries, by his lights, was the one set down on July 16, 1843. That's when Haiti ended its occupation of Santo Domingo and the DR gained its independence: according to the legal principle of *uti possidetis juris*, when one nation's territory is made from another's, their borders should remain in place until such time as a formal treaty abrogating their contours is executed. The 1844 line was based on coordinates set down by Napoleon's troops forty years before, Georges said, and included vastly more territory for Haiti than even Poujol charted in 1908. It touched the island's north shore as far east as Columbus's old colony at La Isabela, by La Plata, and its south coast near Barahona.

* * *

THE ELECTION RESULTS, when they were announced the next afternoon, didn't provoke an uprising—at least not yet. They indicated no clear winner: the Banana Man had predictably come out in front. He'd won 32 percent of the vote. Jude Celestin, with 25 percent, was second. Jean-Charles Moïse received 14 percent. There would be a runoff election, in a few months. Before then, the trailing candidates would launch a formal complaint over alleged ballot stuffing and such. Their supporters, in Port-au-Prince's streets, would burn their share of tires, and a few people. I asked Georges Michel how he thought all this might affect the ethnic Haitians now living in camps by the border—many of them having come from parts of the DR that, as his map showed, had once been Haitian. "The only thing that can happen with those camps," he said, "is that after the Dominican elections, and after ours here, those people will be allowed to go back to where they lived." About that, I wasn't sure: antagonisms had just reached a new low, with Martelly's minister of commerce announcing a misguided ban, in response to calls for a larger Haitian boycott of the DR, on importing many Dominican goods over the land crossings where Haiti's Madam Saras bring across beans and spaghetti on which many Haitians depend to eat. But Georges was insistent: "This game's poses are as old as politics here."

To see how the new import ban was playing on the south coast, I headed the next morning down past the cemetery to find a bus to Jacmel. The mood on the street remained tense: a pickup truck careened around a corner, with people in the back, and a young man with whom I'd been waiting for the bus dashed for cover, crying, "Lavalas!" But we managed to depart smoothly, in any case, and soon found ourselves heading south over a winding mountain road, to roll toward Jacmel.

Built with riches from the super-alkaline coffee still grown on surrounding slopes, Jacmel's downtown rings an aqua bay, and is even more reminiscent than Le Cap, these days, of New Orleans. Its grander dark-iron columns and balconies evoke Louisiana—where many of Jacmel's creole merchants migrated after the revolution—and were also strong enough, unlike many of its newer cinderblock homes, to withstand the earthquake that killed thousands here, too, and left the face of the clock on the town's cathedral stuck, since 2010, at 4:53, when the temblor struck and a mini tsunami pushed all the water from Jacmel's bay out to sea. Haiti's "City of Arts" is famous for its vibrant pre-Lenten carnival and the beautiful papier-mâché masks its participants craft to make a swirling theater, more high-minded than debauched, of the street. The town's artists mix scraps of cardboard with paste made from manioc flour, in alleys and ateliers around the city, to make masks that, once hardened and painted in vivid colors, can be human-sized and larger. Flamingos and monkeys, dragons and ghouls, *lwa* and historical figures who are often the same thing—these figures take over Jacmel's streets, during carnival, in explosions of color and wit punctuated by only-in-Jacmel stock figures like the Chaloska: an aggressive figure in

a Penzance hat whose cartoon-big lips and teeth evoke Charles-Oscar
Etienne, an infamous loudmouthed police chief from the era of the first
U.S. invasion, and who was turned into a carnival staple by an artist here
called Lamour. The one time I made it to Jacmel for carnival proper, I
swam through the crowd to join some friends on a rooftop overlooking the Avenida Barranquilla. I watched packs of giraffes and gazelles
pass beneath, and a trio of Chaloskas, their mouths big and chattering, who followed a troupe of dark-colored pigs—symbols of the hearty
cochon creole who were horribly killed off en masse by misguided U.S.
aid workers in the 1980s, after a swine flu outbreak. Dust-covered boys
and girls scraped the pavement with shovels, pushing wheelbarrows
carrying friends who, playing victims from the earthquake's rubble, also
played dead. Another young man, this one coated in coal, was hunched
over and weaving through the crowd—and dribbling a basketball. The
hens and goblins were no match for him as he spun and then performed
a little juke, shook past a big Baron Samedi, and shot off down the lane.

Jacmel carnival is spectacular. But this was November. Lent's end
was a ways off. And the woman I was keen to see just now lived not in
Jacmel proper, in any case, but along the southern coast road that René
Préval built for some of his remoter constituents here in the 1990s.
This paved road, which connected once-inaccessible villages to the
south coast's main city, ended in the commune of Marigot. This was
where Madam Diamette, the woman I was going to see, lived. Marigot,
despite lying sixty miles short of the DR border, is the closest one can
get on good roads to the crossing. This means it's the place where sixty-
foot wooden boats, leaving nightly, carry goods and people and Madam
Saras between here and the Haitian border town of Anse-à-Pitres. It
was on Marigot's pebbly beach, one early morning when the boats were
returning, after a six-hour overnight float from Anse-à-Pitres, that I
met Madam Diamette.

I had arrived before dawn, that morning, to watch the boats approach
in dim light from the east. They chugged along at half speed to conserve
fuel, their bright sides painted with pious slogans in Haitian French that
read like prayers the vessels wouldn't sink: "CONFIANCE EN DIEU,
CHRIST CAPABLE, SAMUEL 7:12" (a passage that ends, "Thus far
the Lord has helped us"). They were so loaded down with supplies and
people that each wave looked like it might overtop them. But they were
carefully packed, and the great mounds of goods on which their passengers sat—big sacks full of beans and hot dogs and spaghetti, plastic-

wrapped mattresses, jugs of cooking oil—remained dry. Some of their passengers, as they approached shore, hopped into the waist-deep waves. These were men returning from seasonal jobs working on the DR's sugar harvest. Or they were people who'd lived across the border for much longer—folks fleeing the worsening climate in small Dominican towns like Moca, featured in that YouTube video showing a pair of Haitians chased from their home by an angry mob. A Haitian man on the beach in Marigot was now pulling his smartphone out as a crowd gathered around, to share that video I'd first glimpsed in a *batey* in La Romana, to explain what he was fleeing from.

For these migrants, the boats were simple transport: the only road between here and the border is a rough dirt track, much slower and more treacherous than the sea. But for passengers like Madam Diamette and her colleagues—women traveling on business—these vessels were mini freighters. The women came ashore, on the backs of local stevedores, to complete journeys that had lasted not six hours but thirty-six. After making their first all-night journey, they'd spent the day across the border in the Dominican border town of Pedernales, acquiring the goods that the stevedores now humped ashore. On the beach, the women stuck around to direct their cargo to waiting tap-taps, bound for nearby storage depots that act as hubs for the small retailers across southern Haiti. The Madam Saras, in a nation where the "informal sector" makes up 85 percent of trade, remain crucial cogs. Madam Diamette told me, that first morning on Marigot's beach, that the job was hard, "but a good living."

She was a short sturdy woman with a round face and warm but tired eyes. She'd been making the journey to Anse-à-Pitres for twenty years, at least once and often twice a week. She told me how she inherited her vocation from her mother, who was a Madam Sara, too, and how the boat she often took, a blue and white number painted with "ERZULIE PROPHET" in the bow and "CONFIANCE EN DIEU" on the side, was captained by a stoic man called Captain St. Philippe. It was named after a nearby restaurant, Le Reference, whose owner owned this boat, too. She told me how, upon boarding, she and the other Saras curled up along the vessel's sides, to sleep among great sacks of avocados and bundles of *pepe* clothing. How they sold their *pepe* to the Dominican merchants whose own livelihoods, in turn, depended on the women. She explained how the women were wholesalers, moving goods from and to places that Haiti's conventional shipping companies weren't able to. And how, like all businesspeople getting their goods to market, the Madam Saras contended with big expenses and shifting obstacles.

Madam Diamette paid Captain St. Philippe 250 Haitian gourdes for her passage to Anse-à-Pitres. She expended a similar amount for each courier there who carried her goods back from the border, and for each bag of freight loaded onto the boat, often thirty or more per trip. Back home, she had to compensate the stevedores and tap-tap drivers as well. The depot where she leased storage space cost her 1,500 gourdes a year. It was a lot of overhead, she admitted. But after a good trip she could clear 10,000 gourdes—nearly US$200. The solidly built concrete home she shared with her four kids, not far from Marigot's beach, had a lovely wooden porch and a nice dinette set that she had brought back from Anse-à-Pitres. "I built this house," she said, "with Madam Sara money."

That first day, Madam Diamette admitted that "sometimes after a trip, I feel it all over." She also explained how her job was getting tougher. A year before, Haiti's government had tried to allay the widespread problem of trash choking its town streets by outlawing the little plastic bags that food vendors use here, and which the Madam Saras often supplied in big bundles from Pedernales. But now there was a larger obstacle looming—the Dominicans' new efforts to "regularize" their borders—which threatened her whole way of life. The DR's new insistence that entering Haitians carry a passport—which she lacked— had led her to begin phoning her Dominican suppliers from the border, to arrange for them to meet her on the edge of town, just past the checkpoint, after she'd slipped the border guards a slightly larger bribe than she used to pay to enter. Even then, reports from the busy crossing at Dajabón-Ouanaminthe suggested that far fewer Saras were streaming into Dajabón for market. Madam Diamette, for her part, didn't think then that these tensions—or Haiti's threats to retaliate by boycotting Dominican goods—could really mess with things. Obstacles, in her business, were nothing new. "If they stop the Madam Saras," she'd said then, "where will people get their beans?"

But now, as I went to see her months later, Madam Diamette's own government had responded to animus from abroad with a misguided policy. The new ban on many Dominican goods crossing into Haiti by land also restricted the number of ports at which they could arrive by sea. The policy's most likely victims, at least in the short term, seemed likely to be Haitian—the Madam Saras and those depending on the essentials that they transport. Which was why, returning to Marigot and finding Madam Diamette on her porch near the beach, it wasn't wholly surprising to find that she was taking a break from boarding Captain St. Philippe's boat. "They're really enforcing these bans," she said of the new customs regime. "It's time for a break."

Madam Diamette had faith that the ban would soon be lifted and she'd return to work. Down by the beach, there were fewer people than usual. But I was glad to find that Captain St. Philippe was ready to sail, as ever. I was keen to return to Anse-à-Pitres, and to the refugee camp of deportees there, and he was the best way to go. Many of the senior Madam Saras did seem to be sitting this week out, but he didn't lack for passengers. Younger women and others directed the stevedores to carry squealing pigs and crates of chicks and *pepes* aboard his boat. Where one hustle was being cut off, others were being seized on or invented. And as a bright moon rose over the pebbly beach, St. Philippe's crew readied *Le Reference*, with its hull pleading the protection of Erzulie Prophet in the bow, to go. I curled up as best I could with my fellow passengers, against a sack of what felt like mangoes. St. Philippe's crew bailed water from the stern and I dozed as their captain, chanting intermittently to his gods, guided *Le Reference* along Hispaniola's southern shore, hopping through the gentle waves and under mystic stars, to Anse-à-Pitres.

PART II

The Lesser Antilles

Sea of Islands

CHAPTER 11

HEADING SOUTH

NOTES FROM A MIDWINTER SWING (modes of transit: planes, ferries, a freighter, and one rich man's yacht) through the Lesser Antilles:

Cayman

LANDED IN GEORGE TOWN, midafternoon. Tidy little airport, fake-wood-and-stucco walls. Reminiscent of a strip mall in Boca Raton. Nearby houses, the bigger ones, also reminiscent of strip malls in Boca Raton. Other houses are older and smaller with sandy yards and real-wood porches, with swings: they feel like New Orleans. The Cayman Islands are three: Grand Cayman, Little Cayman, Cayman Brac. To refer to the three in toto, locals never say "the Caymans"; they say "Cayman." Cayman's capital has a big Burger King and a big Royal Bank of Canada. George Town also has other buildings that look like banks, and a post office with a bank of metal PO boxes, opening onto the street. They're owned both by shell firms from Qatar and local humans like the sixtysomething black man who tells me, as he's grabbing his mail, that when he first came here from Barbados to work for Barclays Bank, in '73, Cayman had eleven thousand people. "Now there's better than 50K," he says in his nice pink shirt, which he wears tucked in. "And we've got traffic between West Bay and town. But Cayman still sleepy as sin."

Two big cruise ships, hulking offshore. One's orange smokestack reads AIDA.de. It's disgorging big orange dinghies from its hold, containing Germans fleeing winter. The other boat, even bigger, has no visible name. But my phone says that "Princess WIFI" is available on George Town's streets: the Yanks are here, too. They move in Bermuda-shorted packs, by the bayfront, passing fishermen and the Cayman Dive-Masters' blue skiff, and line up to board another boat, the HMS *Atlantis*, through whose Plexiglas hull tourists unschooled in scuba but still coveting coral can ogle it during an hour-long "harbor cruise" for the bargain price of US$89. At Margaritaville, I ask two young women staffing the gift shop in fake grass skirts where they're from. Their wide-set eyes and squat size suggest not the islands but the Spanish Main, to which Cayman's been joined since even before banana boats streamed between here and Honduras. The young women say, "Nicaragua." We chat for a minute, in Spanish, about life in Cayman (*Aburrido*—okay) and where they go for unboring times when they're not at work (Burger King, often, though also a good time, sometimes, is karaoke night at the Mango Tree, out by the airport). Past Swarovski, next door, a colonial-style house contains the Cayman Museum.

Its empty rooms suggest that cruise shippers prefer crystal shopping to history. But inside, the museum's obscure objects and captions recount how Columbus, struck by Cayman's abundant turtles in 1503, first dubbed the islands "Las Tortugas"; how another Italian, the author of the famed Turin Map of 1523, grew sick of the admiral's confounding fondness for naming islands for turtles (there were others), and labeled these ones "Los Logartos" (The Lizards) instead; and how mariners and mapmakers then both agreed, by the 1530s, that the big crocodiles sunning on their beaches were, in fact, these islands' notables, and settled on "Caiman." How they had no record of human residents, maybe because of those crocs, before the sixteenth century; how they were then first settled, fleetingly, by a couple of Welsh castoffs from Oliver Cromwell's army called Watler and Bodden, who came over from Jamaica in 1656; how that first Bodden's grandson, Isaac, then became their first lasting resident; how old Isaac Bodden was soon joined by pirates and slaves and Jews fleeing Spain's Inquisition; and how the new society's historical scorn for taxes (says local lore, if no clear record) was born when a convoy of British vessels crashed against the reef off Gun Bay in 1794, and a grateful George III, who'd seen loved ones saved by Cayman's sons, exempted them thenceforth from both conscription and taxmen. The museum also contained a room of detritus and photos relating to the century and more, from the middle 1800s, when hunting the still-abundant sea turtles, and building the handsome schooners used to catch them, was Cayman's lifeblood. People here still nurse nostalgia for those days, and I'd hear more about them that night, after the Swarovski-hunting hordes were back on their floating hotels, drifting away from this again-sleepy port, toward wherever was next.

Onshore I find my way to a room that is, according to Hotwire.com, the cheapest around. The hotel's a mile from town, set amid big round storage tanks for Rubis gasoline. Room still not cheap. Nothing in Cayman cheap. But the aqua water across the sharp coral shore, out past the oil tanks, is so clear that when I look down and a Technicolor parrotfish by the sandy bottom turns its big eye up, I'm pretty sure we catch each other's gaze. Cayman's where the Caribbean Sea is shallow and sheltered and unrubbed by Atlantic waves. It feels it. It feels like Cozumel. Except that bills from Cayman's banks' ATMs have Queen Elizabeth on them, and they're worth more—not far less, like their Jamaican neighbors' funny money—than U.S. cash. The hotel's manager, who wears a black polo shirt advertising Seven Fathoms Rum, checks me in. "Come by the bar," he says, "for your welcome drink." His shirt's logo is in the same Treasure Island font as the black flag, also touting the stuff, hanging out front. The shirt and flag of the hotelier, who's short and white and says his name is Jason, aren't the sole signs evoking pirates here. Right by the HMS *Atlantis* in town, you can also board an "authentic pirate ship." It looks, bobbing garishly with actors leaping from the poop deck, fake swords clanging, like a Happy Meal toy. But the ship, like Jason's signage, recalls how, for a while before England claimed Cayman in 1730, and for a while afterward, Black Beard's ilk loved raiding off its reefs. Jason comes not from Wales but Wisconsin. He is stout with a stubbly face and a lazy eye; he wears a canvas cap with the short brim favored by Fidel, and Hootie of Blowfish fame. It's impossible not to think, as he waves out toward where the sky is turning six hues of pink, and, maybe, toward Wisconsin ice beyond, that Jason looks like a pirate, too. "Why be in winter," he asks, "when you could be here?"

His place's bar faces a row of underwater stools, on one side, in the concrete pool; the other, facing the concrete deck, is peopled by a couple of sun-dazed Germans and also by a fellow who eases onto his stool, as the sun falls, in a way that screams "regular," and whose super-groomed dreadlocks are those less of a Rasta than a pedant. He orders wine and starts reasoning loudly, with his pirate-barkeep pal, about death and love and why his "baby mama" is pissed off again. He pauses his lecture, whose timbre may answer his question, when I ask them why, in this hardly-Third-World place with none of the stray cats or hairless dogs you see in those, there seems to be one species of feral fauna—chickens—gone amok. "Hurricane blew down big farms by East End—cocks been running free since." The pirate, before I go, insists I try his rum punch. "None of that store-bought mixer here," he says, pulling out a plastic bottle of Ocean Spray and another of Sprite. "Just the good stuff."

I'd heard about Gimistory, the Cayman Islands International Storytelling Festival, from a friend in Trinidad who knew the director, an East Indian from Guyana based in Cayman but likewise girding strong ties, like many impresarios of culture in the Lesser Antilles, to their most southern member. Trinidad is the island from whence came the two musical styles—calypso and steel pan—that dominated the other islands' soundscapes after the war, and before reggae's rise. "My father," Stephen Mootoo says, "was one of the famous Mootoo brothers. Backed all calypso's greats." And now his yearly festival, toasting oral traditions of the Indies, convenes kerchiefed recallers of tales about why the moon's in the sky, or "how agouti lost him' ears," and at least two representatives, as any summit of Antilles "folk culture" must, from the old guard of Trinidad pop. Here these are Lord Relator, a surly old singer who won Trinidad's Junior Calypso Monarch competition in 1965, before taking the full crown in 1980 with his smash hit "Food Prices"; and Black Sage, a veteran exponent of ex-tempo, the calypso style whose singers improvise lyrics, on any subject, over an old minor-key melody from when Trinidad was overrun with French Catholics in the early 1800s. To win the public approval signaled, after an especially cutting or virtuosic display (ex-tempo men traditionally battle each other), they sing an exclamation of "No mercy!" in French: *Sans humanité!* The festival runs for ten days, and includes free shows in each of Cayman's parishes, including "the 'Brac" and Little Cayman. Tonight it's happening in Bodden Town, twenty minutes away.

Arrival in Bodden Town, 8 p.m. A seaside village, *sleepy as sin*. A crumbled stone wall, facing the sea. It looks like it was built by the town's founder. Sitting on the wall: bored young men, pretty in tank tops. They look also like they were maybe built, in another way, by old Isaac's kin. "In Cayman," a spike-haired woman says, "Bodden' like Smith and Jones combined." The old bonds here, convivial or coerced, among ex-slaves and Welsh debauchees, have possibly bequeathed to Cayman more kinky-haired people who are also natural blondes, per capita, than any nation on earth. The blond Afroed boys point down a dirt track to a sandy park. It has almond trees by a stony ruined church, lit with tiki torches for the night. A small steel band plays. Food vendors dispense "fish frittas" and plastic cups of viscous "swanky" limeade, made with brown sugar. The night's MC, a local radio deejay with Cayman-olive skin, begins with a joke.

"A Caymanian, a Bajan, and a Jamaican walk into a bar." He pauses. "Let me rephrase. A Bajan and a Jamaican walk into a bar." Beat. "The Caymanian—he already there." Guffaws.

We in the crowd, bathed in tiki light and stories sure to be better than this, are happy. We laugh and smile along as a vaunted Jamaican teller in Miss Lou mode, another must at summits like this, and resplendent in yellow against cocoa skin, recounts how Anansi the trickster spider caused Crab to have eyes on the sides of his head. And then the calypsonian Lord Relator, red-brown in complexion and gruff of mien, cuts his surly mode with a jangly guitar and riotous-corny tune, "The Eating Competition," recounting how the winner of same ate "ten quart of bread and ninety pounds of cheese, six bits sponge-cake, four tons of beef pie . . . and up to now, he still not satisfy." Black Sage, the extempo man, begins his mini set by riffing on his crowd and its women. He delivers one punch line about "horses I'd like to ride" and manages, in a half-dozen verses, to hit on more of them than that. Then he asks for topics from us. Someone cries, "Barack Obama!" Black Sage smiles and hums. Then he launches into a series of rhymed couplets after ex-tempo's template. "I really love President Obama," he begins, "but these days, the fella under pressure." (Rhymes in ex-tempo need not be exact.) And then he turns home:

> In fact I find the situation sad
> I find them Republicans treating him bad
> The Republicans, I have to admit
> I believe they are a set o' stone hypocrite'
> Out of the White House they want to give [Barack] a push,
> But he still ten times a better president than . . .

He halts the line for us to finish it. We do.
"Bush!"
Mic drop. *Sans humanité*. Delighted applause.

It continues as a beige-black guy in a blue Hawaiian shirt and scuffed cowboy boots, the night's last teller, sidles mic-ward. He's one of those island people, his boots and Stetson say, reared on Kenny Rogers and Dolly Parton. But Dexter Bodden, local hero, went further than the legions of rum-drunk singers across the Antilles who attempt Rogers's "The Gambler" on karaoke nights like the one in St. Lucia where, once, I saw three men do it in a row. He'd gone so far as to move to America and scratch a living for a couple of decades, honing his twang in honky-tonks from Texas to St. Paul. "It sure is good to be at Gimistory again," Dexter Bodden says, grinning at his Gibson. "Here's one of my favorite songs." He offers a lovely cover of Gordon Lightfoot's "House You Live In," twangy and strong.

He's got all the easeful grace of a man who still makes rent, back home, strumming the classics at Cayman's closest thing to a honky-tonk once a week. But it's for one of his own tunes, the one that Stephen Mootoo and his crowd wait for, that Bodden gets invited to play "folk festivals" like this. And it's thanks to America's Department of Homeland Security that he's here to accept: Bodden was forced home when he caught a felony, in suitably country-ballad fashion, for covertly taping the calls of a two-timing lady. How he felt about his deportation, and about gigging now at Donna Myrie's Roof Top Lounge in George Town, wasn't clear from the story on him I dug up in the local paper. Up north "he even played gigs at Nashville's world famous Tootsie's Orchid Lounge," said the article, "where the likes of Charlie Pride and Willie Nelson would hang out." But in Nashville, Bodden never scored a hit like the tune he intros now, known to all in Cayman of a certain age, with a happy sigh.

"I wrote a song a few years ago," he says, "about a schooner we used to have around here."

He doesn't need to tell them. Either about the boat or the song. The schooner *Goldfield* was built for turtle hunting, but then repurposed for other sorts of trade crucial to Cayman and its neighbors in the time before frequent freighters and planes. But somehow it ended up at a marina in Washington State—where its return to Cayman, no matter rumors that it was haunted by a ghostly "entity," became a cause célèbre in the 1980s. And that's when Dexter Bodden penned the song that he starts now, with a hard strum and a tap of his pointy-booted toe.

> They sailed her away, a long time ago
> To Bluefields and Barranquilla
> To San Andres and to Mexico

Trading coconuts for tequila
All the way up to Seattle
Through the snow, sleet, fog, and hail
All the sailors always talked about, how the *Goldfield* she could
    sail
Now were her sails full of wind, I wish she was coming home
    again
To the shorelines of the Cayman isle
Where many years ago, before they sailed her away I know
The *Goldfield* to our people was a blessing in disguise.

The boat, after Bodden's song came out, was bought by a wealthy
guy who endeavored to sail, with the help of her "entity," five thousand miles through the Panama Canal and home from Seattle. The
endeavor, as everyone here knew, ended sadly: the famed schooner with
its mahogany bones and Egyptian cotton sails did make it home, but
sank soon after. Now it's a dive site under the Cayman waves. But the
nostalgia, as they swayed to Dexter Bodden's island twang, was as real
as nostalgia, or the idea thereof anyway, gets.

She was more than just a schooner
Back when things were hard to find
Before we thought of Cayman Airways, Kirk Thompson's ship-
    ping line
She was more like a savior, to our grandmas and grandees
She'll always be a lady, of the oceans and the seas
And were the sails full of wind, I wish she was coming home
    again
To the shorelines of the Cayman isle
Where many years ago, my grandma told me it was so
The *Goldfield* to our people, she was a blessing in disguise.

Barbados

"A BAJAN WILL ALWAYS help you," my friend Baz says, "but given
his choice, he'll sooner regulate you."

We're rolling over the gentle dales of a low grassy island whose people call themselves Bajans and whose nickname for their little limestone home—Little England—more than fits a landscape whose hedge-lined walls, crossing kempt fields, echo Baz's thrust. Gray stone parish churches dot the heath. So do little wooden "chattel houses," so called because they're as movable as chattel slaves. The houses are owned by those slaves' progeny here, on land they still don't own. Their inhabitants project an air that's usually stoic, and sometimes kind, but seldom betrays much to be mistaken, by a stranger or their kin, for effusive warmth. A Bajan will certainly emerge from one of them, should Baz's little Honda have a flat, to furnish practical aid. But on this, the West Indies' first great sugar island, shaped in the image of those old Brits whose slaves pulled brutal fortunes from its soil, the landscape's will to order mimics the constable who tapped Baz on the shoulder, at a concert here once, just when the music got good. "Excuse me, sir," the Bajan bobby said, "but you are dancing in too boisterous a fashion."

Baz laughs at the memory. "Too boisterous a fashion! If that doesn't sum up Barbados, nothing does."

Baz is Trinidadian. Which is to say: his views of this Anglo island smaller than his own should perhaps be taken, as any Bajan would advise, with some salt. Trinidadians love condescending to their uptight neighbors whose clipped Welsh-sounding accents aren't their sole trait to lack the sexy rhythm of a Trini's trademark lilt. Such joshing is a pastime to rival any Trini's love for "wining down to the ground," during his island's famed yearly carnival, a sport Baz was exampling when the constable tapped his shoulder. But Baz is also a keen island journalist who, though wearing a gold hoop in one ear and favoring T-shirts touting the Clash, is also a keen appreciator of the life he's enjoyed here for years, writing for the *Barbados Nation* as well as for papers back home. When Baz and his partner became parents, they fled Trinidad's rampant crime for a place where their kids could be left to play outside in the afternoons, and where they could sleep, at night, not behind the iron bars that guard all Trinis' homes nowadays, but behind open Demerara windows in the lovely house they built here in St. Philip parish. Rules, as even a hip Trini with a hoop earring can admit, have their place. But far be it for any objective hack, like this one who also leaves his adopted home every chance he gets, to dissent from Patrick Leigh Fermor's verdict after he alighted here, in 1948; waxing aghast, he described an island whose culture "reflects most faithfully the social and intellectual values and prejudices of a Golf Club in Outer London."[1]

Because it's still true. And not because Bajans nurture some demotic fondness for golf (unless you're talking about those sugar barons' heirs and rich Brit vacationers who've built several links-style courses, naturally, onto the old sugar fields whose profits once staked Barclays and other City firms tending their stocks). Barbados is set a ways off in the Atlantic from the Antilles' volcanic chain; it's a low coral island built not by rising magma but by billions of busy zoophytes. But geography isn't all that sets it apart from those Lesser Antilles once claimed for Spain by Columbus, as the general pattern went, but then retained by the Carib for a time, before being fought over, for a couple of centuries at least, by French and Dutch and English and Danes desirous of their own spots in the sun. For Barbados only ever had one colonial master. When Captain John Powell arrived here in 1625, the only large mammals he found were feral pigs left behind by Portuguese sailors who'd visited just long enough, some years before, to christen the island with a curious name, meaning "the bearded ones," which was perhaps inspired by the island's odd-looking fig trees. In 1625, Powell claimed Barbados as a dominion of England's king—and it stayed that way, clear from Elizabeth's age until 1966.

Native son George Lamming described the island world those centuries made in his great novel of village life here, *In the Castle of My Skin*. It was one where Queen Victoria's birthday remained a holiday of holidays long after she died, and where when the villagers saw the landlord's light go out by their little crossroads, where "life went on flowing happily or stupidly like the sea," they knew it was time for them to go to bed too.[2] The struggle faced by the book's bright kids, to transcend the mores of grown-ups who adopted "the language of the overseer, the language of the civil servant," but who hated nothing so much as "seeing their people get on," mirrored the experience of Lamming.[3] First leaving Bimshire for Trinidad at seventeen, he then made his way to "the desolate, frozen heart of London, where at the age of twenty-three" he tried not merely "to reconstruct the world of my childhood," he'd recall, but also "the world of a whole Caribbean reality."[4] That Lamming's book succeeded in both aims, when it first appeared in 1953, is evinced by the fact that its author became the keystone figure for the first generation of West Indian students who both invented something called the West Indian novel, in postwar London, and wrote books that sought, in Lamming's words, "to restore the West Indian peasant to his true status of personality."[5]

That a Bajan played that leading role among the islands' "scholar-ship boys" in the metropole, in those years, was in some ways surpris-ing: it's a fair bet that Lamming—a dignified figure whose hairstyle and dark suit, of his old appearances on British TV, aren't all that remind one of Frederick Douglass—was teased for the usual things, by mem-bers of that cohort like the Jamaican host of the BBC's *Caribbean Voices* program, Andrew Salkey, and by Trinidadian pals like Samuel Selvon and John La Rose. (This was the scene from which V. S. Naipaul, with his work betraying slightly different aims, also emerged.) But it also makes a certain sense: who better than an exponent of "the oldest and least adulterated of British colonies" to write his era's crucial book on the psychic damage inflicted by the empire on its Caribbean subjects?[6] Especially since that was an era when the West Indies' cricket capital also gave the islands' less lettered citizens their own heroes to love: after the mighty West Indies cricket team beat Mother England for the first time in 1963, and then began beating up on the Aussies and Paki-stan and everyone else, were awakened a sense of pride and "status of personality" among West Indians everywhere that no book ever could. The great cricketing stars that Little England furnished to "the Wind-ies" in those years are still recalled with mournful joy from Antigua to St. Lucia to Tobago and St. Kitts. Even Trinidadians sang along to the Mighty Sparrow's calypso hailing Sir Garfield "Garry" Sobers, the aptly named Bajan all-rounder whose international test record of 365 runs ("Who's the greatest cricketer on Earth or Mars?" Sparrow sang)[7] stood for thirty-six years. And today one still sees, flying into Bridgetown, round cricket ovals dotting its outskirts like crop circles.

On the ground, one may now be as likely to see kids chasing big soccer balls, across those ovals' dusty grass, as little cricket ones. In Little England today, more young Bajans dream of playing for Man-chester United than of playing for the Windies. And everyone dreams of one day joining their cousins in Brooklyn, who can afford, at Christ-mas time, to send them cardboard parcels full of Barbies or Air Jordan sneakers from another country over whose pop culture one of Barba-dos's own daughters—Rihanna—now improbably presides as a kind of rotten junior queen. But still, it's not merely by Bimshire's cricket ovals, or at sites like the St. John's parish church where Baz and I pause our roll, that Barbados's air still bears the imprint of the lasting moment when, as Lamming put it, "Little England met Big England and Little England, like a sensible child, accepted."[8] The church's cornerstone says it was first erected in 1645. The pair of old mahogany trees out front recall when its island was cloaked with such dense vegetation, as an early visitor wrote, as to be "growne over with trees and undershrubs, without passage."[9] But that description hasn't obtained since Captain Powell's servants, hoping to copy the success of the Jamestown colony, up in Virginia, chopped down its trees to plant tobacco instead.

We wind along the old Bourne Highway on the island's rough Atlantic shore, hugging a stretch of coast whose roiling waves at Bathsheba are now favored by visiting surfers, but that is still best known, by Bajans, for the salt-wind "sea blast" that turns everyone's refrigerators or TVs to rust. In Bath Beach nearby, some of those with rusty fridges are poor whites known as "red legs." They're akin to those other sunburned Scots, in backwoods Tennessee, known by a similar slur. But these figures' forebears, unlike America's rednecks, didn't come here as Daniel Boones spouting self-reliance. They arrived here, rather, as quasi-slaves at a time when Britain's indigent or imprisoned could seek new life by enlisting to board a ship, in Bristol or Glasgow, bound for the hellish Indies, with the promise of performing three to nine years of hard labor in exchange. Many of the red legs arrived like this. Others didn't have a choice: in 1630s England, beggars or street toughs press-ganged onto Indies-bound ships were said to have been "Barbadoed"; the practice of snatching such peons' kids, to the same ends, birthed the English term "kidnap." It's a testament both to this community's scorned insularity, three centuries later, and to the proscriptions of Barbados's "colour bar," that they're still managing, on this mostly black island, to have kids with blond hair (and to have kids also possessed of similar telltale jawlines, if you credit those here who say you can always spot a white Bajan by same). It was these poor whites' ancestors, in the Barbados colony's lean toddlerdom, who settled a tropical hell from where one aristocrat on a scouting mission came away, in 1631, impressed by eating a pineapple "unto a great white strawberry"[10] but also aghast at a place whose drunken inhabitants were much given to sodomy and sheep fucking and in whom "ye Deuill ye spirit of discord haue great power."[11]

This rough colony was okay for producing exotic foodstuffs and shitty tobacco. But it wasn't the society that built the grand granite edifice that Baz and I find just up from Bath Beach; at the end of a long drive reminiscent of Scarlett's Tara but with royal palms in place of mossy oaks sits a Jacobean hall that looks, looming over its stately grounds, like it's been plopped here from Oxford. A plaque on its wall says that Codrington College was built as a school "of Chirurgery and Physic and also Divinity." Starting in 1714, it was made with a fortune left to this end by Christopher Codrington. The local patriarch of an illustrious Gloucestershire clan, he became a key protagonist here in building the industry responsible for producing not merely buildings like this in the Indies, but many other Downton Abbey–like places and families' fortunes back home (to say nothing of the library at Oxford's All Souls College, likewise built with his money). That industry, of course, was Big Sugar. And the man most responsible both for bringing it to the Caribbean and for importing the people—African slaves—who were relied upon to cut it here was Codrington's cousin, James Drax (who also became, when he married Codrington's sister, his brother-in-law). Drax realized that neither tobacco nor cotton was the way to get rich in Barbados's humidity. He traveled to Brazil in 1640 to see how Recife's Portuguese planters, staked by Holland's Sephardic bankers, were making incredible fortunes. Drax was wowed by the opulence of his Portuguese hosts—men given to throwing lavish banquets in their baronial homes, with entertainment furnished by orchestras that, though trained by European conductors, were comprised of thirty black slave girls playing violins. He also absorbed the hugely exacting process by which these planters' *ingenios* turned a big grass from New Guinea into the grains of "white gold" on which Europe was then growing hooked. In Brazil, Drax arranged for the delivery to Barbados, by Dutch traders, of the great iron rollers and stills and copper pots required for the job. And he was determined. Which is to say that he also soon realized, along with his kin and other large-holders here, that producing sugar in huge quantities—which they soon began to do—would require the labor of people other than the bonded red legs who'd cleared their fields.

So arduous was the work of cutting cane, and so debased the condition of those performing it, that even Britain's most destitute couldn't be recruited or even coerced, in sufficient numbers, to do it. In England's age of civil war, some of its nobler minds had concluded that trading in African slaves—a business then dominated by the Dutch and Portuguese—was "un-English."[12] But this didn't stop Drax from asking his Dutch suppliers for another commodity they could deliver, on demand, in whatever number required. Neither Drax nor his cousins were romantic Latins; they never went in for slave girl orchestras. But strong fieldhands and grinder operators and boilers were another story.

Some of the slaves they procured, when faced with this killing work, hung themselves; they hoped, after death, that they might be reborn in "their own Countrey."[13] To dissuade others inspired by their model, wrote a white observer, at least one of Drax's planter peers impaled a suicide's head on a twelve-foot spike around which other slaves were made to march in hopes that this "sad, yet lively spectacle" would persuade them that the poor soul's body couldn't possibly have traveled home.[14] Thus was established the productive engine of an island whose landscape was dominated by "dark satanic mills," as its best historian wrote, two centuries before England's was.[15] And thus were launched, too, the twirling perversions of a society whose owners sought, in building places like Codrington College, to implant in the same people whose heads they put on spikes a belief in their English God and a joined will, come what may, to "live comformably to the laws of the Gospel."[16]

Amid the silk cotton trees outside Codrington College, the ghosts of this monumental violence aren't hard to conjure. Nor is the reason so many people who grew up amid them gleaned that leaving this small place, as Lamming's narrator does in *In the Castle of My Skin*, was the only way to "strike an identity."[17] To see Little England plain, one has long had to leave it—whether by heading for Trinidad, where George Lamming learned that Bajans belonged to "a Caribbean reality affecting all its territories," or by going to New York, like one of his schoolboys in *In the Castle of My Skin* who returns to Bimshire to tell his friends that though "I didn't know it till I reach the States . . . we're all part of the Negro race."[18] To improve the small place, or oneself, one must leave it: true for the exceptional "scholarship boys" who went to London, this has also been so for its commoner emigrants—those striving women and men who after World War I began boarding steamers bound not for England but for New York and then settled on the city's poorer fringes "like a dark sea nudging its way onto a white beach and staining the sand," as the Brooklyn-born writer Paule Marshall wrote in another classic of modern Bajan letters.[19] Those emigrants were armed with a proud command of the King's English and ingrown respect for the rules by which they hoped to emulate their Jewish landlords—new arrivals themselves, not long before, who'd managed by their own will to excel at business and at school, to "buy house" in America.[20] And many of their kids did just as well as Marshall's hero in *Brown Girl, Brownstones*, Selina Boyce, who escaped her mum's insular outer-borough world to matriculate at City College. An elder Bajan friend of mine in Manhattan, who did the same after arriving in the United States from the dirt-floored chattel house where she was born, became the executive at *Sesame Street* responsible for ensuring, in the 1970s and '80s, that every one of the pioneering kids' show's ads or catalogs featured kids of all colors.

In New York City, such Bajan immigrants' successes and ways are familiar to anyone attuned to West Indians' role in the larger drama of race in America. Marshall, years after *Brown Girl, Brownstones* first appeared in 1959, said that it was a book that aimed "to make the immigrant story applicable to blacks."[21] It did just that—heralding a new kind of book in American letters that finally became, in the age of Barack Obama, a belated staple of Manhattan's publishers and prize committees. But such émigré Bajans have been even more crucial to the old island of their parents. When Barbados won its sovereignty from Britain in 1966, it was one of Marshall's Bajan Brooklyn peers who composed its new national anthem, as that composer, Irving Burgie, recalled to me in a café in Greenwich Village, near where he got his start as a folk-calypso singer here, in the 1950s, who called himself Lord Burgess.

Alert and prosperous at eighty-five, Burgie parked his shiny Buick on Macdougal Street and told me how he'd managed to make it in show biz as a short man with big eyes and a soft voice who lacked the charismatic talents of that Village folk scene's breakout star in the '50s, Harry Belafonte. Burgie had a talent for smoothing old island folk songs into forms palatable to U.S. whites. He served Belafonte as his chief songwriter-cum-arranger on the landmark 1956 suite of those tunes, *Calypso*, that became history's first million-selling LP. Burgie was credited with the lyrics to "Jamaica Farewell"; and he also managed, more crucially for his bank account, to register the U.S. copyright for his and Belafonte's slight reworking of an old Jamaican work song called "Day'O." "Whenever 'Day'O' plays in those NBA arenas," Burgie explained over our cappuccinos, "I'm the guy to whom they send the check!" Burgie and Belafonte fell out, perhaps unsurprisingly. But not before *Calypso*'s success prompted 20th Century Fox to produce a film that built on their collaboration's popularity. Released in 1957, *Island in the Sun* was mostly shot at and around the Farley Hill great house in Barbados by whose ruins Baz and I roll en route to the island's calm Caribbean shore, and my onward plane.

The film, *Island in the Sun*, was based on Alec Waugh's novel of the same name—a risqué tale of race-mixing romance that inspired Chris

Blackwell, in Jamaica, to name his music label Island Records. It starred Belafonte as a singing island folk hero who's equal parts crooning heart-throb and fiery labor leader. It played on his stature as America's first black pop star to be as widely desired for his body as for his music, and found Belafonte sharing an implied dalliance, in the film, with Joan Fontaine. The script didn't allow the two ever actually to kiss: their liaison's consummation was only suggested, on a bluff near Farley Hill, by their drinking from the same coconut. The film was a provocative exporting out, to a fantasy island milieu, of U.S. racial mores and anxieties. Notoriously banned across much of the U.S. South, it was an important milestone there in the run-up to the fight over civil rights. But it was also a big deal here in Barbados, where Bajans crowded Bridgetown's cinemas to see their own world captured on a big screen, for the first time, in magical Technicolor. And it was also a picture whose soundtrack's theme song, penned by Burgie, is a staple of local bar bands still. "I see woman on bended knee," went his lyric to its title tune, "cutting cane for her family,"

> I see man at the water-side
> Casting nets at the surging tide
> Oh island in the sun
> Willed to me by my father's hand
> All my days I will sing in praise
> Of your forest, waters, your shining sand.

The timbre of Burgie's movie tune was perhaps a touch secular, in this God-fearing land, to serve as new national anthem after the island followed Trinidad and Jamaica in winning its independence. But free Barbados's first prime minister, Grantley Adams, loved Burgie's work; when Little England finally wrenched itself from Big England, he asked him to compose the tune "In Plenty and in Time of Need," which sounded in November 1966, when the Union Jack was lowered for a final time outside Bridgetown's Government House—or rather moved to another flagpole, a few feet away—to hail the change. Today when Barbados's blue and gold banner is raised outside Government House, over the old slave port through which Baz and I stop for a farewell tipple, it's still Burgie's pious hymn that plays.

Since the days when Bridgetown's wharf was the first stop for any letter from England bound for Boston, or New York, its pier has rather declined in import. But back from the seafront spots that sling fish and chips for tourists, and along the town's premodern alleys, it's not hard for Baz and me to find a little rum bar, with a more local clientele, that's perfect for a final bit of Bimshire anthropology. In Barbados, as across the empire, the Brits enforced a law against abusive language. "Can you imagine such a law," wrote the Antiguan writer Jamaica Kincaid of this policy in the Caribbean, "among people for whom making a spectacle of yourself through speech is everything?"[22] In Barbados, that urge to spectacle may be smaller than on any of the West Indies. But perhaps it's for that reason that the Bajan fondness for cursing—even if it's expressed more by muttering unspeakables about mothers and body parts under one's breath than by yelling in the street—is so pronounced. Because that's the thing about a society built on rules. Every Bajan knows it. From my older friend in Manhattan, Jeannette, alongside whose *Sesame Street* mementos in her kitchen she's also hung an antique sign warning that "Whoever is laft at Breakfaft to clear the Table, shall forfeit," to whoever's hung a similar sign, over this Bridgetown bar, depicting two cartoon friars warning patrons to "LOVE THINE ENEMY and THINE ENEMY IS DRINK"—it's a thing that every Bajan knows well: the rules-loving society is also a society whose members grow extra intimate, in absorbing its strictures, with the joys of their flouting. And it's that intimacy, and Bajans' linked love for cursing, on which Baz's and the barman's story plays in the little bar when our conversation turns, beneath its sign of drink-loving monks, to Barbados's best known rule breaker now: Rihanna.

The barman looks like one of the squat friars on the sign, save for his cocoa skin; he puts a couple of local Banks beers on the bar. I ask Baz how Rihanna is viewed here. He says that her parents are known and respected in the community, and that most people think "Riri's a good girl"—even if the svengali from LA who found her modeling here at sixteen helped her to forge a new image for herself as she grew famous. Baz allows that this native daughter's cinnamon skin matches almost no one on her island, where, a half century after *Island in the Sun*, the color bar's force still feels far stronger, indeed, than in Baz's Trinidad, where lively-ing up the gene pool seems as key to the mating ritual as "wining down to the ground." Baz sips his Banks. "They do say that there are only two hot red women in Barbados. And Rihanna's one of them."

The barman, laughing, concurs. "But do you remember, spar, when she went to church?"

"At Christ the Redeemer?"

"Yes, spar!" The barman turns to me to explain. "She did walk right into that church, with a big gold necklace. The necklace said 'CUNT.' And we do love her for it."

Grenada

"IT TAKES A REVOLUTION," the sign says, "to make a Solution."

It hangs from a wooden balcony on the little "spice island" southwest of Barbados that was best known, before its revolution, for nutmeg. The sign's words are painted red, green, and gold; they're illustrated with the face of the reggae king whose words they are. But the colors aren't merely those of Bob Marley's Rasta mores. They match the flag of an island that had only become a free state some six years before this sign, photographed in June 1980, was nailed together. And there's another face on the sign's boards. It's light-brown like Marley's, but with a kempt little Afro and beard. Its handsome owner is the man, Maurice Bishop, who became first the leader, and then the martyr, of what Bishop and his comrades here aptly touted as "the Anglo West Indies' only Revolution."

If you do a Google image search for "Grenada Revolution," a photo of this Rasta-colored sign is one of the first you'll see. Most of the others will show Bishop addressing his people, or other of his "Revo's" propaganda placards, or both. "FORWARD EVER!! BACK-WARD NEVER!" says one of the most common. "EDUCATION IS A RIGHT," states another. You understand what V. S. Naipaul meant when, in 1983, he turned up here after Bishop's cause fell apart and, observing these still-hanging placards, judged that "[t]he Revolution was a revolution of words." The words "were a shortcut to dignity," Naipaul wrote; they were "too big; they didn't fit."[23] Some disagree. (Of what but assertive words, joined to action, is dignity made?) But either way, the defining episode in Grenada's modern story produced an archive of images befitting a moment and leader who still looks, viewed from the distance of thirty years, like a stupendous synthesis of two pillars of Caribbean style, and of the 1970s everywhere. Maurice Bishop really was Marley and Castro, the pictures say, rolled into one righteous spice island spliff.

His Revo's fire, in the event, didn't burn. Bishop's government, which took power in 1979, imploded less than four years later. But the photos of its salad days—they're really something. They show black people in tight 1970s T-shirts, "preparing the People's Budget." Cheering at rallies. Working hard. Helping their grans or uncles, as volunteers with the Popular Education Brigade, in the countryside learn to read. They're snapped before the signs with their shoulders pushed back, lending the signs human form, and force. "EDUCATION IS A RIGHT," says the one with the country tutors. "THE PEOPLE ARE THE MILITIA, AND THE MILITIA IS THE PEOPLE," the one with soldiers. "FORWARD EVER!! BACKWARD NEVER!" "FREEDOM IS: FEEDING OURSELVES."

"IT TAKES A REVOLUTION, TO MAKE A SOLUTION."

One photo on my laptop screen, as I google away on the quiet terrace at the Heliconia guesthouse, just down the road from the Maurice Bishop International Airport was taken on its then-new tarmac. The airport is a bit of infrastructure whose building by Bishop's friends from Cuba, in some ways, augured his cause's demise. It shows some of his people, still wearing the Revo's T-shirts but with their hands up. They're being questioned by invading U.S. Marines. This is the endgame. But the happier shots, from before that, show hirsute "international volunteers" with inspired locals; they've felled an order that deserved to be felled. Eric Gairy, the leader whose regimes they deposed, was a former labor leader who first won the support of Grenada's black farmers and fisherfolk back in the 1950s, and then won them independence. Once in power, though, he'd become an admirer of Pinochet, and Papa Doc. He had a private army to keep Grenadians in line; his foreign policy, as head of one of the UN's newest and littlest states, included urging its general assembly to name 1977 "The Year of the UFO." To bright Grenadians educated abroad, like Bishop, Gairy was both embarrassment and menace. Bishop's New Jewel Movement, founded in the early '70s, was, at first, forcibly repressed by Gairy's goons; when they tried winning power by electoral means, they were rebuffed. So New Jewel (the name was an acronym: the New Joint Endeavor for Welfare, Education, and Liberation) took another tack. In March 1979, Gairy was again away to address the UN. On a quiet morning at dawn a few dozen men took his island by surprise. They seized control of Grenada's main army barracks, and its radio station. Over its airwaves, the men's leader addressed the island. "Brothers and Sisters," he told his people, "this is Maurice Bishop. The dictator Gairy is gone. This revolution," he intoned, "is for work, for food, for decent housing and health." And the people, by and large, were glad.

Their leader's larger outlook was glimpsed in his decision, upon taking power, to name his baby son Vladimir Ilich. How many of his people backed the economic aims that this implied depends on whom you ask. But this young leader was handsome and articulate; his own father, Rupert, had been killed by Gairy's police. He possessed that crucial Caribbean quality, charisma; he was certainly loved. He became a figure who felt, both to Grenadians and to the grad students and lefties crowding his speeches in London and New York, not only like a heady mix of Marley and Castro; he felt like a lover and a democrat, besides. He didn't seem like someone in whom Castro's occasional dreams of atomic war, as the macho head of a macho-sized island that made Grenada look like Lilliput, could ever take. Utopian dreams, on a lush small Antille with weed and waterfalls from Eden, won new weight. Grenada's new socialist economy, like its old capitalist one, would be based in a trade no less groovy than roasting nutmeg for eggnog, and export.

At least one key person, though, found that mix's prospect not only not appealing but noxious. And sadly for Bishop's Revo, that person became the leader of the Free World just after Bishop became the leader of ninety thousand Grenadians to whom he promised "to make democracy not a once-every-five-years-thing, but an everyday event." This, to Ronald Reagan, wouldn't do. Reagan's Marines began rehearsing an invasion, on Vieques's beaches, soon after he took office. He was determined to snip Bishop's Revo in its heady bud. And when Bishop accepted Castro's offer of helping him build a tarmac able to handle jets larger than prop planes (and perhaps Soviet jets worried Reagan's minders ready to back the Sandinistas or menace Panama's canal), Reagan grew more determined still. His invasion needed a better pretense than a few Cuban contractors pouring concrete. But he didn't have to wait long. The Revo, soon enough, furnished one itself.

It turned out running a state-run economy was harder than painting signs. So was dealing, for the Revo's young leaders, with their own peers' contending ideas about doing so. Certain of Bishop's ministers thought that responsibility for running their party should be shared. Its Central Committee decided—with Bishop's consent and just before he left for a long-planned tour of Soviet Europe—that party leadership would henceforth be split between Maurice and his old lieutenant. Bernard Coard was as uncharismatic as Bishop was charming; he was also married to a foreign woman—a haughty Jamaican, worse—notably disliked by that crucial entity called, in the Revo's patois-flavored populist nomenclature, "the people." When Bishop returned from his trip in the fall of 1983, he informed his colleagues that he was not, any longer, in favor of sharing power. He was placed under house arrest; the people, unsurprisingly, wouldn't have it. Thousands gathered in St. George's; hundreds marched on Bishop's house. They managed, soon enough, to spring him free—but only got him as far, for reasons that still remain hazy, as the old fort guarding its harbor. Built by the French in 1705, the fort had been called Fort George for most of its life, but it had recently been renamed, in a Shakespearean stitch to this story with no shortage of those, for Bishop's martyred dad, Rupert.

Why and how what happened in Fort Rupert's bright yard on October 19, 1983, has been debated by pedants and partisans here ever since. With rumors and Bishop backers swirling outside its walls, soldiers of unplain fealty kept tabs on Bishop, along with his partner, Jacqueline Creft, and seven others. An order came down. Or it didn't. Either way, the soldiers directed Bishop's cohort to face its coral-stone wall. "I wish to face front," he's supposed to have said. He looked his killers in the eye. His body was never found. And then Grenada's trauma was compounded. Five stormy days later, Reagan's Marines swooped in on their Sikorsky choppers, with the 82nd Airborne. They invaded a "little island in the sun" that had never seen anything like the thundering A-7 attack jet that, lacking actual military targets, bombed a psychiatric hospital. Its twenty-one slain patients, in this peaceable place whose people had been behaving unpeaceably indeed, became the saddest casualties of the Cold War's oddest chaplet.

The Americans had an official reason for coming. They said they had to secure the safety of three hundred American medical students who'd come here to earn degrees and tans at the St. George's University of Medicine—and whose safety, of course, was never much troubled. The Americans' truer mission was to confront the Cubans. Fidel Castro, taking a leaf from Khrushchev's missile crisis playbook, had managed to turn a country smaller than his own into Cold War provocation and pawn. In Grenada, the Americans hunted down the sparse Cubans in situ. Then they stayed to toss the seventeen Grenadians they blamed for their trouble—Bishop loyalists and Coard backers alike—into steel crates baking on the Navy boats they'd brought down from Guantánamo. And then the Americans, who transferred "the Grenada 17" to a local jail, went home. Grenada's sorting-out was handled by the country's eastern Caribbean neighbors and the Brits. But thirty years later, those sunny weeks' surreal traumas still hover over St. George's bowl-shaped bay and the sloping streets that rise prettily from its sides. Each one seems to be topped by a stone church, or its roofless ruin.

Grenada lies way down in the southern Caribbean, mostly sheltered from the path of hurricanes coming in off the Atlantic. Its capital's bay-front drive, which is faced with Georgian buildings and a restaurant called the Nutmeg, is built mere feet over sea level. But back in 2004, Hurricane Ivan did hit here; it was easier, people say, to leave the old churches' ruins be than to haul them down. The same ethic didn't obtain with regard to signage from the revolution. But by the iron-railed steps leading up to Fort Rupert, the Revo's love for national colors and idealist cant remains. There, a red, green, and gold banner, reading "ONE NATION, ONE PEOPLE." Another homier sign, nearby, makes overt the reggae tinge of post-Revo Grenadian patriotism. It advertises a "NATIONAL COLORS FETE" hosted by the Twelve Tribes of Israel, a Rasta sect. It's set for February 7—Bob Marley's birthday. By the bay, a group of men stand in back of a pickup truck that's backed up, at the seawall, to a tub-like little schooner with a metal mast. The men are unloading cartons from the truck and into the boat. The boxes are full of plastic jugs of cooking oil, and corn flakes. One of the men wears an Atlanta Hawks T-shirt. He tells me where they're heading.

"Carriacou."

Carriacou is twenty miles to the north. It's the largest of the Grenadines—those specks of snorkeling heaven beloved of yachtsmen that reach from Bequai through Mustique, up to St. Vincent. But Carriacou, as the first or last of the chain, belongs to Grenada. And boats like this are how Carriacou gets its corn flakes. There's a reason Paule Marshall opened her *Praisesong for the Widow* on the deck of one such vessel, steering from St. George's to the little-sister isle that in the larger cosmos both of Grenada and Marshall's novel is a site for undiluted *folk*—the place in whose annual Big Drum Dance a hurting black woman can come to eat "bambam an' smoke food" and be asked, as she comes to a seat of Africanity purer than anything up north, whether she's "Coromantee? Igbo or Manding?"[24] That's Carriacou. Or was. But those 1970s pieties seem far from the concern of two young men I chat with, in the next boat down, with big fishing poles lining its gunwales and its name, *DELIVEROUS II*, painted in red across its hull. The young men wear too-big Dinkies shorts and wifebeaters, and fondle green bottles of Stag beer. It's unclear whether their workday is done or not yet begun. It's 11 a.m. "Jackfish, yellowfin, snapper," says the one with gold fronts when I ask what they catch. "All dem. Shark, too." He grins at his pal. "But not shark big so', like these fat women here."

None of the women climbing the stairs to Fort Rupert, still over-looking the sparkly bay, is fat. The fort's name has been tweaked back to the Brits' moniker—Fort George. Some of its buildings' roofs, claimed by Ivan and then by ferns, have gone the way of the churches'. But still the site of the Revo's killing is maintained for tourists and students met by the polite woman shelling peas, in a booth outside, who takes my two dollars to enter its courtyard. This is the place where it hap-pened—a half basketball court behind whose rusty rim there's an iron plaque stuck to the wall. "TO THE EVERLASTING MEMORY OF PRIME MINISTER MAURICE BISHOP," along with the names of seven comrades, it reads, "KILLED AT THIS FORT, OCTOBER 19, 1983. THEY HAVE GONE TO JOIN THE STARS AND WILL FOREVER SHINE IN GLORY."

The fort is no longer a barracks, doesn't have the feel of a place used by soldiers to exercise. But it's still got a little gym, says a loud clang off to the side, where a couple of friendly fellows lean sweatily on rusted weights beneath a wrinkled sign that's printed on yellowed Xerox paper. "MEMBERS—REQUIRED ONLY 3 WORKOUTS PER WEEK," it says. It's unclear whether this connotes a limit or a minimum, as to how often one may pump iron with Maurice Bishop's memory. But the price one of the men quotes, when I ask him how much membership costs before I walk back down the hill, is a bargain either way. I have an appointment tomorrow with one of Bishop's closest aides not killed in 1983—which is to say a member of New Jewel's Central Committee implicated, along with Coard and the others, in his murder, and who was only recently freed, after serving twenty-six years, from prison. Selwyn Strachan, New Jewel stalwart, served New Jewel as its minister of mobilization and labor. Today, though, I want to catch a maxi up to the northern town of Gouyave, home to Grenada's main Nutmeg Cooperative.

I chat by the bus stop with a sixty-ish woman in a blue dress whose features, from South Asia, are what people in the southern Caribbean call East Indian. She tells me, as a maxi called FREE UP—not the one we need—passes by, and another dubbed NOTHING YET does the same, that her name's "Fletcher, Azra Fletcher," that she lives by the Concord Waterfall, and that she's never been to New York, but that she has a sister in Brooklyn "who does send barrel" (that is, who sends economy-sized care packages here by freighter, full of needed foods and

Brooklyn things). Azra also tells me she has two daughters in Trinidad, "both pretty," and that she herself lived in Trinidad once, but then came home to quiet Grenada "because in Trinidad, they kill people so." I recall, when she does, a tabloid front page from the last time I was in Trinidad. Its fifty-point headline blared over a lifted-from-Facebook photo of a pretty Indian girl, slain by a jealous lover. "16 STABS," it said. Trinidad, it's true, is a place where "they kill people so"—its fractious polity of a million souls is divided by color and class and contends for power and oil money and drug money and all the rest; coups and crime and political violence are as common as roti. It's the kind of place, unlike Grenada, in which what happened in Grenada in 1983 would make sense. Grenada is a place where, climbing aboard the maxi we need, this one named NOT GUILTY AGAIN, I'm wedged happily between two church ladies in big hats, who politely cry "Conductor!" when they have to get out, before we greet their replacements, with a chorus of "Good afternoon"s. We wind north along the lovely coast, over the driver's chosen soundtrack of Lorde and Eminem and pass a mural, painted on a cement bus shelter, honoring "The Mighty Sparrow—Calypso King of the World." (Sparrow made his name in Trinidad, as every West Indian knows, but it was in Grenada where he was christened with a birth name—Slinger Francisco—that's even better than his sobriquet.) We then pass another bus shelter whose two sides hail Grenada's history with both simple pride and what seems a typically Grenadian squashing of its tensions: one of its sides depicts ERIC GAIRY, 1973–1979, in a dark suit; the other shows the bearded MAURICE BISHOP, 1979–1983, in a guayabera. We reach Gouyave. It's a tidy seaside town on whose main street, past a shop called Chubby's Price Cutter Boutique, there's an airy three-story building, which smells both better and subtler than Hershey, Pennsylvania. The Gouyave Nutmeg Cooperative has a shellacked photo, hanging by its door, of a sci-fi-looking off-yellow fruit that's splitting open around a dark-orb pit inside, wrapped with a crimson web of mace.

"We've got 40 percent of the world's trade now," says the plant's foreman. He's a nutmeg-colored man named Aston, who explains how nutmeg, not native to the Caribbean, was brought here from Java as a test in 1843 ("When the fruit opened its own," he says, "they knew it'd work"). He also explains how every one of Grenada's five thousand nutmeg farmers ("Before Ivan, there were seven thousand") belongs to this co-op and how those farmers bring their mace and seeds to a scale out front, and are paid EC$4 (about US$1.50) per pound for each; how the unshelled seeds, which can stay fresh for ten years in that state, are laid out to dry for six weeks on the big drying racks we walk among upstairs; how the dried seeds are sorted, with metal racks through whose golfball-sized holes the smaller ones fall; how the optimal-sized seeds then bounce down a chute and into a great bowl on an octagonal wooden table downstairs around which the workers Aston calls "the ladies"—the nutmeg shellers of Gouyave—sit on vinyl-covered chairs to shell seeds by hand under a sign reading "WORKERS! BRING GOD'S PEACE INSIDE AND LEAVE THE DEVIL'S NOISE OUTSIDE"; how "the ladies," who earn EC$40 a shift (about US$15), then drop each seed into a vase of water, by their station, to glean its density and fate ("If it sinks, it's food grade; if it floats—aftershave"); how the now-dried seeds, hulled and destined either for kitchens or to be used in scents, are bagged in baby-hippo-sized burlap sacks weighing 142 pounds apiece; how those bags, once full and ready for shipping, are brought to the co-op's stencil shop, its racks hung with copper plates cut with the block-stencil names of the bags' destinations (ANTWERP, TRIPOLI) and a few words to be imprinted in dark ink on every one (GRENADA CRACKED NUTMEG, QUALITY). Aston, back outside, says farewell with some recent history. "During that revolution time," he says, "government did take the co-op over. So we very happy, when it' give back again."

Selwyn Strachan, back in town, will disagree. He's a dignified sixty-six-year-old man who's called Sello by his comrades and Breeze by his friends. He served Bishop's government first as its minister of communications and works and labor, and then, in a slightly less wordy recasting of the same expansive office, as its minister of mobilization and labor. Strachan was a fixture in the Revo's visual record—a tall and slim figure, in those days, with cocoa skin and a Bishop-ite beard who helped the leader lead rallies, and once even stood in for him as Grenada's representative to the UN, in New York in 1981, to address the General Assembly not about UFOs but about their island's "transition to socialism." He was a New Jewel stalwart, as close to both Bishop and Coard as anyone. He knows whereof he speaks, there on the guesthouse porch. He pooh-poohs Aston's beef. "In the transition to socialism," he says, "one of our great priorities was bolstering the cooperative sector." He has arrived at the guesthouse with profuse apologies for being late; his old car, he explains, is in the shop and he had to catch a ride with a friend. He's still recognizable from the photos. The height remains; so does the beard, though now it's snowy; the cheekbones are even more prominent, on a face gone prison-gaunt. His once-bright eyes have lost some spark. But serving twenty-six years in jail didn't extinguish them. Sello was responsible, before Bishop's death, for overseeing the Revo's "ideology and agitprop"; he was the man behind the signs and slogans, in other words, on which Naipaul so effusively shat after Grenada's "transition to socialism" came to grief in 1983. During his visit here, Naipaul didn't see Strachan. The Grenadian revolution's chief propagandist and its sharpest critic didn't meet: Strachan, in early November 1983, was padlocked in one of those sweltering crates on a Navy ship offshore. He was to be tried and convicted, that winter, by an ad hoc court of dubious probity, for his role in the chaos that saw his comrades killed. He was sentenced to hang. Six years later, when Grenada's pre-Revo constitution was restored in 1989, he and his fellow members of the Grenada 17, whose case became a cause célèbre for Amnesty International, saw their sentences commuted to life. It took another twenty years of endless appeals, after that, to win their release. "It's been a very long struggle," he tells me as he puts down his phone. "But it's good to be outside." And his struggle isn't through.

Sello Strachan, tapping at his BlackBerry, has things on his mind. He excuses himself right after we sit. "Pertaining to which matter?" he says into his phone. "We need to file, before steps are taken." He was trained as a lawyer while in prison; it's as a lawyer that he works now. But he's still not allowed, he explains, to do certain things—like argue cases in court. Convicted felons aren't looked on kindly, dodgy convictions or no, by the Solicitors Regulation Authority, the UK body still empowered to judge, in the semi-sovereign states of the British West Indies, whether applicants are of suitable character to be admitted to the bar. "I still have some matters to deal with," he says, "related to the exceptional circumstances of my political historical background." For Sello Strachan, the past's heavy matters weigh on his days not merely in the way you'd expect of a man still living on the same small island where he served years in prison, as every Grenadian knows, for his role in the death of their best-loved son. The narrative he unspools, about his effort to prove the "exceptional circumstances" of his case, and his life, to the Solicitors Regulation Authority, to a length sufficient for him to become Selwyn Strachan, QC, is a story he spent days and years alone in his cell at Richmond Hill prison, it's clear, rehearsing.

He tells me about how he passed those days, in Grenada's one prison, along with sixteen others who were convicted of abetting Bishop's killing—among them, fellow members of New Jewel's Central Committee, including Bernard Coard, and the soldiers who actually pulled their triggers; about how he taught English courses in the prison's education program for two decades; about how he studied for, and earned, that law degree by correspondence, from the University of London; about the hardest weeks inside, when he thought he'd be hung ("We could hear the gallows being built"); about how when Hurricane Ivan blew Richmond Hill's roof off, it was he and Bernard Coard who convinced the other inmates, rushing to escape onto an island with nowhere to hide, to stay put and "earn their release the right way"; about the joy he felt, when, on "the seventh of February, 2007," a special Privy Council order from London caused the resentencing of the Grenada 17 and a release that finally came on "the fifth of September, 2009. I bear moral responsibility for the prime minister's death." He's had thirty years to distill his point. "My name has to be attached. But a legal responsibility and a moral responsibility are completely different things."

His segue into how this responsibility should be apportioned, for "the prime minister's death," is smooth like eggnog. He recounts the debates enjoined within, and challenges faced by, the New Jewel's Central Committee as they tried to effect "socialist transformation" on an island of farmers and fishermen and a few wealthy merchants whose economy's "orientation was capitalist" but which was "pre-capitalist in its mode of production." He explains how, given that Grenada "didn't have what's known, scientifically, as a national bourgeoisie," they thus had "to pursue a mixed economy, state-sector dominant"; how the "programmatic platform" tied to building that economy did manage, "by the time the revolution imploded, to start forty-four state enterprises in sectors from fisheries to concrete"; and about how those enterprises also managed "to reduce unemployment from 49 percent to 14 percent," without "necessarily providing a massive wage for every job, but with a massive social wage"—free education, and the like—"built in"; and also how running all these programs, especially after the revolution's "hero phase" waned, became hugely difficult. "The leadership thus had to rock back. To analyze, prioritize, and rationalize." It was in the context of these discussions that "the aim of marrying Maurice and Bernard's respective strengths, and leaving their weaknesses behind"— the proposal for dividing the prime minister's responsibilities—was first introduced and then, with Maurice and the Central Committee in full assent, affirmed as "the decision," says Sello, "which pure and simple, led to the implosion of the revolution."

"And you know," he continues, "Maurice did have reservations. He had to be reassured that it wasn't a vote of no-confidence. That it was about saving the revolution; but he was reassured. When on September the fourteenth, 1983, we finally had the vote, it was a sigh of relief. We went up to Maurice's for a round of drinks. But the whole problem was that he was scheduled to leave the next day."

"The whole problem," Sello explains, wasn't necessarily that Maurice was gone; it was those pulling the PM's ear while on his plane to Havana and Prague. "Because he found himself in the hands of people who used the occasion to put a lot of things in his head. To prey on Maurice's genuine weakness, which you see a lot in leaders, to want to please everybody."

"Like Obama," I suggest.

"Precisely. And on this trip Maurice was surrounded by these people—his press secretary and his protocol officer, his chief of security, the chief mischief maker, who were running these things through his head. Telling him that it was all a plan; that the next step was to remove him from leadership. And for the first time in the entire revolution, Maurice never contacted Bernard Coard or myself from the road. To keep abreast of developments. He's our leader. But for the first time, not a word. Which was instructive. He'd left in the midst of a party crisis. But—nothing, right up until he returned." Sello pauses, looks at his BlackBerry. Then he continues. "I was called out of a breakfast meeting. I was seeing visitors from the United States, discussing our radio station, modernizing equipment. But in the middle of this meeting, my security detail came; they'd just received word that the prime minister was returning. So I rushed to the airport. But nothing was happening there—not for hours. Until the Cuban chargé d'affaires showed up. The Cubans had the right schedule, which was also instructive. It was evening now. And Maurice's plane arrived—a private plane that the Cubans had donated to us, for traveling around the region. Maurice and I, as usual, rode back to St. George's in the same car. And he told me then that he'd been reflecting. He told me then that he'd changed his mind. That he wasn't in accord now with what we'd voted on. That he wanted to go back to the leadership. I told him, I understood where he was coming from. 'This is not a light decision,' I told him. 'But by all means, I will go back to the leadership, to inform them of the need for an emergency meeting, so we can discuss it.' And that was that." But the chain reaction, say both Sello's rising tone and use of the passive voice, went from there.

"So we met. Maurice put forth his decision. We broke for lunch.

And that's when it hit—a rumor. All over the country. The rumor that Bernard Coard and his wife were planning to kill Maurice Bishop. The rumor, it was clear, had been planted before the meeting. It hit the ground. Took like fire. And that was the beginning of the end, as different decisions were taken." He anticipates my question. "Different entities were taking decisions. The decision to put Maurice under house arrest—that was taken by the security. But we had to endorse it. And it was a bad decision. Because Maurice was the link to the people. The people want their leader. So, soon there are thousands in the streets— the most from at any time in the revolution. And you see where the thing is heading. One decision. Then another. And another." Until, Sello's tailing-off voice says, people end up dead.

I have to ask. "Do you, given all that happened, and the death of your friend, have any regrets?"

His look says I'm mad. "Absolutely not! The revolution is the greatest thing that ever happened to this country. The greatest. Life has shown that. A black revolution, in the West Indies. It was earth-shattering! We raised literacy to 99 percent. We lowered unemployment, in four years, from 49 percent to 14 percent." The first statistic is likely fair. His well-loved second may have the ring, depending, of being produced by a onetime chief of agitprop. But this New Jewel stalwart and Man of the People so down for the cause that he saw friends slain for it is sticking to his guns. "The revolution," he insists, "never lost its support. Across all classes and strata, the programs of the revolution, in the people's heart of hearts, remains."

In this member of the people's heart, anyway, that's true. Whether it's also so for the boys on *DELIVEROUS II*, or for Azra Fletcher, may be another story. But the Grenadian revolution's chief both of poetry and prose has flashing eyes and a firm handshake. He looks at once steadfast and as confused as anyone, about how his island's effort to better its lot had to end, as he stands out by the road, still hopeful, waiting for his ride.

Barbuda

BARBUDA: I ALWAYS DID want to go. Both because of how it's an island apart, and because of how it's not. Barbuda bobs off the Leewards' northeast shoulder like a long-bodied fly; it looks, on maps, like an afterthought. It belonged once to the British crown. Now it belongs to the nearby island the crown used as the Leewards' administrative capital and whose name, Antigua, now lends itself to an island nation, "Antigua and Barbuda," comprised, as a kind of administrative hangover from that fact, of not one substantial island but three. The first of these is Antigua, an amoeba-shaped Antille whose drought-wracked coves once sheltered pirates but now host beached tourists tended to or resented, or both, by its eighty thousand residents. The second, Redonda, is a guano-covered rock whose sole residents are booby birds. Barbuda is the third: a low coral place, thirty miles to Antigua's northeast. In photographs it seems to resemble, with its arid aspect and wandering feral cows, a slice of old Utah plopped in the Caribbean. Barbuda, like its near namesake, Barbados, began its colonial life claimed by Britain. In 1674, though, the crown leased all its acreage to Barbados's Codrington family, for the annual rent of "one fat sheep (if demanded)"—and it remained a private preserve of the Codringtons, who also owned substantial plantations in nearby Antigua, from then till the nineteenth century.

Barbuda's limestone is covered by a thin layer of sandy soil; it was never much use for plantation-scale agriculture. The Codringtons' estate managers made brief stabs, with the slaves they brought to tend the place, at growing cotton and sugar. They also tried, and abandoned, aloe and ginger and cochineal. But the main use to which Barbuda was put, from the start, was as a place to grow provisions for the Codringtons' plantations in Antigua, and for grazing the livestock which became the forebears of those semi-wild cattle and mules still wandering its scrub. Scarcely more oversight was applied to Barbuda's human inhabitants. Some of the Codringtons' agents, at different times, lived here with one or two overseers; others simply sailed over, on occasion, to check in and then return to Antigua with a hogshead of yams or a sheep. Barbuda's slaves, like their peers on the littler Grenadines or in Grand Exuma, enjoyed a level of autonomy over their own affairs, on their desert island, far greater than those unfortunates cutting cane on Antigua and on other islands, for whom they grew provisions and whose Hobbesian lives, as a general rule, were both brutal and short.

Barbuda became a place, for this reason, to which myths attached. From early on, the island—whose residents were surrounded by plentiful sources of protein walking and swimming all around them—

attracted attention, from the Codringtons' agents and their visitors, for having "Negroes . . . far better fed, stronger, and more healthy" than any in Antigua.[25] It also became known for the astonishing way in which those Negroes didn't merely reproduce themselves, after the last addition of new arrivals from Africa here in the mid-1700s, but substantially grew their number. These islanders' health and vim had far more to do with their conditions of life, as compared to the grim standards of the sugar islands, than with their owners' aims. But that didn't stop Barbuda from becoming the main Caribbean locus of a myth that also became, in the antebellum United States, a persistent staple of the racial imagination. Where Americans nurtured lurid fantasies of Virginia stud farms—places where Mandingo supermen were bred like horses and stood ready, in Yankee minds twisting with bigotry and desire, either to vanquish white honor or enact its fantasies—so did similar stories circulate about Barbuda. These tales, propagated in history books even now, spoke of a remote island where "Christopher Codrington dreamed up the practical idea," as one popular account put it, "of developing a race of . . . king-sized slaves."[26]

There's no evidence that Christopher Codrington, of Codrington College fame, ever wrote or said anything about what he "dreamed up" in this regard. The same goes for any of his progeny or agents, none of whom left behind anything as suggestive, even, as the sole misty quotation to which historians in the United States once pegged the Mandingo myth—a hardly clear but oft-quoted speech by an obscure state legislator, in 1832, who described Virginia as a "grand menagerie where men are to be reared for market."[27] That the image of this menagerie, based on no more documentary proof than that, should have lodged so deeply in the American mind, and sprouted a thousand paperbacks and porn flicks, has of course said more about the weird eros attending America's "peculiar institution," and the varied lusts its whites projected onto enslaved blacks, than it has about the actual history of Virginia. The same holds, no doubt, for Barbuda. But one interesting thing about Barbuda's breeding myth, at least from afar, is the way that Barbudans themselves, like the members of the island's main fraternal organization in New York, the Barbudan Brotherhood Social Club, have also embraced it. "Barbuda was used as the experimental breeding ground for slaves," says that organ's charter, with pride, "thus producing some of the strongest slaves in the West Indies." My curiosity about how Barbuda's fifteen hundred inhabitants now approach its myths is part of

why I'm keen, at the start of a week's stop through Antigua and its satellites, to catch the small ferry, in Antigua's grim little capital of St. John's,
over to Barbuda's sole town of Codrington. The ferry departs most days
for the sister isle, which, to judge by the two stories about Barbuda in
the *Daily Observer* I pick up at the Antigua airport, still nurtures a feel
of the Wild West.

One story reports, "Barbuda's Power-Outage Set to Continue." The
other is related: "Thieves apparently took advantage of the electricity
load-shedding," it says, "to steal what is initially estimated as a quarter-
million dollars from the Barbuda Council."[28] These are Eastern Caribbean dollars, not U.S.—250,000 of them equals some 80,000 greenbacks.
The money had been flown into Codrington on Thursday from Antigua and stored in a safe ahead of being distributed, on Friday's payday,
to the many Barbudans who work for their government. Mysterious
bandits, the story reports, took advantage of the fact that "electricity
was intermittent overnight, leaving the island pitch black . . . with no
moonlight last night," to make off with the safe, which "weighs several
hundred pounds, requiring a team of people to lift it." The immediate facts, in both stories, are intriguing. More telling about those facts,
though, are the deeper ones they imply—the truth that Barbuda and
its civil servants are dependent on their neighbor, both for electricity
and jobs; that even those Barbudans with good jobs as civil servants,
it seems, are paid in cash, which, should they wish to put it in a bank,
they'll have to take over to Antigua.

For Antigua, whatever it lacks, doesn't lack for banks: indeed, banking of the "offshore" kind, along with that other "industry" that's not
an industry, tourism, is the main source of income for an island that
seems to have piracy in its blood. This is a place where in the free tourist
magazine called *The Antiguan* that's stacked in the airport, there are ads
describing how, "by making a US $250,000 donation (nonrefundable) to
the National Development Fund, foreigners can apply for Antiguan citizenship." It's also an island where the first thing you see, upon leaving the
airport, is a manicured mini-cricket oval with tulips in the outfield, and
pricy-looking Florida-style condos across the street. These were all put
here by Allen Stafford—the disgraced Texas financier who paid his quarter million U.S. dollars to Antigua's government, before placing many
of his ill-gotten assets in Antigua's banks (though he was still busted by
the U.S. feds in 2009 for his Ponzi-style frauds). Stafford's Potemkin village's welcome-tableau is a comfort, one suspects, for the many foreign

visitors here who, after blinking at his cricket ovals' canned charm from behind a tour bus's tinted windows, won't come fully awake again until they're deposited by similarly landscaped oases, with imported flowers and wasteful green lawns, at one of Antigua's many all-inclusive resorts. But if you're heading into St. John's proper, where Antiguans live, this tableau falls away to reveal a poor town whose pocked streets are all named for "English Maritime criminals" like Hawkins and Drake. As native daughter Jamaica Kincaid put it when she returned to where she grew up on Horatio Nelson Street, after twenty years away, and wrote her masterpiece on the uniquely stale air of this place, "all the ways there are to acquire large sums of money are bad ways."[29]

Most tourists who arrive to Antigua by air head straight to the new Sandals outside town, or cross the island's scrubby central hills to the marina by English Harbour, and never see St. John's at all. There is a place to stay in town, though, by the one spot here that many foreigners do see—the cruise ship dock. It's built, at that dock's end, into a desultory complex that's called Heritage Quay but whose buildings are wood and plastic facsimiles which, though meant to evoke the 1780s, look like they were built in the 1980s instead, and haven't been much maintained since. At the Heritage Hotel, the woman behind the desk stands before a sign proclaiming St. John's aim to become "the best brand in Caribbean tourism, and life." She gives me a room on the third floor. Its cracked concrete balcony overlooks a long cement jetty to whose sides are moored two immense cruise ships. By the entrance to the jetty, a pair of booths are set up to welcome such boats' passengers. The booths' sign informs visiting gringos that they can get their hair braided into little faux dreadlocks right here, by a member of the Antigua Hair-Braiders Association ("$5 US ONE BRAID," it says, "$30 US FULL HEAD") or head straight for one of Antigua's corners where white folks flock, with a licensed driver from the Antigua Taxi-Drivers Association ("STANDARD RATES," the sign says, "SANDALS/DICKINSON'S BAY US $20, ENGLISH HARBOUR US $35"). My hotel room may not call to mind "the best brand in Caribbean tourism, and life," but it would be perfect for a visiting member of Interpol needing to look out for a dodgy banker coming off one of these boats to alight here and become Antiguan, perhaps, with a suitcase full of cash.

"Just come tomorrow, eight a.m.," says the woman down the quay, by where the Barbuda ferry docks. I've told her that I don't want the package tour she's evidently obliged to offer all white people here (it includes "a lobster beach lunch and a horseback ride"), but do want a simple ferry ticket that will let me visit the island for a couple of nights and then return. The woman, who has white skin and a French accent and the air of someone who landed here as part of some expat's island fantasy, maybe, but ended up peddling package tours by St. John's ugly wharf, says "No problem." I thank her and, heading past the shuttered hair braiders and off of Heritage Quay, walk into St. John's near-deserted streets to look for dinner at a place whose hand-painted sign says "ELENA'S SNACKETTE, SERVING THE PUBLIC FOR MANY YEARS." I'm surprised to find, inside, not a West Indian woman but a smiling brown-skinned one, speaking Spanish, who says her name's not Elena but Marisol, and that the place is under new management. Marisol's clientele are all male and all Dominican like her. They drink green bottles of Presidente beer and tell me over watery stew and white rice and a couple of cold Presidentes, which are the meal's best part, that "there are plenty Dominicans here now, to work! We're everywhere." Heading home, I pass on the empty street shuttered shops whose names suggest they're owned by the "Syrians" or Chinese who own much here, and an ominous sign warning, "This place may not be burglarproof but you are not bulletproof." In my room over the cruise ship dock, I find a superb view of the dredging boat, which rumbles slowly back and forth across the bay all night, to ensure that it will remain deep enough for the next day's hulking cruisers, and shining its spotlight back and forth across my room's wall over the bed till dawn.

The myth of Barbuda's breeding past, says the best scholarly article on the subject, was so widespread that one of that article's authors, a geographer eminent among Caribbean scholars, acknowledges that he himself repeated it often, like most of his peers, before completing the research detailed in "The Past of a Negro Myth." David Lowenthal, and his colleague Colin Clark sifted through a few centuries of the Codrington family's archives in Gloucestershire, along with a key store of their plantation managers' surviving letters and records housed on microfilm at the University of Texas. Their study's findings were conclusive: "There was never a deliberate program of slave-breeding in Barbuda," they say, "nor did the Codringtons contemplate this as a possibility."[30] But just as interesting as the myth Clark and Lowenthal's research destroyed, of course, was what the archives they studied revealed about the society that did emerge on Barbuda—and about how that society's unique traits, especially in the years surrounding the end of slavery in the British Antilles in 1835, fed the great myth about it.

Barbuda's population of blacks, records show, increased between 1750 and emancipation, eighty-five years later, from barely two hundred to over five hundred. Records also show that this growth, which was not tied to any interventions by the island's owners, was instead attributable, in those owner's own eyes, to the island's "virtual self-sufficiency." This was a place where blacks were "constantly engaged in hunting" and in entrepreneurial activity, too, and who enjoyed such power vis-à-vis their owners, in a place supposedly built to breed them for export, that in fact "no persuasion [could] induce any of them to leave." It was an island where, even before emancipation, they were spending most of their time "harvesting firewood, fish and livestock to sell," not for the Codringtons, but for themselves.[31] Barbuda was an island, in other words and as one of the family's agents opined after visiting in 1826, whose slaves "in reality have little more of servitude in their condition than the name"[32]—and who unsurprisingly couldn't be convinced after emancipation, either, to leave settled lives for the promise of sketchy jobs as paid "apprentices" on an Antigua plantation. It was this fact that prompted the Codringtons, who claimed of Barbuda's blacks that "nothing can alone take them from that island," to ask for extra compensation from the crown for their property lost to emancipation.[33] And it was at this moment, too, when Barbuda's imagined past was born, propagated for acquisitive reasons by some of the Codringtons' allies, and for more prurient ones by those prepared to believe a tale whose twin thrusts were perhaps summed up best by a Codrington agent. In 1837, with illuminating candor about his attractions, he judged that "a large number of the men are tall, upright, athletic, and well-proportioned, and the women very many of them the finest figures I ever saw—barring their colour I should call them perfectly magnificent!"[34]

Barbudans, in 1837 as today, were no more likely than any West Indian to be over six feet than under. But even more true: their owners who barely owned them had nothing to do with it, either way. Yet the widespread sense that these people—under slavery—bore the carriage of persons both proud and well fed, rather than degraded and hungry, had real historical causes and real historical effects. And those effects in particular, one suspects, have shaped its modern history in ways suggested by the Barbudan Brotherhood's charter in New York, but sensed more strongly by the small-island pride evinced by its own political party, the Barbuda People's Movement, whose leader, Mr. Mackenzie Frank, features prominently in the *Observer*'s new story the next morning on the power outage still ongoing.

I read the story with my instant coffee at the Heritage Hotel. It says the outage may soon be over: a new motor was just shipped to Codrington, for Barbuda's little power station, from St. John's. But Mr. Mackenzie Frank of the Barbuda People's Movement is losing patience. "They brought a generator over from Camp Blizzard," Frank says in the story, "but it mashed up. It can't carry the load." Frank also says that perishables are going bad in Codrington's market. The blackout has caused other casualties: two thousand tilapia at the Barbados Research Complex, a fish farm whose aquaponic system failed because of the blackout, have died. Mr. Frank, for his part, is "en route to Antigua in search of what he described as 'peace of mind and comfort.'"[35]

There is some good news from his island: the safe removed from the local government offices by thieves, it seems, has been recovered. The bandits hadn't made it far, on a desert island with few escape routes. The safe was found in an abandoned house, a hundred feet from the council, with the cash still in it; the bandits had tried to break it open, but didn't succeed. Barbuda's civil servants would be paid. And to guard against future incidents, the regular delivery of cash to Barbuda would be changed up, according to an official the paper identifies as National Security Minister Steadroy "Cutie" Benjamin. "There will not be consistent monies movement at particular points in time," Mr. Benjamin says. "We will make sure that we put an end to any regular behavioral pattern."

On the quay, few of those waiting for the ferry to Barbuda look much concerned. Few of them, in fact, look Barbudan. Most of them tote snorkels and folding chairs and speak German or British English—they've booked the package tour. A power outage won't hinder their "lobster lunch" or snorkeling: anyone staying over in Barbuda will lodge at one of the little luxe spots whose owners, no doubt, don't trust their livelihoods to Antigua's dodgy power company, and have their own generators. The Frenchwoman who told me to turn up at 8 a.m. is toting a clipboard in her sundress. She's harried now, less optimistic about my getting on the boat. These people with snorkels, she says, have bought the package tour. "And whatever tickets are left for walk-ups"—she gestures toward the only nonwhite people in the waiting area—"will go to them." The group includes a young mother, carrying big rice-paper bags full of stuff and two young kids; and two young men, one "king-sized" and one not, wearing sneakers and shorts. "It's their home," the Frenchwoman says. "They get dibs." There's no arguing with that. Nor with the fact that this bit of transit infrastructure, like many such services in the Caribbean, caters first to tourists who'll pay full freight, and then second, if its operators are so disposed through their own compunction or government subsidies, to actual locals who need them to get around. The prospects, for an odd solo traveler who's neither of these, aren't good.

The woman with her rice-paper sacks tells me that she is indeed from Barbuda; she's come over for the shopping and to see her sister. Perhaps, once upon a time, an old Englishman on tour could have described her, and the mellow fellows with her, as people "perfectly magnificent." But they are just people now, trying to get home. When I ask her about the theft of the council's safe, she waves the incident away. "Silliness," she says, before offering an utterance—"All' them thief!"—whose subjects at first seem clear, in context, but whose thrust is also marvelously expansive and whose tone makes one feel she could be referring to the bandits, the government, or all men everywhere. Except maybe the men with her this morning, who are also her cousins, one of whom is helping her carry a big electric fan, in its cardboard box. As they board the boat I tell them that I hope the power comes back on soon. She allows that she does, too, so she can plug the fan in.

I don't make it to Barbuda. At least not on this trip. Luckily, though, there's a little plane leaving that afternoon for another of Antigua's neighbors. I want, before heading home, to sink deeper in St. John's depths. But for now, and for a few days, a visit to another island once ruled from here, if thirty miles in the opposite direction from Barbuda and as volcanic and lush as Barbuda is flat and dry, sounds just right. A few hours later, I roll past Allen Stafford's cricket complex once more, and board the little eight-seat aircraft which—after taking off from Antigua's V. C. Bird International Airport and banking over Redonda's guano-covered mass that rises from the sea like a huge sperm whale with whitecaps flicking its barnacled sides—glides on toward Montserrat.

Montserrat

THE STAMP, WHEN THE kind-faced woman at the little airstrip by the ocean lowers her dark brown hand, flipping your passport to an empty page, is a four-leaf clover. Its glowing green ink bleeds through the page. It isn't a nod to local flora; northern clovers don't mix, on Montserrat's lush slopes, with pink hibiscus or the big local frogs that local humans call "mountain chickens." Nor does the stamp, on this luckless isle, signify luck: Montserrat's luckless people, within a few brief years in the 1990s, watched Hurricane Hugo decimate their homes and then saw their volcano blow its top. The clover, rather, recalls some older settlers here: Irish indentured servants, Catholics expelled from their homeland or from nearer-by Nevis, in the late seventeenth century, who came to pick sea cotton on this pear-shaped Antille. Ten miles long, it was named by Columbus for a Catalan hill. Today, Montserrat's "Irish presence" is akin to Rip Van Winkle's in once-Dutch New York. But the stamp's shape and hue still feel fitting, if you've flown over in an eight-seat Piper from the burned-brown neighbor whose name, allege Antiguans wearied of their island's incessant drought, derives from Columbus calling it *Anti-AGUA*. Montserrat, rising steeply from the white-flecked sea, looks like Eden as you rattle toward it at eight thousand feet. And it keeps looking that way when, banking down toward the short runway on a bluff by its northern tip, you absorb why no plane bigger than this eight-seater flies here, and you worry, until you bump to a stop and collect your clover stamp, that it won't be big enough for this one either.

"This airport, sir, only dates from the volcano crisis." The taxi man says his Christian name is Sylvester but his business card cites a moniker—"LA BUMBA"—that matches the one stuck on his Corolla. "Persons do just call me that here," he explains, "from long time." La Bumba has a round, brown face and gentle manners. He also has a Victorian-sounding name he doesn't often use, like many Montserratians, and a predilection for invoking the "volcano crisis," of 1995–97. That event still defines the lives of Montserratians, who were forced by the crisis to leave their homes in the island's old capital of Plymouth. "Square one, sir," is how La Bumba describes the place from where he and his mother had to restart their lives, in the new community of Little Bay, here by this British Overseas Territory's once-deserted northern tip after leaving their old home down by the Soufrière Hills' explosive feet. "All this is new." He waves over a hillside of prefab houses built, like the new airport, by the UK's overseas development agency whose acronym name—DFID—is a word you hear here as often as "volcano crisis." There is a little dock, down by a once-deserted black sand beach where the freighter-cum-ferry from Antigua now docks and a shiny new red-roofed building "that's our new Community Centre, sir, just built by Sir George." Sir George Martin, the producer of every Beatles record, explains La Bumba, "has been a friend to Montserrat from long time."

We wind south along Montserrat's one main road. We pass the painted-white cinderblocks of the Anglican church La Bumba attends with his mum and the general store, Osborne's M.S.O., where they get salt cod and mops ("Mr. Osborne, sir, is our chief importer"). We also pass a spring, gurgling from under Jurassic ferns, about which there is a suitably Celtic-sounding legend: if you drink from it, you'll always return to Montserrat. On the car radio, an announcer for Radio Montserrat is touting the approach of St. Patrick's Day. Black Montserratians, whose forebears came here as slaves to join the Irish on English-owned plantations, toast their ancestral pride with Guinness each year on March 17, too. The announcer also lets us know about a can't-miss event this weekend. Montserrat Idol is a local singing-contest riff on the popular U.S. television show. It is staged at a bar in Little Bay, and its original eleven contestants have been trimmed, he tells us, to eight. "Before the volcano crisis, Montserrat did have ten thousand people," says La Bumba. "Now it's five."

The crisis didn't claim five thousand lives—immediate fatalities numbered no more than a dozen: twelve poor farmers who chose the wrong day to ignore evacuation orders and check their plots on Soufrière's slopes. But many of those who lost homes in the eruption left for new ones in Toronto or England. La Bumba never considered leaving; his one stint off-island, working construction, was enough. "Antigua, for nineteen months," he says without warmth. "I helped build the new Sandals." But that was that, and now he's back on this island with no Sandals or any such resort. He drops me by a shaded lane that leads to the old plantation house that Sir George Martin bought in the '70s, after coming to Montserrat on vacation and perhaps drinking from that storied spring at Runaway Ghaut. Sir George still visits Olveston House for some weeks each winter, to stay near where he ran a recording studio here in the '80s. But Sir George's place now functions, when he's not in residence, as a tasteful inn whose wraparound porch and gnarled island-apple trees help it look, with its air of faded gentry and photos of Sergeant Pepper's '60s, about how you'd expect Sir George Martin's house to look. It's one of the few places where visitors to Montserrat can now lodge; most of the island's old hotels are now ruined. They were located in what's now the "exclusion zone"—the no-go zone, where no one's allowed to live. Olveston House is managed, when Sir George is away, by two gracious white women in their sixties, who are presiding, this Friday supper, over a veranda full of guests who all call one another Mister or Miss. "Can Mr. Wilson"—one of them gestures toward the bar—"fix you a drink?"

Mr. Wilson wears a starched shirt against his dark skin and not merely a tie around his neck but a pewter rooster on a string. "The key to excellent rum punch," he says, "is nutmeg." Mr. Wilson's rum punch is excellent. So is the company, at the table where I'm seated with a Professor Pulsipher, from Tennessee, and her archaeologist mate. They've been coming to Montserrat for forty years, explain the professor and her white-bearded husband, Mac, to study Montserrat. "Before the volcano crisis," Lydia Pulsipher says, "some hypothesized that the fossils of pre-Columbian people crouching with their heads between their knees, up by Little Bay, were the remains of a sacrificial rite. But that's exactly the pose in which they found those poor people in St. George's after the crisis. It's the pose taken by people, it seems, facing a fast-moving pyroclastic flow."

"Pyroclastic flow" is a phrase, like "volcano crisis" and "DFID," that every Montserratian knows. At the Volcano Observatory here, you can even get a T-shirt that's screen-printed with a photo of the erupting island and the words "WARNING! PYROCLASTIC FLOW INSIDE." A pyroclastic flow is a roiling river of noxious gas and ash, explains the excellent video the observatory screens for visitors, extra deadly when speeding downhill. It's one of these flows that emerged—after two years of sporadic eruptions, beginning in July 1995, that saw Plymouth evacuated; and Montserratians grow used to waking, many mornings, to find their cars coated in ash like snow—from a great magma dome, on Soufrière's southeast shoulder. Bursting that dome's shell on the day after Christmas in 1997, the pyroclastic flow buried their capital and pushed a big chunk of adjacent St. Patrick's Parish, for good measure, into the sea.

Professor Pulsipher, a small blond woman whose southern manners mirror Montserrat's and whose pedagogue's tone reflects a career spent mentoring undergrads at the University of Tennessee, explains that for years she centered her research around a site in St. Patrick's, an old Irish-run plantation called Galway. In 1997, Galway's ruins were buried. But by then, Lydia and Mac had collected years' worth of its detritus, hundreds of ziplock bags full of shards of its old denizens' pottery and bones, which are now stored in the basement of the Montserrat National Trust. They're still coming here from Knoxville, for several weeks each year, to keep piecing together Galway's story in the back garden of the grand old home, just down from Sir George's, where the trust is housed. And it's from there, the next morning, that they take me as far down toward Plymouth as we can go. The short drive passes the now-shuttered AIR Studios where Sir George helped Elton John and Sting's Police make hits back in the '80s. (This is where the Police shot their bohos-in-paradise video for "Every Little Thing She Does Is Magic," too.) Across a dry riverbed, by the road, a big white sign bears a warning in red block letters. "WARNING," it says. "ZONE V. ENTRY BEYOND THIS POINT IS STRICTLY PROHIBITED."

"It's okay," Professor Pulsipher says. "We can go as far as Richmond Hill."

Mac pulls their rental SUV to a stop by a round stone tower: the remnant, they say, of an old sugar plantation. It's now surrounded by ruins of newer age—small houses and larger dwellings with louvered wood windows, some grand and others humbler, but all now in some state of reclamation—by climbing lianas and by rot and clumps of ferns growing from their roofs—by nature. Visible a couple of miles distant, on a slope rising gently from the sea, the ghost buildings of Plymouth sit silent. Mac and Lydia recall walking through town with volcanologists, in January 1998, mere weeks from the burying. The ashy mud was piled so thick around the Catholic church, they recall, that you could walk up and touch the steeple. The surface was cool enough to walk on, they say, but down just six inches, it was four hundred degrees. It's not possible now—or legal anyway, without a hard-to-get permit—to go so far as Zone I, by that buried steeple. But La Bumba is down to go, as far as Richmond Hill's base, at least, after he's done delivering DFID's meals on wheels for Montserrat's seniors.

We pass the Zone V sign again and press past another placard that touts a failed scheme to harness geothermal power here. Reaching an empty straightaway, La Bumba guns the Corolla's four little cylinders. "People does use this here," he allows, "for racing." That, and grazing cattle, he explains after we pass a man meditating on his brown beast, by the road, whom La Bumba greets in patois and for whose cell phone number he asks by saying, "Me glad me see you. How yuh say yuh number?" We find the grounds of the old Vue Point Hotel not far away.

What was once Montserrat's grandest lobby is now caked with three feet of ashy mud under a mostly gone roof. Out back, what looks like a rectangular pond is full of green reeds and frogs. "This pool was once the deepest in Montserrat," says La Bumba. By what seems an old manager's office, I pick up an old plastic case to a VHS tape called "Quality Service Skills, Part II." La Bumba inspects the ash-gray beach below. "When I use' to come here with my gran," he says, pointing to the green trees a hundred yards back from the water, "the sea came all the way there." Montserrat's population may be shrinking. But in size the island is growing, thanks to the same underground tumult that forced the gaseous earth upward and pushed the old residents of St. Patrick's, like the old friend of Lydia Pulsipher's whom we go to see the next day, from their homes.

Miss Sissy lives up by the airport, like most such people, in the hills over Little Bay. But en route to see her, we pass through the exclusion zone's edge and by an old plantation that Lydia says showed up on a 1673 map of Montserrat she's studied and that was home, in the '70s, to an eccentric old American lady, very dear, who bought its house to live her dream of seeing out her days drinking gin in the tropics.[36] Miss Dolores's arrival here in the 1970s previewed the more conventional snowbirds whose arrival, starting in the '80s, made them a still-prominent part, especially in the winter, of Montserrat's social mix. Miss Dolores and her old house have both gone back to jungle now. But by the place's overgrown drive, there's an old man carrying an empty rice-paper sack, who bids us good day. "I' looking for guavas," he says.

"Did you look by Miss Dolores's place?" Lydia asks. "She had guava bushes there."

He had. "I grew up by St. George's Hill, but now all I find"—he invokes a variant of local tree—"is these ginip here."

We wish him luck. Lydia, as we roll away, shakes her head. "So many of those who relocated, after the crisis, are still at sea. DFID moved them into these new houses up north—they're well built, but they've got nothing to do with how Montserratians live; with the old social structure here, and with homes they built to fit it." The social structure she invokes is the "matrifocal yard"—a cluster of wooden homes, once common to Montserrat's warm glens, centered on the house of the oldest able woman, and run by sisters and daughters not necessarily partnered with their children's dads. "In a fluid mating system, men were always sort of portable," the professor says. Which is why the women, traditionally vested with running their yards rather than tromping the hills to hunt fresh guavas or mates, whose lot has perhaps been most changed by moving into a prefab concrete home, up by the new airport, like the one where we find Miss Sissy.

She's frail looking and with glaucous eyes beneath her bright head wrap. But when she rises to say hello in her airless kitchen, her handshake feels like Iron Man's. The room is dominated by a large photograph of one of her daughters, now living in Georgia, who sits with her corn-fed Georgia husband and their chubby-handsome kids, for what looks like a portrait shot at Walmart. "She did marry a white man there!" says Sissy, less with disapproval than wonder. The world figured in the photo, like the one contained in this new home several miles north of where she lived for seven decades, feels many more miles than that from the island where she grew up. But out in her little yard, Miss Sissy brightens among plants she knows as well by touch as by sight. "This' aloe, yes. Good for jaundice. Doctor Dyett"—a low plant with purplish blooms—"does lower your pressure. But I ninety-three years of age! And I no dead yet." The little tree she shows us next is the key. "But when you do it"—she breaks off a leaf—"you don't put the front. Put the back. Just rub it so."

Miss Sissy isn't among those who turn up that night for Montserrat Idol. But few others in Little Bay, suggests the crowd that starts arriving at sunset to find good seats, are passing on an event put on by an expat American couple with matching blond hair and leathery tans who run the Soca Cabana beach bar from September to May. The man's name is Tommy, and he says, in his Hawaiian shirt, that he's got a band called Tommy and the Bahamas. His place fills with Little Bay locals and aid workers and a woman who tells me she's La Bumba's cousin. They sip rum-and-Cokes from plastic cups as Radio Montserrat's staffers ready microphones to broadcast the action live. The judges are two deejays from the station, and a handsome fortysomething man wearing a jaunty Kangol cap. He goes by the nom-de-Idol "Kulcha Don," and his authority to pass judgment on its hopefuls—he's been cast in the acerbic-buffoon Simon Cowell role—rests on his having spent a stint working in New York, in some hazy capacity, in the music business. He doesn't go easy on a young woman who begins her performance of "Skyfall," Adele's contribution to the recent James Bond film, with her back to the crowd. The woman, who has charmingly poured her un–Bond Girl figure into a tight black dress, wobbles her way through the tune before

Kulcha Don tells her, as she holds back tears, that voice lessons could be wise. The whooping patrons' clapped support for her effort is sincere, though, in the group-therapy way karaoke always is, and the warm vibe continues for a pink-skinned fellow who I gather is DFID's new head here. He's an energetic Oxbridge sort whose air-guitar-heavy rendition of "Summer of '69," complete with him doing the splits, seems straight from the charming-the-natives-by-playing-the-fool school of foreign aid work. A bespectacled woman with a church-strong voice, choosing a tune perhaps a touch elegiac for a bar, tries that bit of Leonard Cohen at his most elegiac, "Hallelujah." I leave before learning who won, in real time, anyway. For the results of Montserrat Idol remain the talk of Montserrat (none of these three contestants was eliminated) for the rest of a weekend that ends, at sunset Sunday. At a more buttoned-up affair, at the residence of the British high commissioner, his dominant tone contains more than its own hint, as one suspects most such official events must, here, of elegy for Montserrat's past.

The event is meant to raise money for the Dr. Howard Fergus Island Scholarship. The award is named for the former island governor and Renaissance man who led Montserrat through the crisis; its winner will go off-island to study. Dressed in blazers and skirts, upstanding Montserrat has come out to the seaside manse of a limey bureaucrat whose station here, in a home backed by an emerald hillside over the waves, is enough to make one want to join Her Majesty's foreign service. I meet a few local civil servants whose salaries, too, are paid by the crown, and then chat by the pool with an elegant black man who, I realize, is not only the same Mr. Osborne who's behind Osborne's M.S.O. but also the longtime husband, it turns out, of one of the not-single ladies running Olveston House for Sir George. Then I find a seat with Professor Pulsipher and Mac, while Tommy and his Bahamas, here as a warm-up act, reminisce from a low stage about the old days at the Vue Point Hotel by performing that old risqué calypso classic, "The Big Bamboo." The higher-brow segment of the evening commences with a woman folklorist, who recites poems in dialect about old yard life, "both he and she, and this and that," before trading proverbs with a dreadlocked fellow plainly cherished here, and with reason on the evidence, as an artist and a thespian and a teacher in the Howard Fergus mold.

The man's segue to recalling "the volcano times," as he takes over the stage, is less maudlin feeling than apt. He recites a funny ode to those fine Montserrat women who during the crisis carried themselves, and continued visiting the beauty parlor, like there was no crisis at all ("Ash in the air, she doesn't care; Ash on the ground, and . . . she wearin' four-inch heels: She steppin'"). He tweaks the tone for a piece directed at those patronizing newscasters from abroad, whose praising of this island's "strength" may have meant well, but began to wear. "I tired," he recites in rhythm. "I tired. Tired of coping, tired of sheltering, tired of prefabbing, tired of stressing. Tired of smiling . . . with ash on my teeth." And then Mr. Chadd Cumberbatch reaches his segment's synthesis and payoff, there by the high commissioner's pool on the "Emerald Isle of the West" whose kinship with Erin may be based less in their history's hurts than in the will to render them as lyric. "Man he go to the mountain," Cumberbatch intones. "And we dance in circles. Mother, brother, sister, all. Dance in rainbow colors." That's the start. But the piece's sung part, hummed at the start and middle and end, riffs on a tune that Dr. King would have called an Old Negro Spiritual and that was made famous by Johnny Cash's Carter Family, but whose words, here, Chadd Cumberbatch has recast for Montserrat. And this is the bit that gets this crowd, moist-eyed by his number's end, and on this island that's as pretty as the Cliffs of Moher but that has lost half its people, where it wants to be.

> I was standing by my window
> On that dark July day
> When I saw those ash clouds rolling
> They were taking my people away
>
> Undertaker, undertaker, won't you please drive real slow
> Cause there's someone special, that you're carrying
> And I sure hate to see them go.

Antigua

TAXI DRIVERS. You meet a lot them when traveling. Especially when visiting small places lacking public transit. You end up, when exploring such places, absorbing more from people who drive cars for a living than from people engaged in any other occupation. There's a reason much "travel literature" and reportage, about such places, can leave the impression that cabbies comprise the majority populace or represent a majority view—that their purpose in life, mirroring their place in reporters' notebooks, is to issue bits of eccentric insight to inquisitive scribes.

Guilty as charged.

But if the figure of the taxi driver in the traveler's tale can be turned into a kind of peak-capped archetype, so too does the figure of the "client"—generally, in the Caribbean, a tourist—blend into what amounts less to a kind of person, for drivers freighting them about for a living, than a generic flow of inputs. The daily stream of pink-faced vacationers disgorged on the curb by the V. C. Bird airport in Antigua, or alighting from cruise ships by its Heritage Quay like melting snow-pack in winter, or slowing to a trickle in spring, grow akin, for the cabbies taking their bags, to widgets on a conveyor belt—animate objects to whom they're supposed to offer a bright "Welcome to Antigua!" as they come off the line.

In St. John's the taxi stand by the cruise port abuts a parking lot behind the Heritage Hotel just down from where members of the Antigua Hair-Braiders Association sit on milk crates to plait hair. The taxi stand, like the hair braiders' booth, has a large sign listing a set schedule of fees to common destinations. The men and a few women who gather around it park rattly Toyotas or newer Nissans nearby, and all wear the standard-issue shirt of the Antigua Taxi-Drivers Association. Their pale peach button-downs are embroidered at the breast with the logo of a syndicate they've joined to have the privilege of waiting here, each day, for dazed visitors to amble off the boats looking for a ride to Jolly Harbour's marina or the tourist beach by Dickinson Bay.

On a few mornings I brought my bad hotel coffee to the wharf, where the association's cabbies gather by 8 a.m. with their own Styrofoam cups. They wait, as does the steel band that sets up on the quay, wheeling their drums onto the wharf, to meet the boats. These boats arrive here after an overnight sail from Martinique or St. Thomas, at around 9. In a place whose economy's main good is tourists, access to that industry's low end is controlled through a union. Most of the drivers had begun paying dues to the association, both figurative and real, many years before. Some had belonged for decades. A few had managed to join its ranks after coming here from less-touristed islands nearby and putting in a few years of friend making. One, a man who went by his nickname, Sprat, had come six years before from Dominica. He delighted in reminiscing about a nice man we both knew in the sleepy village of Calabishie, on that mellow island's north shore, and had affixed a warning on his van's front door in what amounted to two languages—"PLEASE DON'T SLAM," and "NUH SLAM UM"—to ensure that, as he said, "all persons know what I mean." A woman driver with olive skin and the corpulence of many people the world over whose working lives involve sitting in place, said her name was Ms. Vieira. She pulled at the gearshift by her van's steering column with calm authority. "I did come here from St. Kitts when I married an Antigua man," she told me. "He was shrewd with the financials, and we did have children, but it didn't last. You know how it go." Ms. Vieira smiled patiently as she told me that many people moved between St. Kitts and here. "All this talk about the new Caribbean community, CARICOM and so— we've been moving among these islands since time. My grandfather was one of thirteen Portuguese brothers, from Madeira. I've got cousins, from where the brothers settled, all across the Leewards; Windies, too." Sprat and Ms. Vieira, though, were the exceptions. Most of the association's members had spent their whole lives on Antigua.

One such drove me across the island to Willikies and furnished a running commentary as we went, in his island's Victorian-sounding Anglo-Antillean patwa, on how slaves in Antigua's scorched-dry fields once drank a beverage, made from brown sugar and water, that they called *brebitch*; on how sour sop fruits mature ("When it ripe, it could hard") but may also cure cancer ("It may slow, but it does work"); and on how eating mangoes in excess can make you "defecate and so—change your body language." He also explained how, though he'd never traveled farther from Antigua than St. Kitts, his son, who had neurofibromatosis, was now living all the way up in Maryland, where he was to get treated, and from where his father was sure "he gon get out, in the process of time." We paused where some friends of his were playing, and then arguing, over the stones-in-a-wooden-tray backgammon-like game that's called mancala in Africa but "warra" here. When we passed Antigua's big cricket ground—the Sir Vivian Richards Stadium looks big enough to hold all the island's people—he admonished me that as great a batsman as Viv Richards was, "you can't forget that man Roberts: he took five wickets." I had no idea what long-ago match he was referring to. The sticker on his car's bumper, though, perhaps offered a clue: it commemorated a test between the West Indies and England, back from the era when the West Indies beat all comers, with the phrase "WE v. THEM." When I complimented the sticker, he said, "It's a West Indies thing. We like to go big, one time!"

On one of my last days in town, I met the Antigua Taxi-Drivers Association's head. He had won his position by dint of seniority, and he gave his name as "Benjamin, Desmond Theophilus Benjamin." He said he'd been driving a cab for fifty years. "Five-zero, since 1963," he said for emphasis. Desmond Theophilus Benjamin had the responsibility of keeping tabs, in his head and with the help of a marble-covered notebook he kept on the passenger seat of his aged Corolla, on all three hundred of the association's members. "Those that don't go out today," he explained, "must be first to queue tomorrow." When I asked his age he said, "I have seven-eight years. But my birthday is U.S.A. tax day—April 15. So soon I'll have seven-nine." When he was young he'd worked cutting sugarcane from 6 a.m. to 6 p.m., each day, he said, for six shillings a day. Then he'd turned to driving a cab. In those days everyone here drove Plymouths, American cars. Now he drove a Japanese one, like most every driver here. In Antigua, people drive on the left, as in England. But since he'd learned to drive in an American car, his Toyota was still a left-hand drive, as in the States. Not that he'd ever left Antigua. (Not even for St. Kitts? *Never.*) Desmond Theophilus Benjamin was still working, and had no plans to retire, "because young people today does wear inch-long fingernails, and trousers way below they waist. They don't want to work." His one-line exegesis of Antiguan history was this: "Once we worked for sugar, now we work for you."

I asked Desmond, which is what he told me to call him after we talked for a while, to take me to a place that wasn't on the association's list of standard fares. The place was just several blocks from the taxi stand, up Market Street, past Drake and on the edge of town. Desmond knew how to get to the Princess Margaret School before I told him the address that I'd found for it. "I know plenty attended Princess Margaret," he said with a half smile that betrayed nothing of the stories behind it except that they were there. We pulled up to a low white building, visible across a drainage ditch. Its front lawn needed mowing. The school's motto was painted on a sign outside: "The World Is in Need of Good Men and Women."

I'd wanted to visit the Princess Margaret School because a woman who went there in the 1950s went on to become as fine a writer of English prose as emerged from the West Indies, or from anywhere, in the last decades of the twentieth century. Desmond wasn't familiar with Princess Margaret's most famous alumna, either from when she was called Elaine Potter Richardson, which was her name when she lived here, or from the books she wrote after leaving Antigua and changing her name later on. But he was glad to wait bemusedly by the car, waving to passing friends, as I took a couple of pictures.

Jamaica Kincaid's first published work, in the magazine where she made her name, was not credited either to her Christian name or to the new moniker she gave herself after leaving St. John's for New York. The work appeared in the September 30, 1974, issue of *The New Yorker*. It was a brief notice about the annual West Indian Labor Day Carnival in Brooklyn, in the magazine's "Talk of the Town" section. It ran without a byline, as was customary for "Talk" pieces at the time, and began by employing a royal pronoun also common to these pieces then. "Speeding across the Manhattan Bridge with our sassy Antiguan friend," the piece began, before then describing "a few of the things one ought to know" about the sights on display on Eastern Parkway that afternoon: the difference between Mighty Sparrow and Lord Kitchener; Jumping Up ("key West Indian concept"); White People who go to Carnival ("many looked as if they were doing fieldwork for an extension course in Intercultural Interaction: the Folk Experience"); and Shabazz Bean Pies ("the number one third world dessert").[37] The column may have run without a byline, but its author was in fact the same sassy Antiguan friend whose views had recently begun to appear in "Talk" pieces penned by the section's lead writer, George W. S. Trow. Jamaica Kincaid was a real-life friend of Trow's whom Trow had begun taking along to the art parties and society dinners that he covered. She was a tall young woman with eccentric style (she favored jodhpurs, short blond hair, and bright red lipstick) who had arrived in New York from Antigua as an au pair a few years before, but had recently determined to become a writer instead, and had given herself a new name to do so. That September, she'd shared with Trow some notes about the Brooklyn carnival they'd attended together. Trow had shown them to *The New Yorker*'s editor, William Shawn, who decided to publish them unchanged. Over the next decade, she contributed dozens of pieces to the magazine whose staff she soon joined.

Her first piece for *The New Yorker* was one of the only ones that dealt explicitly with the city's West Indians. But the presence of her voice and vantages in the famously WASP-y magazine signaled the larger role of Caribbean people in its eponymous city: as its most notorious new "ethnic" presence in the postwar era. By the 1970s they had not merely seen their Tower Island Patties gain the metropolitan status Kincaid described in that "Talk" piece—"You know an ethnic group has made it when you can get its foods at the local grocer's"—but they had built an annual carnival that still draws over a million revelers each Labor Day weekend from across the Manhattan Bridge, and beyond, to Brooklyn's Eastern Parkway.

Once she also began writing books a decade later, Kincaid marked crucial trails for the wealth of writers, in our new century, who've made the voices and stories of browner immigrants in Manhattan's outer orbit "matter"—in new ways—to its publishers and prize committees. But if New York provided the necessary stage and launching pad for her career as a reporter, it was her sad childhood in Antigua, and a hard relationship with the emotively distant woman who raised her, that comprised the well she drew from to write sterling novels like *Annie John* and *Lucy* and *The Autobiography of My Mother*. Kincaid's fiction, set on the little British island where she grew up, was unique for the devotion it attracted both from literal-minded critics of colonialism and from literary critics who built her earned repute as one of her generation's most subtly inventive stylists.

But it was in her first book of nonfiction—an essay that got its start as a piece rejected by *The New Yorker*'s then editor, Robert Gottlieb, for being "too angry"—that Kincaid described the weed-choked little school, outside of which I now stood with Desmond Theophilus Benjamin. It wasn't long before she became a student at the Princess Margaret School there, she wrote, that it began to accept students who'd been born outside of marriage ("In Antigua it had never dawned on anyone," she explained, "that this was a way of keeping black children out of this school").[38] When she was a student here, skipping to class from her mum's home on Nelson Street, down Hawkins to Drake and past other byways named for English criminals, the school hired a new headmistress, sent by the colonial office:

> This woman was twenty-six years old, not too long out of university, from Northern Ireland, and she told these girls over and over again to stop behaving as if they were monkeys just out of trees.[39]

The book where Kincaid recalled the Princess Margaret School, and that new headmistress, was called *A Small Place*. It described her first trip back to Antigua after nearly twenty years away. The book's tone may have been stinging, but its sentences' timbre was far less "angry" than matter-of-fact. They parsed the particular wounds of a colonial youth to approach more general failures, of the corrupted leaders and people of an island sometimes called "postcolonial," to salve those wounds' legacies in an iniquitous world. It described returning to a kind of jail whose cell bars were this school's untruths. It recorded the experience of "walking through my inheritance, an island of villages and rivers and mountains and people who began and ended with murder and theft and not very much love."[40]

It involved being reminded of what life in a small place, where "not only is the event turned into everyday but the everyday is turned into an event," was like.[41] Of returning to a place where

[o]n a Saturday, at market, two people who, as far as they know, have never met before, collide by accident; this accidental collision leads to an enormous quarrel—a drama, really—in which the two people stand at opposite ends of a street and shout insults at each other at the top of their lungs. This event soon becomes everyday, for every time these two people meet each other again, sometimes by accident, sometimes by design, the shouting and the insults begin.[42]

Where

[t]he people in a small place can have no interest in the exact, or in completeness, for that would demand a careful weighing, careful consideration, careful judging, careful questioning. It would demand the invention of a silence, inside of which these things could be done. It would demand a reconsideration, an adjustment, in the way they understand the existence of Time. To the people in a small place, the division of Time into the Past, the Present, and the Future does not exist.[43]

Walking the streets of her girlhood, all those alleys named after criminals, Kincaid despaired of how, though Antigua may have changed from a colony into a country (and a country, no less, that would soon change some of those street names to honor black cricketers rather than white pirates), it still remained a place where "all the ways there are to acquire large sums of money are bad ways."[44] She tried to visit the lovely old library whose books provided her, when she was a girl, with a

Way Out; but she found it sitting empty and shut with a sign out front reading "THIS BUILDING WAS DAMAGED IN THE EARTH-QUAKE OF 1974. REPAIRS ARE PENDING." This was the 1980s. She wrote of how the problems of Antigua were the problems of a place where "eventually, the masters left, in a kind of way," and where "eventually the slaves were freed, in a kind of way," but also of how they were the problems of a place where these slaves' descendants, the people now in charge, were having to contend with the troublesome truth, vis-à-vis those who once owned them, that "once you cease to be a master, once you throw off your master's yoke, you are no longer human rubbish, you are just a human being, and all the things that adds up to."[45] And similarly, the enslaved who by simple dint of being enslaved, were held up as noble, had reached a new role, too. "Once they are no longer slaves, once they are free, they are no longer noble and exalted; they are just human beings."[46]

She reflected on how, long after leaving this school, she had learned more of the princess for whom it was named:

> Years and years later, I read somewhere that this Princess made her tour of the West Indies (which included Antigua, and on that tour she dedicated my school) because she had fallen in love with a married man, and since she was not allowed to marry a divorced man she was sent to visit us to get over her affair with him. How well I remember that all of Antigua turned out to see this Princess person, how every building that she would enter was repaired and painted so that it looked brand-new, how every beach she would sun herself on had to look as if no one had ever sunned there before (I wonder now what they did about the poor sea? I mean, can a sea be made to look brand-new?), and how everybody she met was the best Antiguan body to meet, and no one told us that this person we were putting ourselves out for on such a big scale, this person we were getting worked up about as if she were God Himself, was in our midst because of something so common, so everyday: her life was not working out the way she had hoped, her life was one big mess.[47]

There had certainly been changes since the era she'd grown up here, in a place where "I met the world through England, and if the world wanted to meet me it would have to do so through England."[48] Now when she went to an event called a "Teenage Pageant," in St. John's, she found teenagers "parading around a stage singing a hideous song called 'The Greatest Love.'" While her generation's young people "were familiar with the rubbish of England," these were kids for whom "the rubbish of North America" was secondhand.[49] But what preoccupied Kincaid most of all, as she flew to Antigua from the prosperous American city where she now lived, and to whom she addressed her essay, were the people from her adoptive home, her fellow passengers on the plane down, whose flight to this small place comprised not a daunting trip to a bygone home, but an escape. To those people, the salient features of her small place were soft sand and three-hundred-plus days of sun per year, three to seven of which, they hoped, would coincide with their holiday—a holiday on which few would be interested in hearing what Kincaid had enough respect for them to tell them plain: "The thing you have always suspected about yourself the minute you become a tourist is true: A tourist is an ugly human being."[50]

Not that the tourist, she hastened to add, was an ugly human being all of the time; "you may be a very nice person," she assured him or her, this tourist. "You may be a person of whom it's true to say," in the place where you're from, that "all the people who are supposed to love you on the whole do."[51] But when you become a tourist, when you step into that role off an airplane, an ugly person is what you become. You become an ugly person because you hope for some of the very things— like sunny heat, every day—that people in this place, those trying to grow food in a desert, don't. Because on the taxi ride to your resort,

> You see yourself taking a walk on that beach, you see yourself meeting new people (only they are new in a very limited way, for they are people just like you). You see yourself eating some delicious, locally grown food. You see yourself, you see yourself . . .[52]

You see yourself. You see yourself. You also see yourself—if you pay attention and look behind the playacting of those who depend on your presence here for a living, or some approximation thereof—to be a sort of person, here, who isn't much liked. And why should you be? Kincaid does the generous thing of telling you this, too:

> That the native does not like the tourist is not hard to explain. For every native of every place is a potential tourist, and every

tourist is a native of somewhere. Every native everywhere lives a life of overwhelming and crushing banality and boredom and desperation and depression, and every deed, good and bad, is an attempt to forget this. Every native would like to find a way out, every native would like a rest, every native would like a tour. But some natives—most natives in the world—cannot go anywhere. They are too poor. They are too poor to go anywhere. They are too poor to escape the reality of their lives; and they are too poor to live properly in the place where they live, which is the very place you, the tourist, want to go—so when the natives see you, the tourist, they envy you, they envy your ability to leave your own banality and boredom, they envy your ability to turn their own banality and boredom into a source of pleasure for yourself.[53]

Of course, there's also this: even in a small place, even in an encounter between a person who's never left that small place, and one who's just visiting, there's also always the prospect, the possibility, of just being human beings. And there's even the reality of that, too, in the moments when Desmond Theophilus Benjamin and I, observing my inability to grasp the rules of cricket or his misadventures in chasing Princess Margaret girls in his youth, made each other laugh. But as we rolled away from the school and back down Market Street toward Drake, all the history shaping how he spent his days and how I was spending mine, was hovering in the car and between us as well, as it always does: our appointed roles here, in this small place, whose strictures could be transcended but where subversion might never feel total. Recalling Kincaid's words on all this, on how it all plays out, I wondered: Has anyone said it better? I thought not.

CHAPTER 12

AU PAYS NATAL:
ON MARTINIQUE
(AND GUADELOUPE)

BUILT ON A BAKING plain of sugarcane near Martinique's drowsy capital city, the Aimé Césaire International Airport can't not impress you with its airy scale, and gleaming construction. The place seems more befitting of some wealthy city in Alsace than a little Antille. The terminal's arrivals board, hung past its prim patisserie, compounds the feeling. This runway receives six transatlantic flights a day from Paris de Gaulle—and not a single one from nearby Miami or Kingston. And your sense of dislocation is made complete by the smooth street outside; its signs are marked with the fonts and numbers of French *routes-nationales*—as if their endpoint were not Fort-de-France but Paris itself.

For all this, there's a reason. This island, like its sister Guadeloupe, is not a sovereign state but rather an overseas *département* of the country that colonized it. That status, and the French treasury checks and EU infrastructure subsidies that come with it, is the most important fact about Martinique today. But what's perhaps most intriguing about the island's modern past is the story of how—or more to the point, by whom—that status was won.

Aimé Césaire was a poet, French-ly enough. But the figure whose ten-foot face smiles sagely down from his *aero-gare*'s wall, bespectacled and cacao brown as on building sides across his island, was much more than that. Born a country clerk's son in 1913, Césaire left home at eighteen to study in Paris. His *Cahier d'un retour au pays natal*, a pamphlet-length poem first published in 1939, made him a favorite of André Breton's—and a hero to his own peers: that remarkable group of black students and aspiring activists from across French West Africa and the West Indies, with whom Martinique's best and brightest evolved the school of thought known as *negritude*. The philosophy of those dashing Frenchmen *des couleurs* was based in rejecting the self-hate that colonial rule had instilled in black people everywhere ("My negritude is not a stone / its deafness hurled against the clamor of the day . . .").[1] It was nowhere more potently distilled than in Césaire's oblique riff on the experience of returning home, as an ex-colored boy now warmed by the metropole's chill lights, to his native land. Which is part of what makes what he did after actually returning there, especially after the war, so interesting.

Fort-de-France's prodigal son became its mayor (a position he'd retain for sixty years). He was also elected his island's first *deputé* in the French National Assembly. "For centuries, Europe has force-fed us with lies and bloated us with pestilence."[2] That's what he wrote in his fervid *Cahier*. But now in his new post in 1946, he changed his line. Empire's eloquent foe pushed to stay party to its rule. "Departmental-ization," he said, "is the normal outcome of a historic process."[3]

Césaire's position derived both from a rising politician's pragmatism and his poet's Francophilia. Which factor was more key to his helping draft the law creating France's *départements et territoires de'outre-mer* (the DOM-TOMs also include Réunion, in the Indian Ocean, and French Guyana) depends on which of his radical friends or restive heirs you ask: they've been debating the question since. But the impress of his inclin-ings toward the metropole are visible at every turn on Césaire's island. He was an artist whose love for Old World culture, and for Breton's epithet for him ("a black man handles the French tongue better than any white today"),[4] were entwined with—not separate from—his belief that "[Europe] is a dying civilization."[5] For lodged by that precept in the poet's mind and ego was a linked idea, just as deeply held. Europe might have been sick. It may have been dying. But it was not, as negri-tude's less subtle exegetes claimed, worthless. Any civilization that pro-duced Balzac and *Les Fleurs du Mal* retained hope. But Europe's hope, he felt, lay outside Europe. Césaire had consummated his love for Old World civilization in the years just before its descent into barbarism; he'd watched its non-Nazi custodians thrill to Josephine Baker's jazzy moves and Picasso's Bantu-ish masks. This may have been a "sick civili-zation . . . morally diseased"[6]; but if it wished not to "[draw] over itself, with its own hands, the pall of mortal darkness it had to galvanize dying cultures or raise up new ones."[7] The sole hope of the Old France he loved, that is, was people like him.

The complex mix of affinity and zeal evinced in Césaire's stance, and its implications' central role in the larger story of the French Fifth Republic, gave him a place in the latter such that when he died at the age of ninety-four, in 2008, he was given a state funeral attended by Nicolas Sarkozy, and a plaque in the Pantheon itself. In his homeland, he became a figure synonymous with its people's modern story to an extent rarely seen beyond North Korea. He also became a model for a larger generation of grand and grandiose political figures across the Caribbean, who to a man—from Eric Williams in Trinidad up to Jamaica's Manleys and old Fidel himself—espoused Césaire's claims about both the African root of Caribbean culture and the leading roles the Caribbean could play, among the emergent nations of the third world, at the coming "rendezvous of victory."[8] His paternal shadow over the region's writers—and especially the French ones—is even darker. For figures like Frantz Fanon, the Fort-de-France kid turned French psychiatrist whose *Wretched of the Earth* became an anticolonial bible for '60s radicals from the Black Panthers to Sartre; for Edouard Glissant, another Césaire pupil at their island's top lycée, whose elegant tracts on the "poetics of relation" turned his teacher's negritude into a thing more subtly equal to the mixed creole core of Antillean life; for Patrick Chamoiseau, the Prix Goncourt–winning novelist whose richly historical fictions are animated more by the creole *oralité* of Martinique's streets than its metropole's tongue—Césaire's is the model with which writers like these, and many others from the Antilles, have had to contend as fount and foil. And his ideas' shadows have been palpably present, too, over polemics surrounding the French Antilles' great human export of now: those other public artists—soccer players—whose goals in World Cup stadia, firing France to victory in a *Coupe de Monde* contested in Paris in 1998, prompted scenes of joy on the Champs-Élysées more massive than any since the Liberation, and forced a country still unaccustomed to seeing itself reflected in the brown and black faces of its colonies to ask pointed questions about what, two centuries after Robespierre's fall, a Frenchman is.

When the autumn after that win I took a college course, like many liberal arts students at U.S. universities around the fin de siècle, on "postcolonial literature," our first assigned text was Césaire's *Cahier*. Long ago translated into English, the poem's ringing-but-ambivalent lines evinced their author's pride both in his island's nature and in his manhood ("my negritude is neither tower nor cathedral / it takes root in the red flesh of the soil / it takes root in the ardent flesh of the sky / it breaks through opaque prostration with its upright patience").[9] They also suggested some more complex ties to some well-sunned isles, beautiful or no, where that pride had still to be found:

the hungry Antilles, the Antilles pitted with smallpox,
the Antilles dynamited by alcohol,
stranded in the mud of this bay,
in the dust of this town sinisterly stranded.[10]

Encountered thus for the first time, Césaire's lines served as entree
for a seminar of future newswomen and hacks, fully grasping them or
no, to parse how the dramas of colony-and-metropole were crucial not
only to most expressive culture dubbed "modernist" by the twentieth
century, but to modernity's *longue durée*. Césaire's "native land," in
the seminar room and on its own terms as well, resounded as abstraction and allegory: a kind of stand-in, in our transient age, for all the
homeplaces of all those ex-colonials whose names dotted our syllabi
and whose kin, in our lifetimes, had blessedly transformed the feel
and sounds of Paris and New York and Milan and Montreal. But the
abstraction was also a place. It figured, in books like *The Wretched of
the Earth*, by then also a staple of American undergrad curricula, as a
mysterious line in an author's bio ("Frantz Fanon was born in Martinique . . ."). Such lines raised questions about an island, which gave way
to an intriguing suspicion. This French Antille, it seemed clear, had
become the fount of more books crucial to the signal geopolitical story
of its twentieth century—the rebirth of the old Third World's colonies,
in the shadow of the Cold War, as independent states—than any such
bit of once-colonized earth.

When years later I finally made it to Césaire's *pays natal*, to spend
time deepening my rough grip of his best-loved tongue, there was only
one thing to reread, on the flight in. "Iles cicatrices des eaux," it goes.
"Iles évidences de blessures."[11]

Islands scars of the water
Islands evidence of wounds
Islands crumbs
Islands unformed
Islands cheap paper shredded upon the water
Islands stumps skewered side by side on the flaming sword of the
    Sun . . .

The sunned stump that the Carib called Madinina, the island of flowers, much resembles its neighbors—St. Lucia and St. Vincent to the
south, Dominica and Guadeloupe up above—in aspect. With a long

windward coast rubbed by Atlantic swells, and its leeward side curving *crevette*-like around the calm Caribbean, its geography is defined by the great cloud-flecked volcano, Morne Pelée, snoozing over its north, and by the little southern city, Fort-de-France, that stands over where the island's shrimp-shaped shore curls in on itself. Fort-de-France's bay front is backed by gaily painted *auberges* and the art deco lines of its handsome Hotel L'Imperatrice. It now looks much as it must have—with the exception of a plastic-looking McDonald's franchise touting "WI-FI GRATUIT"—when Césaire reapproached it on a transatlantic steamer, at the age of twenty-six in 1939, to launch his grown-up life.

Not that I had the pleasure of seeing as much, upon first arrival, from the sea. For that, I had to wait until a few days later. After visiting the stone ruins, across the bay, of the old plantation where Napoleon's Empress Josephine spent a colonial girlhood amid flamboyant blooms and her daddy's slaves I took a bobbing *vedette* back to town. But the tableau at Césaire International was striking enough. Especially since I arrived on a little LIAT flight from St. Vincent, fresh from a few hours' layover by the low-slung hovel, on that poor nearby island, that's the main entrepôt for a place whose banana-and-weed-based economy has limped along, since being willingly cast from Britannia's rule, with a gait not unlike that of the bored customs agent who perfunctorily stamped my passport, in his blue uniform faded from royal to baby from too many washes, before wandering off, mumbling to himself, for some assignation up the road by which I'd bought a bit of coconut bread from a round-faced woman who told me, as I ate with a Coke by the road's pocked side, about how her son lived in a section of Brooklyn with which I was familiar, and about "All him up to there, Lord!" The round-faced woman seemed, along with a goat munching on some dust, until the customs man returned, like the airport's sole staff. But that was there. And this here, with its rigid gendarmes in de Gaulle–style cap and blinding-white shirts, was different.

"Êtes-vous familier, monsieur," one of them said, glancing at my passport's U.S. cover with unique disdain, "avec tout les implicacions de le traité de Schengen?" Was I familiar with all the implications of the Schengen Treaty, which created the EU? His index finger's rise, as he invoked said *implicacion*s, matched his voice.

I wasn't sure. I said "*Oui.*"

Gainful employment, for *les Américaines* in this eurozone, was verboten. "*Oui.*"

He lowered his stamp. I passed the terminal's big Césaire face; its glass pâtisserie case of flaky *chaussons*; a pretty newsagent who wore a tangerine scarf as she placed new issues of *Psychologies* magazine and nine-euro packs of Gauloises in plastic sacks for her patrons. On the smooth taxi ride into town: shiny Peugeot dealerships; Carrefour *supermarchés*; tidy apartment blocks with a small white dish stenciled with the logo of CANAL-PLUS congruently angled on every balcony, like so many Francophilic sunflowers, toward an orbiter over Paris. It was France in the tropics. And well it should be. For though France's Antillean ventures reached their spectacular but doomed apogee in Saint-Domingue in the eighteenth century, it was the older colony of Martinique—which Paris has been able to hold uninterrupted from the 1630s to today, save for a few years of British occupation in the 1790s—that has always remained, in other ways, the core of the French Antilles.

When in 1635 the chartees of Cardinal Richelieu's new *Compagnie* of American Isles set out for the forbidding Lesser Antilles, the islands they made for were nominally owned by the Spanish. Their actual inhabitants, though, were the Carib, who'd dominated this stretch of the chain since arriving from the Orinoco a few centuries before. The first Frenchmen to brave Martinique's beaches to confront the Indians found the same fate as Spain's friars who went before: they didn't come back. Soon enough, though, a group of colonists with bolstered resources and determination succeeded in pitching a camp beneath Morne Pelée's peak. They drove Madinina's *Carib* toward the island's rough Atlantic shore and then fell back to the sheltered bay around which they harvested dyewood. By the time Richelieu's Compagnie was liquidated in 1651, its members had managed to found sizable settlements not merely in Martinique, but also on nearby Guadeloupe, St. Lucia, and, farther south, in Grenada. (Dominica and St. Vincent, still Carib-dominated for now, were another story.) That year those holdings were sold off to private investors: the Knights of Malta ended up with St. Barts; the Sieur d'Houel got Guadeloupe; the best-developed French island, Martinique, became the property of the du Paquet family. For the sum of sixty thousand livres, the du Paquets bought Grenada and St. Lucia, too. Martinique's new owners moved haltingly, with their planter friends, to build lives from old Madinina's flowers and trees.

At first, they relied on the toil of poor white *engagés*—debt peons from the metropole, many of them expunged Protestants. But after

France won its *asiento* from Philip V to enter the slave trade in earnest in 1701, that all changed. The French advantaged this new era, most famously, in Hispaniola's remote northeast. Saint-Domingue, during its scarce ninety-year life, made the merchants of Bordeaux and Nantes rich, brought nearly a million slaves to the New World, and augured its young history's most astounding event. But if the Haitian Revolution comprised the most famed fallout from France's island ventures, its other sugar *îles* also experienced huge growth—and revolutionary drama—before the long eighteenth century's stormy end.

Of Paris's two smaller pearls in the Lesser Antilles, it was Guadeloupe—and especially the butterfly-shaped island's flat eastern wing of Grand-Terre—that was best suited to growing sugarcane. Martinique, though, was no slouch. And with its better infrastructure and larger populace of rich planters invested in making Antillean lives, it was the picturesque town they built here at Morne Pelée's feet, St. Pierre, that became "the Paris of the Antilles." Together, the two islands were so dear a prize that in the 1760s France let the Brits have Canada in exchange for keeping them. Martinique developed as a sophisticated colony which, in the age of Diderot, was subject to an encyclopedic census that noted a population in 1798 of 83,020 slaves, 9,811 *blans*, 9,349 free people of color, and some 11,000 cows. (The document also counted mules and ceiba trees.) All these inhabitants were convulsed during France's Age of Revolution, first by a Republican government's decision in Paris to end slavery in the colonies, and then by Napoleon's determination, after declaring the First Republic's end, to see slavery returned to the French Antilles by the loyal generals he dispatched to that end, with better than fifty thousand troops, in 1802. Napoleon's brother-in-law Leclerc's eventual defeat in Saint-Domingue heralded the Haitian Revolution's final victory. But the empire's mission, like its old slaves' resistance, wasn't limited to Haiti. And Napoleon's General Richepanse, dispatched to Empress Josephine's home islands, met the Lesser Antilles' own answer to Toussaint and Dessalines. The *nègres* of Martinique and Guadeloupe were infected with the same rhetoric of liberty as Haiti's Black Jacobins, and had no desire to be enslaved once more. Their struggle, which centered around the port town at the base of Guadeloupe's own great volcano, Basse-Terre, came to a head in late May 1802, with Basse-Terre ringed by Richepanse's boats.

Inside the town's fort, a ragtag force of freedmen and *nègres*, four hundred strong, defied his advance. Their leader was a free mulatto named Louis Delgrès. He'd grown up in St. Pierre, but then come here to uphold Republican ideals against the empire's aims. From inside Basse-Terre's fort, he issued a "last cry of innocence and despair," that he addressed to "the universe entire."[12] "These are the greatest days of a century that will always be famous for the triumph of enlightenment," wrote this former French officer, beloved by his men for rallying them by playing his violin. "And yet in the midst of them is a class of unfortunates." He concluded bravely, "And you, posterity! Shed a tear for our sorrows, and we will die satisfied." For ten days, his men repelled the siege. But then, overwhelmed by Richepanse's forces, they retreated to the lower slopes of Basse-Terre's peak, and laid stores of gunpowder around a last lair. Richepanse's men approached; Delgrès's brave men waited. And then they lit the fuse. Every one of them died. So did three hundred of Bonaparte's wool-breeched troops. But slavery returned to the French Antilles.

A stone hailing Delgrès's greatness, placed in 1998, now sits in the Pantheon near Césaire's. In Guadeloupe, the penitent French state has paid to have Basse-Terre's old fort redone as a *musée* of homage to his cause, complete with holographic models of his heroic men. But these are recent developments. And if Delgrès's memory is now ingrained in the mind of every Antillean school kid, one can glean much from the fact that these islands had to wait another 150 years to win their version of self-rule; it's not the fiddling freedom fighter whose name became the default eponym for their schools. That honor belongs instead to the enlightened Frenchman—Victor Schoelcher—who finally forced France to outlaw slavery, in 1848. Schoelcher was an abolitionist and a politician and the first biographer of Toussaint L'Ouverture. His name now is affixed not merely to the main museum in Guadeloupe's modern capital, Pointe-à-Pitre, and to Fort-de-France's main suburb, but to the city's premier place of learning, the Lycée Victor Schoelcher. It is also attached to the library-cum-tourist-attraction downtown, the Bibliothèque Schoelcher, a place first built in Paris but then shipped here like the Statue of Liberty, in 1893, to stand as a kind of melancholic monument, cast in colored-metal gingerbread, to the Lumières' spirit in the tropics.

* * *

FOR GENERATIONS, Antillean school kids heard little about their own history; they instead absorbed France's litany of revolutions and republics alongside the oeuvres attached to those Montesquieus and

Voltaires whose names ring the Bibliothèque Schoelcher, and French
school atlases showing their islands to float someplace off of Brittany,
like odd rocks in the English Channel. School curricula have progressed.
But now the old geographic confusion is compounded. These islands
are no longer merely French. They are a part of Europe, full stop. For
people on the islands themselves, the fact carries benefits: any citizen
with sufficient will and cash can visit Rome or hunt for jobs in Zurich.
The founding of the European Union drew their French rafts farther
out into the Atlantic. For better or worse, it has also increased the
French Antilles' distance, in economic terms, both from nearby islanders (many of whose own job hunting brings them here) and *Américaine*
visitors with whose currency the euro, that winter of my stay especially,
was wiping the Atlantic's floor. In a city where a cod *macadam* and salad
lunch for two, in the Imperatrice's quayside café, ran about 36 euros,
my cabbie did not deposit me that first day outside the swish establishment evoking *To Have and Have Not*, the old Bogie-and-Bacall film set
here in 1944. We stopped instead by a highway overpass on downtown's
outskirts. The steep hill before us, cloaked in what looked at first like
tumbledown huts, resembled Rio's favelas.

   The slope's solidly built buildings, fastened hard to the hill, seemed
to exude the same healthful cheer as the smiling young woman who
emerged from a concrete two-story building and waved us down. The
young woman's name was Rebecca and her complexion was root beer.
She showed me into the simple top-floor flat that had emerged, on the
internet, as the cheapest listed lodging in Fort-de-France. Rebecca had
grown up here before spending her school-age years, she said, in the
immigrant filled *banlieues* outside Paris. She'd stayed there for a couple
of years to teach school, before returning home to raise the adorable
baby girl she now held on her hip. She'd also spent a semester at Antioch
College, in Ohio, which explained her good English and the fact that,
having worked out how to list her family's extra flat on Airbnb, she'd
evidently cornered a market on visiting grad-student types from America, drawn to cogitating in situ on Césaire's poetics or the dialectics of
postcolonialité. She laughed at my presentation as such, knowingly. And
then she showed me how to open the thick wooden windows, which,
when ajar, looked over the old bidonville—tin-can city—where she'd
grown up. "This larger district is called Trenelle," she said, gesturing up
the hill. "But to us and now the city planners, too, this is La Cascade."

   This waterfall of habitation may have looked, at first glance, like a favela. But its homes' reinforced concrete, like the fresh pavement on its steeply winding streets, lacked a typical ghetto's air of menace and suggested the concerned presence of a state whose guiding mores, at least in intent, remain social democratic. The shop in the TIGER gas station down the hill, when its employees weren't on strike, Rebecca said, stocked fresh baguettes and cheap Bordeaux. And as if I needed to feel more pleased about this corner of the realm that evening: a knock to my door. I opened it to find my host's grandmother, up from her flat downstairs and smiling shyly in her antique skirt as she proffered a pink plastic plate onto which she'd placed a little pile of fresh, hot *accras*—fried cod fritters—fresh from her stove, onto their paper-towel bed. She'd repeat the trick often many times, in ensuing weeks, often turning up with a bowl of coconut *glacée*, too.

It was a good job, given those comforts, that my Fort-de-France life involved so much walking, as I made my way daily between La Cascade and the little Formation DOM-TOM language school, in a low office building way down by the water, where I relearned the subjunctive mood from a poised young woman named Odalis. Odalis favored lime-green ballet flats and explained *les Antilles*' baroque taxonomy of color, to my earnest German classmate and me, by pointing to her own cinnamon arm: "*Je suis métisse.*" The route to Odalis's lessons, through the old working-class district of Terre-Sainville, passed boulangeries dispensing island coffee; streets named for Hugo and Flaubert; a parking garage, between the Theatre Césaire and the Parc Culturel Césaire, named for Lafcadio Hearn (the eccentric American who spent a couple of years here, in the 1880s, writing a book—*Two Years in the French West Indies*—evidently more recalled here than in the States).

In the evenings, passing groups of young men manning Terre-Sainville's corners in too-big Dinkies shorts, I listened to them talk shit in a rhythmic tongue whose vocabulary I could at times make out (*sa ou fè?! mwen neg!*), but whose grammar plainly diverged from that of Odalis's lessons. One night as one such group egged on their friends on bright scooters, in creole, zooming over wet pavement, I heard a predictable skid. When I reached the crowd gathering a couple of blocks up, the ambulance was already there. A Vespa lay on its side; a little Peugeot's hatchback door, nearby, bore a deep dent. The kid responsible for both, though, thankfully more dazed than hurt, leaned against a doting EMT's knees in this town with its ready first responders and purring Renault buses, that in those ways felt worlds, rather than islands, away from San Juan or Kingston. When another evening I took one of those buses out to the seaside suburb of Schoelcher, I watched a retinue of distinguished-looking Martinicans—the men in double-breasted suits in butter white; the ladies, bright dresses with foulard head scarves or Jackie O–style hats—parade across a hotel veranda worthy of Cap d'Antibes. They were joining a reception whose purpose, said a white-gloved *garçon* refilling their flutes of brut, was toasting heroic local vets of the Free French Air Force. That night on the rue Hugo, heading home, I heard not scooter skids but faint cheers up ahead, before I saw their target: a vibrant throng of bicyclists, zooming down the traffic-free road in bright spandex. They looked like they'd rolled here from the Tour de France—except that it was past 10 p.m., and the peloton was comprised not of wiry Italians or Basques but of men whose skin tones were all Africa. Racing road bikes is as favored a pastime here as in France—just not in the day's heat, when no one in their right mind would willingly exercise.

This town's namesake country was everywhere. But Fort-de-France is also a black city, closer to New Orleans and New York than Paris. And these linked facts, here as elsewhere in an era when the look and styles of American blackness have furnished a template for kids from Brazil to Ghana seeking a new negritude more usable than Césaire's, are very evident. "Wall Street Junior" is where its would-be thugs cop their Dickies and kicks; "So Sexy" and "Santa Monica" are patronized more by the stylish young women who may no longer favor their forebears' foulards or layered skirts but whose eye for bright patterns and bias-cut lines still demands admiration. Outside the shop where I found jeans to replace my worn Levi's, a sign touted their source. "Direct of San Diego," it promised, over an image of two jet-dark fists, bumping hello beneath its name: "Black Style."

* * *

FORT-DE-FRANCE IS A TOWN where you can often feel, strid-ing past blinking-green pharmacy crosses or the block-letter signage atop the building still housing the "Parti communiste martiniquais," like you're walking from the 1950s to the '70s and back again. What you don't feel as often, in a town whose built environs and politics feel so mid-century modern, is much of a colonial past—which makes sense, given that the island's spectacular capital from colonial days, St. Pierre, was destroyed in 1902. The "Paris of the Antilles," over the two-plus centuries before a fateful day, in May of that year, grew into a genteel hotbed for culture. The town's monied *bekés*—white slave owners—built a marble copy of Bordeaux's opera house and flocked to balls where old Hearn penned odes to brown-skinned *mulâtresses* whose clothes combined madras cloth with French couture to such spectacular effect that the place's owners passed sumptuary laws limiting their use. This was a capital where "all that was precious morally, materially, intellectually and politically [was] centralized," as one visiting writer put it.[13] But then Morne Pelée, just past 9 a.m. on May 8 in 1902, blew its top.

Within minutes of the eruption, some thirty thousand people lay buried under lava or ash. The town's sole known survivor was a condemned thief named Syparis. Saved from molten death by the town jail's thick stone walls, he became a sideshow attraction in P. T. Barnum's circus, as a living monument to "The New World's Pompeii." When Patrick Leigh Fermor turned up here in 1948, his considered view was that its people "still ascribe[d] to this event nearly all the handicaps under which the island now labours." That view is less held now, by Martinicans, than it maybe once was. But St. Pierre's loss was certainly their second city's gain. The island's new capital, though largely eschewed by its *békes*—those old French masters who'd once bought its slaves, and still own its real estate—was built up by their slaves' heirs, who left the countryside in ever-growing numbers in the years before and especially just after World War II, to grow a settlement whose figurehead was one of them. It was as a schoolboy that old Césaire, born in the little plantation town of Basse-Pointe, on the north Atlantic coast, first arrived in the city where he launched a life story now celebrated, not only in the monikers of its theater and airport, but also on its Museum of Ethnology and History's billboard-sized facade that traced his face's lines—his nose said "l'universelle fraternité"—in bits of verse.

"C'est son centenaire," explained the handsome man seated at the front desk inside, when I asked him why, in this town with no shortage of Césaire-ia, a history museum saw fit to hail him, too. The man had salt-and-pepper hair and a plastic name badge saying "ANDRÉ." His tone conveyed no boredom, as he explained that the previous spring had marked one hundred years since the great man's birth, taking my five-euro entry fee and ushering me into the museum's first room. It was decorated with wall-sized photos of his island's splendor—Morne Pelée's peak; a waterfall tumbling from its heights; a miles-long white-sand beach—all overlaid with snippets from Césaire's poems ("from Trinité to Grand-Rivière / the hysterical grand lick of the sea!")[14] extolling Martinique's beauty in florid white script and in ways far less ambivalent than his *Cahier* ever was. Around many of these images was wrapped a long pink flower. "C'est le fleur de les progressistes," said André. The symbol of Césaire's party: the balisier flower that he'd insisted on taking Breton to see when he visited him here, André said, and that he described as "un triple coeur haletant au point d'une lance."[15] I worked out a translation: "a triple heart panting at the point of a lance." The learned guard showed me how to spell "balisier." And then we stepped into a room whose glass cases displayed the curated detritus, beneath large signs, from the seasons of his hero's life.

There in a case marked "ETUDIANT": a copy of *L'Étudiant noir*, the magazine he started in Paris with Leopold Senghor of Senegal and Léon Damas from Guyana, at the prestigious Lycée Louis-le-Grand. Also, an essay by his remarkable future wife, Suzanne Roussi, whose impressions shaped Césaire's own that the surrealists' "radical belief in the image" (and rejection of Old Europe's mores) could find special resonance in their region fecund with what Alejo Carpentier would soon call the "marvelous real." A case marked "L'OUEVRE POETIQUE": a letter from Breton (return address: Manhattan) about Breton's promise to write his famous preface for the 1947 edition of the *Cahier*, which made Césaire's name in France; in it the great surrealist extolled *un grand poète noir*'s gifts by claiming them, and Césaire, for *surrealité*'s cause. A copy of that edition here, adorned with the abstract images of the Cuban painter Wifredo Lam, was splayed open to the famous scene where the poet, on his Paris commute, encounters a fellow black—"a nigger big as a pongo, trying to make himself small on the street-car bench"—and is at first reviled, before winning an ecstatic moment, in accepting this man, no matter his circumstance, as kin.[16] The lines that follow—"I accept, I accept . . . without reservations, I accept"[17]—in ensuing decades would be taken up, allied to brighter ones about tom-tom playing and "black genius," by certain African intellects and heads of state given to funding research sarcophagi and seeking "African solutions to African problems," by extolling

> Those who invented neither powder nor compass
> those who could harness neither steam nor electricity
> those who explored neither the seas nor the sky
> but knew in its most minute corners the land of suffering[18]

The lines were Césaire's. Thankfully, though, he himself wasn't much for sarcophagi or mystics, as the next case, "HOMME D'ÉTAT," made plain. It contained a ballot from the 1945 election that saw the poet, entering the deeply un-surreal realm of politics, become a mayor and a *député;* a copy of his "Lettre à Maurice Thorez," from 1956, wherein the poet mayor renounced his membership in the French Communist Party after Stalin's invasion of Hungary; a founding document from the Parti Progressiste, founded soon after, that he turned into its dominant political organ.

Next, "L'OUEVRE DRAMATIQUE." Here were original notes and finished scripts representing the poet politician's decision, in the 1960s, to turn to an art form more accessible, he hoped, to a provincial public than was experimental verse—a script for *La Tragédie du roi Christophe* (1963), his didactic drama about the pratfalls of free Haiti's first monarch, seeking to mimic French kings rather than absorbing his subjects' African ways; for *Une Saison au Congo* (1965), his Rimbaudian treatment of the rise and demise of Patrice Lumumba, Kinshasa beer seller turned anti-colonial martyr; and for *Une Tempête* (1969). The latter's title page outlined the aims of a play, "an adaptation of Shakespeare's *Tempest*— for the Black Theatre," that transmuted the bard's imagined Caribbean into a historical one wherein Ariel is a kind of tragic mulatto and Caliban a black nationalist who rejects Prospero's congratulating himself for teaching his slave to speak: "You didn't teach me a thing. Except to jabber in your own language so that I could understand your orders."[19] The last glass case, by the back of the room and before the entrance to its permanent exhibition, was labeled "PÉDAGOGUE." It contained a squib of self-appraisal from a man who identified as Caliban's heir but who here adopted the master's voice: "I was a teacher," it said.

> I trained a lot of young people—they're men now—and some became friends, others enemies, not that that matters much. They all came out of me, out of my teaching. I was a teacher, and quite an effective one it seems, and I undoubtedly influenced a whole generation.[20]

The aggrandizing-but-humble words, at once megalomaniac and true, of an un-humble man. Césaire's time as a tutor at Fort-de-France's top school, before he entered politics and made his town his fief, lasted just four years. But during those brief terms at the Lycée Schoelcher, he indeed left a mark. Perched on a chair and commencing class with

declamations like "Rimbaud: the power of revolt!" he recited cascades
of verse from memory. Wearing a green-checked suit, he won a fond
nickname from his charges of "the Green Lizard" and a reputation "as
a man who awakened consciences," recalled one of his great pupils,
Edouard Glissant. "For the first time," recalled another, "we saw a lycée
teacher, and therefore an apparently respectable man, saying that it is
fine and good to be a nègre."[21] Copying down his lectures on Lautré-
aumont and Malraux in their best handwriting, they passed around his
lessons like love notes.

One suspects, from that remark's ring about "enemies and friends,"
that the teacher's best-recalled pupils were those who stuck around his
little hothouse-*île* to offer affronts or acquiescence, as adults, to his ego's
intents. He never had much to say, at any rate, about the most famed
by far of all the boys to pass through his classes. And Frantz Fanon was
similarly quiet about the master whose model was key to the journey that
eventually produced books giving the student's name a notoriety, after
he left Martinique for the world, wider even than his teacher's. But the
one glancing mention of "CÉSAIRE: PÉDAGOGUE," that appears in
Fanon's published work says much: that line about a man who showed
his students "it was fine and good to be a nègre," is from his *Black Skin,
White Masks*. The son would find a fair amount with which to quarrel in the father's negritude—a philosophy that amounted, said Fanon
in that same book, to a "black mirage replacing a white mistake."[22]
But this doesn't change the key role his sixth-form teacher played in
opening a door onto the best of all thought. In their shared language,
he stepped through that door to write a book that examined race and
colonial violence through panes evolved by Sartre and Merleau-Ponty,
that's still read far beyond the streets he skipped along between the
Lycée Schoelcher and its namesake library, where he did homework
after school.

* * *

FRANTZ FANON WAS RAISED with seven siblings by a customs officer dad with whom he never got along, and an ambitious cloth merchant
mum who ensured that his homework was done. His childhood address
was mere blocks from the museum. Stopping by where M. and Mme.
Fanon's home stood, though, you wouldn't know. Their old wood house
at 33 rue de Republique was at some point replaced by a big shoe store

called Mil Chaussure. Its walls bear no plaque to Fanon's memory but are lined by what indeed look like a thousand pairs of pumps and flip-flops. There the young woman behind the counter, wearing a T-shirt with a familiar logo but saying "COMME DE F*CK DOWN," had no knowledge of, and even less interest in, what I proffered in asking if she knew who'd once slept here. "Mais nous avons tennis' Puma," she said, brightening, to tout her Puma sneakers. "Très chic." Her ignorance wasn't shocking, on an island where the most prominent marker to Fanon's memory that I glimpsed was in the little Atlantic coast town of Le François. It's a place where young Frantz spent some time, living with an uncle and playing soccer for the local club. (Club Franciscan remains one of the best in Martinique's league.) But though the frayed pink banner hanging from the town police station looked plenty old, it didn't date from the 1940s or hail the middling footballing prowess of a teenager recalled by his brother as "an energetic but limited attacker." The banner, looking like someone had just forgotten it was there, instead hailed "La Journée Frantz Fanon: 1982." This was in 2013.

That Martinique's most famous son abroad isn't nearly so touted as the mentor who stayed comes mostly down to one fact: the place that inspired the man who supplanted Césaire as the globe's most notorious scourge of colonial rule, in the '60s and since, wasn't the country in which he grew up. It was the one with whose people's plight and cause he identified to his core after settling there in the early '50s. His old teacher put it simply: "He chose. He became Algerian. Lived, fought, and died Algerian."[23] Césaire's description bore more than the simple sourness of an elder patriot. It described something real in both the life and the thought of a pupil whose ideas about *identité*'s sources and use were deeply opposite those of negritude's father. The wellspring of the self, for the evolved psychiatrist and avid student of Sartre's *phénoménologie*, wasn't some historic essence. It was human experience. And that category was early marked, in the life of a young man recalled by his lycée classmates as *un écorché vif*—"an open nerve"—by his decision to leave home, at eighteen, to join the Free French Army and kill Nazism dead with ideals he'd absorbed in Schoelcher's iron temple to Voltaire. And then it was shaped: as he won medals for courage in the mud-and-snow-filled theater of the Bois de Grappes, by his learning Free France's contradictions first from serving in a segregated unit always picked, by his officers, for the most dangerous missions, and then from being scorned by their daughters, during parties after Liberation, who preferred necking with Yankee GIs who didn't know Voltaire from Volvo; by his years as a medical student given to pondering the problem—of "being a black man in white society"—on which he wrote his first book; and then, after he went to help run a hospital in an old French colony in North Africa, by his being scandalized by colleagues who still felt that all their patients' ailments sprang from some mysterious aspect of "the Arab mind." Those ills, he felt instead, perhaps had something to do with the daily violence of a country whose every occupying police-man was growing familiar with the sinister uses to which their big field telephone batteries, nicknamed the *gégène*, could be put when clipped to the pinkies or scrotums of the scores of traumatized men. Fanon saw a great deal of these men, many of them involved in the Algerian resis-tance but many of them not, in his Bilda clinic.

Practicing psychiatry in a place occupied by French soldiers since 1830 and used by French industry as a source for raw materials, Dr. Fanon came of professional age in a country in which two-thirds of adults couldn't sign their names; where those people practiced a reli-gion scorned by occupiers who didn't speak their language; where they lived in cordoned-off medinas, or other jobless zones, where "you are born anywhere, anyhow," and "die anywhere, from anything."[24] This is the country, not Martinique, in which, in the autumn of 1954, the victims of structural violence began placing bombs in Algiers's cafés to better their lot. It is the country that launched the famed diagnosis, and putative cure, comprising the first volley in his most famed work:

> National liberation, national reawakening, restoration of the nation to the people or Commonwealth, whatever the name used, whatever the latest expression, decolonization is always a violent event.[25]

Written amid the longest and most deadly war attending France's imperial decline, *Les Damnés de la terre* described a war that was launched with those café bombs of November 1954 and that didn't end until after another eight years had passed and a million had died. The cause for Fanon's conclusion-as-lead was the motor that he saw bracketing all ties between "colonizer and colonized" ("Their first confrontation was colored by violence and their cohabitation . . . continued at the point of the bayonet and under cannon fire")[26] and the daily coercion he saw thereafter, as key to the continuance of colonial violence "which only gives in when confronted with greater violence."[27] The doctor who parsed this coercive motor, and how it might perish by its own means, also dilated on the psychic and other effects of such revolts ("at the individual level," he said, "violence is a cleansing force").[28] This was salutary. It didn't stop him from becoming the caricature known, to both his admirers and foes, as the murder lover of Hannah Arendt's starkly off-base appraisal, in a much-read early commentary on Dr. Fanon as a champion of "violence for its own sake."[29]

But his thesis was earned: he wrote what he saw, and what he saw was horrific. It was through his narration of a nation suffused with violence that Fanon became the progenitor of a new ideology, Third Worldism. And this ideology saw—in the social geography of a country whose poor masses lived in jobless shanties ringing its *colon*'s country clubs and cafés—a metaphor and model for the entire globe. That metaphor and model, in 1961 as today, fit Fanon's hometown in many ways: Fort-de-France is a place whose bidonvilles and unindustrialized rim are still full of people hanging on, as Patrick Chamoiseau wrote, in "the city's thousand survival cracks."[30] But there were also various ways—from the finer lot those folk enjoyed, as compared to their neighbor, to their identifications with Hugo and Rousseau—that made it different. And Martinique's general reception of Fanon's work, then as now, was perhaps well captured in the one review of *Les Damnés* to appear in local press that year:

> Fanon denounces with extreme rigour all the ugliness of old Europe's policy of colonization, without ever taking into account what the France of the Rights of Man and the Citizen, republican and secular France, has done for the country he came from: the French West Indies, for Fanon is Martinican. It was as a result of his noble freedom as a free and independent Frenchman that he felt himself obliged to side with the FLN and to place his science and conscience at its service.[31]

Not that he cared. A scourge as much of France's lefty leaders as its right-wing colonels, it didn't take Fanon until the betrayals of '56 to reject their old Marxist assumption that the revolution would have to happen first in those parts of the world developed enough, in industrial terms, to have a real proletariat. He saw that this line left little space, in colonies founded to furnish First World factories with their oil or zinc, for anyone interested in winning a better life for those colonies' people—many of whom didn't belong to the world of formal labor at all. In this, he wasn't alone; after Césaire left the French CP in '56, he said the same things. But it was the doctor's synthetic brilliance as a rhetorician that saw him ground his insights in Maghreb particulars before rendering them global, in the apocalyptic tones of Engels ("The Third World is today facing Europe as one colossal mass"). His book appeared in English just as Che Guevara began speaking of creating "two, three, many Vietnams": it became a master narrative for which the world's loathers of "Empire," and "The Man," were perfectly primed.

The Wretched of the Earth was the kind of work whose polemical force—its declarative verve and its dealing in ideal types; its evidence only invoked *en passant*—is also its weakness. "I am trying to reach my reader affectively," he once remarked of his prose style, "or in other words irrationally, almost sensually."[32] In this, he succeeded to a remarkable degree. But his rational prescriptions and models were scarcely applicable to Red China's satellites or the caudillo-led client states of South America. His polyglot Antilles strained to breaking his vision of "native" culture and its ties to the "nation's liberation." As revolutionary Algeria began to experience the usual predations and problems of life in a one-party state—a state run by the FLN, in whose employ as propagandist Fanon worked—it became all too easy for his critics, borrowing from the playbook of lazy minds attributing the thuggery of Pol Pot, say, to Marx's exegesis of capital's works, to confound apt diagnosis with off-kilter cures. But part of what makes Fanon both so magnetic and so slippery is the zealotry he seemed to share, with a simpler admirer, for his models and ideas. When a few months before his hounded martyrdom from cancer, at just thirty-six, news of a little riot in Fort-de-France met his ears, he rejoiced that his homeland was at last launching its anticolonial war. But the "riot," which arose from a white motorist running into a black stevedore's Vespa, amounted to what the powers that be described as "a response to a banal traffic accident."[33] In 1961, Martinique was even further from Fanon's sovereign ideal, if anything, than when he kicked his football past where that tawdry sneaker shop staffed by Ms. COMME DE F*CK DOWN now looms.

* * *

AN ANTILLEAN MAN unchained from the Antilles: Frantz Fanon was that, by the end. But he was Antillean indeed. And that accident

of birth mattered to a man who may have won global icon status but
who always did "enjoy rum, accras, and the beguine," wrote his most
thorough biographer. Fanon's own prose was never scrubbed completely clean of homeland idioms like the local creature Fanon invoked
in his most autobiographical work, to insist that in matters of intellection, "adopting a 'crabe-ma-faute' attitude is pointless."[34] The *crabe-
ma-faute*—"my-fault crab," in creole—is native to Martinique's coastal
mangroves. Beloved as an ingredient for stews, the *ma faute* is distinctive
for having one claw longer than the other, which it often waves about,
as any Martinican but few others could tell you, like a man beating his
chest in a mea culpa: a pose to which Dr. Frantz Fanon, like many of
his countrymen, was never much given. But if the impress of his island's
fauna and feel never left him, so too that of the green lizard who served
as a model early on—Césaire—and some of his ideas.

Negritude wasn't one of these. Dismissing Césaire's philosophy as
that "black mirage replacing a white mistake," Fanon here disagreed
with his intellectual hero as an adult, Jean-Paul Sartre. In his "Orphée
Noir" essay from 1949, Sartre argued that negritude comprised the
requisite weak stage in a dialectic whose eventual synthesis, once this
"antiracist racism" did its work, was a new and equal world. The Sartre that Fanon loved was the inquisitor of lived ennui whose work and
tone he borrowed in describing, in *Black Skin, White Masks*, his own
moment of racial awakening on a metropolitan trolley—a scene that
no literate Martinican can read without thinking of Césaire's streetcar
("I accept / I accept / Without reservations . . . I accept"). But where
that scene in Césaire's *Cahier* narrated a feeling of felt kinship with his
brothers, Fanon's streetcar was a scene of alienation. Stilled in the gaze
of a white boy and his mum ("Look ma, a Negro!"), he described the
nausea brought on by being made to "feel responsible" for a race tied,
in that boy's mind, to "cannibalism, mental retardation, fetishism, racial
taints, slave-traders and above all, above all, 'Y a bon banania.'"[35] (The
last: a reference to omnipresent ads for tropical fruit, in France, that
featured a grinning darky like America's Uncle Ben.) What was at stake
for Fanon were the psychic costs for any person made to exist in the
dimension of himself that Sartre called "being-for-another." What he
was rejecting, beyond the violence of a little boy's gaze, was the imagined sameness of the "black mirage" that some of his fellows, following
Césaire, supplied as antidote.

And yet: Césaire stays present. When in *Les Damnés de la terre* Fanon
sought to underscore his central argument, about how "the colonized

man liberates himself in and through violence," the writer he finally turned to wasn't an American like Chester Himes, from whose proto-blaxploitation detective tales (the books that Himes wrote, that is, after *If He Hollers, Let Him Go*) Fanon pulled dubious truths about Black American life. Nor was it the new work of some North African writer whose great works, he said, would during the anti-colonial era emerge to forge a *littérature de combat* illuminating the Struggle in real time agit-prop that would also, somehow, be good art. Unsurprisingly, no such books yet existed. So to illustrate his core thesis, the student turned instead to his teacher's little-read early play *Et les chiens se taisaient* (*And the Dogs Fell Silent*). He quoted from the climactic action in Césaire's allegoric oratorio about an imagined slave revolt, in Martinique. The scene finds a slave called the Rebel entering his master's house. Rebel meets with the chance to remake his world; and he doesn't flinch:

> I went in. It's you, he to me very quietly. It was me, it was indeed
>   me.
> I told him, me, the good slave, the faithful slave, the slavish slave,
> And suddenly his eyes were like two frightened roaches on a
>   rainy day . . .
> I struck a blow and blood flowed: that is the only baptism I can
>   remember today.[36]

* * *

WHETHER HE LEVERAGED it or not, what separated Fanon, like all West Indians raiding intellectual circles of Europe in those days, was his homeland's history. It was the sense of dignity in Fort-de-France's *pointe de nègres:* the place by the quay where slavers once unloaded human chattel and that was now marked with a monument to the kind of moral largesse long since imbued, in liberal culture worldwide, in the suffering slave. Fanon wasn't like most every wannabe Left Banker steeped in Hegel's ideas about how humans gain their sense of self only in relation to an Other. He hailed from a place where the old dialectician's metaphor of master and slave registered not as abstraction but as historical prompt: he was a writer who could ask whether the real-life masters who'd flayed his forebears' backs were actually more concerned with gaining the slave-Other's "recognition" than with extracting his labor. He was, in other words, Caribbean. That history and root, no matter his Algerian ventures, colored everything he wrote about freedom and violence alike. It couldn't not. But if the fact and legacies of "slave days" hover over his prose and his homeland alike, there's another era more palpably key to both Fanon's life and the ambience persisting around the point *nègre* today. Called *An Tan Robè* in creole—"the Robert time"—it's the era when *les Antilles'* streets were filled with more French soldiers than at any time since the day of Delgrès.

Named for Admiral George Robert, high commissioner for the French West Indies and commander in chief of the West Atlantic Fleet, Robert's age began when in June 1940 he pledged his men's loyalty not to de Gaulle's Free French cause but to the collaborationist state being set up in Nazi-run Paris. The admiral built a mini Vichy regime enforced by white-uniformed men who'd run Martinique for the next four years. With trenches dug into Savane for repelling attacks that never came, this black and creole city was made full, as the price of oil for cars and cooking both shot skyward, of *blan* soldiers who couldn't leave. Crucial to shaping the racial consciousness of Fanon's generation—boys who saw their town's streets made not theirs just as they passed puberty—*An Tan Robè*'s end also augured Césaire's notorious choice: in 1945 the prospect of joining with the new Gaullist Republic forming in Paris was rather more attractive than "staying French" looked before the departure of Robert's men. At the outset of *Black Skin, White Masks*, Fanon ironically hums, "Adieu foulard," it goes, "adieu madras."

Adieu graine d'or, adieu collier chou,
Alas, alas, it is for ever,
My sweetheart has gone.
Alas, alas, gone for ever

Such *"doudouiste"* tunes were a defining feature of Martinique's beguine songbook well before *An Tan Robè*. But the era's end witnessed a constant replaying of its guiding dynamic and scene: the comely Martinican *mulâtresse* bidding a teary farewell, by the quay in her twisted head scarf and checked skirts, to a white *doudou* lover, whom she'll never see again, heading home to his wife. In those years when Martinique was overrun with such fellows, winning one as a lover became, for a certain class of island ladies, a key goal—as the era's notable novelist, Mayotte Capécia, explored in *Je Suis Martiniquaise* and *La Negresse Blanche*.[37] Which is part of why it's unfair that Capécia's books—excavating the era's degraded eros and real emotional life with at-times purplish prose, but also sensitive wit—are now best recalled for the gusto with which Fanon decried their author as a writer of "third-rate books" who "asks for nothing, demands nothing, except for a little whiteness in her life."[38] The doctor was no literary critic. His ungenerosity toward Capécia, if born of teen-boy sorrows back home, was of a piece with his marshaling-cum-misreading of Chester Himes, whose white women characters, Fanon thought, all evinced a secret desire to be raped. His own marriage to a white woman from Lyon, who took the dictation that became his books ("When my . . . hands caress these white breasts, I am making white civilization and worthiness mine") hardly struck him, as Capécia's heroines desires did, as an "abdication" of personality.[39] He was as masculinist as his times. But none of this alters the phrase-making force that made *Black Skin*'s closing line—"Oh my body, always make me a man who asks questions"[40]—a go-to choice for clever college students of radical bent—since he became a staple on the syllabi—who think it's a good idea, at age nineteen, to get tattoos. Nor does it change how the intellectual trek begun during *An Tan Robè*—and then brought to fruition in France's defining colonial war—would shake the entire French world when it appeared in Paris's bookshops, in late 1961, with a preface by its author's hero.

That *The Wretched of the Earth* was better known in France, at least at first, for Sartre's preface than for Fanon's text would have vexed a man who'd bewailed his professor's ties to his own *blan* booster ("[T]here is no reason why M. Breton should say of Césaire: 'And he is a black man who handles the French language better than any white can handle it today' ").[41] But no white man anywhere, in 1962, could have not caught flack for publishing this: "[K]illing a European is killing two birds with one stone" (he explained: "eliminating in one go oppressor and oppressed").[42] That this particular white man was his era's most famed intellectual, now made "the most hated man in France," both helped Fanon's book's cause and occasioned the finest public quip of de Gaulle's reign, when in reply to those urging Sartre's arrest, he said, "One does not arrest Voltaire." The kerfuffle caused by Fanon's book signaled the centrality of its subject—the Algerian War—to France's postwar era. De Gaulle saw the writing on the wall. The longest and deadliest of Africa's anti-colonial wars didn't merely bring down the Fourth Republic and send de Gaulle and a million *pieds-noirs* home. It also blared a hundred lessons still studied both by admirers of the FLN's bomb-planting guerrillas and those unlucky soldiers charged with waging "asymmetric warfare" in Gaza or Iraq today. It makes sense that when Pentagon strategists recently faced an insurgency in the latter country, they screened *The Battle of Algiers*, Gillo Pontecorvo's now-classic film: they wanted to try to understand how an occupying force willing to use all tools at its disposal, including torture, can at once suppress an insurgency and lose a nation's hearts and minds—and with them, a war. The world born in the Algiers of Pontecorvo's Colonel Mathieu and Ali La Pointe, and that Fanon descried with unexcelled verve in *The Wretched of the Earth*, is the one we live in still.

And it's also the war—barely acknowledged as it happened, and only incrementally reckoned with since—whose ghosts hover over the *banlieues* ringing Paris and Marseille, where the commingling of Frenchmen from North Africa and the Antilles, with one another and with metropolitan life at large, has in many ways defined French culture since that famous World Cup victory in 1998. Then two million revelers bounced down the Champs-Élysées, streaming beneath an Arc de Triomphe lit with the proud image of a son of Berber immigrants who, like all Algerians who arrived here in the 1950s, gave a portion of their earnings to the FLN. Zinedine Zidane's chiseled face became the icon *par excellence* for certain French liberals, of the hopeful new multiculture born in those scenes. But in an intriguing echo of the past, one of their cause's key footballing spokesmen, against right-wingers who still insisted that "France cannot recognize itself" in the face they toasted on the Champs-Élysées, was from the Caribbean. In the metropole of the '60s, the Antilles' Fanon became Africa's signal voice. Now Zidane's great teammate Lilian Thuram, the elegant Guadeloupe-born defender, emerged as one of modern France's most eloquent foes, in the years after his goals fired his team to that win in 1998, of Vichy's racist heirs. "What can I say about Monsieur Le Pen?" Thuram said of the National Front politico. "He is unaware that there are Frenchmen who are black, Frenchmen who are white, Frenchmen who are brown."[43] When he then curated a well-received exhibition called "Human Zoos: The Invention of the Savage," at Musée du quai Branly, which traced its subject from the first so-called cannibals brought home by Columbus through to the vulgar lingo of a *bon banania*, the footballer who's traded his cleats for a nice suit made its inspiration plain. "You have to have the courage to say that each of us has prejudices," he said in a catalog published on the fiftieth anniversary of Fanon's death, "and these prejudices have a history."[44]

That the names of Antillean footballers like Thuram and Thierry

are today far more revered, in the Antilles, than Thuram's hero's is perhaps a fact most attributable to the wider public's greater interest, in
general, in sport than in books. But Fanon's dim star in his homeland
surely has to do, too, with the now-cemented outlook of islands whose
bonds with *le metropole* were likely secured for all time when the socialist François Mitterand rose to power, in 1981, reciting rhetoric about
the DOM-TOMs' "right to difference." In reply, Césaire decreed then
that any discussion of Martinique's making a formal break with Paris,
a resurgent cause in the 1970s, was to be tabled for a decade, and then
offered, as his sole contribution to his old pupil's Journée de Fanon, the
next year, a rather phoned-in homily:

> You lash the iron
> You lash the prison bars
> You lash the gaze of the warriors
> Silex-warrior
> spat
> From the mouth of the snake in the mangrove-swamp[45]

Today's visitors to the old Librairie Papet, on the corner of the *silex-
warrior*'s childhood block, just down from that shoe shop on the rue de
Republique, can certainly still find Fanon's books. Shelved in a little
section marked "LOCAL INTEREST," they're right there alongside Césaire's plays, Glissant's poems, and the estimable novels of the
émigré Guadeloupeans Daniel Maximin and Maryse Condé. Like all
authors winning his kind of fame, he is fated to be as misunderstood
by his admirers as by his foes: this fierce critic of "black nationalism"
has seen many followers of that school, around the world, name their
kids "Fanon." Few if any of those followers, though, would seem to hail
from Martinique. Whatever "local interest" his books retain, it derives
neither from their implied political program nor from their vision of an
ongoing encounter between "colonizer and colonized," whose relationship, as well as its continuance, means violence. It derives, of course,
from something simpler: his provenance. And that provenance, if you
know where to look, is all over his work. But on a Sunday afternoon in
February 2013 in his home city, his conception of authentic culture as
deriving only from a nation's "natives," and of "liberation" tied solely to
their armed revolt, felt very far indeed from his dear Savane as a parade
of *vidés*—carnival bands—rounded its green expanse.

Mardi Gras proper was still a couple of weekends off, but Martinique is a self-respecting outpost of the Catholic New World's saints and festivals belt: Martinicans begin their carnival warm-up while signs wishing them "Joyeux Noël" still hang over the streets. A *vidé* composed of middle-aged men dressed as Maryan Lapo-Fig—a stock carnival character here, in the Empress Josephine mold—passed, ahead of a troupe led by teen girls in green leotards spinning chrome batons. This group of twirlers, comprised of both women and men, first caught my attention for their banner. Printed in madras, it touted a restaurant—Le Goût des Antilles—whose tablecloths, I knew from passing it daily in Terre-Sainville, were cut from the same vinyl cloth. With their feathered caps and shiny buttons and faces comprising a chromatic study in the color brown, each member of this Taste of Antilles troupe seemed to challenge, in their way, the old antinomies of gender and race around which the political history of this place, like so many, has turned. But it was their leader, a young man, strikingly pretty, with slim hips and wearing heeled boots like a *chabine* majorette's, who really buried them. His white Dumas-style cap was stuck with red and green feathers, his permed hair tumbling in bouffant waves to his shoulders. His eyebrows were dark arches expertly penciled onto his shiny-beige face. And with each rolled hip and pranced step he took, there beneath the cobalt sky and around the Savane, he seemed to push the ego-driven dramas tied to Fanon's fear of emasculation, and that shame's hoped-for overturning with violence, ever further into the past.

Even in Fanon and Césaire's day, of course, and long before, there was plenty of evidence, for those willing to look, that much of what's emerged in the Caribbean has represented something new—"not African, not European," indeed—and not requiring a manifesto or frame supplied from either of the Old World's continents to explain. But in this place, like all others in its region, in the past couple of decades, the novels and books filling the "Local Interest" shelf, like Chamoiseau's *Solibo Magnificent*, say, have exemplified the fact. Composed in the same piquant mix of French and creole one hears on Martinique's streets, the breakthrough work by a writer later peddled to worldly readers as "the Garcia Márquez of the Antilles" begins at the tipsy end of a carnival day. A town policeman's logbook already includes "seven rum-drunks picked by patrol, three Rastas whose charges were yet to be drawn up, [and] . . . a quimboiseur [sorcerer] caught desecrating a tomb."[46] His evening grows more interesting, though, when on a corner of the Savane where I

had watched M. Goût des Antilles gambol past, a creole storyteller from
the old school gathers a group of revelers to his tongue that "knew the
road to all ears," with the traditional call-to-story—"É kri!" he calls; "É
kraa!" they reply—before then keeling over, mid-tale, to die by the suitably magic-realist means of choking on his words. The ensuing murder-
mystery-cum-meta-literary riff sets the French voice of officialdom (the
investigating police) against Solibo's creole-speaking witnesses and kin
("Saki tué'y?" they rhetorically ask the cops: What killed him?). It's a
novel whose form and concerns embody what Chamoiseau and the two
friends with whom he composed a manifesto in 1986, calling for a literature tied to life as it was actually lived in Martinique, meant when they
insisted that "Creoleness is the cement of our culture."[47] And it is one
of the main reasons, too, that I determined, before leaving his island for
Guadeloupe, to go speak with a writer who often refers to himself in his
books, with typical wordplay, as the "Oiseau de Cham."

Few large countries, let alone little ones, boast the literary riches
allowing one to trace the whole modern arc of their culture, and the
contours of that culture's conflicts, through those of its books. But in
Martinique you can—and you can even do so while reading the books
against the diagnoses and prescriptions penned by Chamoiseau and the
two friends with whom he wrote *Éloge de la Créolité*, the linguist Jean
Bernabé and fellow scribe Raphaël Confiant. They wrote for a generation to whom the aim of "handling the French language better than any
white man" was, to them even more than for Fanon, an irrelevant goal.
A manifesto: what's more French than that? But their *Éloge*'s opening
line—"Neither Europeans, nor Africans, nor Asians, we proclaim ourselves Creoles"—evinced an old Oedipal drama, now made new. "We
are forever Césaire's sons," they stated. "Césairian negritude is a bap-
tism, the primal act of our restored dignity." But then they held up an
alternate idol, from among the ranks of the *père*'s pupils, who insisted on
the necessity in the Antilles of forging a literature that "attempts to construct itself at the frontier of the written and the spoken word." Their
definition of what they called Créolité carried programmatic implications both artistic ("Créolité is a literary project designed to keep the
Creole language alive") and political ("Our solidarity is first with our
brothers of the neighboring islands and secondly with the nations of
South America"). Forging a literature in creole was part and parcel of
rejecting France.

But the books they wrote, more than mere pedants' workouts, have
long rivaled even global hits like *Twilight* and soft-core S&M literature

that are as popular here as everywhere, in the sales ledgers of Papet and
other local bookshops. Works like Confiant's written-in-creole account
of *An Tan Robè*, *Le Nègre et l'Amiral*, are staples of every lettered Martinican's home. Confiant's vehemence vis-à-vis old Césaire ("You show
once more your true face: a hopeless Frenchman, an inveterate enemy
of independence") goes yet further, perhaps not coincidentally, than the
manifesto he cowrote with Chamoiseau.[48] But neither Confiant nor any
modern writer from *les Antilles* has equaled the international splash of
the friend whose books (unlike Confiant's) have been translated into
English, from their creole and French, and touted by their U.S. publisher as written by "the García Márquez of the Antilles." Chamoiseau's
larger reception and repute, in the world republic of letters, was perhaps distilled in Derek Walcott's encomium to the Martinican writer's
most outsized achievement, the 1992 novel *Texaco*. "A great novel has
been written," intoned the modern Antilles' own Nobel, "one with [a]
melodic voice and amplitude of heart."[49] And so *Texaco* was, and is, a
garrulous masterwork whose achievement equaled its ambition not so
much to trace the deep past and lived presents of a bidonville built amid
oil-storage tanks on Fort-de-France's edge, but to emplace its denizens'
tales within the larger New World epic. Its main narrator, a woman
called Marie-Sophie Laborieux (Chamoiseau's names are never innocent), has deep recall not only of the tales of forebears who left the
cane fields to crowd the city's swampy edge, but of those neighbors
whose lives and stories remain peopled with spirits called *dorlis* and *sou-
cougnan*, some sent by *quimboiseurs* at night, who shape their lives with
metaphysic forces either malevolent or good. This creole voice is once
again set against the official French of a civil servant sent to "renovate"
the shanties (she says, "In his scientific language that really meant: to
raze it"). But in *Texaco* we also hear from a humble "word-scratcher"
who endeavors to write all this down while also nursing a piquant self-
consciousness (he wonders whether the writing amounts "to tak[ing]
the conch out of the sea and crying: here's the conch!") and relaying the
thoughts, while he's at it, of an enlightened urban planner ("The Creole
city needs the chaos of its fringes").

Which all may help explain why the shiny office building I approached
on the morning of my appointment with the Oiseau de Cham—a glass-
and-brick number that wouldn't have looked out of place in the Maryland suburbs—felt a bit incongruous. But the great *escrivaine*, like most
cultured Martinicans of a certain class, works for the French state. He
has for years, in fact—first as a youth counselor in Fort-de-France, but

more recently as a kind of presiding eminence at the Conseil Régional (Martinique being a region of France)—been charged with overseeing an ambitious project to turn the island's old capital, "Le Gran Saint-Pierre," into a new tourist magnet with official UNESCO designation, as humanity's patrimony. Thus far the project's sole result has been a cluster of abstract totem poles placed at Saint-Pierre's entrance. Carved from big logs of island greenheart, it was described by more than a few with-it young people, like my landlord-friend Rebecca, as more risible boondoggle than worthy art. If the new generation's whispers, though, bothered the cherubic man in a white linen shirt who welcomed me to his air-conditioned office, it didn't show.

With the round glasses and amused smile of a lyric intellectual, the author of some of the more ambitiously fine novels published anywhere in recent decades bid me sit down. And then, apologizing graciously for his nonexistent English, proceeded to answer my questions, just as graciously and in precise island French, about his work (yes, he confirmed, the urban planner in *Texaco* was his friend Serge Latchmi, who from his roots in the former bidonville of La Cascades, where I was staying, had gone on since the book to succeed Césaire as Fort-de-France's mayor; no, he hadn't considered changing the name of the book's Césaire character, who is first described by Texaco's people as "our revenge on the bekés and the big-wig mulattoes," before then making them false promises); about the strides the creole tongue had made on an island where its formal orthography, only evolved in the '70s, is now learned in school by kids who grow up both fully bilingual and glad for the fact; about his enduring attachment to Glissant's insistence that though the "poetics of relation" may exist everywhere on earth, the "rhizomed" region of the Caribbean, crisscrossed with the entwined roots and pasts of many lands, is a place "represent[ing] the anticipation of the relation of cultures . . . the future world whose signs are already showing."[50] On that point, I pressed him. The creolists had rejected their forebears' embrace of the idea that all people came from a singular root—whether African or European. That stance was surely progressive in its day. But what was its use in a century when the point that we're all shaped by meetings with difference, and the melding of many cultures, is little more than banal, for such exceptionalism? Were the Antilles really special? He insisted they were—and weren't. "It's not that the Antilles are different. But these are islands"—he was quoting Glissant—"where the poetics of relation make themselves especially visible."

How, then, might we apply that view to Fanon? "Well, he chose." His reply echoed Césaire—and then not. "He became Algerian—but you see, that's the poetics of relation, too! To imagine, and live, the multiplicity of your affinity." He smiled. An assistant padded over and handed him a note. "My affinity is to Martinique," he said, "but I write with that principle, too." He looked at the note. He would have to excuse himself shortly, he explained with great politesse, to get on a call with some UN colleagues in New York.

I readied to tell him farewell. But before I did I had to ask the great writer about more prosaic politics. His and Confiant's *Éloge* had insisted that "our solidarity is first with our brothers of the neighboring islands and secondly with the nations of South America." But what did he think of that line now, in the realm not of feeling and art, but of realpolitik? Was the old idealist dream of cross-Caribbean confederation, to say nothing of separating from the metropole, still worth discussing (especially after the stiff defeat dealt that question by his peers in the last referendum on it, in 2010)? Most people in *les Antilles*, by now, can recite the creolist's contentions about how their island's dependence on Paris has contributed to ills both economic and psychic. Among these are all the ways the islands can't afford to feed themselves—farmers unable to make a living, food shipped from the metropole to a fertile island that could well grow all its own, to stock grocery stores owned by the same *beké*s who also run banana plantations they deliberately plant before hurricane season, so their crops will be ruined and replaced with something better: a big check from the French Department of Ag. Many more Martinicans, though, whether or not they know those truths, have come to rely on a distant state's cosseting hands, throughout their working lives and after—and know well, too, that no one on nearby islands has their comforts, or roads. "Is it possible," I asked the once-radical scribe in his wireless specs, "that Césaire, on pragmatic grounds, was right about independence?"

The gentle author smiled. And then he sighed. He was sitting in a plush office afforded by a civil service whose presence here Césaire, fellow aging lefty and man of letters both, had ensured. His eyes twinkled. And then he rose, with a mischievous spring in his step, to shake my hand.

C'est compliqué.

Walking out of the Conseil's office, and turning toward where the aqua Caribbean looked "pensive as a cemetery," as Chamoiseau once wrote, I passed a crowd of people whose presence in the hot sun, gathered outside a low-slung apartment building, was mysterious. Then I saw the white and blue sign overhanging a door—"SECURITÉ SOCIAL," it said—from which young mums and older men emerged, periodically, with envelopes in hand. I continued on my way to the quay downtown, and the big twin-hulled ferry on whose gangplank I heard a weathered-looking fellow say that the trick to this ride on plainly proletarian transport (any *beké*s going between the two islands go by plane) was to choose between getting wet and getting sick. Chugging out of Fort-de-France's harbor, and up Martinique's leeward coast past Morne Pelée's peak, we entered the thirty rough miles between here and Dominica, known as the Martinique Passage. Here the Atlantic's roiling swells come rushing into the Caribbean, and I learned my weathered friend's meaning.

Crew inside the cabin handed out plastic barf bags as a dubbed-in-French version of *Teen Wolf* blinked on little TVs. Outside, gray waves like hillocks mirrored skittering clouds; the heavy seas' spray mingled, on deck, with big raindrops plunking down. I followed my friend's advice. Keeping hold of the outside deck's rails wasn't easy. And it was decidedly soaking. But focusing on Martinique's receding slopes, and then on the steep peaks of Dominica, as the latter's sides rose into view as on a painting with gaily painted houses affixed to their sides it was decidedly better than the smell inside, as not a few passengers put those sacks to use. But once we passed Dominica's tip and my shirt dried on my back, the boat flowed past honey-lit shores to find brighter skies and smaller seas and a stretch of water that puts one in mind, perhaps more than any in the region, of the archipelagoes of Homer and Mead. There off to the left, as we approached Guadeloupe, were the jagged teeth of the Saints—those little out-islands once settled by a sunburned tribe of inbred Bretons who comprised a community, Leigh Fermor wrote, "as odd as any of the odd ethnological rock-pools of Europe."[51] To the right was the low-slung turtle of Marie Galaint, half-obscuring the coffin-shaped mass of the little satellite isle from where the soccer star Thierry Henry's people hail, and that Columbus himself dubbed "La Desirade"—the desired—in 1498. And there straight ahead, looming over the whole scene, was the imposing height of Basse-Terre, its volcanic peak piercing clouds over where Delgrès issued his "last cry of innocence and despair." We sailed north, toward where the two wings of Guadeloupe's butterfly—towering Basse-Terre to the left, low-slung

Grand-Terre to the right—meet over the brackish river by which its modern capital, Pointe-à-Pitre, bestrides the twin isle's cloaca. Alighting in the city that at once welcomes cargo to its streets and expunges their shit, I passed shops hawking flip-flops and madras cloth I'd just left behind—Pointe-à-Pitre resembles Fort-de-France, but lacks some of the latter's Frenchy self-regard; its people are blacker—and found a room in a little quayside hotel, where I awoke to rent a little Renault hatchback the next morning and rolled out of town.

I passed banks of eight-story housing projects resembling the *banlieues* where their residents' cousins live in Paris; a roundabout in whose grassy center a cow chewed its cud; a roadblock manned with masked men—they were dancing; it was nearly carnival time now—who stopped each car to ask its driver for coins. And then, bypassing the overrun resorts of Grand-Terre's south coast, where French tourists of a certain age dance to dated disco hits and quaff rosé-and-Sprite spritzers by the sea, I drove bumpily inland across vast sugarcane fields toward Grand-Terre's northern tip and the sleepy town of Anse-Bertrand, where a couple of friendly little fish restaurants pushed their bouillabaisse on signs also touting Corsair beer.

Outside the place's little rum store, which sat conveniently next door to the bookie's shop touting wagers on horse races in distant Chantilly, Anse-Bertrand's older gents were passing the blazing morning with little glasses of strong, sweet coffee or strong, sweet *tafia*—the raw white sugar liquor that cane cutters long imbibed not merely at their torrid days' ends, but in the morning as a *décollage*—a takeoff—to launch their toil and its salving all at once. I asked one of them, dark as his forebears and well into his cups at 10 a.m., about my purpose here. "Do you know Monsieur Thuram?" Anse-Bertrand is where the great footballer was raised, with five siblings, by a mother who was back cutting cane in the fields, with little Lilian strapped to her back, a week after his birth.

My interlocutor brightened. *Je suis Thuram!* He looked mischievously at a friend, who chuckled into what looked to be the French edition of *Racing Form*.

I played along. *Un plaisir.* I extended my hand. His trousers looked like they'd once belonged to someone's suit. The angle of his head mirrored that of the framed hologram picture of a kitten inside. He took my hand. "You look just as well," I said, "as when you played for Barcelona."

He cackled. And then he moved to put his elbow on his knee just like Thuram did in a World Cup goal celebration citing Rodin's *The Thinker*. But when I said something about Sarkozy, his interest seemed to fade.

"Lilian's my cousin." He returned to his *tafia*. "Go talk to his sister. *La bas*."

What degree of kin the round woman with kind eyes was whom I found *la bas* was unclear. But there down the block she too smiled at Lilian's name and gestured past the little beach, by the town's edge, to where "the most expensive defender in history" (the powerful Italian club Juventus once paid rivals Parma $36 million for her Lilian's services), she said, stays when he's home. And to there I walked until coming to a stop by the turquoise sea and before a cluster of concrete bungalows that were the closest thing, in this untouristed sugar isle, to a hotel. They certainly didn't look like a great sportsman's manse. A healthy-looking fellow, passing by in shorts, confirmed as much. This was a holiday center owned by the French electrical workers' union—sometimes full, but plainly not now, of wire jockeys from Lyon. "Lilian lives there." The shirtless fellow pointed to a grander manse, up on the hill.

"He comes for Christmas—he was just here, stayed many weeks." He pointed to where Lilian liked to take sea baths when he was in town, and gestured toward a little stand, done up in Rasta colors and called Zion Train, where Lilian liked to get coconut water.

"But he just went away." We considered this a moment.

"Un grand homme," I said.

The fit fellow looked at me. And then he gave a perfunctory nod. He ambled off down the beach, leaving me to recall how after winning that World Cup in 1998, Thuram slipped away from the festivities in Paris. His kin and people here were raising thimblefuls of proud cane liquor to his name, no doubt, here by the beach and the rum shop's hologram kitten. And when a reporter asked Thuram why, as the toast of France, he'd slipped away to board that domestic flight home, his explanation was simple. "The procession along the Champs-Élysées was fabulous," he said. "But these were my people."

CHAPTER 13

THE LAST OF THE CARIB: DOMINICA

LATE IN THE WARM West Indian winter of 1948, Patrick Leigh Fermor alighted on Dominica's northern shore and exhaled deep. Midway through his months-long Caribbean swing, he came to a place that suited him. Here was an island home outfitted not merely with "the sort of library one sighs for everywhere," but also "drinking equipment of almost Babylonian splendor"[1]—all that one could require to enjoy what Leigh Fermor's host, the Scottish-born writer and politician Elma Napier, called "a bohemian life in the colonial West Indies."[2] Pointe Baptiste was sited on a green bluff by the sea. Built by Mrs. Napier and her husband in 1934, after they resolved to make a life here, their home's gracious veranda hosted guests like Noël Coward and Princess Margaret. Since Mrs. Napier's death, her family has maintained the home as a rustic holiday rental. And Pointe Baptiste's cultured charm—those books still line the wall, alongside Leigh Fermor's sketches of its cove—still tugs at bohemians of a certain caste. The day before I visited, Napier's grandson told me, one such had stopped through: Mick Jagger, his yacht moored nearby, wanted to look in on a place of which he, too, harbors fond memories.

It wasn't hard to see why. Behind the frangipani and other blossoms perfuming Pointe Baptiste's garden, green peaks rose into wispy clouds that help make rainbows here an every-afternoon event. There's a reason Dominica always fares well in any most-lush-of-the-Antilles debate. With its high waterfalls and sparse populace and "a river for every day of the year," Dominica is a Candy Land for lovers of nature and calm. But what had most drawn me here was a more bookish rock star who also once sipped rum at Pointe Baptiste—but whose life traced an opposite arc from those Brits who've come here chasing tropic dreams. That star was the novelist who remains Dominica's best-known export to the world, and whose best-known book, *Wide Sargasso Sea*, has won her a place on good bookshelves everywhere.

Jean Rhys's masterpiece mined her memories of an island girlhood to invent a prequel for *Jane Eyre*. Imagining a backstory for the West Indian "madwoman in the attic" who comes to grief after wedding Mr. Rochester in Charlotte Brontë's classic, Rhys's tale of doomed love plays against a backdrop of looming reprisal from newly freed slaves on the island where it's set. *Wide Sargasso Sea* won its author notice in *The New York Times*, before she died, as our "best living English novelist"[3]; it was later included on everyone's Best Novels of the Century list. But what's always attracted Rhys's fans to the author, as much as her extremely wise and shapely prose, is a life story as filled with drama and sadness as her books.

Born in Dominica to a Welsh doctor and his Scots-Cuban "creole" wife in 1890, the girl who became Jean Rhys was sent away to school in England at sixteen. Forced to drop out when her father died, the future writer with un-English-looking cheekbones and what seems an innate sense for glamour chose not to head back home. She became a chorus girl instead, twirling for workmen in gray Brighton and Leeds before heading to Paris and joining the demimonde. She had an eruptive affair with Ford Madox Ford, who praised her "singular instinct for form" and became her sponsor.[4] Then she published four novels, in the 1920s and '30s, that evoked the louche worlds she traversed as an exotic enigma from an island no one knew. Those books won her praise from critics and peers, but had meek sales—and sent their discouraged author, by the 1940s, to a penurious life in rural Devon. Rhys grew so reclusive that even many of her Left Bank friends thought she'd died. Her books fell out of print. When *Wide Sargasso Sea* appeared from nowhere in 1966, its author was seventy-six. Depressive and alcoholic, she didn't get to enjoy its success much, even as she became a fixture at London hotspots like Ronnie Scott's, the famous jazz club, wearing her trademark pink wig. But the old eccentric has certainly laughed last. Nowadays, *Wide Sargasso Sea* dots more college syllabi and may even sell more copies, if one credits the figures on Amazon.com, than *Jane Eyre*.

The sad-but-triumphal tale of a struggling artist whose vision finally won: the built-in allure is plain. And alluring is certainly what Rhys had been for me since I first encountered *Wide Sargasso Sea* in college—and as I then read the earlier novels of an author who became an artist, in books like *Voyage in the Dark* and *Good Morning, Midnight*, by lending precise language to the emotional texture of the "bohemian life" she made for herself, and suffered from, in England and Paris. My trip to Dominica was partly animated by a question not unlike the one that informed her attraction to the story of Brontë's madwoman in the attic: What was that remote little island, which this always-unsettled writer called "the only home I ever had," really like, and how had it shaped her?

Such is the basic wondering with which one comes to any place that features in the biography of someone you admire. More intriguing than that basic query were others raised by the truth that Rhys never returned to Dominica, after that one visit in 1936. Her native island may have been the home that made her, and that she loved. But it wasn't a place where she ever felt very comfortable as a girl; she felt even less well there as a woman. In the ways in which she wrote of the years that she spent there—and those that she didn't—lay something crucial about understanding whiteness in the West Indies, and also its close relation: the lived experience of being a white West Indian in Europe, which Rhys shared with her "mad" heroine in *Wide Sargasso Sea*. She was a woman whom Old World men like Mr. Richardson, as she renames Mr. Rochester in her book, could never quite understand (or countenance, for that matter, as ever quite "white"). The critic Hilton Als once praised Flannery O'Connor for "the originality and honesty of her portrayal of Southern whiteness. Or, rather, Southern whiteness as it chafed under its greatest cultural influence—Southern blackness."[5] The same could be said, and in even stronger terms, about whiteness in the West Indies. Jean Rhys knew this well: it was a fact key to her art and that informed her discomfort in Dominica, and is one of the most intriguing things about her. But what most discomforted and intrigued Rhys about her one trip home—a trip highlighted by her visit to the island's Carib Reserve—was the truth that Dominica isn't an island populated solely by whites and blacks and their offspring. Jean Rhys's island, alone among the Antilles, is an island where the indigenous people who lend the Caribbean its name aren't just an abstraction but remain an actual human presence.

* * *

DOMINICA'S DIFFERENCE from its neighbors is visible even before one lands. Wedged between its far more populous French kin, the island's volcanic *mornes* rise sharply from the sea. Banking into its little airport, you see little but green flora and stately palms; scarcely a house or road breaks the verdure. And once your commuter-sized plane touches down—the short runway can't handle jetliners—that first impression of the "Nature Island" changes little. The roller-coaster road ringing its thirty-mile length passes sleepy hamlets and nary a plush hotel. The feeling is of a Caribbean from before the era when tourism led even little St. Lucia, nearby, to build an airport able to receive big 747s carrying tourists and celebrities. They alight there for a stint of rehab, or to soak in a private infiniti pool at the Jade Mountain or one of the others overlooking its famed Pitons. Neither 747s nor infiniti pools are the thing in Dominica.

Dominica was first spotted by Columbus during his second voyage in 1493. The admiral claimed the island—which he first saw on a Sunday, *Domingo*—for Spain. But for the next two centuries, it was left largely untouched. When King Ferdinand asked its finder to describe this place he'd named for the Sabbath day, Columbus explained the first reason why: "Like this," the admiral said, crumpling a piece of parchment at his feet. With mountains rising to nearly five thousand feet from rocky shores, Dominica's geography made it both foreboding to settle and unsuited to the big sugar plantations that became its neighbors' raison d'être. Also foreboding were the people whom Columbus dubbed "Carib" and who called themselves "Kalinago"—and who had no interest, either way, in letting white men onto an island they called "Waitukubuli," meaning "tall is her body." On almost every other island in the sea named for them, the Carib were wiped from sight soon after the Europeans' arrival. But not in Dominica. When Spanish friars came to set up missions, the Carib killed them in their tracks. France's pirates and England's planters fared no better. The contending powers grew so fed up that they signed a treaty, in 1660, agreeing to leave Dominica to the indigenous people, in perpetuity, as neutral territory.

Paris and London's treaty, being a pact concerning the Americas' First Nations, didn't last. But it colored the halting colonization of an island first settled by the French in the early 1700s, but then seized by the British, fifty years later, during the same war that won them Canada. Sugar plantations did arrive here, but they were restricted to a few coastal valleys. Limes were a better fit, but Big Agriculture, in general, never was. And with the Carib still controlling a large portion of the island well into the nineteenth century, its mountain forests also came to host large numbers of runaway Maroons from nearby islands whose ancestors, on this longtime British isle, still speak a French creole.

When Dominica finally won its full independence in 1978, it had scarcely a dozen hotel rooms on the whole island: Pointe Baptiste was about the only guesthouse catering to foreign holiday makers. In recent years and as "ecotourism" takes off, new tourism development has notably spiked. But on an island still lacking big all-inclusives or a single hotel run by a foreign chain, the norm remains small-scale. And with many old sugar and banana estates now turned back to the jungle, this is a place that is today even more green than it was when a young Jean Rhys, standing barefoot in the grass here after it rained, learned to love a smell, "unbelievably fresh and sweet," that she always said she could never forget.[6]

* * *

THE TOWN WHERE Ella Gwendolyn Rhys Williams was born in 1890, Roseau, sits on the sheltered southwest tip of the island's leeward shore. Dominica's capital is a tumbledown little port with a reputation for "Caribbean vernacular" architecture—which, in a place founded by the eighteenth-century French and built up by an assortment of creole planters and freed slaves and Syrian and Chinese merchants, isn't a label connoting any single style. Roseau's gabled roofs and corrugated zinc mix with old stone churches and painted-wood jalousies. Its pacific streets, near a guesthouse whose name, Ma Bass, matches its proprietor's, were filled with people whose gracious manners reflected Victorian schooling. It has the mellow ways of a place too small to be overtaken by the crime now afflicting bigger islands. Its downtown feels in many ways unchanged from when a young creole Rhys gazed out from behind those jalousies during carnival a century ago, and longed to dance with the black masqueraders below—"as life surged up to us sitting stiff and well-behaved," as she later recalled.[7] It didn't take long, ambling Roseau's jangling streets on a weekend two weeks before the start of this still-Catholic island's pre-Lenten carnival, to find her childhood home. Down a block on which dreadlocked vendors sold CDs beneath loudspeakers booming soca and reggae, 48 Cork Street was a faded two-story dwelling with a tailor's shop on the ground floor, with paint peeling from its walls. That the nineteenth-century house was still standing evinced the slow pace of change here. But its deteriorated aspects suggested how change does occur. The jalousies through which a young Jean gazed onto the street were still there, but now they're nailed shut, plastered over by posters advertising a carnival fete called "Black and White Thang."

As a white creole girl born to Dominica's slave-owning class not long after slavery's end, Rhys's childhood bore a conflicted mix of loving black culture and her island without belonging fully to either. That she found escape in books is unsurprising. And strolling Roseau's waterfront now, it was gratifying to find the beautiful Carnegie Library, built on a bluff over the sea, where she read as a girl. With the uniformed schoolchildren who studied and flirted with each other at its tables, I spent a deeply pleasant afternoon with the library's copy of *Smile Please*, and its descriptions of carnival and rain-fresh grass and of how after happening, as an awkward nine-year-old, upon a photo of herself from a few years before, Rhys grew aware for the first time "of time, change and the longing for the past."[8] Published six months after Rhys's death in 1979, *Smile Please* was put out by Rhys's trusted friend and editor Diana Athill. After Rhys was found and rescued from obscurity by a BBC presenter in 1956, it was Athill—also editing V. S. Naipaul at the time—who spent a decade coaxing a completed version of *Wide Sargasso Sea* from her, after myriad rewrites and hospitalizations and other trouble. In an introduction to *Smile Please*, Athill described the book's genesis in relation to Rhys's other books, novels in which Rhys feared she had already "used up" most of her life's more resonant episodes. By this Athill meant that Rhys was a writer who drew from her own life, as all writers must—but that Rhys did so to the special degree of a deeply unhappy woman whose novels "happened to her," in such a way that she felt impelled rather than driven, through their writing, to lend prosodic shape to her life's deeper heartbreaks. Her books "were not autobiographical in every detail, as readers sometimes suppose they were, but autobiographical they were," Athill wrote, "and their therapeutic function was the purging of unhappiness."[9]

Jean Rhys was as unsparing of herself as she was of such modern pieties as the "therapeutic"; she might not have put it that way. But the books that she wrote about being a woman abroad in the world, after she largely disconnected from family at eighteen, all described the grief to which she came by attaching to men whom she loved or loathed or came to resent. In *Voyage in the Dark*, her book about the life of a colonial showgirl in Edwardian England, her heroine, Anna, claims that "the thing with men is to get everything you can out of them and not care a damn."[10] But in that book and her three novels about the glam uncertainties of Paris between the wars, her heroines were markedly modern: women untrammeled by convention, and unmoored by propriety, Rhys's women lived according to their affinity and will. But they weren't "feminist," in a form we'd recognize as such. They didn't fear depending on a man; they craved it. They craved pretty dresses and liked wearing makeup, too, and were less scornful than canny about the transactional aspect of all human relations, especially when sex is involved. But they weren't shallow.

That these desires could coexist in a complex dance with a deeper wish to be cared for and loved was an insight presented by Rhys not as some kind of revelation but as simply true to her experience. Unsubtle readers could perhaps be forgiven, absorbing her accounts of courtship and marriage gone wrong in *Quartet* (1928) and *After Leaving Mr. Mackenzie* (1930), for viewing those books as cautionary tales about the risks of attaching to the wrong men. But Jean Rhys was about as far from a moralist as it's possible to be. And by the time she wrote *Good Morning, Midnight* in 1939, the technical and emotive tour de force she published before disappearing for nearly twenty years, she offered no option but for her readers to see clearly what she'd been up to all along: a mode of writing at once unsparing of her protagonists' delusive contradictions and accepting of them as real. She captured with frightening vividness, moving between a continual present tense and passages rendered in a dreamlike past, of a woman on the verge. Trapped in drink and sorrow she confronts the part she also may have deserved in her reply to the question animating all her heroines: "Why must I suffer?"

If the first books "used up" the life experience of young adulthood, in *Wide Sargasso Sea* she returned to her childhood—and moved beyond her own experience. Writing about a time before she was alive—the 1830s—she also narrated half her book in the voice of a male narrator, Mr. Richardson, akin to the English men dotting her earlier books as n'er-do-well causers of feminine grief. The challenges of doing so were a big part of why the book took so long to write ("that man is making me very thin," she remarked).[11] But the psychic state and emotive world at its core—the inner life of a woman whose past on an island, and formative traumas experienced there—were her own. And so was the plantation, as she recalls in *Smile Please*, where its action unfolds. In *Wide Sargasso Sea*, the place is called Coulibri and is located in Jamaica. But it is modeled on her maternal family's estate, Geneva, on Dominica's south coast, where she spent much time as a girl. Once the second-largest estate on the island, Geneva's burning by Dominica's newly freed slaves in 1844 was also the model for what happened to Mr. Richardson's Coulibri in *Wide Sargasso Sea*. Rhys's resistance to doing an autobiography, deriving partly from the feeling that she'd "used up" her life, was about literary form as well. "I like shape very much," she said. "A novel has to have a shape, and life doesn't have any."[12] But thankfully she got over those resistances to craft a book, all but finished when she died, whose vignettes of childhood were as succinct and lapidary as you'd imagine from Jean Rhys. And it furnished a brilliant lens into the girlhood that shaped her, and her relation to difference, as that odd sort of person once called a "colonial": that peculiar fruit of empire that was produced in abundance from, say, the beginning of the nineteenth century until the first half of the twentieth, but not before or since. Too old to belong to the group of people who colonized these islands, she was also too young to belong to the "bohemian" class of people like Leigh Fermor who turned up later, and for whom engaging with difference was the point of hanging out here. Allured by and sheltered from the kinds of difference that attracted her but that she couldn't quite belong to, she was also the girl, when she arrived at school in England, who by dint of her background was expected to know how "coon songs" went.

* * *

IN *SMILE PLEASE*, Rhys wrote of a dear if distant father whose passion was cards and politics but who, when "talking to women, especially pretty ones, . . . had a gentler, teasing way," and who liked his daughter Gwen, too, to the extent that he "stopped the hated plate of porridge my mother suddenly expected me to eat every morning, and arranged that I should have an egg beaten up in hot milk with nutmeg instead."[13] She described her mother as a woman "who loved babies, any babies, including black ones, but didn't much care for her elder daughter once she had a littler one, and who then grew "middle-aged and plump and uninterested in me."[14] She wrote, too, about growing up in a Caribbean household full of "[s]weet sugar stolen on the sly; frizzy hair and the swizzle-stick and the clinking of crushed ice against the glass, which still means the West Indies to me."[15]

   She wrote of how as carnival passed, "I used to long so fiercely to be black and to dance, too, in the sun, to that music."[16] She recounted a "riot" during which her mother woke her and brought her down to their parlor in the middle of the night, but of how her father said,

> "Why do you want to wake the children up at this time of night? It's ridiculous."
>
> I heard far away a strange noise like animals howling but I knew it wasn't animals, it was people, and the noise came nearer and nearer.
>
> My father said: "They're perfectly harmless."
> That's what you think.[17]

She recounted how a certain wariness crept into her views of black people for a time—but so did envy. "I decided that they had a better time than we did; they laughed a lot though they seldom smiled. They were more alive, more a part of the place than we were."[18]

She also described how black people were not symbols nor extractions in her girlhood. They were also "individuals whom I liked or disliked."[19] One of those in the latter camp was her nurse Meta, "a short, stocky woman, very black and always . . . brooding over some unforgettable wrong," who teased her young charge, teaching her to be hysterically afraid of cockroaches ("She said that when I was asleep at night they would fly in and bite my mouth and that the bite would never heal"), and of all the other creatures stalking Dominica's woods— zombies, *soucriants* (succubi), and the *loup-garou* (werewolves) said to haunt all the old slave colonies of the French Indies from Haiti down to here.[20] She wrote of how Meta was a woman whose every story was "tinged with fear and horror," and all ended by her saying

> So I went to the wedding and they say to me, "What you doing here?" I say, "I come to get something to eat and drink." He give me one kick and I fly over the sea and come here to tell you this story.[21]

She wrote of how Meta took out her experience of the world's rejection on a young charge whom she was forbidden to slap, but whom she took by the shoulders and shook violently as the young Jean, hair flying, yelled, "Black Devil, Black Devil, Black Devil!" But who, in any case, showed Rhys "a world of fear and distrust," as she wrote, that "I am still in."[22]

She wrote also about an older girl at the Catholic convent school where her parents, unlike most Brits in Dominica, sent her to be educated with the mostly "colored"—mixed-race—girls who went there:

> I was young and shy and I was sitting next to a girl much older than myself. She was so tall and so pretty, and she spoke in such a confident way, that she quite awed me. She had aquiline features, large flashing eyes and a great deal of not too frizzy hair which she wore in a loose, becoming way. She didn't look coloured but I knew at once that she was. This did not prevent me from admiring her and longing to be friendly . . .
>
> Without speaking, she turned and looked at me. I knew irritation, bad temper, the "Oh, go away" look; this was different. This was hatred—impersonal, implacable hatred. I recognized it at once and if you think that a child cannot recognize hatred and remember it for life you are most damnably mistaken.
>
> I never tried to be friendly with any of the coloured girls again. I was polite and that was all.
>
> They hate us. We are hated.[23]

But she wrote also of a black girl she loved, "whose stories were quite different, full of jokes and laughter, descriptions of beautiful dresses and good things to eat."[24] And which also began with a ritual.

> Francine would say "Tim-tim." I had to answer "Boissêche," then she'd say "Tablier Madame est derrière dos" (Madam's apron is back to front). She always insisted on this ceremony before starting a story and it wasn't until much later, when I was reading a book about obeah, that I discovered that Boissêche is one of the gods. I grew very fond of Francine and admired her; when she disappeared without a word to me I was hurt. People did disappear, they went to one of the other islands, but not without saying goodbye.[25]

Francine was a person, she recalled in *Smile Please*, about whom "she wrote elsewhere"—a reference most directly to *Voyage in the Dark*, in which Francine is a servant of Anna's parents, back in the Caribbean, whose gay songs she recalls as the most happy-making aspect of her life back home (but whose parents, in the novel, sent Francine away). But it was also, perhaps, a reference to other of her black women characters. Antoinette's caring surrogate mother Christophine introduces her to Obeah and the black cultures and natural world of the Caribbean; it's to her that the mad creole lady—and the novel's readers—turn to understand its world. In her short story "Let Them Call It Jazz," which Rhys based on her own experience of being remanded to the psychiatric wing of Holloway Prison, after she was convicted of assault for drunkenly slapping her neighbor in 1949, her narrator protagonist is a West Indian immigrant named Selina Davis who says that "if they treat you wrong over and over again the hour strike when you burst out."[26] If it was black women who brought her into the world of distrust and hate, they also introduced her to affection and stories. And as her biographer Carole Angier put it, "whenever she was hurled most low, she found a black woman from her islands to speak for her."[27] Which is another way of saying: Francine appeared in the books of this woman from an island where "people did disappear"; Meta did not.

If the people of Roseau, and the black women who shaped her experience of Dominica, featured strongly in her reminiscences of the island, the scary but wondrous "interior" did, too. It is in writing of the shabby rural estate her father bought their family in the hills over Roseau—a place she described as "very beautiful, wild, lonely, remote"—that she waxes most lyrical about the magic and terror of Dominica's thunderstorms in August; the smell of wet grass through which she walked barefoot in those storms' wake; the hibiscus and pink-flowered frangipani trees which "if you broke a branch bled copiously, not red blood but white."[28] She described gazing up at the mist-ringed peak of Dominica's highest point, Morne Diablotin—a place whose French name suggested its repute as a home to malevolent beings. "I believed that Diablotin was eight thousand feet high," she wrote, "and that it had never been climbed because its summit was rock. Round it flew large black birds called Diablotins (devil birds), found nowhere else in the West Indies or the world."[29] She was entranced by the island's beauty, and wanted to be of it. She walked barefoot—a pleasure not allowed by white parents but indulged in anyway. She also ate with her "fingers out of a Calabash as the Negroes did [because] food seemed to taste better that way."[30] But there was something in her, too, of Mr. Richardson's abiding distrust of this island's lushness, and the disquiet it evoked when he fretted that here there was "too much blue, too much green."[31]

* * *

ON THIS LITTLE-TOURISTED ISLAND where the restaurants always feel half empty, and where any hotel with more than three rooms is called "big," the countryside remains the point—with the difference from Rhys's day being that the interior is less to be gazed at, these days and by visitors especially, than explored. This is a volcanic land where you can, for example, trek through a Martian wasteland called the Valley of Desolation; visit a Boiling Lake (a water-filled crater, bubbling with underground heat); or snorkel at Champagne Beach (where undersea sulphur springs cause little bubbles to rise from the reef). I settled, my first time in Roseau, for a short hike to famed Trafalgar Falls, where twin 180-foot cascades spill down from a jungle crevice. Scrambling over the boulders to a pool at the falls' base, I waded into bath-warm waters, fed from the same subterranean source as the Boiling Lake, whose milky look resembled unfiltered sake. No less toothsome was lunch at the nearby Papillote Wilderness Retreat, the garden restaurant and lodge that, when it opened thirty years ago, became a signpost for an "eco-friendly" approach to tourism that Dominica—and many places in the Caribbean, and worldwide—have adopted since.

But these weren't places one went in the 1890s. In those days the main mode of transportation between Roseau and Portsmouth, which lay thirty miles apart on the northern and southern ends of its calm leeward shore, was steamship. Traveling to the wild Atlantic coast was only achievable over steep mountain trails, on horseback or foot. Until the arrival, anyway, of an energetic colonial administrator who looms large both in Dominica's modern history and in Jean Rhys's emotional life.

Sir Henry Hesketh Bell's endeavors to know and improve this island foreshadowed a long career in the colonial service that was perhaps highlighted by a World War I–era stint running Uganda, when he succeeded in eradicating sleeping sickness there. He was a man whose good imperial works made him a poster child for the kind of bighearted Brit called to mind by mourners of the empire's passing. Bell didn't cure any diseases in Dominica. But one of his achievements was convincing Andrew Carnegie, the American philanthropist, to fund the building of the lovely library by the waterfront that's still in use now. He also convinced the Rose's lime juice company to set up shop here, and got its banana trade under way. But the endeavor for which he's best recalled in Dominica—and that most caught a young Jean Rhys's fancy—was his triumph in conceiving and building an "Imperial Road" through the island's interior and to join its two coasts, whose first main section Bell opened to much pomp and ceremony in 1904. A potent and glamorous figure from her girlhood, "Mr. Hesketh" was an administrator who wore a gold-laced uniform and "went his own active way and did what he liked."[32] He didn't merely bring Dominica modern roads but hosted a fancy-dress ball for children where he asked her to dance and gave the fourteen-year-old Rhys not merely the best night of her young life but also something akin, in waltzing with this powerful and charming man who "like all good dancers . . . made his partner feel she too was an expert," her sexual dawn.[33] Bell's Imperial Road remains the way to cross Dominica today—at least the seventeen miles he was able to complete, winding steeply up out of Roseau to the island's centerpoint, at a place called Pont Cassé, if not all the way to Carib people for whom Bell was an enlightened advocate, too.

Rhys wrote in *Voyage in the Dark* of her memories of the reserve that Hesketh Bell, her teenage crush, made for Dominica's Indians. Her antiheroine in that book, Anna, lies on her bed in an Eastbourne rooming house and writes a letter recalling them:

> The Caribs indigenous to this island were a warlike tribe and their resistance to white domination, though spasmodic, was fierce. As lately as the beginning of the nineteenth century, they raided one of the neighboring islands, under British rule, overpowered the garrison and kidnapped the governor, his wife and three children. They are now practically exterminated. The few hundreds that are left do not intermarry with the negroes. Their reservation, at the northern end of the island, is known as the Carib quarter.[34]

Looking up from the page, Rhys-as-Anna exclaims, "They had, or used to have, a king. Here's to Mopo, King of the Caribs!" The young Caribbean immigrant in England, lonely and alienated, doesn't merely invoke the Carib of her native land. She identifies with them. One thinks of the famous first lines from *Wide Sargasso Sea:* "They say when trouble comes close ranks, and so the white people did. But we were not in their ranks."[35] Perhaps the Carib, as one academic commentator put it, were for her "a symbol of loss, defeat, and passivity; like her, a victim of European domination."[36] Whatever one makes of that, it wasn't until 1936 when Rhys, for the one and only time as an adult, actually visited the Carib Territory herself.

During that visit—a return home more full of disappointment than rapture—Rhys was saddened by the truth that the old Lockhart estate at Geneva was now a ruin. She hated that the eastern sections of old Hesketh Bell's road had become impassable. The crystal rivers she'd drunk from as a girl, according to her guide, were now too dirty to drink. But one venture she did manage to complete was to at last visit the Carib Territory she'd written of in *Voyage in the Dark*. She described her visit there in a short story with the suggestive title "Temps Perdi," a phrase evoking days past in Proust's sense, but which in the "patois" of her homeland, she's careful to underscore, "does not mean, poetically, lost or forgotten time, but, matter-of-factly wasted time, lost labor." This was a concept with a special resonance on an island that was said to be "one of those places hostile to humans, that knows how to defend itself"; a place which had a way, whether by hurricane or crop sickness, to create "more West Indian ruins and labor lost."[37]

In that story, she wrote of how "[a]ll my life I had been curious about these people because of a book I once read, pictures I once saw."[38] She described an illustration very much like one her parents had hung in their dining room in Roseau, called *Homme Caraibe Dessiné d'après natur par le Père Plumier*, and depicting a figure with

> Bow and arrows in his right hand, club in his left, a huge, muscular body and strange, small, womanish face. His long, black hair was carefully parted in the middle and hung smoothly to his shoulders. But his slanting eyes, starting from their sockets, looked wild and terrified. He was more the frightened than the frightening savage.[39]

Determined to find this fellow or his kin, she and her husband had a hard time finding someone willing to take them to the Carib Territory, a 3,700-acre parcel whose borders had been formalized by Hesketh Bell in 1903. They arranged, though, for horses and a guide. They made the trek down from the north, discussing the rumor that Carib women spoke a different language from the men (true, at least in those days; now they all speak English), and wondered if they would actually encounter any of these people who "live all separated from each other, and all hidden in the bush."[40] They didn't encounter many. Instead, they visited the territory's new police station—whose opening here, the policeman inside told them, had occasioned bad riots. The disturbance had been set off when the government's men arrived here not to build a hospital, as the Carib had asked for, but a constabulary instead. The Caribs burned the first station, and then part of the second. When Rhys asked the policeman if anyone was hurt, he replied, "Oh no, only two or three Caribs were killed."[41] And then he directed them, if they wanted to meet an actual Carib, to visit a beautiful Carib girl, just down from the police station, whom he said people liked to go see, bearing small gifts since she was not only beautiful but also crippled, and to take photographs of.

They found the girl in a house whose one room was decorated with pictures cut out from newspapers, "and coloured cards of the Virgins, saints, and angels."[42] Rhys chatted with the girl's mother, who "looked like an old Chinese woman," and who'd spent time in service in Martinique, even traveling to Paris with her employers before returning here. The girl was beautiful indeed, with white and lovely teeth and "thin, lovely hands," and "[s]he dragged herself across the floor into the sun outside to be photographed, managing her useless legs with a desperate, courageous grace."[43] Rhys and her party took a few photos of the girl, whose "skin in the sun was a lovely colour." And then they left. She'd begun her day in the Carib Territory with the hope that she might understand something of what it felt like to "be a savage person—a true Carib."[44] The day ended, back at the estate known as Temps Perdi, in a kind of fever dream lying on her back, reminded that "it is at night that you know old fears, old hopes, that you know unhappiness, turning from side to side under the mosquito net, like a prisoner in a cell full of small peepholes."[45]

* * *

IT'S A LOT EASIER to reach the Carib Territory today, as I found in heading there from Roseau, than it once was. By one of the Syrian-owned department stores, I found where the silver or green Nissan minibuses lined up to traverse Hesketh Bell's old Imperial Road to the Atlantic coast. There by where Dominicans buy their flip-flops and washing machines, a woman carrying a wooden box of smoked cod from Canada pointed the way. Dark-skinned and stocky with startling green eyes, she said she was heading to the village of La Plaine and just to follow her lead. The maxis waiting to fill up with passengers had names like "PUTTING UP RESISTANCE" and "LIZARD LICK," and, more mysteriously, "LOVE AND HATE CAN'T BE GREAT."

My friend with her cod told me to sit tight, though, as one of the few minibuses without a name on it, whose older driver she knew well, readied to leave. Rolling from town some minutes later, we turned up into the mountains and traced the steep switchbacks of Hesketh Bell's road. "Alex, you know every one of these curves," someone exclaimed to our aged driver. "I do," he replied, "but you best hope I don't forget any."

He didn't, and after a brief break so that Alex could buy bananas from a stand by Dominica's high crossroads at Pont Cassé, we continued to its wilder coast. Winding through lush river valleys to pass the old banana estate at Rosalie, we reached the sleepy village of La Plaine. There I slept that night in a tent by the banks of the Picard River, at a place that would become dear to me—a little restaurant, run by some Frenchies from nearby Guadeloupe, that was hard by the stony current and had the best callaloo and river bathing you could ever want. And then, walking into La Plaine and greeting the green-eyed woman with her cod who was sitting on its main street, hawking her fish in Kreyol, I found a ride back up to Pont Cassé, and from there another lift north and east to the Carib Territory. The latter lift came from a pale American fellow, well fed and well groomed, who confirmed what his van's sides, which touted the Church of the Nazarene, suggested. He was an evangelical from Kentucky, leading an expansive new mission here. He pointed up into a field just before we entered the Carib Territory, gesturing at what looked like a big white tent but which he said was his church. Then he dropped me by the road's edge, high over the island's Atlantic shore, and continued on his Christian way.

As Dominica has turned to making tourism a more central part of its economy, the government has moved to secure the patronage of one subset of travelers—hikers—not much targeted by other islands. The Waitukubuli National Trail was formally opened in 2010. It's a hundred-mile trek from the island's southern tip to its north. The trail wends over and through Dominica's valleys and peaks, joining new trails to old footpaths first blazed by the island's Maroons and natives. Many locals seem suspicious of whether the trail will ever attract enough hikers to stay viable. But for now, its route offers a grand way to see an island whose alluring profile, as Anthony Trollope wrote when he turned up here in 1856 and rather disagreed with Jean Rhys's Mr. Richardson, "fills one with an ardent desire to be off and rambling among those green mountains."[46] I set out from the edge of the Carib Territory to ramble over a few miles of the trail near where the Kalinago watch over its turns. Skirting oceanside cliffs, the trail snaked down through fecund gullies to deposit me at rocky beaches whose grapefruit-sized stones looked as if they'd need a few more millennia of the ocean's pummeling to become sand. This Jurassic isle's Atlantic shore can still feel like the world's end. Apart from one or two small brown men to whom I waved hello by the main road, I didn't see another soul for the forty minutes it took to stroll down to the rocky edge of what's known here as L'Escalier Tête Chien—the "Staircase of the Boa Constrictor": a broad formation of hardened magma, ridged like stairs and emerging from the crashing Atlantic, which in Kalinago lore marks the place where a great snake came ashore, after swimming here from their own ancestral home by South America's Orinoco River, to found their first settlement here.

Today the Carib Territory boasts new houses built by Hugo Chávez and the Chinese, both of whom have taken an interest in the Kalinagos' fortunes. Visitors can tour a traditional village showcasing how its inhabitants' ancestors lived after arriving here in dugout canoes from the mainland. Educational as it may be, the village bears about as much resemblance to modern Carib life as Colonial Williamsburg does to that of suburbanites in Richmond. The Caribs' struggles to balance economic development and cultural pride, and to combat alcohol abuse and other ills, are familiar to observers of North America's reservations. But it's not a place absent people and leaders aiming for something different, as I found when I entered the village of Crayfish River and found Charles Williams, who had served as the elected chief of the territory from 2004 to 2009. Williams runs a small guesthouse here, where I found him sitting in a linoleum-floored office furnished with a rickety bookcase mostly filled with knickknacks and old newspapers but also two books: a worn copy of Jared Diamond's *Guns, Germs, and Steel* and a vinyl-covered volume that resembled a high school yearbook but whose spine's embossed title read *Unsung Heroes of the Caribbean, 2003–2011*. Williams was a short and wiry man with his people's copper skin and prominent cheekbones who worked a mention of both books into what amounted to an opening monologue he directed at my willing ears after he gleaned that I was both keen to stay at his guesthouse for a few days and keen to hear his story.

"I received that book at a meeting of indigenous leaders at the Organization of American States in Washington, D.C.," he said, gesturing at the Diamond volume. "And those three things, the guns and germs and steel, are what Europeans used to exterminate us across the continent.

Here in Dominica, they also gave us blankets infected with mumps and measles. But we survived, and we still survive, and that is why we are here today. And that is why it is important to defend our rights and our integrity to this day." He paused in his worn polo shirt to look at his visitor. "You read about me on the internet?" I told him I had, which made him smile. "Then you know about what landed me in this book, too?" He pulled out the *Unsung Heroes of the Caribbean* book.

I nodded. "Is it to do with when the Disney company came to Dominica to film *Pirates of the Caribbean*?"

"That's right," he said. "And you know I gave them hell." That film's production had issued an open call for extras to play members of a "cannibal village" afflicting Johnny Depp's crew, at a rate of a few dollars a day. Chief Charlie led the protests. "When Columbus arrived here," he said, "he portrayed us as cannibals. But it wasn't true then, and it never has been. So I said: We're not going for that." The production eventually opted to fly in, from the Philippines, its own brown-skinned extras.

* * *

WHEN I ASKED WILLIAMS if he thought he'd like to be chief again, he didn't pause.

"I think so, yes. I am an active man, and . . ."

"Like hell you will!" I'd heard Charlie's wife come home a few minutes before. Now she walked across the cement patio from the kitchen and said hello. She was a squat woman with a great round face who generally gazed at her husband with a look of wry bemusement. Margaret paused to greet me before returning to him. "Charl-o, you know this—being chief is just one big headache." He smiled wanly. She showed me to my windowless room and I threw my pack onto a thin foam mattress covered with flower-print sheets, commencing a visit with the first couple of the Kalinago nation that furnished as much of a glimpse into their fractious domestic idyll as it did the lives of their people in toto—but which provided plenty of the latter, too.

That evening, as on each of the next, Margaret laid out a feast on their plastic table, beneath one of those harsh-white halogen bulbs that provide all light nowadays in humbler tropical homes, and that was comprised—like much that's called "creole food" in the islands, but which Margaret called "Carib food" here—of four or five types of starch: boiled plantain and macaroni and slaw and sundry sorts of pumpkin and tuber mashed with garlic and inevitably including the fibrous dasheen (or taro) root known throughout the Caribbean's old sugar islands as "ground provision" but also often called, due to the purplish hue it takes on when cooked, "blue food." Joining me for this repast as Margaret busied herself in the kitchen, Charlie looked out at the sea through the lengths of rusty rebar onto which he one day hoped to extend his patio. He pointed with pride at his stands of plantain and pumpkin vines on the slope below. "All 3,783 acres of the Carib Territory are collectively owned," he explained. "We have no title here. But everyone knows whose holding is whose."

As I began to press him on how this system of land tenancy actually worked in practice, we heard a cry from the road.

"My chief!"

We walked over to the road to find a small glassy-eyed man, drunk and carrying a pitchfork.

"How are you going there?" Charlie greeted the drunken man. The drunken man hugged his chief. Charlie looked at him indulgently. "Planting dasheen tonight?"

"Yes, my chief," he slurred. In the hand not holding the pitchfork he toted a mostly empty little plastic bottle of clear white rum I grew used to seeing in the hands of men here: the bottles seemed to be the main item on sale, apart from beer and stale cheese puffs, from the little tin-roofed store down the way.

"Full moon tonight," Charlie observed as the man ambled off. "Right time for planting dasheen." He shook his head sadly, when I remarked upon the man's state. "If you think Stanton's bad, you should have seen his dad."

Over the next few days with Charlie, walking the byways of the territory, it wasn't uncommon for tipsy men to hail him as "chief"—or for Charlie to lament, as those men stumbled off, the twin ills of alcohol and the fact that the area was not, as he put it, "commercially active." And so it wasn't: its villages' main visible economy seemed to consist of women who sat by the road as elegantly composed as the drunken men were sloppy. They spent their days hoping a curious visitor or two would stop through the territory and buy one of their beautiful woven baskets. Charlie described his ambitious plans, if he could raise the capital, to start another enterprise here: "I wanted to produce coconut and essential oils," he said. "That's a resource we have." He insisted that whatever Margaret thought, he wanted to be chief again. "Oui, man"—

this was his one Kreyol phrase—"I like challenges. I like, you know, to overcome the fucking thing! And the man who's in there now is a scamp. Nothing but matter, taking up space." Charlie's rapid step, as he hiked up a slope called the Horse Back Ridge, was anything but that of a man who was merely matter. "I'm gonna run again."

Charlie loved having a diplomatic passport and going on trips to Washington, D.C., too. I knew, though, from Margaret and from some of the drunks by the rum shop, that not all his moves as chief had been popular. "People say that you asked all the black people from the territory to leave," I said by way of asking him what happened.

"I'm not trying to interfere in anyone's private life," he replied. "I simply said that any time a man from outside wants a wife in the Carib Territory, he must take his wife and go. That is the traditional rule, and that stands. Since the United Nations came together and signed the Declaration on the Rights of Indigenous People, all traditional law stands." The principle was clear enough. But the challenge of enforcing any laws that aren't also national laws, in a territory that doesn't have its own police force ("Police cost money," Charlie explained), was large. And so was the basic demographic and social fact that many of the three-thousand-odd members of Dominica's Kalinago Nation by now possess families and family trees as richly tangled as anyone's in the Caribbean. Charlie delighted in recounting the era when Jolly John, the chief in the 1930s, led the skirmish with the Brits that's wryly called "the Carib War" in Roseau, and of which Jean Rhys learned when she visited the Carib Territory in 1936. It was during that episode, after his people burned the government's police barracks down, that the Brits took the dramatic step of sending a gunboat around the island from Portsmouth to shine its blinding spotlight onto his hometown from sea. Charlie loved such stories of Kalinago autonomy and pride. But as became clear one afternoon when we drove his little Nissan up to Marigot, twenty minutes north of the territory, to buy some fish to accompany our tubers, that didn't mean his own family wasn't mixed, too. The woman by the pier from whom we bought a fat snapper had a complexion like Grace Jones's. But after she greeted him warmly, Charlie hailed her as "the Black Carib." Their ensuing conversation—about some shared cousin from St. Kitts, with the surname Williams—was hard to follow, but the shared affection was palpable. Charlie's own daughter, as he admitted with some chagrin but also evident pride, had gone to work as a lawyer for the government in town; the likelihood that she'd settle with a Carib man, back home, wasn't great.

Charlie told me, driving back to the territory that afternoon, that he wanted to show me one of its beauty spots that few people knew. He turned up a steep road before we reached Crayfish River. We crested a hill whose peak must have been eighteen hundred feet above the water below. Charlie pulled to a stop by our destination: a little thatch-roofed bar with open sides and a hand-painted sign out front that read "ELVIS' HIGH RISE." The view, over the Carib Territory and the whole north of Dominica, was sublime. The place's eponymous proprietor was a shirtless man with copper-black skin and a tremendous round belly and twinkling eyes.

"How you going, Elvis?" Charlie shook our barman's hand as he handed us a couple of green-bottled Kubuli beers. His place's main decor was comprised of posters touting the beer we were drinking, plastered with the slogan "Che Bé Sa'w!" ("That's Kreyol for 'Get yours!'," Elvis explained), and a rather effective piece of found art made from the cheese grater–like metal cylinder from an old washing machine. We took our beers outside to chat with the pair of small Kalinago men who were mixing concrete in the dirt.

One of the men seemed to be an old pal of Charlie's. It became clear as they talked that his half-empty rum bottle, and current station, belied a flashing and worldly intelligence. He and Charlie recounted the recent debate in the Carib Council that had resulted in the blond leader of the Church of the Nazarene being denied permission to build his church on Kalinago land—a good thing, they agreed. Charlie voiced a new aim: he wanted to print five hundred copies of the United Nations Declaration on the Rights of Indigenous People—enough copies, if he could convince the government to fund the printing, for every household in the territory. ("What is more expensive, five hundred copies of this thing, or this whole region of islands we used to have from Puerto Rico to Trinidad?") The man mixing concrete with rum nodded that this might be a good idea, but looked unconvinced. The part of Charlie's riff with which he agreed was signaled by his remarking, apropos of the Kalinagos' proud past, about how when he'd gone to Venezuela, "the people there by the Orinoco, it's true, was just like we!"

And then Charlie, at a brief pause in the conversation, asked his old pal the question that was really on his mind. "What you think, I should run and be chief again?"

The man took a swig of rum. "You can do, Char-lo. But you know to win you have to make sure that when you speak, people feel you speak for them, too."

* * *

CHIEF CHARLIE, in the event, did made it back into office: I wasn't shocked to learn, in 2014, that he'd run and been reelected. But the problems of the Carib Territory weren't dissimilar to those of Dominica as a whole: a largely powerless country in the world economy that, since the World Trade Organization declared its preferential trade ties with Britain null in the 1990s, has found being "commercially active" a big challenge. Once many of its large estates were under sugar; then they were under bananas. Their current decay (or their turning into "eco-resorts") is down to forces beyond Dominica's control.

I went to see how these forces were playing out at Geneva, the old estate by the island's southern tip that was so key to Jean Rhys's stories. En route there, I stopped off to see another Dominican whose knowledge of the island's past, and of its favorite daughter's work and its indigenous past, too, is unexcelled. I found Lennox Honychurch at the site of a project to which he's devoted much of the past twenty years: the old British fort that overlooks strategic Prince Rupert Bay, off of Portsmouth, which Honychurch's team has spectacularly restored to resemble its eighteenth-century glory. Dominica's leading historian and exponent is a tall and eloquent man with salt-and-pepper hair whose name has long been notorious to West Indian schoolchildren as the author of a classic textbook, *The Caribbean People*, which he wrote when he was in his twenties but which has now been a staple of grade-school curricula, from Antigua to Trinidad, for thirty years. At home in Dominica, Honychurch is celebrated as a national encyclopedia. Visitors to the website of the island's tourist board are directed, if they wish to learn more about Dominica, to visit lennoxhonychurch.com. He traces his West Indian roots back to the seventeenth century, in Barbados on his father's side. His mother was a daughter of Elma Napier, the madame of Pointe Baptiste. Apart from being Dominica's leading historian, he is also, in typical small-island fashion, its leading broadcaster and leading archaeologist and an advocate for preservation. He also paints his own book covers. When Honychurch went to England to do a late-in-life PhD at Oxford in the 1990s, he produced an important thesis on Dominica's pre-Columbian past, based on years of fieldwork on the island, that helped shape the current consensus about when and how subsequent indigenous groups settled the lush river valleys: the Ortoiroids, who made their way to the Antilles from South America, beginning in roughly 5000 BC; the Arawak, who rode the South Equatorial Current here from the Orinoco's mouth around 100 BC; and the Carib, who turned up to vanquish the Arawak in around AD 1200, and to whose modern cause and interpretive materials, in the model village in the Carib Territory, Honychurch has been a key contributor and ally. "It's not always easy living on this island," he reflected as we looked out from the Cabrits at a turquoise bay bobbing with fishing boats and pleasure craft. "I'm a lover of theater and film living on an island without a cinema. But Dominica is my passion."

Honychurch is a new kind of white West Indian not around in Jean Rhys's day or in the immediate post-independence era either: he's a devotee of his island who is neither a nostalgic "colonial" nor a government huckster (involved in the immediate post-independence government of Eugenia Charles, he long ago forswore the sad indignities of groveling before the IMF for more awful loans, or before the Chinese for more aid), and who remains here despite the debilitating sense of fatalism infecting a place where, as puts it, "There's always been the sense here of: Why do anything if it's just going to be washed out, you know, in the next storm? We in Dominica are just accustomed to things disappearing and being destroyed." But life on the Caribbean's "nature island," if Honychurch is anything to go by, makes you nothing if not philosophical. "There are all these elements Dominica does not have," he explained. "Yet one also has to feel a bit like Dr. Pangloss in *Candide*, absorbing these terrible situations but going on, at the same time, about the best of all possible worlds. Because the fact that we can't build an airport that takes international jets, no matter that many people *want* an international airport, is also preserving the country—protecting our security, and our relation to the land." The end of those preferential trade deals with Britain, he said, turned a small island into an entity ill-equipped to compete in the world market. "That slope used to be covered in banana plantations," Honychurch said, gesturing toward a lush hillside behind Portsmouth. "Dominica is now more forested than it's been at any time since the eighteenth century." But about this, Honychurch felt fine. "If people want to go live in the Miami suburbs, I say let them go. Let them go and return for their nostalgic holidays and leave those of us who remain here struggling, to struggle. It's not GDP that measures quality of life."

I asked Honychurch about his island's most famous scribe, and he told me about how Rhys wrote a cutting letter about his grandmother, after visiting Elma Napier in Point Baptiste, in which she mentioned having encountered a "semi-literary woman" near Calibishie whom she didn't much like. ("Jean Rhys's husband at the time was an editor in London—and my grandmother was quite taken up with him, wanting to publish her novel.") Honychurch had a theory, based on a discovery he'd made in Henry Hesketh Bell's papers in the Royal Commonwealth Society Library in Cambridge, about a woman named Mary Pruitt, arrested for practicing Obeah in 1904 at Geneva; he thought she must be the model for Christophine in *Wide Sargasso Sea*. In Bell's papers he also found a trove of photos of the Lockhart family, and of a young Jean Rhys, which are those that have graced every book about Rhys since his find.

On a visit to England in 1978, Honychurch went to find the woman herself in Devon; he managed "only to see her," as he put it, "but not meet her." After traveling to the village of Cheriton Fitzpaine, Honychurch knocked at the door of the little garden cottage. Jean Rhys's assistant opened her door. He explained to her that he was from Dominica and that he brought best wishes to Jean Rhys and just wondered if he might see her—only to be told by the assistant, to his surprise, "Well, somebody came from Dominica yesterday, and she's a little tired." Honychurch watched as the assistant padded off down the hall. Looking over her shoulder down the corridor, he could see a white-haired woman sitting in an armchair to whom the assistant spoke and whom he heard say, "Oh, I'm just too tired to see anyone." Honychurch asked the assistant who else from Dominica could possibly have made this pilgrimage. He was chagrined to hear the name of an American academic who had made herself the world's self-appointed main Rhys scholar, but who was not, in fact, Dominican. Apart from getting in the way of his own visit, her apparent false claim of being from the island didn't earn her affection from Lennox Honychurch, bemused author of *The Dominica Story*, who now chuckled at the memory.[47] "I went on this whole adventure into the Devon countryside. I heard her voice. I saw this sort of ghostly figure at the end of the corridor. But that was my time seeing Jean Rhys."

Honychurch gave me a ride into Portsmouth to catch my onward ride down to Roseau. We said farewell by the workshop of a friend who was readying costumes for the approaching carnival. Like all good West Indians passionate about politics and current affairs but critical of government, Honychurch would play *mas* in Roseau the following week. The costumes his friend was crafting for their band were made from muslin and wire. Their white and orange zebra stripes made them resemble a creature—the invasive lionfish, which had been introduced to the Caribbean some years before from the South Pacific, Honychurch explained, and had wreaked havoc on its reefs. When I asked him what lettered Dominicans made of how Jean Rhys wrote so lovingly of an island to which she never returned to live, he replied by quoting a poem that another Dominican author, Phyllis Shand Allfrey, penned on the subject. "Love for an island is the sternest passion," that verse began.

pulsing beyond the blood through roots and loam
it overflows the boundary of bedrooms
and courses past the fragile walls of home.[48]

Those lines, antique but affecting, lingered in my ears as I headed south toward Geneva.

There in its wide valley encircled by lush peaks and facing the sea, it was easy to see why the young Jean Rhys was so taken with this place's "strong atmosphere of age, melancholy, and adventure."[49] It was also easy to understand why her rendering of this estate, built not for pleasure but for profit, was so racked with foreboding in *Wide Sargasso Sea*. The novel's climactic fire may have been modeled mostly on what happened here after emancipation, when Rhys's great-grandfather's former slaves rioted in the vicinity of Geneva's first great house, burning the family's possessions. But it also evoked another fire, when those slaves' own grandkids burned down the house Rhys had known as a girl, during labor unrest in the 1930s and just before her return to the island. After that fire, Honychurch had told me, the last Lockharts never fully rebuilt. They sold Geneva in 1949 to the most prominent of Dominica's Lebanese families, the Nasseifs, and moved to Trinidad.

Approaching the property's ruins, I was met by an affable Rasta whose black hair was draped in ropes about his head. He told me how his ancestors had worked these lands—but then repeatedly torched their masters' homes for "revolution and 'ting." My guide led me past crumbling stone walls, showing me a plaque noting that Geneva has recently been named, with the help of funding from the European Union and Dominica's ecotourism initiative, a "heritage park" for reflecting on the island's past. This was a place, like many in the Caribbean, where history's weight rests heavy: that Jean Rhys knew this, and gave it voice in her novels, was key to her genius. That it was also key to her sadness, vis-à-vis the home to which she could never return except in words, seemed plain, too.

As carnival alighted on Dominica that weekend, Roseau's streets were taken over by festivities that partly copied the bikini-and-bead vulgarities of the carnival mainstream, these days, on other islands, but whose dominant strain seemed stuck, like so much in Dominica, some decades in the Caribbean past. Alongside artful *mas* ensembles like Lennox Honychurch's school of darting lionfish, many people wore traditional costumes like the rag-and-hemp Snuffalufagus *sensay*—a mop-like character who often wears cow horns atop his head and whose roots lie in ceremonial costumes of West Africa's Twi people. Heading out to the southeastern village of La Pleine, I found the cod saleswoman with the striking green eyes, along with not a few other faces I'd learned in my days there, bouncing to soca and sipping rum on the village's main street while menaced by a half-dozen masqueraders in coal-black paint. Playing devils or overseers or both, they demanded coins from revelers before expressing their menace, or themselves, by cracking their long black whips on the ground. Their mix of melancholy and joy was no less artful than a Jean Rhys sentence, enacting a pathos as old as the island.

The next day as I made for the airport in a soft drizzle, I found the maxi called LIZARD LICK to head for Melville Hall. Its driver, usually, would have taken the old imperial road north from Pont Cassé to skirt the Carib Territory. But that route, he said, had been washed out in a recent storm. We would be rolling, instead, through the territory itself—even though that road on Ash Wednesday, he explained, could be blocked up by the Kalinagos' traditional carnival wind-down. And sure enough, as we passed the trail down to the Staircase of the Boa Constrictor and neared Crayfish River, a din was audible down the road. Sounding softly in the mist at first, it grew louder as my driver slowed to a stop by the side of the road. Around a bend ahead came a troupe of a few dozen small people with copper skin, banging on pans and bells and small handheld drums. Some were dressed in straw hats and white clothes; others wore no costumes at all. A couple of these Carib, on their creolized island, were dressed as *sensay* chickens not from the Orinoco but Ghana. Most carried green leaves. And as they neared where we sat, I could see a group in the middle of the throng holding a cloth-covered coffin on their shoulders. Passing slowly and taking up the road in such a way that we couldn't pass, they were on their way to effect the ritual of Téwé Vaval—their festive burning of this coffin, as the sun set, would symbolically bury the spirit of carnival for another year. Pausing to let the procession pass, we rolled slowly past its stragglers, some of them banging on the van's sides as we did. As we drove past the Carib Territory Guest House, in the land to which Ella Gwendolyn Rhys Williams always returned in her books but not in body, I could see chief Charles Williams and his queen, Margaret, standing out in front. Charlie had his arms crossed. He was taking in the scene.

CHAPTER 14

RETURN TO EL DORADO: TRINIDAD

BEYONCÉ IS GOLD. Gold like the burned grass of the Queen's Park Savannah at dry season in Port of Spain. Like the lamé costumes and corded locks of the masquerade band that, two days before she performed in Trinidad's capital city, strode around this same park to claim top honors during its famed yearly carnival. Like the twenty Grammys she's scooped by now. And gold, too, like her glittered bodysuit and shining skin and hair as she emerged, on the largest concert stage ever built in the Caribbean, to close a triumphant ten-month world tour at the bottom of the Antillean chain.

Port of Spain is a steaming oil town wedged between the sea and the island's high northern mountains. This post-carnival concert, once upon a time, wouldn't have occurred here, for religious reasons. In the land of calypso, Fat Tuesday's excesses are meant to connote a Farewell to the Flesh. "No calypsos were heard for the whole 40 days of Lent," the Trinidad-born actor and artist Geoffrey Holder recalled of his 1940s boyhood in Port of Spain. "You heard only sacred music, classical music, 'refined music.'"[1] Now concerns of theosophy had been replaced with more secular worries—over whether people who save for much of the year to afford carnival costumes costing upwards of US$1,000 would pony up, just after carnival's end, for tickets to Beyoncé's show, which ranged in cost from US$70 for general admission to $160 for VIP to $250 for "VVIP," if you wanted to be in real sight of the actual stage. Many commentators had urged the island's main cell phone company, TSTT—the show's prime underwriters—to withdraw their support for an event they saw as competing directly with carnival. Cultural power brokers like Brian MacFarlane, the masquerade designer of the lamé costumes that had won him his third straight carnival crown that year, protested that "that same money could have been spent on promoting our local culture."[2]

The controversy had taken over the opinion pages and airwaves for weeks. But as dusk approached and showtime neared, the press of people around the Savannah's southwest edge showed that enough tickets had been sold. Most years in Port of Spain, the day after Ash Wednesday is a time for VD tests and groggy naps. This year, Lent's start found tout Trinidad out for a last lap around the Savannah.

Groups of brightly dressed young women queued along roads still stained with the paint from J'ouvert—the pre-dawn celebrations of the Monday before when many of these same people, coated in mud and cocoa powder, stormed the city's center flinging bright colors on one another. This year, like every other, J'ouvert's "dutty mas" had given way to the "pretty mas" of Carnival Tuesday, with swarms of feathered revelers in sneakers and thongs marching and "wining" (gyrating alone or with a partner) behind trucks belching diesel exhaust and booming soca in corresponding measure. Now the sneakers had given way to high heels wobbling on dusty ground. Tan lines left by carnival tops accented strapless dresses. Unsubtle makeup accented faces that—in their striking rhymes of Benin bone structure and Kerala hair—suggested something of the complex past that had given Trinidad's people a particular beauty not unlike that of the creole superstar about to perform. This was a place to see and be seen. And everyone was here—not just those young women from Port of Spain's monied classes who could be counted on all along, but Indians from the countryside, grown-ups of all kinds. Young men, too. All, it seemed, were welcoming the chance, in the afterglow of carnival's lowered inhibitions, to button up (at least partway) and parade oneself with a boo or at least move in on one in more elegant fashion than humping her thigh on a paint-spattered street. This was an Event.

It was also a concert. As dusk fell, the hundred-plus members of Silver Stars—crowned the island's top steel band during carnival's Panorama competition—wheeled their pans onto the vast metal stage erected by the Savannah's western edge. Mallets beat out the ringing tones of the national anthem on their round metal drums. Most of the crowd remained outside the fences that had sprung up around the park's perimeter. Sucking down plasma-rich water from a fresh green coconut procured from a salesman across the street, I lingered with friends in front of the stately Queens Royal College, the prestigious

Victorian school where the island's overclass had long sent their boys to study Shakespeare and God. The alma mater of leading island lights like V. S. Naipaul and C. L. R. James, this is also where James worked as a teacher in the 1930s, where students included future leaders of the island's struggle for self-rule, like Dr. Eric Williams—the scholar politician who, after heading to Oxford to write *Capitalism and Slavery*, a famous scholarly indictment of England's selfish reasons for ending slavery, became Trinidad's first prime minister. Now on the same patch of grass where all three once played cricket, Beyoncé's trailer sat.

Trinidad was first claimed by Christopher Columbus for Spain in 1498. It takes its name from the three mountain peaks Columbus glimpsed on spying an island that is, geologically speaking, an extension of Venezuela. It spent most of its colonial history as a thinly settled backwater, used by the Spanish as a launching place for expeditions seeking El Dorado, the mythic city of gold said to lie on the nearby Main. In the late eighteenth century, the Spanish crown sought to bolster Trinidad's population by offering land grants to French Catholic planters. The result, in short order, was a Spanish colony whose populace and culture were majority French. And the island's ultimate seizure by the English in 1797 marked no end to the complexity of its cultural history, which continued to be shaped, thereafter, by the French slaves and planters who remained on the now-British island. After slavery's end in 1835, indentured workers from India were imported by the British to toil on the cocoa and sugarcane estates. Finally, in the years during and after World War II, came the U.S. Navy. Their base and soldiers on the island, apart from corrupting local women with those GIs' cash, bequeathed to the culture the fifty-five-gallon oil drums from which local musicians crafted what is here plausibly termed the "only acoustic instrument invented in the twentieth century"—the steel pan drum. Grouped together in great orchestras like Silver Stars and Phase II, the "pan" has been celebrated as the national instrument since Trinidad and Tobago (so-called for Trinidad's administrative joining with its smaller island neighbor) gained its independence in 1962 and secured its unique and lasting stature in the larger cosmos of the once-British Antilles.

As an island whose oil wealth has spared it the indignities of the tourist trade, Trinidad has also long served as a destination for "small islanders" who've come here hunting work or to make it in the arts. Across the cultured Caribbean, Port of Spain has been known as the place where Derek Walcott came from St. Lucia to launch his Trinidad

Theatre Workshop and where Beryl McBurnie, the choreographer and folklorist, "invented West Indian dance" at her Little Carib Theatre in the 1940s. This is where Peter Minshall, elaborating a new form of masquerade in the carnival street that's now called *mas*, crafted storied pieces of public theater, with thousands of participant-performers in the street, with names like Paradise Lost and Dance Macabre. It's also where the musical forms that dominated the Anglo Antilles before the rise of Jamaican reggae—calypso and steel bands—were born. It's the place whose proponents formed the prime model and motivation for the builders of northern carnivals, from London to Toronto to Brooklyn, that represent those cities' largest yearly public gatherings. These days it also plays host to the region's leading literary and film festivals, and is home to more than a couple of visual artists of international repute. But alongside (and not unrelated to) those cultural riches, it's also a place whose remunerative but volatile petro-economy has made a society run by shadowy forces much less interested in art or tradition than in a big flow of cash and status.

Down the road, a row of Victorian mansions known as the "Magnificent Seven" were being allowed to conspicuously crumble: symbols, perhaps, that the government of this "emerging" nation may be less interested in preserving the colonial past than in building monuments to the future, such as the monstrous glass structure visible across the Savannah. This was the just-finished National Academy for the Performing Arts, an out-of-all-scale knockoff of the Sydney Opera House, purposed to someday house a symphony orchestra in a country with no tradition of or affinity for classical music. Chinese designed and built, and with no evident utility in a city whose perfectly serviceable concert hall is full to capacity only a dozen times a year, the spaceship-like building had been built, according to the consensus view, largely to serve the megalomania of Eric Williams's latest heir as head of the People's National Movement (PNM), Patrick Manning. The PNM of today, like many Third World parties legitimized by little more than the faint memory of their heroic role in liberating the nation, rarely shows the intent or need to consider a people perhaps less in need of a concert hall than of a government committed to battling the corruption and crime that bedevil Trinidadian life—or one committed, at least, to supporting the riches of its performance culture in the streets.

"Local culture" is as loaded a phrase in Trinidad as anywhere: one man's "local culture" is another woman's dead art. The maker of those gold lamé costumes that won top prize in 2010, Brian MacFarlane, was considered by many to be lamely derivative of *mas* design's great innovator, Peter Minshall. And of course the Beyoncé show's backers, staked by a cell phone company's billions, had their own gloss on "local culture": the need to put on a show for which enough locals would buy tickets that they'd recoup their investment. Beyoncé and her eighty-strong brigade of stylists and roadies and dancers, with whom she arrived by private plane, fresh from a triumphant series of dates in Brazil, don't come cheap. TSTT added a bankable local star, the soca legend Machel Montano, to the bill. The kinetic brand of "soul-calypso" that has been Trinidad's de facto national music since the late 1970s incorporates aspects of Indian and electronic music and is played at deafening volume during carnival, from sound trucks on the streets. Montano, one of the form's leading lights, had taken this year's carnival off and not appeared in any of its fetes: the buzz provided by his presence now would, the organizers hoped, sell the tickets they needed to cover Beyoncé's rider. It may have.

Montano is a former child star with a singing voice at once tuneful and gruff, and ideally suited to bringing revelers to crescendos. He's not unused to big crowds: he's filled Madison Square Garden with émigré "Trinis" who've made parts of Brooklyn's Flatbush Avenue as Trini-feeling as jangling Frederick Street in Port of Spain. But being the champion of this small island and the champion of the world are different things. What quickly became plain, as Montano ran through a bevy of familiar hits, was that for this diminutive dreadlocked figure in silver pants, commanding this huge stage purpose-built for Beyoncé's act was a task too tall.

The real show began when velvet curtains dropped across the stage and spotlights raked the scene. The curtains parted, and her goldenness emerged at the top of a staircase. Beyoncé shimmied down those stairs in the way of someone who'd been honing her act for a year, and took the stage with her dancers. The number was "Crazy in Love." The sidelong pumping of chest and pelvis was fierce. And Sasha Fierce—as Beyoncé was then calling the stage-queen persona she enacts in concert—belted and stomped her way through an anthem that, with its music video featuring the first couple of "urban music" leaving the city like Bonnie and Clyde, will be forever associated with her pop-epochal marriage to Jay Z. Her crack backing band was made up entirely of black women, the Sugar Mamas, whose name and appearance are seemingly meant to provide the "authentic" backdrop for Beyoncé's straightened-haired ability to "cross over." She moved smoothly into "Baby Boy," another high-energy duet whose recent music video had found her writhing on a Caribbean beach, lending the song the feel of a *How Stella Got Her Groove Back*–style paean to reigniting one's libido on a tropical isle like this one.

Now clothed in leopard-print leotard, the band slinked from the brilliant Timbaland-produced bounce of "Irreplaceable" ("To the left / to the left"), into the name-making hit from her Destiny's Child years— "Say My Name." It was lent a certain new élan by the fact that few could imagine forgetting the name of the woman mouthing these words. After singing "Ave Maria" in an elaborately cantilevered white wedding dress, she disappeared. Reemerging in the aviator eyeshades and black-studded garb of an S&M leather queen, she accented "If I Were a Boy" with wry quotes from Alanis Morisette's "You Oughta Know" and Tupac Shakur's "California Love." "This show is very special to me," she said into the hot night air during an early pause. "[It's] my first time performing here, and I can see you all can party." She had the crowd even before that.

The sources for this world star's act, as precise a distillation of what was going on in world pop as one could imagine at that time, were many. As a stage show, it may have its most crucial antecedents in the kinds of pop spectacle made famous by Madonna and Michael Jackson. Her planeload of costumes were by the French designer Thierry Mugler, best known for creating the shoulder-padded "power bitch" look of the 1980s. Her choreography is informed by "J-Setting"—the lead-and-mimic step dancing first evolved by gay black youth in Atlanta. She knew, just as Madonna did a generation ago when she brought voguing from New York's queer ballrooms to the mainstream, where to get what she needs. Absorbing her own brand of masquerade, it was hard not to think, too, of the New Orleans roots of a performer named for the maiden surname of her creole mother, born of French, African, and Amerindian ancestry in a city sometimes termed the "northern edge of the saints and festivals belt."[3]

Trinidad's own carnival, like Brazil's and New Orleans's, was born in a joining of the masquerade balls that French Catholics used to celebrate *carnevale* (farewell to the meat) and the festive traditions of their slaves. In the case of Trinidad, this meant those practices used to mark the Africans' harvest festival of Canboulay (from *canne brulée*, burning of the cane): limbo dancing, stickfighting, and the ensemble drumming that begat the steel bands of today. Carnival here was from the start a time for "turnabout": for landed whites to doff their heavy suits and dance shirtless like the dark-skinned and poor who, during carnival, donned powdered wigs and crowns. As it grew into the grand mixed party that it remains, a number of stock characters emerged who still roam Port of Spain's streets each year: "King Sailor," with his cane and naval epaulettes; "Fancy Indian," in his Crazy Horse headdress; "Dame Lorraine," with her French parasol and petticoats (often played by a man, with pillows stuffed fore and aft). If you're picturing a gay disco band in Greenwich Village of a certain vintage, you're not far off. The explicit joys of masquerade may have migrated from queer subcultures into the "mainstream" of American pop only since the 1970s, but in carnival cultures like Trinidad's, the public joining of gender play and sexual license is as old, literally, as sin. On the Fat Tuesday that year before Beyoncé's show, I'd ended my Carnival Tuesday in a large club whose entrance was festooned with a rainbow flag. There, sailors and dames grinded and vogued beneath the stars, in the open-air space off an avenue that had served as one of the main drags for masqueraders earlier that day. In some ways Trinidad's culture is just as homophobic as that of any other island in the West Indies. But it was hard not to think that the presence of this space—still unthinkable in Jamaica, say, with its centuries of Anglican rule and gay-bashing norms—was at least partly due to a particular tolerance. Bred across two centuries of life on this island, Trinidad's inhabitants, as the saying goes, are at all times either "playing carnival, reminiscing about last year's, or preparing for the next."

This was a vibe, in any case, that Beyoncé clocked for her show's crowning moment. The rhythm switched to one this crowd had heard a few hundred times in the weeks before, and Beyoncé and her dancers pogo-ed left and right, energetically aping the dance that went along with the song: "Palance," which had won this year's Carnival Road March title as the year's soca anthem.

"Palance" is little more than a catchy jingle repeated and joined to the gleeful exhortation of its creators—two affable soca deejays called JW and Blaze—to perform their tune's eponymous dance ("Watch we palancing / Watch we palancing"). Bygone are the days when calypso masters like Mighty Sparrow and Lord Kitchener beguiled with their wordplay, and everyone on the island knew not just the choruses from each year's favorites, but entire verses spun around layered metaphors as likely to reference geopolitics as sex (and often touching on both). That soca has never gained the same sort of international reach as Jamaican reggae is perhaps unsurprising: heard out of context, the charms of many of these songs—with their frantic tempos and shouted hooks—can be obscure. To understand the effect of Beyoncé's dancing along to "Palance" as she closed out this year's carnival season, one has to understand the singular relationship her audience had developed with the song by this time, and how that relationship had come to be: a process of annual hit making that begins, at the start of carnival season, with hundreds of songs contending for airspace. Over the two months of near-nightly fetes running from New Year's to Shrove Tuesday, these are winnowed down first to a few dozen, then to ten, then to one Road March champion whose status is based on its ability to meet a single purpose: to get people to drink rum, "jump up," "wine," and "trip down the road" all at once from dawn till dusk beneath the broiling sun. Its singular purpose, in other words, is to feed a kind of collective delirium within which revelers can "get on bad." For people who'd heard "Palance" at top volume dozens of times on Tuesday alone, seeing this famous body and person affirm their way of doing so was a potent gesture of generosity and presence.

Carnival, as performance studies scholars like to point out, is a unique form of spectacle for collapsing all distinctions between performer and spectator: it is a folk culture, wrote its most famous theorizer, Mikhail Bakhtin, "that knows no footlights." Beyoncé's performance knew not merely footlights but air jets blowing out that golden hair. And she was a foreigner. But a people that knows so well the power of spectacle and the joy of shaking your ass understood they were seeing a performer who knew more than a bit about both. Fireworks exploded above the Savannah, red and white against the dark mountains beyond, and Beyoncé embraced her dancers. In the days following, newspaper stories about her show were full of complaints about long lines for the "free" corn soup that came with VVIP tickets. But no one could be found saying a bad word about a performance that, all seemed to agree, had actually justified the sky-high cost of its ticket.

Those papers and the conversations of the chattering classes were full, too, of the annual debates about what the year's carnival might suggest about the state of a nation that, for its half century of independence, has grown accustomed to looking at its near-naked self through this particular lens. Some hailed J'ouvert's ability, with its mud-covered revelers erasing their ethnic identities, to unite this sometimes fractious nation. The lamé maker Brian MacFarlane announced that he wouldn't be presenting a band the following year, lending fuel to those who see, in the continuing descent of masquerade arts into bikinis and beads, a symbol of the nation's larger decline. Others rejoined the annual debate about whether and how carnival's fleeting joys relate to the political trajectory of this country. Its course, in the following weeks, many hoped would be altered by the ascendance of an impressive woman of Indian descent (soon to be the first such person to lead Trinidad) to a leadership role in the opposition party. By the time I left the country a month later, signs were growing that the PNM of Patrick Manning—hamstrung by the news that his great performing arts center was not even usable due to shoddy construction—might soon be on the way out. Despite the lack of rain to wash away the J'ouvert colors that still stained Port of Spain's streets, Carnival 2010 was fading into memory. "Palance" had died a rapid death on the nation's soundscape.

But Beyoncé was still everywhere. And so were the questions that her visit prompted, in a country obsessed with thinking about itself through the lens of its parties. To invoke or describe something as "modern" can connote many things. In Trinidad, it may refer to pride at being "multicultural" before the rest of the world knew what that was, or to the fact that this island's million people display rates of internet usage higher than any other on earth. What one also finds here, though, is many people who'll nod along to what the island's most famous writer meant when he returned after some years away, in the 1960s, to describe a place where "[a]mbition—a moving hand, drink being poured into a glass—was not matched with skill, and the effect was Trinidadian: vigorous, with a slightly flawed modernity."[4]

* * *

FOR THE VISITOR WHO turns up here knowing that line of V. S. Naipaul's or disposed to affirm it, there's a lot of "flawed modernity" to be seen in Port of Spain. Here where gasoline is cheap and every Trini seems to own at least one car and often two, treeless streets are choked with traffic. Dingy signs on decaying 1930s buildings tout "X-RAYS PERFORMED (BY MEDICAL DOCTOR)." This town's name may evoke Havana-esque fountains and antique squares fronting an aqua bay, but the view from the ugly new Hyatt downtown offers naught but rusty tankers dotting the mud-gray port.

But Port of Spain's charms have never lain in its physical plant. Patrick Leigh Fermor got it right when he turned up here from prim Barbados in 1948 and, absorbing the zoot-suit wearing "saga boys" by the Savannah and the wry wit of calypso singers and street-corner nutters alike, praised "a forcefulness and a vulgarity that are almost pleasing."[5] Port of Spain may have been covered in concrete and dust, but those saga boys wore their billowing suit legs with "pleats like scimitars." This was a place whose singular chutney of a culture was hard to experience for long without coming to feel that "all [the] curious threads in the fabric of the Trinidadian world," Leigh Fermor wrote, "invest the social life of the island with a colourfulness, a lack of inhibition, and a dashing cosmopolitan atmosphere that turn the fading recollection of Barbados into something parochial and grey and fiercely Anglo-English."[6]

The modern visitor who alights here now, and absorbs Trinidad's thriving cultural scene as against Barbados's staid mores, could hardly disagree. I certainly haven't, from the first time I landed here, at twenty, to fulfill an errand nominally scholarly in nature—I'd come down to research an undergraduate thesis, about the role of ethnicity and difference, on this singularly diverse Caribbean island, during its postcolonial "nation building" project. I had also by that time adopted C. L. R. James as a kind of intellectual hero and style icon alike. For the late adolescent aiming to synthesize a certain set of political instincts with more cultural affinities—for soccer and for John Coltrane and for John Berger's essays—it was hard to imagine a more enticing model than James. Here was a scholar activist who wrote with equal verve and brilliance about the Haitian Revolution and the game of cricket, Hegelian philosophy and Hollywood movies, Herman Melville and calypso music—and whose synthetic aptitude for doing so, moreover, found him placing all those subjects within the larger telos not only of modern capitalism but also of humanity's struggle for democracy reaching back to the Greeks. He was a man who liked to watch cricket matches, at the Queen's Park Oval here in Port of Spain, toting a print of Picasso's *Guernica* to examine between innings to see how the two spectacles compared. He was my first big intellectual crush. And he himself had claimed that his outlook on the world had come from being born to a place uniquely "experienced in the ways of Western civilization and most receptive to its requirements."[7] It was a place I had to see. I went the first chance I got.

And Trinidad didn't disappoint, though, try as I might—sitting in the same stand where James contemplated his masterpiece on the game and its import to the world and to his own life, *Beyond a Boundary*— the charms of cricket, to my American mind, remained opaque. Still, I left that first trip convinced that any country where the street food was doused in curry and the rhythms were African and there were signs up, all over town, with piquant bits of witty or mysterious English speech—"C TRU," "PRISON'S SALTY," "SHORT IS THE GLORY OF THE BLUSHING ROSE"—was the place for me. And I left only more impelled to understand something more of the history, both older and new, of a country that has long been "at once a western nation, an immigrant nation, and a Third World nation."[8]

Trinidad's history as an "international nation," whose mix of people from the four corners vexed those seeking to rule it, reaches back to colonial days. When in 1797 the British took over the island from Spain, they were confronted with a colony quite unlike any of their others. Here was a place where not only did free people of color outnumber whites, but where the white populace of French, Spanish, Corsicans, and Germans outnumbered the Brits. In an 1810 memo to Trinidad's colonial governor, the British secretary of state noted of these people that "the greater part of them must be wholly ignorant of the British Constitution and unaccustomed to any frame of government which bears any analogy to it," before going on to wordily opine that

> [t]he circumstances on the Island of Trinidad are in many respects so materially different from those of all the West India Colonies, that supposing the system of Government established in those colonies to be the best could be afforded them in their situation, it would not follow that the same system could be rendered applicable either in justice or in policy to the Island of Trinidad.[9]

And that was before the mass influx of indentured Indians, which began in 1845.

More lately, and in the postcolonial "nation building" phase attending independence, there's been no shortage of reasons for the profusion of jokes here about Trinidad being a "heaven for social scientists." Politicians and academics argued, for years, over whether or not, for example, M. G. Smith's "plural society theory" of Caribbean governance, which held that one ethnic group necessarily had to control a split society like Trinidad's, had merit. East Indians fought for their role in Dr. Eric Williams's PNM—and then founded their own party.

But meanwhile, and in a move that also marked Trinidad as different, Williams's government supported calypso and steel band as intrinsic to the nation they set out to forge in the 1950s—even though the role of calypsonians, like their "chantwell" forebears from colonial days, was always partly to critique power and comment on current affairs. The result, beginning in 1956, was the emergence of musical figures like Lord Melody and his upstart rival Mighty Sparrow—the youngster from Grenada who took the first Calypso Monarch crown, that year, with a tune that endures as the signature calypso song of Trinidad's independence era. "Jean and Dinah," Sparrow sang, "Rosita and Clementina! Round the corner posin'." He praised Trinidad's lovelies, he hailed the truth that their charms were now once again in reach of a young islander like him, and concluded his first signature tune with a flourish: "De Yankees gone, Sparrow take over now!"

Trinidad is a place, no small thanks to those figures' wordplay and erudition, that began to exhibit what Derek Walcott termed "extreme literacy." It remains a country where a man named "Sprangalang" would not only become the head of an organization called the Trinbago Union of Calypso Organizations (now the Trinbago Unified Calypsonians Organisation), but would be quoted, in serious newspaper stories, commenting that "[y]ou can't pass a law to decide what is a nation building song. At what point will the song be banned, at the time of writing, in the tent, or at Dimanche Gras?"[10]

It's a place, in other words, where the emergence of C. L. R. James begins to make sense. From the village of Tunapuna, where he watched white-jerseyed men bowl and bat on the dusty green each afternoon, he grew into a radical who said "*Vanity Fair* holds more for me than *Capital*." And while understanding this from afar is one thing, absorbing his attachments to the idea of the "dramatic personality" in Trinidad, a place where being a "dramatic personality" is almost a national duty, is different indeed.

In *The Black Jacobins*, James described Toussaint L'Ouverture as "[o]ne of the most remarkable men in a period rich in remarkable men," as an individual whose person and story embodied the essential tensions of his age.[11] The question of how and where "individual personality" might bear on revolution, and of how capitalism repressed not only the abstract mass but its constituent individuals' capacity for self-expression, was the core of James's politics. It was thus that his Marxism—at a time when many on the doctrinaire left were still advocating for "socialist realism"—anticipated not only the move among

Marxism's later academic adherents toward "cultural studies," but also the utopianism of Herbert Marcuse and the 1960s New Left. "Politics, art, life, love in the modern world all become so closely integrated," he wrote his American wife, Constance Webb, in the summer of 1944, "that to understand one is to understand all."[12]

James's outlook seemed unique in 1940s Los Angeles—but his way of speaking, as I was reminded when I visited the woman who delivered his eulogy here in 1989, was less so in Trinidad. Pat Bishop was an august black woman with close-cropped hair: a painter and a classicist and a musician who conducted vocal choirs and the famous Despera-does steel band, too. She was a Renaissance woman and also a political leftist in the James vein, and when I went to see her in her Wood-brook home, the walls of which were painted with starry constellations, I found her receiving a visitor from the Oil Field Trade Workers Union. She broke from their strategizing to address me. "Nello understood what we must," she said, referring to C. L. R. by his nickname among his friends, "that Aeschylus drew from the same well as do our calypso and steelpan." Pat Bishop recalled how she'd brought her own bands on tour to Europe and New York. "We have never been afraid, in Trinidad, to ready ourselves for history."

* * *

OF COURSE, ONE OF the interesting things about Trinidad's trade-mark cultural forms, as opposed to, say, Jamaican reggae or Cuban-ish salsa, is their comparative *lack* of visibility on the world stage. Pat Bishop may have managed to bring a few dozen players from Despera-does to Carnegie Hall, but hearing one of Trinidad's great steel bands in full effect has been, in the main, an experience reserved for those who visit Trinidad itself: you can't really tour a 110-piece band whose instru-ments alone would require a big cargo plane to transport. The Mighty Sparrow did transcend Trinidad to the extent of becoming a hallowed name in West Indian homes from St. Kitts to Brooklyn. But he's earned a living playing club dates for West Indians abroad and heading home for carnival. He has never been a Bob Marley–like figure, selling out stadiums in Tokyo or Berlin. Calypso, apart from during its early and ersatz adoption by Harry Belafonte, never crossed over.

And its soca offspring's frenzied beats, more recently, are anything but suited—in their tracks' total unsuitability to accompanying a relaxing drive or urbane dinner party—to the task. Trinidad, despite a dynamism across a myriad of arts that far outstrips Jamaica, never had its Marley moment. It never had its *Harder They Come*.

Which isn't to say that it didn't try—or produce, in the same era that saw "reggae go global" with *The Harder They Come*, a film whose stylish portrait of a young striver making his way in a corrupted postcolonial island shared much with Jimmy Cliff's Jamaican opus. That Trinidadian film, *Bim*, was shot in and around Port of Spain in 1974. With a script by one of Trinidad's leading journalists, the playwright and reporter Raoul Pantin, *Bim* was directed by Hugh A. Robertson—a Brooklyn-bred film editor of Jamaican extraction whose credits included *Shaft* and *Midnight Cowboy* (for which he was nominated for an Oscar). Robertson, when he made *Bim*, had recently turned up in Trinidad to launch a film school here. His feature was ambitious in scope and beautifully shot: its spare cinematography has the Italian neorealist influence also glimpsed in *The Harder They Come*. It tells the story of an Indian boy from the sugarcane fields of southern Trinidad, who after the murder of his trade unionist father is sent to live with an aunt in town. Bim is teased for his "coolie" heritage by black schoolmates; he stabs one of them to make it home from school and is forced, thereafter, into a life of crime that eventually finds him fleeing back to the Indian south. There he at last avenges his father's killing and, rising to prominence as a union leader himself, returns to Port of Spain to confront the black political leaders there who were taking over the country from its old colonial leaders. He tries to win for Indians a modicum of power in their shared land before meeting an inevitably tragic end.

With its outlaw hero and terrific script and Caribbean setting, *Bim* bears more than a passing resemblance to its Jamaican cousin. It also had a terrific score, by Trinidad's leading jazz-folk and steel pan musical polymath, André Tanker. It didn't have Jimmy Cliff or the Melodians singing reggae classics, though. And if *Bim* is a fondly recalled piece of Trinidadian lore for islanders of a certain age, and is often cited as a classic of Caribbean cinema by West Indian cinephiles, it has barely been screened outside Trinidad. With only a couple of prints of the film in existence until it was finally digitized a couple of years ago, I didn't manage to see it myself until a special fortieth-anniversary screening. Held in an auditorium at the Eric Williams Financial Complex in downtown Port of Spain, the screening featured a Q&A with the film's charismatic star, Ralph Maraj, and the author, Raoul Pantin. (Maraj worked for years as a schoolteacher and playwright, but is now a respected politician associated, ironically enough, with the nominally "African" PNM.) The conversation, as at many such gatherings here where a microphone is present, largely devolved into a state-of-the-nation debate, in which every questioner seemed to ask: "Why can't we make films like this anymore?" But it also found Pantin, a journalist who'd written crucial accounts of most of the key events in Trinidad's modern political history—and who would die suddenly just a few months after that screening, at age seventy-one—singing the film's praises in the context of the present. Pantin, a slim man with light brown skin and a distinctive bulbous nose, claimed that "at the risk of self-praise, I think you'll agree that this film is still as relevant today as when I wrote it."

One felt disposed, given the film's quality and its textured rendering of the Trinidadian world, to agree with him. But what precisely Pantin meant wasn't easy to say. Since the *Bim* era, things had changed a great deal in Trinidad—and in Port of Spain in particular—for Indo-Trinidadians. To many, the rise to power of the island's first Indian head of state in 1995—Basdeo Panday, who was a former unionist from "south"—represented something akin to the ascent to power of Bim himself. Divides between "creole" Port of Spain and an Indian south thought to be more rural and poor have lessened considerably. But as we saw there in the Eric Williams Financial Complex, it was also the case that Trinidad's politics remained shot through with ethnic and geographic rivalry. With Kamla Persad-Bissessar now in power for four years, there had been a notable increase in public spending and infrastructure projects funneled to contractors in the island's rural south. There was a reason that political wags down at classic bars like Smokey and Bunty, and across the island, could be heard proclaiming a generally accepted truth: "Is India time now." Which was another way of placing ethnic rivalry at the core of Trinidadian politics, still, but also of suggesting that corruption remains the driving force in this place that has always had a Wild West feel. The entwinement of Trinidad's political establishment with its underworld began a grave new era after 1990. That's when a group of Islamist radicals called Jamaat al Muslimeen attempted to overthrow the government by launching an armed attack on parliament and holding members of the assembly and of the media—including Raoul Pantin, who was held for six traumatic days in the offices of Trinidad and Tobago Television—hostage. The island's

authorities were exposed as weak. The coup's leader, a once-powerful figure on Trinidad's streets named Abu Bakr, was jailed. But his revolt heralded a new era of impunity and warfare between gangs vying to control the huge flow of drugs passing through here from Venezuela. (Pantin wrote a book, *Days of Wrath: The 1990 Coup in Trinidad and Tobago*, which remains the essential account of Bakr's coup attempt.)[13]

There's a reason today that even most patriotic Trinis who love their country view their government, and the shadowy others who run their island, with suspicion. But long before the current nadir, not everyone—and especially not every Indian—bought into the "nation-building project," and the larger love for Trinidad, espoused by the calypso-loving intellectuals and urbane blacks of Eric Williams's PNM. When V. S. Naipaul won his Nobel Prize in 2001, he said the prize was "a great tribute to both England, my home, and India, the home of my ancestors."[14] He didn't mention Trinidad. This suggested his vexed relation to an island where he always viewed the accident of his birth, as he once told an interviewer, as "a great mistake."[15] But it also evinced his most Trinidadian quality: the trickster's delight he has always taken in verbal provocation or in "playing old *mas*" to upset his fellows, as one of his legion of West Indian foils, George Lamming, put it.[16] Naipaul certainly did become one of those Indo-Trinidadians, not un-numerous by now, who, after parting from this island for England or Toronto or New York, have come to regard Trinidad as a mere "stopover" on their way from their ancestors' land to the one where they wanted to raise their kids (or, in the case of Naipaul, on his way to his vision of being a writer meant becoming an English writer in the Wiltshire countryside). But what bonds him to Trinidad, as lettered Trinidadians all know and as one suspects he does on some level, too, is the truth that though he produced as huge and varied an oeuvre as you'd expect of a Nobel winner, with books set all over the world, the books he wrote about growing up in Trinidad—*The Mystic Masseur* (1957) and *Miguel Street* (1959) and *A House for Mr. Biswas* (1961) in his early phase; *A Way in the World* (1994) later on—have remained in many ways unexcelled both in their vivid rendering of a society's audible surface and in their grip of its internal dynamics.

Born poor in 1932 in the central Trinidadian market town of Chaguanas, Vidiadhar Surajprasad Naipaul was the grandson of a Brahmin pundit, from northern India, who'd obscured his caste to enlist to come here and cut cane for eight cents a day in 1894. That pundit,

the patriarch of Naipaul's maternal family, the Capildeos, was eventually "cut" from indenture, perhaps by a local potentate who learned that he could read. The pundit became a successful merchant in whose shop on Chaguanas's main street his daughter met Seepersad Naipaul. Naipaul was a Brahmin, too, but not from a family of means; he was a struggling journalist who became the Trinidad *Guardian's* Chaguanas correspondent, but who was long frustrated by having to depend on his wife's family for support. He determined that his children should have more—and moved them, when Vidia was a boy, into Port of Spain. It was in absorbing Seepersad's own thwarted ambition as a writer, and his standard-issue animus toward Trinidad's blacks, that the young Vidia formed both his own literary aims and the retrograde racial attitudes that often peppered his work. After graduating from Queen's Royal College and earning a scholarship to Oxford, he launched a precocious literary career, in London, that really took off when, at the age of twenty-nine, he published his expansive novel—*A House for Mr. Biswas*. That still remains, a couple of dozen books and several decades later, his mostly fully realized work of fiction.

Inspired by the travails of his own dad, *Mr. Biswas* tells the story of a cultured provincial from Trinidad's illiterate countryside. His struggles to make a living as a sign painter and an assistant to a Hindu priest eventually lead him to become a newspaper reporter penning stories with headlines like "White Baby Found on Rubbish Dump." But his larger ambitions for his life, and his image of himself, rub against both his dependence on his in-laws and the petty tyrannies, and creeping stasis, of the late colonial Caribbean. The book was hailed in the London *Observer* for "having the unforced pace of a master-work: it is relaxed, yet on every page alert."[17] But its larger resonance in the West Indies, at the time, is suggested by the full-page spread that the Trinidad *Guardian* ran, with an article by the St. Lucian poet and playwright Derek Walcott (who was then living in Port of Spain and directing the Trinidad Theatre Workshop, and had yet to fall out with the fellow Nobel laureate he would later take to calling "V. S. Nightfall") under the headline "A Great New Novel of the West Indies." Decades later, one grows used to hearing Trinidadians of all hues insist that it's a book whose depiction of the intricate workings of color and petty corruption in Trinidad contains more of worth on those subjects than every academic study to have appeared here since. And no less popular here, at least among those who care more about literary merit than patriotism, is *Miguel*

Street. That earlier book, built from characters Naipaul observed as a boy in Woodbrook, is a slighter achievement. But as any literate wag at Smokey and Bunty's bar can tell you even now, *Miguel Street*'s warmly hilarious rendering of a certain kind of dissipated Trini manhood and diction ("What happening there, Bogart?") grant it a place alongside C. L. R. James's *Minty Alley* and Earl Lovelace's *Dragon Can't Dance* (a great book on identity trouble in a city defined by its love for carnival masks) as one of the three essential Port of Spain novels.

But if Port of Spain's more cultured barflies claim Naipaul, his more conflicted ties to establishment leaders whom he's mostly dissed or ignored, down the years, are glimpsed in the story of the old Naipaul house in St. James. When the house recently came up for sale—this was the home that served as both motor and conclusion to *A House for Mr. Biswas*—Professor Kenneth Ramchand had to fight long and hard to convince the government's Ministry of Arts and Multiculturalism to buy the property, as an important piece of Trinidad's national patrimony. To do so, he'd founded a group called the Friends of Mr. Biswas. Once Ramchand, eminent author of the landmark 1970 study *The West Indian Novel and Its Background,* convinced the government to buy the place, with the purchase price going to Vidia's sister Savi, the one of his siblings still residing in Trinidad, the group still had some work to do. "There was still an old Naipaul family retainer living here," Ramchand explained to me as he showed me around the place on a hot afternoon. It was an unremarkable two-story frame house on a treeless St. James side street. "It took twelve thousand more dollars plus the bailiffs to get him to go. But we got it done." Dr. Ramchand, a small and gentle Indian man wearing an orange polyester shirt, pushed open the door.

"This is the house that Seepersad Naipaul built to get out of Chaguanas, and the Lion House of the Capildeos," he said. "So it is, really, the House for Mr. Biswas." We were standing in what once would have been its parlor. Its sole furniture was a pair of walnut Morris chairs, which were, Ramchand said, once a prized possession of Seepersad Naipaul. The parlor had been lovingly cleaned, the wood floor buffed and its walls decorated with family photos whose captions said things like "Though small by today's standards, this house was home to two parents and seven siblings," and a touch more awkwardly, things like "Full of family and love, the house was described as a happy and pretty house." By whom it was described as such is perhaps hard to say, but tidy and well kempt, anyway, the place certainly was now. Ramchand explained that though the government had bought it, his group wasn't receiving any funds to keep it up. He didn't have any budget for regular staff to keep it open, so tours like mine were only by appointment. His hope and aim for the Friends of Mr. Biswas was that donations and events honoring accomplished Caribbean writers, who would be named "Distinguished Friends of Mr. Biswas," could help make up the short-fall. He was supporting these efforts himself: he'd paid for the case of bottled water and a carton of plantain chip packets he'd bought for the group's meeting that week from his own pocket. And this, certainly, was important to a man who had not only praised *Mr. Biswas* as the "great West Indian novel" but also understood that its last lines were applicable to all West Indians, regardless of color or past, who, in this society at the apex of New World sensibility, were making their own version of a modern future as they went along. Mr. Biswas craved not just to move out of his in-laws' but also reflected, in the house in town he did manage to build, upon "how terrible it would have been . . . to be without it . . . to have lived without even attempting to lay claim to one's portion of the earth; to have lived and died as one had been born, unnecessary and unaccommodated."[18]

Among Naipaul's later books, his Uganda novel *A Bend in the River* has its deep merits; so does the formally inventive mélange of reportage and fiction, *In a Free State*. But it's hard not to suggest that the best of his later work was not the at-times ponderous and ill-tempered travel books but, rather, the long-form essays he produced beginning in the 1970s, mostly for *The New York Review of Books*. Those essays, every crafter of what's now called, somewhat pretentiously, "literary nonfiction" revere for a reason. This writing found him alighting in places like Maurice Bishop's Grenada or the declining Argentina of Eva Perón, and then endeavoring, after spending a few days or a few weeks absorbing such places' idiosyncrasies, to parse with unsparing incisiveness the delusions and disappointments of all those people, all across what was then called the Third World. With an eagle eye for manipulation and cant, he had a special love for ridiculing the hoped-for Redemption that's long been key to black politics. He summed up Jamaica's Rastafarians like this: "These islanders are disturbed. They already have black government and black power, but they want more. They want something more than politics. Like the dispossessed peasantry of medieval Europe, they await crusades and messiahs."[19] He also delighted, of course, in those days of Black Power and radical chic, in picking at the white liberals who fell for such scripts.

Which all helps to explain, perhaps, why his one sustained engagement with Trinidad's postcolonial era, rather than the late-colonial muddiness of his youth, came in the wake of street protests that shook Port of Spain, following carnival in 1970—inspired by the rhetoric of Stokely Carmichael, a local kid who, after being raised in Belmont here, moved to the Bronx and coined the phrase "Black Power." And why it came, more specifically, in his following a richly flawed character from that world: a fellow Trinidadian of mixed racial descent who was born Michael de Freitas in the same Belmont neighborhood where Carmichael was raised, but who then fashioned himself, in swinging '60s London, into a fair-skinned apostle of Black Revolution, streetwise and celebrity savvy, named Michael X.

Having arrived in London as a seaman in 1957, Michael X had worked as a pimp and a hustler in Notting Hill, and then as strongman and debt collector for Peter Rachman, a notorious slumlord. His move into politics in the 1960s, as the civil rights movement reached a crescendo in the United States, came as England's emergent counterculture craved its own vision of racial justice. Changing his name first to Michael X and then, after embracing Islam, to Michael Abdul Malik, he founded an organization called the Racial Adjustment Action Society—RAAS. To Naipaul, he was simply an opportunist: "He sensed that in England, provincial, rich and very secure, race was, to Right and Left, a topic of entertainment. And he became an entertainer."[20] To Naipaul, he was a con man and an artifact of his time: "He was the X, the militant, the man threatening the fire next time; he was also the dope peddler, the pimp."[21] Others had different versions. Malik was much more a mimicker, to be sure, of orators like Carmichael, than an originator of ideas himself. But he said some things that some people wanted to hear. He also said some things, building his cred with those admirers, that the establishment didn't. He landed in jail after giving a speech urging the killing of any white man seen "laying hands" on a black woman, charged under Britain's new Race Relations Act. Once freed, he helped found a counterculture educational outfit called the London Free School. With the help of wealthy backers, he also started a commune, called the Black House. The latter was partly funded by John Lennon and Yoko Ono, who donated locks of their hair for Malik to sell at auction. Malik and his associates got into trouble after luring a Jewish businessman to the Black House and forcing him to wear a spiked slave collar until he backed their cause. When Malik was indicted for extortion, John Lennon posted bail. But England was getting too hot. In February 1971, Malik fled for Trinidad.

The plan there, as presented to his English backers and as Naipaul put it with withering scare quotes, was "to revolt against 'the industrialized complex' . . . and 'do agriculture'" on a new commune.[22] The reality, in the quiet town of Arima, eighteen miles to Port of Spain's east, was a bland house in a sleepy subdivision where he and his followers kept a little vegetable garden. Having left Trinidad an unknown in his twenties, he returned at thirty-seven as a London celebrity and a victim of racist persecution who had turned himself, by his lights anyway, into "the Best Known Black man in this entire white western world." Malik gave an interview to Raoul Pantin, at the Trinidad *Express*, in which he said, "The only politics I ever understand is the politics of revolution. The politics of change, the politics of a completely new system."[23] But mostly, in Arima he bided his time. And he was soon joined there by Hakim Jamal, an American radical from Boston who had also spent time in London.

Like Malik, Jamal had plenty of schemes for "[converting] race into money."[24] In London, he'd peddled his plans for a string of "Malcolm X Montessori schools," and described himself to *The Guardian* as "excruciatingly handsome, tantalizingly brown, fiercely articulate."[25] He also became the lover of Naipaul's editor at André Deutsch, Diana Athill (a fact one imagines Naipaul privately delighting in, given his sometime frustration with Athill and his loathing for Jamal and Malik). Now Jamal turned up in Trinidad with a rather less substantial English girlfriend. Gale Benson was the twenty-something daughter of a Tory MP who wore dashikis and worshipped her black king in a more-than-metaphoric way. She had changed her name, by the time they reached Arima, to "Hale Kimga"—it sounded vaguely African, but was in fact an anagram of "Gale Hakim").

In February 1972, Malik's house mysteriously burned down. In shallow graves nearby, two bodies were found; one lay beneath a freshly planted bed of lettuce. The bodies belonged to a young man from Belmont, Joseph Skerritt, who'd joined Malik's "Black Liberation Army" but evidently fallen afoul, in some way, of its leader or his lieutenants, and to Gale Benson. Both had been hacked to death by machete. Benson had been buried while she was still breathing.

The "Black Power Killings," and their brutality, scandalized Trinidad. They also prompted a great hue and cry from abroad, once a fleeing Malik was captured in Guyana and a half dozen of his followers were indicted for their roles in the Arima murders, to free Malik or at least save him from the hangman. (Hakim Jamal and a mysterious "coworker," whom he allegedly flew down from Boston to do his and Malik's dirty work, were back in the United States.) Angela Davis and John Lennon and Kate Millet joined the Save Malik Committee. Naipaul did not. He spent a few months in Trinidad investigating what had happened. Interviewing Malik's neighbors and associates and attending the trial, he produced an account of the whole affair that was brisk and thorough and laced with typically piquant Naipaulian aperçus ("He was everybody's Negro, and not too Negroid"). It also contained not a few conclusions about what actually happened in Malik's back garden in Arima and why those have been debated since. But given the horrid deaths that his "project" here resulted in, in the sad denouement of a very Trinidadian life—"so many names, so many personalities, so many ways of presenting himself to people: that was his great talent," Naipaul wrote[26]—it's also hard not to affirm, with Naipaul, that other Trinidadian trickster who pulled Malik's story apart, that in a small country whose real problems rendered "racial redemption as irrelevant for the Negro as for everybody else," Malik turned the rhetoric of Black Power into little more than a "sentimental hoax."[27]

Within a year of the murders, Hakim Jamal, back in Boston, would himself be murdered, by enemies he'd made in a black nationalist group called De Mau Mau. Malik, charged and then convicted of Skerritt's murder, though not Benson's, was jailed and then hanged in Port of Spain's Royal Gaol in 1975.

But it's hard to deny the ghosts that still linger in Christina Gardens, as I found when I drove out to Arima one humid November day, turning off the traffic-choked main road that leads into the center of this old mission town at the base of the Northern Range. The development's smooth streets and large homes were guarded by metal gates and faux-marble plastic columns in the Trini-riche style. This was a zone of the well-to-do. But there was no landscaping on the crescent-shaped street; scrub grass and trash rubbed its lots' edges. The overall feel, as in much of this frontier society, was less of an affluent place than a poor one with rich people in it, tending to their own behind high walls. Outside the house that now stands where Malik's acolytes once hacked up Gale Benson and Joseph Skerritt with machetes, an expensive-looking sportscar was parked in the drive. When I asked a pair of workmen painting its gate if they knew the name Michael X and about what had once happened there, their eyes flashed with recognition. But they declined, in that West Indian way of being obsessed by death but not fond of invoking it, to say more.

* * *

IN THE DECADES SINCE the Michael X affair, and especially in this new century as Trinidad has taken a growing role in the drug trade that makes the hemisphere's shadow economy tick, the feel of an island run by its outlaws has only grown. Here where the noir films of Bogart became icons, and where a young nation's steel bands adopted the names of western heroes, this still-young nation retains the ambience of the O.K. Corral; and that ambience isn't helped by macabre newspaper headlines that accompany their daily reports on Laventille gun deaths or shootouts in Curepe with a grim ticker citing the mounting body count ("the 371st and 372nd killing of the year . . ."). Part of this climate derives from geography: with a wild and poor stretch of Venezuela lying a mere seven miles across the Dragon's Mouth, the arrival of small pirogues from the mainland to Trinidad's remoter beaches—whether full of impoverished Venezuelans simply coming to buy toilet paper and milk, or more sinister types bringing prostitutes or blocks of cocaine— has long been a feature of Trinidadian life. And it's hardly surprising, given the place's strong links by air and sea to Europe and America and West Africa, too, and with first the Colombians and now the Mexicans needing ever more ways to get their drugs to market, that Trinidad has become such a key transshipment point in their networks. Some of this is of a petty scale: there's a reason, looking out your plane's window onto the tarmac at Piarco airport, that you now see security officers patting down baggage handlers before they're allowed near the suitcases they're loading into your plane's belly. "What easier than that," a man who'd been one of those handlers explained to me, of how he used to ship kilos of coke north to JFK. "You just text your man in New York who's working the night for JetBlue there and tell him: 'Side pocket, green bag,' and he take out what you put there. Matta' fix."

But that kind of small smuggling, like the poor kids who shoot each other up in port-adjacent neighborhoods like Beetham and Sea Lots, whether in the name of gangs like Rasta City or for area dons with names like "Spanish" and "Chemist," is hardly the problem's root. The blame for Trinidad's becoming a key node in the global drug trade, and for all the crime that's come with that, lies less in the government's inability to stop it than in the generally agreed-upon truth that the Trinidadian elite, inclusive of its richest businessmen and officials from that government alike, are in fact profiting from, if not outright coordinating, that trade themselves. This corruption, for example, takes the shape of Coast Guard and police officers paid to look the other way as drugs arrive on small crafts, or of port officials looking on as yachts and freighters loaded with drugs packed in juice cans or false holds leave the marina at Chaguaramas for England or Accra.

But Trinidad is a place rife with rumors about nameless "big fish" who wash the drug trade's profits with bunkered oil from offshore rigs, owned by BP, or who build highways for a government from whose leaders they've long since bought immunity. The opaque world of these characters is one that's rarely seen. A few years ago the news emerged of a spectacular discovery by the police, in one of the faux-rococo mansions lining the highway in Valsayn, of a Dr. Evil–like lair whose owner wasn't merely keeping cartons of automatic weapons in his garage, and sitting on a pharmacopeia of different strains of high-grade marijuana, but who had also set up a sophisticated lab to produce "high-end exotic hallucinogens" in his den. You might think, after this revelation, that news of charges or convictions, related to the case, would appear in the paper. None did, beyond the news that the deceased's accused wife and son had been freed on bail. And not one Trinidadian was surprised when, the next time the name Hafeez Karamath Ltd. appeared in the newspapers here, it was in relation to a lucrative government contract to build a new cricket stadium and "judicial center" by the Trincity mall.

Trinidad is today a country with a First World GDP but decidedly Third World rule of law. And if that feeling of lawlessness occurs near its modern heart, it only makes sense that it should abide in the more marginal parts of the country, like the one where I visited the site of the horrible crime that had that fall of 2014 dominated the papers for weeks. *Newsday* and the *Express* emblazoned the front pages with daily updates on a nationwide manhunt for a skinny brown-skinned fellow whose unbecoming mug shot appeared under the headline "Trinidad's Most Wanted." The young man with matted hair and the blank stare was neither a big businessman nor a drug runner. He was a thug, simply put, who also seemed to be something of a sadist. Azmon Alexander had been in and out of jail since his early teens, on charges of assault and thieving and attempted murder, and had escaped custody several months before the crimes he was accused of now. Landing in a remote village at the end of a winding road that leads up into the Northern Range's rainforest from Arima, he had sheltered with cousins there, in the village of Brasso Seco, before some mysterious plot or desire had led him to do what he was accused of now: setting upon a young mother and her baby and then dragging them into the forest, for reasons unknown, before murdering them both and killing an old man in the village as well. When I ventured up into the mountains over Arima, to visit Brasso Seco, where these unspeakables had taken place, Azmon was still at large, rumored to be sheltering in the wild woods here, on an island whose forests share their ecology with the forests of South America. A friend from the area told me that "the bush, for certain, will handle him." For now, though, no one knew where Azmon was.

And so it was that we set out from Arima, an old mission town in whose surrounding hills many people trace their ancestry to the Carib and other indigenous groups who lived here before the Spanish. We wound our way up toward Brasso Seco and through a landscape whose denizens didn't need this case to show them the total absence of the state's interest or presence in their lives. Passing a quarry once run by the Jamaat al Muslimeen, we turned upward through the forest, through acres of sloping plots covered with low green vines hanging with squash-like fruit called christophine: this land was nominally owned by the government, but "the Christophine man" had, by some arrangement with someone in power, been able to set up a large agribusiness concern on what was meant to be protected forest. Soon enough we reached Brasso Seco, an impoverished little place in a spectacular setting. Its townspeople were gathered in an open-walled community center surrounded by lush hillsides and anthurium blooms, to discuss this recent trauma with a delegation of officials from Port of Spain.

The people of Brasso Seco—friendly Rastas, soft-spoken folk with Carib cheekbones, and bored youngsters biding their time before they could escape to the city—sat in folding chairs. An advance team for the nation's chief of police and their member of parliament had erected a cardboard backdrop, bedecked with the police's Star of David logo, behind a podium so that when the chief arrived, along with camera crews from each of the country's news stations, his care for this community would be broadcast across the island. Much of the meeting consisted of townspeople, teary or indignant, mourning their neighbors who'd been so brutally killed by an interloper from outside. Many issued calls for the building of a police station in their remote community, "or at least an occasional patrol," so that wanted fugitives wouldn't want to come hide in plain sight here. Others lamented Brasso Seco's lack of jobs. One woman complained that it was "very terrible" to have to go all the way to Arima, nearly an hour away, to get her mail. All were united in their hope that the police, aided by the search parties from here who knew these forests better than any police, would capture the outlaw soon. (As it happened, they got their wish when Azmon, unable to hack it in the wilderness, soon emerged in Arima to find some food and was promptly arrested.) The police chief, after an hour of listening and nodding along with an earnest look on his face, took to the microphone and, reminiscing about how "I was raised in what persons call a rural community myself," offered his condolences and thanked them for their proposals. Next up was this zone's member of parliament, an unctuous man with his face fixed in a permanent half smile who wore a pressed polyester suit and the concerned look of the priest he had once been. He offered similar platitudes but went further by insisting to his constituents, preposterously and perhaps channeling a bit of his old Jesus talk, "that though you may not see me, I am here all the time, sometimes in the middle of night."

Such speech making, if not such absurd statements, were perhaps to be expected at a sad occasion like that. But what highlighted the true functioning of this government, or its performance, came when I encountered the same MP at an event in Port of Spain the next night—a literary occasion, hosted by Dr. Kenneth Ramchand and the Friends of Mr. Biswas, meant to honor a fine poet who, though long resident in Guyana, was Trinidadian by birth and was tonight being made a Distinguished Friend of Mr. Biswas. The MP for Arima and its wild hinterland, it turned out, was also the current minister of arts and multiculturalism. And in that capacity, he was now here to give a practiced speech about how the poet being honored—a genteel white-haired man named Ian McDonald who'd graduated from Queen's Royal College before moving to Guyana—would "always be a Trini, in our book." He then trotted out some hoary and self-congratulating lines, of the sort that holders of his office have no doubt delivered thousands of times in recent decades, about how "we are blessed to live in a land where we have people from every place, where we can go all to the beach, and be beautiful and enjoy this island together."

It was hard not to think of a Naipaulian line about Trinidad's government's empty gift for "congratulating itself on its multiculture." Because if that was true in the 1970s, it's even more true now. The election of Kamla Persad-Bissessar, the island's first Indian woman head of state, brought not a new era of transparency or progress, but the new corruptions signaled by "Is India time now." Soon enough, the local sports official and kingmaker widely credited with helping her win office, Jack Warner, was indicted by the U.S. Department of Justice on charges of racketeering and fraud for his central role in the FIFA corruption scandal. As a small-island soccer bureaucrat who'd managed to become a huge player in the world game's governing body, Warner would the next spring become a global symbol of what Trinidadians call *bobol*—corruption—and would see him trumpet, as he fought extradition, that "there is no U.S.A. that would carry me from here."[28] The prime minister who owed her office to him, and who like everyone here had long known of the ways and means behind Warner's ill-gotten largesse, bewailed that the world's attention was focused on Trinidad "not for the good and great things, but because of the actions of one man."[29]

But indictment of "Trinidad Jack" wouldn't happen for a few months. And the big story on the island that fall, apart from the evil of the outlaw Azmon (from whose saga, and from inane details like "Azmon Asks Mum to Bring Him KFC in Jail," the press got mileage for months), was to do with another large-scale "development" project—the building of a big highway to a new natural gas deposit, in the country's south. The project had been approved, typically enough, with little concern for the mangrove swamp it would destroy and the people it would displace. That this plan had also gone through with the awarding of a no-bid contract to a government-friendly firm was, of course, business as usual. But what had made it a story, interestingly, was the movement that had cropped up to stop it—a movement that, like so many other successful ones here, showed that what's great in Trinidad often has nothing to do these days with the state.

The Highway Re-route Movement coalesced around an earnest lecturer at the university who, in an effort to force Kamla's government to consider halting construction, had embarked on a hunger strike, the veracity of which was sometimes questioned (he went over 100 days). Camped outside the prime minister's office, Dr. Wayne Kublalsingh gathered much of bien-pensant Trinidad, and most of its artists, carnival and otherwise, to his cause. And the moment the movement reached its height came during a vigil-cum-rally, outside a hospital where after some fifty days of surviving on nothing but coconut water and tulsi leaves, Kublalsingh had been interned to be fed by an IV. The crowd outside was, someone said, "very uptown." But they chanted slogans about how Trinidad's aims to develop—to grow modern—had to include "Mediation now!" Kamla had refused, no matter Dr. Kublalsingh's worsening state, to change the government's plans. When a convoy of black SUVs pulled up to the hospital, with the middle one carrying the prime minister—she had come, she said, to express "her concern and friendship for Dr. Kublalsingh"—there was a debate as to whether the demonstrators should block her access to their leader. A cry went up: "Kamla playin *mas*!"

And so she was: the prime minister, as any Trini could spot, was up to some tricks.

But here was a crowd, and a nation, that can give like for like. On the grass outside the hospital that night, the island's greatest "mas man" took the microphone. Peter Minshall hadn't been seen during carnival for ten years. Depressed by the course his beloved carnival had taken, or depressed about other things, he hadn't put out a band in years. Now, though, he seemed to be getting some energy back. The next year's carnival would mark a triumphal return: Minshall's carnival king, the "Dying Swan," a moko-jumbie-cum-ballerina in drag, which sent the crowd here into raptures, marked the reminder to all Trinis, according to a much-loved local columnist, that "we once had the depth and gumption and self-esteem to view the whole world as our stage and our palette."[30] The scene outside the St. Clair Medical Centre, that night of the vigil, was hardly about the world stage. But the speech that Minshall gave, referencing the struggle of Kublalsingh and of everyone present, in terms of his own storied *mas* characters from the past, was classic Trinidad. "Kamla is the mama of Mamaguy," he intoned. "And Mancrab is this government—it is Mancrab's greed, his love for money and his lust for power, now enabled as never before by technology, incarnate. But we have, in Dr. Wayne, our own callaloo. He is all the good things of this country—he is the Callaloo from my band of that name. The Callaloo who went to speak to God about the evils of Mancrab. Callaloo became tired during his journey and sat on the back of a Morocoy, lamenting that the journey was long. But Morocoy urged him on, reminding Callaloo that he was strong."

This particular riff required knowing Minshall's oeuvre. But Trinidad's gift to the world is its gift for "working out" these tensions and the course of their mixed-up nation, through the theater of the carnival street. And it's perhaps that gift that Trinidad, above all, has given to the world, not least through people like the Trinidadian, Junior "Jay" Telfer, who became by the end of my journey my guide to all things great and good about this island, and to much else. We first met at the suggestion of our shared friend Peter Doig, the Scots-Canadian-Trinidadian painter who said that I had to meet Telfer if I was interested in C. L. R. James, to say nothing of the Notting Hill carnival and modern Trinidad's impacts on the world.

About this I knew he was more than correct nearly from the moment that Jay Telfer strode into the old Woodbrook home of Boscoe Holder, where Doig was then living with his family. Jay, who knew Holder from when they both danced in Beryl McBurnie's Little Carib Theatre, was a slim man with copper-brown skin and gorgeous manners. And he was dressed in what I would soon learn was the uniform he'd worn each day for decades. On his head was a red turban. His white cotton tunic was freshly pressed; his black pants, bespoke. All of which combined to make him a walking Trini flag—which was certainly part of the point for this island patriot whose favorite soca from the twenty-first century was Benjai Garlin's "I'm a Trini." But on that first occasion in Jay's presence, I was crass enough to ask him, in a town where fashioning oneself as a character is a kind of duty, why he dressed as he did; and he offered his explanation, in the same softly patient tones to which I would grow accustomed, of the more piquant personal symbology his garb conveyed: "Red is for living with passion," he said. "And white is for a pure heart"—his heart was never far from his guru Sai Baba's locket. "But from here down," he chuckled gently at his waist, "it's pure niggerdom."

* * *

THAT FIRST NIGHT, Jay Telfer opened a holster-like metal case that was affixed to his belt, and pulled from it a thin white spliff. I thought of Derek Walcott's poem about this place and its people's theatric ways: "All Port of Spain is a 12:30 show." Jay lit his spliff. And then, pulling deeply, he fixed me with a gentle smile. "So you've been reading your C. L. R. James."

Jay's James story, it turned out, derived from the era when both he and James had returned to Trinidad to work for Eric Williams's first PNM government. Born in Port of Spain in 1929, Jay had gone away to attend college in New York in the 1950s: after a stint working in Port of Spain for his father, the Trinidad representative of RKO Pictures and a well-known presenter of films, he became one of New York University's first-ever students in the then-new field of marketing. Returning to his home island shortly after independence, Jay took a job in its new government's Economic Planning Unit—a position in which he oversaw such key construction projects, for the nation, as extending its north coast road as far as Las Cuevas, and building the new Hilton hotel by the Savannah. He had bonded with James, when he returned to edit the PNM's paper, over their shared love for cricket and Shakespeare. "C. L. R. was an elegant and empathic man," said Jay, to whom both qualities meant a lot. "And with the intellect! But I did always tell him, you know, that Trinis would never go for that Trotsky stuff. This is a country with *orishas* and Krishna and carnival—what do we want with a little Russian Marxist? But that, of course, is why he had to leave."

When James's predictable falling out with Eric Williams came, as the PNM's leader wearied of his old teacher's unhelpful agitating for socialist revolution at a time when Williams was trying to win respect and not antagonism from Washington, Jay was more on the side of their shared boss. But Williams's move to push the old lefty from his employ, and, more than that, to place James under house arrest, wasn't one Jay could abide. Personal ethics, like personal style, were for him much more important than politics. He went to Williams and told Trinidad's first prime minister that whatever his disagreements were with James, this was not the way to treat a mentor. This Williams didn't like. It was only because Jay was an old friend of Williams's attorney general, Carlton Phillips, that he called and told him to pack and be ready to leave the country in an hour—officers were coming to arrest Jay as well. In late 1961, Jay left Trinidad—where he wouldn't return to live for good for eighteen years. He headed for London, partly because his younger brother Mervyn, who would become key to the launch of TV back in Trinidad, had gone there with the first Trinidadian pan ensemble, the Dixieland Steelband, to establish them as a touring act. But London turned out to be precisely the right place, both for Jay and for London's West Indians, to be.

He was employed for a time as a lighting tech at the Saville Theatre ("Of course I'm a creature of the theater," he said. "I'm Trinidadian").

He enjoyed meeting Laurence Olivier there, but he wanted more. With his brother's efforts to establish Dixieland languishing, Jay seized on the idea of finding a place where the band could be in residence. He found a florist's shop for rent in the Queensway, right across from the Bayswater tube. And then in early 1964 he opened a nightclub and restaurant called the Ambience, with the help of investors including Sir Learie Constantine. The eminent cricketer, whose biography C. L. R. James had helped write in the '30s, had now become Trinidad and Tobago's first chief of mission in the UK. With folk singers upstairs and London's first resident steel band in its basement bar, Jay employed waiters from Claridge's and an Italian maître d' named Bruno whose attention to the place's patrons was, like the cuisine, "impeccable." Jay's place became a crucial meeting place for the generation of West Indians. During those years in London, as Stuart Hall put it, "we became consciously West Indian."[31] Jay's place was where everyone hung out—from dancers like Boscoe Holder and company members like Sylvia Wynter, to writers ranging from George Lamming to Samuel Selvon to Naipaul and all those other figures clustered around the Jamaican Andrew Salkey's *Caribbean Voices* show on the BBC. More than that, his stylish club soon had a strong claim to being *the* swinging-est spot in swinging-'60s London. With its avowedly interracial clientele, this was a place whose list of habitués soon grew to include sundry Rolling Stones and minor royals and Marcello Mastroianni. Musical guests included "all three of the blind bards—Ray Charles, Stevie Wonder, and Jose Feliciano."

As if introducing such figures to the wonders of steel pan weren't enough, Jay's heyday at the Ambience also saw him play a crucial role: shortly after he opened the club, a local schoolteacher and activist named Rhaune Laslett came to him to ask for help in raising the funds and getting the neighborhood's merchants on board for a new Notting Hill carnival—in launching what soon became the biggest street party in Europe.

"But that, brother, is a story for another night." So Jay said as we parted after three hours that had felt like three minutes, that first night at Boscoe's, and he went home with his customary farewell ("Blessings") and an invitation, seconded by his cherished wife, Ruth, to come see them in their home in the Cascade Valley up above Port of Spain.

Which is what I naturally did, a couple of days later—and what I continued to do, each time I was in Trinidad, for the next eight years.

Already near eighty when we met, Jay was still spry: dancing remained his passion. Whether on his patio when a record he loved came on the stereo, or keeping an old nighthawk's schedule by going out to clubs with friends a third his age, he moved with sage grace. A fixture at the panyard of his beloved Phase II (his oblique explanation for their name: "We're way beyond a Phase I"), he remained their literal flag waver at Panorama for years. But it was on his patio surrounded by orchids, as Jay sipped cocoa tea and bid me listen to the mad melodies of a songbird he called Charlie Parker, that I learned his life story. It was the story of a man who was a kind of West Indian Forrest Gump: he had met everyone who mattered in the high cultural world of the Black Atlantic over the second half of the twentieth century, more from dumb luck than brains and depth, and with more than a smidge of splendid karma he won during the years he spent in India in the 1970s.

Born in 1929 to a squarely middle-class couple from the island's "red" bourgeoisie, Jay grew up on the same convivial Woodbrook streets where Naipaul set *Miguel Street*. His father worked as the Trinidad representative for Hollywood's RKO Pictures; he was responsible for bringing American films to Trinidad—and, on one memorable occasion during the war, for bringing Orson Welles here, too. Jay's mother was a music teacher who also played organ in Woodbrook's Catholic Church. Jay was sixteen on VE Day in 1945, when he stepped out with the neighborhood's great steel pan group—the Invaders—which, like the Desperadoes and others, was named for tropes from American films. He spent his late teens dancing in the company of Beryl McBurnie—the "mother of West Indian dance," whose Little Carib Theatre was just down the block from the Telfers' in Woodbrook. Among his peers in McBurnie's company were Boscoe Holder, the painter and pianist and dancer whose company became so crucial in London in the 1950s, and Boscoe's younger brother Geoffrey—the less talented of the pair, by Jay's lights, but the better known today because he went to New York. Geoffrey launched his career with a lauded bow in Truman Capote's show *House of Flowers* (1954), in whose cast he met his stupendous wife Carmen de Lavallade, before later playing the villain Baron Samedi opposite James Bond in the 1970s.

Once Jay left Trinidad to attend NYU in the early '50s, he put his dance training to use while working as a busboy at storied Greenwich Village jazz spots like the Village Vanguard and the Village Gate. Meeting Harry Belafonte just as he was getting his calypso act together with the help of Louise Bennett, he also befriended John Coltrane and Thelonious Monk—who told him, "Man, you're the only cat I've ever known who can dance to my music."

Jay's stint in Eric Williams's independence government, once he returned home, may have come from a sense of national duty (Williams asked Jay to use his marketing expertise to sell his development plan to the nation); but as one of those who helped secure the "steel band movement" an officially sanctioned role in the new state, he used the connections thereby forged, once he reached London, to organize his resident steel pan ensemble at the Ambience—and then to draw on that network, again, when the Notting Hill carnival jumped off.

The larger birth of that festival is a story that has been told and debated in different versions, with a certain disagreement about who "founded" the yearly gathering that came to convene all of Merry Old England—whether in harmony or conflict—under the sign of a Trinidad-style carnival, and that has served as both flashpoint and touchstone for going on a third generation now, to work out just what and how its new multiculture will be—whether the restive riots of 1976, or the EDM-and-reggae fueled bacchanal of today where a new and evolved England can congratulate itself on how well everyone gets along (until someone gets stabbed). But the political subtext, or overt nature, is no accident when you consider that the tradition of West Indian carnival was born in direct response to a watershed event in the racial history of postwar Britain. The Notting Hill riots of August 1958, which saw white teddy boys go "nigger hunting" in the streets by Ladbroke Grove, roiled England a decade after the arrival of the SS *Empire Windrush* marked the symbolic arrival of Britain's postwar blacks. The carnival born in that year was the brainchild of a Trinidadian communist, Claudia Jones, who'd spent her formative years in the United States, in Harlem, before falling afoul of its McCarthyite mores in the red-scare '50s; like C. L. R. James, she was imprisoned at Ellis Island en route to being expelled from the United States for her Marxism.

In London, Jones cofounded Brixton's *West Indian Gazette* with the express aim, as a veteran of more developed battles against racial injustice in the United States, of cohering Britain's disparate blacks around their common experience of racism. Her idea for a carnival was expressly allied with those aims and purposed, after the riots, to "get the taste of Notting Hill out of our mouths."[32] Her first carnival was held in January to coincide with the festivities back in Trinidad. It was held indoors, in the St. Pancras Town Hall, and featured a revue of calypsonians and other music makers under the direction of the Trinidadian Edric Connor. Like Jay, a veteran of Beryl McBurnie's Little Carib Theatre, he was a performer perhaps best known outside Trinidad, if not by name, for singing "Hill and Gully Rider," the old Jamaican folk song, in his role as the harpooner Daggoo in John Huston's classic film version of *Moby Dick* starring Gregory Peck, from 1956. Claudia Jones's carnival would be repeated each year until her death in 1964. But it was some time before the cultural politics of carnival—the large-scale statement that Briton's blacks were here, and here to stay—made it to the streets of Notting Hill. And it was someone else entirely in that neighborhood, with no connection to Jones, who made it happen: an educator and community activist who came to see Jay Telfer at his club about helping to get the community and police aboard her plans to do so.

Rhaune Laslett was a Londoner of Native American and Russian extraction who worked in the then-poor neighborhood of Notting Hill as a schoolteacher. One evening at the Ambience, Jay's headwaiter told him someone was there to see him. Laslett's been sent, she said, by Sir Learie Constantine. They said that if she really wanted to get the area's West Indian artists behind her plan, she should speak with Jay. He invited her to sit for a meal, and she described her plan. "She said she was interested in doing a children's carnival; the Trinidad mission had told her to come speak with me—they knew I had experience with the Carnival Development Commission in Trinidad, and with bringing out bands in Trinidad." Her concept wasn't necessarily for a West Indian–themed event; it was, rather, for a weeklong street fair—open to and featuring all the people in the area, Portuguese and African and Ukrainian and Caribbean—culminating in the August bank holiday weekend, "to prove that from our ghetto there was a wealth of culture waiting to express itself, that we weren't rubbish people."[33] Jay was immediately on board.

Contributing funds and agreeing to help get all the merchants in the Notting Hill area to agree, he enlisted a streetwise friend—Michael X—to go with him from store to store enlisting support. Having worked for years as a thuggish debt collector for local slumlord Rachman, Michael had founded his RAAS organization and was also readying, with the support of some of the rock stars who hung out at Jay's club, to launch the London Free School. "He did have his ways of making it clear to those shopkeepers," Jay recalled, "that they didn't really have a choice." Their first carnival, in August 1965, went off without a hitch near Portobello Road.

More than just playing that role in making it happen, Jay had also been essential to shaping the carnival's West Indian flavor. Advising Laslett that if children were to be involved, adults should be, too, he enlisted members of Le Flambeau, and also urged her to contact Sterling Betancourt and Russell Henderson—the great steel pan player who'd gotten his start playing the piano at the Little Carib, and whose walkabout with his pan trio, from their first carnival's starting point, turned it into a parade. For the second carnival, Jay called a dear friend of his from Trinidad who was then working in London as a costume designer for the theater because, as Jay put it, "we needed to raise the tone of the carnival." The result, in 1966, was Peter Minshall's original version of "Paradise Lost."

As the carnival grew into something far larger than the original children's fair envisioned by Laslett, a great many other people grew involved in the committee putting it on. Among those who today argue about how key their role was are stalwart figures from the world of West Indian London, in those days, like the pan man and educator Selwyn Baptiste, who later became the first official head of the Carnival Development Corporation, and the first chairman of the group that came before. Telfer resisted ever being their chairman for reasons he outlined sitting on his Indian cushion in Port of Spain. "The only chairman I like to be is the man in my chair right here. All my life I've been there as a support and an activist, but my personality's not given to being in charge of a group." During those years his work as an impresario was devoted to finding new spaces for "Caribbean culture, and Third World culture at large, in London"; he once put on a gala show featuring Byron Lee from Jamaica and Trinidad's Mighty Sparrow at London's Olympia Hall. His role behind the scenes remained crucial, though, as the carnival's reputation for danger also grew.

Many people in the neighborhood became decidedly uncomfortable about the parade of revelers whose "white participants apart from my wife in those days," Jay said, "I could count on one hand." Internal tensions had also emerged in the shape of certain Trinidadians resistant to Jamaicans especially, with their reputation for bad behavior and unawareness of Trinidad tradition. Telfer, though, was a crucial voice in favor of the carnival maintaining a space for all. "This is *not* a Trinidad carnival," he recalled insisting to his colleagues, "and it was never meant to be. The principal creativity, the spark, came from Trinidad. But like most cultural things, you have to adapt, to the conditions, and the different cultures that will be supportive of what you're doing." But calling a friend at the BBC to come film the carnival with Minshall's great costumes, he also made sure, with his marketers' mind, to direct the camera crews away from a gang of Jamaican kids he knew who liked to try to pick revelers' pockets under the Westway.

By 1971, Telfer was growing weary of working till 5 a.m. six nights a week, at an establishment that, although popular, never made much money. ("Paying the best staff in town and keeping a seven-piece band playing every night of the week was for me the utmost," he said, "but it's not the way to make money.") The scene he'd worked to build, like the larger counterculture in that year that witnessed the death of Jimi Hendrix (also a regular at his club, naturally), was entering a new and grimmer phase. Michael X was drawn up on extortion charges, and his Black House, having been the scene of the "slave collar affair" that involved assaulting a Jewish businessman, mysteriously burned. Freed on bail posted by John Lennon, Michael chose to leave London for Trinidad. Jay closed the Ambience. During the club's final years in operation, he was involved in the production of Marcello Mastroianni's *Leo the Last*, which was partly shot in the club; he also dabbled in promoting prizefights, collaborating with a Saudi prince to try to arrange a title bout involving Muhammad Ali (Jay's line on the day he spent with the champ: "We enjoyed each other deeply") in Jeddah; but Elijah Muhammad ultimately failed to allow Ali to go to Saudi because he recalled what had happened when Malcolm X went there.

Having strenuously urged Michael X not to return to Trinidad— "that plan can lead nowhere good," he'd told him—it was the awful deaths of Gale Benson and Joseph Skerritt, and the subsequent jailing of the old friend whom Jay insisted on calling Michael Abdul Malik, that led to Jay's first return to Trinidad in over a dozen years. Still persona non grata to Dr. Eric Williams in 1975, he gained special permission to return with the help of friendlier parties in his government and sought, alongside friends working to abolish the death penalty in Trinidad and Tobago, to at least save the life of a friend to whom he remained loyal. It was for the simple reason that "Michael had deep flaws and mistaken ways," as he told me, "but he was a person to whom I owed a deep debt for helping me know who I am—in moving me from my upbringing as a middle class 'red nigger,' in Port of Spain, to absorb the African part of

my heritage, to understand myself as a black man in the world." Recalling the last time he saw Michael in Royal Gaol, Jay wept softly on his
porch, forty years after the fact of going to tell him in person that he'd
done what he could, but they were determined to hang him. "Michael
put his hands up to the bars and I told him, 'Your spirit, my brother, is
not in this place. You don't need to know which way is east.'" When I
asked him about Naipaul's book on the whole affair, he scowled into his
tea. "Vidia wrote that Hakim Jamal killed Gale Benson—rubbish," he
said without elaborating. His larger appraisal said more. "Mr. Biswas,
of his books, was exquisite. But Vidia became a person with no affection
for Trinidad or Trinidadians, so why should I have affection for him?"

Soon after his brief trip home to try and fail to forestall the hanging
of his friend, he and his wife, Ruth, the beautiful New Zealander who
became a fellow follower of Sai Baba, left London for India. The pair
spent several seasons on Sai Baba's ashram in Puttaparthi, near Bangalore, and also lived for a time by the beach in Goa. Transporting hashish
down from Kashmir in his pant legs, Jay sold his "smoke" to visiting
hippies and read their palms while Ruth peddled banana bread; he also
"trained with the stickfighter Boom Shaka." It was 1979 when Jay and
Ruth returned to Trinidad for good. Arriving home in the uniform he
was still wearing thirty years later—he'd adopted the turban, in the days
of the Ambience, when he met a Sikh man on a London street whom
he took to be his double, and enlisted to learn the technique—some of
his friends ribbed him about his look. ("Have you become some sort of
Moroccan policeman?" went one comment Jay loved to repeat.) But he
wasted no time in shaping a new era of carnival arts back home.

In addition to managing the careers of the great calypsonian Black
Stalin, the conscious author of such Calypso Monarch–winning tunes as
"Caribbean Man" (1979) and "Bun 'Em" (1987), in which he urged St.
Peter to cast the likes of Cecil Rhodes and Ronald Reagan and Margaret Thatcher into hell (1987), and "Black Man Feeling to Party"(1999),
Jay was also a close associate of Roy Cape, the exemplary saxophonist
who became Trinidad's greatest modern bandleader. When it came to
steel pan, Jay was a devotee of Len "Boogsie" Sharpe, of whose Phase II
panyard he and Ruth became fans. He and Ruth led the fight to reopen
and relaunch the Little Carib Theatre, a few blocks from his childhood
home in Woodbrook, and he spent the rest of his time on the patio of
the lovely home, up in Cascade, dispensing bon mots about love and
loyalty to the many members of a "pumpkin-vine family," women and

men who benefited from his talent for friendship. One truism of Baba's that he recited every time I went to see him there, whenever returning to Trinidad, about being a man at once sincere and charming, went like this: "Do not speak untruth, no matter how pleasing. Do not speak truth that is displeasing. Only speak the truth that is pleasing."

One year when I returned to see him after attending the Notting Hill carnival, he delighted in hearing that I'd spent an evening on All Saints Road, one of his old zones, watching the Magnolia Steel Band play a wicked arrangement of one of his favorite Trinidadian soca tunes of recent years—Bunji's "Differentology." My report from the area around the old Mangrove Restaurant struck him as surreal; the Mangrove had been a notorious hangout for the Black Power set, after many of his patrons migrated there once the Ambience closed, and had been surrounded by flats rented by Rachman for two pounds a week; nowadays, a good apartment would run you a million quid at least. That the humble Notting Hill carnival had so grown, though, was clearly a point of pride. Another time, I brought him the Smithsonian's newly remastered version of Emory Cook's recording of "Calypso Carnival" from 1956. He knew, leaping up to dance before I even told him, what it was. "It's Invaders, playing 'Back Bay Shuffle'! No one before or after has captured, on record, what it feels like to be out with a steel band on the street—where the music was born, where we belong." His grin was beatific. "Listen!"

During the last months of Jay's life, I had the good fortune, while spending a semester on the island as a visiting scholar at the university, of living in Jay and Ruth's spare apartment in Cascade. Eighty-six by then, Jay had slowed down a bit. Troubled by shortness of breath—not helped, no doubt, by his insistence that copious ganja smoking wasn't part of the problem—he spent most of his time sitting down, and his favorite line to quote was from Rabindranath Tagore: "I have scaled the peak and found no shelter in fame's bleak and barren height. Lead me, my Guide, before the light fades, into the valley of quiet where life's harvest mellows into golden wisdom."[34] Still, though, he was liable to leap up, when the mood struck, and demonstrate how his uniform's black leather belt had a utility beyond the sartorial. "You see," he'd say as he wrapped its length around his palm and whipped it out. "An assailant can't get near. I just give licks!" Down at the panyard, he was still good for a few suave twirls before taking a seat. During the evenings, though, as we sat on the patio drinking coconut water, he kept his TV tuned to the Arts Channel and rhapsodized about the exquisite playing of Andrés Segovia or the exquisite plié of some bygone dancer in the Ballets Russes. Retiring to my own quarters next door, an airy flat decorated with the art of Boscoe Holder and of Jay's brother Henry, I often worked late into the night—and would hear Jay shuffling around on the wall's other side. He'd always kept a nightclub owner's schedule. "You and I know the magic hour," he'd say.

One night when we both went to sleep rather earlier than dawn, and while Ruth was away on a visit to New Zealand, my love and I awoke to hear rapid breathing from through the wall. It was Jay, unable to catch his breath. Rushing him into a car, we drove at 3 a.m. to Mt. Hope hospital, outside Port of Spain, and checked him into the ER, beneath the sign reading "Gunshot and Chop Wounds This Way." With a little oxygen and a half hour or so hooked up to one of the breathing machines with which asthmatic kids from the nearby ghetto, in the dingy ward, were also catching their breath, he was soon okay. But when a couple of weeks later two young kids robbed us both at gunpoint, on Jay's once-peaceful block—his trusty old German Shepherd, Raja, was soon to be put down himself; he snoozed through the whole event—it seemed the writing was on the wall.

The kids with their pop guns, taking account of this mixed-race crew with a man in a turban, had said as much when they asked: "What kinda' people you?"

Jay replied, "Trinis like you, bredren."

When early the following spring I got an email, back home in New York, that Jay had passed on, it wasn't a surprise. Nor was the word that his funeral, which I couldn't get down for on short notice, was an occasion to best all, with a great funeral pyre by the Caroni River and Hindu rites accompanied, in perfect Trini fashion, by Orisha drummers and flower petals and great wafts of ganja smoke rising to the heavens.

The last time I saw Jay, though, wasn't on his porch. Nor was it on Port of Spain's streets, even though it was Carnival Tuesday and that stage, to this street-dramatist *par excellence*, was a second home. Having taken ill days before, Jay had checked into Port of Spain General. He'd been unable to wave the flag for his beloved Phase II during Panorama; what little of carnival he'd caught was through his ward's open window by the Savannah, across which I walked to visit him, dodging last-lap revelers on Tuesday afternoon. But propped up there in bed, Jay was utterly himself: quoting Tagore and *Julius Caesar*; charming nurses he called "sister"; trading verses from old Midnight Robber songs with an ailing man, one bed over, whom he called "my true pardner." As he lay there, perking up as the sounds of a passing steel band drifted up from below, his turban was still in place, his tunic impeccable. And when I remarked on this, he didn't miss a beat. "You know the other reason I dress like this," he murmured. "It's so that when I'm coming, you know I'm me—that this man, here, is different from the rest."

We knew—those who knew him. And I thought, walking out of Port of Spain General and past a little eatery called We Foods, that maybe I knew something about why he could only have come from here, too, and nowhere else.

ACKNOWLEDGMENTS

The debts amassed in completing this book accrue most to those who crossed tracks with my questions and who trusted me with their time and replies. To name every person who has made this project real over the past fifteen years would beggar the limits of tact and space here. I hope all those who shared so generously of their lives with me, and who may not be mentioned here but know who they are, will understand that my massed THANK YOU now is offered in deep gratitude and with the sincerest hope that this book, above all, does their stories honor. Any errors of interpretation or fact are down to me alone. It just remains to thank those who made this project possible, in its development as a PhD thesis in UC-Berkeley's mighty department of geography, and in the years before and after that phase of life, too.

Thanks due, with feeling: To Professor Michael Watts, comrade and chair, who abided my happenstantial career as a Berkeley geographer from the off, and to a dissertation committee that comprised a scholarly dream: Nadia Ellis, Percy Hintzen, Jake Kosek, and Jocelyne Guilbault. To Alan Pred and Donald Moore, also in Berkeley, whose humane brilliance has marked so many, and to John Gillis and David Lowenthal, who paved the way. To the Social Science Research Council, and the DPDF Fellowship group in Black Atlantic Studies, led by Andrew Apter and Percy Hintzen, that got my research started. To the National Science Foundation, and the Graduate Research Fellowship that kept me fed for the time it took. And to the American Council of Learned Societies (and a Dissertation-Completion Fellowship), for finishing it.

To the makers, back in 1998, of Yale's new program in Ethnicity, Race, and Migration, where I had the great fortune to land and where Alicia Schmidt-Camacho, Stephen Pitti, Patricia Pessar, and Gil Joseph made the questions feel worth asking, and where Michael Denning,

Vera Kutzinski, and Paul Gilroy guided how I do so in ways that endure. To the Parker Huang Fellowship, from Yale, that got me to Cuba. To the Yale Center for International and Area Studies, for funding my first trip to Trinidad in 2001, and to the Fulbright Flex Fellowship, thirteen years later, that let me return to the University of the West Indies at St. Augustine. To Dr. Patricia Mohammed and all of her esteemed colleagues at UWI's Institute for Gender and Development Studies; and to the gracious librarians in the West Indiana and Special Collections division of the UWI Library, who steward the C. L. R. James Papers and other treasures with invaluable care.

To the John Carter Brown Library, Ted Widmer, and the Jeannette D. Black Memorial Fellowship in cartographic history that afforded a crucial summer of work in Rhode Island. To the New Orleans Center for the Gulf South at Tulane, and to Joel Dinerstein and Rebecca Snedeker. To the Headlands Center for the Arts, and to Brian Karl and Holly Blake, for the gift of getting to work in Marin's rare air amid the friendship and inspiration of Chinaka Hodge, Ben Ehrenreich, and Brett Goodroad, and the supreme harmelodics of Jamaaladeen Tacuma. To Raul Fernandez and the UC-Cuba group. To the Caribbean Studies Association, and to Holger Henke and Anton Allahar. To the Institute for Public Knowledge at NYU, where the beneficence of Eric Klinenberg, Gordon Douglas, and Siera Dissmore, along with the whole IPK massive, has made a home in the city. And to Rebecca Solnit, essayist and force of nature and culture nonpareil, from whom I've learned so much about how to write about place, and with whom collaborating has been a vast boon.

To the kind people at the Library for the Spoken Word at University of the West Indies, Mona. And, also in Jamaica, to Annie Paul, Nicole Smythe-Johnson, Storm Saulter, Brad Klein, Ralph A. Smith, Herbie Miller, Junior Lincoln, Shirley Hanna, and Cathy Snipper. To Carlos and Dagdelay Goicechoa, in Havana, and to Nehanda Abiodun, Joseph Mutti, Joel Saurez, Conner Gorry, and the Centro Memorial Martin Luther King. To Ana de Santiago Ayón, always. To Bridget Wooding and Allison Petrozziello at OBMICA, in Santo Domingo; to Gustavo Toribio at Solidaridad Fronteriza, in Dajabón; to Ana Maria Belique and to everyone at Centro Bono and who bravely make Recononici.do go. To Richard Jacques Miguel, Daniel Morel, Jean Ruid Sénatus, Giles Clarke, Richard Fleming, and Faubert Pierre. And also in Haiti, to David Belle and Kathryn Everett and everyone at Artists Institute; to Cassia van der Hoof Holstein, *Dokta* Paul Farmer, and Partners in Health; to Jean-Baptiste Azolin at GARR. To Dave Eggers, for getting me to Jacmel, to Regine Chassagne and Win Butler for pointing the way, to the indomitable Elvens Brevil, for going the distance. To B. C. Pires, Selwyn Strachan, Lydia Pulsipher, and Mac Goodwin. To Patrice Glondu and Patrick Chamoiseau, in Martinique, and to Lennox Honychurch, Mark Steele, Polly Pattullo, Chief Charles Williams, Margaret Williams, and Anne and Hervé at the Riverside Café in Dominica, B.W.I. To Ray Funk, the calypso king of Fairbanks, Alaska. And in Trinidad: to Peter Doig, Tracy Assing, Jonathan Ali, Melanie Archer, Bonnie Kennedy, Katinka Bukh, Catherine Emmanuel, Matt Ross, Charlotte Elias, Terry Perry, Robert Bos, Ruth Telfer, and the late but ever-great Everest C. "Jay" Telfer, Jr., whom we miss each day.

To Bob Silvers, Vendela Vida, John Palatella, Jeremy Keehn, Nicholas Laughlin, Carin Besser, Gemma Sieff, Deirdre Foley-Mendelsohn, Pru Pfeiffer, Michael Shae, Franklin Bruno, and Matthew Specktor—editors, all, to whose sense I owe much. To Chaz Reetz-Laiolo, Nathaniel Rich, Ash Ferlito, Suketu Mehta, Eric P. Brown, Alex Vazquez, Alan Audi, Mark Beasley-Murray, Jon Lee Anderson, Joe Boyd, Jodi Weinstein, and Sarah Levitt. To Zsofia Jilling, Vaughn Sills, and Lowry Pei—island people, too. To Zoë Pagnamenta, my dear agent and dear friend, who is simply the best. To Nicholas Thomson, unflappable and on it, and to Jess Purcell and everyone at Knopf who I know less by their names than by the deep skill and care with which they make exemplary books. And to Erroll McDonald, my editor, whose grace abided this one, and whose brilliance shaped it.

To Jamie Byng, who knows why the revolution still won't be televised, and to Francis Bickmore and to everyone at Canongate who make publishing joy. To the late great loco David Sullivan, who did make it to Havana. To Mark Danner, mentor and friend, for true shelter and true support, and to Jeanette Neff for same. To Hilton Als, for sending me a well-loved copy of *Brown Girl, Brownstones*, once, and for his Olympian gifts for brotherhood, generally. To Eli Jelly-Schapiro, my first friend and finest reader. To Garnette Cadogan, indefatigable and very often inspired, who read every line, way more than once, and made a ton of them better. And to Mirissa Neff, who holds my heart and holds me upright, whose eyes and wisdom are all over these pages, and who both brought this project home and made it possible, as she does the gift of our life together, in all the ways that matter.

It is to my beloved parents, Katherine L. Jelly and Steven A. Schapiro, to whom I owe all. This book is for them—and for those it's about.

NOTES

Introduction

1. Tariq Ali, "A Conversation with C. L. R. James," *Socialist Challenge*, July 3, 1980, 8–9.
2. Interview with James Baldwin, *Paris Review* 91 (Spring 1984).
3. Wilson Harris, jacket copy on *Special Delivery: The Letters of C. L. R. James to Constance Webb, 1939–1948*, ed. Anna Grimshaw (Oxford: Blackwell, 1996).
4. James, "From Toussaint L'Ouverture to Fidel Castro," in *The Black Jacobins: Toussaint L'Ouverture and the San Domingo Revolution* (New York: Vintage, 1963), 391.
5. Ibid.
6. Ibid.
7. Ibid., 392.
8. Ibid.
9. Alex Dupuy, *Haiti: From Revolutionary Slaves to Powerless Slaves* (New York: Routledge, 2014), 1.
10. James, "From Toussaint L'Ouverture to Fidel Castro," 410.
11. See David Scott, "Modernity That Predated the Modern: Sidney Mintz's Caribbean," *History Workshop Journal* 58 (2004): 191–210.
12. Thomas Jefferys, *The West-India Atlas, Or, a Compendious Description of the West Indies: Illustrated with Forty Correct Charts and Maps, Taken from Actual Surveys: Together with an Historical Account of the Several Countries and Islands Which Compose That Part of the World, Their Discovery, Situation, Extent, Boundaries, Product, Trade, Inhabitants, Strength, Government, Religion, &c.* (London: Printed for Robert Sayer and John Bennett, 1775), iv. As discussed by Carl Ortwin Sauer, *The Early Spanish Main* (Berkeley: University of California Press, 1966), 4.
13. Christopher Columbus, "Journal of the First Voyage of Christopher Columbus," as copied by Bartolomé de las Casas and collected, e.g., in Julius E. Olson and Edward Gaylord Burns, *The Northmen, Columbus, and Cabot, 985–1503: Original Narratives of Early American History* (New York: Charles Scribner's Sons, 1906).
14. Edward Said, *Orientalism* (New York: Vintage, 1978), 3.
15. Bob Marley, "Slave Driver," the Wailers, *Catch a Fire* (London: Island Records, 1973).
16. Pedro Mir, *Contracanto a Walt Whitman* (Guatemala: Ediciones Saker-Ti, 1952). Translation mine.

17. Edouard Glissant, *Poetics of Relation*, trans. Betsy Wing (Ann Arbor: University of Michigan Press, 2000). Stuart Hall described the Caribbean as the "home of hybridity" on the BBC and as re-sounded in *The Stuart Hall Project*, John Akomfrah, dir. (2014).
18. Alejo Carpentier, "Lo Real Maravilloso," *Tientos y Diferencias* (Montevideo, UR: Arca, 1967 [1949]).
19. Sylvia Wynter, "1492: A New World View," in *Race, Discourse, and the Origin of the Americas*, ed. Vera Lawrence Hyatt and Rex Nettleford (Washington, DC: Smithsonian, 1995).
20. C. L. R. James to Randolph Rawlins, October 4, 1960, C. L. R. James Papers 1901–1989, West Indiana and Special Collections, the University of the West Indies Library, St. Augustine, Trinidad and Tobago.
21. C. L. R. James to Morris Philipson, December 10, 1960, C. L. R. James Papers 1901–1989, West Indiana and Special Collections, the University of the West Indies Library, St. Augustine, Trinidad and Tobago.
22. Derek Walcott, "The Spoiler's Return," in *The Fortunate Traveller* (London: Faber & Faber, 1981) ("All Port of Spain is a 12:30 show, / Some playing Kojak, some Fidel Castro.")
23. Patrick Leigh Fermor, *The Traveller's Tree: A Journey Through the Caribbean Islands* (New York: New York Review Classics, 2010 [1952]), xxiii.
24. V. S. Naipaul, *The Middle Passage* (London: André Deutsch, 1962), 29.
25. Sauer, *The Early Spanish Main*, 4.
26. Leigh Fermor, *The Traveller's Tree*, xxiii.
27. Antonio Benítez-Rojo, *The Repeating Island: The Caribbean and the Postmodern Perspective* (Durham, NC: Duke University Press, 1996), 4.
28. Leigh Fermor, *The Traveller's Tree*, 50.
29. Brent Dowe and Trevor McNaughton, "The Rivers of Babylon," as performed by the Melodians, *The Harder They Come*, soundtrack album (London: Island Records, 1972).
30. Simone Weil, *The Need for Roots* (London: Routledge, 1952 [original French, 1949]).
31. Bob Marley, "Exodus," Bob Marley and the Wailers, *Exodus* (London: Island Records, 1977).
32. John Gillis, *Islands of the Mind: How the Human Imagination Created the Atlantic World* (New York: Palgrave Macmillan, 2004), 26.

Chapter 1: Branding

1. Tim Layden, "Bolt Adds to Developing Legacy with Second Straight Gold in 100 Meters," *Sports Illustrated* online, August 5, 2012.
2. Oshane Tobias, "Burrell: Jamaica Will Benefit from Olympic Success," *Jamaica Observer*, August 25, 2012.
3. Lisa Hanna, MP, "A Positive Nation on a Mission to Achieve," Jamaica 50 Secretariat, 2012.
4. Tig Padgett, "Jamaica at 50: Island Nation's PM Talks About the Queen, the Caribbean and Usain Bolt," Time.com, August 5, 2012.
5. Portia Simpson-Miller, remarks at Jamaica 50 gala, reprinted in *Caribbean Journal*, August 6, 2012.
6. "Prime Minister Portia Simpson-Miller's Inaugural Address," printed in full in the *Gleaner*, January 5, 2012.

7. Simon Anholt, *Brand Jamaica Feasibility Study*, 2006.

8. Jamaica Tourist Board, "JTB History—Chapter 1: Come to Jamaica (1955–1963)," http://www.jtbonline.org.

9. Jan van Riebeeck, unsourced anecdote as quoted, e.g., by Edward Long, *The History of Jamaica, or General Survey of the Antient and Modern State of That Island with Reflections on its Situation, Settlements, Inhabitants, Climate, Products, Commerce, Laws, and Government* (London: T. Lowndes, 1774).

10. Charles Leslie, *A New History of Jamaica, from the Earliest Accounts to the Taking of Porto Bello by Vice-Admiral Vernon* (Cambridge: Cambridge University Press, 2012 [1739]), 91.

11. K. C. Samuels, *Jamaica's FIRST President: Dudus, 1992–2010* (Kingston, Jamaica: PageTurner Publishing House, 2011).

12. Adidja Palmer (a.k.a. Vybz Kartel) with Michael Palmer, *The Voice of the Jamaican Ghetto* (Kingston, Jamaica: Ghetto People Publishing, 2012).

Chapter 2: Badness

1. Patrick Leigh Fermor, *The Traveller's Tree: A Journey Through the Caribbean Islands* (New York: New York Review Classics, 2010 [1952]), 335.

2. Roger Steffens and Peter Simon, *Reggae Scrapbook* (San Rafael, CA: Insight Editions, 2007), 100. Palace Theater scene and concert as discussed by Colin Grant in *The Natural Mystics: Marley, Tosh, and Wailer* (New York, Norton, 2011), 61.

3. Peter Tosh in *Stepping Razor: Red X*, documentary film based on Tosh's audio diary, the Red X Tapes, Nicholas Campbell, dir. (1993).

4. M. G. Smith, Roy Augier, and Rex Nettleford, "The Ras Tafari Movement in Kingston, Jamaica" (Mona, Jamaica: Institute of Social and Economic Research, University of the West Indies, 1960).

5. James Baldwin, "Alas, Poor Richard," in *Nobody Knows My Name* (New York: Dial, 1961), 43.

6. Vincent Brown, *The Reaper's Garden* (Cambridge, MA: Harvard University Press, 2008).

Chapter 3: Redemption Songs

1. Laurie Gunst, *Born Fi' Dead: A Journey Through the Jamaican Posse Underworld* (New York: Holt, 1996).

2. " 'Fat Head' Survives Head Wound," *Gleaner*, December 23, 2012.

3. Katherine Dunham, *Journey to Accompong* (New York: Holt, 1946).

4. Annie Paul, " 'No Grave Cannot Hold My Body Down': Rituals of Death and Burial in Postcolonial Jamaica," *Small Axe* 23 (June 2007): 158.

5. See Joshua Jelly-Schapiro, "Queen of the Dancehall," *Believer* (July/August 2010).

6. Diana McCaulay, "Does Jamaica Really Have a Strong Local Brand?," Facebook post, July 18, 2013.

7. FutureBrand, *Country Brand Index, 2012–2013* (London: FutureBrand.com, 2013), http://www.futurebrand.com/images/uploads/studies/cbi/CBI_2012-Final.pdf.

8. Adidja Palmer (a.k.a. Vybz Kartel) with Michael Palmer, *The Voice of the Jamaican Ghetto* (Kingston, Jamaica: Ghetto People Publishing, 2012), 248.

Chapter 4: Cuba Sí

1. Thomas Jefferson to James Monroe, October 24, 1823, *Memoirs, Correspondence and Private Papers of Thomas Jefferson, Late President of the United States* (London: Colburn & Bentley, 1829), 391.

2. T. J. English, *Havana Nocturne: How the Mob Owned Cuba and Lost It to the Revolution* (New York: William Morrow, 2008), 19.

3. Fernando Ortiz, "Los factores humanos de la cubanidad," *Revista Bimestre Cubana* XLV (1940), as discussed by Patricia Catoira, "Transculturation à la *Ajiaco:* A Recipe for Modernity," *Cuban Counterpoints: The Legacy of Fernando Ortiz,* ed. Mauricio Font and Alfonso W. Quiroz (Lanham, MD: Lexington Books, 2005).

4. Alejo Carpentier, *El Amor a la Ciudad* (Madrid: Alfaguara, 1996), 101; as quoted in Alfredo José Estrada, *Havana: Autobiography of a City* (New York: Palgrave Macmillan, 2007), 165.

Chapter 5: Cuban Counterpoints

1. Tomás Robaina Fernández, *El Negro en Cuba* (Havana: Sciencias Sociales, 1990).

2. José Martí, "Mi Raza," *Patria,* April 16, 1893; collected as "My Race" in *José Martí: Selected Writings,* trans. and ed. Esther Allen (New York: Penguin Classics, 2002), 319.

3. C. L. R. James, "From Toussaint L'Ouverture to Fidel Castro," in *The Black Jacobins: Toussaint L'Ouverture and the San Domingo Revolution* (New York: Vintage, 1963), 395.

4. Fernando Ortiz, *Hampa afro-cubana. Los negros brujos (apuntes para un estudio de etnologia criminal), con una carta prólogo del Dr. C. Lombroso* (Madrid: Librería de Fernando Fé, 1906).

5. James, "From Toussaint L'Ouverture to Fidel Castro," 395.

6. Fernando Ortiz, "Por la integración cubana de blancos y negros," lecture at the Club Atenas, Havana, December 12, 1942, printed in *Ultra* 13 (1943): 69–76.

7. Ibid.

8. Fernando Ortiz, *Cuban Counterpoint: Tobacco and Sugar* [1940], trans. Harriet de Onis, introduction by Bronisław Malinowski (New York: Knopf, 1947), 98.

9. Fernando Ortiz, *Los instrumentos de la música afrocubana,* 2 vols. (Madrid: Editoral Música Mundad Maqueda, D.L., 1996), 24.

10. Bartolomé de las Casas, *Historia de las Indias,* vol. 3 (Madrid: Impr. De M. Ginesta, 1875 [1561]), 99.

11. Ortiz, *Cuban Counterpoint,* 281.

12. Ortiz, *Los negros brujos,* 10.

13. Lydia Cabrera, *Reglas de Congo—Palo Monte Mayombero* (Miami: Peninsular, 1979), 50.

14. Alfredo José Estrada, *Havana: Autobiography of a City* (New York: Palgrave Macmillan, 2007), 101.

15. José Martí, "Nuestra America," *El Partido Liberal* (Mexico City), January 20, 1891; as collected in *The America of José Martí: Selected Writings of José Martí,* ed. and trans. Juan de Onis (New York: Minerva, 1954), 141.

16. Ibid., 150.

17. *New York Journal*, August 17, 1897; as quoted in Louis A. Pérez Jr., *Cuba in the American Imagination: Metaphor and the Imperial Imagination* (Chapel Hill: University of North Carolina Press, 2008), 3.

18. "The Platt Amendment," *Statutes at Large of the United States*, XXI (Washington, DC, 1902), 879–98.

19. John Quincy Adams to Hugh Nelson, April 28, 1823, in U.S. Congress, House of Representatives, *Island of Cuba*, 8; as quoted in Pérez, *Cuba in the American Imagination*, 39.

20. *Congressional Globe*, January 15, 1855, 33rd Cong., 2nd sess., vol. 31, Appendix, 92; as quoted in Pérez, *Cuba in the American Imagination*, 39.

21. Young quoted in Walter Mills, *The Martial Spirit: A Study of Our War with Spain* (Cambridge, MA: Literary Guild of America, 1931), 362.

22. *Havana Post*, September 19, 1925; as quoted in Pérez, *Cuba in the American Imagination*, 235.

23. Consuelo Hermer and Marjorie May, *Havana Mañana: A Guide to Cuba and the Cubans* (New York, 1941), 3–4; as quoted in Pérez, *Cuba in the American Imagination*, 235.

24. José Martí to Manuel Mercado, May 18, 1895, in *Selected Writings* (2002), 395.

25. Desi Arnaz, *A Book* (New York: William Morrow, 1976), 56.

26. Ned Sublette, *Cuba and Its Music: From the First Drums to the Mambo* (Chicago: Chicago Review Press, 2004), 444.

27. Pérez, *Cuba in the American Imagination*, 238.

28. Sublette, *Cuba and Its Music*, 504.

29. Alexandra T. Vazquez, *Listening in Detail: Performances of Cuban Music* (Durham, NC: Duke University Press, 2013), 149.

30. Max Salazar, "Who Invented the Mambo?," Parts 1–2, *Latin Beat* 2: 9–10.

31. Helio Orovio, "Arsenio Rodríguez y el son cubano," *Revolución y cultura* (la Habana), no. 7, July 1985.

Chapter 6: Autumn of the Patriarch

1. Milan Kundera, *Life Is Elsewhere*, trans. Peter Kussi (New York: Penguin, 1986), 162.

2. Janos Kornai, *The Socialist System: The Political Economy of Communism* (Princeton, NJ: Princeton University Press, 1992).

3. Donald E. Schulz, *The United States and Cuba: From a Strategy of Conflict to Constructive Engagement* (Carlisle Barracks, PA: United States Army War College, 1993), 18.

4. Colin Powell et al., "Commission for Assistance to a Free Cuba: Report," May 6, 2004, http://www.cafc.gov/rpt/index.htm.

5. Daniel P. Erickson, *The Cuba Wars: Fidel Castro, the United States, and the Next Cuban Revolution* (New York: Bloomsbury, 2008), 102.

6. Fidel Castro Ruz, "Proclama del Comandante en Jefe al Pueblo de Cuba," *Granma*, July 31, 2006, available online in English at http://www.granma.cu/granmad/secciones/siempre_con_fidel/art-017.html.

7. "Speech by the First Vice-President of the Councils of State and Ministers, Army General Raúl Castro Ruz, at the main celebration of the 54th Anniversary of the attack on Moncada and Carlos Manuel de Céspedes Garrisons, at the Major General Ignacio Agramonte Loynaz Revolution Square in the city of

Camagüey, July 26th, 2007, 'Year 49 of the Revolution,'" *Granma*, July 27, 2007, http://www.granma.cu/ingles/2007/julio/vier27/Raúl26.html.

8. José Martí, "Nuestra America," *El Partido Liberal* (Mexico City), January 20, 1891; as collected in *The America of José Martí: Selected Writings of José Martí*, ed. and trans. Juan de Onis (New York: Minerva, 1954), 148.

9. Wil S. Hylton, "Casualty of War," *GQ*, October 30, 2006.

10. Louis A. Pérez Jr., *Cuba in the American Imagination: Metaphor and the Imperial Imagination* (Chapel Hill: University of North Carolina Press, 2008), 11.

11. Raúl Castro Ruz, "Statement by the Cuban President," December 17, 2014; available online in English at http://en.cubadebate.cu/news/2014/12/17/statement-by-cuban-president/.

12. "Con un pueblo como este se puede llegar al año 570 de la Revolución," *Granma*, December 20, 2014.

Chapter 7: Boricua and the Bronx

1. Lola Rodríguez de Tió, "A Cuba," in *Mi Libro de Cuba* (1893).

2. Rita Moreno, *Rita Moreno: A Memoir* (New York: Celebra, 2014), 13.

3. José Luis González, *Puerto Rico: The Four-Storeyed Country and Other Essays*, trans. Gerald Guinness (Princeton, NJ: Marcus Wiener, 2013 [1980]), 5.

4. Theodore Roosevelt to Henry Cabot Lodge, May 19, 1898, in Charles F. Redmond, ed., *Selections from the Correspondence of Theodore Roosevelt and Henry Cabot Lodge, 1884–1918* (New York: Scribner's, 1925) 1:299.

5. González, *Puerto Rico*, 21.

6. New York Times, February 22, 1899; quoted in Nelson A. Denis, *War Against All Puerto Ricans* (New York: Nation Books, 2015), 16.

7. Ibid., 57.

8. Sidney W. Mintz, *Worker in the Cane* (New York: Norton, 1974 [1958]); see also Mintz, *Sweetness and Power* (New York: Penguin, 1986).

9. Denis, *War Against All Puerto Ricans*, 99–100.

10. Ibid., 245.

11. Bernardo Vega, *Memoirs of Bernardo Vega: A Contribution to the History of the Puerto Rican Community in New York*, ed. César Andrea Iglesias and trans. Juan Flores (New York: Monthly Review Press, 1984 [1977]).

12. César Miguel Rondón, *The Book of Salsa: A Chronicle of Urban Music from the Caribbean to New York City*, trans. Frances R. Aparicio with Jackie White (Chapel Hill: University of North Carolina Press, 2008 [1980]), 15.

Chapter 8: The Massacre River

1. Consuelo Varela, "La caída de Cristóbal Colón: El juicio de Bobadilla," Edición y transcripción de Isabel Aguirre, Series: *Estudios* (Madrid: Marcial Pons Ediciones de Historia, 2006).

2. Junot Díaz, *The Brief Wondrous Life of Oscar Wao* (New York: Riverhead, 2007), 1.

3. Michelle Wucker, *Why the Cocks Fight: Dominicans, Haitians, and the Struggle for Hispaniola* (New York: Hill and Wang, 1999), 75.

4. Ibid.

5. Ibid., 74.

6. Jean-Jacques Dessalines, *Constitution d'Haïti* (Aux Cayes, 1805), as discussed, e.g., in *The World of the Haitian Revolution*, ed. David Geggus and Norman Fiering (Bloomington: Indiana University Press, 2009).

7. Joaquín Balaguer, *La isla al réves: Haiti y el destino dominicano* [1983], in *Obras selectas: Tomo VIII: Textos históricos* (Santo Domingo: Editorial Corripio, 2006), 209, 69, 77.

8. Frank Moya Pons in "Haiti and the Dominican Republic: An Island Divided," episode of *Black in Latin America*, PBS; exec. prod. Henry Louis Gates Jr., 2011.

9. Díaz, *Oscar Wao*, 225.

10. Ibid., 3.

11. Ibid.

12. Wucker, *Why the Cocks Fight*, 48.

13. Díaz, *Oscar Wao*, 225.

14. "A Museum of Repression Aims to Shock the Conscience," *New York Times*, September 12, 2011.

15. José Ramon Fadul, in "Dominican Republic to Deport Illegal Aliens Beginning June 15," May 25, 2015, DominicanToday.com.

16. Jacques Stephen Alexis, *Compère Général Soleil* (Paris: Gallimard, 1955); as quoted in Wucker, *Why the Cocks Fight*, 48.

17. "Persiguen a dos haitianos acusados de matar pareja de esposos en Las Petacas de Neyba," *Hoy* (Santo Domingo), November 23, 2013.

18. "JCE revela documentos de Ana Maria Belique presentan irregularidades," *Noticias Sin*, July 9, 2015.

Chapter 9: The Citadel

1. "Ministro de Cultura: RD sigue con 'especial interés' supuesto hallazgo de la Santa María," *El Nuevo Diario* (Santo Domingo), May 14, 2014; "Expertos dudan hallazgo de la 'Santa María,'" *El Día* (Santo Domingo), May 15, 2014.

2. Michel-Rolph Trouillot, *Haiti, State Against Nation: The Origins and Legacy of Duvalierism* (New York: Monthly Review Press, 1990), 60.

3. Voltaire, *Candide*, ed. and trans. Theo Cuffe (New York: Penguin, 2005 [1759]), 69.

4. C. L. R. James, "From Toussaint L'Ouverture to Fidel Castro," in *The Black Jacobins: Toussaint L'Ouverture and the San Domingo Revolution* (New York: Vintage, 1963), 392.

5. Ibid.

6. "Hérard Dumesle, Voyage dans le nord d'Hayti; ou, révélation des lieux et des monuments historiques" (Aux Cayes: Imprimerie du Gouvernement, 1824); as quoted in Laurent Dubois, *Haiti: The Aftershocks of History* (New York: Metropolitan, 2012).

7. Mark Danner, "To Heal Haiti, Look to History, not Nature" *New York Times*, January 22, 2010.

8. Trouillot, *Haiti, State Against Nation*.

9. C. L. R. James, *The Black Jacobins: Toussaint L'Ouverture and the San Domingo Revolution* (New York: Vintage, 1963), 88.

10. Jean-François Brière, *Haïti et la France, 1804–1848: Le rêve brisé* (Paris: Kharthala, 2008), 27.

11. M. J. Mavidal and M. E. Laurent, eds., *Archives parlementaires de 1787 à 1860, premiere serie (1787–1799)* (Paris, 1962); as cited by Laurent Dubois, *Avengers of the New World: The Story of the Haitian Revolution* (Cambridge, MA: Harvard University Press, 2004).

12. Madison Smartt Bell, *Toussaint L'Ouverture: A Biography* (New York: Pantheon, 2007), 18.

13. Guillaume Thomas Raynal, *Histoire Philosophique et politique des établissements et du commerce des Européens dans les Deux Indies* (Geneva: 1780), 3, 204–05.

14. James, *The Black Jacobins*, x.

15. Ibid., 86.

16. Ibid., 198.

17. Ibid., 197.

18. Jean Casimir, *La culture oprimée* (Delmas, Haiti: Lakay, 2001); as discussed by Dubois, *The Aftershocks of History*, 122.

19. William Wordsworth, "Toussaint Louverture," originally printed in the London *Morning Post*, 1802; reprinted, e.g., in Wordsworth, *The Complete Poetical Works* (London: Macmillan, 1888).

20. Patrick Leigh Fermor, *The Traveller's Tree: A Journey Through the Caribbean Islands* (New York: New York Review Classics, 2010 [1952]), 294.

21. James, *The Black Jacobins*, 292.

22. Ibid., 271.

23. Bonaparte to Leclerc, July 1, 1802, in Paul Roussier, ed., *Lettres du Général Leclerc, commandant en chef de l'armée de Saint-Domingue en 1802* (Paris: Société de l'Histoire des Colonies Françaises et E. Leroux, 1937), 306–07; as cited by Dubois, *Avengers of the New World*, 255.

24. Leclerc to the First Consul, September 27, 1802; as cited by James, *The Black Jacobins*, 353.

25. James, *The Black Jacobins*, 108.

26. Leclerc to the Minister of Marine, July 6, 1802; as cited by James, *The Black Jacobins*, 337.

27. James, *The Black Jacobins*, 364.

28. Ibid., 372.

29. Ibid., 289.

30. Hubert Cole, *Christophe, King of Haiti* (New York: Viking, 1967), 190.

31. Earl Leslie Griggs and Clifford H. Prator, eds., *Henry Christophe and Thomas Clarkson: A Correspondence* (Berkeley: University of California Press, 1952), 134–35.

32. Ibid.

33. Jean-François Brière, *Haiti et la France, 1804–1848: La rêve brisé* (Paris: Kharthala, 2008), 19; as translated and cited by Dubois, *Aftershocks of History*, 168.

Chapter 10: Haiti Cherie

1. Charles Onians, "Scientologists 'Heal' Haiti Quake Victims Using Touch," *Agence France-Press*, January 22, 2010; as cited by Jonathan Katz, *The Big Truck That Went By: How the World Came to Save Haiti and Left Behind a Disaster* (New York: Palgrave Macmillan, 2013), 68.

2. Laurent Dubois, *Haiti: The Aftershocks of History* (New York: Metropolitan, 2012), 3.

3. Edwidge Danticat, *Create Dangerously: The Immigrant Artist at Work* (Princeton, NJ: Princeton University Press, 2010), 139, 148.

4. Katherine Dunham, *Island Possessed* (New York: Doubleday, 1969), 8.

5. See, e.g., Georges Michel, *Autour des constitutions républicaines haïtiennes* (Port-au-Prince: Fardin, 1986); *Les chemins de fer d'île d'Haïti* (Port-au-Prince: Le Natal, 1989); *Panorama des relations haïtiano-dominicaines* (Port-au-Prince: S.n., 1999); and Michel's sole book to be translated into English, *Charlemagne Péralte and the First American Occupation of Haiti* (Dubuque, IA: Kendall/Hunt, 1996).

Chapter 11: Heading South

1. Patrick Leigh Fermor, *The Traveller's Tree: A Journey Through the Caribbean Islands*, introduction by Joshua Jelly-Schapiro (New York: New York Review Classics, 2010 [1952]), 134.

2. George Lamming, *In the Castle of My Skin* (Ann Arbor: University of Michigan Press, 1991 [1953]), 69.

3. Ibid., 27.

4. Ibid., xxxviii.

5. George Lamming, *The Pleasures of Exile* (London: Joseph, 1960), 39.

6. Lamming, *In the Castle of My Skin*, 17.

7. Mighty Sparrow, "Sir Garfield Sobers" (Trinidad: National Recording Company [2], 1966).

8. Lamming, *In the Castle of My Skin*, 37.

9. Father Andrew White, "A Briefe Relation of the Voyage Unto Maryland, By Father Andrew White, 1634," in *Narratives of Early Maryland*, ed. Clayton Colman Hall (New York: Scribner's, 1910), 37; as quoted in Mathew Parker, *The Sugar Barons: Family, Corruption, Empire, and War in the West Indies* (London: Windmill, 2011), 16.

10. Sir Henry Colt, "The Voyage of Sir Henry Colt" (1631), in *Colonising Expeditions to the West Indies and Guiana, 1623–1667*, ed. Vincent T. Harlow (London: Hakluyt Society); as quoted in Parker, *The Sugar Barons*, 24.

11. Colt, "The Voyage," 67; as quoted in Parker, *The Sugar Barons*, 25.

12. Richard Jobson, *The Golden Trade; Or, A Discovery of the River Gambra and the Golden Trade of the Aethiopians* (London: Speight and Walpole, 1623).

13. Richard Ligon, *A True and Exact History of the Island of Barbados* (London, 1657), 51.

14. Ibid.

15. Parker, quoting Blake, in *The Sugar Barons*, 360.

16. Thomas Wilkie, 1727, collected in Frank Joseph Klingberg, *The Codrington Chronicle: An Experiment in Anglican Altruism on a Barbados Plantation, 1710–1834* (Berkeley: University of California Press, 1949), 99; as quoted in Parker, *The Sugar Barons*, 361.

17. Lamming, *In the Castle of My Skin*, 261.

18. Ibid., 295.

19. Paule Marshall, *Brown Girl, Brownstones* (New York: The Feminist Press, 2006 [1959]), 4.

20. Ibid., 11.

21. Paule Marshall as quoted in Felicia R. Lee, "Voyage of a Girl Moored in Brooklyn," *New York Times*, March 11, 2009.

22. Jamaica Kincaid, *A Small Place* (New York: Farrar, Straus and Giroux, 1988), 25.
23. V. S. Naipaul, "Heavy Manners in Grenada," *Sunday Times Magazine* (1984): 23–31; collected in Naipaul, *The Writer and the World* (New York: Knopf, 2012).
24. Paule Marshall, *Praisesong for the Widow* (New York: Plume, 1983), 167.
25. Christopher Bethel Codrington to William Codrington, June 16, 1790, Codrington Correspondence, University of Texas microfilm 106; as quoted in David Lowenthal and Colin G. Clark, "Slave-Breeding in Barbuda: The Past of a Negro Myth," *Annals of the New York Academy of Sciences* 292, no. 1 (December 2006): 510–35, 515.
26. Sidney Clark with Margaret Zellers, *All the Best in the Caribbean* (New York: Dodd, Mead, 1972), 252.
27. Thomas Jefferson Randolph as quoted in Fredric Bancroft, *Slave-Trading in the Old South* (Baltimore: J. H. Furst, 1931), 69–70.
28. "Thieves Take Quarter of Million Dollars from Barbuda Council," *Antigua Observer*, February 20, 2015.
29. Kincaid, *A Small Place*, 59.
30. Lowenthal and Clark, "Slave-Breeding in Barbuda," 512.
31. Cristopher Bethel Codrington to Sir George Murray, February 11, 1830, Public Record Office 7/30; as quoted in ibid., 524.
32. Henry Nelson Coleridge, *Six Months in the West Indies in 1825*, 2nd ed. (London: John Murray, 1826), 276.
33. Christopher Bethel Codrington to E. G. Stanley, June 1, 1834 (draft), Codrington mss., Gloucestershire County Archives E 36; as quoted in Lowenthal and Clark, "Slave-Breeding in Barbuda," 525.
34. J. Liggins to Christopher Bethel Codrington, April 5, 1837, Codrington Correspondence JL 452; as quoted in Lowenthal and Clark, "Slave-Breeding in Barbuda," 515.
35. Mackenzie Frank quoted in "Power Outage Causing 'Chaos on Barbuda,'" *Antigua Observer*, February 23, 2015.
36. Lydia Mihelic Pulsipher, "Assessing the Usefulness of Cartographic Curiosity," *Annals of the Association of American Geographers* 77, no. 3 (September 1987): 408–22.
37. Jamaica Kincaid, unattributed "Talk of the Town" column, *New Yorker* (September 1974); collected in Kincaid, *Talk Stories* (New York: Farrar, Straus and Giroux, 2001), 15–24.
38. Kincaid, *A Small Place*, 29.
39. Ibid., 26.
40. Kincaid, *Autobiography of My Mother* (New York: Farrar, Straus and Giroux, 1996), 88–89.
41. Kincaid, *A Small Place*, 56.
42. Ibid., 56.
43. Ibid., 54.
44. Ibid., 59.
45. Ibid., 81.
46. Ibid.
47. Ibid., 33.
48. Ibid.
49. Ibid., 44.

50. Ibid., 14.
51. Ibid., 15.
52. Ibid., 13.
53. Ibid., 19.

Chapter 12: Au Pays Natal

1. Aimé Césaire, *Notebook of a Return to the Native Land*, ed. and trans. Clayton Eshleman and Annette Smith (Middletown, CT: Wesleyan University Press, 2001 [1939]), 35; original French, "Cahier d'un retour au pays natal," *Volonté* 20 (1939).
2. Ibid., 44.
3. Aimé Césaire in *Rapport, séance du 26 février 1946*, JORF, Documents de l'Assemblée, no. 520, 519; as quoted in Gary Wilder, *Freedom Time: Negritude, Decolonization, and the Future of the World* (Durham, NC: Duke University Press, 2015), 279.
4. André Breton, "Un grand poète noir," first published in *Tropiques* (May 1944); in English as the introduction to the first bilingual edition of Aimé Césaire's *Cahier d'un retour au pays natal/Memorandum on My Martinique* (New York: Brentano's, 1947).
5. Aimé Césaire, *Discourse on Colonialism*, trans. Joan Pinkham (New York: Monthly Review Press, 2001), 31; original French, *Discours sur le colonialisme* (Paris: Présence Africaine, 1955).
6. Ibid., 39.
7. Ibid., 78.
8. Césaire, *Cahier,* 46.
9. Ibid., 35.
10. Ibid., 1.
11. Ibid., 42.
12. Louis Delgrès, *À l'Univers entier, le dernier cri de l'innocence et du désespoir, Proclamation au fort Saint-Charles*, Guadeloupe, May 10, 1802.
13. Patrick Leigh Fermor, *The Traveller's Tree: A Journey Through the Caribbean Islands* (New York: New York Review Classics, 2010 [1952]), 72.
14. Césaire, *Cahier,* 8
15. Breton, "Un grand poète noir."
16. Césaire, *Cahier*.
17. Ibid., 39.
18. Ibid.
19. Aimé Césaire, *A Tempest: Based on Shakespeare's* Tempest: *An Adaptation for the Black Theatre*, trans. Richard Miller (New York: Ubu Repertory Theatre, 1992), 11; original French, *Une Tempête* (Paris: Seuil, 1969).
20. Jacqueline Leiner, "Entretion avec Aimé Césaire," *Tropiques* I, x; as quoted in David Macey, *Frantz Fanon: A Biography* (London: Verso, 2000), 68.
21. Frantz Fanon, "Antillais et Africains," *Esprit* (February 1955); reprinted in English in *Toward the African Revolution*, trans. Haakon Chevalier (New York: Grove, 1994).
22. Ibid.
23. Aimé Césaire, "La Révolte de Frantz Fanon," *Jeune Afrique*, December 13–19, 1961, 24.

24. Frantz Fanon, *The Wretched of the Earth*, trans. Richard Philcox (New York: Grove, 2004), 4; first published as *Les Damnés de la terre* (Paris: Maspero, 1961).
25. Ibid., 1.
26. Ibid., 2.
27. Ibid., 23.
28. Ibid., 51.
29. Hannah Arendt, *On Violence* (New York: Harcourt, Brace, 1970), 65.
30. Patrick Chamoiseau, *Texaco*, trans. Rose-Myriam Réjouis and Val Vinokurov (New York: Pantheon, 1997 [1992]), 316.
31. Marius Larcher, "Le Livre de Frantz Fanon," *L'Information*, May, 22, 1962; as quoted in Macey, *Frantz Fanon*, 13.
32. Francis Jeanson, "Reconnaisance à Fanon," in the 1965 edition of *Peau noire, masques blanc* (Paris: Seuil, 1952); as quoted in Macey, *Frantz Fanon*, 157.
33. *Le Monde*, December 24, 1959; as quoted in Macey, *Frantz Fanon*, 415.
34. Fanon, *Peau noire*, 10; as discussed in Macey, *Frantz Fanon*, 30.
35. Fanon, *Black Skin, White Masks*, trans. Richard Philcox (New York: Grove, 2008 [1952]), 92.
36. Fanon, *Wretched of the Earth*, 46.
37. Mayotte Capécia, *Je Suis Martiniquaise* (Paris: Editions Corréa, 1948); published in English in *I Am a Martinican Woman & the White Negress: Two Novelletes*, trans. Beatrice Stith Clark (Pueblo, CO: Passeggiata Press, 1998).
38. Fanon, *Black Skin, White Masks*, 25.
39. Ibid, 45.
40. Ibid., 206.
41. Ibid., 22.
42. Jean-Paul Sartre, preface [1961] to Fanon, *Wretched of the Earth*, iv.
43. "We are Frenchmen Says Thuram, as Le Pen Bemoans Number of Black Players," *Guardian*, June 30, 2006.
44. Angelique Chrisafis, "Paris Show Unveils Life in Human Zoo," *Guardian*, November 29, 2011.
45. Aimé Césaire, "Par tous mots Guerrier-Silex," *Le Progressiste*, March 24, 1982.
46. Patrick Chamoiseau, *Solibo Magnificent*, trans. Rose-Myriam Réjouis and Val Vinokurov (New York: Pantheon, 1999 [1988]), 25.
47. Jean Bernabé, Patrick Chamoiseau, and Raphaël Confiant, *Éloge de Créolité* (Paris: Gallimard, 1989), bilingual French-English edition, 87.
48. Raphaël Confiant, "Letter from a Thirty-Year-Old Man to Aimé Césaire," as referenced in Lucien Taylor, "Creolité Bites: A Conversation with Patrick Chamoiseau, Raphaël Confiant, and Jean Bernabé," *Transition* 74 (1997): 124–61, 139.
49. Derek Walcott, "A Letter to Chamoiseau," *New York Review of Books*, August 14, 1997.
50. Edouard Glissant, *Poetics of Relation*, trans. Betsy Wing (Ann Arbor: University of Michigan Press, 2000), 11.
51. Leigh Fermor, *Traveller's Tree*, 33–34.

Chapter 13: The Last of the Carib

1. Patrick Leigh Fermor, *The Traveller's Tree: A Journey Through the Caribbean Islands*, introduction by Joshua Jelly-Schapiro (New York: New York Review Classics, 2010 [1952]), 103.

2. Elma Napier, *Black and White Sands: A Bohemian Life in the Colonial Caribbean* (London: Papillote Press, 2009).

3. A. Alvarez, "The Best Living English Novelist," *New York Times Book Review*, March 17, 1974.

4. Ford Madox Ford, introduction to Jean Rhys, *The Left Bank* (London: Jonathan Cape, 1927), reprinted in Rhys, *Tigers Are Better Looking* (London: André Deutsch, 1968), 148.

5. Hilton Als, "This Lonesome Place," *New Yorker*, January 21, 2001; collected in *White Girls* (San Francisco: McSweeney's, 2013), 113.

6. Jean Rhys, *Smile Please: An Unfinished Autobiography* (New York: Harper & Row, 1979), 15.

7. Ibid., 42.

8. Ibid., 14.

9. Diana Athill, foreword to *Smile Please*, 4.

10. Rhys, *Voyage in the Dark* (London: Constable, 1934), 44.

11. Rhys, letter to her daughter Maryvonne Moerman-Langlet, May 7, 1964, *Jean Rhys Letters, 1931–1966* (London: Deutsch, 1984).

12. Rhys as quoted in Athill in her foreword to *Smile Please*, 7.

13. Rhys, *Smile Please*, 58–59.

14. Ibid., 33.

15. Ibid., 17.

16. Ibid., 43.

17. Ibid., 37.

18. Ibid., 39–40.

19. Ibid., 38.

20. Ibid., 22.

21. Ibid., 23.

22. Ibid., 24.

23. Ibid., 39.

24. Ibid., 23.

25. Ibid., 24.

26. Jean Rhys, "Let Them Call It Jazz," in *Tigers Are Better Looking*, 47–67, 65.

27. Carole Angier, *Jean Rhys: Life and Work* (London: Faber & Faber 1991), 81.

28. Rhys, *Smile Please*, 16.

29. Ibid., 15.

30. Ibid.

31. Rhys, *Wide Sargasso Sea* (London: André Deutsch, 1966), 41.

32. Rhys, *Smile Please*, 73.

33. Ibid., 74.

34. Rhys, *Voyage in the Dark*, 105.

35. Rhys, *Wide Sargasso Sea*, 1.

36. Evelyn Hawthorne, "'Persistence of (Colonial) Memory': Jean Rhys's Carib Texts and Imperial Historiography," *ARIEL* 32, no. 3 (July 2001): 94.

37. Jean Rhys, "Temps Perdi," collected in *Tales of the Wide Caribbean* (London: Heinemann, 1985), 144–61, 155.

38. Ibid., 156.

39. Ibid., 157.

40. Ibid., 159.

41. Ibid.

42. Ibid., 160.

43. Ibid.

44. Ibid., 161.

45. Ibid.

46. Anthony Trollope, *The West Indies and the Spanish Main* (London: Chapman and Hall, 1859), 160.

47. Lennox Honychurch, *The Dominica Story* (London: Macmillan Caribbean, 1995).

48. Phyllis Shand Allfrey, "Love for an Island" (1973), collected in *Love for an Island: The Collected Poems of Phyllis Shand Allfrey* (London: Papillote Press, 2014).

49. Rhys, *Smile Please*, 26.

Chapter 14: Return to El Dorado

1. Geoffrey Holder, *Geoffrey Holder's Caribbean Cookbook* (New York: Viking, 1973), 2.

2. "Fed-up MacFarlane: No More Competition for Me," *Trinidad Express*, February 18, 2010.

3. Garnette Cadogan interview with Ned Sublette, *BOMB* (May 2008).

4. V. S. Naipaul, *The Middle Passage* (London: André Deutsch, 1962), 35.

5. Patrick Leigh Fermor, *The Traveller's Tree: A Journey Through the Caribbean Islands*, introduction by Joshua Jelly-Schapiro (New York: New York Review Classics, 2010 [1952]), 154.

6. Ibid., 159.

7. C. L. R. James, "From Toussaint L'Ouverture to Fidel Castro," in *The Black Jacobins: Toussaint L'Ouverture and the San Domingo Revolution* (New York: Vintage, 1963), 410.

8. C. L. R. James as quoted by Stefano Harney, *Nationalism and Identity: Culture and the Imagination in a Caribbean Diaspora* (London: Zed, 1996), 163.

9. Eric Williams, *From Columbus to Castro: The History of the Caribbean 1492–1969* (New York: Vintage, 1970), 395.

10. Dennis "Cultural Sprangalang" Hall, *Newsday* (Trinidad), February 27, 1997; as cited by Selwyn Ryan, *The Jhandi and the Cross: The Clash of Cultures in Post-Creole Trinidad and Tobago* (St. Augustine, Trinidad: ISER, University of the West Indies, 1999), 134.

11. C. L. R. James, preface to *The Black Jacobins: Toussaint L'Ouverture and the San Domingo Revolution* (New York: Vintage, 1963), x.

12. James to Constance Webb, June 14, 1944, in *Special Delivery: The Letters of C. L. R. James to Constance Webb, 1939–1948*, ed. Anna Grimshaw (Oxford: Blackwell, 1996), 123.

13. Raoul Pantin, *Days of Wrath: The 1990 Coup in Trinidad and Tobago* (iUniverse, 2007).

14. "V. S. Naipaul Wins 2001 Nobel Prize," *Guardian*, October 11, 2001.

15. *The Listener*, June 23, 1983; as quoted in Patrick French, *The World Is What It Is: The Authorized Biography of V. S. Naipaul* (New York: Knopf, 2008), 9.

16. French, *The World Is What It Is*, 5.

17. Colin MacInness, "Caribbean Masterpiece," *Observer* (n.d., 1961).

18. V. S. Naipaul, *A House for Mr. Biswas* (London: André Deutsch, 1961), 14.

19. V. S. Naipaul, "Power to the Caribbean People," *New York Review of Books*, September 3, 1970.

20. V. S. Naipaul, "Michael X and the Black Power Killings in Trinidad," in *The Return of Eva Perón, with The Killings in Trinidad* (New York: Knopf, 1980), 23.

21. Ibid.

22. Ibid., 5.

23. Ibid., 21–22.

24. Ibid., 55.

25. Ibid., 5.

26. Ibid., 15.

27. Ibid., 70.

28. "Jack: Moonilal Asked Brazilian Company for $50m," Trinidad *Express*, July 2, 2015.

29. "Kamla Walks Out on Warner," Trinidad *Guardian*, June 6, 2015.

30. B. C. Pires, "From Hummingbird to Dying Swan," Trinidad *Guardian*, February 12, 2016.

31. Claire Alexander interview in *Stuart Hall and "Race"* (London: Routledge, 2014).

32. Gary Younge, "The Politics of Partying," *Guardian*, August 17, 2002.

33. Ibid.

34. Rabindranath Tagore, *Stray Birds* (London: Macmillan, 1919).

BIBLIOGRAPHY AND FURTHER READING

For a full bibliography and suggestions for further reading,
see http://www.joshuajellyschapiro.com/islandpeople/bibliography.

TEXT PERMISSIONS

A NOTE ABOUT THE AUTHOR

Joshua Jelly-Schapiro is a geographer and writer whose work has appeared in *The New York Review of Books, New York, Harper's, The Believer, Artforum,* and *The Nation,* among many other publications. Educated at Yale and Berkeley, he is the coeditor, with Rebecca Solnit, of *Nonstop Metropolis: A New York City Atlas.* He is a visiting scholar at New York University's Institute for Public Knowledge. This is his first book.

A NOTE ON THE TYPE

This book was set in Janson, a typeface long thought to have been made by the Dutchman Anton Janson. However, it has been conclusively demonstrated that these types are actually the work of Nicholas Kis (1650–1702), a Hungarian, who most probably learned his trade from the master Dutch typefounder Dirk Voskens.

Composed by North Market Street Graphics,
Lancaster, Pennsylvania

Printed and bound by Berryville Graphics,
Berryville, Virginia

Designed by M. Kristen Bearse